Windows 11 Inside Out

Ed Bott

Windows 11 Inside Out
Published with the authorization of Microsoft Corporation by Pearson Education, Inc.

Copyright © 2023 by Ed Bott

All rights reserved. This publication is protected by copyright, and permission must be obtained from the publisher prior to any prohibited reproduction, storage in a retrieval system, or transmission in any form or by any means, electronic, mechanical, photocopying, recording, or likewise. For information regarding permissions, request forms, and the appropriate contacts within the Pearson Education Global Rights & Permissions Department, please visit *www.pearson.com/permissions*. No patent liability is assumed with respect to the use of the information contained herein. Although every precaution has been taken in the preparation of this book, the publisher and author assume no responsibility for errors or omissions. Nor is any liability assumed for damages resulting from the use of the information contained herein.

ISBN-13: 978-0-13-769133-3
ISBN-10: 0-13-769133-5

Library of Congress Control Number: 2022952040

155 2024

Trademarks
Microsoft and the trademarks listed at *http://www.microsoft.com* on the "Trademarks" webpage are trademarks of the Microsoft group of companies. All other marks are property of their respective owners.

Warning and Disclaimer
Every effort has been made to make this book as complete and as accurate as possible, but no warranty or fitness is implied. The information provided is on an "as is" basis. The author, the publisher, and Microsoft Corporation shall have neither liability nor responsibility to any person or entity with respect to any loss or damages arising from the information contained in this book.

Special Sales
For information about buying this title in bulk quantities, or for special sales opportunities (which may include electronic versions; custom cover designs; and content particular to your business, training goals, marketing focus, or branding interests), please contact our corporate sales department at corpsales@pearsoned.com or (800) 382-3419. For government sales inquiries, please contact governmentsales@pearsoned.com.
For questions about sales outside the U.S., please contact intlcs@pearson.com.

Editor-in-Chief: Brett Bartow
Executive Editor: Loretta Yates
Technical Editor: Carl Siechert
Sponsoring Editor: Malobika Chakraborty
Development Editor: Charlotte Kughen
Managing Editor: Sandra Schroeder
Senior Project Editor: Tracey Croom
Editorial Services: The Wordsmithery LLC
Indexer: Cheryl Lenser
Proofreader: Sarah Kearns
Editorial Assistant: Cindy Teeters
Cover Designer: Twist Creative, Seattle
Compositor: Bronkella Publishing LLC
Graphics: tj graham art

Pearson's Commitment to Diversity, Equity, and Inclusion

Pearson is dedicated to creating bias-free content that reflects the diversity of all readers. We embrace the many dimensions of diversity, including but not limited to race, ethnicity, gender, socioeconomic status, ability, age, sexual orientation, and religious or political beliefs.

Books are a powerful force for equity and change in our world. They have the potential to deliver opportunities that improve lives and enable economic mobility. As we work with authors to create content for every product and service, we acknowledge our responsibility to demonstrate inclusivity and incorporate diverse scholarship so that everyone can achieve their potential through learning. As the world's leading learning company, we have a duty to help drive change and live up to our purpose to help more people create a better life for themselves and to create a better world.

Our ambition is to purposefully contribute to a world where:

- Everyone has an equitable and lifelong opportunity to succeed through learning.

- Our products and services are inclusive and represent the rich diversity of readers.

- Our content accurately reflects the histories and experiences of the readers we serve.

- Our content prompts deeper discussions with readers and motivates them to expand their own learning (and worldview).

While we work hard to present unbiased content, we want to hear from you about any concerns or needs with this Pearson product so that we can investigate and address them. Please contact us with concerns about any potential bias at *https://www.pearson.com/report-bias.html*.

Dedication

To Judy, who has been by my side every step of the way

Contents at a Glance

Table of Contents

Acknowledgments

For this edition of the book, like many before it, we're fortunate to have an experienced production crew that has worked together as a team for multiple editions in this series. Led by executive editor Loretta Yates, the team includes technical editor Carl Siechert (who was a co-author on earlier editions), proofreader Sarah Kearns, compositor Tricia Bronkella, and indexer Cheryl Lenser. Together, they asked the right questions and made excellent suggestions to help turn a collection of Word files and screenshots into the visually compelling, tightly organized, technically accurate volume you're reading now. Thanks, too, to Andrew Warren, who provided much-needed help with the enterprise-focused chapters.

And we've saved a special tip of the hat to our longtime colleagues Charlotte and Rick Kughen. This book would never have gotten into your hands without their production magic.

About the author

Ed Bott is an award-winning author and technology journalist who has been researching and writing about Microsoft Windows and PC technology, in print and on the Internet, for more than two decades. Much of that work has appeared in *The Ed Bott Report* on ZDNet (*zdnet.com/blog/bott*), where his signature hands-on advice columns and buying recommendations have been a fixture through at least a half-dozen Windows versions. Ed has written more than 30 books, all on Windows and Microsoft Office, which have been translated into dozens of languages and read worldwide.

You can catch up with Ed's latest opinions and get hands-on advice in his newsletter, Ed Bott's READ ME; for details, visit *edbott.com/newsletter*. You can also connect with him on Twitter (@edbott) and on the open source Mastodon network (*mastodon.social/@edbott*). Ed and his wife, Judy, live in Atlanta, Georgia. They are currently between dogs.

Introduction

I've spent most of my professional career chronicling the ups and downs of Microsoft Windows and, more importantly, helping human beings make sense of its fabulous features, weird idiosyncrasies, and occasional frustrations.

By my unofficial count, this is the sixteenth release in the *Inside Out* series since we kicked off the franchise in 2001 with a volume covering what was at the time the newest member of the Microsoft operating system family, Windows XP.

The world has gone through a few changes in the 20-plus years that have passed since the publication of *Windows XP Inside Out*. Back then, detailed technical information was hard to come by, Now, *reliable* information is a scarce commodity, especially when it comes to an ever-evolving product like Windows.

For those early *Windows Inside Out* editions, we had the reassurance of knowing that each new release from Microsoft would have a lifespan of at least three years. That's no longer the case, with Windows 11 getting new feature updates yearly and Microsoft now reworking even core features as part of its monthly updates.

In combination, those two factors have dramatically influenced how this book is organized. Where we once might have devoted a page or more to a table listing command-line switches for an essential utility, for example, we now have the luxury of posting a link to the complete (and authoritative) online documentation. That frees us to spend more pages explaining how a feature works and how to integrate it into your personal workflow.

One bedrock fact we've discovered over the past two decades is that the core features of Windows change very slowly. The fundamentals of NTFS security and the registry, for example, have remained reassuringly consistent throughout many generations of Windows. But there's also plenty that's new in Windows 11, some of it obvious (the new Start menu), some familiar from Windows 10 features (Windows Hello), and some existing almost completely under the covers (hardware-based security).

Our team started this revision in 2021, shortly after Microsoft announced the first Insider Preview release of Windows 11. We consciously chose to keep working for more than a year as Microsoft prepared the first major update to Windows 11, version 22H2. Every page in this book has been tested and fact-checked using that release.

We know there will be further updates, but we're confident that this book will be relevant for several years to come.

— Ed Bott, January 2023

Who this book is for

This book offers a well-rounded look at the features most people use in Windows. It serves as an excellent starting point for anyone who wants a better understanding of how the central features in Windows 11 work. If you are a Windows expert-in-training, have a day job that involves IT responsibilities, or are the designated computer specialist managing computers and networks in a home or small business, you'll discover many sections we wrote just for you. And if you consider yourself a Windows enthusiast—well, we hope you'll find enough fun and interesting tidbits to hold your attention because, after all, we're unabashed enthusiasts ourselves.

Assumptions about you

This book is not for beginners. It was written for people who have experience with Windows and are comfortable with and even curious about the technical details of what makes Windows work. It touches only briefly on some of the basic material that you'll find covered in more detail elsewhere.

Whether you've been working with Windows for a few years or a quarter-century, we expect that you're comfortable finding your way around the desktop, launching programs, using copy and paste operations, and finding information in a web browser. We don't assume that you're a hardware tinkerer, hacker, hardcore gamer, or developer.

How this book is organized

Part 1, "Windows 11 essentials," offers an overview of what's new in this version, along with details on installing, configuring, and personalizing a PC running Windows 11. It also covers the Windows 11 app landscape, which has changed dramatically just in the past two years, with one full chapter devoted to the new default web browser, Microsoft Edge. Finally, we explain how to make best use of local and cloud-based storage, with a special emphasis on a core Windows 11 tool, File Explorer.

Part 2, "Managing Windows 11," starts with a detailed guide to keeping your user accounts and devices secure. Additional chapters cover tools and techniques for measuring and improving your computer's performance, keeping your network connections fast and secure, and configuring hardware. The section closes with advice on how to back up your important files, how to recover quickly from problems, and how to troubleshoot issues when they arise.

Part 3, "For IT professionals and Windows experts," leads off with a chapter that introduces Windows Terminal and PowerShell, tools that take some effort to master but pay huge dividends for automating repetitive administrative tasks. An additional chapter covers Hyper-V, a powerful virtualization platform built into Windows 11 Pro and Enterprise editions. In the final chapters, we cover the unusual Windows subsystems for Linux and Android and offer pointers for administrators working in enterprise environments.

Finally, we provide three appendixes of reference information: a concise look at the differences between Windows 11 editions, a hands-on guide to the Windows Insider Program, and an overview of help and support resources.

Stay in touch

Let's keep the conversation going! We're on Twitter: *https://twitter.com/MicrosoftPress*.

Errata, updates, and book support

We've made every effort to ensure the accuracy of this book and its companion content. You can access updates to this book—in the form of a list of submitted errata and their related corrections—at

https://MicrosoftPressStore.com/Windows11InsideOut/errata

If you discover an error that is not already listed, please submit it to us at the same page.

For additional book support and information, please visit

MicrosoftPressStore.com/Support

Please note that product support for Microsoft software and hardware is not offered through the previous addresses. For help with Microsoft software or hardware, go to

https://support.microsoft.com

Everything you need to know about Windows 11

Microsoft officially released Windows 11 on October 5, 2021, after an unusually short testing period. It represents the first major upgrade to Windows since Windows 10, which was released more than six years earlier. It's built on the same core code as its predecessor, and in many important respects it resembles a feature update to Windows 10.

But don't let the incremental change in version number fool you into thinking this is an insignificant upgrade. Windows 11 introduces some fundamental changes in familiar elements of the core Windows experience, including the Start menu, the taskbar, and the Settings app. It also enables some sophisticated security features that take advantage of new features found only in modern hardware. Over time, the differences between Windows 11 and its predecessor will be even more pronounced, thanks to a steady stream of feature updates to Windows 11 as well as changes in apps included with the newer operating system.

Historically, Microsoft has emphasized backward compatibility as one of the defining characteristics of Windows. That's still mostly true with Windows 11. With rare exceptions, legacy desktop programs and apps from the Microsoft Store that worked with Windows 10 will continue to run as expected on Windows 11, and most of the productivity shortcuts you've mastered over the past few years will still work.

The emphasis on backward compatibility doesn't continue on the hardware side, however. Minimum system requirements for Windows 11 are significantly more stringent than those for any previous Windows version; the most important change is a CPU compatibility list that specifically excludes most processors released before 2018. As a result, hundreds of millions of PCs that currently run Windows 10 are not eligible for Windows 11 upgrades.

NOTE

It's possible to work around these compatibility restrictions and install Windows 11 on hardware that falls short of the minimum system requirements. You'll find details on how to override compatibility restrictions and install Windows 11 on unsupported hardware in Chapter 2, "Setting up a new Windows 11 PC."

CHAPTER 1

The new hardware compatibility requirements mean that many legacy configurations are no longer supported. In this book, we assume you're running Windows 11 on hardware that meets the minimum compatibility requirements, with appropriate guidance on how to overcome issues that you're likely to encounter when upgrading from Windows 10.

The purpose of this introductory chapter is to provide an overview of Windows 11, with a special emphasis on what's new and what's changed from Windows 10.

What's new in Windows 11?

If you're familiar with Windows 10, you'll probably adapt fairly quickly to Windows 11, because the two operating systems share a significant amount of core code. And not all of those changes are immediately obvious. Microsoft's engineers continue to make steady and significant improvements in memory and storage management, for example, which results in faster start-ups and more efficient management of running processes, although the differences might be so slight that you'll need a stopwatch capable of measuring in fractions of a second to quantify the improvements.

Some new features that are apparent on your first boot after upgrading to Windows 11 include changes to the user experience and a major update to the Microsoft Store, including options for third-party developers to make Windows desktop apps available for secure downloads through the Store. We discuss those in more detail later in this chapter.

A few features that were new in Windows 10 are carried over into Windows 11 mostly intact. You can monitor system performance in Task Manager, for example, a utility that has been part of Windows for decades. Press Ctrl+Shift+Esc to open Task Manager, and then click the Performance tab to see detailed information about the most important aspects of how the operating system is using available resources. In Windows 11 version 22H2, this familiar tool receives a visual refresh that replaces the horizontal tabs with a vertical layout, as shown in Figure 1-1.

> ➤ For an in-depth look at how Task Manager works, see Chapter 14, "Performance and power management."

In another significant enhancement to a core Windows utility, the primary file management tool, File Explorer, gets several significant changes in Windows 11. The Microsoft Office–style ribbon from Windows 10 is gone, and the sometimes-overwhelming shortcut menu is simplified, although the full menu is still available by clicking Show More Options. Figure 1-2 shows the new-look File Manager in action.

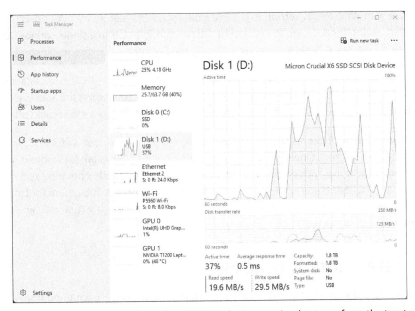

Figure 1-1   Beginning with version 22H2, Task Manager's tabs move from the top to the side, adopting a visual style that matches the Settings app.

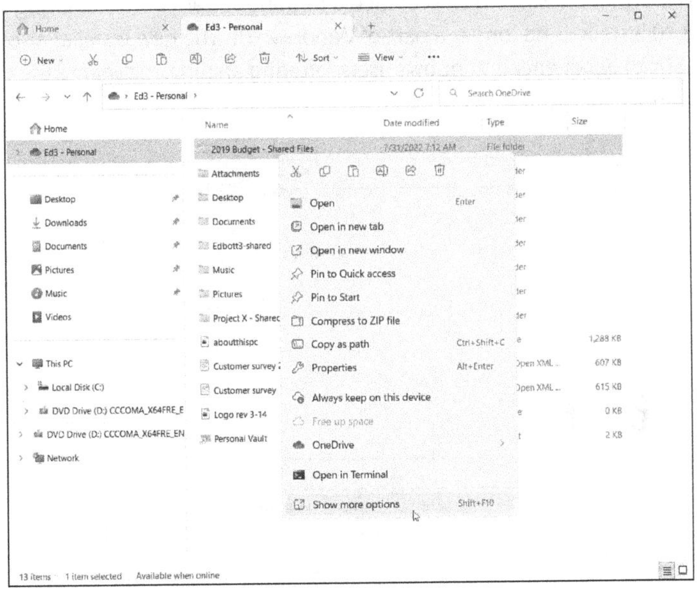

Figure 1-2   In Windows 11, File Explorer gets a simpler menu bar and a shorter shortcut menu. Version 22H2 adds a long-requested feature: an interface with multiple tabs.

Effective with Windows 11 version 22H2, File Explorer adds a feature that Windows users have been requesting for decades: the option to display multiple tabs in a single window. We cover these new features in detail in Chapter 9, "Using File Explorer."

Hardware-assisted security features, which were optional in Windows 10, are now enabled by default. That means Secure Boot, device encryption, and other advanced features are available the first time you turn on a Windows 11 PC, offering protection against increasingly sophisticated attackers.

Windows 11 also includes some new features designed to help Windows PCs work with alternative operating systems. One such feature is a new Windows Subsystem for Android, which allows you to install and run apps originally written for the Android mobile operating system on a Windows 11 PC; that feature goes hand in hand with the Windows Subsystem for Linux, which enables developers and administrators to work with Linux apps in a virtual machine that's tightly integrated with Windows.

Setup, updates, and upgrades

Windows 10 introduced an image-based setup process that makes upgrading from a previous Windows version fast and resilient. The Windows 11 Setup program, which powers both clean installs and upgrades, is functionally similar but offers a redesigned visual appearance that is noticeably cleaner and less chatty than its predecessor. ("Less chatty" is not just a figure of speech, either. The Cortana voice, which provided a running stream of wisecracking commentary during Windows 10 installs, is no longer a part of Windows 11.) The new installer also addresses a frequent request from experienced Windows users, offering an option to name the device during a clean install, as shown in Figure 1-3.

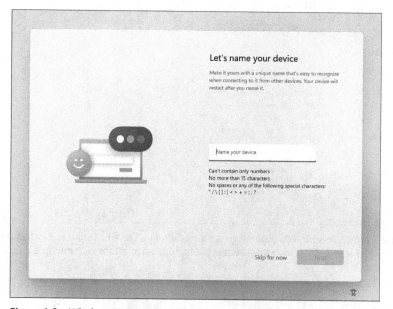

Figure 1-3   Windows 11 Setup is marked by a visual design that's noticeably cleaner and less chatty than its predecessor.

Many familiar aspects of Windows Setup are unchanged. You can install Windows 11 without entering a product key, and activation occurs automatically when reinstalling the operating system on hardware where it was previously activated. Most people purchasing new PCs from the retail or small business channels choose one of two editions: Home or Pro. In corporate and academic environments, administrators have the choice of Enterprise and Education editions, which offer some specialized management features.

The image-based setup also powers the recovery tools, shown in Figure 1-4; the Reset This PC option allows you to reinstall Windows without having to search for installation media or product keys, with the option to keep your personal files or wipe the system clean. For more details, see Chapter 15, "Troubleshooting, backup, and recovery."

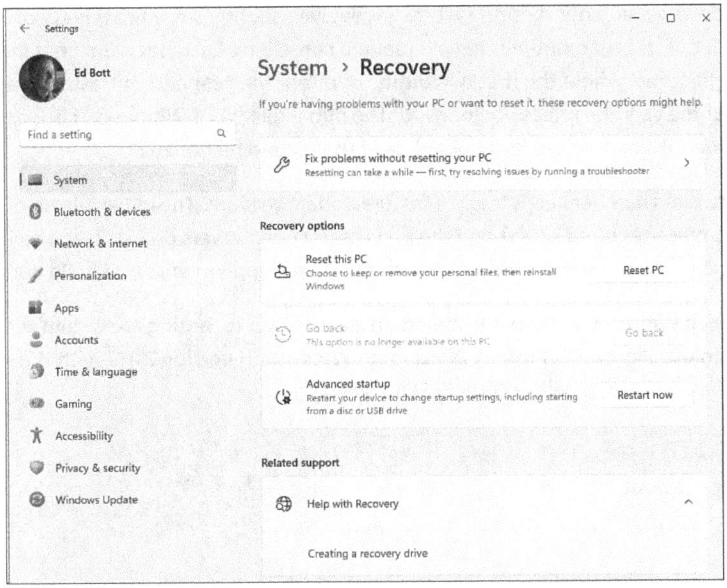

Figure 1-4   The Recovery options in Windows 11 allow you to reset a PC without requiring separate installation media or wiping out your personal files.

As far as updates are concerned, Windows 11 offers a few changes compared to what Windows users and administrators have come to expect in recent years. Monthly updates intended to address security and reliability issues still arrive on a predictable schedule, delivered via Windows Update on the second Tuesday of each month. Feature updates, which represent the equivalent of a full version upgrade for Windows, are another story.

Before the initial release of Windows 10, Microsoft declared its intention to treat Windows as a service, making feature updates free for anyone running a supported version of the operating system. "Windows as a service" eventually turned into a twice-yearly feature update cadence for Windows 10, which turned out to be unsustainable for developers and customers alike.

With Windows 11, Microsoft has committed to a more reasonable annual delivery schedule for feature updates, with those updates arriving predictably in the second half of the calendar year.

Retail editions include 24 months of support, with Enterprise and Education editions qualifying for 36 months of support.

➤ The sole exception to the preceding discussion of feature updates is the Long Term Servicing Channel, available only for Windows Enterprise editions. You can read more about this unusual variant in Appendix A, "Windows 11 editions and licensing options."

ABOUT WINDOWS 11 VERSIONS

Which version of Windows 11 are you running? Like so many questions that involve the internal workings of Microsoft Windows, the answer is far from simple.

The Windows version numbering system has evolved slightly since the release of Windows 10 in 2015, but its broad outlines have remained consistent. Each new version is identified by a four-digit string, where the first two digits represent the year and the last two represent the half of the year the release belongs to. The initial release of Windows 11, for example, was version 21H2, reflecting its launch date in the second half of 2021.

A separate build number keeps track of feature update versions. The initial release of Windows 11, for example, was build 22000, and the first feature update, version 22H2, was build 22621. A version identifier for each monthly cumulative update is appended to that build number.

To see which Windows version is installed on a device, go to Settings > System > About. The example in Figure 1-5 shows a PC running Windows 11 version 21H2 with the July 2022 cumulative update (OS Build 22000.675) installed.

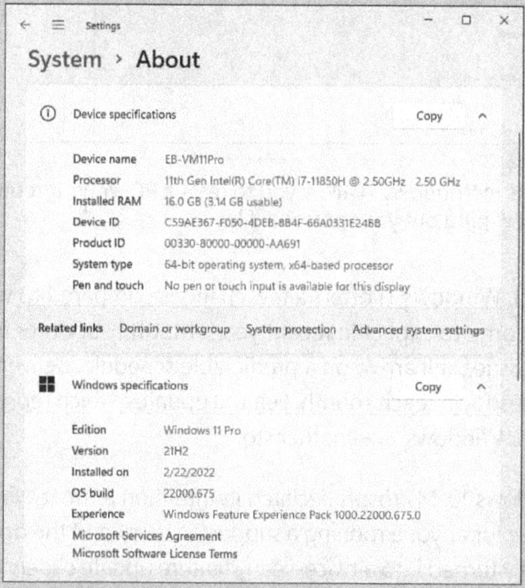

Figure 1-5   The Version and OS Build fields on this page show which feature update is currently installed; the number following the decimal point identifies which monthly cumulative update is installed.

You can also check version information by running the Windows Version Reporter app, Winver.exe, which displays the version string and build information in a classic Win32 dialog. If you prefer a command line, you can run the Ver command from a Command Prompt session; that returns the full Windows NT version string—on the system shown earlier in Figure 1-5, that command returns the version 10.0.22621.232. And no, that's not an error. Windows 10 and Windows 11 share the same Windows NT version, 10.0, a reflection of just how similar the two operating system versions are at their core.

Any device running any edition of Windows 11 is eligible for feature updates. After Microsoft declares a new feature update complete, the new version goes to PC manufacturers and to the general public through Windows Update in a gradual release that can take months to complete. Each feature update appears first as an optional update, with Microsoft offering the new release to devices that its algorithms identify as most likely to have a problem-free upgrade. Throughout the rollout, Windows engineers use diagnostic data and feedback from the first wave of installations to identify and resolve issues, widening the rollout as it identifies and fixes compatibility and reliability issues associated with specific hardware and software configurations. In business settings, network administrators can set their own deployment schedules, using Group Policy settings to defer both monthly updates and feature updates from being installed automatically while they test for compatibility issues.

The new update process also allows Windows users to opt in to the Windows Insider Program, which allows them to receive feature updates ahead of the general public. Insider builds are delivered in different channels that allow Microsoft to collect feedback about new features and identify bugs and compatibility issues before they reach the General Availability channel.

NOTE

Since the dawn of the Windows 10 era, Microsoft has changed the terminology for its public Windows release channels so many times, even we have trouble remembering the twists and turns. Previously, consumer and business releases were on separate timetables, called the Current Branch and Current Branch for Business, respectively. These were renamed to the Semi-Annual Channel (Targeted) and Semi-Annual Channel, and then the two channels were combined into a single Semi-Annual Channel. With the move to annual feature updates comes yet another name change: The one and only release channel for Windows 11 is the General Availability Channel.

Microsoft's developers receive unprecedented levels of feedback that shape the development effort in real time. That feedback comes from automated data collection (known formally as *diagnostics* and informally as *telemetry*) as well as from a Feedback Hub app, shown in Figure 1-6, which is installed with every Windows 11 release.

CHAPTER 1

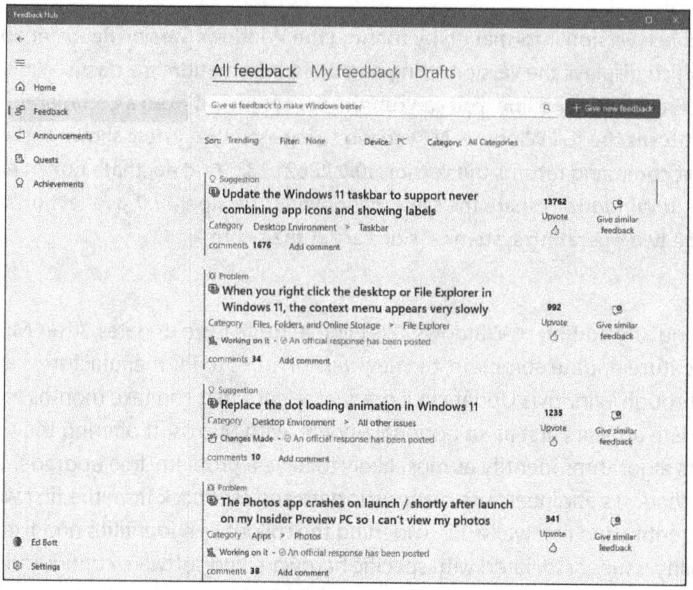

Figure 1-6   The Feedback Hub app allows anyone using Windows to report bugs and offer suggestions directly to Microsoft.

> ➤ **For more details on how Windows preview releases work, see Appendix B, "The Windows Insider Program."**

User experience

We devote two full chapters (3 and 4) to using and customizing the Windows 11 user interface, but we offer a quick overview here. Our lightning tour of the Windows 11 user experience starts at the lock screen, which hints at a few of the security features we talk about later. Note that instead of entering a password here, we can use a PIN assigned to this device, as shown in Figure 1-7. On devices that support Windows Hello biometric authentication, you can skip that step completely and sign in automatically using facial recognition or a fingerprint.

After you successfully sign in, you're taken to the desktop. The taskbar runs along the bottom, as it has in every Windows version since the beginning of time, but in Windows 11 the taskbar is centered rather than being aligned on the left. At the left side of the taskbar is the familiar Start button, represented by a stylized Windows logo. Clicking that button opens the Start menu, as shown in Figure 1-8.

CHAPTER 1

Figure 1-7   The Windows 11 lock screen offers the option to sign in using a PIN instead of a password. The profile pictures on the left allow for switching between user accounts.

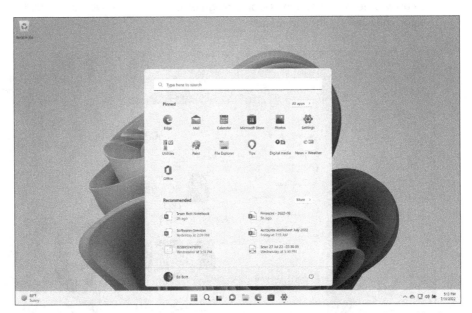

Figure 1-8   The Windows 11 menu is radically simple compared to earlier versions, with a bare minimum of customization options.

In comparison with earlier incarnations, the Windows 11 Start menu has a radically simple lay-out, with a search box along the top, a Pinned section that holds shortcuts for pinned apps, a Recommended section that holds shortcuts to recently opened files, and a bottom row that holds only a profile picture and a power button by default. Beginning with version 22H2, you can combine multiple pinned apps into named folders to help keep icon overload in check. Clicking the All Apps button leads to an expanded list of installed apps, which you can open, pin, or uninstall.

The size of the new Start menu is fixed and can't be adjusted, and it's possible to make only the most minimal changes to the Start menu layout. You can adjust the relative size of Pinned and Recommended sections, and you can add shortcuts to commonly used data folders in the space to the left of the power button, but that's about it.

Clicking the search button on the taskbar has the same effect as clicking in the search box at the top of the Start menu. The Pinned and Recommended items disappear, replaced by a list of recent searches and documents. Typing a word, name, phrase, or question in the search box replaces its contents with the results for that search box, delivered using Microsoft's Bing search engine. (And no, it's not possible to choose an alternate search engine for this feature.)

In many cases, you can get the answer you're looking for without having to open a web browser, as in the example in Figure 1-9. The expanded search results pane can also be used to look up weather forecasts, sports scores, biographies, currency conversions, a full-featured cal-culator, and even a built-in translator.

Figure 1-9   Typing a word, phrase, or question into the search box on the Start menu produces instant results, often obviating the need to open a web browser and look any further.

At the leftmost edge of the taskbar, in the spot where the Start menu used to sit, is an icon that shows the weather for the current location. Clicking that target opens a large Widgets pane like the one shown in Figure 1-10, filled with news headlines, an expanded weather report, stock quotes, and other tidbits of information.

Figure 1-10   Click the weather icon at the far left of the taskbar to open this Widgets pane.

The Widgets pane is customizable, with the ability to add calendar items and tasks from the Microsoft To Do app, build custom stock watchlists, and fine-tune news headlines. If you find the taskbar shortcut distracting, you can remove it and summon the Widgets pane with the keyboard shortcut Windows key + W.

Another key part of the Windows user experience has received a major visual reworking in Windows 11. The Settings app debuted in 2012 with Windows 8, and its evolution accelerated under Windows 10. Over nearly a decade, Microsoft's designers and engineers have been steadily moving user controls from the old Control Panel to their new home. That work continues in Windows 11, accompanied by a new design that moves the major categories to a navigation pane on the left and arranges subcategories in sliding panels to their right. The Bluetooth & Devices pane, shown in Figure 1-11, is a particularly elegant example of the new design.

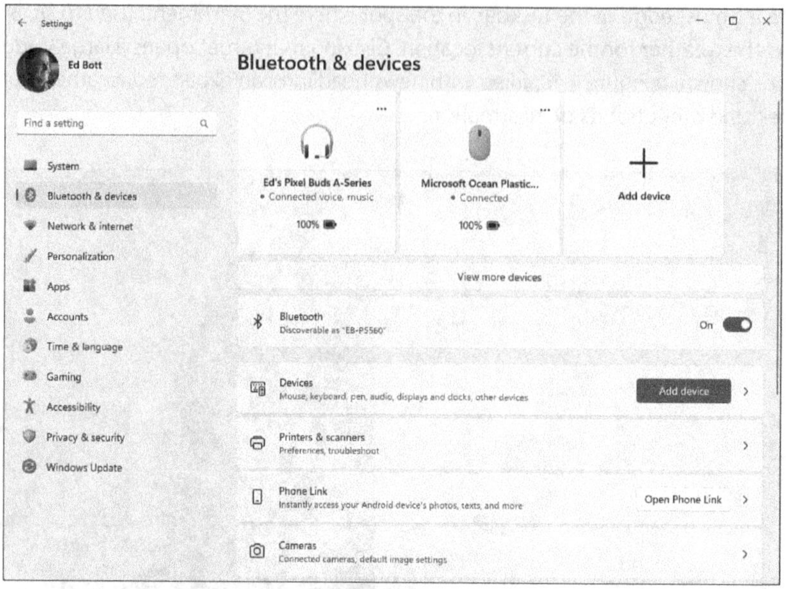

CHAPTER 1

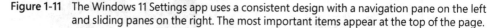

Figure 1-11   The Windows 11 Settings app uses a consistent design with a navigation pane on the left and sliding panes on the right. The most important items appear at the top of the page.

One significant new feature of Windows 11 that isn't immediately obvious is a set of controls that help you arrange multiple windows for maximum efficiency. Hover the mouse pointer over the Minimize button in the upper-right corner of any window to see your options, as shown in Figure 1-12. You can position windows side by side, move a window into a specific quadrant, or even snap three windows into vertical arrangements of differing sizes. (The available arrangements depend on the screen real estate, with larger displays offering maximum flexibility.)

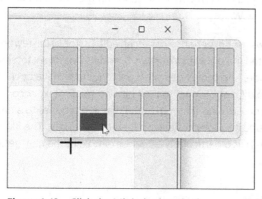

Figure 1-12   Click the Minimize icon in the upper-right corner of any window to display this list of window arrangement options. (Exact choices vary depending on available screen real estate.)

Windows 11 and the web

With Windows 11, Microsoft has finally retired one of the oldest members of the Windows family. The Internet Explorer desktop application, which debuted more than a quarter-century ago as the default web browser in Windows 95, is disabled in Windows 11. If you try running its familiar executable, Iexplore.exe, from a command line, you're redirected to Microsoft Edge, the new default web browser for Windows.

This change represents the final step in the transformation of Internet Explorer. The browser began its slide into obsolescence with the release of Windows 10 in 2015, when Microsoft released a new browser called Microsoft Edge, which was based on the same rendering engine as Internet Explorer. That legacy version of Microsoft Edge was then replaced in 2020 by a completely new browser using the same name but built on the open-source Chromium codebase, which is at the core of Google's Chrome browser.

If all that sounds hopelessly confusing, you're not alone. (Good luck using your favorite search engine to uncover the differences between the new Edge and the legacy Edge.)

From a usability perspective, however, the transformation makes the web-browsing experience notably less painful. Because the new Edge shares a codebase with the popular Google Chrome, it should feel familiar to longtime Chrome users; more importantly, that common codebase means browsing with Edge won't result in the kind of compatibility problems that plagued the legacy Edge.

So, what makes the new Microsoft Edge different from Google Chrome? The most striking feature is a set of strong privacy controls that prevent websites from tracking your movements online. You can see a portion of the Edge Settings page for this set of features in Figure 1-13.

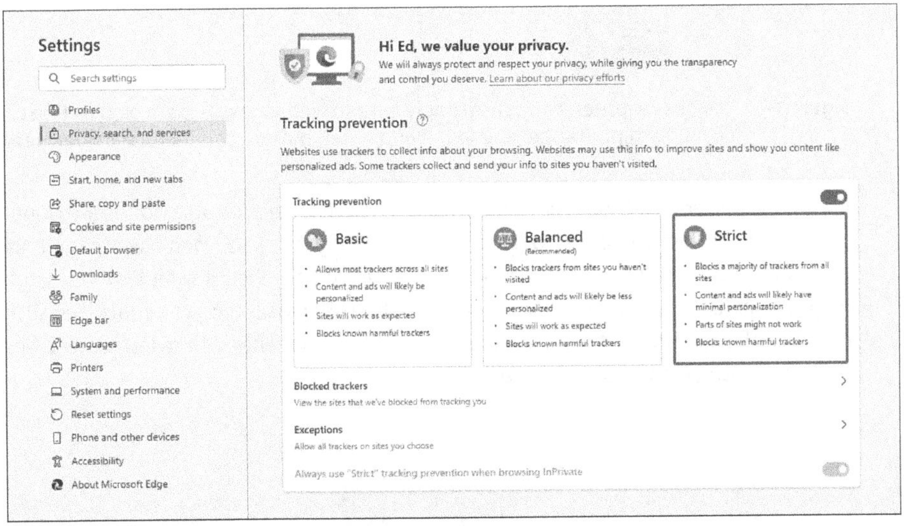

Figure 1-13   The new Microsoft Edge includes these tracking prevention controls. With Strict mode on, the feature functions as an effective ad blocker.

The new Edge browser is updated regularly, with a new version in the Stable channel arriving roughly every four weeks. (Enterprise customers have the option of an Extended Stable option that uses an eight-week release cycle.) You can also expand the browser's capability through the addition of extensions, which you acquire from the Microsoft Store or directly from Google's Chrome Web Store.

The new Edge also includes an intriguing feature called Collections, which enhances your ability to perform web-based research. This feature offers a way to organize shortcuts to websites, snippets of text, product details, images, and other web-based content that can then be shared easily with other people. Figure 1-14 shows an example of a collection pinned to the Edge sidebar.

Figure 1-14   Unlike Favorites, which are simply links to webpages, items in a collection can also include snippets of text, images, and notes, making this feature an ideal research tool.

Internet Explorer may be officially deprecated, and its obvious entry points are gone for good, but it's not completely banished from Windows 11. If you try to open a webpage that requires Internet Explorer, Edge can open it in IE Mode, which uses the Internet Explorer rendering engine in an Edge tab, complete with support for otherwise defunct capabilities such as ActiveX controls. This feature is of most use in enterprise deployments, where legacy web applications survive for use on company intranets.

Because Microsoft Edge is such a rich, full-featured product, we've devoted an entire chapter to it. Even if you prefer another browser, we recommend reading through Chapter 7, "Using Microsoft Edge," to learn more about its inner workings.

Cloud connections

Throughout this book, we assume most of our readers are signing in to Windows 11 with a Microsoft account (free to individuals) or an Azure Active Directory account associated with their organization. Although it's possible to sign in using a local account and avoid cloud-based services completely, using an online account managed by Microsoft unlocks access to a variety of valuable cloud services.

Some of the benefits of signing in with a Microsoft account occur automatically, with no effort required on your part. For example, the system drive is automatically encrypted on a device that supports Modern Standby, and the encryption recovery key is backed up to cloud storage using the Microsoft account. In addition, saved passwords, language preferences, and other Windows settings automatically sync across devices, making setup easier when you sign in to multiple devices. You can also opt to sync the contents of the Windows Clipboard between devices that sign in using the same Microsoft account.

In addition, you'll need a Microsoft account to download apps (free and paid) from the Microsoft Store. As we explain in Chapter 5, the Store has been completely redesigned for Windows 11, and apps available through the Store include not just so-called modern apps but also many traditional Windows desktop apps that previously required manual downloads and updates.

When you create a free Microsoft account, the package includes access to Outlook.com email and calendar services with 15 GB of free storage. That same account includes an additional 5 GB of free cloud storage in OneDrive. If the account is associated with a Microsoft 365 subscription, the OneDrive allocation increases to a total of 1 TB of cloud storage for personal files. That's a lot of online storage space.

The OneDrive synchronization client installed with Windows 11 supports connections to cloud storage from the consumer version of OneDrive and its professional counterpart, OneDrive for Business, with synced files and folders available in File Explorer. That sync client supports a feature called Files On-Demand, which allows you to see all cloud files in File Explorer, even if they're not synced to the local device. By default, Windows 11 syncs the contents of the Desktop, Documents, and Pictures folders to OneDrive, as shown in Figure 1-15. Having those backup files saved automatically makes recovery easier after a hardware failure or even when a PC is compromised by a ransomware attack.

Figure 1-15   Signing in with a Microsoft account enables automatic backup of these key data folders to OneDrive.

> ➤ For more information about how OneDrive and Windows 11 work together, see Chapter 8, "Managing local and cloud storage."

Windows 11 apps and the new Microsoft Store

Longtime Windows users are familiar with two types of Windows apps. Legacy desktop apps (sometimes referred to as Win32 apps) still account for much of the productivity work people do on PCs and are fully supported on Windows 11. This category includes stalwarts like Microsoft Word, Microsoft Excel, and other members of the Office family, as well as a practically endless list of third-party apps.

A handful of legacy desktop apps, in fact, are included with a default installation of Windows 11, including Windows Media Player, Microsoft Paint, and WordPad. Most of those legacy apps are in maintenance mode at this point and haven't changed in more than a decade; they remain a part of Windows largely because of inertia and because some Windows users have long-established workflows that depend on them. In Windows 11, the Windows Accessories and Windows Administrative Tools folders, where most of these legacy apps were filed in previous Windows versions, are no longer on the Start menu; to find legacy desktop apps, you'll need to use the Search box.

A second category of apps includes those designed and packaged to work on any device running Windows 10 or Windows 11. Some of these apps are provisioned automatically with a new

Windows installation; others are downloaded from the Microsoft Store. In either case, because these apps can be updated automatically via the Store, they can incorporate new features and bug fixes without requiring a separate installation, as is usually the case with legacy desktop apps.

It's tempting to think of legacy apps and Store apps as living in separate universes, but that's no longer the case. Over time, Windows application programming interfaces (APIs) have evolved, allowing developers of traditional desktop apps to deliver and update those apps through the Microsoft Store; the list of apps that have been repackaged in this fashion includes some mega-hits like iTunes and Spotify Music, as you can see in the Store listings in Figure 1-16.

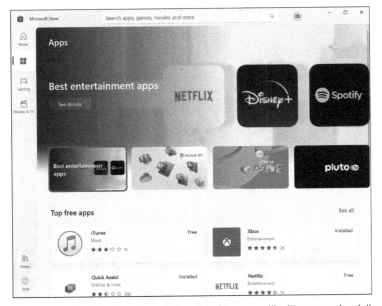

Figure 1-16 In Windows 11, traditional desktop apps like iTunes can be delivered and updated through the Microsoft Store.

An additional set of APIs supports *Progressive Web Apps*, which are built on the same foundation and open standards as the web but allow features that aren't available in a browser—working offline, for example, or accessing hardware directly. You'll find more details about all of these app types in Chapter 5, "Installing and configuring apps."

Windows 11 includes a lengthy list of productivity, entertainment, and news and information apps as part of a default installation. These apps can also sync settings and data between devices where you're signed in with the same Microsoft account. When you set up a new Windows 11 device, this feature allows you to switch devices and pick up where you left off without having to reconfigure accounts or import data.

CHAPTER 1

The productivity apps provisioned with Windows 11 include the Mail, Calendar, and To Do apps that are also part of Windows 10. New in Windows 11 is a consumer-focused version of Microsoft Teams that allows you to chat with other Teams users (on PCs and mobile devices) and participate in video calls and online meetings, even with people who aren't using Microsoft Teams. Figure 1-17 shows the screen you see when setting up an online meeting using the free version of Microsoft Teams.

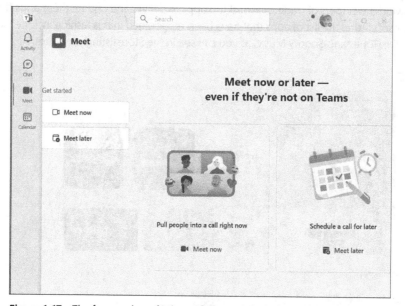

Figure 1-17   The free version of Microsoft Teams is included with Windows 11 and allows a wide range of communications, including online meetings with live video and audio.

Windows 11 also includes an assortment of entertainment apps and casual games (the Microsoft Solitaire Collection is included with every edition). A noteworthy addition to Windows 11 is the Media Player app, which replaces Windows 10's Groove Music app. (Confusingly, it's not related to the legacy Windows Media Player app, which is also included with Windows 11.)

One common misconception about Windows apps from the Microsoft Store is that they're light and underpowered. That might have been a valid criticism of Store apps in the Windows 8 era and even in the early days of Windows 10, but the Windows API now allows developers to build full-featured Store apps using a variety of tools. By design, those apps are more secure and easier to update than Win32 apps that require a separate download and installation.

➤ For more information about apps and utilities included with Windows 11, see Chapter 6, "Using and managing built-in Windows apps."

Security

Windows 11 incorporates many of the same hardware-based security features built into Windows 10, with a notable difference: Those features are no longer optional but are instead incorporated into the hardware requirements for Windows 11. They are also, in most cases, enabled by default.

From a security standpoint, the most prominent part of the new hardware lineup is a cryptographic processor called a Trusted Platform Module (TPM), which can be embedded on a motherboard as a discrete chip or integrated into a CPU or chipset as part of a system design. In Windows 11, the TPM serves as a secure repository for cryptographic keys that are used for encrypting data, supporting hardware-based authentication, and ensuring that the operating system hasn't been tampered with—by malware, for example, or by an attacker trying to bypass Windows security to access data on the device.

Modern hardware designed for Windows 11 starts up from a Unified Extensible Firmware Interface (UEFI) rather than an old-fashioned BIOS. That hardware design, in turn, enables a Windows security feature called Secure Boot, which protects your PC from an insidious form of malware called *rootkits*. After successfully booting, Windows uses virtualization-based security to protect crucial parts of the operating system, including user credentials, from being compromised by malicious exploits.

Most of these hardware-dependent features are essentially invisible in operation. To monitor their activity and to provide tools for troubleshooting potential security issues, Windows 11 includes a utility called Windows Security. Its dashboard, shown in Figure 1-18, provides an overview of security subsystems, with a green check mark confirming that things are running smoothly and red or yellow indicators highlighting potential problems.

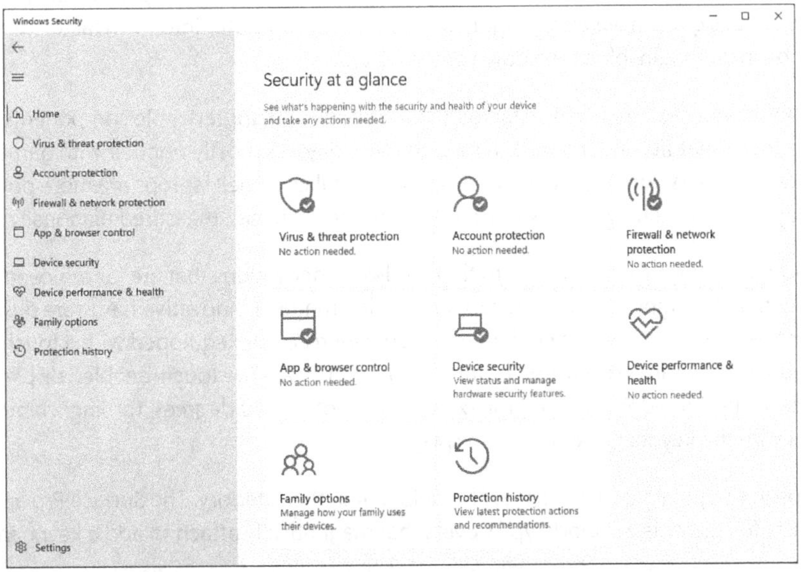

CHAPTER 1

Figure 1-18   You can monitor and configure the full set of user-facing security features from this dashboard in the Windows Security app.

Each of the categories listed here can be configured with minimal technical knowledge, making this the primary window into security on Windows 11 PCs running in homes and small offices where a full-time IT department isn't available. Corporate customers can use Microsoft Defender for Business, which provides additional monitoring and management tools for multi-platform environments.

Other core security features of the operating system are enabled by default, including the antivirus software included with every installation of Windows 11. (If you or your organization have installed an alternative security software solution, Microsoft Defender Antivirus steps aside gracefully.)

More advanced security options include multifactor authentication options for PCs as well as BitLocker Disk Encryption, which is available on PCs running Windows 11 Pro or Enterprise editions. (Modern PCs running Windows 11 Home provide device encryption for the system drive, but only if the user signs in with a Microsoft account.)

Privacy options in Windows 11 are extensive, with the most confusing choices revolving around the diagnostic data (sometimes referred to as telemetry) that Microsoft collects as part of its product improvement efforts. Recent feature updates include a new tool called the Diagnostic Data Viewer, which allows you to inspect the diagnostic data being sent to Microsoft under your current privacy settings. We discuss all of these topics in detail in Chapter 12, "Windows security and privacy."

Windows 11 and hardware

Mobile devices have made it possible to accomplish tasks that once required a desktop computer, but smartphones and tablets have yet to replace the PC. In the past decade, however, hardware designers have transmogrified the personal computer into form factors that would have been unimaginable at the dawn of the PC era.

The traditional desktop PC form factor is still around, with upgradeable components installed into a tower that fits under a desk, although these days it's mostly popular with gamers and corporate customers. Among retail buyers, conventional clamshell laptops are more popular, with displays that typically range in size from 13 inches to 17 inches, measured diagonally.

But you don't have to look too far to find hardware innovations that are far removed from those conventional designs. Windows 11 supports a wide range of innovative hardware designs that break the traditional mold, including so-called *hybrid devices*, equipped with a touchscreen and a keyboard that can be detached or folded out of the way. The touch-enabled displays in Lenovo's perfectly named Yoga series, for example, can rotate 360 degrees, turning a laptop into a tablet with the keyboard behind the display.

Microsoft's popular Surface devices also help define the category. The Surface Pro and Surface Go, for example, support Type Covers that magnetically attach to add a keyboard and a precision touchpad. The Surface Book series looks and acts like a traditional laptop until you push the Detach button and remove the screen from the base. When you remove the keyboard from the display, a Surface device becomes a tablet; add a Surface Pen and that tablet becomes a sketchbook or notepad.

The defining characteristic of these next-generation Windows devices is a touchscreen. On touchscreen-equipped laptops, you can choose to perform a task by tapping the screen or by using the keyboard and touchpad. Removing the keyboard automatically increases the spacing between taskbar items, making it easier to use them as touch targets; that action also displays the touch keyboard icon in the notification area and automatically pops it up when you tap in a box where you're expected to enter text.

Windows 11 fully supports PCs powered by Arm processors, which use chips more commonly found in mobile devices like smartphones rather than Intel and AMD CPUs from the x86 family. Arm-powered PCs like the Surface Pro 9 run most Windows desktop apps in x86 emulation mode and are likely to have issues with hardware drivers that haven't been compiled for the Arm architecture.

Regardless of form factor, every Windows 11 PC includes a core set of hardware components that occasionally need adjustment, including display, audio hardware, and network connections. One new feature on the Windows 11 taskbar is intended to simplify the task of adjusting those common settings without having to open the Settings app. Clicking or tapping any of the three icons to the left of the system date opens a compact mini control panel like the one shown in Figure 1-19.

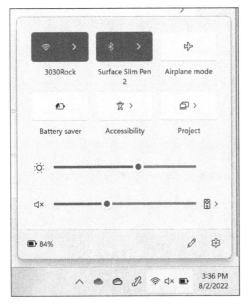

Figure 1-19   This compact Quick Settings panel offers easy access to a wide range of useful settings and can be customized.

From here, you can adjust the display brightness and audio volume, change network settings, and get an instant readout of remaining battery life on a laptop.

We offer details on how to be productive with the Windows 11 user experience on traditional PCs and touchscreen-equipped devices in Chapter 3, "Using Windows 11." Our coverage of customization options is in Chapter 4, "Personalizing Windows 11."

CHAPTER 2

Setting up a new Windows 11 PC

Setting up a Windows PC is not something most people are likely to do often. Many people, in fact, encounter the Windows Installer (Setup.exe) only once every few years, during the upgrade from one major Windows version to the next or when turning on a new PC for the first time and going through the brief Out Of Box Experience (OOBE). In either case, the process is relatively quick and uncomplicated.

That's certainly not the case for those who manage, deploy, repair, and tinker with Windows PCs. If you count yourself among that group, a handful of Windows 11 installation programs are an essential part of your management and troubleshooting toolkit, and you'll benefit from knowing about some of Setup's advanced options in a variety of scenarios.

This chapter covers the two most common Windows 11 installation scenarios: upgrading a device that is currently running Windows 10 and performing a clean install on a new or freshly formatted disk. (You'll also find details on how to perform an edition upgrade—from Windows 11 Home to Pro, for example.)

Although Microsoft tries to discourage customers from installing Windows 11 on older, unsupported hardware, you can indeed accomplish that task. In fact, Microsoft's support pages helpfully document exactly how to do so, as this chapter explains.

And, of course, no discussion of Windows installations would be complete without a thorough examination of product keys, digital licenses, and the ins and outs of Windows product activation. But first, let's make sure you've prepared your PC for a successful installation, starting with a hardware check.

Backing up data and settings

Having an up-to-date backup of important files is, of course, good advice for any time. But it's especially important when you're upgrading an operating system.

The simplest way to back up your data files is to sync them to a cloud storage service, such as OneDrive, Dropbox, or Google Drive. With your files saved in the cloud, you can sync them to a new PC at your convenience, after the upgrade is complete.

With large file collections or slow internet connections—or if you just prefer not putting your files in cloud storage—a sufficiently large USB flash drive or an external hard drive makes a perfectly good target for a local backup. You can use any backup app, including the legacy Windows 7 Backup And Restore tool (which is included with Windows 10 and Windows 11). If you're more comfortable with a third-party backup app or even with the command-line-driven Robo-Copy, by all means use those tools. The most important consideration is to carefully test your backups to confirm that you really can restore your files (For a complete look at your options, see Chapter 15, "Troubleshooting, backup, and recovery.")

If you're upgrading from Windows 10 and you signed in with a Microsoft account, some of your personalized settings are already being synced to OneDrive, as are settings for apps installed by way of the Microsoft Store. For other apps, the simplest solution is to reinstall and reconfigure them manually. Although you can find third-party utilities that promise to accomplish this task, it's usually just as fast (and less risky) to re-create that handful of settings than it is to mess with transfer utilities. A far more important task is to ensure that you have product keys or other license details for any third-party software that might require reinstallation or reactivation.

Downloading and creating installation media

Regardless of which installation scenario you choose—clean install or upgrade—you need Windows installer files. For an online upgrade, the simplest option uses the Windows 11 Installation Assistant, which automatically downloads those files to a temporary folder and discards them after the upgrade is complete. For a clean install, you need physical installation media, typically a bootable USB flash drive. (You can also use a bootable DVD, although this option is unnecessary on modern hardware.) For upgrades and reinstallations, you can use physical media or download an ISO file and mount its contents as a virtual DVD drive.

NOTE

An ISO file (sometimes referred to as an *ISO image*) contains the contents of an entire optical disc in a single uncompressed file. The ISO name is shorthand for the file system originally used with CD-ROM media, which was designated ISO 9660 by the standards-setting body that published it. These days, an ISO image file is more likely to use the UDF file system (ISO/IEC 13346), which is commonly found on larger-capacity optical media such as DVDs and Blu-ray discs. Although physical DVD data discs are rarely used these days, ISO files are still useful for sharing installation media, especially when setting up virtual machines.

You can still buy a physical copy of Windows 11 in a package that includes installation files on a bootable USB flash drive or a DVD. In the modern era, this option offers few advantages. Given the annual feature update schedule for Windows 11, that physical media will most likely be out of date on the day it's purchased. On even a modest broadband connection, it takes little time to download the latest version and create your own fresh installation media.

NOTE

Microsoft makes only the most recent versions of Windows 11 and Windows 10, in retail editions, available for download on its public website. IT pros, software developers, and Volume License customers can download a much wider range of ISO image files, including older Windows versions and specialized editions. If you have a Visual Studio subscription or a Microsoft Partner Program membership, you can access this expanded selection after signing in to the online portal for the respective service. Volume License customers will find ISO files for Pro, Enterprise, and Education editions at the Volume Licensing Service Center.

To get started, go to the Download Windows 11 page (*https://aka.ms/downloadwindows11*), which supports three options:

- **Windows 11 Installation Assistant**   This simple tool is designed for upgrading PCs that are running a supported version of Windows 10 (version 2004 or later). Download the tool and click Run to perform a compatibility check. If the hardware meets Microsoft's requirements, the app downloads the most recent release of Windows 11 and performs the upgrade.

- **Create Windows 11 Installation Media**   Use this option to download the Windows 11 Media Creation Tool, which helps you create a bootable USB flash drive containing the most recent installation files for Windows 11. You will, of course, need to supply a USB flash drive with a capacity of 8 GB or more. (You'll find more details on how to use this tool later in this chapter.)

- **Download Windows 11 Disk Image (ISO)**   If you know how to work with ISO files, this option is incredibly versatile, allowing you to access the files as a virtual DVD drive on any device or to copy them to a bootable device such as a USB flash drive. And you can back up the file for later use, saving time and bandwidth if you have multiple PCs to upgrade.

Using the Media Creation Tool

The Media Creation Tool is a small file (less than 10 MB in size) that takes only seconds to download and runs a bootstrap version of Windows Setup. If you've used the Windows 10 version of this utility, you already know that it offers minimal options; for Windows 11, it includes even fewer choices. After running the tool and accepting a license agreement, you should see a screen with two dropdown options—one for language and another for edition—as shown in Figure 2-1.

CHAPTER 2

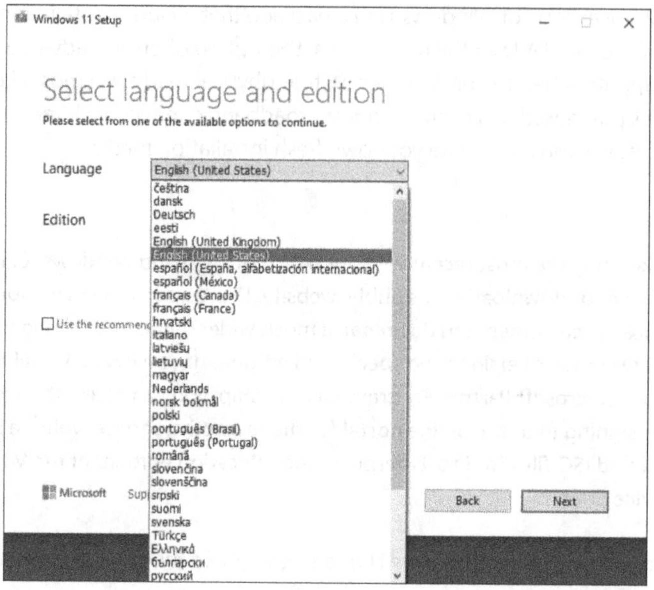

Figure 2-1   When downloading Windows installation files, choose the base language that matches your regional settings. You can add other languages after installation is complete.

Windows 11 is available in a large number of base languages that determine how Windows displays menus, system messages, and other parts of the core user interface. After installation is complete, you can add language interface packs to change regional settings (such as time and date formats and currency) and to translate text that's displayed in commonly used wizards, dialogs, menus, and other items in the user interface; however, you can't change the base language except by reinstalling Windows using an edition built for that language.

For most people, the correct response is to click Next and move on. In the unlikely event you're downloading a version of Windows to install in a region other than the one where your PC is currently situated, clear the Use The Recommended Options For This PC checkbox and then select your preferred language settings. Then click Next.

Regardless of your language settings, this option takes you to the step shown in Figure 2-2.

> ➤ Note that you can download installation files regardless of whether you have a Windows license. For more about the intricacies of Windows licensing, see "Activating Windows," later in this chapter.

Insert a USB flash drive with a capacity of at least 8 GB. (Before proceeding, back up any important files on the drive, as the Media Creation Tool will format the drive as part of its operation.) Click Next and follow the prompts to select your drive and create the bootable installation media. Label the drive and keep it in a safe place for future installation-related tasks.

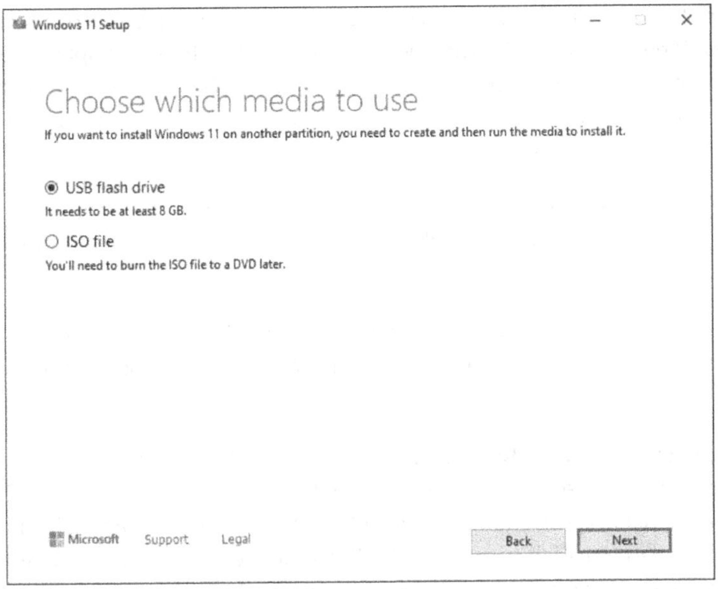

Figure 2-2   Use the default Media Creation Tool options to create a bootable USB flash drive that will allow installing Windows 11 on any modern PC.

Working with ISO files directly

The Media Creation Tool takes much of the drudgery out of creating bootable Windows installation media. But it's not the only way to acquire the files needed to run Windows Setup. As an alternative, use the third option on the Download Windows 11 page to retrieve the installation files in a single file, saved using ISO format.

The biggest advantage of an ISO file is that it's easy to access from a local drive, which can be advantageous if your internet connection is slow or you're subject to a data cap. You can save an ISO file in the Downloads folder on your primary PC; from there, you can archive it to an external hard drive, sync it to a cloud service like OneDrive, or transfer it over a local area network. The next time you need to lay your hands on Windows 11 installation files, you don't need to wait for it to download from Microsoft's servers.

What can you do with an ISO file? The three most productive ways to put your ISO download to use are to mount the file as a virtual DVD drive, burn it to a DVD, or use it to create a bootable USB flash drive.

Every supported Windows version allows you to double-click an ISO file to mount it as a virtual DVD drive. The mounted drive appears in File Explorer with its own drive letter. You can run Windows Setup directly from a mounted drive, or copy files from that location to a fixed or removable drive for later use.

CHAPTER 2

It's also possible to burn a Windows 11 ISO to a DVD, which then can be used as bootable instal-lation media. There are few modern hardware configurations where that option makes much sense, but if you're so inclined, you can choose this option in File Explorer in Windows 10 or Windows 11. The Burn Image option is on the right-click shortcut menu and on the ribbon (Win-dows 10) or the command bar (Windows 11).

With an ISO file and a PC running Windows 10 or Windows 11, you can create your own instal-lation media with ease, using a process that is more versatile and quicker than using the Media Creation Tool.

You can't simply copy installation files to a USB flash drive and use it to perform a clean install, however. First, you have to make the disk bootable. When creating a bootable drive, you need to consider two factors:

- **Partitioning scheme: MBR or GPT?**   You can use a flash drive formatted using either scheme with a Unified Extensible Firmware Interface (UEFI) system; older BIOS-based systems are typically able to recognize only MBR partitions. (For an explanation of the dif-ference and a discussion of the new MBR2GPT tool, see "Setting up hard disks and other storage devices" in Chapter 8, "Managing local and cloud storage.")

- **Disk format: NTFS or FAT32?**   Installing Windows 11 on a modern UEFI-based system requires that the boot files reside on a FAT32 partition on the flash drive. If the drive is for-matted using another file system, the PC will not recognize the device as bootable.

One of the simplest ways to create a bootable install drive is to use the built-in Recovery Media Creator tool, RecoveryDrive.exe. To run the Recovery Media Creator tool, type RecoveryDrive in the search box and then choose the Recovery Drive app from the search results. (Or, if you pre-fer, search for the Create A Recovery Drive option in Control Panel or Settings.) Figure 2-3 shows this tool in operation.

In both Windows 10 and Windows 11, the Back Up System Files To The Recovery Drive option can be used to create a bootable drive that includes the recovery partition provided by the OEM. If you performed a clean install of Windows, or if you previously removed that recovery partition to reclaim disk space, this option has no effect, and the recovery drive includes only the most essential repair tools.

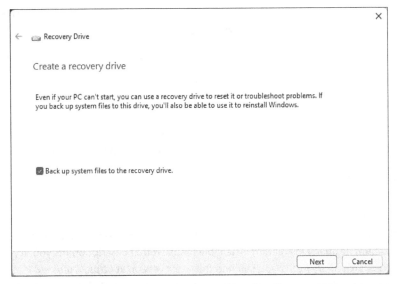

Figure 2-3   Choose the option to back up system files if you want to create a recovery drive using a Windows image preinstalled by an OEM; you can use that image later to reset the current system.

TROUBLESHOOTING

You are unable to create installation media because the Windows image file is too large.

Installation files you download using the Media Creation Tool are specifically designed for use with USB flash drives. If, however, you are trying to use custom installation images, including those downloaded as ISO files from Microsoft's official Visual Studio subscription site, you might encounter a frustrating compatibility issue related to the FAT32 disk format used by bootable flash drives.

To perform a clean install on a device that uses UEFI firmware, the bootable USB flash drive must be formatted using FAT32. But the FAT32 disk format limits file sizes to a maximum of 4 GB. Because many ISO downloads from Microsoft's Visual Studio subscription site include Windows Image (.wim) files that are larger than 4GB, they won't fit on a USB flash drive that's formatted using FAT32.

There are solutions, although none are particularly appealing. You can create a multipartition USB drive, for example, using advanced Windows deployment tools. Or you can store the installation image on a separate removable drive, formatted using NTFS, which might require you to boot from a FAT32-formatted recovery drive, start Setup.exe, remove the recovery drive, and plug in the new drive containing your installation media. Or you can store the installation image on a network location or split the image files.

For the daunting but detailed instructions for all these scenarios, see
https://bit.ly/deploy-single-usb-drive.

CHAPTER 2

On a PC running Windows 10 or Windows 11, you can use a downloaded Windows 11 ISO file to make your own bootable installation media, following these steps:

1. Create a blank recovery drive using the steps described earlier, skipping the option to copy system files to the drive.

2. Double-click the ISO file to mount it as a virtual DVD.

3. Use File Explorer to drag all files and folders from the virtual DVD to the USB recovery drive. (If prompted, choose the option to overwrite files on the destination drive.)

4. Label the USB drive and store it in a safe place.

NOTE

Although it's not necessary for most purposes, some people and organizations want maximum flexibility in creating installable media. If that description fits you, try the free, open-source utility Rufus; you can find the latest version at *https://rufus.ie/*. It allows precise control over partitioning, formatting, and copying installation files to a USB flash drive. If you encounter difficulties using the built-in Windows tools, this alternative can offer an easy solution.

Because the recovery drive is bootable, you can use it to access the Windows Recovery Environment on any Windows 10 or Windows 11 PC. And there's nothing wrong with copying other useful files to the recovery drive, including downloads of installation files for utilities you regularly use when setting up a new PC for the first time or performing maintenance tasks on an existing PC.

Windows 11 minimum hardware requirements

Microsoft publishes detailed minimum hardware requirements that PC makers must follow when building PCs to run Windows 11. Devices that meet these requirements should have no problem running Windows 11 and should perform acceptably with mainstream Windows apps and services.

As with previous versions, Windows 11 sets the bar fairly low for processor speed and memory, but you'll notice some increases compared to Windows 10, including a higher disk space requirement:

- **Processor**   1 gigahertz (GHz) or faster, 2 cores or more, from a supported processor generation and model.

- **System memory**   4 gigabytes (GB).

- **Storage**   64 GB or more.

- **Security**   Trusted Platform Module (TPM) 2.0, with UEFI Secure Boot enabled.

- **Display**   Microsoft DirectX 12 graphics device with WDDM 2.0 driver; integrated displays must be larger than 9 inches (measured diagonally) with a minimum resolution of 720p.

- **Connectivity**   Wi-Fi or Ethernet is required; on portable devices, Bluetooth is required.

- **Hardware buttons**   Power, Volume Up/Down.

- **Connectors**   At least one USB port, video output.

Two very big changes are worth noting here, representing a major shift from previous Windows hardware requirements. First is the requirement that a PC have a Trusted Platform Module (TPM) that meets the TPM 2.0 standard. Previous Windows versions recommended but did not require TPM support. Second, the PC's CPU must be included on Microsoft's list of supported processors; that requirement effectively eliminates most CPUs that were introduced before 2018.

On a PC running Windows 10 or Windows 11, you'll find CPU details in Settings > System > About, under the Device Specifications heading. To confirm that a processor is compatible with Windows 11, look for it on one of the following lists:

- Supported AMD Processors at *https://bit.ly/win11-compatible-cpu-amd*

- Supported Intel Processors at *https://bit.ly/win11-compatible-cpu-intel*

- Supported Qualcomm Processors at *https://bit.ly/win11-compatible-cpu-qualcomm*

These requirements don't just apply to new PCs. The Windows Installer (Setup.exe) blocks installation of Windows 11 when you try to upgrade a PC that falls short of those minimum requirements. (In some cases, you can override that block and install Windows 11, a topic we get to in a moment.)

If you buy a new PC with Windows 11 preinstalled from a Microsoft partner, you can be confident it meets those specifications. If you're upgrading a PC that was originally designed for Windows 10 or an earlier version, checking Windows 11 compatibility is a more challenging task. Save yourself the hassle of tracking down detailed spec sheets and use Microsoft's PC Health Check app to perform an automated compatibility inspection. Download the app from *https://aka.ms/GetPCHealthCheckApp* and then run the installer. Click the Check Now button under the Windows 11 heading to generate a report like the one shown in Figure 2-4.

CHAPTER 2

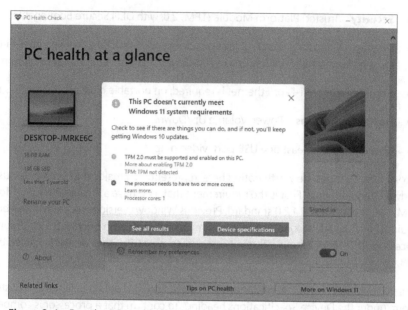

Figure 2-4   Run the PC Health Check app to identify potential hardware compatibility issues before trying to upgrade a Windows 10 PC.

That initial report is a simple pass/fail dialog that tells you whether the PC meets the minimum requirements for Windows 11. Click See All Results to view a detailed report.

Inside OUT

Watch out for software incompatibilities, too

If you're concerned about potential incompatibilities with installed software on a machine you plan to upgrade, the PC Health Check app won't offer much help. System utilities, including security software and low-level disk tools, are the most likely to inter-fere with an upgrade. In some cases, even otherwise benign drivers or utilities can cause problems. Before upgrading, it's a good idea to check the Windows release information status dashboard (*https://aka.ms/windowsreleasehealth*) for issues that are specific to your configuration.

Bypassing hardware compatibility issues

If Windows Setup stops after performing its initial compatibility check and informs you that your PC doesn't meet the minimum system requirements for running Windows 11, don't give up right away.

Some compatibility issues are strictly temporary. If Setup fails because of inadequate disk space, for example, you might be able to unblock the upgrade just by clearing out your Downloads and Videos folders. You can resolve some other compatibility issues by changing settings in your PC's firmware. On some PCs, for example, a TPM is installed but disabled by default. In that case, changing the TPM settings in firmware (and turning on Secure Boot, if needed) should allow the upgrade to proceed.

Even in more extreme compatibility issues, you have options. If your older PC has a processor that isn't on Microsoft's list of supported CPUs and has a TPM 1.2. version instead of the required TPM 2.0, you can still install Windows 11 using either of the following techniques:

- Boot from Windows 11 installation media and do a clean install. In this scenario, the Windows Installer skips the CPU check completely and accepts an older TPM version. Because this is a clean install, you can't migrate any apps or settings, and you have to restore data files from a backup.

- The second option allows you to upgrade from Windows 10 by modifying the registry; the technique is officially documented in a Microsoft support article, "Ways to install Windows 11," found at *https://bit.ly/override-win11-compat-check*. It bypasses the checks for CPU family and model but requires a TPM version 1.2 or later. The usual caveats apply when editing the registry—incorrect modifications can result in data loss or a system that fails to boot; make sure you have a backup first. In Registry Editor, go to the following key:

  HKEY_LOCAL_MACHINE\SYSTEM\Setup\MoSetup

  Add a new DWORD value, with the name **AllowUpgradesWithUnsupportedTPMOrCPU**, and set its value to **1**.

Restart your PC and try upgrading by opening installation media in File Explorer (a mounted ISO works fine). You see a stern warning, like the one shown in Figure 2-5.

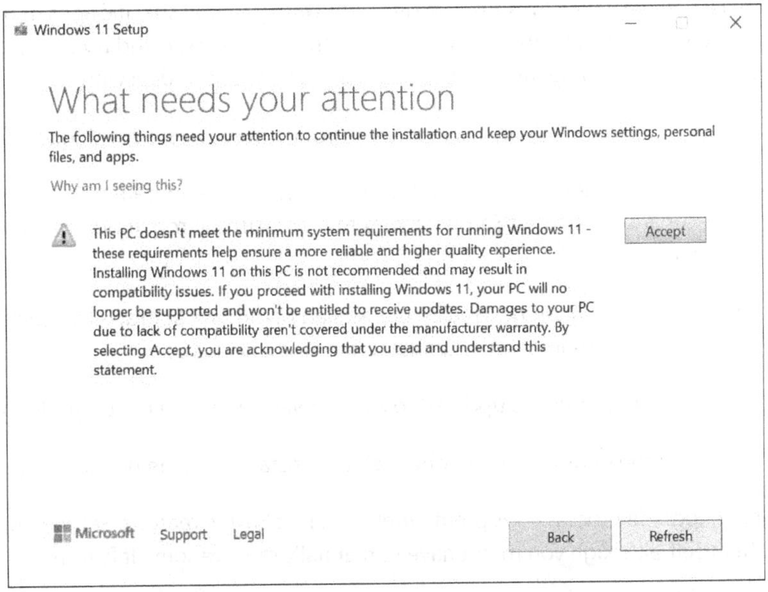

Figure 2-5   You need to read and acknowledge this warning before upgrading to Windows 11 on a PC whose hardware falls short of Microsoft's compatibility requirements.

Installing Windows 11

You use the Windows Installer (Setup.exe) for both in-place upgrades and clean installs. For upgrades, the installer is streamlined, offering a minimum of options. Booting from Windows installation media offers a much more complete set of options: choosing a specific physical disk for use in dual-boot (or multiboot) scenarios, creating and formatting partitions, and setting up unattended installations, for example.

This section covers both options. It doesn't include step-by-step instructions to document every possible upgrade or clean installation scenario. Given the nearly infinite number of combinations of PC hardware, providing comprehensive instructions would be impossible. But the Setup wizard is straightforward enough to allow for easy navigation under most scenarios.

How Windows 11 Setup works

The Windows Installer works in multiple stages, the details of which vary depending on whether you're performing an in-place upgrade or a custom installation. The process is extremely robust and is capable of recovering from a failure at any stage. If you've previously installed Windows 10, the general steps in Windows 11 should feel familiar, although the visual design is different.

Setup first performs a hardware compatibility check as discussed previously in this chapter. During this phase, Setup also inventories hardware and confirms that critical drivers are available (for storage and networking devices, for example). If any critical drivers are unavailable, or if Setup detects a BIOS or driver version that is known to cause errors, the installation process stops immediately and rolls back.

For less severe issues, Windows Setup might warn you that specific apps or devices might not work correctly. You might be given the option to fix the issue and try the upgrade again. In these cases, the compatibility checker offers instructions to deal with specific issues:

- You might need to install updates to your current version of Windows before continuing.

- You might need to suspend disk encryption before upgrading. (For common upgrade scenarios, Windows Setup handles this task without requiring any intervention on your part.)

- Some apps might need to be uninstalled before the upgrade can continue. (In most cases, they can be reinstalled after the upgrade is complete.)

- Some apps must be updated to a newer version before the upgrade can be completed.

- After the upgrade, you might need to reinstall language packs.

If the upgrade process ends prematurely for any of these reasons, Setup generally cleans up after itself, although you might have to manually remove some leftovers.

In either type of installation, the lengthiest stage occurs with Setup running offline in the Windows Preinstallation Environment (Windows PE), during which it backs up the previous Windows installation (if one exists) into a Windows.old folder and applies the new Windows 11 image.

The remaining stages of installation run after a restart, with the final stage consisting of what's known as the Out Of Box Experience (OOBE), where the user signs in and either creates a new profile or migrates an existing one as part of the upgrade. The most important part of the OOBE process is the creation of the primary user account, a topic covered in greater detail in Chapter 10, "Managing user accounts, passwords, and credentials."

For an upgrade, Setup uses several temporary folders:

- **C:\\$Windows.~BT**   This hidden folder contains the files used during both the online and the offline phases of installation. When you launch Setup from the Windows Installation Assistant, the initial phase of Setup creates this folder and copies the installation files to it for temporary use.

- **C:\\$WinREAgent**   During an upgrade or update, Setup creates this hidden folder, which stores files needed in case a rollback is necessary. If the installation is successful, these files are automatically deleted.

- **C:\Windows.old**   You'll see this folder, which is not hidden, only when you perform an upgrade or do a clean install on a volume that already contains a Windows installation. During upgrades, Setup uses this folder as a transfer location to hold files and settings that are moving from the old installation to the new one. After Windows Setup completes its work, the folder holds system files from the previous Windows installation as well as any user files that were not migrated during Setup.

  ## NOTE

  These temporary installation files are saved for 10 days, as is your previous Windows installation in Windows.old, allowing you to roll back to the previous version or recover files if necessary; after that time, they are deleted automatically. On systems with limited free disk space, you can remove these files using the Disk Cleanup utility or tools in Settings > System > Storage. We describe this process in more detail in Chapter 8.

If you poke around in the root of the system drive, you might notice additional hidden folders with similarly cryptic names: $Windows.~WS, for example, is created by the Media Creation Tool when you download Windows 11 installation files, and $GetCurrent is created when installing feature updates.

CHAPTER 2

Upgrading from Windows 10

A streamlined wizard walks you briskly through an upgrade from Windows 10. The process is fast, even on systems with a large number of files. No major upgrade is ever risk free, of course, but the Windows 11 installer, like its predecessor, is designed to be robust enough to roll back gracefully in the case of a failure.

From a PC running Windows 10, you can begin the upgrade process by going to the Download Windows 11 page (*https://www.microsoft.com/software-download/windows11*) and running the Windows 11 Installation Assistant. That option downloads the full installation file and then runs Windows Setup immediately, downloading additional installation files on the fly. As an alternative, you can use bootable installation media or an ISO file mounted as a virtual drive.

Inside OUT

Upgrade directly from an ISO file

Obviously, this option won't work for a clean install on a freshly formatted drive, but it's ideal for upgrades and feature updates. When you double-click a saved ISO file in the Windows 10 File Explorer, its contents appear as a virtual CD/DVD drive in the Devices And Drives area of File Explorer, as in Figure 2-6.

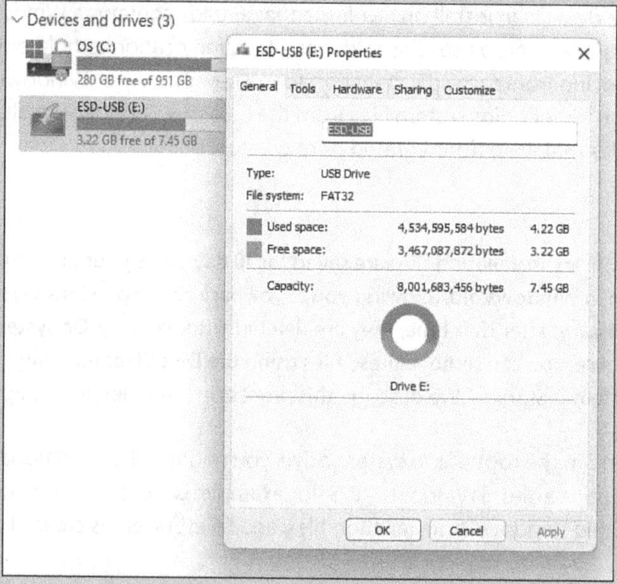

Figure 2-6   In this File Explorer window, drive C is a physical drive, but drive E is a virtual drive created by double-clicking and mounting an ISO disc image file.

Double-click to open the mounted disk, and then double-click Setup to kick off an upgrade. When you no longer need the virtual drive, right-click its File Explorer icon and click Eject.

When you run the Windows 11 Installation Assistant from the Download Windows 11 page on a PC that is currently running Windows 10, the upgrade process preserves all your files and apps. To choose an alternative option, you must run Setup from installation media or a mounted ISO file. If you previously created Windows 11 installation media, open the USB flash drive or DVD in File Explorer; if you have a Windows 11 ISO, double-click the file to open it as a virtual DVD drive. Then double-click Setup to launch the installation process.

The resulting wizard walks you through several steps that aren't part of the streamlined online upgrade. The most important of these is the option to transfer files, apps, and settings. When you reach the Ready To Install page, click Change What To Keep, which displays the options shown in Figure 2-7.

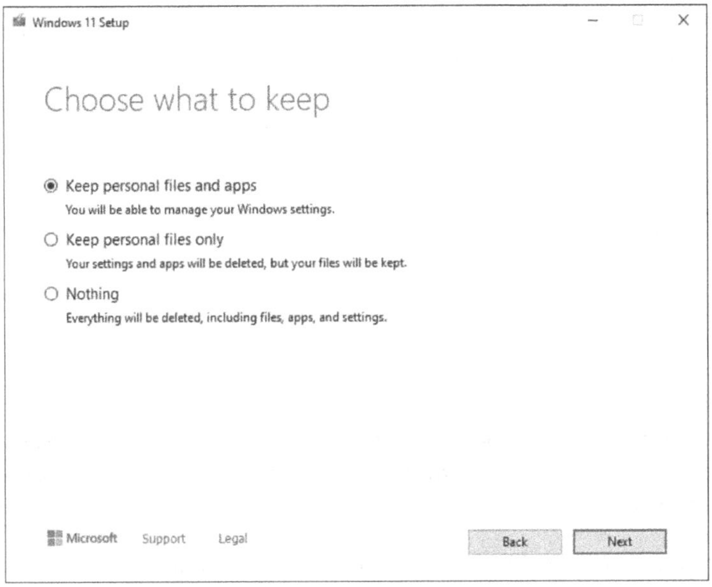

Figure 2-7   When you upgrade from Windows 10 to Windows 11, these three options are at the beginning of the installation process.

Here's what happens with each option:

- **Keep Personal Files And Apps**   All Windows desktop programs and user accounts are migrated. After the upgrade is complete, you need to sign in with your Microsoft account to install apps from the Microsoft Store and sync saved settings.

- **Keep Personal Files Only**   This option is the equivalent of a repair installation. Each user's personal files are available in a new user profile that otherwise contains only default apps and settings.

- **Nothing**   Choose this option if you want to perform a clean install, with your existing installation moved to Windows.old. Note that the descriptive text, "Everything will be deleted," is misleading. Your personal files, as well as those belonging to other user accounts in the current installation, are not deleted. Instead, they are moved to the Windows.old folder, where any user with administrative permissions can recover them by using File Explorer.

After the initial prep work, Setup restarts in offline mode, displaying a progress screen that is simpler than the one from the initial release of Windows 10.

In this mode, you can't interact with the PC at all. Your PC is effectively offline as the following actions occur.

Windows Setup first moves the following folders from the existing Windows installation on the root of the system drive into Windows.old:

- Windows

- Program Files

- Program Files (x86)

- Users

- ProgramData

During this offline phase, Setup extracts registry values and program data from the files it just added in the Windows.old folder, based on the type of upgrade, and then prepares to add this data to the corresponding locations in the new Windows 11 installation. Third-party hardware drivers are also copied from the old driver store in preparation for the new installation.

Next, Setup creates a new set of system folders for Windows 11 using the folder structure and files from the compressed Windows installation image. After that task is complete, Setup moves program files, registry values, and other settings it gathered earlier.

Moving folders minimizes the number of file operations that are required, making upgrade times consistent even when individual user accounts contain large numbers of files. To further speed things up, the Windows Installer uses hard link operations to move files and folders from the transport location to the new Windows 11 hierarchy. Not having to physically move the file improves performance and allows for easy rollback if something goes wrong during the upgrade.

Setup moves folders associated with individual user accounts as part of a default in-place upgrade. The entire folder is placed within the fresh Windows 11 installation unchanged; every file in the folder and all its subfolders are preserved. (Note that organizations using corporate deployment tools can override some of this behavior, excluding some files or subfolders and merging the contents of default folders with the contents of existing folders from the source operating system.)

This activity is accompanied by several restarts and can take more than an hour, depending on your hardware, although an upgrade on modern hardware typically goes much faster. At the conclusion of this process, you're confronted with a sign-in screen. That's followed by a series of screens that prompt you to review privacy settings and, optionally, connect to other Microsoft services.

If you're upgrading from a PC that was configured with a local user account, you need to sign in using the credentials for that account. After that, you have the option to link your account to a Microsoft account or to continue using a local account.

By signing in with a Microsoft account, you can continue setting up Windows 11 by using your synced settings. The most current version of each preinstalled app is downloaded from the Store before you sign in.

➤ **For more information about your options when setting up a user account, see Chapter 10.**

Performing a clean install

Among some PC traditionalists, it's a badge of honor to wipe a newly purchased PC clean and then set up Windows from scratch. Even if you're not so fastidious, a clean install is sometimes unavoidable; it's the only option for PCs you build yourself and for virtual machines, and it's sometimes the fastest way to get back up and running after a disk failure.

> ## Inside OUT
> ### The easiest route to a clean install
>
> The time-tested road to a clean install involves starting up from a bootable USB flash drive containing the Windows installation files and removing all traces of the currently installed Windows version before proceeding to run Setup.
>
> This is still a perfectly valid installation method, but it's no longer the only option, nor is it always the best. For a system that's already running any supported version of Windows, the easier alternative is to start Setup from within Windows and choose an upgrade install; at the Choose What To Keep screen, choose Nothing. After the installation is complete, you can use Disk Cleanup Manager or the tools in Settings > System > Storage to remove the old Windows installation. The result is functionally identical to an old-fashioned clean install.
>
> For a thorough discussion of how the so-called push-button reset option works, see Chapter 15, "Troubleshooting, backup, and recovery."

This section describes the steps for a clean installation on the simplest of all PC configurations: one with a single storage device (hard disk or SSD) containing unallocated space ready to be automatically partitioned for use as the system drive. This is the configuration you encounter if you build a new PC or replace the hard drive on an existing PC. It's also where you find yourself if you've wiped the system drive clean on a PC that you plan to give away, sell, or reassign to another employee or family member.

For those scenarios, you need to boot into Windows Setup from a USB flash drive. You might need to read the manual for your device to learn the magic combination of keystrokes and firmware settings that make it possible to start up using a bootable Windows disc or drive.

When you boot from that media, you pass through a few introductory screens. After confirming the language and regional settings you want to use for your new installation and clicking Install Now, you're asked to enter a product key. If you have a product key, you can enter it here and Setup automatically installs the Windows edition (Home or Pro, usually) that's associated with that key. You also have the option to choose I Don't Have A Product Key, as explained later in this chapter.

After completing those preliminaries and accepting a license agreement, you eventually reach the Windows Setup dialog shown in Figure 2-8. You're asked to choose an installation type— Upgrade or Custom. Be aware: Which Type Of Installation Do You Want? is a trick question.

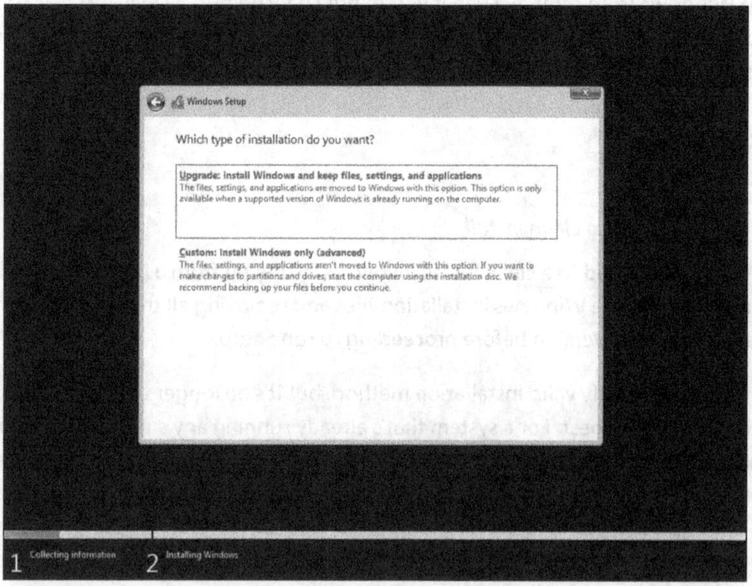

Figure 2-8   When you boot from a USB flash drive or DVD to perform a clean install of Windows, the only option that works from this screen is Custom.

Choosing the Upgrade option leads to an error message. You can upgrade Windows only if you start Setup from within Windows.

The Custom option allows you to continue, and you're presented with a list of available disks and volumes. Figure 2-9 shows what you see on a system with a single drive that has not yet been partitioned and contains only unallocated space.

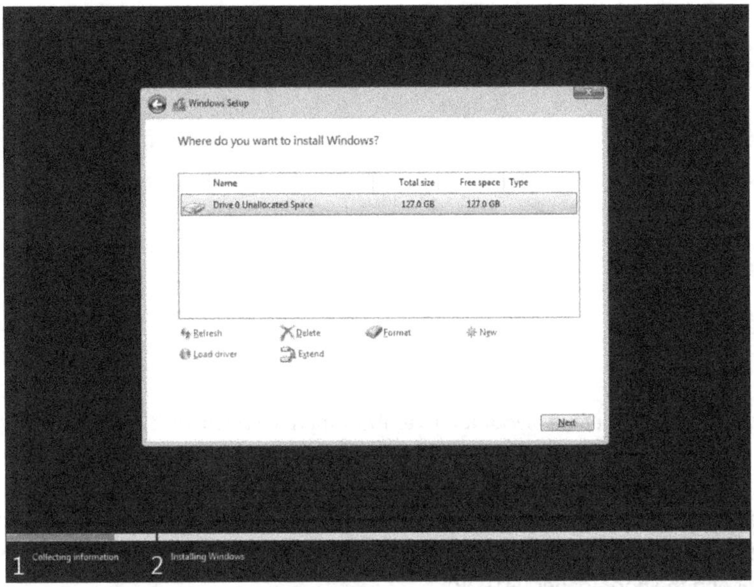

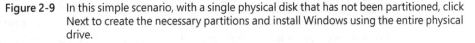

Figure 2-9 In this simple scenario, with a single physical disk that has not been partitioned, click Next to create the necessary partitions and install Windows using the entire physical drive.

Inside OUT

How Windows 11 divides a disk

If you install Windows 11 on a UEFI-based system with a single unformatted disk, Setup creates a default disk layout. Three of its partitions are visible in the Disk Management console and in a new display, visible when you go to Settings > System > Storage > Advanced Storage Settings > Disks & Volumes. Figure 2-10 shows an example from a freshly created Hyper-V virtual machine running Windows 11.

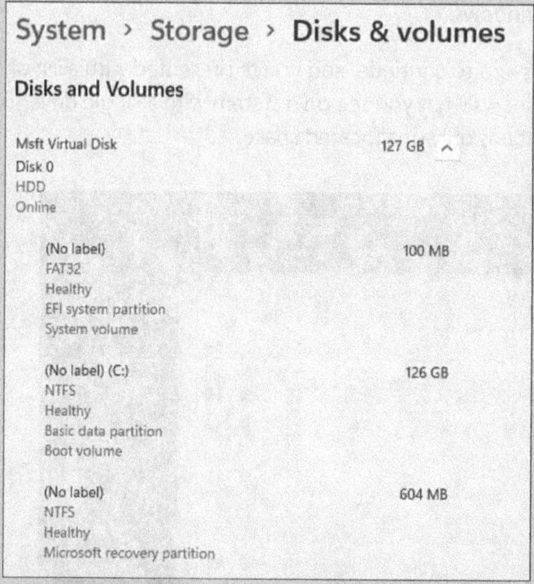

Figure 2-10   The default layout for a freshly formatted system disk looks like this. PC makers can and do introduce more complex partitioning schemes.

The EFI system partition at the start of this disk occupies a mere 99 MB. It contains the files required for the system to start up, including the Windows Hardware Abstraction Layer and the boot loader (NTLDR).

The small (604 MB) recovery partition at the end of the disk in this example contains the Microsoft recovery partition, which allows the system to boot for repair and recovery operations. (This partition might be a different size and in a different location on your PC.)

The largest partition is the primary partition, formatted using NTFS, which contains Windows system files, the paging file, and all user profiles.

A fourth partition, required for every GPT disk, is hidden and not visible in any of Windows 11's disk utilities. This partition, MSR (Reserved), resides between the EFI system partition and the primary partition and is used for post-installation tasks, such as converting a basic disk to a dynamic disk. It's visible when you use DiskPart or the partitioning tools available with a custom installation.

PC makers have the option to add custom OEM partitions to this layout, with those volumes containing files that are part of a custom installation. In addition, some PCs include a second recovery partition at the end of the drive, which contains proprietary utilities and files you can use to restore the original system configuration.

When you start a clean install on a PC whose system drive contains an existing Windows instal- lation and user data, you have a variety of disk management options. You can keep the existing partitions, in which case the existing Windows installation is moved into a Windows.old folder. If you want a truly fresh start, you can use the tools beneath the list of available drives to manage partitions to select each partition and click Delete until only unallocated space remains. You can also use these tools to create one or more new partitions, format an existing partition, or extend a partition to include adjacent unallocated space.

With a new internal storage device or an existing one, you might have any of several good reasons to tinker with disk partitions. You might prefer to segregate your operating-system files from your data files by placing them on separate volumes, for example, or you might be planning to set up a dual-boot or multiboot system. In any event, it's always easier to make partitioning decisions before installing Windows than it is to resize and rearrange volumes after they're in use.

You can choose to install Windows 11 to any fixed internal drive. You cannot, however, install Win- dows to an external drive connected via USB or IEEE 1394 (FireWire) or to any form of removable media. (External drives connected via eSATA connections appear as internal drives and are eligible for installation, although this configuration is rare. Some third-party utilities are also available that allow external disks connected through a Thunderbolt port to appear as internal drives.)

To make adjustments to existing disk partitions, boot from Windows 11 installation media and run through Windows Setup until you reach the Where Do You Want To Install Windows page. Figure 2-11 shows a system that contains two physical drives. Drive 0 contains a standard parti- tion layout, with Windows installed on Partition 4. (Partitions 1 and 2 for this drive have scrolled out of view.) Drive 1 is a newly added SSD that has not yet been partitioned or formatted.

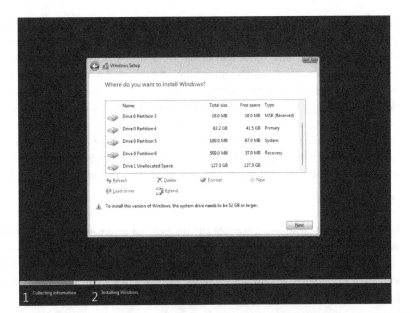

Figure 2-11   Use the disk-management tools in this phase of the Windows 11 installation process to manage disk partitions for more efficient data storage and multiboot configurations.

You can accomplish any of the following tasks here:

- **Select an existing partition or unallocated space on which to install Windows 11.**   Setup is simple if you already created and formatted an empty partition in preparation for setting up Windows, if you plan to install Windows 11 on an existing partition that currently contains data or programs but no operating system, or if you want to use unallocated space on an existing disk without disturbing the existing partition scheme. Select the partition or unallocated space and click Next.

- **Delete an existing partition.**   Select a partition, and then click Delete. This option is useful if you want to perform a clean installation on a drive that currently contains an earlier version of Windows. Because this operation deletes data irretrievably, you must respond to an Are You Sure? confirmation request. After deleting the partition, you can select the unallocated space as the destination for your Windows 11 installation or create a new partition. Be sure to back up any data files before choosing this option.

- **Create a new partition from unallocated space.**   Select a block of unallocated space on a new drive or on an existing drive after deleting partitions, and click New to set up a partition in that space.

  By default, Windows Setup offers to use all unallocated space on the current disk. You can specify a smaller partition size if you want to subdivide the disk into multiple drives. If you have a 4 TB drive, for example, you might choose to create a relatively small partition on which to install Windows and use the remaining space to create a second volume with its own drive letter on which to store data files such as music, pictures, documents, and videos.

- **Extend an existing partition by using unallocated space.**   If you're not happy with your existing partition scheme, you can use the Extend option to make a partition larger, provided that unallocated space is available immediately to the right of the existing partition in Disk Management, with no intervening partitions. If the manufacturer of your PC initially divided a 128 GB hard disk into system and data volumes of equal size, you might decide to rejoin the two partitions when performing a clean install. After backing up your files from the data volume to an external drive or to cloud storage, delete the data partition, select the original system partition to the left of the newly freed space, and click Extend. Choose the total size of the extended partition in the Size box (the default is to use all available unallocated space) and click Apply. You can now continue with Setup.

CAUTION

In both the Disk Management console and the disk-management tools available via Windows Setup, it can be confusing to tell which partition is which. Confusion, in this case, can have drastic consequences if you inadvertently wipe out a drive full of data instead of writing over an unwanted installation of Windows. One good way to reduce the risk of this sort of accident is to label drives well.

➤ **For a full inventory of all disk-management tools and techniques available in Windows 11, see Chapter 14, "Performance and power management." For details about partitioning a drive and managing data storage, see Chapter 9, "Using File Explorer."**

Alert observers will no doubt notice that one option is missing from that list. Unfortunately, Setup does not allow you to shrink an existing disk partition to create unallocated space on which to install a fresh copy of Windows 11. The option to shrink a volume is available from the Disk Management console after Windows 11 is installed, but if you want to accomplish this task before running Setup, you need to use third-party disk-management tools.

After you click Next, the installation process switches into a lengthy unattended phase in which it partitions and formats the disk (if necessary), copies the clean Windows 11 image to the system partition, installs device drivers, and starts default services. When those operations are complete, you arrive at a series of screens where you select the default region and keyboard layout and can give the new device a name.

If you do a clean install of Windows 11 Pro using bootable media, you're faced with one additional choice immediately after Setup completes these initial installation tasks. The dialog shown in Figure 2-12 asks you to choose whether you want to set up the device for personal use or as part of an organization. For an installation of Windows 11 Enterprise or Education, the dialog asks whether you want to join Azure AD or join a domain. (This portion of Setup has undergone numerous changes since the initial release of Windows 10, all in the interest of reducing confusion when setting up a work PC.)

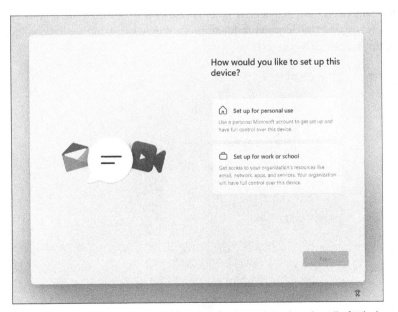

Figure 2-12   This option is available only when you do a clean install of Windows 11 Pro.

If you own the device, or if it is a company PC that will be joined to a Windows domain, choose Set Up For Personal Use and click Next to continue.

If the PC will be managed by your organization using something other than a Windows domain on a local network, choose the second option, Set Up For Work Or School, and click Next. You're prompted to enter the username and password for your workplace or school account; those credentials are managed in Azure Active Directory and can be linked to services such as a Microsoft 365 account at a workplace or university. If your organization requires additional authentication, such as responding to a Microsoft Authenticator prompt or providing a smart card or other hardware token, you need to complete those tasks to proceed.

With those duties complete, you're ready to go set up your default user profile.

> ➤ **For more information about setting up user accounts and user profiles, during Windows installation or afterwards, see Chapter 10.**

Performing an edition upgrade

To gain access to features that aren't available in the currently installed edition of Windows 11, you need to upgrade to a different edition. You're most likely to encounter this scenario when you purchase a new PC with Windows 11 Home Edition preinstalled (or upgrade a PC that originally shipped with Windows 10 Home Edition) and want to take advantage of advanced features available in Windows 11 Pro.

On a system with a properly activated copy of Windows 11 Home, go to Settings > System > Activation and expand the Upgrade Your Edition Of Windows section. In that configuration, you see the options shown in Figure 2-13.

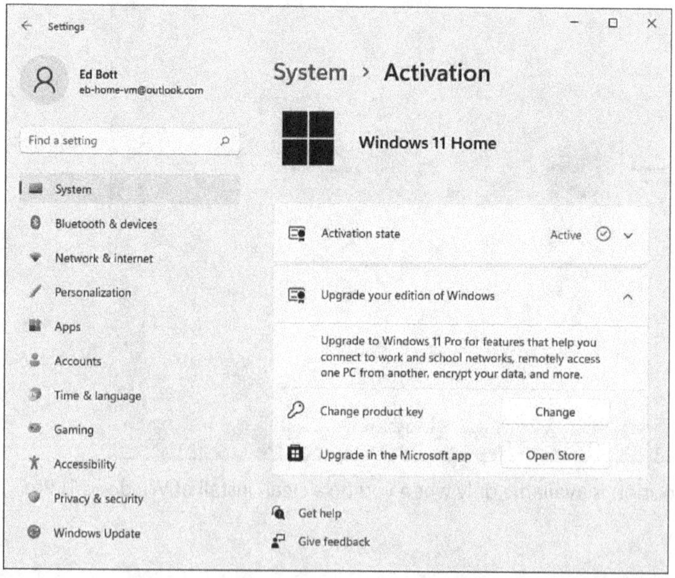

Figure 2-13   Use the options here to upgrade a PC from Home Edition to Pro.

If you have a product key for Windows 11 Pro, you can use that product key to complete the upgrade. Click Change to open the dialog shown in Figure 2-14.

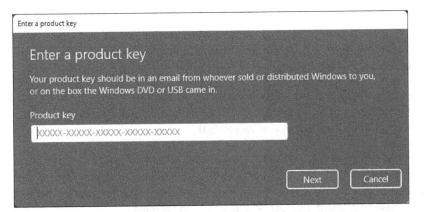

Figure 2-14   If you skipped the option to enter a product key when installing Windows 11, you can enter it here.

Enter the 25-character product key and click Next to begin the upgrade process. If you don't have a valid key and you're willing to pay for an instant upgrade, click Open Store and follow the prompts to buy and install an upgrade to Windows 11 Pro or Pro Workstation.

Inside OUT

Use a product key from an earlier Windows edition

If you have a Windows 10 product key, you can use it to activate the corresponding edition of Windows 11. That's true for clean installs, version upgrades, and edition upgrades. So, for example, on a new PC running Windows 11 Home, you can use the Change Product Key option described in this section to upgrade to Windows 11 Pro by entering a Windows 10 Pro product key. In fact, you can upgrade to Pro using a valid product key from Windows 7, Windows 8, or Windows 8.1. The effect is the same as if you had upgraded your original version of Windows to Pro and then used the free upgrade options to move to Windows 10 and then to Windows 11, minus all those intermediate steps.

On a PC running Windows 11 Pro, the Change Product Key option is the only one available in this section. Enter a valid Pro Workstation, Enterprise, or Education product key to perform an upgrade.

CHAPTER 2

Activating Windows

For more than two decades, desktop versions of Windows have included antipiracy and anti-tampering features. Through the years, Microsoft has used different names for these capabilities: Windows Activation Technologies and Windows Genuine Advantage, for example. In Windows 10 and Windows 11, these features are collectively referred to as the Software Protection Platform.

The most visible part of the Software Protection Platform is Windows Product Activation, an action that occurs shortly after you sign in for the first time on a new PC or on an older device running a freshly installed copy of Windows 11.

Typically, activation involves a brief communication between your PC and Microsoft's licensing servers. The activation process is anonymous and does not require that you divulge any personal information. If everything checks out, your copy of Windows is activated silently, and you never have to deal with product keys or activation prompts.

After you successfully activate your Windows installation, your hardware is still subject to periodic antipiracy checks from Microsoft. This process verifies that your copy of Windows has not been tampered with to bypass activation. It also detects attempts to "clone" a disk for use on a different PC than the one on which it was originally activated. In rare cases, Microsoft can revoke the activation for a computer when it determines after the fact that the original activation was the result of product tampering or that a product key was stolen or used in violation of a volume licensing agreement.

These checks and challenges are, at their core, enforcement mechanisms for the Windows license agreement. This agreement is displayed during the process of installing or deploying the operating system, and you must provide your consent to complete setup. Figure 2-15, for example, shows the license screen that appears when you perform a clean install of Windows 11.

I'm not a lawyer, so I won't attempt to interpret the terms of this legal document. I do, however, recommend that you read the license agreement, which is written in relatively plain language compared to many such documents I've read through the years.

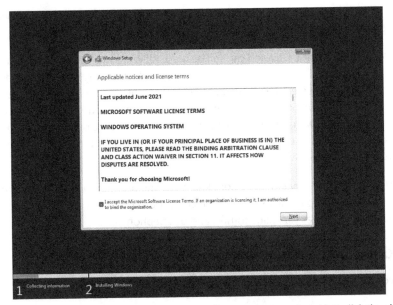

Figure 2-15   Most people never read the license agreement and just click the checkbox to accept it; it's worth reading the full agreement at least once.

NOTE

It's important to understand a potentially confusing concept here: The legal and contractual restrictions imposed by license agreements are completely independent of technical restrictions related to installation.

Licenses are assigned to devices. If you upgrade a system to Windows 11 and then the system's hard disk fails, you can replace the storage device, perform a clean install of Windows 11, and still be properly licensed. Conversely, it's technically possible to install and activate Windows on a computer that doesn't have an underlying license; the fact that activation succeeded doesn't necessarily translate to a valid license. This distinction is especially crucial for businesses (even small ones) that could be the target of a software audit to verify proper licensing.

You can find the license terms for the currently installed Windows edition by going to Settings > System > About. Under the Windows Specifications heading, click Microsoft Software License Terms.

The activation mechanism is designed to enforce license restrictions by preventing the most common form of software piracy: casual copying. Typically, a Windows license entitles you to install the operating system software on a single computer. If you're trying to activate Windows 11 using a product key that has previously been activated on a second (or third or fourth) device, you might be unable to activate the software automatically. In that case, you see a watermark on the desktop alerting you to an issue with activation.

A Windows PC that is not activated can still be used. All Windows functions (with the exception of personalization options) work normally, all your data files are accessible, and all your programs work as expected. The nagging reminders are intended to strongly encourage you to resolve the underlying issue. Some forms of malware can damage system files in a way that resembles tampering with activation files. Another common cause of activation problems is a lazy or dishonest repair technician who installs a stolen or "cracked" copy of Windows instead of using your original licensed copy.

Links in the Windows Activation messages lead to online support tools, where you might be able to identify and repair the issue that's affecting your system. Microsoft also offers free support for activation issues via online forums and by telephone.

Windows licensing options

Every copy of Windows is licensed, not sold. Windows 11 supports the following license types:

- **OEM**   An OEM (original equipment manufacturer) license is one that's included with a new computer. This license is locked to the computer on which it's installed and cannot be transferred. OEM System Builder packages, which include installation media as well as the license, are intended for use by small PC makers but are often used by consumers and hobbyists. The system builder is required to provide support for OEM Windows along with the device on which it is installed.

- **Full**   A full license is sold directly to retail customers as an electronic distribution or a packaged product. With a full license, Windows can be installed on a computer that was not sold with Windows 10 or Windows 11 originally. You need a full license to install Windows in a virtual machine, on a Mac, or on a computer that you build yourself. A full license can be transferred to a different computer; the underlying copy of Windows on the original PC must be removed for the transferred license to be valid.

- **Volume**   Volume licenses for Windows are sold in bulk to corporate, government, nonprofit, and educational customers and are available as an upgrade on machines that already have what Microsoft calls a "qualifying base license," such as an OEM license for Windows 10 or Windows 11 Pro.

- **Cloud**   Businesses can purchase upgrades to Windows 10 or Windows 11 Enterprise using a subscription option (E3 or E5); licenses purchased through this channel are associated with an Azure Active Directory account in that organization and are managed by the organization. This type of Windows license can be activated on up to five PCs simultaneously by signing in with the Azure AD credentials of the licensed user.

If you inspect the activation status of a Windows 11 PC, you might see a reference to a *digital license*. This terminology replaces the certificates of authenticity and stickers that were required with older Windows versions. The details of a digital license can be linked to a Microsoft account, allowing for easier troubleshooting of activation issues, as described later in this section.

Do you need a product key?

If you're building your own PC or installing Windows 11 in a new virtual machine, you need to enter a 25-character alphanumeric product key before you can successfully activate your new installation. You won't need a product key if you buy a new PC built by one of the industry's big OEMs (Dell, Lenovo, HP, Acer, and ASUS account for the overwhelming majority of PCs in this category) and sold with a copy of Windows 10 or Windows 11 already installed. On those devices, Windows can retrieve the embedded license information from the computer's firmware and activate automatically.

Smaller OEMs (in Microsoft's parlance, these are called System Builders) purchase individual copies of Windows that require a product key for activation. The System Builder is required under the terms of the OEM license to include that key as part of the Windows installation and to provide an official copy of that key to the purchaser of the PC.

If you skip the opportunity to enter a product key during a clean install, or if the key you enter fails activation (perhaps because it has been used on another PC), you can go to Settings > System > Activation and click the button to the right of the Change Product Key label. Enter a valid product key for the currently installed Windows edition using the dialog shown in Figure 2-16.

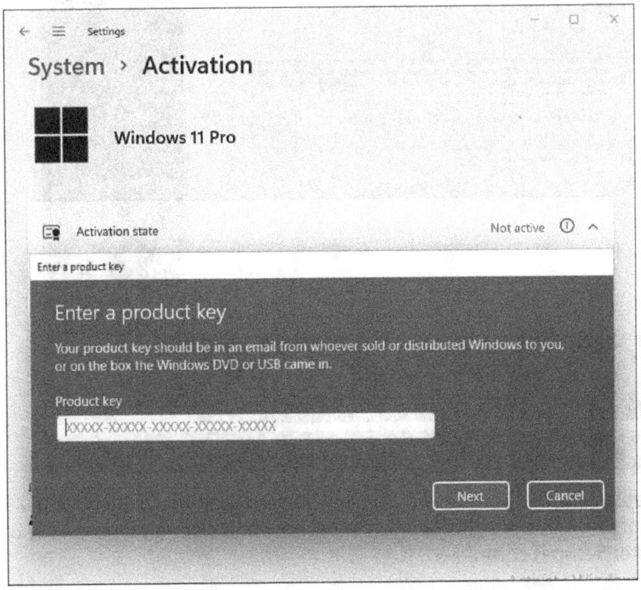

Figure 2-16   When you enter a 25-character alphanumeric product key here, Windows automatically checks its validity and prompts you to complete activation.

CHAPTER 2

Here are some important facts you should know about product keys:

- **A custom product key is stored in firmware on any copy of Windows that is prein-stalled on a new PC by a large computer maker.**   This configuration is called System Locked Preinstallation (SLP). On a PC that has been configured this way, you can reinstall the original edition of Windows and reactivate without having to enter a product key.

- **Your product key matches your edition of Windows.**   When you enter a product key as part of a custom install of Windows, the key identifies the edition to be installed. If you purchase a boxed copy of Windows 10 or Windows 11, the installation media (a DVD or a USB flash drive) contains a configuration file that automatically installs the edition that matches the product key included with that package.

- **Windows 10 product keys work with Windows 11, and vice-versa.**   The product key matches a specific Windows edition and will activate the corresponding Windows 11 edition (assuming your hardware is compatible with Windows 11, of course).

- **You are not required to enter a product key when performing a clean install of Windows 11.**   When you perform a clean installation of Windows 11 by booting from a USB flash drive or DVD, Windows Setup prompts you to enter a product key, as shown in Figure 2-17. If you don't have a product key handy, you can defer this step by clicking I Don't Have A Product Key, just to the left of the Next button.

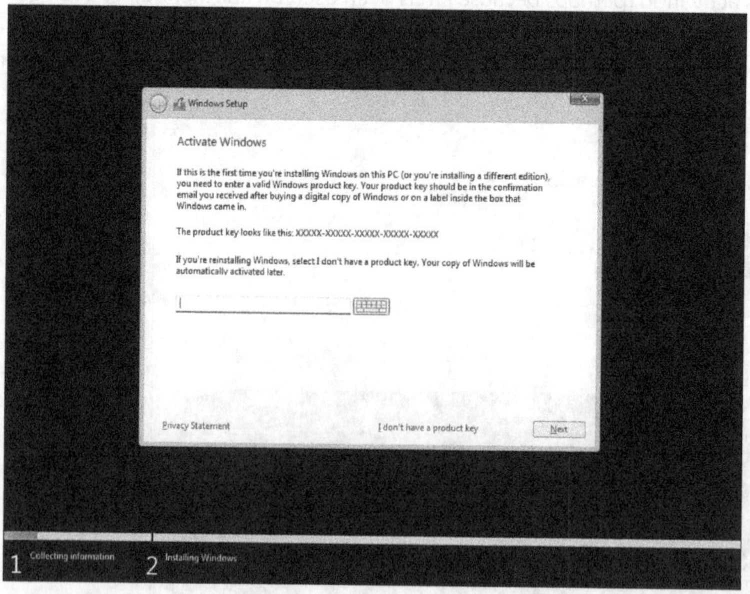

Figure 2-17   Setup automatically installs the Windows edition that matches the 25-character alphanumeric product key you enter here and attempts to activate using that key after Setup is complete.

- **When you reinstall Windows 11, you don't need to enter a product key.**   If you previously activated Windows 11 as part of a clean install or an upgrade, a record of that activation is stored along with the device's hardware ID on Microsoft's activation servers. When you reinstall the previously activated edition (Home or Pro), you can skip past the prompt to enter a product key. After Setup is complete, Windows is activated automatically.

Clicking I Don't Have A Product Key allows Setup to proceed but might require that you select a specific Windows edition to install. Be sure to choose the edition that matches the one that was previously installed and activated on this PC or that matches the product key you plan to use later for activation.

Managing Windows activation

Shortly after the release of Windows 10, Microsoft created a new activation mechanism as an alternative to the traditional product key. That mechanism applies to Windows 11 as well. On PCs upgraded to Windows 10 or Windows 11 from a properly activated Windows installation, the Microsoft activation server generates and stores a Windows license certificate (Microsoft initially called it a *digital entitlement* but later changed the nomenclature to *digital license*) for the corresponding edition, Home or Pro. You also receive a digital license if you purchase Windows 11 (or a Windows 11 Pro upgrade) from the Microsoft Store or if you install an Insider Preview release of Windows on a properly activated PC.

That digital license format is stored in conjunction with your unique installation ID on Microsoft's activation servers. The unique installation ID is essentially a fingerprint of your PC, based on a cryptographic hash derived from your hardware. That hash is not reversible and not tied to any other Microsoft services. So, although it defines your device, it doesn't identify you. But it does make it possible to store activation status for that device online.

(You can read more details about digital licenses and other activation issues at *https://bit.ly/win11-activation*.)

Once that online activation status is associated with your hardware ID, you can wipe your drive clean, boot from Windows 11 installation media, and install a clean copy (skipping right past the prompts for a product key); at the end of the process, you'll have a properly activated copy of Windows 11.

At any time, you can check the activation status of your device by going to Settings > System > Activation, as shown in Figure 2-18.

CHAPTER 2

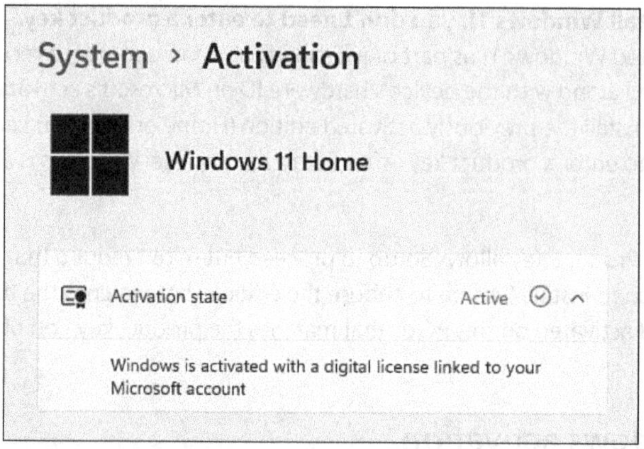

Figure 2-18   Most Windows 11 PCs are automatically activated, with the successful activation status shown in this dialog.

One detail worth noting in Figure 2-18 is the connection between the digital license and the current Microsoft account. Doing so creates a record of the digital license that can be retrieved for troubleshooting purposes, as discussed in the next section.

Troubleshooting activation problems

When you install Windows 11 on a new PC, it attempts to contact Microsoft's licensing servers and activate automatically. Under most circumstances, activation over the internet takes no more than a few seconds. If Windows is unable to reach Microsoft's activation servers, perhaps because of connectivity issues, it continues to attempt activation for three days. If activation fails, you see several indications that there's a problem. The first is a faint gray Activate Windows watermark that appears in the bottom-right corner of the display and is visible at all times. In smaller text below that message is the instruction Go To Settings To Activate Windows.

You'll also find a Windows Isn't Activated link at the top of the System page in Settings, with a handy Activate Now link to its right. If you open the Personalization page in Settings, every option is grayed out and unavailable, with a message at the top that reads You Need To Activate Windows Before You Can Personalize Your PC.

The most obvious reminder of all appears, naturally, if you click Settings > System > Activation. Alongside the Activation State heading, you see the words Not Active, with a bright red exclamation point alongside and an error message, also in red, beneath it. Figure 2-19 shows an example of this message.

If you're confident you have a valid Windows license, click Troubleshoot to try to fix the problem. The activation troubleshooter can resolve some simple problems and is especially well suited for activation errors that result from hardware changes or from situations where you inadvertently installed the wrong Windows edition (Home instead of Pro, for example). In fact, if the troubleshooter is unable to resolve your issue, it offers an I Changed Hardware On This Device Recently option, as shown in Figure 2-20.

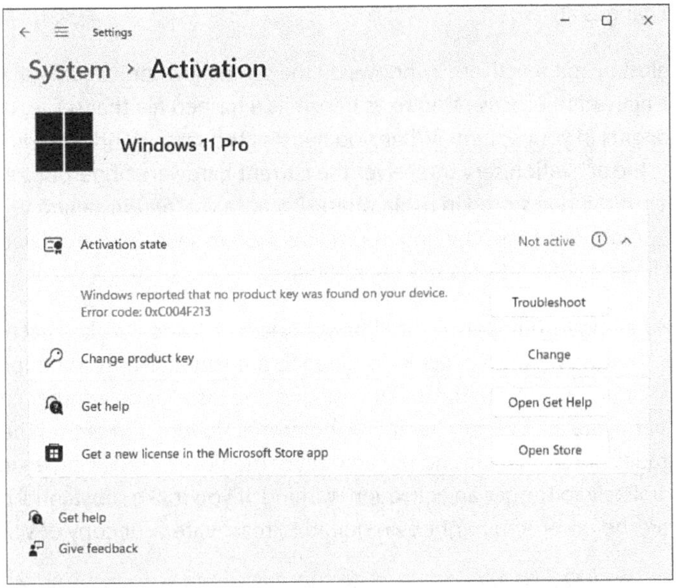

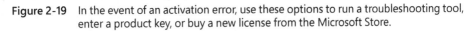

Figure 2-19   In the event of an activation error, use these options to run a troubleshooting tool, enter a product key, or buy a new license from the Microsoft Store.

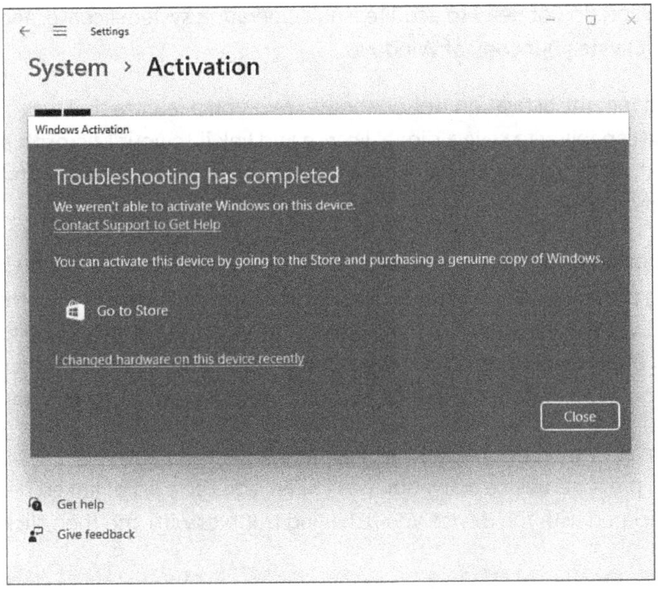

Figure 2-20   If the activation troubleshooter is unable to resolve the issue because you recently changed hardware, it offers one additional resolution option.

Why are hardware changes an issue?

You're allowed to reinstall and reactivate Windows on the same hardware an unlimited number of times. During the activation process, Windows transmits a hashed file that serves as a "fingerprint" of key components in your system. When you reinstall the same Windows edition you activated previously, the activation server receives the current hardware fingerprint and compares that value against the one stored in its database. Because you're reinstalling Windows on hardware that is essentially the same, the fingerprint your system sends to the activation server matches the stored fingerprint, and activation is automatic.

A copy of the hardware fingerprint is also stored on your hard disk and checked each time you start your computer. This activation process is designed to prevent attempts to tamper with the activation files or to "clone" an activated copy of Windows and install it on another computer. If you upgrade the hardware in your computer, the fingerprint no longer matches the stored version. Minor upgrades, such as increasing the amount of memory or replacing an internal storage device, are unlikely to trigger an activation warning. If you make substantial changes to your system hardware, however, you might be required to reactivate your copy of Windows.

You can upgrade almost all components in a system without requiring a new license. Replacing the motherboard on a PC is the most certain way to trigger the activation mechanism, because the activation server assumes you tried to install your copy of Windows on a second computer. If you replaced a defective or failed motherboard with one that is the same model or the manufacturer's equivalent, you do not need to acquire a new operating system license, and you should be able to reactivate your copy of Windows.

To help with this scenario, the activation troubleshooter relies on a feature that was introduced with Windows 10: the capability to save a digital license and link it to your Microsoft account. This step isn't mandatory, but it's handy if you make major changes to a system with a digital license and need to reactivate.

If the PC in question was previously activated and its digital license was associated with a Microsoft account, you can run the activation troubleshooter to make the match that Microsoft's activation servers can't. Click the Troubleshoot link at the bottom of that Settings page to launch a tool that tries to find the activation record for the PC you're using. If you're not signed in with a Microsoft account, you need to do so, using the account you used previously to activate this PC.

Figure 2-21 shows the activation troubleshooter in action. After signing in with the Microsoft account to which the previous device activation was linked, you see a list of linked devices. Select the name associated with the device you're having troubles with and then click Activate.

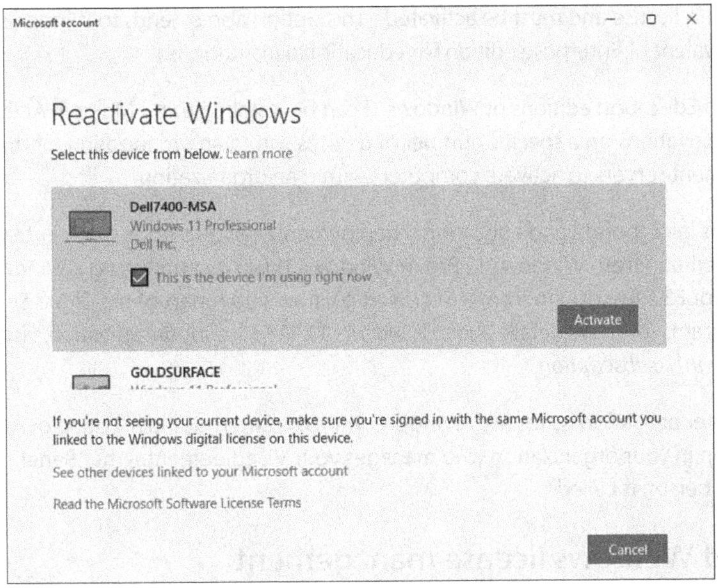

Figure 2-21   Using the activation troubleshooter, you can choose a digital license from a previously activated device to resolve issues that occur if you make significant hardware changes.

If all else fails, your only remaining option is to contact the telephone-based activation support center, explain the circumstances, and—assuming that the support representative accepts your claim—manually enter a new activation code. (If you replace a failed motherboard with one that is functionally identical, you're entitled to transfer the existing license to the new device. However, if you upgrade your PC with a new motherboard, Microsoft considers the end result to be a new PC and might require a new license.)

The license agreement for a retail copy of Windows 11 allows you to transfer it to another computer, provided that you completely remove it from the computer on which it was previously installed. An OEM copy, by contrast, is governed by a different license agreement, which restricts the license to the computer on which it was originally installed. You can reinstall an OEM copy of Windows an unlimited number of times on the same computer. However, you are prohibited by the license agreement from transferring that copy of Windows to another computer after it has been assigned to a device.

Product activation and corporate licensing

Businesses that purchase licenses through a Microsoft Volume Licensing (VL) program receive access to VL media and product keys that require activation under a different set of rules from those that apply to retail or OEM copies. Under the terms of a volume license agreement, each computer with a VL copy of Windows 10 or Windows 11 Enterprise edition installed must have a

CHAPTER 2

valid underlying license and must be activated. (This option also extends to Windows 11 Education, the equivalent of Enterprise edition for educational institutions.)

Enterprise and Education editions of Windows 11 can be installed using Multiple Activation Keys, which allow activations on a specific number of devices within an organization, or they can use Key Management servers to activate computers within an organization.

Administrators in corporate and educational deployments can also upgrade to Enterprise or Education edition from Windows 10 Pro or Windows 11 Pro by purchasing a Windows 11 Enterprise E3 or E5 subscription from a Microsoft partner who is part of the Cloud Service Provider program. For more details about Windows 10/11 subscription activation, visit *https://bit.ly/win11-subscription*.

If you encounter activation issues with Windows 11 Pro or Enterprise in a VL deployment, contact the person in your organization who manages your VL agreement—the "Benefits Administrator," as this person is called.

Advanced Windows license management

For dealing with basic activation tasks, the relevant Settings page has everything you need. Administrators who need more granular control over licensing and activation can use the Windows Software Licensing Management Tool (Slmgr.vbs). Use this Windows Script Host–based utility to examine the licensing status of a PC, change its product key, and perform other activation-related tasks.

Although this feature is primarily intended for automating volume tasks associated with volume license activation and administration, you can also run the script interactively. Open a Command Prompt or Windows PowerShell window with administrative privileges and then run the command Slmgr.vbs. If it's run without parameters, this command shows its full syntax in a series of dialogs. (Note that it's not necessary to use the .vbs extension to run this command.)

Use parameters with the Slmgr command to accomplish specific tasks. For example, to display the current licensing status for a device, use the command slmgr /dli. That parameter opens a dialog like the one shown in Figure 2-22, which displays the status of a device running an OEM version of Windows 11 Pro that has been properly activated.

```
Windows Script Host                           ×


Name: Windows(R), Professional edition
Description: Windows(R) Operating System, OEM_DM channel
Partial Product Key: CKCKC
License Status: Licensed



                              [   OK   ]
```

Figure 2-22   This output from the Windows Software Licensing Management Tool shows a system that is properly licensed. If you see an error code here, you need to do some troubleshooting.

For a much more detailed display of information, use the same command with a switch that produces verbose output: slmgr /dlv. Use slmgr /ipk <product_key> to install the 25-character product key you provide following that switch. The /upk switch uninstalls the current product key, and the /cpky switch removes the product key from the registry to deter attempts to steal and reuse a key. To see all available switches, enter the Slmgr command by itself.

Using multiple operating systems on the same PC

If your computer already has any version of Windows installed and you have a second disk partition available (or enough unallocated space to create a second partition), you can install a clean copy of Windows 11 without disturbing your existing Windows installation. At boot time, you choose your Windows version from a startup menu, like the one shown in Figure 2-23. Although this is typically called a *dual-boot system*, it's more accurate to call it a *multiboot configuration*, because you can install as many copies of Windows or other PC-compatible operating systems as your system resources allow.

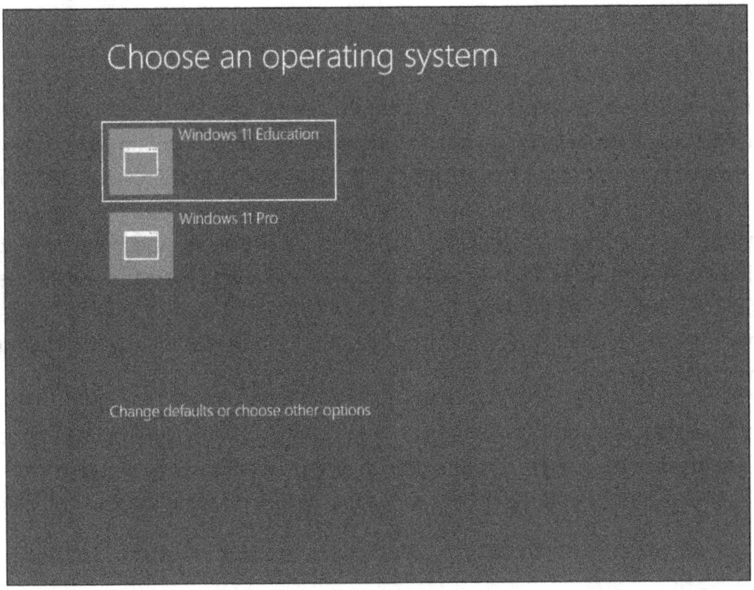

Figure 2-23 This system is configured to allow a choice of operating systems at startup.

CHAPTER 2

> ### TROUBLESHOOTING
>
> **After installing Windows 7, you see a text-based boot menu**
>
> The preferred way to build a multiboot system is to install the most recent version last. If you follow that order when setting up a PC with Windows 11, you get that operating system's graphical boot menu. If you install Windows 7 as a second operating system on a PC that is currently running Windows 10 or Windows 11, you get Windows 7's black-and-white, text-based boot menu instead. To change the boot menu so that it uses the graphical version, start Windows 11, open an Administrative Command Prompt, and run the following command: **bcdboot c:\windows**. Restart and you should see the familiar blue-and-white menu.

Having the capability to choose your operating system at startup is handy if you have an app or device that simply doesn't work under Windows 11 and can't easily be run in a virtual machine. When you need to use the legacy app or device, you can boot into your earlier Windows version without too much fuss. This capability is also useful for software developers and IT professionals who need to be able to test how programs work under different operating systems using physical (not virtual) hardware.

For experienced Windows users, installing a second copy of Windows in its own partition can also be helpful as a way to maintain a completely clean environment, separate from confidential work data. It's also useful when you need to experiment with a potentially problematic hardware/software combination without compromising a working system. After you finish setting up the second, clean version of Windows 11, you see an additional entry on the startup menu that corresponds to your new installation. (The newly installed version is the default menu choice; it runs automatically if 30 seconds pass and you haven't made a choice.) Use the new installation to experiment with the software or hardware and see how well it works. If your experiments produce satisfactory results, you can add the new app or device to your primary Windows 11 installation.

To add a separate installation of Windows 11 to a system on which an existing version of Windows is already installed, first make sure you have an available volume (or unformatted disk space) separate from the volume that contains the system files for your current Windows version.

Inside OUT

Use virtual machines whenever possible instead of hassling with multiboot menus.

You can create truly elaborate multiboot configurations using Windows versions that date back a decade or more. But unless you're running a hardware testing lab, there's no good reason to do that. The much simpler, smoother alternative is to use virtual hardware that faithfully re-creates the operating environment. Installing Windows 11 in a virtual machine also allows you to capture details of several crucial tasks and processes that can't easily be documented on physical hardware, and takes only minutes to roll back changes in a virtual machine, a process that can take many hours when backing up and restoring Windows on physical hardware.

The simplest option is Microsoft's Hyper-V virtualization software, which is a standard feature in Windows 11 Pro, Enterprise, and Education and on current Windows Server versions. (For more information about Client Hyper-V, see Chapter 17, "Running Windows 11 in a virtual machine or in the cloud.")

To run Windows 11 on a Mac, try Parallels, available at *https://parallels.com*. For other operating systems, check out VMware (*http://bit.ly/vmware-personal*), which offers excellent virtualization software for use on desktop Windows machines and servers, and the free VirtualBox package from Oracle (*https://virtualbox.org*).

Using any of these solutions, you can install even the most ancient Windows version. Backing up a machine's configuration and restoring it is usually as simple as copying a few files. Of course, you need a license for every operating system you install in a virtual machine. If you have a license to use Windows for evaluation purposes, the option to run Windows in a virtual machine can be a tremendous time-saver.

CHAPTER 2

The target volume can be a separate partition on the same physical disk as the current Windows installation, or it can be on a different hard disk. If your system contains a single disk with a single volume used as drive C, you cannot create a multiboot system unless you add a new disk or use software tools to shrink the existing partition and create a new partition from the free space. (The Disk Management console, Diskmgmt.msc, includes this capability on Windows 10 and Windows 11; you can also use third-party software for this task. For details, see "Shrinking or extending an NTFS volume" in Chapter 8.) The new partition does not need to be empty; if it contains system files for another Windows installation, they are moved to Windows.old. Run Setup, choose the Custom (Advanced) option, and select the disk and partition you want to use for the new installation.

Windows Setup automatically handles details of adding the newly installed operating system to the Boot Configuration Data store.

And how do you edit and configure the Boot Configuration Data store? Surprisingly, the only official tool is a command-line utility called Bcdedit. Bcdedit doesn't offer a user interface; instead, you perform tasks by appending switches and parameters to the Bcdedit command line. To display the complete syntax for this tool, open an elevated Command Prompt session (using the Run As Administrator option) and type the command **bcdedit /?**.

For everyday use, most Bcdedit options are esoteric, unnecessary, and risky. In fact, the only option you really need to remember is the command to change the text for each entry in the boot menu. By default, Windows Setup adds the generic entry "Windows 11" followed by a volume number for each installation. If you set up a dual-boot system using two copies of Windows 11 (one for everyday use, one for testing), you'll find it hard to tell which is which because the menu text is essentially the same for each. To make the menu more informative, follow these steps:

1. Start your computer and choose either entry from the boot menu. After startup is complete, make a note of which installation is running.

2. Right-click Start, or press Windows key+X, and choose Windows Terminal (Admin) from the Quick Link menu. Click Yes in the User Account Control box to open an elevated session.

3. Type the following command: **bcdedit /set {current} description *"Menu description goes here"*** (substituting your own description for the placeholder text and making sure to include the quotation marks). Press Enter.

4. Restart your computer, and note that the menu description you just entered now appears on the menu. Select the other menu option.

5. Repeat steps 2 and 3, again adding a menu description to replace the generic text and distinguish this installation from the other one.

A few startup options are available when you click or tap Change Defaults Or Choose Other Options at the bottom of the boot menu. Doing so leads to the Options menu shown in Figure 2-24.

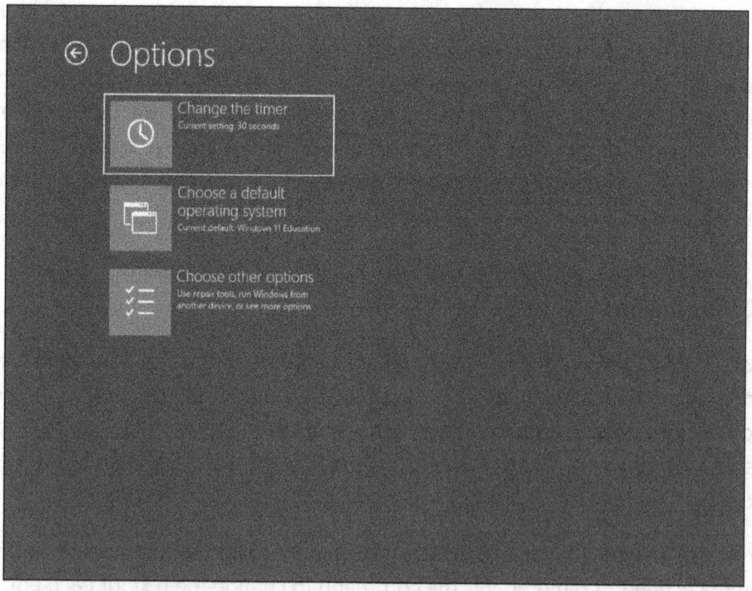

Figure 2-24   Use these options on a multiboot Windows configuration to specify how long Windows should wait for you to choose from the boot menu and which installation should run when that timer is up.

You can choose which installation is the default operating system (this is where descriptive menu choices come in handy) and change the timer that determines how long you want to display the list of operating systems. The default is 30 seconds; you can choose 5 seconds (allowing the default operating system to start automatically unless you quickly interrupt it) or 5 minutes, if you want to ensure you have a choice even if you're distracted while the system is restarting. These options write data directly to the Boot Configuration Data store.

For slightly more control over the boot menu timer, use the System Configuration utility, Msconfig.exe. You can use the Boot tab to change the default operating system and set the Timeout interval in any amount between 3 and 999 seconds.

Inside OUT

Installing Windows 10 and Linux in a multiboot configuration

The availability of the Windows Subsystem for Linux and Hyper-V virtualization makes it far less necessary to run Linux in a multiboot configuration with Windows 11. If you choose this option, however, you'll find that it works much like the Windows multiboot setup described on the preceding pages. You can set it up to use the Windows 11 boot menu or, if you prefer, you can use a Linux boot loader (most commonly, GRUB). The procedure is a bit more complex than the procedure for installing another version of Windows, and it varies somewhat depending on which Linux distribution you use and which Linux tools (such as partition editors, boot loaders, and the like) you prefer. It's generally easier to set up such a system if the Windows partition is set up first, but it can be done either way: Windows and then Linux, or Linux and then Windows.

An internet search for "dual boot Linux Windows" turns up plenty of detailed instructions, and if you add the name of your Linux distribution to the search input, you're likely to find the specific steps needed to make it work with Windows 11.

Tweaking and tuning your Windows installation

When Windows Setup completes, you're signed in and ready to begin using Windows 11. For upgrades and clean installs alike, use this checklist to confirm that basic functionality is enabled properly:

- **Check Windows Update.** Depending on how you chose to start your installation or upgrade, you might need additional updates, including the most recent feature update and additional security updates. Those updates should arrive automatically within 24 hours. Checking for updates manually allows you to install them at your convenience and avoid a scheduled overnight restart or an inconvenient delay.

- **Look for missing device drivers.** Open Device Manager and look for any devices that have a yellow exclamation mark over the icon or any devices that are listed under the Other category. This is also a good time to install any custom drivers supplied by the device maker that might unlock additional features not available with the class drivers provided through Windows Update. For more information on working with device drivers, see "How device drivers and hardware work together" in Chapter 13.

- **Adjust display settings.** Confirm that the display is set for its native resolution and that any additional tasks, such as color calibration, have been completed.

- **Check your network connection.** Go to Settings > Network & Internet to view and change current network connections. Click the Properties icon (at the top of the page, just to the right of the connection name) to adjust advanced network settings (such as DNS server addresses) or to switch from a public network to a private network and allow local file sharing.

- **Verify security settings.** Open Windows Security and look for any required actions; if you use third-party security software, install it now and get the latest updates.

- **Change default programs.** Use this opportunity to install and configure your preferred browser, email client, music playback software, and so on.

- **Adjust power and sleep settings.** The default settings are usually good enough, but they're not always a perfect match for your preferences. Now is a good time to adjust when your device sleeps and whether it requires a password when it wakes.

Using Windows 11

This chapter covers the core features of the Windows 11 user interface—all the things you tap, click, drag, and drop to make Windows do what you want it to do.

If you're like most of our readers, you're coming to Windows 11 after spending the past few years learning how to work with Windows 10, and you'll find plenty of familiar elements here, with some new twists. The two most important pieces of the Windows 11 user experience—for example, the Start menu and taskbar—work roughly the same as their predecessors, but the tools for customizing them are very different indeed, as we document in this chapter.

To make things even more confusing, Microsoft has decided to build Windows 11 in a way that allows it to release new features at any time. Those features might be included with one of the operating system's annual feature updates—the 22H2 release we used as the basis for this book includes a major update to File Explorer, for example, that adds a multitabbed interface for the first time ever. (We cover that change in Chapter 9, "Using File Explorer.")

But new features can also arrive along with monthly security and reliability updates or as part of the many apps that are included as part of a default Windows 11 installation. The upshot? You're almost certainly looking at a later version of Windows 11, with a slightly different set of features than those we document here. It's possible that some of the screenshots and step-by-step instructions you find in this book may not match exactly the system you're working with. We hope that our descriptions are clear enough that you'll be able to take those small changes in stride.

An overview of the Windows 11 user experience

Before we dive into detailed descriptions of individual features, please join us for a brief tour of Windows 11. Our goal is to introduce the different parts of Windows, new and old, so that we can be sure we're on the same page.

Figure 3-1 shows the two most important building blocks of Windows 11 and offers a hint of its signature visual style.

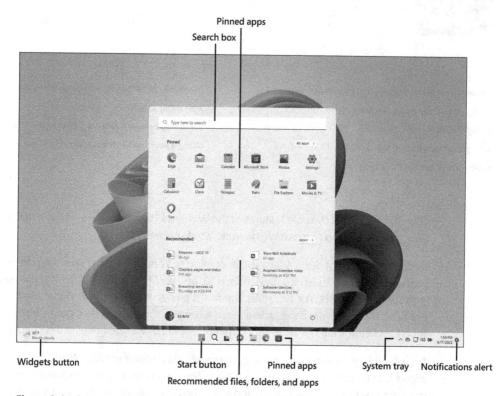

Figure 3-1 Compared to its predecessor, the Windows 11 Start menu is radically simplified.

When you first start up a PC running Windows 11, you see the familiar Windows desktop and taskbar. Clicking the Start button—the Windows logo at the left of a row of buttons centered along the bottom of the display—opens the Start menu.

Conceptually, the Windows 11 Start menu is similar to its immediate predecessor, but it differs dramatically in some key details. The most obvious difference is its position on the screen—centered at the bottom of the display rather than in the lower-left corner. But that's just one of many important changes. Here's a list of what else is changed from the Windows 10 Start experience:

- There are no resizable tiles, live or otherwise. In Windows 11, all app buttons are the same size.

- You can switch between a grid containing pinned apps and a scrolling All Apps list, but you can't see both at once. In Windows 10, by contrast, the All Apps list is visible alongside the pinned app tiles.

CHAPTER 3

- The Power button, user profile picture, and shortcuts to common data folders are in a row along the bottom of the Start menu rather than in a thin vertical strip on the left side.

- The Windows 11 Start menu is a fixed size. You can't drag its borders to change its dimensions, and there's no option to use it in full-screen mode.

- A search box appears at the top of the Start menu, above the grid containing pinned apps. Tapping the Start button and then typing a search term (or clicking in the search box or clicking the search button on the taskbar, just to the right of Start) opens a different view of the Start menu that includes suggested web searches.

MICROSOFT ACCOUNTS AND WINDOWS 11

Although it's possible to use Windows 11 with a local account, the Windows Setup program requires the use of a Microsoft account for most clean installs. That requirement pays off when you set up a new PC or device using the same Microsoft account you used previously on a different device. If you configured that device to sync your personalized settings, your new device picks up synced settings such as desktop backgrounds and colors, making it feel familiar right away.

If you sign in to a corporate network, your personalized settings roam according to policies defined by your network administrator. (If your organization allows you to, you can attach a Microsoft account to your domain account, and both your personal and work settings roam together as you switch between devices.)

When you allow your Microsoft account to sync settings between devices, you don't have to go through a tedious process of tweaking the default settings to match those preferences; instead, your visual themes, notification settings, and saved Wi-Fi passwords appear exactly as you expect. If your Microsoft account is connected to OneDrive, your online files and photos are available, too.

Also new in Windows 11 is the Widgets button, which appears by default at the far left of the taskbar. The button itself offers a quick view of the temperature and weather in the current location; clicking that button (or using the keyboard shortcut Windows key+W) opens the Widgets pane, which can be customized to show an expanded weather forecast, news headlines, stock prices, and tasks and calendar events from an associated Microsoft account, as shown in Figure 3-2.

CHAPTER 3

Figure 3-2   The Widgets pane displays news headlines, sports scores, weather, and other tidbits of information. It's customizable, and its button can be removed from the taskbar if you find it distracting.

We discuss how to customize the Widgets pane (or hide it completely) later in this chapter.

On the far-right side of the taskbar, just to the right of the clock, Windows displays a subtle icon (a number in a circle, whose color matches your Windows accent color) that alerts you to any notifications you have received from apps, services, or Windows itself. Click that icon to display the notifications pane, shown in Figure 3-3. (If you have no unread notifications, click the clock to open this pane.)

You can fine-tune the list of apps that are allowed to interrupt you, but even with all that attention, the notifications pane still contains ample opportunities for distraction, as meeting requests, email messages, and reminders compete for your attention. As a counterbalance, the Windows 11 notifications pane includes not one but two features designed to suppress those interruptions and allow you to work. We cover the Do Not Disturb and Focus features later in this chapter.

As with previous versions, Windows 11 offers multiple ways to switch between tasks. You can click the Task View button on the taskbar or use the keyboard shortcuts Windows key+Tab or Alt+Tab to quickly switch between apps. Windows 11 also offers much richer tools than its predecessor for arranging open windows in predetermined layouts on the screen. Allowing the mouse pointer to hover over the Minimize button, for example, offers a variety of "snap" options that are considerably more versatile than the Windows 10 equivalents.

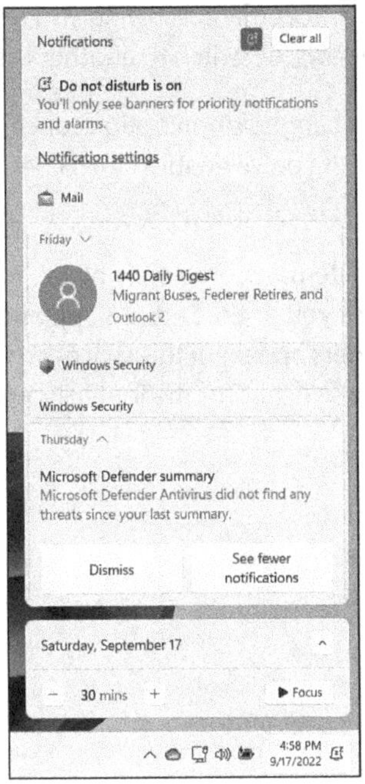

Figure 3-3 You can curate the list of apps and services allowed to interrupt you with notifications in this pane. You can also turn on a pair of features to temporarily suppress those interruptions and allow you to focus on work.

Using and customizing the Start menu

The interface element popularly known as the Start menu has gone through some drama in recent times, including a brief banishment in the Windows 8 era. In Windows 11, its core remains intact, with a dramatically simplified focus compared to its recent predecessors.

To open the Start menu, click the Windows logo—the leftmost button in the center of the taskbar—or press the Windows key. In Windows 11, Start is divided into a series of horizontal regions. At the top is the search box, where you can enter search terms and see matching results from local content, from cloud accounts, and from the web.

Below that are two large regions, labeled Pinned and Recommended. The first contains icons for apps installed on the current PC; you can add, remove, and rearrange these pinned apps to match your working style. The Recommended block displays shortcuts to files you've opened recently, which Windows quite logically thinks you might want to work with again.

At the very bottom of the Start menu is a horizontal region that, by default, contains only two controls. On the left is a picture (and username) that matches the account with which you signed in to Windows. Click that picture to display a shortcut menu allowing you to change the settings for your account, lock the PC, sign out of Windows, or switch to another user account.

On the right is a power button, which you can click to change sign-in options or choose one of three additional options: Sleep, Shut Down, or Restart. (If you've enabled the Hibernate option, you see it here as well.)

On a default installation, the space between those two items is completely blank. You can choose to fill it with up to nine shortcuts, one that takes you to the Settings app and the remainder from your user profile. To choose which folders appear in this space, go to Settings > Personalization > Start > Folders, and then turn on the switches for the folders you want to see, as shown in Figure 3-4.

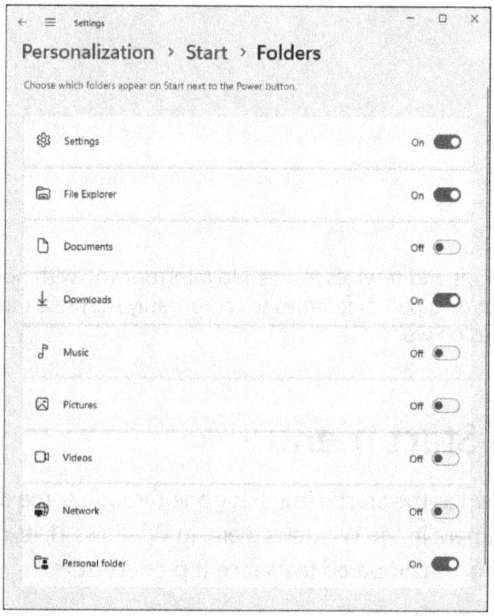

Figure 3-4   Use the switches on this Settings page to tell Windows which folder shortcuts you want to see on the bottom of the Start menu.

Inside OUT

Change your Start picture

The picture that appears alongside your username in the lower-left corner of the Start menu is the one associated with your user account (the one that also appears on the Welcome screen). If you're not happy with that picture, click it, and then click Change Account Settings. That takes you to the Settings page for your account, where you can choose a different picture or snap one with a webcam.

Customizing the contents of the Start menu

In sharp contrast to its predecessors, the Windows 11 Start menu is lean, with a minimum of customization options. As we noted earlier, the menu itself is fixed in size and divided into two regions: the top for pinned program icons and below that a place for recommended shortcuts to files and apps.

Inside OUT

Using Start to search

You can launch any pinned app or document shortcut on the Start menu by tapping or clicking it. Alternatively, if you're comfortable typing, you can skip all the scrolling, tap the Windows key, and then begin typing the name of an item you want in the search box, at the top of the Start menu. What you're looking for soon appears at or near the top of the search results. This approach is especially handy when third-party installers store a collection of related apps in folders on the All Apps menu.

This same technique works if you want to search for content on the web. Windows 11 uses the Bing search engine to deliver search results in the same space where it displays your pinned program icons and shortcuts to recently used files.

You can't change the search engine associated with this functionality; if you prefer the results you get from another search provider, you should skip Start and go directly to your browser to search for online answers.

The Start menu's most important function is to organize shortcuts to installed apps. Windows pins a selection of apps to the list by default. You can pin any installed app to that list by right-clicking its executable file or an app shortcut and choosing Pin To Start Menu. To remove a pinned app, right-click and choose Unpin From Start. You can rearrange pinned shortcuts by clicking and dragging them from their current position to the one you prefer.

Initially, the Pinned and Recommended regions are configured to be roughly the same size, with three rows of shortcuts in each. You can change the relative allocation of space by going to Settings > Personalization > Start and choosing More Pins or More Recommendations from the Layout section at the top of the page, as shown in Figure 3-5. (You can also get to this page by opening the Start menu, right-clicking the blank area at the bottom of the menu, and choosing Start Settings.)

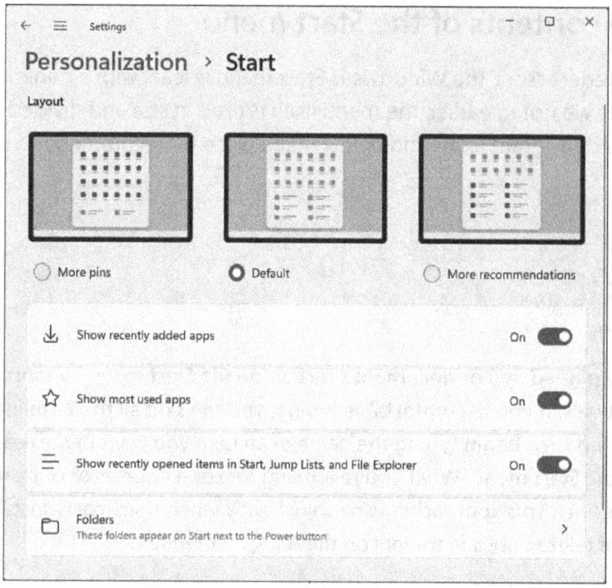

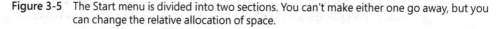

Figure 3-5   The Start menu is divided into two sections. You can't make either one go away, but you can change the relative allocation of space.

You can't hide the Recommended section, but you can make it shrink to almost nothing. If you prefer to use the Start menu exclusively for app shortcuts, choose the More Pins option and then turn the three switches on that page to the Off position. That configuration hides all short-cuts from the Recommended section and shrinks it to a minimal size.

Both regions include a button at the top right that takes you to an expanded list of items from that category. Clicking the All Apps shortcut reveals an alphabetical list of every installed app, in a format that should be familiar to anyone who's used any version of Windows in the past two decades. Clicking More (to the right of the Recommended heading) displays an expanded list of recent documents. In either case, you can use a Back button to return to Start.

Inside OUT

Use the powerful "other" Start menu

Every Windows power user knows the maxim: When in doubt, right-click. Testing that principle on the Start button is especially rewarding, as it reveals the hidden Quick Link menu. (You can also summon this menu using the keyboard shortcut Windows key+X.) Figure 3-6 shows the options available as of Windows 11 version 22H2.

Figure 3-6 The Quick Link menu, which appears when you right-click Start, contains an impressive assortment of system management tools.

Alas, the Quick Link menu isn't customizable, but it's still exceptionally useful. Most of the major system management and troubleshooting tools are on this menu, including Disk Management, Event Viewer, and the Computer Management console. At the top of the list is a useful shortcut to the Installed Apps page in Settings.

Windows traditionalists will appreciate the fact that the Shut Down Or Sign Out menu item is here, along with links to Settings and Task Manager. The menu also includes links to Windows Terminal, where you can use your favorite command-line shell: Windows PowerShell or Command Prompt.

Arranging pinned apps into folders

Pinned apps can be combined into folders, with or without folder names. A folder containing two or more pinned apps takes up the same space as a single app, with miniature versions of the first four app icons displayed in the folder.

To create a folder, drag one app icon and drop it on top of another. To give a folder a descriptive name, click the heading at the top of any open folder and start typing. To drop additional apps into the folder, drag them to the existing folder. When you click or tap a folder, the folder opens to reveal the individual apps contained within. You can click any pinned app in the folder to open that app.

To remove an app from a folder while leaving it pinned to the Start menu, open the folder and then drag the pinned app to the place where you want it to appear.

Using the Start menu to search

Search is built into Windows 11 as an integral feature that gets prime real estate. Unlike its predecessor in Windows 10, however, the search box isn't built into the taskbar. Instead, it exists as an alternative view of the Start menu, which you can trigger by tapping the Windows key or clicking the search button (to the right of Start if you have opted to show it using Settings > Personalization > Taskbar) and then typing your search request. If the Start menu is already open, just click in the search box at the top of the menu to change the view.

For most simple tasks, such as searching for an app or a setting, the fastest route to success is to tap the Windows key and begin typing. The results, as shown in Figure 3-7, are businesslike and efficient, with no personality.

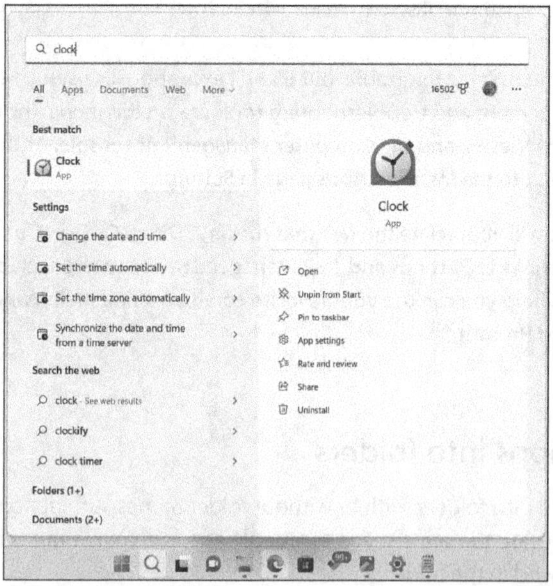

Figure 3-7   Type a word or phrase in the search box, and you get a categorized list of results that match the search term, including apps and settings. Use the options at the top to change the search scope.

The list on the left shows search results by category, including results from the web, with a Best Match item at the top if Windows believes it knows exactly what you're looking for; the larger pane to its right shows details for the currently selected item from the results list. That list also includes local files available to the currently signed-in user as well as files stored in OneDrive or OneDrive for Business. Click the profile icon in the top right to search using a different OneDrive account.

If you click Search without entering a search term, you see a list of recent searches on the left, with a Today view to its right. That view shows a highlight from the Bing search engine if you've selected a Microsoft account from the profile menu; choosing an Azure AD account shows search results from your school or workplace, including recently edited files and comments by coworkers to shared work files.

As mentioned earlier, you can narrow the scope of the search by choosing a category from the list above the results pane. The Apps, Documents, and Web categories are visible by default; click More to expand the list of available categories to include Email, Folders, Music, People, Photos, Settings, and Videos. Choosing one of those categories immediately changes the search results list to show only the category you selected.

Choosing a category has a simple but powerful action: It inserts a prefix in the search box, before the search term. If you're more comfortable with the keyboard, you can accomplish the same result by typing the category prefix manually: **folder:** or **photos:**, for example.

Windows highlights the top item on the results list, but you can use the arrow keys to scroll up and down through the list. You can also use the mouse to select the arrow to the right of any entry and make its properties or Jump List options visible on the right side of the results pane.

When you enter a word or phrase in the search box, results from the web can appear directly in the results list in a panel that pops out to the right of the initial display of search results in Start. This feature enables you to get instant answers to questions in a wide array of categories. If your question is clear and unambiguous and you have a working internet connection, your answer appears immediately, as shown in Figure 3-8.

CHAPTER 3

Figure 3-8   When the best match for a search term is on the web, you might see a detailed info box like this one to the right of the results list.

You can use this same technique for the following types of queries:

- **Dates and times**   Use the search box to check the dates of upcoming holidays and events. ("When is Thanksgiving this year?" and "What time does the Super Bowl start?")

- **Biographical details**   If someone is famous enough or holds a public office, you can ask for more information. ("How old is Bill Gates?" or "Who is Governor of New Mexico?")

- **Definitions**   Not sure of the meaning of an unfamiliar word? You can view a definition in the results pane, with an option to hear the word's pronunciation or jump to an online dictionary. ("What does phlegmatic mean?")

- **Sports scores**   You can see scores and standings for any team or league, even for games that are in progress.

- **Stock prices**   To get the current price and a chart for any stock or index on a major exchange, enter a dollar sign followed by the ticker symbol: $MSFT, $DJIA.

- **Weather**   Type **weather** followed by a city name to see a five-day forecast that can help you decide whether to pack an umbrella or extra sunscreen for an upcoming trip.

The expanded results pane can also display interactive controls. Enter an arithmetic problem, and Windows search shows the result in a calculator where you can continue your number-crunching. If you ask how to convert units of measurement, the resulting display enables you to choose from an enormous number of conversions, including length, volume, and even fuel efficiency. Figure 3-9 shows a conversion that might not be as practical as gallons to liters but could help settle a bet over your favorite space opera.

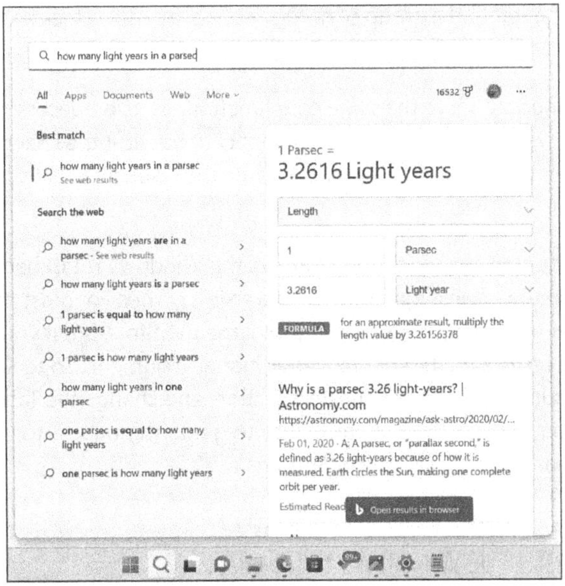

Figure 3-9   An interactive widget appears in the search results when you ask a question that involves calculation or conversion.

Besides conversions, you can also do basic math by entering an appropriate query in the taskbar search box. Enter any valid mathematical format—addition, subtraction, multiplication, division, exponentiation, and more, with support for using parentheses to group operations—and see the answer directly in the results pane.

The search box is also able to look up current exchange rates and convert any amount in one currency to its equivalent in another. Specify the amount and the target currency—for example, **$195 in GBP**—and then use controls in the widget to change the amount, choose a different currency, or enter a new value in the second box to reverse the conversion.

The results can change with every character as you type, so feel free to use the backspace key and change your input slightly to help Search understand what you're asking.

Using and customizing the taskbar

The taskbar is the valuable strip of real estate along the bottom of the screen. The taskbar made its debut in Windows 95, and in the years since, it has added features and buttons without changing its basic shape.

In Windows 11, Microsoft has rewritten the taskbar code from scratch, stripping away nearly three decades' worth of cruft and starting fresh with a design that is deliberately clean and simple. Its initial arrangement contains a group of buttons in the center, with (from left to right) the Start button, a group of system shortcuts, and then a group of buttons representing apps; the Widgets button is on the far left and a group of notification icons and a clock are on the far right.

The Windows 11 taskbar continues to serve the same core functions as its predecessors—launching apps, switching between apps, and providing notifications—but the changes from its Windows 10 predecessor are profound. (For a partial list, see the sidebar, "What you can't do with the Windows 11 taskbar.")

The most obvious change is the starting position. By default, the Windows 11 taskbar is centered on the bottom of the display rather than aligning to the lower-left corner. For most people, the new position quickly becomes second nature, especially on large monitors; but if you'd rather not adapt, it's easy enough to restore the taskbar to its traditional alignment. Go to Settings > Personalization > Taskbar, expand the Taskbar Behaviors section, and change the Taskbar Alignment menu option from Center to Left. (An even faster way to get to this page is to right-click any empty space on the taskbar and choose Taskbar Settings.)

WHAT YOU CAN'T DO WITH THE WINDOWS 11 TASKBAR

Earlier Windows versions offered a staggering number of options for customizing the taskbar, many of them dating back to the earliest appearance of this feature in Windows 95.

As part of a comprehensive rewrite of this and other core elements of the Windows user experience, Microsoft has removed many of those customization options. If you've grown accustomed to extensively tweaking the taskbar in Windows 10 and earlier versions, you're in for a bit of a shock.

Here's a partial list of advanced taskbar options that are not available in Windows 11:

- You can no longer move the taskbar from its default position at the bottom of the screen. If you prefer to dock the taskbar at the top (a configuration that's similar to Apple's MacOS) or to either side, you need to use a third-party utility.

- Previous Windows versions allowed you to expand the height of the taskbar to accommodate two or more rows of buttons. That option is not available in Windows 11.

- There's no longer an option to use smaller taskbar buttons.

- A legacy taskbar option, one that dates back to the earliest days of Windows, allowed the addition of optional toolbars that were hosted entirely within the taskbar, in a space just to the left of the notification area. Windows 11 does not support additional toolbars.

- When you have multiple windows open for an app, earlier Windows versions allowed you to configure the taskbar so that each of those windows has its own button. Windows 11 always combines those Windows into a single taskbar button, without labels.

- You can't drag file or folder icons from File Explorer and drop them onto the taskbar to pin them to a taskbar icon's Jump List, as you could in Windows 10.

And one more thing: If you're used to right-clicking an empty space on the taskbar to see additional options, you've no doubt grown accustomed to a long menu packed with options: a long list of taskbar items you can show or hide, as well as options for arranging open windows. You might want to sit down before you right-click the Windows 11 taskbar to reveal its shortcut menu, which includes only two options: Taskbar Settings and a shortcut to Task Manager.

If you find the prospect of giving up those classic taskbar features unacceptable, you have an alternative: Install a third-party utility to restore the missing functionality. Start11 (*https://www.stardock.com/products/start11/*) is a commercial product that brings back the Windows 10–style Start menu. If you'd rather not pay, consider the free, open-source alternative ExplorerPatcher (*https://github.com/valinet/ExplorerPatcher*).

CHAPTER 3

Every running app with a user interface has a corresponding taskbar button. (Apps that run exclusively in the background don't offer a taskbar button.) When you close that app, the button vanishes as well, unless you pinned it to the taskbar. A short line appears underneath the icon for a pinned app that is currently running, and the app with the current focus has a longer line and a subtle but noticeable transparent shadow to identify it.

The Windows 11 taskbar offers a limited (but useful) selection of customization options, available through Settings > Personalization > Taskbar (or by right-clicking any empty space on the taskbar and clicking Taskbar Settings). Figure 3-10 shows an expanded view of the first two groups of options available on that page.

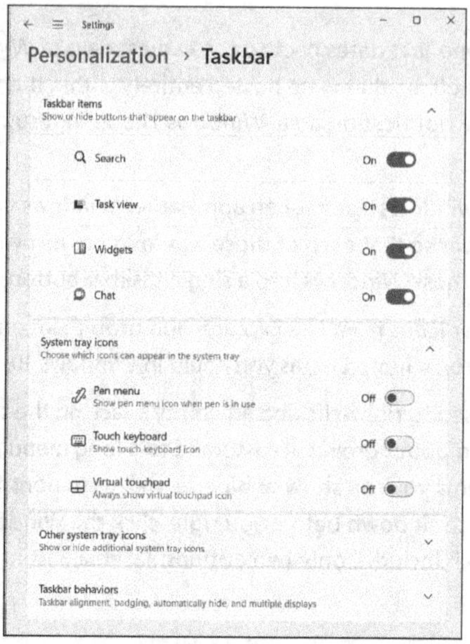

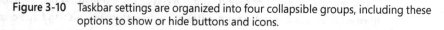

Figure 3-10 Taskbar settings are organized into four collapsible groups, including these options to show or hide buttons and icons.

Here's a rundown of the available taskbar customization options:

- **Taskbar Items**   The four items in this group allow you to show or hide items that appear on the taskbar independently of app buttons: Search, Task View, Widgets, and Chat. If you don't use one or more of these features, it might make sense to suppress their appearance on the taskbar. In the interest of saving space, you might even choose to hide the button for a feature you use occasionally and just rely on its keyboard shortcut instead. For example, you can hide the Widgets button and press Windows key+W when you feel the need to check news headlines or see the local weather forecast.

- **System Tray Icons**   On systems that are equipped with the requisite hardware (a pen and/or touchscreen), you can configure Windows so that the Pen Menu, Touch Keyboard, and Virtual Touchpad icons are always visible. We cover these features in more detail later in this chapter.

- **Other System Tray Icons**   Third-party apps (including some from Microsoft) can add their own icons to the system tray, which is the region just to the left of the clock in the taskbar. By default, most of these icons are hidden and available only in an overflow area visible when you click the upward-pointing arrow at the left of the system tray, as shown in Figure 3-11. You can drag icons from the overflow area onto the system tray (or vice versa), or use the switches on this Settings page to show or hide individual icons.

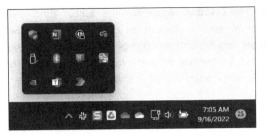

Figure 3-11   Drag icons out of this overflow area and onto the system tray to make them always available for notifications and access to shortcut menus.

- **Taskbar Behaviors**   The final section on this page (shown in Figure 3-12) contains a limited selection of options you can use to manage the appearance of the taskbar as well as the behavior of taskbar buttons.

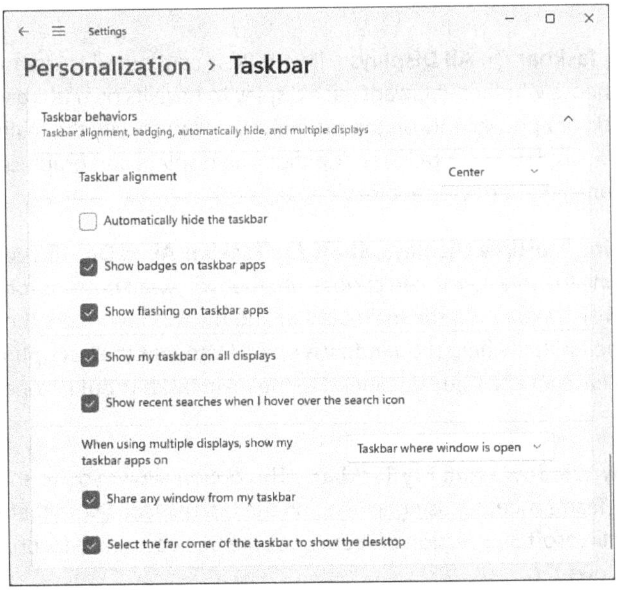

Figure 3-12   Use the Taskbar Alignment setting to move the Start button to the left. Note that some options shown here are available only on PCs with multiple displays.

The following is a rundown of the options shown in Figure 3-12:

- **Taskbar Alignment**   By default, the Windows 11 taskbar buttons are centered at the bottom of the display, with the Start button on its left. Change this option to Left if you want the Start button to appear in the lower-left corner, with taskbar buttons appearing to its right, as in previous Windows versions.

- **Automatically Hide The Taskbar**   By default, the taskbar remains visible at all times. If that's inconvenient for any reason, you can tell it to get out of the way. With this option set, the taskbar retreats into the bottom edge of the desktop whenever a window has the focus. To display the hidden taskbar, move the mouse pointer to the bottom of the desktop. On a touchscreen, swipe from that edge toward the center of the screen.

- **Show Badges On Taskbar Apps**   Badges are small circular notifications that can appear over taskbar buttons to indicate that something in that app needs your attention. Badges on the Clock icon, for example, indicate that an alarm has been set, while badges over the To Do and Mail buttons indicate that you have overdue tasks and unread messages, respectively.

- **Show Flashing On Taskbar Apps**   This option allows Windows to flash a taskbar button when it requires immediate action on your part to proceed. If you turn this option off, the taskbar button changes color to alert you, without calling any additional attention to itself.

- **Show My Taskbar On All Displays**   If your PC is configured to use multiple displays, you can choose whether you want each display to have its own taskbar. If this option is off, the taskbar appears only on the main display. (You specify the main display in Settings > System > Display. For details, see "Configuring displays and graphics adapters" in Chapter 13, "Managing hardware and devices.")

- **When Using Multiple Displays, Show My Taskbar Apps On**   If you've chosen to show taskbars on all displays, you can choose whether you want buttons for running apps to appear on all taskbars, on the main taskbar and the window where the window is open, or only on the taskbar where the window is open. Note that the last option can be confusing if you have an app's button pinned to the main taskbar, but it's open on a secondary window.

- **Share Any Window From My Taskbar**   This option allows you to share a window in a Microsoft Teams meeting using a menu on the taskbar icon. Note that this feature works with the Microsoft 365 version of Teams, not the free consumer-focused version included with Windows.

- **Select The Far Corner Of The Taskbar To Show The Desktop**   With this option (called Peek in previous Windows versions) on, clicking in the lower-right corner of the display (beyond the Notification Center button) hides all open windows, giving you the opportunity to see the underlying desktop. Click again to restore the previous arrangement.

Pinning apps to the taskbar

Pinning apps to the taskbar makes it easy to find and run favorite apps without the need to open Start or use the search box to find the app's shortcut. To pin an app to the taskbar, simply drag its icon or a shortcut (from Start, from the desktop, or from any other folder) to the taskbar. Alternatively, right-click a pinned app (in any location) or the taskbar button for a running app and then click Pin To Taskbar.

To remove a pinned app from the taskbar, right-click the pinned app and then click Unpin From Taskbar. This command also appears on other shortcuts to the app, including those on the desktop and on Start.

You can use taskbar buttons to launch an app that's not currently running or to switch from one running app to another. You can also click a taskbar button to minimize an open window or to restore a minimized window. If those features sound too obvious, here's a trick you might not know: You can open a new instance of an app that's already running—a new Microsoft Word document, for example, or a fresh File Explorer window—by right-clicking the taskbar button and then clicking the app name; alternatively, hold Shift and click the app's taskbar button.

Changing the order of taskbar buttons

To change the order of buttons on the taskbar, drag them into position. Pinned apps retain their order between sessions, allowing you to quickly find your most used apps in their familiar (to you) location.

CHAPTER 3

Inside OUT

Use shortcut keys for taskbar buttons

The first 10 app buttons on the taskbar (not counting the Start button or the optional Search, Task View, Widgets, or Chat buttons) are accessible by keyboard as well as by mouse. Press Windows key+1 for the first, Windows key+2 for the second, and so on (using 0 for the tenth). Using one of these shortcuts is equivalent to clicking the corresponding taskbar button: If the app isn't running, it starts; if it has a single open window, you switch to that window; if it has multiple open windows, Windows displays previews of all windows and switches to the first window. Press Shift+Windows key+*number* to open a new document in the associated app.

Hold down the Windows key and tap the number key repeatedly to cycle between all open windows for that app.

Note that when you change the order of a taskbar button, you also change the Windows key+*number* combination that starts that particular app.

Another useful shortcut key is Windows key+T, which brings focus to the first app button on the taskbar. At that point, you can repeatedly press Windows key+T, Shift+Windows key+T, or the arrow keys to select other taskbar buttons. When a taskbar button is selected, you can press the Spacebar to "click" the button or press the Menu key to display its Jump List.

Using Jump Lists for quick access to documents and folders

A Jump List is the official name for the set of additional menu options that appear when you right-click a taskbar button for an app that supports this feature.

For Microsoft Office programs, Adobe Acrobat, and other document-centric apps, Jump Lists typically include links to recently opened files as well as pinned shortcuts to files and folders. In Microsoft Edge, these groups are labeled Top Sites and Recently Closed. Jump Lists can include shortcuts to common tasks that can be performed with that program, such as New Window or New InPrivate Window on a Microsoft Edge Jump List, and New Email Message or New Appointment on the Jump List for Microsoft Outlook.

Figure 3-13 shows the default Jump List for File Explorer.

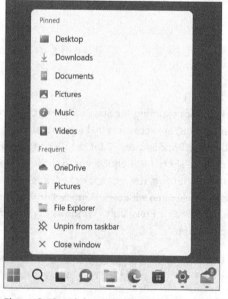

Figure 3-13   Right-click a taskbar button, such as File Explorer, to see a Jump List showing recently opened files and folders with the option to pin items for quick access.

Individual files and folders can't be pinned directly to the taskbar, but you can add them to Jump Lists on any program that supports this feature. Opening a file or folder from File Explorer adds an entry for that to the Recent list in the app where it opened. Right-click the taskbar button, point to its entry, and click the pushpin icon to move the file or folder to the Pinned section of the Jump List:

- To open a pinned document or folder, right-click the taskbar button and then click the name of the document or folder.

- To remove a pinned document or folder from the Jump List, right-click the taskbar button and point to the name of the document or folder to be removed. Click the pushpin icon that appears.

Customizing the Quick Settings pane

Three icons on the right side of the taskbar behave differently than their neighbors. The network, volume, and battery icons sit between the system tray and the clock and cannot be hidden or moved.

Right-clicking any of these three icons reveals a shortcut menu specific to that icon's function. Clicking any part of the region, however, opens the Quick Settings pane, which is shown in Figure 3-14. As an alternative, use the keyboard shortcut Windows key+A to open Quick Settings.

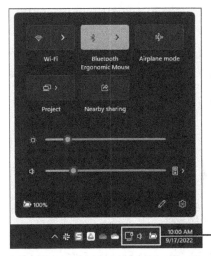

Click here to open Quick Settings

Figure 3-14   The Quick Settings pane includes a wide-ranging assortment of tools for efficiently managing common system settings.

This compact pane packs an impressive collection of controls into its small space. On the example shown in Figure 3-14, each of the five buttons at the top of the pane allows direct control over common system settings without having to open the full Settings app. Two slider controls below that control screen brightness and system volume, respectively. Clicking the battery icon opens the Power & Battery page in Settings, where you can change the power mode or turn on Battery Saver mode.

The playback controls above the Quick Settings pane are available for apps that don't include these functions on the taskbar item itself, as is the case with a Progressive Web App that uses Microsoft Edge as its engine.

Quick Settings controls that have an arrow on the right allow you to choose an additional option for that control. Click the arrow to the right of the volume slider, for example, to direct sound output to a different device. Both the Wi-Fi and Bluetooth controls offer a split button, with the left side turning the feature on or off. Click the arrow on the right of the Wi-Fi control to select from a list of available Wi-Fi networks; click the arrow on the right of the Bluetooth button to display a list of paired Bluetooth devices that are available for connection, as shown in Figure 3-15.

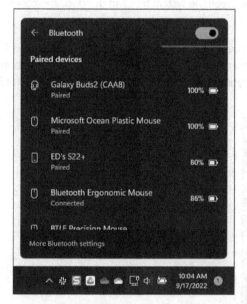

Figure 3-15   Click the arrow to the right of the Bluetooth button in Quick Settings to open this list and connect to a previously paired device.

The gear icon in the lower-right corner of Quick Settings opens the full Settings app. Click the pen icon just to its left to add, remove, or rearrange the controls at the top of the pane, as shown in Figure 3-16. Click Add to display a list of available controls that can be pinned to this region; click the unpin icon next to any control to remove it. Drag icons to change their order.

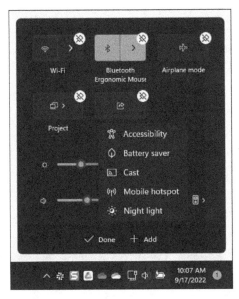

Figure 3-16   You can add, remove, or rearrange controls on the Quick Settings pane using these options.

Managing notifications and eliminating distractions

Windows 11 is capable of displaying notifications from apps, services, and Windows itself, alerting you to incoming messages, alarms, and events that require your attention. These notifications can pop up as banners in the lower-right corner of the primary display; they also show up in the notification center, a pane that appears at the right side of your screen when you swipe in from the right (on a touchscreen), press Windows key+N, or click the clock on the right of the taskbar. In addition to hosting notifications, this pane includes a collapsible calendar as well as a pair of features that you can use to eliminate distractions caused by, among other things, notifications.

Figure 3-17 shows the notification center with two notifications and Do Not Disturb turned on. Notifications are grouped under headings corresponding to the notifying applications.

CHAPTER 3

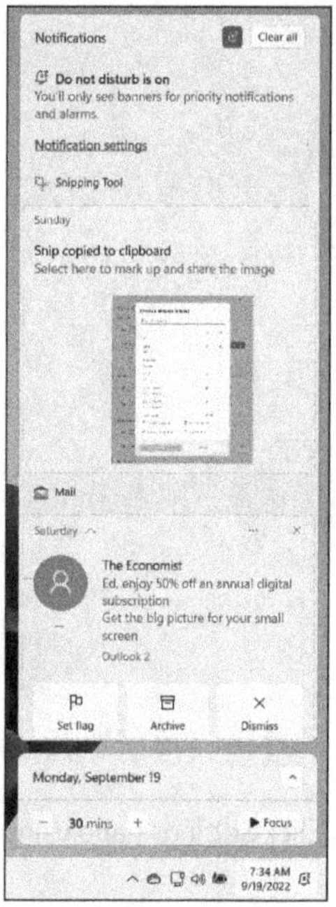

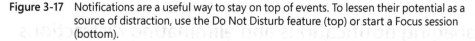

Figure 3-17   Notifications are a useful way to stay on top of events. To lessen their potential as a source of distraction, use the Do Not Disturb feature (top) or start a Focus session (bottom).

You can respond to notifications in various ways. If you hover the mouse pointer over a notification, a Close button appears in its upper-right corner, with a Settings button (three dots) just to its left. Click Close to dismiss the notification. If you click on the body of the notification, the relevant action occurs. For example, clicking on an email message opens it in the associated app (Mail or Outlook, for example); clicking on a message from Snipping Tool telling you that you've successfully captured a screenshot opens the Snipping Tool app with the capture available for immediate editing. Acting on a notification in this fashion removes it from the notification center immediately.

If there are more notifications from a single app than will fit in the notification center, a small message at the bottom lets you know how many additional alerts are available. Click that message to expand the list and see all available notifications. You can click the Close button to the right of any heading to close all notifications in that group.

Click Clear All, in the top-right corner of the notification center, to clear all notifications immediately.

Customizing notifications

The options for controlling which apps and services can deliver messages to the notification center are available in Settings > System > Notifications, as shown in Figure 3-18. The Notifications section at the top of the page contains an On/Off switch that allows you to shut off all notifications. If you leave notifications enabled, use the checkboxes below that switch to eliminate sounds associated with notifications and to control whether messages are displayed on your lock screen.

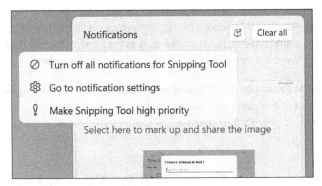

Figure 3-18   Use the switch at the top of this page to suppress all notifications.

Turning off all notifications is a fairly drastic step. A more measured approach if you find the volume of notifications excessive is to adjust settings for each source. You can make this adjustment directly from the notification center by clicking the Settings button to the right of a group heading. That action opens a menu like the one shown in Figure 3-19.

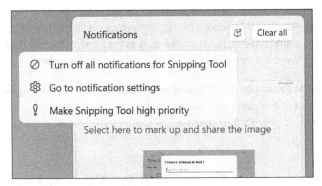

Figure 3-19   Use this Settings menu to quickly adjust notification options for a group that's currently visible in the notification center.

CHAPTER 3

If you decide you don't really need to see notifications from Snipping Tool, for example, click its Settings button and then choose Turn Off All Notifications For Snipping Tool. If, on the other hand, you want those notifications to be treated with high priority so that you see them above other notifications, even when Do Not Disturb is turned on, choose Make Snipping Tool High Priority.

For more granular control over notifications on an app-by-app basis, click Go To Notification Settings from this menu. That opens a page like the one shown in Figure 3-20.

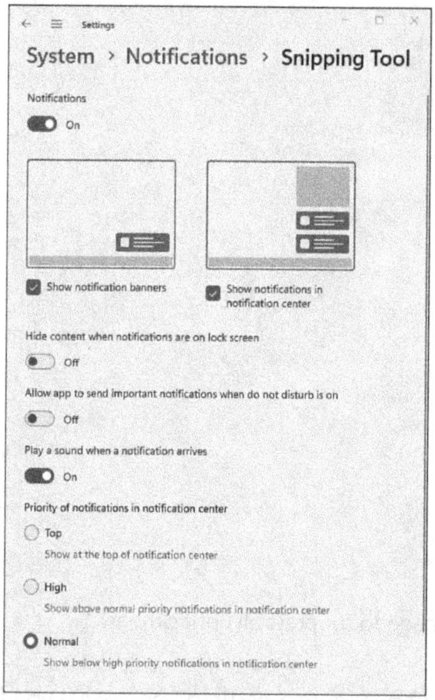

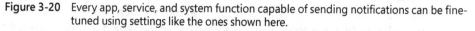

Figure 3-20   Every app, service, and system function capable of sending notifications can be fine-tuned using settings like the ones shown here.

Most of the options in this page are self-explanatory. If you don't want notification banners to appear briefly in the lower-right corner, clear the Show Notification Banners box. (A jargon note: Windows calls this type of alert "toast," because of the way it pops up, like a slice of bread from a toaster.) Conversely, if you want to see notification banners as they arrive but you don't need to see the ones you missed, clear the Show Notifications In Notification Center box.

The three options under the Priority of Notifications In Notification Center heading allow you to roughly sort the contents of this pane by importance. Set your must-see notifications to the Top option; use High for those you want to see near the top; everything else is categorized as Normal.

On a well-used Windows 11 PC, dozens of apps and services, as well as Windows features such as USB and Bluetooth, are capable of sending you notifications. You can curate what you see in the notification center by scrolling through the entire list at the bottom of Settings > System > Notifications. Turn the switch to Off for any app you never want to hear from, and then go through the individual settings to adjust the behavior of alerts from those that are allowed to send notifications.

Eliminating distractions

Notifications are designed to get your attention. That's a mixed blessing if you're trying to do something that demands your undivided attention, like finish a high-priority work project or play a game against a skilled online rival.

For those instances, two features are especially useful: Do Not Disturb and Focus.

Do Not Disturb does exactly what its name promises: When you click the Do Not Disturb button at the top of the notification center (or go to Settings > System > Notifications and turn on the corresponding switch), Windows temporarily suppresses toast-style notifications, sending them directly to the notification center. The only exceptions are incoming voice and video calls (including VOIP calls), reminders (you don't want to miss an appointment because you were busy playing Halo), and notifications from any app you set as High Priority. To adjust these settings, open the Notifications page in Settings and click Set Priority Notifications.

Windows 11 can turn on Do Not Disturb automatically. By default, it does so when you're duplicating your display (on the theory that you're probably delivering a presentation and don't want your audience to be distracted by your notifications), when you're playing a game, or when you're using an app in full-screen mode. Do Not Disturb is also on automatically for the first hour after a Windows feature update, when the system is busy doing housekeeping tasks.

You can adjust these settings and also specify times when you want Windows to remain quiet. You'll find these options on the Notifications page in Settings. Expand the Turn On Do Not Disturb Automatically section and configure the options you see there. In Figure 3-21, for example, we've told Windows to turn on Do Not Disturb between 11:00 PM and 6:00 AM.

The Focus feature (which was known as Focus Assist and before that as Quiet Hours in Windows 10) is a productivity-focused feature designed to minimize interruptions from your computer for a specific period of time while you concentrate. The idea is that you will focus your attention, uninterrupted, for a burst of productive activity.

Figure 3-21   Windows turns on Do Not Disturb automatically when it senses you don't want to be bothered. You can set your own "quiet hours" here.

To start a focus session, open the notification center and look for the controls at the bottom of the pane, below the calendar. By default, a focus session lasts 30 minutes. Use the plus and minus buttons to change the time, if necessary, and then click Focus. If you set a session for more than 30 minutes, as we've done in Figure 3-22, Windows offers to give you breaks.

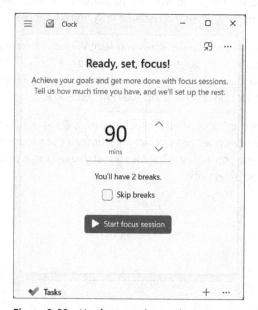

Figure 3-22   Use focus sessions to increase your productivity by hiding notifications and other distractions for a set period of time.

When you're in a focus session, Windows turns on Do Not Disturb automatically and suppresses notifications and badges on taskbar buttons. To help you stay focused, Windows displays a minimalist view of the Clock app with a small timer and a Stop button that allows you to end the session early. By default, this timer shows a simple circular progress indicator; you can click to expand it to show the full time remaining in your session. When your focus session ends, Windows lets you know by interrupting your train of thought with (naturally) a notification.

To configure these options, go to Settings > System > Focus. Note that you cannot adjust these settings while you're in the middle of a focus session.

Managing and arranging windows

Windows 11 includes a host of keyboard shortcuts and gestures that greatly simplify the everyday tasks of resizing, moving, minimizing, arranging, and otherwise managing windows. The most useful trick is a collection of "snap" techniques that have been around for several Windows versions; Windows 11 supercharges these options.

The simplest window-snapping scenario is a PC with a single display, where you want to arrange two windows side by side. You might want to compare two Word documents; move files between the Documents folder and an archive, each open in separate File Explorer windows; or do financial research in a web browser and plug the numbers into an Excel spreadsheet.

Drag a window title bar to the left or right edge of the screen, and it snaps to fill that half of the display. Drag a window title bar to any corner of the screen, and it snaps to fill that quadrant of the display. As soon as you let go of the title bar, the window snaps into its position, and Windows helpfully offers thumbnails for all other open windows to help you choose what to run alongside your first snapped window.

In Figure 3-23, for example, we've just snapped a File Explorer window to the right side of the screen and now have a choice of seven other running windows to snap opposite it. (If you don't feel like snapping a second window, just press Esc or click anywhere except on one of those thumbnails. They vanish immediately and retain their previous size and position.)

An even easier window-snapping technique, new in Windows 11, allows you to quickly snap a window into one of several predetermined layouts by pointing and clicking—no dragging and dropping required. To get started, hover the mouse pointer over the maximize button on the window you want to rearrange. That displays a list of available layouts like the one shown in Figure 3-24.

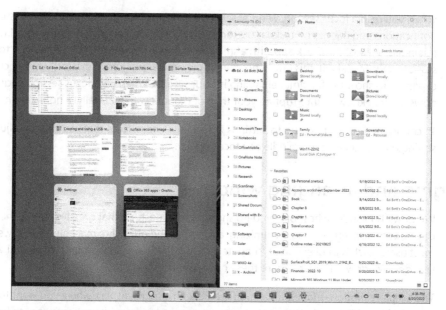

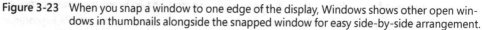

Figure 3-23   When you snap a window to one edge of the display, Windows shows other open windows in thumbnails alongside the snapped window for easy side-by-side arrangement.

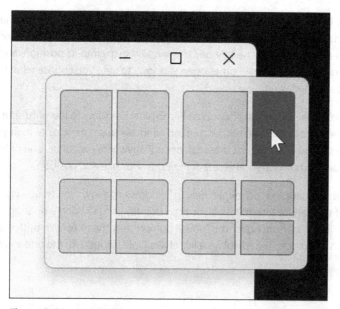

Figure 3-24   Hover the mouse pointer over the maximize button to expose this menu of available snap layouts. Click to immediately snap the window into the chosen position.

A variation of this feature, first available in Windows 11 version 22H2, makes window snapping easier on a touchscreen device. Drag the title bar up until you see a menu of available layouts drop down from the center of the display's upper edge, as shown in Figure 3-25.

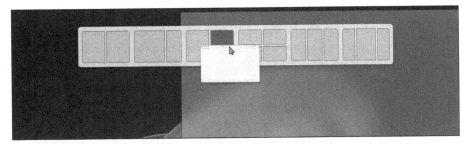

Figure 3-25   On a touchscreen device, you can drag a window's title bar to the top of the display to choose from available snap layouts.

Inside OUT

Expand your selection of window-snapping layouts

Alert readers might notice that Figure 3-25 contains an expanded selection of layouts, with options to position three windows side by side, rather than two. Those options are available only on wide displays, those with an effective resolution of at least 1850 pixels in width. (To calculate effective resolution, divide the display's native resolution by its scaling factor. The native resolution of a Surface Pro device, for example, has a width of 2880 pixels, but at the recommended scaling factor of 200%, its effective resolution is 1440 pixels wide.)

If your effective display resolution is too narrow to support the larger selection of window-snapping layouts in Windows 11, you have an option. Use the FancyZones utility, which is part of the Microsoft PowerToys package. Full documentation, including a download link, is available at *https://learn.microsoft.com/windows/powertoys*.

As soon as you begin dragging a snapped window away from the edge of the screen, it returns to its previous size and position.

If you drag the top window border (not the title bar) to the top edge of the screen, or drag the bottom border to the bottom edge of the screen, the window snaps to full height when you reach the edge, without changing its width. When you drag the border away from the window edge, the opposite border snaps to its previous position.

CHAPTER 3

Inside OUT

Snap side-by-side Windows at different widths

Although Windows automatically arranges side-by-side windows at equal widths, you don't have to settle for symmetry. On a large desktop monitor, for example, you might want to arrange a news feed or chat session along the right side of your display, using a third or less of the total display width and leaving room for Word or Excel to have a much larger share of the screen real estate.

If you have a large enough monitor, you can choose this option from a predetermined layout. But regardless of the effective display resolution, you can change the relative width of snapped windows with ease. The secret is to snap the first window and immediately drag its inside edge to adjust the window to your preferred width. Now grab the title bar of the window you want to see alongside it and snap it to the opposite edge of the display. The newly snapped window expands to fill the space remaining after you adjusted the width of the first window. To readjust the division of space between the two windows, you can drag the border between them; when doing research on the web, for example, you might opt for a wider Microsoft Word or OneNote window to hold your notes with a relatively slim window for your browser alongside.

The rules work the same with multimonitor setups. With two side-by-side monitors, for example, you can snap a window to the inside edge of a display, allowing for two pairs of equal-size windows lined up from left to right. By dragging the title bar, you also can move a maximized window from one screen to another on a multimonitor system.

Inside OUT

Shake to minimize distractions

An ancient Windows feature called Aero Shake, introduced with Windows Vista, survives in Windows 11. Grab the window's title bar and quickly move it back and forth a few times. Suddenly, all windows retreat to the taskbar except the one whose title bar you just shook. This move takes a bit of practice, but it's worth learning. It requires only three smooth "shakes"—a left, right, left motion is best—not maniacal shaking. If this feature isn't working, you might need to turn it on. Go to Settings > System > Multitasking and turn the Title Bar Window Shake switch to the On position.

Windows 11 includes keyboard shortcuts that correspond with the preceding mouse gestures. These (and a few extras) are shown in Table 3-1.

Table 3-1   Keyboard shortcuts and gestures for resizing and moving windows

Task	Keyboard shortcut	Gesture
Maximize window	Windows key+ Up Arrow	Drag title bar to top of screen
Resize window to full screen height without changing its width	Shift+Windows key+ Up Arrow	Drag top or bottom border to edge of screen
Restore a maximized or full-height window	Windows key+ Down Arrow	Drag title bar away from screen edge
Minimize a restored window	Windows key+ Down Arrow	Click the Minimize button
Snap to the left half of the screen	Windows key+ Left Arrow*	Drag title bar to left edge
Snap to the right half of the screen	Windows key+ Right Arrow*	Drag title bar to right edge
Move to the next virtual desktop	Ctrl+Windows key+ Left/Right Arrow	Three-finger swipe on precision touchpad; none for mouse
Move to the next monitor	Shift+Windows key+ Left/Right Arrow	Drag title bar
Minimize all windows except the active window (press again to restore windows previously mini-mized with this shortcut)	Windows key+ Home	"Shake" the title bar
Minimize all windows	Windows key+M	
Restore windows after minimizing	Shift+Windows key+M	

* Pressing this key repeatedly cycles through the left, right, and restored positions. If you have more than one monitor, it cycles these positions on each monitor in turn.

The Windows 11 taskbar also exposes some traditional window-management menus. The secret? Hold the Shift key as you right-click a taskbar button. For a button that represents a single window, the menu includes the following commands: Restore, Move, Size, Minimize, Maximize, and Close.

Window snapping is one of our favorite Windows 11 features. But if you prefer to arrange windows manually, go to Settings > System > Multitasking. Turning the Snap Windows switch to the Off position disables this feature completely. If you'd like to adjust some of the available options (turning off snap layouts that appear when you drag a window to the top of the screen, for example), use the checkboxes beneath this switch.

CHAPTER 3

Switching between tasks and desktops

As in previous Windows versions, you can switch to a different app by clicking its taskbar button. And if you're not sure which icon your document is hidden under, hover the mouse pointer over a taskbar button to display a thumbnail image of the window (or windows) above the button.

If the live thumbnail isn't enough to help you select the correct window, hover the mouse pointer over one of the preview images. That action brings the window to the forefront, temporarily masking out the contents of all other open windows.

On a modern PC, with ample memory and disk space, the number of open windows can become overwhelming, making it cumbersome to manage those windows manually. To simplify that task, Windows 11 offers two features that can make the management process simpler: Task View and Virtual Desktops.

Using Task View to switch between windows

Task View is a time-tested alternative to manual hunt-and-click window management techniques. It displays large, live thumbnails of each open window on the current display so that you can switch with confidence.

To begin, click the Task View button or use the Windows key+Tab shortcut. On a touchscreen-equipped device, you can swipe in from the bottom of the display using three fingers. Figure 3-26 shows the results on a system with seven windows available.

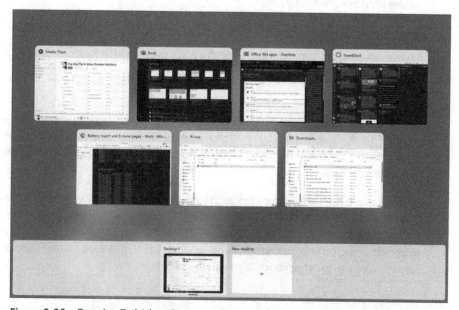

Figure 3-26   Opening Task View shows running programs using their windowed dimensions. Clicking or tapping any thumbnail opens it in its current position.

Those thumbnails remain open until you do something, usually by clicking or tapping a thumbnail to switch to that window or by pressing Esc to return to the current window.

If there are too many open windows to fit as thumbnails on the display, use the up and down arrows at the bottom of the screen to scroll through the full list.

The old-fashioned Alt+Tab task switcher, familiar to every Windows user of a certain age, is still available as well. The concept is similar, but the thumbnails appear only as long as you continue to hold down the Alt key. Hold down Alt and tap the Tab key to cycle (left to right, top to bottom) through all open windows. When you've highlighted the window you want to bring to the front, release the Alt and Tab keys.

When using Task View, you also have the option of closing a window by clicking the X in the upper-right corner of the preview or, if your mouse scroll wheel supports clicking, by middle-clicking anywhere in the preview image. Other basic window tasks are available on the shortcut menu that appears when you right-click the preview image.

Switching between virtual desktops

The idea of virtual desktops is straightforward: Instead of arranging program windows on a single desktop, you create a second, third, fourth, and so on. On each desktop, you arrange individual apps (or combinations of related apps) that you want to use for a specific task. Then, when it's time to tackle one of those tasks, you switch to the virtual desktop and get right to work, without being distracted by the unrelated programs running on those other desktops.

To create a new desktop, allow the mouse pointer to hover over the Task View button and then click the New Desktop shortcut. (If you've hidden the Task View button, or if you just prefer keyboard shortcuts, press Windows key+Tab to make the list of currently configured desktops and the New Desktop icon visible.)

Virtual desktops show up as a row of thumbnails along the bottom of the Task View window, as shown in Figure 3-27.

Figure 3-27   Arranging groups of open windows into separate virtual desktops can help you focus on specific tasks without being overwhelmed by unrelated windows.

Right-click a virtual desktop to give it a new name or background.

The system depicted in Figure 3-27 has two virtual desktops. Windows draws a bright border to indicate which desktop is active, and it dims the others. A New Desktop thumbnail makes it easy to expand the layout. You can switch from one virtual desktop to another by clicking its thumbnail. You'll notice that your taskbar changes to reflect the makeup of the current desktop. To close an existing virtual desktop, select its name and click the Close button that appears. If any windows are open on the desktop you are closing, they are transferred to the preceding desktop—from Desktop 2 to Desktop 1, for example.

To change the name of a virtual desktop from its generic default—for example, from *Desktop 2* to *Annual Report Project*—right-click the thumbnail and choose Rename.

Using a keyboard and voice input in Windows 11

If you need to enter text in an app or dialog in Windows 11, you have a variety of options. Most of the time, you type on a physical keyboard attached to your PC. If you're using a touchscreen device, you have the option of using a virtual keyboard where you can tap or swipe on the screen. And in a new feature, added to Windows 11 in version 22H2, you can also quite literally tell your PC what to do by using voice commands and dictation. We cover all three forms of input in this section.

Customizing and using a physical keyboard

For the most part, becoming more productive with a desktop or laptop keyboard is a simple matter of adjusting to the different "feel" of each physical device. The very limited set of options for fine-tuning how the keyboard works are still in the old-style Control Panel and haven't made it to the modern Settings app. To find these options, type **keyboard** in the Search box and then click the result that appears under the Settings heading. That action opens the dialog shown in Figure 3-28.

The repeat delay—the amount of time Windows waits as you hold down a key before repeating that key—is set, by default, a bit long for the tastes of some proficient typists. You can make it shorter by dragging the slider to the right. On the other hand, if you sometimes find that Windows gives you an unwanted string of repeated characters, you can drag the slider left. You might also then want to reduce the repeat rate.

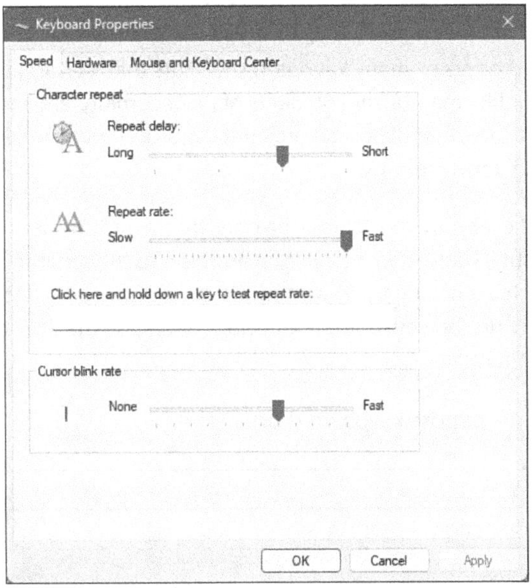

Figure 3-28   Adjust these options if you find that your keyboard occasionally repeats characters without your permission.

Inside OUT

Reconfigure the Caps Lock key to avoid shouting

If your fingers occasionally slip and accidentally strike the Caps Lock key, causing your emails to LOOK LIKE YOU'RE SHOUTING and proper nouns like nEW yORK cITY to appear in completely mixed-up case, there's a solution.

Although it's possible to edit the registry to disable the Caps Lock key, this technique is needlessly complex. The much safer, simpler alternative is to enlist the help of a software utility to make this change. We've successfully used SharpKeys (a free download from *https://github.com/randyrants/sharpkeys*) to turn off the Caps Lock key; you can use it to remap or turn off any key. We can also recommend the Microsoft PowerToys utility package, which includes a keyboard remapping module. You'll find it at *https://learn.microsoft.com/windows/powertoys/*. For documentation and to report any issues, go to *https://github.com/microsoft/PowerToys*.

Increasing productivity with keyboard shortcuts

Like its predecessors, Windows 11 offers so many keyboard shortcuts that learning them all would be a remarkable feat, a bit like memorizing 80 digits of pi. Becoming familiar with a handful (or several handfuls), on the other hand, can definitely improve your productivity without being a burden on your long-term memory.

Table 3-2 presents a selection of everyday shortcuts—the ones that we use most often and would have trouble living without. (These are, of course, in addition to the separate table, earlier in this chapter, of keyboard shortcuts having to do with window management.) Because your own needs probably differ from ours, however, you might want to peruse the truly exhaustive list at *https://aka.ms/keyboard-shortcuts*.

Table 3-2   A short list of general-purpose keyboard shortcuts

Shortcut	Action
Ctrl+C	Copy selection
Ctrl+X	Cut selection
Ctrl+V	Paste Clipboard contents
Ctrl+Z	Undo
Ctrl+Y	Redo
Ctrl+N	Open new window (in many apps)
Ctrl+S	Save
Ctrl+W	Close current window (in many apps)
Ctrl+P	Print (in many apps)
Ctrl+A	Select all
Ctrl+Shift+Esc	Open Task Manager
F2	Rename (in File Explorer)
F3	Search (File Explorer and most web browsers)
F5	Refresh (File Explorer and most web browsers)
Alt+F4	Close current window
Alt+Enter	Display the properties dialog for the currently selected object
Windows key	Display Start
Windows key+E	Open new File Explorer window
Windows key+I	Open Settings
Windows key+R	Open the Run command
Windows key+X	Open the Quick Link menu

A shortcut for emojis and more

Windows 11 offers an impressive tool for entering characters that aren't available on a standard keyboard. Press Windows key+. (period) or Windows key+; (semicolon) in any window that accepts text input to open the emoji keyboard. That name, unfortunately, doesn't even begin to hint at what this versatile input tool can do for you. Yes, it allows you to enter any character from the standards-based emoji library, but it does much more. Choosing one of the characters along the top row changes the input type to the following:

- **Emoji**   Emojis are arranged by category (smiley faces, food, people, and so on). To change the skin tone of an emoji in the people category, click one of the six colored dots alongside the category heading.

NOTE

For a full list of officially supported Windows-compatible emoji characters, see *https:// emojipedia.org/microsoft-emoji-list/*.

- **GIF**   Use this tool to search for animated GIFs and insert them into social media posts or presentations.

- **Kaomoji**   These are combinations of text characters that take on expressive facial characteristics, with one of the most famous being the shruggie: ¯_(ツ)_/¯.

- **Symbols**   This panel is extraordinarily useful when you need to enter unusual forms of punctuation, currency symbols, Latin characters with diacritic marks, and other characters that would otherwise require obscure keyboard shortcuts or the ancient Character Map utility.

- **Clipboard History**   If you've enabled this feature, the 25 most recent items copied to the Clipboard appear here. To open this panel directly, use the keyboard shortcut Windows key+V; you can then scroll through the list and click any item to paste it at the current insertion point.

The emoji library is also accessible via the Touch Keyboard, and we discuss its use later in this chapter (see "Using the Touch Keyboard").

Using alternative keyboard layouts

Windows 11 offers keyboard support for more than 300 languages. Most of these languages are available as full language packs, and installing a language pack changes the entire Windows user interface—menus, dialogs, and all—to the selected language. But you can also simply install a keyboard layout for another language, without changing the user interface. This might prove handy if you work in an international environment and occasionally need to dash off an email to, say, a Ukrainian-speaking colleague or customer.

CHAPTER 3

To install another keyboard, go to Settings > Time & Language > Language & Region. When you click Add A Language, the entire set of available languages appears, as shown in Figure 3-29, and you can make your choice. When the keyboard is installed, it becomes available through the Input Indicator system icon, which typically lives on the taskbar, adjacent to the clock. Clicking there pops up a menu of available keyboards, along with a Language Preferences command.

Figure 3-29   After you install an additional language, you can switch the keyboard layout to support that language.

To remove a language, make it the default, or set options relating to the language, return to Settings > Time & Language > Language & Region, and then click on the language.

Inside OUT

For emojis, accented characters, and language assistance, use the Touch Keyboard.

The primary purpose of the Touch Keyboard, as its name suggests, is to facilitate input on a touch-enabled device. (We discuss this feature in the section that follows this one.) But it's invaluable for certain kinds of input on any computer—which is why it's also available on machines that lack a touch display.

To display the emoji panel above the Touch Keyboard, click on the heart icon in the upper-left corner, above the Esc key. To enter a character with a diacritical mark, click and hold the unadorned character; your choices will appear in a pop-up window. Hold the *n*, for example, and the option to type ñ will appear. Hold the *o*, and you'll have the opportunity to enter variants like ò, ö, ô, and even œ. If you've ever labored to memorize ANSI codes or wandered through Character Map in search of the accent you need, you'll certainly appreciate this feature.

As for language assistance, suppose you're a whiz touch typist in English but you hunt and peck in Russian. When you select Russian as your input source, the Touch Keyboard turns to Cyrillic. You can use it as a visual layout guide while you type with your standard keyboard. Or you can use the Touch Keyboard to do the pecking as well as the hunting.

Using the Touch Keyboard

As we noted earlier, the Touch Keyboard is available on any device, even one without a touchscreen. (In this configuration, you need to use a mouse to "tap" the virtual keys.) But the Touch Keyboard is most useful, indeed indispensable, on a touchscreen-equipped device, especially one where you've temporarily detached the physical keyboard. Use it to enter text or provide other forms of keyboard input in dialogs, web forms, your browser's address bar, documents, the search box—anywhere you would normally need a physical keyboard to provide input.

To make the Touch Keyboard visible, tap its icon in the system tray. If the icon isn't visible, go to Settings > Personalization > Taskbar and slide the Touch Keyboard switch to the On position.

Figure 3-30 shows the standard Touch Keyboard layout.

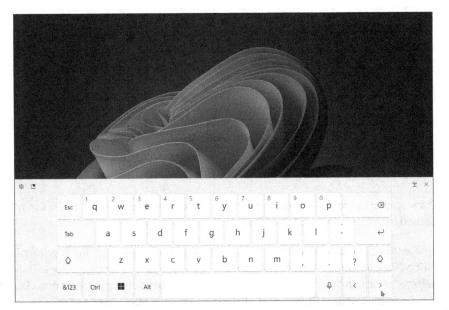

Figure 3-30   Use the gear icon in the upper-left corner of the Touch Keyboard to change the layout.

When no physical keyboard is attached, tapping in any location that accepts text input should cause the Touch Keyboard to appear automatically. (To turn this feature on or off, go to Settings > Time & Language > Typing and expand the Touch Keyboard section. There, you can also find options to add key sounds as you type, automatically add a period when you double-tap the spacebar, and capitalize the first word of a new sentence.)

Clicking the gear icon in the upper-left corner allows you to choose an alternative layout. Choose Default if you want to see a virtual keyboard that contains all the characters on a standard 103-key keyboard, including backslashes, square brackets, and the separate row of numbers, among others. To display function keys (F1 through F12), switch to the Traditional layout and tap Fn.

The Small layout shrinks the Default layout to roughly a quarter of its width. You can then drag that keyboard to any location on the screen, which is handy if the larger layout is interfering with your ability to see a complex document such as a form.

Choose the Split layout if you're working with a tablet-style device and you want to be able to enter text using your left and right thumbs.

On the default layout, you can enter numbers by pressing and holding the respective key on the top row (Q for 1, W for 2, and so on). That technique isn't productive if you need to do extensive numeric input, of course. In that case, tap the &123 key in the lower-left corner to replace the standard QWERTY layout with one that includes numbers and special characters, as shown in Figure 3-31.

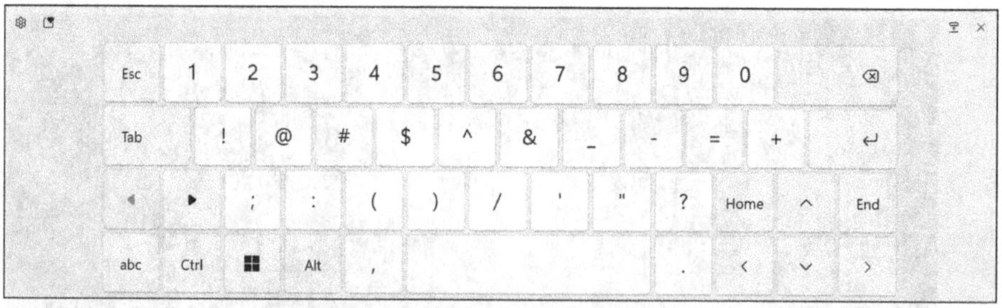

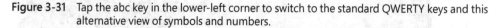

Figure 3-31   Tap the abc key in the lower-left corner to switch to the standard QWERTY keys and this alternative view of symbols and numbers.

If the symbol you're looking for isn't visible, tap the right arrow key just above Ctrl to display a second layout containing additional symbols.

Unlike their physical counterparts, the Ctrl, Alt, and Windows keys on the Touch Keyboard are "sticky." Tapping any of those keys causes the key you tapped to change color to indicate it's selected; its action takes effect when combined with whatever key you type next. Thus, to copy text using the standard Ctrl+C shortcut, tap Ctrl and then tap C. To open File Explorer, tap the

CHAPTER 3

Windows key and then tap E. (To open the Start menu when the Touch Keyboard is covering the taskbar, tap the Windows key twice.)

In some respects, the Touch Keyboard is more versatile than its physical counterparts. Entering a typographic symbol like the interrobang (a character consisting of an exclamation point superimposed on a question mark) or an emoji doesn't require the use of ANSI codes. Instead, you can enter characters directly. To enter an interrobang, for example, click (or press) and hold either the question mark or the exclamation point. Relevant special-character options appear in a panel above the character you clicked. Use the same technique to enter, for example, an accented vowel.

Inside OUT

Swipe to type

If you find hunting and pecking is onerous and slow, draw your words instead. Using either the compact or the wide (default) layout of the Touch Keyboard, you can create words by drawing a line from one letter to the next. Windows does an excellent job of recognizing your intentions, and where it cannot, it proposes alternative possibilities (just as it would if you misspelled using conventional typing methods). Mobile phones have had this "swipe to type" capability for some time, and if you've texted this way on a hand-held platform, you'll find it much the same on your Windows tablet.

With all these layouts, you can take advantage of Microsoft's superb text-prediction engine in apps that support it, such as Microsoft Word. As soon as you finish a word (and sometimes before), likely continuations appear in a row at the top of the keyboard. So, for example, to write "Give me a few minutes to get the money," all you need to type is the first two letters. You can click your way through the rest of the sentence. If you're sending input to an app that understands emojis, the engine suggests those as well as text continuations.

One additional option that appears when you tap the gear icon is Handwriting, which replaces the keyboard with an input panel where you can enter text. This panel is most useful with devices that support pen input, but you can also use your fingertip to enter text. Windows automatically translates your printing or cursive input into characters for entry at the current insertion point.

If your handwriting is so sloppy that even you have trouble deciphering it, you might be in for a surprise. In the unlikely event that the panel can't figure out what you meant, you can select from a row of suggestions that appears at the top of the window.

Using voice commands and dictating text

If you'd rather not type, why not talk instead? Position the insertion point in any place where text input is available, and press Windows key+H to turn on voice typing. If the Touch Keyboard is visible, tap the microphone button to begin.

The first time you use this feature, you're prompted to install device-based speech recognition components. When that installation completes, you see a microphone button that you can click or tap to begin dictating.

You can pause or stop dictation using voice commands like "Pause dictation" or "Stop listening." In addition to words, you can dictate punctuation symbols and such editing instructions as "delete last ten words" or "new line."

Beginning with Windows 11 Version 22H2, you can also turn on a feature called Voice Access, which enables you to control every Windows function using your voice. To get started, run the Voice Access app, which downloads the required components and prompts you to set up your microphone. Voice Access adds a bar to the top of the display with a microphone button and a gear icon to adjust settings. To turn the feature on, say "voice access wake up." To see a list of commands you can use, say "what can I say?"

Voice Access has a rich command set and some surprisingly powerful features. For example, you can ask it to add numbers to the screen identifying every possible object that can be clicked and then say "click 14" instead of trying to describe the button you want to interact with. For people who have difficulty interacting with a physical keyboard or mouse, Voice Access is worth mastering.

Using a pen with Windows 11

On PCs designed to work with a pen, including Microsoft's line of Surface Pro tablets, a pen can be a powerful input tool. You can use it in place of a mouse, to point and click with more precision than you can get from a fingertip. You can also use it to draw and to input text directly in apps that support it.

To make it easier to access apps that provide pen support, consider adding the Pen menu to the system tray. (You'll find this setting under Settings > Personalization > Taskbar > System Tray Icons. Tap the Pen icon to open this menu, and then tap the gear icon and choose Edit Pen Menu to see a list of pen-compatible apps that you can pin here.

Options relating to your pen are located at Settings > Bluetooth & Devices > Pen & Windows Ink. In the lower portion of that settings page is a set of options for configuring pen shortcuts. (See Figure 3-32.) These options, which require a pen with a shortcut button, govern what happens when you press that button once, press it twice in quick succession, or press and hold.

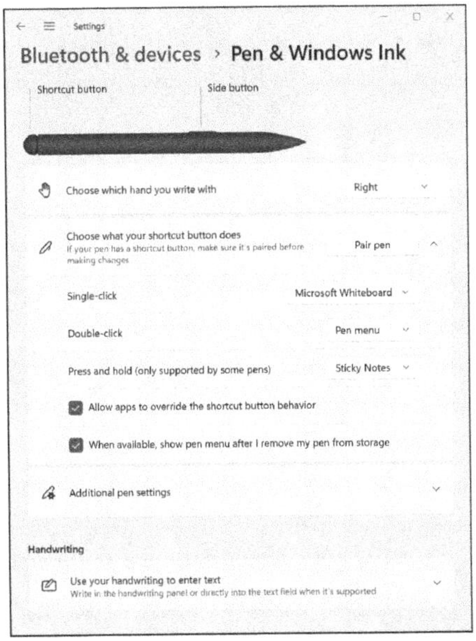

Figure 3-32   You can train your pen to launch a program, perform a screen capture, or open the Pen menu when you use one of its shortcut buttons.

Within the three sets of dropdowns are options to launch programs, capture screens, and more.

Personalizing Windows 11

Like every previous version of Windows, Windows 11 offers you innumerable options for personalizing your workspace. These are the choices that make your computing device feel like it's truly your own, embodying your own design preferences as well as choices that make your interaction with Windows work for you. Most of these customizations have only an incidental effect on your productivity. But creating an aesthetically pleasing workspace makes you more comfortable with your PC, and when you're more comfortable, you're more productive.

With that goal in mind, we introduce the extensive lineup of personalization features in Microsoft Windows 11. Most of the features we discuss in this chapter will be familiar from earlier Windows versions, but there are enough changes in the way these features are implemented that we recommend reviewing this chapter to see what's new. In particular, it's worth noting that almost all personalization options have now moved into the modern Settings app; only a few legacy options, such as the option to customize system sounds, remain in the old-style Control Panel.

If you use multiple Windows PCs and sign in using the same Microsoft account or Azure Active Directory (Azure AD) account, you can choose to have your customizations apply to all such devices. To control this feature, go to Settings > Accounts > Windows Backup and expand the Remember My Preferences section.

Check the Passwords and Language Preferences boxes to control whether those preferences are synced between devices. Settings that are synchronized when the Other Windows Settings option is selected include themes, accessibility options, and notification preferences. Note that settings are synced on a per-user basis. Settings that apply to all users at your computer, such as screen resolution, are not included in the current theme or other synchronized settings. Settings associated with a local user account are not synchronized with other computers.

Browser settings are not synced with your Windows account. To configure synchronization in Microsoft Edge, open the Edge Settings page and choose Profiles > Sync. (We cover the Sync features in Microsoft Edge in more detail in Chapter 7, "Using Microsoft Edge.")

CHAPTER 4

Customizing the look and feel of Windows

The most obvious way to personalize your Windows experience is to modify its visual appearance—the desktop background, lock screen picture, accent colors, and so on. These options are neatly arranged under the Personalization heading in Settings.

Selecting the desktop background

You can perk up any desktop with a background image. Your background can be supplied by a graphics file in any of several common formats: BMP, GIF (static only, not animated), JPEG, PNG, and TIFF. If you can't settle on a single image, set up a slideshow of images from your own collection of saved photos or from Microsoft's curated Windows Spotlight collection. And if you find pictures too distracting, just pick a background color. (That last option might prove especially useful if you like to populate your desktop with files, folders, and app shortcuts; those icons are easier to recognize without the distraction of a background image.)

To get started, go to Settings > Personalization > Background. The default choice on the Personalize Your Background dropdown is Picture, which displays the options shown in Figure 4-1.

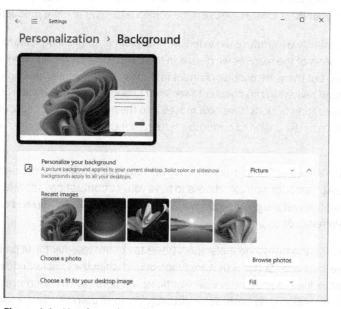

Figure 4-1   Use the options shown here to choose a single image and use it as your desktop background.

Here's what you can do with each of the options on the Personalize Your Background menu:

- **Picture** displays a single image of your choice, scaled to fit the resolution of your display. Windows 11 includes a default selection of images, and PC makers often include additional selections. Click Browse Photos to choose one of your own pictures.

- **Solid Color** covers the background with a color you select from a palette of two dozen shades. You can also create a custom color, and that color then becomes the twenty-fifth item in your palette. Click the View Colors button to the right of the Custom Colors label, and then click or tap in the color picker that appears to specify the color you want, as shown in Figure 4-2.

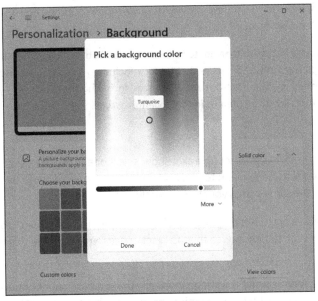

Figure 4-2   Use the color picker tool to create your own custom color if none of the 24 standard colors seems quite right.

Choose a color from the square at the top; then use the slider below to adjust its intensity from dark (left) to light (right). The vertical bar on the right shows the result of your current selection at the top and the current custom color (if any) below it.

- **Slideshow** is like the Picture option, but with a twist: At an interval you select (at one of six preconfigured intervals ranging from 1 minute to 1 day), Windows changes the desktop background to a new picture from the folder you select. Unless you specify otherwise, Windows uses the Pictures folder in the current user profile as its source. For best results, we recommend that you select a group of properly sized images, copy them to their own folder, and then click Browse to replace the default choice with your custom folder. Note that on a multimonitor setup, this option uses a different image on each display.

  Two additional options allow you to shuffle the picture order and to let the slideshow run even if your PC is on battery power. Both of these options are off by default.

- **Windows Spotlight** displays a new image on the lock screen each day. Windows downloads the images from an online collection curated by Bing. There are no additional configuration options available in Settings, although administrators can manage the behavior of Windows Spotlight using Group Policy or mobile device management software.

Inside OUT

Restore the photographs furnished with Windows

When you click Browse Photos and select a new picture, your selection replaces the rightmost of the five current picture choices. But what if you decide you'd rather go back to one of those terrific photos provided with Windows? Getting any one of them back is simple, but not obvious.

Click Browse Photos and navigate to C:\Windows\Web\Wallpaper. You'll find a handful of nice pictures in subfolders of that folder—including the ones you displaced. If you downloaded any themes from online sources, including those offered by Microsoft, you find pictures for those themes in that location as well.

After you choose an image or set up a slideshow, select one of the six options on the Choose A Fit For Your Desktop Image menu to let Windows know how you want to handle images that are not exactly the same size as your screen resolution:

- **Fill** stretches or shrinks the image so that it occupies the full screen, cropping the image in one or both dimensions so that no blank space remains on the sides or the top and bottom.

- **Fit** reduces or enlarges the image to exactly the width or height of the display without changing its aspect ratio or cropping the image; this option might result in letterbox bars (using the current background color) on either side or above and below the image.

- **Stretch** reduces or enlarges the image so that it fits both dimensions, distorting the image if necessary. If there's a significant mismatch between the aspect ratios of the image and the display, the effect can be unpleasant.

- **Tile** repeats the image at its original size to fill all monitors. This option is most effective for abstract backgrounds or for simple, small images (such as a corporate logo) where the repeated design looks like a pattern.

- **Center** displays the image at its original size in the center of the screen, without stretching. If the image is smaller than the display resolution, this can leave blank space on the sides or at the top and bottom; if the image is larger than the display, some parts of the image might be cropped away to fit.

- **Span** works like Fill to display a single image across multiple monitors. On a single-monitor PC, choosing this option has the same effect as choosing Fill.

Inside OUT

Assign separate images to multiple monitors

Of the six fit options we describe in this section, only Span is specifically intended for use with systems that have additional monitors attached. For the remaining five options, the image you select and the fit options are repeated on each display, and there's no obvious way in Settings to assign a different image to each monitor.

Even though it's not obvious, there's a secret menu that allows you to specify that you want to use an image with a specific monitor. The images you want to use must be available in the list of five thumbnails on the Background page in Settings. Right-click each thumbnail in turn to display a menu like the one shown in Figure 4-3, with options for each available monitor.

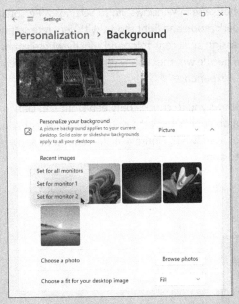

Figure 4-3   On a PC with more than one monitor, you can right-click any thumbnail from the Recent Images list to assign that image to a specific monitor.

For even more control over multimonitor configurations, we recommend the third-party utility DisplayFusion (*https://displayfusion.com*). The software is available in a free version that supports a wide range of per-monitor background image options; a paid Pro version is also available.

CHAPTER 4

Here are some other ways to change the desktop background:

- Right-click an image file in File Explorer and choose Set As Desktop Background.

- Open any image file in Paint, open the File menu, and choose Set As Desktop Background. A submenu lets you position the picture using Fill, Tile, or Center options.

- Use the Photos app to open an image file, and then right-click and choose Set As > Background.

- If a slideshow is running, right-click any empty space on the desktop and choose Next Desktop Background to skip to the next image in the collection.

Selecting colors

As we noted in the previous section, you can choose to assign a solid color to the desktop background. To adjust colors everywhere else in Windows, go to Settings > Personalization > Colors. Here, you can choose between dark mode and light mode, with separate settings for apps and for Windows itself. You can also assign an accent color and specify where you want that accent color to be used. Finally, you can decide whether you want to apply transparency effects to various surfaces in the Windows user experience.

The Choose Your Mode option allows you to choose between Light and Dark modes for Windows and for apps (the latter option applies to all the default Windows apps, including Settings). Choose the Custom mode, as shown in Figure 4-4, if you want to apply one mode to Windows and a different mode to apps.

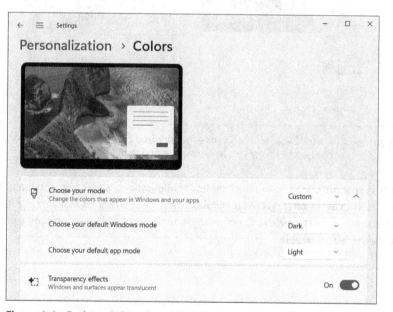

Figure 4-4   Dark mode is easier on the eyes in dimly lit environments. Light mode offers a more traditional view of the Windows interface.

Dark mode options are useful for conserving battery life on portable devices, but another important benefit is to prevent eyestrain, especially in dim or dark environments. By changing the selection in the dropdown from Custom to either Light or Dark, you can apply those mode choices to both Windows elements and apps. Setting the Transparency Effects switch to On allows display elements behind the foreground window to bleed through faintly.

The next set of options on the Personalization > Colors page allows you to select a complementary accent color and specify where and how to use it. In Windows 11, you're allowed to choose one and only one accent color from a palette of 48 solid colors (or one and only one additional color of your own making if you click View Colors), as shown in Figure 4-5.

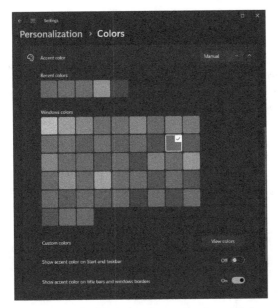

Figure 4-5   The Manual option on the Accent Color menu allows you to pick an accent color of your own; choose Automatic if you want Windows to pick an accent color to match your background.

Changing the Accent Color menu option from Manual to Automatic is useful if you've configured a slideshow for the desktop background. With this setting on, the accent color changes each time the background picture changes, minimizing the chances that a particular image will represent a poor contrast with a background color you choose manually. On the other hand, be prepared to see garish accent shades of purple, pink, and yellow, depending on the image. (To change your mind, you don't need to change that switch back to Manual. Just choose a different color and Windows changes it for you.)

The accent color you choose appears in some places automatically—in text links in built-in apps like Mail and Settings, for example, and on the desktop when a background image doesn't fill the display fully.

If you've configured Windows to use Dark mode, you can enable the Show Accent Color On Start And Taskbar option. (This switch is grayed out and unavailable if you've selected Light mode for Windows.) Choosing this setting applies your accent color as a background to the taskbar and the Start menu, when they're visible. With this option turned off, those areas have a neutral background that matches the selected mode. A separate option, Show Accent Color On Title Bars And Windows Borders, turns color on or off for the title bars in desktop apps and in Store apps that don't specify a custom color.

Customizing the lock screen and sign-in screen

The lock screen is a security feature that prevents someone from seeing or accessing your account when you step away from the computer while you're signed in. To display the lock screen, click Start and then click your account picture, where Lock is on the menu of available options. Naturally, there's a faster way to lock the screen: Use the keyboard shortcut Windows key+L.

Just as you can customize the desktop background, you can change the lock screen to your liking by adding custom images and specifying which notifications appear on the lock screen when you're away. Go to Settings > Personalization > Lock Screen to see your options, as shown in Figure 4-6.

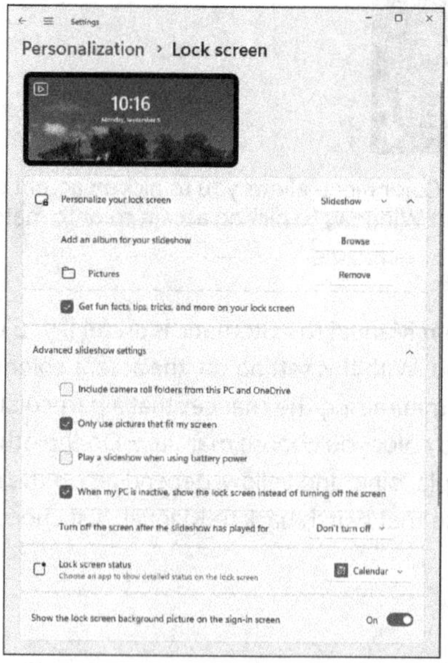

Figure 4-6   As with the desktop background, you can choose a slideshow to use as your lock screen instead of a static picture.

These settings closely resemble those for the desktop background. Under the Personalize Your Lock Screen menu, you'll find Picture options that work exactly like those under the Background headings, so we're not repeating the detailed instructions here.

The Slideshow option includes several options that aren't the same as those for the desktop background, however. Notably, you can choose to use only pictures that match your display resolution, so you're not greeted with a distorted image when you try to sign in. You can also configure the system to keep the slideshow visible when your PC is inactive, with an additional option to turn off the screen if you're away longer than a specified interval.

The Windows Spotlight option supplies a new background image each day, along with captions to identify the image location and a pair of icons to indicate whether you like or dislike a particular image—that feedback goes into the algorithm that serves future images to you.

Turning on the Show Lock Screen Background Picture On The Sign-In Screen option makes it possible for you to clear the lock screen—by clicking, swiping, or tapping any key—and see the box to enter your credentials with the same image behind it.

NOTE

Windows uses the custom lock screen image for the user who last signed in. On a PC with multiple user accounts and different lock-screen settings, the result might be that you see a lock screen image configured by another user. If you sign out completely and then restart, Windows might display the default sign-in screen instead.

Inside OUT

What ever happened to screen savers?

Screen savers don't save screens, and they certainly don't save energy compared to simply blanking the display.

In the distant past, when screens were invariably CRTs and many offices displayed the same application at all hours of the working day, having an image move about during idle times probably did extend the service life of some displays. Today, this legacy feature is strictly for nostalgia buffs who want to compute like it's 1999.

By default, Windows 11 does not configure a screen saver, although it includes a handful of old favorites. To see what's available, go to Settings > Personalization > Lock Screen, scroll to the bottom of the Lock Screen page, and then click Screen Saver.

Unless you're desperate to recapture the nostalgic glow of running the Windows 95–era 3D Text or Bubbles screen saver, however, we suggest ignoring those old options and using the modern alternative. Configure your lock screen to display a slideshow and lock your PC by pressing Windows key + L when you step away.

You can allow one or more apps to display their current status—such as the number of new email messages, upcoming appointments, and so on—on the lock screen. You can also see alarms and reminders here. Depending on your personal preferences, these notifications are either a convenience or a potential privacy issue; if you don't want anyone who passes by your desk to see notifications, go to Settings > System > Notifications. Expand the Notifications section and then turn off Show Notifications On The Lock Screen and Show Reminders And Incoming VoIP Calls On The Lock Screen.

If you choose to use lock-screen notifications, you can configure a single app to display detailed status messages (the time, title, and location of your next appointment, for example, or a weather forecast for your location). From Settings > Personalization > Lock Screen, use the Lock Screen Status menu to choose which app gets this preferred treatment.

Assigning sounds to system events

Decades ago, when Windows was new, custom sound schemes were a popular form of personalization. Microsoft and third-party developers offered collections of beeps, gurgles, and chirps that Windows and various apps played in response to various system and application events.

Those sound schemes have gone the way of Pet Rocks, Beanie Babies, and other once-popular fads. In Windows 11, Microsoft's designers have curated a collection of system sounds that are subtle but distinctive and are designed to be helpful without being intrusive.

In fact, you won't find an option to adjust system sounds in the modern Settings app. Instead, these controls live on in a legacy dialog that hasn't changed in 30 years. To get there, go to Settings > Personalization >Themes and click the Sounds box below the thumbnail at the top of the page. That opens the dialog shown in Figure 4-7.

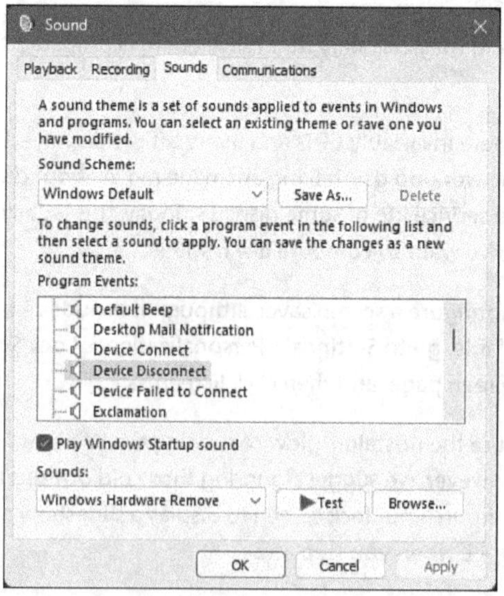

Figure 4-7 It's unlikely you'll have any need to change the sounds associated with system events, but the controls are available here just in case.

A new installation of Windows comes with only a single scheme, called Windows Default. If you can find and install a custom sound scheme, you can choose it from the Sound Scheme list, or you can customize the current sound scheme to match your preferences.

To see which sounds are currently mapped to events, scroll through the Program Events list. If an event has a sound associated with it, its name is preceded by a speaker icon; select the event name and then click Test to hear its sound. To switch to a different sound, scroll through the Sounds list or click Browse. The list displays .wav files in C:\Windows\Media, but any .wav file is eligible. To remove the sound associated with an event, select the event and then choose None, the item at the top of the Sounds list.

If you rearrange the mapping of sounds to events, consider saving the new arrangement as a sound scheme. (Click Save As and supply a name.) That way, you can experiment further and still return to the saved configuration.

Inside OUT

Mute your computer

If you like event sounds in general but occasionally need complete silence from your computer, choose No Sounds in the Sound Scheme list when you want the machine to shut up. When sound is welcome again, you can return to the Windows Default scheme—or to any other scheme you have set up. Switching to the No Sounds scheme doesn't render your system mute (you'll still be able to play music when you want to hear it), but it does turn off the announcement of incoming mail and other events.

If you want to control sound levels on a more granular level—perhaps muting some applications altogether and adjusting volume levels on others—right-click the volume icon in the notification area and choose Open Volume Mixer. Volume Mixer provides a volume slider (and a mute button) for each output device and each app that produces sounds or audio output of any kind.

Customizing mouse pointers

Over the course of the past few years, Microsoft's designers have been moving personalization options from the classic Control Panel to the new Settings app. Although this migration is nearly complete, a few remnants of the old-style Control Panel remain. Such is the case with options to change the appearance of the mouse pointer.

You might want to change the size and color of the mouse pointer to make it easier to see. These options are especially helpful if you're using a large, high-resolution display, where the default white pointer can be difficult to locate against a light background.

To quickly change the pointer size and color, go to Settings > Accessibility > Mouse Pointer And Touch, where you see the options shown in Figure 4-8.

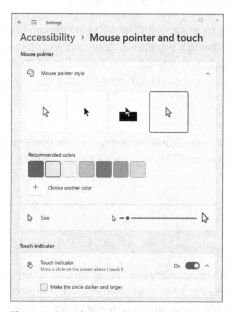

Figure 4-8   A larger pointer, especially one in a bright color, can be easier to pick out on a large display.

The first option under the Mouse Pointer Style heading is the standard white pointer with a thin black outline. Choose the second or third option to change the pointer style to solid black or to an inverted pointer that shifts from dark to light depending on the background. Choosing the fourth box reveals a row of seven bright colors (with a Choose Another Color option if you want to pick your own shade); in our experience, the fluorescent green and pink options work surprisingly well at helping you find a pointer even on a large display.

Adjusting the Size slider makes the mouse pointer larger or smaller. The Touch Indicator controls enable you to customize visual feedback when using a pen or a finger on a touchscreen.

Meanwhile, you can find a completely separate entry point to a closely related group of options by going to Settings > Personalization > Themes and clicking the Mouse Cursor option beneath the thumbnail at the top of the page. That action opens the old-style Mouse Properties dialog shown in Figure 4-9, where you can choose from pointer schemes that match those found in the Mouse Pointer And Touch section of the Settings app. If you bump the pointer size up one notch and choose the Inverted pointer style, you've chosen one of the ready-made system pointer schemes—in this case, Windows Inverted (Large).

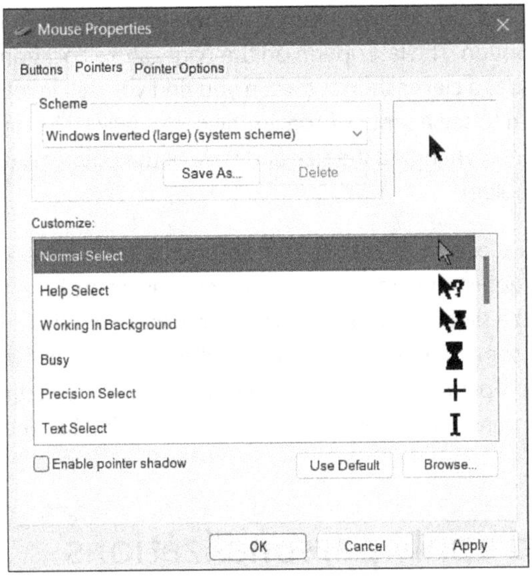

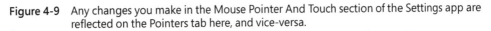

Figure 4-9 Any changes you make in the Mouse Pointer And Touch section of the Settings app are reflected on the Pointers tab here, and vice-versa.

Although it's possible to change the shape of any pointer listed in the Customize box, we don't expect many people to take advantage of this option on a Windows 11 PC. Those options are left over from the Windows 95 era, when custom themes supported goofy cursor options. (The Browse button takes you to C:\Windows\Cursors and displays files with the extensions .cur and .ani. The latter are animated cursors.)

A few additional settings of interest are available on the Pointer Options tab, shown in Figure 4-10.

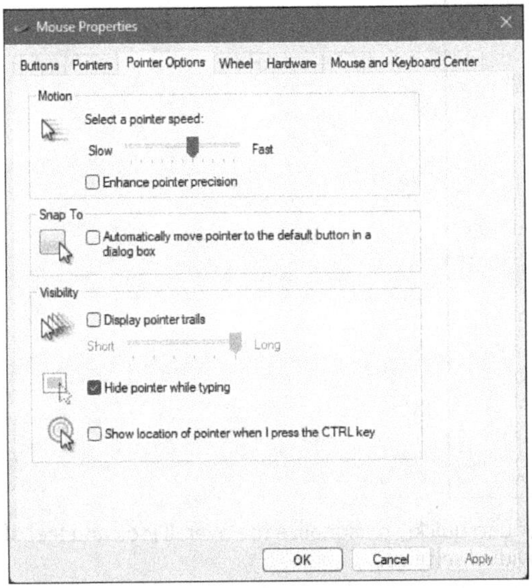

Figure 4-10 Use these old-school pointer options to make the mouse pointer easier to spot as it moves.

If you sometimes struggle to find the mouse even after you've moved it slightly, consider turning on the Display Pointer Trails option. The last option on the page, Show Location Of Pointer When I Press The CTRL Key, provides a clever shortcut when you find yourself involuntarily playing "Where's the pointer?" Tap Ctrl to see a series of concentric circles where the mouse pointer is currently hiding. In our experience, changing the size and style of the pointer is usually a more effective way to deal with this problem.

You'll find several additional mouse options in the modern Settings app (Settings > Bluetooth & Devices > Mouse). The option to adjust the mouse pointer speed is available here, for example. You'll also find an odd switch with a slightly confusing name: Scroll Inactive Windows When I Hover Over Them. This behavior, sometimes known as "focus follows mouse," will be familiar to those who've used Linux-based operating systems. Although it takes some getting used to, we've found that it can eliminate unnecessary mouse clicks when switching between windows, especially on large displays.

Using themes to save and apply personalizations

A theme is a named collection of personalization settings that includes background images, color settings, system sounds, and mouse pointers. Windows 11 includes a small collection of ready-made themes, along with a link to a much bigger collection of free themes in the Microsoft Store. The page at Settings > Personalization > Themes shows thumbnails of all the themes that are currently installed and available; to apply one, simply click it. Figure 4-11 shows the themes available on a default installation of Windows 11, with the Light Bloom theme in use.

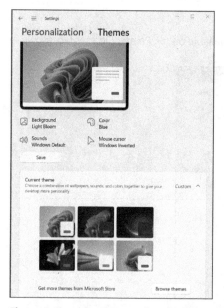

Figure 4-11   Using themes allows you to quickly personalize the overall look and feel of Windows without tweaking individual settings.

If you've tweaked the look and feel of Windows, you can save your work so you can return to it later. To save the current settings as a theme, go to Settings > Personalization > Themes. Near the top of the page, you'll see a summary of your current settings; click the Save button and give your theme a name.

Custom theme settings are saved as a plain text file with the .theme file name extension in your %LocalAppData%\Microsoft\Windows\Themes folder. (Visit *https://bit.ly/windows-theme-format* for complete details about the format of .theme files.)

Perhaps more important than the ability to name your own customizations, the Themes page includes a link to the Microsoft Store that gives you free access to hundreds of beautiful themes created by professional and amateur photographers all over the world. You can find a full listing on the web at *https://www.microsoft.com/store/collections/windowsthemes*. Most of these are slideshows; a few include sounds as well. After installing a theme from the Store, apply it by selecting it at Settings > Personalization > Themes. If you apply a theme as a slideshow, you can configure the change interval at Settings > Personalization > Background, just as you would for a slideshow of your own photos.

Fine-tuning visual options

Windows 11 includes a few legacy customization options that give you fine-grained control over small aspects of the user experience. None of the options we discuss here have made the transition to the new Settings app, but they're worth knowing about anyway.

Configuring desktop icons

A fresh, cleanly installed Windows 11 desktop (as opposed to one generated by an upgrade installation) includes a single lonely icon—Recycle Bin. If you want to display other system icons, go to Settings > Personalization > Themes and click Desktop Icon Settings. That opens the dialog shown in Figure 4-12, which provides checkboxes for five system folders—Computer, User's Files (the root folder of your own profile), Network, Recycle Bin, and Control Panel.

If you're really into customization, you can change any of the five icons that appear in the large box in the center; this, too, is an option left over from the earliest days of Windows, and we expect that very few people will take advantage of it. Note that the Control Panel icon does not appear in this center box even if you select its checkbox; Windows doesn't provide a way to change it.

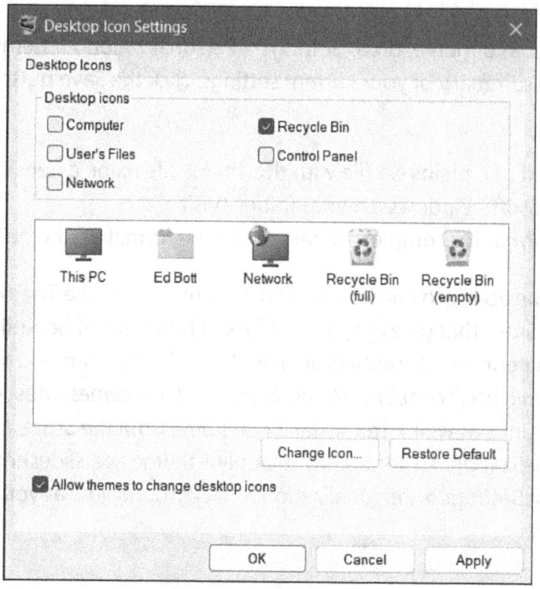

Figure 4-12   Use the checkboxes at the top of this dialog to show or hide specific icons from the desktop.

To change an icon, select it in the center box and click Change Icon. By default, the Browse button displays the selection of alternative icons from the file C:\Windows\System32\Imageres.dll. (Be sure to use the horizontal scroll bar to see them all.) If none of these suits you, try browsing to C:\Windows\System32\Shell32.dll.

After you populate your desktop with icons, you might want to control their arrangement. Right-click the desktop to find two commands at the top of the shortcut menu that can help in this endeavor. To specify that you want icons to shift and close up the empty space when you delete an icon from the desktop, click View > Auto Arrange Icons. To ensure that each icon keeps a respectable distance from each of its neighbors (and that the whole gang stays together at the left side of your screen), click View > Align Icons To Grid. And if you don't want desktop icons to get in the way of your gorgeous desktop background image, click View and then clear the check mark to the left of Show Desktop Icons. (Return to this option if you decide you miss those desktop icons.)

To change the sort order of desktop icons, right-click the desktop and click Sort By. You can sort on any of four attributes: Name, Size, Item Type, or Date Modified. Sorting a second time on any attribute changes the sort order from ascending to descending (or vice versa).

Making other small visual tweaks

Windows is alive with little animations, such as when you open or close a window. Along with other effects, these can help to direct your focus to the current window or activity. But some folks find them annoying, and they arguably have an impact on PC performance, especially on underpowered hardware. As with so many things Windows, you have the option to turn off these effects.

In the search box of Settings or Control Panel, type **performance** and then choose Adjust The Appearance And Performance Of Windows. That action opens the Performance Options dialog, shown in Figure 4-13, where you can control animations and other effects on a granular level.

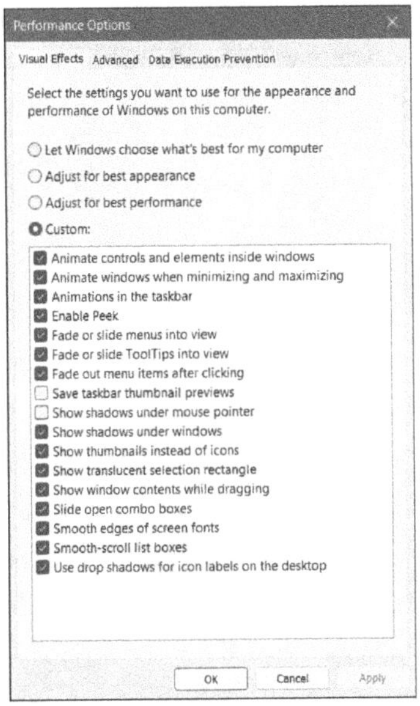

Figure 4-13   In general, it's best to choose the first option here: Let Windows Choose What's Best For My Computer.

On modern hardware with even a moderate graphics processor, these options make little or no difference in actual performance. The loss of animation can be disconcerting, in fact, as you wonder where a particular item went when you minimized it. These options offer the most payoff on older devices that weren't designed for use with Windows 11 and have underpowered graphics hardware. If you had to bypass installation restrictions to run Windows 11, these options are worth exploring.

Setting date and time, currency, and other regional options

A personalized experience requires Windows to know some things about where you reside, including basic information about how other people in your part of the world display the date and time, currency symbols, and preferred number formats, such as whether to use a comma or a period as a separator.

In Windows 11, some language options are determined by the base Windows version. Windows configures additional regional settings using your location (with your permission).

In most cases, Windows picks the right regional settings during setup. You might need to customize some of these options if you prefer settings from one region (your home, typically) but Windows insists on applying settings for a different region, such as one you're visiting. Your first stop is Settings > Time & Language > Date & Time, where you can change time zones and make other time-related settings, as shown in Figure 4-14.

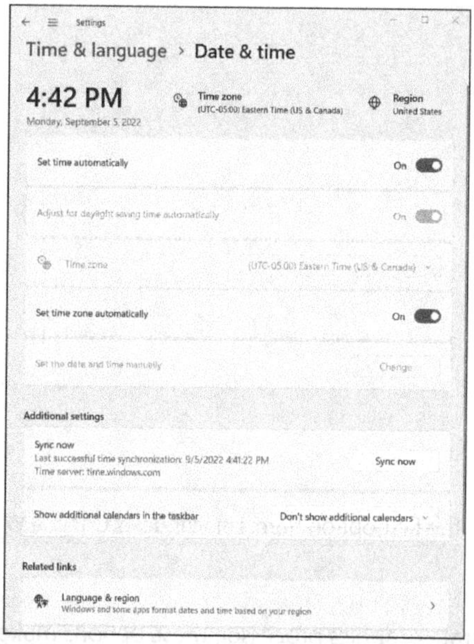

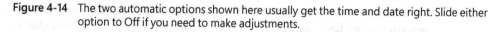

Figure 4-14   The two automatic options shown here usually get the time and date right. Slide either option to Off if you need to make adjustments.

If you have an always-on internet connection, we recommend leaving the Set Time Automatically and Set Time Zone Automatically options enabled. Windows 11 uses your location (and that of your internet provider) to determine your time zone and periodically synchronizes your computer's clock to an internet-based time server, fixing any "drift" if your PC's clock isn't working correctly. (On a domain-based network, this setting is controlled by the domain server.)

In some cases, Windows might not detect your time zone properly. This might happen if you're using a satellite-based internet service provider, for example. In that case, you can manually set

CHAPTER 4

the PC's time zone by turning off the automatic setting and selecting the correct location from the scrolling Time Zone list.

If you frequently communicate with people in other time zones, you might want to add one or two clocks to Windows, with each one displaying the time in a relevant time zone when you hover the mouse pointer over the clock in the taskbar. (The additional times also appear just above the calendar when you click the time display at the right side of the taskbar.)

To make this tweak, click Settings > Time & Language > Date & Time. Under Related Links, click Additional Clocks. This opens a dialog in which you can configure one or two clocks, selecting a time zone and a display name for each one.

Current versions of Windows 11 also support the Traditional Chinese and Simplified Chinese lunar calendars. To install either, go to Settings > Time & Language > Date & Time, and then choose which lunar calendar you want from the list labeled Show Additional Calendars In The Taskbar. Your calendar then displays the lunar dates below the corresponding Gregorian dates.

Windows uses your country/region and language settings to provide some personalized content and for regional formats such as the way dates, times, and numbers are displayed and the preferred measurement system. To adjust these formats, go to Settings > Time & Language > Language & Region. There, you can change the Windows display language, add a language pack (only if you're running Windows 11 Pro, Enterprise, or Education), change the current country or region, and view and adjust regional formats.

Figure 4-15 shows this Settings page with the Regional Format section expanded to show current regional formats.

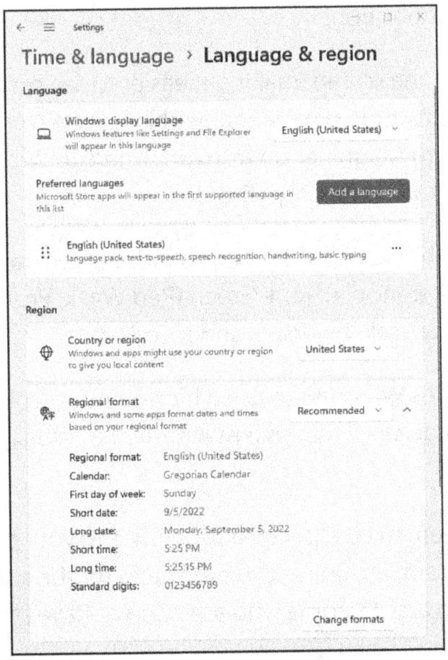

Figure 4-15 Expand the Regional Format section on this page to see (and, if necessary, change) how Windows formats dates and times.

To adjust the preferred display format (so that File Explorer shows 2022-09-05 instead of 9/5/2022, for example), click the Change Formats button and choose from one of the available options.

Overcoming challenges

Microsoft has a long-standing commitment to making computing accessible and easier to use for persons with vision, hearing, or mobility impairments. Windows 11 groups these options into the Accessibility section of Settings. (Alternatively, you can press Windows key+U to open this page directly.)

The options at Settings > Accessibility are organized in three groups: Vision, Hearing, and Interaction. Any of the settings can be used alone or in conjunction with others.

Vision options include the following:

- **Text Size**   On this page, you can use a slider control to adjust the size of text for most Windows interface elements.

- **Visual Effects**   Use these settings to prevent scrollbars from automatically hiding and to adjust transparency and animation effects. A separate control allows you to configure how long Windows waits before dismissing notifications.

- **Mouse Pointer And Touch**   See the previous discussion in this chapter ("Customizing mouse pointers") for details about the settings available here.

- **Text Cursor**   On this page, you can change the thickness and color of the text cursor to make it easier to find your current text position.

- **Magnifier**   This tool enlarges part of the screen, making it easier to see small text, icons, or other elements. Use settings here to automatically enable this feature when you sign in and to configure its zoom levels. To turn Magnifier on from anywhere in Windows, press Windows key+Plus. To turn it off, press Windows key+Esc.

- **Color Filters**   These are designed to help users with color-blindness. Available filters include Red-Green (Green Weak, Deuteranopia), Red-Green (Red Weak, Protanopia), Blue-Yellow (Tritanopia), Grayscale, Grayscale Inverted, and Inverted.

- **Contrast Themes**   This tool configures Windows to use a high-contrast color scheme (by default, white text on a black background) that makes it easier for visually impaired users to read the screen.

- **Narrator**   This tool converts on-screen text to speech and sends it to your computer's speakers. An enormous variety of options, including custom voices for the speech-to-text portion of this feature, are available to assist people who are blind or have severe vision impairments to use Windows.

Hearing options include an Audio page, where you can turn on monaural audio or configure visual behavior to accompany audio alerts. For example, you can choose to make the title bar of the active window, the entire active window, or the entire screen flash in response to an audio alert. Also in the Hearing section is a Captions option, which lets you configure the appearance of closed captioning in videos.

The Interaction section includes the following:

- **Speech**   On the Speech page, you can interact with your PC by setting the Voice Access switch to On and, optionally, setting this feature to turn on automatically. A separate Windows Speech Recognition switch allows you to dictate text, system commands, and editing commands by speaking instead of typing. When you first enable this feature, a wizard guides you through some simple setup steps and leads you to a Microsoft support page where, among other things, you can view and print a table of recognized editing commands.

➤ **For more details about these features, see "Using voice commands and dictating text," in Chapter 3, "Using Windows 11."**

- **Keyboard**   This collection of tools provides alternative means for Windows users with impaired mobility to enter text using a pointing device. Options that appear when you click Options in On-Screen Keyboard let you control how it works—you can choose whether to select a letter by clicking, for example, or by allowing the pointer to pause over a key for a specific amount of time. Other tools on the Keyboard page allow users with impaired mobility to deal with key combinations and repeated keystrokes more easily.

- **Mouse**   This page enables the numeric keypad to move the mouse pointer so you don't have to use a mouse.

- **Eye Control**   Windows supports the use of eye tracking devices, which allow users to manipulate the mouse and keyboard, and to turn narration on or off, by means of the eyes. (Support is currently provided for a variety of Tobii Eye Tracker, EyeX, and Dynavox devices as well as the EyeTech TM5 Mini. The EN-US keyboard layout is the only one supported at this time. Support for additional keyboard layouts and hardware devices is promised for the future.)

The easiest way to configure your computer for adaptive needs in one fell swoop is to click Start, type **Ease Of Access**, and then click Let Windows Suggest Ease Of Access Settings. That action launches a wizard, shown in Figure 4-16, that walks you through the process of configuring accessibility options.

CHAPTER 4

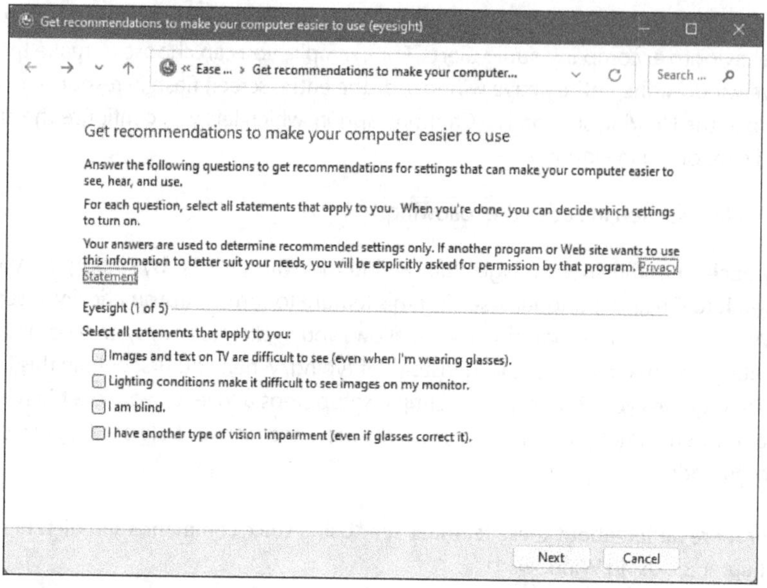

Figure 4-16   Use this dialog to automatically apply accessibility options that make Windows easier to use.

If you want accessibility options to be available at all times, even before signing in to the computer, click the up arrow from that page and then click the Change Sign-In Settings link in the left pane of the Ease Of Access Center in Control Panel. This option, shown in Figure 4-17, enables you to specify any changes that you want to make to the sign-in desktop.

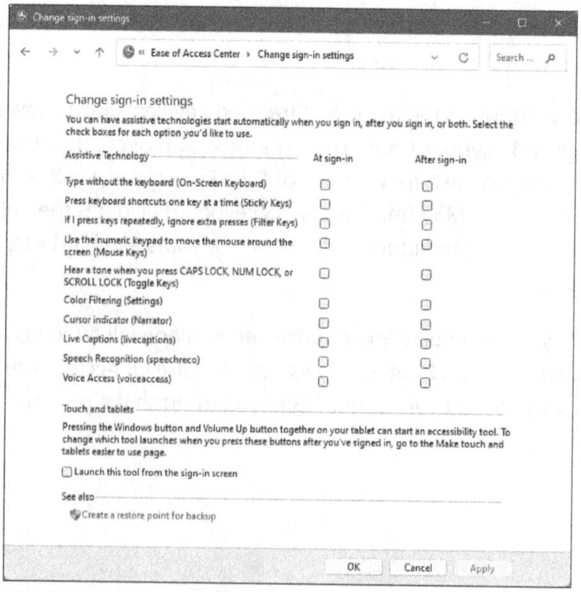

Figure 4-17   Use this old-style Control Panel option to automatically apply accessibility settings when you sign in to Windows.

If you choose not to enable this option, you can still turn accessibility features on or off at the sign-in screen; click the small Ease Of Access icon in the lower-right corner of the sign-in screen to display a list of available settings. Press the Spacebar to enable each one.

Working with fonts

Microsoft Windows includes an extensive library of fonts representing more than 60 font families, all designed to make text more legible in any language supported by Windows and to enable the display of special characters that aren't a part of any alphabet, such as Wingdings and emoji. (If you're curious about the technologies that go into rendering fonts in Windows, you'll find a tremendous amount of information at the Microsoft Typography website: *https://learn.microsoft.com/typography/*.)

To view all available fonts, install new fonts, or manage font settings, go to Settings > Personalization > Fonts. That opens a page like the one shown in Figure 4-18.

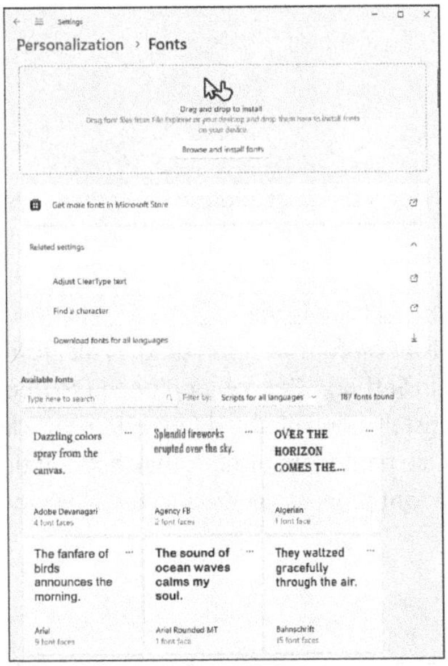

Figure 4-18   No more "quick brown fox"—Windows 11 uses a variety of clever text snippets to preview installed fonts.

Use the drop target at the top of the page to install fonts by dragging them from File Explorer. A link below that transports you to the Microsoft Store, where additional fonts are available.

Under the Available Fonts heading, a preview box displays the number of fonts available for each installed font family. Click any box to see a full list of font faces, with additional metadata information about the font version and designer, as well as licensing, copyright, and trademark details. Figure 4-19 shows all nine members of the Arial family on a system where Microsoft 365 has installed additional font faces alongside those included with Windows.

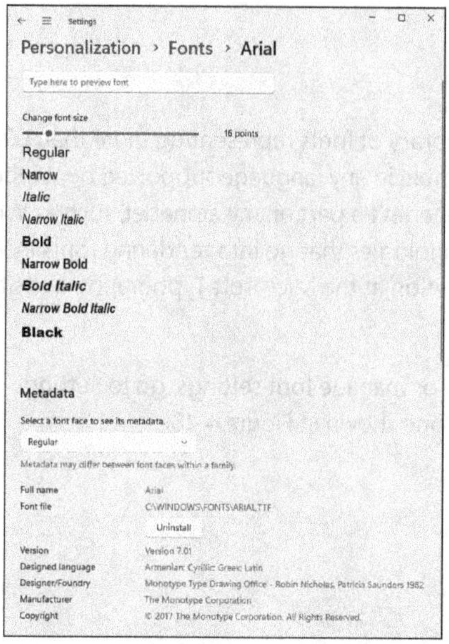

Figure 4-19 Each of the font faces listed at the top of this page represents a different font file in the same family—in this case, Arial.

The font format used by Windows is OpenType—a font format "superset" that encompasses TrueType and PostScript Type 1 fonts. To install a new font, you can drag its file from a folder or compressed .zip archive to the Fonts page in Settings. But you don't need to open Fonts to accomplish this task; an even simpler way to install a downloaded font is to right-click its file in File Explorer and choose Install. Because font file names are often somewhat cryptic, you might want to double-click the file, which opens the font preview window, to see what you're getting. If it's a font you want, click the Install button.

NOTE

PostScript Type 1 fonts normally consist of two or three files. The one you use to install the font—regardless of which method you use—is the .pfm file, whose file type is shown in File Explorer as Type 1 Font File.

Making text easier to read

If you like to work at high screen resolutions but find yourself straining to read the text, you can try the following:

- Look for scaling ("zoom") commands in the text-centric apps you use. Most modern word processors, for example, include these scaling features. Scaling text up to a readable size is a good solution for particular apps, but it doesn't change the size of icon text, system menus (such as Start), or system dialogs.

- To enlarge part of the screen, use the Magnifier tool. (For more information, see "Overcoming challenges" earlier in this chapter.)

- Use the scaling options in Display settings. Adjusting the scaling to a higher level enables you to have readable text at higher screen resolutions.

There's no supported way to change the Windows 11 system font, and we don't recommend using any of the registry hacks available online that offer to help you make this adjustment. You can, however, change the size of text everywhere, without changing the overall scaling of your system. Go to Settings > Accessibility > Text Size and move the dot on the Text Size slider to the right. The Text Size Preview window shows you how large your text will become, and a Screen-Tip over the dot displays the percentage of magnification, from 100 to 225 percent, as shown in Figure 4-20. Click Apply to accept the changes.

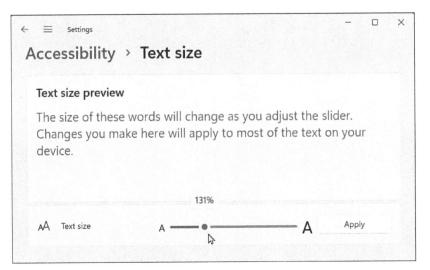

Figure 4-20 By moving this slider, you can magnify the size of text throughout Windows.

Using font smoothing to make text easier on the eyes

ClearType is a font-smoothing technology that reduces jagged edges of characters, thus easing eye strain.

To check or change your font-smoothing settings, open the Fonts page in Settings, expand the Related Settings group, and then click Adjust ClearType Text. Doing so opens the ClearType Text Tuner, which allows you to turn on ClearType and then adjust its settings using a series of optometrist-style choices ("Which Is Better, Number 1 or Number 2?"). If you have more than one monitor attached, the ClearType Text Tuner goes through this exercise for each one.

Windows includes seven fonts that are optimized for ClearType. The names of six of these—Constantia, Cambria, Corbel, Calibri, Candara, and Consolas—begin with the letter *c*—just to help cement the connection with ClearType. If you're particularly prone to eye fatigue, you might want to consider favoring these fonts in documents you create. (Constantia and Cambria are serif fonts, considered particularly suitable for longer documents and reports. The other four are sans serif fonts, good for headlines and advertising.) The seventh ClearType-optimized font, Segoe UI, is the typeface used for text elements throughout the Windows user interface. (Windows also includes a ClearType-optimized font called Meiryo that's designed to improve the readability of horizontally arrayed Asian languages.)

➤ **For information about how ClearType works, visit Microsoft's ClearType site at** *https://bit.ly/ClearTypeInfo.*

CHAPTER 5

Installing and configuring apps

Apps make it possible to get things done with Microsoft Windows. That's true for businesses of all sizes, which use productivity apps like Outlook, Word, and Excel to enable employees to create, collaborate, and communicate. Large organizations often rely on a mix of custom line-of-business applications and off-the-shelf accounting and management software, some of it written decades ago. And apps aren't just for work, as the success of PC-based games and streaming media services makes clear.

A default installation of Windows 11 includes dozens of apps. In Chapter 6, "Using and managing built-in Windows apps," we provide instructions on how to be more productive (or have more fun) with some of the most useful ones. But the real strength of Windows is its ability to add and run a truly astonishing range of old and new applications, many of which are available through the Microsoft Store, which is itself a Windows app.

Later in this chapter, we cover the tools and techniques for installing, configuring, troubleshooting, and uninstalling third-party apps. Those tools are especially useful for dealing with the legacy desktop apps that are still the mainstay of many Windows PCs.

We start with a discussion of how those old-fashioned programs, many written for earlier Windows versions, are able to coexist happily alongside more modern apps.

Understanding the Windows app landscape

As far as most apps are concerned, Windows 10 and Windows 11 are functionally identical. And both of those operating systems were designed with backward compatibility as a prime directive. Taken together, those two statements help to explain the broad outlines of the Windows app landscape.

If you've been using Windows for more than a few years, you probably think of *apps* and *desktop programs* as separate beasts. In the first few years after the release of Windows 10, in fact, the operating system applied different labels to "trusted Microsoft Store apps," which were acquired from the Store, and "desktop apps," which had to be downloaded and installed separately. In the Windows 11 era, those lines have been erased: When you search for a program, the tile that appears in the search results list is labeled simply "App."

That's not just a semantic distinction. Instead, it reflects the significant changes in the Windows app landscape over the past few years. You can still download legacy desktop apps that were originally written years ago and set them up by double-clicking on an installer package. But developers now have the option to distribute desktop apps securely through the Microsoft Store, which has itself been significantly redesigned for Windows 11. In addition, developers can turn websites into Progressive Web Apps (PWAs) that function like native apps. You can find some PWAs packaged for delivery through the Store; in addition, you can also use Microsoft Edge to install a supported website as a PWA.

In Windows 11, Apps has its own top-level heading in Settings, which we discuss in more detail later in this chapter. There, you find settings for every installed app, regardless of its origin.

In the remainder of this section, we look more closely at the differences that define legacy desktop apps, Store apps, and PWAs.

Inside OUT

You don't need Control Panel anymore

Microsoft has made admirable progress in migrating controls from the legacy Control Panel to the more modern pages in the Settings app. That's certainly true when it comes to apps. From Settings > Apps > Installed Apps, you can examine version information for any app, see how much storage space it's using, modify its installation (if the installer allows), and uninstall the app. Those functions are available for apps acquired from the Microsoft Store, as well as for PWAs and legacy desktop apps.

For legacy Win32 apps, a Programs And Features page still exists in the old-style Control Panel. But it offers only one tiny capability not available in the corresponding modern Settings page: Apps that include a website address as part of their app information have a clickable link that takes you to that address. If you're absolutely stumped by the provenance of a desktop app installed on your system, that might be a reason to open Control Panel. But aside from that one exception, there's no reason to leave Settings.

Legacy desktop apps

The oldest category consists of Windows desktop apps that were developed using the Win32 application programming interface (API). Don't let the name fool you: This API has its roots in 16-bit Windows versions but over the years evolved to support 32-bit and then 64-bit Windows versions, which is one reason its formal name is now simply the Windows API.

These legacy apps, sometimes called Win32 apps, are designed to run on all versions of Windows, using whatever features and capabilities are available in the version on which they're running. Traditionally, they have been delivered as self-contained packages that can be downloaded and installed by anyone with administrative rights on a Windows PC.

Windows 11 continues to support these traditional apps, which make it possible for PC owners to remain productive with apps that have proven their utility for a decade or more, through multiple Windows versions. These legacy applications are designed, for the most part, for use with a keyboard and a mouse, and many of them first came into being during the era when desktop machines dominated the computing landscape.

Beginning in May 2022, Microsoft began allowing developers of Win32 apps to distribute those apps through the Microsoft Store. Apps delivered through this channel are subject to certification by the Store, a process that includes a variety of security checks as well as confirmation that the app can be installed silently, with no activity required by the user, and that it can be uninstalled cleanly, without leaving behind any files, folders, or stray registry entries.

Apps distributed in this fashion work exactly as they would if they were downloaded and installed from the web; they are not subject to the same restrictions as native Store apps, nor are they eligible to receive automatic updates through the Store. Although developers can submit updated versions of desktop apps to the Store, those updates are not automatically installed.

CHAPTER 5

Inside OUT

How to prevent users from installing unsafe apps

Conventional Windows app installers downloaded from arbitrary sources, running with administrative rights, can create and run Windows services, install files in protected system folders, and add junk to the Windows registry. Because that same installer app is responsible for the uninstallation process, there's no guarantee it will clean up after itself if you decide you no longer want that app on your system. And there's a possibility that a downloaded installer can include malware or additional, unwanted software.

Apps delivered through the Microsoft Store have been vetted to confirm that they do not subject the user to these potential risks. The conclusion is obvious: A PC running Windows will be safer if users are allowed to install only certified apps delivered through the Store.

Some OEM PCs are delivered with Windows 11 Home edition running in S Mode. On those systems, only apps installed from the Store are eligible for installation, even by administrators. Installing legacy desktop apps is forbidden, and system apps that operate at the command line, including Cmd.exe and PowerShell, are also prohibited from running. The net effect of those prohibitions is to dramatically increase system stability.

On a PC running a stock version of Windows 11, you can create a similar configuration by going to Settings > Apps > Advanced App Settings; the four choices under the Choose Where To Get Apps heading, shown in Figure 5-1, allow you to configure the system so that standard users are prohibited (or discouraged) from installing apps from sources outside the Store. The most extreme option (listed as Recommended) allows only apps from the Microsoft Store.

Apps > Advanced app settings

Choose where to get apps	Anywhere
	Anywhere, but let me know if there's a comparable app in the Microsoft Store
Share across devices Continue app experiences on other devices	Anywhere, but warn me before installing an app that's not from the Microsoft Store
	The Microsoft Store only (Recommended)
App execution aliases	>
Archive apps Save storage space and internet bandwidth by archiving apps automatically	>
Related settings	
Uninstall updates	>
How to install a program	⬀

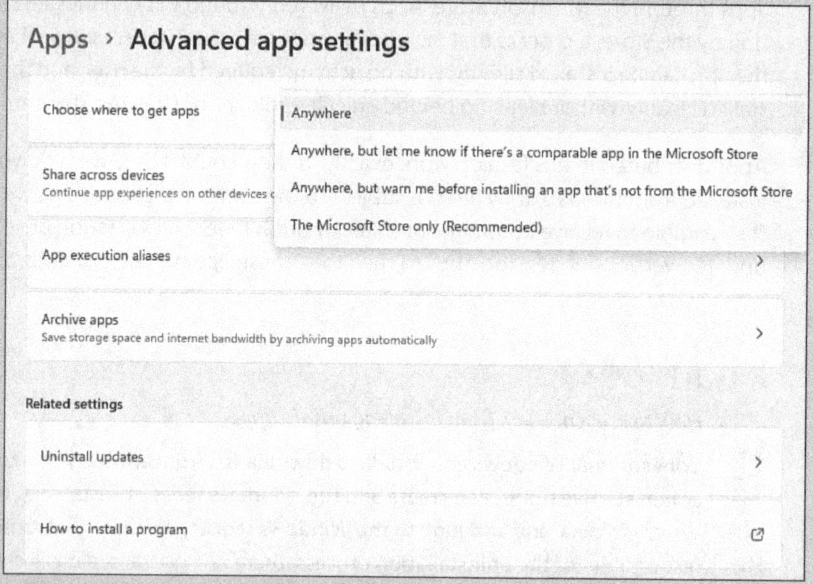

Figure 5-1   These settings allow an administrator to configure Windows 11 to allow installation of apps only from the Microsoft Store.

What makes this configuration more versatile than the extremely strict Windows 11 in S Mode is that it allows you (as an administrator) to download and install a handful of trusted legacy apps that you know to be safe before locking down app installation privileges. That allows even standard users to run those apps while preventing them from inadvertently compromising the system by installing other legacy desktop apps from outside the Store.

Windows apps

The second category consists of apps that were written and compiled to run only on Windows 10 and Windows 11. This category includes many of the built-in apps included with Windows 11 as well as third-party apps delivered through the Microsoft Store (previously known as the Windows Store). Apps in this category are delivered as packages and installed to secure locations in the file system that are not readily accessible to users. They are also "sandboxed," which means they run in secure isolation, free from potentially hazardous interactions with other running processes.

The earliest generation of apps delivered through the Store were optimized for use on touch-screen-equipped mobile devices running Windows 8. Later, Microsoft developed a subset of Windows APIs specifically targeting Windows 10 devices called the *Universal Windows Platform (UWP)*.

Today, UWP is mostly deprecated. Developers have a new set of tools called the Windows App Software Development Kit (SDK) that they can use to build desktop apps for Windows 11. This SDK provides a common user experience framework called the Windows UI Library (WinUI 3); apps built using these tools support native Windows 11 features but can also run on Windows 10 version 1809 and later.

Windows apps built using these tools can be distributed through the Store using a package format called MSIX. (The name is derived from a combination of the Win32 Microsoft Windows Installer format, MSI, and the UWP-era Windows application package file format, APPX.) These apps combine the capabilities of traditional desktop apps in a package that is installed and licensed like a UWP app and is updated through the Microsoft Store. Desktop apps packaged in this fashion must meet strict standards, including the ability to run as a standard interactive user, with no reliance on kernel-mode drivers or Windows services.

Packaged desktop apps are most commonly installed from the Microsoft Store, but they can also be delivered as standalone packages that you can install by double-clicking. When installed in this fashion, the app behaves just as if it had been acquired from the Microsoft Store.

> ➤ **For more details on the Windows App SDK and the Windows UI Library, see the developer-focused documentation at** *https://docs.microsoft.com/windows/apps/windows-app-sdk* **and** *https://docs.microsoft.com/windows/apps/winui.*

Progressive Web Apps (PWAs)

Modern website developers can use an assortment of interesting open web technologies (Service Workers, push notifications, Fetch networking, Cache API, and Web App Manifest, to name just a few) to make websites work very much like native apps. With a few fairly simple additions, a developer can transform that work into a packaged Progressive Web App that runs on just about any platform, just as if it were a native app. (Why are they called *progressive?* Because the user experience scales up or down depending on the capabilities of the device on which they're running.)

Unlike a website, a PWA works even when a device is offline. PWAs run in their own window, independent of the browser, and can be pinned to Start and to the taskbar. They can interact with hardware (a built-in webcam and microphone, for example), access user resources (such as a calendar, saved documents, or local music files), and send push notifications to Windows while still under the control of the same Windows security features that keep packaged apps safely sandboxed.

Developers can submit PWAs to the Microsoft Store as packaged UWP apps, but Microsoft also uses its Bing App Crawler to identify sites that include a Web App Manifest and makes some of those apps available in the Store. (You can spot these apps easily—the publisher is listed as Microsoft Store.) In addition, sites that work as PWAs can be installed using the Apps menu in Microsoft Edge.

> ➤ For more details on Progressive Web Apps in Microsoft Edge, see the support article "Overview of Progressive Web Apps (PWAs)" at *https://bit.ly/edge-pwa-overview*. For more on how PWAs work, see "The user experience of PWAs" at *https://bit.ly/edge-pwa-ux*.

Installing, managing, and uninstalling apps

As we noted in the previous section, you can acquire and install legacy desktop apps directly from software publishers, from third-party stores, and even, unfortunately, from dodgy websites. All other apps typically arrive through the Microsoft Store (or, in the case of PWAs, through a browser). In this section, we look at how these different installation methods determine where program files are located, how apps are allowed to interact with other system resources, and how to uninstall an app.

For an inventory of available apps, you can look in two places. Go to Settings > Apps > Installed Apps (or right-click Start and choose Installed Apps from the Quick Link menu) for a list of every app installed on the current system. This list, which we explore in more detail later in this section, includes not just apps but program libraries, driver installers, update managers, notification tools, and other utility apps that you might not recognize, typically because they're installed as part of a larger package.

You'll find a smaller, more focused list of apps by clicking Start and then clicking All Apps. The resulting list includes every app that accepts user interaction. Utility apps that work exclusively in the background and don't have a user interface don't appear here. For example, Microsoft Edge Update and Microsoft Update Health Tools are both included with a default Windows 11 installation and are in the Installed Apps list; because they have no user-accessible functions, you won't find them on the Start menu.

Any item on the All Apps list can be pinned to Start, to the taskbar, or to both locations. Right-click any app icon on Start or in the All Apps list to see a shortcut menu that includes a limited set of management tools. An Uninstall menu option is available for every app that allows you to remove it. (Windows system apps and some provisioned apps do not include the Uninstall option.)

➤ **For a list of Windows system and provisioned apps, see "Apps included with Windows 11," in Chapter 6. For more on how to organize app icons, see "Using and customizing the Start menu," in Chapter 3, "Using Windows 11."**

As mentioned earlier, the most complete list of apps is available in Settings > Apps > Installed Apps. Each entry initially displays the name of the app, the name of the app's developer (if available), the date on which the app was installed, and the amount of disk space it's currently using (including any data that is saved as part of the app's local data store but not data files stored in the user's profile).

The list is arranged in alphabetical order by default, but you can use the Sort menu at the top of the list to change the order to Size (to identify potential disk hogs for removal when storage space is tight) or Install Date (to quickly remove one or more apps you recently installed for evaluation and decided not to keep). Figure 5-2 shows the default List View, with the Sort By option set to Size (Large To Small).

Figure 5-2   The Installed Apps list includes legacy desktop apps alongside apps from the Microsoft Store. Sorting the list by size, large to small, shows which apps are using the most disk space.

CHAPTER 5

You can also filter by drive, in the unlikely event you have apps installed on a secondary drive in addition to your system drive.

If the list feels too unwieldy to scroll through, try filtering its contents by using the search box. Note that the results include matches for the app name and the developer name; the latter option is a particularly effective way to see all the apps preinstalled by the PC's manufacturer.

The options in the top-right corner of the Installed Apps list allow you to switch from the default List View to a more compact arrangement that drops the version number and developer name from each entry, allowing multiple items in each row. Tile View is the most space-efficient arrangement; Grid View, shown in Figure 5-3, displays each entry as a square tile with an Uninstall link beneath the app details.

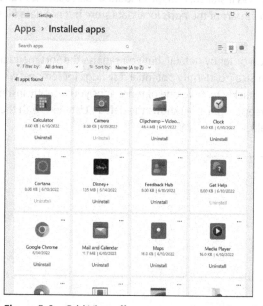

Figure 5-3   Grid View offers a more compact view of the Installed Apps list, with the Uninstall option available beneath each app listing.

Regardless of which view you've chosen, you can click the three dots at the right of any entry on this list to see additional options for managing that app. What you see in this expanded listing varies depending on how the app was installed.

For desktop apps, the shortcut menu includes Modify and Uninstall options that launch the installer registered for that app. If the Modify option is grayed out and unavailable, it means the installer for that app doesn't include a so-called maintenance installation option in which you can add or remove features or otherwise change the current configuration.

For packaged apps and PWAs (but not desktop apps) that were installed through the Microsoft Store, the shortcut menu includes three choices: Advanced Options, Move, and Uninstall. We look more closely at these options in the next section.

Using and managing Store apps

The Microsoft Store is an emporium where you can purchase a wide-ranging variety of digital goods and services: games, movies, TV shows, and apps. (It's not an ever-expanding marketplace, however. In the years since the introduction of Windows 10, Microsoft has stopped selling music and ebooks through the Store, and most TV shows and movies are purchased or rented by owners of Xbox consoles; those consoles run a variant of Windows 10/11 and use the same Microsoft Store to deliver digital content.)

But focusing only on commerce risks missing the real point of the Store, which serves as a secure channel for distributing apps, including those that are preinstalled with Windows. Part of that security comes from the fact that apps have to go through a vetting process to be distributed through the Store; it's unlikely that a malicious app can survive that vetting process, and in the unlikely event that a bad app managed to sneak into the Store, it would be shut down as soon as its misbehavior was discovered.

An equally important part of the Store's security model is the way it manages the installation and updating of app packages—a highly structured process that installs files to a restricted hierarchy in the file system, marks their contents as read-only, locks everything down using file permissions, and keeps them up to date without requiring any user intervention. That combination prevents Store apps from contributing to "Windows rot" and degrading system performance. They can also be uninstalled cleanly, without leaving digital detritus behind.

The executable file (along with supporting files) for a desktop application is normally stored in a subfolder of %ProgramFiles% or %ProgramFiles(x86)%. By contrast, packaged apps are stored in a hidden folder called %ProgramFiles%\WindowsApps. This folder is locked so that only the Microsoft Store app or the Windows System account can view, run, or modify its contents. Although that might frustrate those who like to crawl through every hidden nook and cranny of their hard drive, there's a good reason for the high security: Instead of signing individual files, as is the case with most desktop applications, the entire app package is signed, making it possible to validate the contents of any or all files in the package. Instead of running an executable file and calling other resources, Windows runs the entire package in a protected app container environment. Because users (including you) and other apps are prevented from making changes, the app files are safe.

Inside OUT

Take a peek at installed Windows packages

If you try to open the WindowsApps folder in File Explorer, you quickly discover that your user account lacks the necessary permissions to browse through that folder's contents. You could, of course, open a Command Prompt window with administrative privileges and browse from the command line. But if you're just interested in seeing what sort of files and resources are stored in that location for a particular app, we can point you to a useful back door. (Don't worry: Although you can view the folder directories, you can't make any changes.) The following steps get you there:

1. After starting the app you want to examine more closely, open Task Manager. (For details, see "Managing apps and processes with Task Manager," later in this chapter.)

2. On the Processes tab, right-click the name of the app of interest. (If a number in parentheses follows the app name, you first need to expand the entry by clicking the arrow on the left side. Then right-click the name of the app in the expanded list.)

3. Click Go To Details. Task Manager switches to the Details tab and selects the app's executable file.

4. Right-click that executable file and choose Open File Location. You're in.

You can't run an app directly from this folder, nor can you make changes to files stored there.

Legacy desktop apps that you download and install from outside the Store can be installed for all users or for a single user. By contrast, Windows apps that are managed by the Store are installed only for the current user account. After installation, you find data files for the newly installed app in a part of your user profile, where they are kept private and can't be tampered with by other apps. You can view these folders (but you can't change their contents) at %LocalAppData%\Packages.

Anyone who signs on to another user account on the same PC can share the installed app files, but only after going to the Store, installing the app for their own account, and setting up their own private data folders. Uninstalling a packaged app is, likewise, a per-user activity that cleans up the data folders for the current user without touching files for other user accounts that have installed the same app. If you uninstall an app that's not in use by any other accounts on the same PC, Windows completely removes the app and its resources from the %ProgramFiles%\WindowsApps folder.

CHAPTER 5

Packaged desktop apps you install from the Store (as well as apps built using the same tools but distributed as standalone packages) follow a similar security-focused installation routine. Unlike legacy desktop apps, which typically require administrative permission to install and can splatter files throughout Windows system folders, these packaged desktop apps follow a rigid set of installation rules that dramatically lessen their ability to mess with the system.

Just as with Windows apps, packaged desktop apps are installed to a well-managed location, with file permissions keeping the package contents safe from tampering. Unlike other Store apps, however, they're not required to run in a sandboxed app container. Instead, these so-called full-trust apps run in the context of the user account that launched them. As a result, they can mimic the behavior of a legacy desktop app.

Behind the scenes, however, these apps are managed in a way that keeps them from interfering with the rest of the system. On Windows 11, the following modifications are made to the file system and registry:

- When the app attempts to write files or folders to the user's AppData folder, Windows intercepts those requests and writes them instead to a private location that is merged with the actual AppData folder when the app runs. This architecture allows apps to uninstall cleanly and avoid "Windows rot."

- Any files that would normally be added to the Windows\System32 or Program Files (x86) folders (such as DLL files) are stored instead in a virtual file system (VFS) folder as part of the app package. These files are dynamically merged with the actual system folders when the app runs, so that the app thinks everything's working as its developer intended.

- App packages contain a registry.dat file, which mirrors the contents of the corresponding branch of HKLM\Software. When the app runs, this virtual registry merges its contents into the registry to allow the app to run as expected.

- When the app makes changes to HKCU, those changes are written to a private location and merged when the app runs, which allows the system to clean this information when the app is uninstalled.

Finding apps in the Microsoft Store

The Microsoft Store app separates its wares using three tabs: Apps, Gaming, and Movies & TV. On the Apps tab, you can scroll through categorized, curated lists to find popular apps or collections of related apps. If you know more or less what you're looking for, you can use the search box to find it. Search by name or publisher, and the search results include entertainment offerings as well as apps. Figure 5-4 shows the Microsoft Store in Windows 11, with the Apps tab selected.

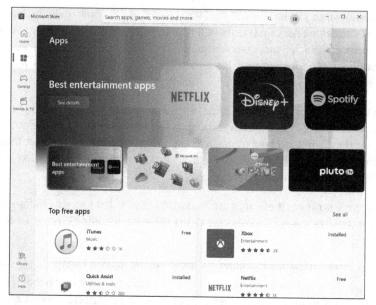

Figure 5-4   Click the Apps icon in the navigation bar on the left side to display a categorized listing of apps available for Windows 11.

Click any listing to see a details page that includes most of the information you need to decide whether an app is worth installing, including the developer's name, a description, screenshots depicting the app in action, and reviews and ratings from other people who've used the apps. Figure 5-5 shows the listing for Adobe Lightroom, a popular third-party app for organizing and editing digital photos.

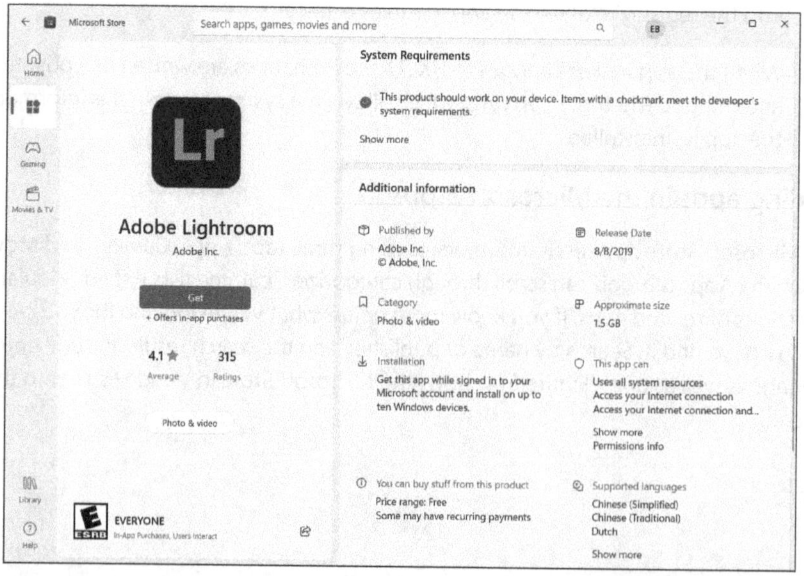

Figure 5-5   The System Requirements section should alert you to any incompatibilities.

Inside OUT

Is it a Store app or a desktop app?

As noted earlier in this chapter, the Microsoft Store allows you to download and install traditional desktop apps. How can you tell this type of desktop app from a UWP app or a packaged desktop app that is managed or updated by the Store? Look at the blue button.

If the blue button displays the word *Get* (or, in the case of a paid app, if it shows a price), the app is managed by the Store. If you see the word *Open*, the listing represents a Store-managed app that you've already installed.

If you see the word *Install*, the listing represents a traditional desktop app. Clicking that button downloads the installer and runs it silently, with no interaction required on your part except to approve a UAC prompt. If you previously installed the app, you don't see a blue button; instead, you see the word *Installed* in faint text on a gray background. We cover techniques for managing installer-based desktop apps in the next section.

The offerings in the Microsoft Store are not organized by price, but if you type **free** in the Search box, you can choose from filtered lists showing only free apps, games, or digital content. When you consider the cost of a so-called free app, however, you should check the (literal) fine print to see if the app listing includes an asterisk and a notation that the app "offers in-app purchases." Some apps offer a free trial but require payment for continued use after the trial period ends. Other apps, including those for streaming video services like Netflix or Disney+, require paid subscriptions to view content. Still others offer a free, ad-supported tier with a paid option to remove ads. When you click on an item, the details page that appears might enumerate the extra offerings.

Scrolling to the bottom of the page usually reveals additional useful details, such as the approximate size of the app, the release date, system requirements, a privacy policy, and the number of devices on which the app can be installed. (This section is also where you can inspect the permissions that the app requires, a topic we cover in more detail later in this section.)

To begin the process of installing a free Store app for the first time, click the blue button labeled Get. That action immediately begins downloading and installing the app. When the installation is complete, the button text changes to Open, and you can click to run the app.

If payment is required, the blue button is labeled with the price, and clicking that button begins the purchase process. The payment itself is managed through your Microsoft account. If you sign in to Windows 11 using a local account or an Azure AD account, you'll be prompted at this point for Microsoft account credentials to use with the Store, and you'll be guided to configure a payment mechanism if you haven't already done so.

Updating and reinstalling Store apps

Clicking the Library icon in the lower-left corner of the Store app opens a page like the one shown in Figure 5-6. Any available updates as well as downloads in progress appear at the top of the page. The lower section shows a list of apps, games, and digital content available in the current user profile. Controls at the top of that list allow you to filter its contents to show only Apps, as we've done here.

Figure 5-6   In its default view, the Library page shows updates and downloads at the top, with a list of available Store apps below it. Note the download icon to the right of Adobe Express, indicating that it's not currently installed.

The Sort control above the list includes Sort By Date and Sort By Name options that work as expected, displaying a list of all currently installed and previously purchased apps. Two additional options on that menu, however, behave in an unexpected fashion. Although the menu options include the word *sort*, they really act as filters:

- **Sort By Installed**   Choosing this option filters the list to show only Store apps and packaged desktop apps that are installed in the current profile, sorted by the date they were last modified. It does not include traditional desktop apps delivered through the Store.

- **Sort By Not Installed**   This option displays a list of all apps that were previously installed or purchased by the signed-in Microsoft account and are not currently installed. The list includes games, browser add-ons, and theme packages installed on any Windows 10 or Windows 11 device but does not include traditional desktop apps delivered through the Store.

The latter view is particularly useful when you're setting up a new PC (or refreshing your Windows installation on an old one). Go through the list to identify any apps you previously acquired; if you don't recognize an app, click its name to go to the details page for that app in the Microsoft Store. Click the cloud icon to the right of any app to download and install the app on your fresh Windows installation.

Inside OUT

Get updates for Microsoft Store apps manually

The Updates & Downloads list at the top of the Library page (shown previously in Figure 5-6) includes a Get Updates button in the upper-right corner that allows you to check for and retrieve updates to Microsoft Store apps at any time. In theory, checking for updates shouldn't be necessary because Microsoft Store apps periodically check for and install updates automatically. But if your computer has been offline for an extended time, or if you just performed a clean install, you might want to oversee the updating process.

The automatic update process works well, and we recommend leaving it enabled. If you prefer to turn off automatic updates, open the Store app, click the icon for your user profile, click App Settings, and slide the App Updates switch to the Off position. Just remember to open the Store app and check for updates regularly.

Inside OUT

Use the Windows Package Manager to install apps from the command line

The simplest way to install packaged apps is to use the Windows Store. But you can also install software packages that are available in a known repository from a command line using the Windows Package Manager command-line tool, Winget.exe.

Winget is automatically installed with Windows 11 and allows anyone to install packages from the Windows Package Manager Community Repository, at *https://github.com/microsoft/winget-pkgs*. Although this capability is primarily of interest to developers who are comfortable with the corresponding package manager in Linux distributions, it's relatively easy for nontechnical users to employ. You can install the latest version of PowerShell, for example, using the following command:

```
winget install --id Microsoft.Powershell --source winget.
```

For full documentation on how to use Winget, see *https://learn.microsoft.com/windows/package-manager/*.

Managing, troubleshooting, and uninstalling Store apps

For packaged apps that are managed by the Store, including UWP apps and packaged desktop apps, Windows includes a variety of tools you can use to perform maintenance tasks, up to and including uninstalling the app.

The easiest way to access these functions is to right-click the app's pinned icon on Start, and then click App Settings. (If the app icon isn't pinned, go to All Apps, right-click the App, and then click More > App Settings.) You can also reach this page from the app's entry in Settings > Apps > Installed Apps: Click the three dots to the right of any entry in the list, and choose Advanced Options. That opens a page like the one shown in Figure 5-7.

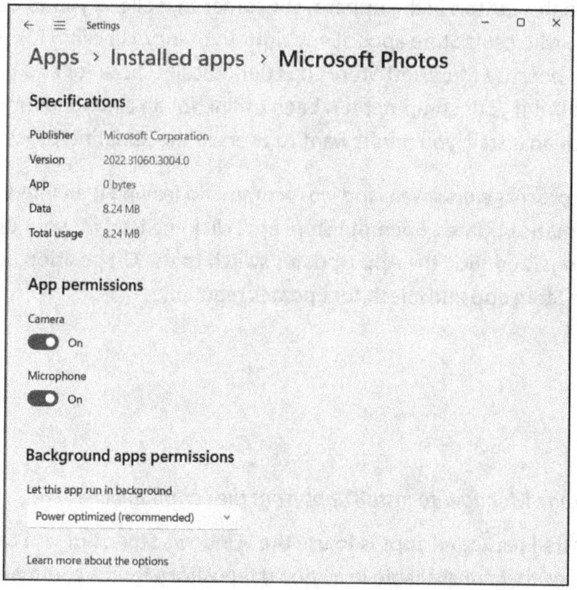

Figure 5-7 The Advanced Options page shows version information and offers maintenance tools for apps that are managed by the Store.

The Specifications section at the top of the page shows the version number and disk space used by the app package. Below that is an App Permissions section, which gives you the option to change the permissions assigned to that app when it was installed. The Background Apps Permissions setting controls whether the app is allowed to run in the background—a setting that can help with battery life on portable devices.

Every app listed in the Microsoft Store is required to disclose which permissions it requires. A packaged desktop app is a "full trust" application, and its Store listing page includes the following permissions info under the This App Can heading: "Uses all system resources." For a full list of the 30 or so available app permissions, see *https://bit.ly/Windows11-app-permissions*.

Scroll down the page a bit and you find two options that are useful when troubleshooting a misbehaving app:

- **Terminate**   On the rare occasions when an app is completely nonresponsive and can't be closed, click Terminate to forcibly close the app and all related processes.

- **Reset**   You find two buttons under this heading. The Repair option attempts to fix any corruption in the app installation without affecting your user data. Reset is a more drastic option that deletes all user data for that app, including sign-in details.

The easiest way to uninstall a packaged app is to right-click its icon on Start and then click Uninstall. An Uninstall button is also on the Advanced Options page. (Note that some apps installed as part of Windows 11 can't be uninstalled. For a full list of these apps, see Chapter 6.)

As noted earlier, packaged apps are installed on a per-user basis, and uninstalling works that way as well; if you've installed an app from multiple user accounts, the app package remains on the system until you uninstall it from all user accounts.

TROUBLESHOOTING

Store apps won't uninstall

If the normal uninstall routine for a Store app doesn't seem to work, you can remove the troublesome item by using Windows PowerShell. (See Chapter 16, "PowerShell, Windows Terminal, and other advanced management tools," for information about PowerShell.) Use the Get-AppxPackage cmdlet to obtain a list of packages installed on your system. Find the one you want to remove and note its *PackageFullName* property. Then supply this property as a parameter to the Remove-AppxPackage cmdlet. Note that you must be working in a PowerShell session with administrative privileges.

Managing legacy desktop apps

With rare exceptions, Windows 11 supports virtually all legacy Win32 desktop applications that are compatible with Windows 7. Any desktop apps you own that aren't available in the Microsoft Store can be installed in the usual ways, by double-clicking an installer file you download from the internet.

Uninstalling a desktop app

When you install a legacy desktop app, the installer provides Windows with instructions for how to uninstall the app (you can find some examples of these instructions in the registry, at HKCU\SOFTWARE\Microsoft\Windows\CurrentVersion\Uninstall). To execute those instructions, right-click the app's icon on the Start menu, and then click Uninstall. If the app included instructions for quietly uninstalling itself (most don't), you're asked to confirm your intention; when you do, the app is uninstalled without any further interaction.

CHAPTER 5

For desktop apps that don't include the switches necessary to quietly uninstall, choosing that option from the right-click shortcut menu takes you to the old-style Programs And Features page in Control Panel. Select the name from the Uninstall Or Change A Program list and then click Uninstall to continue.

If you'd rather skip the side trip to Control Panel, start in Settings > Apps > Installed Apps. Find the entry for the app you want to remove, click the three dots to the right of its name, and click Uninstall.

Running desktop apps as an administrator or as another user

Windows 11 includes an assortment of Win32 apps used for system management tasks, including some management tools that have been part of Windows for decades. These apps, and similar third-party system utilities, must be run with an administrative token. To edit the registry, for example, you need to run Registry Editor (Regedit.exe) as an administrator. You can run most apps as an administrator by right-clicking the executable file or any app shortcut (on Start or elsewhere), choosing Run As Administrator, and satisfying the User Account Control (UAC) prompt with either consent or credentials. (This option does not work for File Explorer, Explorer. exe.) Here are two additional ways to accomplish the same result:

- Start a Command Prompt or PowerShell session as Administrator. From that console, you can type the name of the executable file for whichever app you want to run, and it will inherit the administrator token from the elevated session.

    To run Registry Editor, for example, type **regedit**. Because you already passed UAC inspection for the Command Prompt session, and because whatever you run from Command Prompt is a child process of Command Prompt, you don't have to deal with any further UAC prompts. (The same rules apply to PowerShell.) This method is excellent for situations where you need to run a sequence of apps as an administrator. Keep one administrative-level Command Prompt or PowerShell window open, and run your apps from the command line.

- Type the name of the app you want to run in the taskbar search box, and then press Ctrl+Shift+Enter.

To run an app under a different user account, you can use the Runas command. You can do this from Command Prompt or PowerShell. The syntax is

Runas /user:*username appname*

After you issue the command, you're prompted to enter the password for the specified user account. Note that the Runas command does not work with File Explorer or with Microsoft Management Console (MMC) snap-ins.

Inside OUT

Use Steps Recorder to troubleshoot misbehaving software

When you need to report details about a software problem to a tech support person, the built-in Steps Recorder tool (Psr.exe) can prove valuable. To locate this app, click Start, type **steps** in the search box, and then click Steps Recorder from the list of search results. Click Start Record, retrace your steps through the problematic app, and then click Stop Record.

Steps Recorder takes a screenshot and time stamp at each crucial juncture (each mouse click or command) and then appends a text description of each step. You can add your own comments along the way. After you stop and save your recording, you can share it with tech support. (Steps Recorder is also an excellent tool for creating documentation to be used by others in your organization.)

Dealing with compatibility issues

Apps that run without problems on Windows 7 should run equally well on Windows 11. Certain older desktop applications might create problems, however. Windows attempts to flag potential compatibility problems when you first run such a program. The Program Compatibility Assistant that appears offers you the alternatives of checking online for solutions (such as downloading a more recent version) or going ahead and running the program.

If you install an app and subsequently run into compatibility issues, a compatibility trouble-shooter might appear. Alternatively, you can run the troubleshooter yourself from Control Panel. You can find it by typing **compatibility** in the taskbar search box. Click Run Programs Made For Previous Versions Of Windows to launch the troubleshooter, and then click past the opening screen.

The troubleshooter begins by scanning for problems it can detect automatically. If it finds none, it presents a list of apps installed on your system from which you can select the one that's giving you difficulty. Select the offending app and follow the prompts to try to resolve your problem.

Managing Progressive Web Apps

Progressive Web Apps (PWAs) can be installed from the Store or directly from a web browser that supports PWAs, including Microsoft Edge and Google Chrome. The only indication that a Store listing belongs to a PWA is a compatibility note that reads "This app requires the latest version of Microsoft Edge." When you use Microsoft Edge to visit a website that is eligible to be installed as a PWA, the App Available icon appears in the address bar. In Google Chrome, an Install button appears in the address bar. Clicking the respective icon or button installs the PWA.

The XML files that make up a PWA are stored in the same protected location as packaged Windows apps, and the management options are identical to those available for apps from the Store.

To see a list of PWAs installed using the Microsoft Store or Microsoft Edge, open Edge and go to *edge://apps*. On this page, you can open any app by clicking Open. To learn more about an app or uninstall it, click Details.

Managing apps and processes with Task Manager

Task Manager is a tool that serves two essential purposes. You can use it to track aspects of your system's performance and to see what apps and processes are running, and you can use it to terminate items when the normal shutdown methods aren't working.

➤ **For information about using Task Manager to monitor system performance, see Chapter 14, "Performance and power management."**

The easiest way to run Task Manager is by means of its keyboard shortcut, Ctrl+Shift+Esc. As an alternative, right-click Start and choose Task Manager from the Quick Link menu. Figure 5-8 shows the Processes tab in Task Manager.

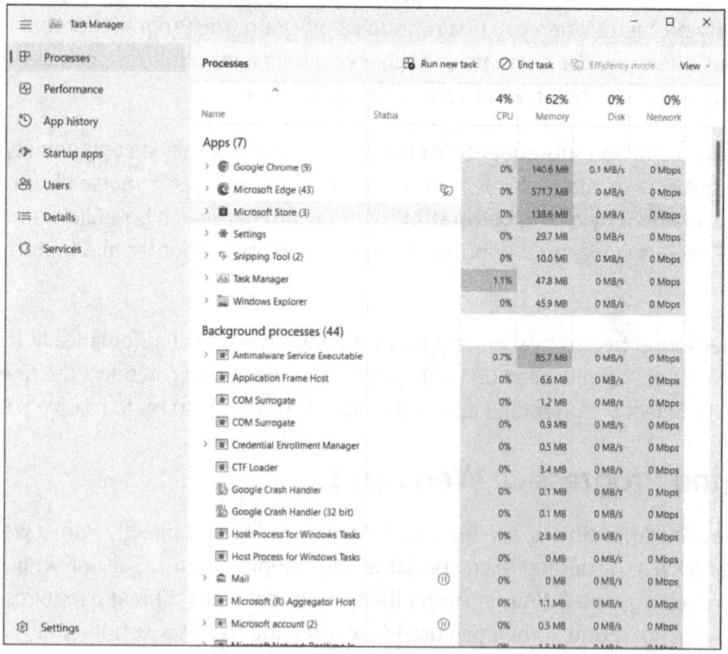

Figure 5-8   Task Manager is useful for terminating recalcitrant applications and processes, as well as for monitoring system performance.

By default, the items listed on the Processes tab are grouped by type—apps at the top, followed by background processes, and then by Windows processes, and so on. Grouping is optional; clear Group By Type on the View menu if you want a single list.

Note that some items in the Apps list have outline controls. You can expand these to see what files or documents are open. The lists are initially sorted by name (within each group if grouping is enabled), in ascending alphabetical order. Click any performance heading to sort by that column, in descending order, an arrangement that allows you to see at a glance which apps or processes are making the greatest use of the resource in that column; click again to reverse the sort. Clicking the CPU heading, for example, gives you a continually updating sorted list showing which apps and background processes are responsible for your laptop fan kicking into action.

Terminating an app with Task Manager

The Processes tab also includes a Status column. (If it's not visible, right-click a column heading and choose Status.) Most of the time, the entries in this column will be blank, indicating that everything is humming along. If an app hangs for any reason, you'll see the words *Not Responding* in this column. In that case, you can attempt to shut down the miscreant by right-clicking its name and clicking End Task. Don't be too quick on the trigger, however; Not Responding doesn't necessarily mean permanently out to lunch. If the app is using every bit of resources to handle a different task, it might simply be too busy to communicate with Task Manager.

Before you decide to end the app, give it a chance to finish whatever it's doing. How long should you wait? That depends on the task. If the operation involves a large amount of data in memory (transcoding a large high-definition video, for instance), it's appropriate to wait several minutes, especially if you see signs of disk activity. But if the task in question normally completes in a few seconds, you needn't wait that long.

Finding detailed information about an app

To see detailed information about the process that's running an app, right-click the app and choose Go To Details. This takes you to a related item on the Details tab.

For each process, Task Manager includes the following information by default: image name (the name of the process), process ID (PID), status (running or suspended, for example), user name (the name of the account that initiated the process), CPU (the percentage of the CPU's capacity the process is currently using), memory (the amount of memory the process requires to perform its regular functions, also known as the private working set), and description (a text field identifying the process). To display additional information for each process, right-click one of the headings and choose Select Columns.

Managing startup apps

The author of a Win32 desktop app can easily set it up to run automatically when you start Windows. Many apps do this during their installation, sometimes without bothering to ask for your consent. Reputable publishers typically offer the option to enable or disable automatic startup within the Settings for the app.

Packaged apps distributed through the Store can also be configured to run at startup. This option is typically configurable in the app's settings, and not in Windows itself.

Win32 apps that set themselves up to run automatically have a great many methods at their disposal. If you find yourself troubleshooting an app that starts automatically and doesn't include a mechanism for preventing it from running at startup, the following list might help you find (and disable) the setting:

- **Run key (machine)**   Apps listed in the registry's HKLM\Software\Microsoft\Windows\CurrentVersion\Run key are available at startup to all users. For 32-bit apps, this data might be stored in HKLM\SOFTWARE\Wow6432Node\Microsoft\Windows\CurrentVersion\Run.

- **Run key (user)**   Apps listed in the HKCU\Software\Microsoft\Windows\CurrentVersion\Run key run when the current user signs in. A similar subkey, HKCU\Software\Microsoft\Windows NT\CurrentVersion\Windows\Run, can also be used.

- **Load value**   Apps listed in the Load value of the registry key HKCU\Software\Microsoft\Windows NT\CurrentVersion\Windows run when any user signs in.

- **Scheduled tasks**   The Windows Task Scheduler can specify tasks that run at startup. In addition, an administrator can set up tasks for your computer to run at startup that are not available for you to change or delete.

- **RunOnce and RunOnceEx keys**   This group of registry keys identifies apps that run only once, at startup. This configuration is typically part of the initial setup for an app. These keys can be assigned to a specific user account or to the machine:

  - HKLM\Software\Microsoft\Windows\CurrentVersion\RunOnce

  - HKLM\Software\Microsoft\Windows\CurrentVersion\RunOnceEx

  - HKCU\Software\Microsoft\Windows\CurrentVersion\RunOnce

  - HKCU\Software\Microsoft\Windows\CurrentVersion\RunOnceEx

- **RunServices and RunServicesOnce keys**   As their names suggest, these rarely used keys can control the automatic startup of services. They can be assigned to a specific user account or to a computer.

- **Winlogon key**   The Winlogon key controls actions that occur when you sign in to a computer running Windows. Most of these actions are under the control of the operating system, but you can also add custom actions here. The HKLM\Software\Microsoft\Windows NT\CurrentVersion\Winlogon\Userinit and HKLM\Software\Microsoft\Windows NT\CurrentVersion\Winlogon\Shell subkeys can automatically launch apps.

- **Group Policy**   The Group Policy console includes two policies (one in Computer Configuration > Administrative Templates > System > Logon and one in the comparable User Configuration folder) called Run These Programs At User Logon that specify a list of apps to be run whenever any user signs in.

- **Policies\Explorer\Run keys**   Using policy settings to specify startup apps, as described in the previous paragraph, creates corresponding values in either of two registry keys: HKLM\Software\Microsoft\Windows\CurrentVersion\Policies\Explorer\Run or HKCU\Software\Microsoft\Windows\CurrentVersion\Policies\Explorer\Run.

- **Logon scripts**   Logon scripts, which run automatically at startup, can open other apps. Logon scripts are specified in Group Policy in Computer Configuration > Windows Settings > Scripts (Startup/Shutdown) and User Configuration > Windows Settings > Scripts (Logon/Logoff).

In addition, packaged apps can programmatically configure themselves to run at startup and can also run utility apps that are installed along with the app package.

Suspending or removing startup items

The problem many users have with startup apps is not with creating them (that's easy, and in many cases, it happens without your explicit consent when the program is installed) but getting rid of them. Having too many startup apps not only makes your system take longer to start, it also has the potential to waste memory. If you don't require an app at startup, you should consider removing it from your list of auto-starting apps.

That task is not always as simple as it sounds, however, because—as we noted earlier—there are many ways by which an app can be made to run at startup.

To see a list of startup processes, open Task Manager and switch to the Startup Apps tab. As Figure 5-9 shows, this tab identifies each item and includes an estimate of its impact on the time required to start your Windows environment.

You can't remove a startup item from this list, but you can disable it so that the item doesn't automatically run each time your computer starts up. To do this, select the item and then click Disable.

CHAPTER 5

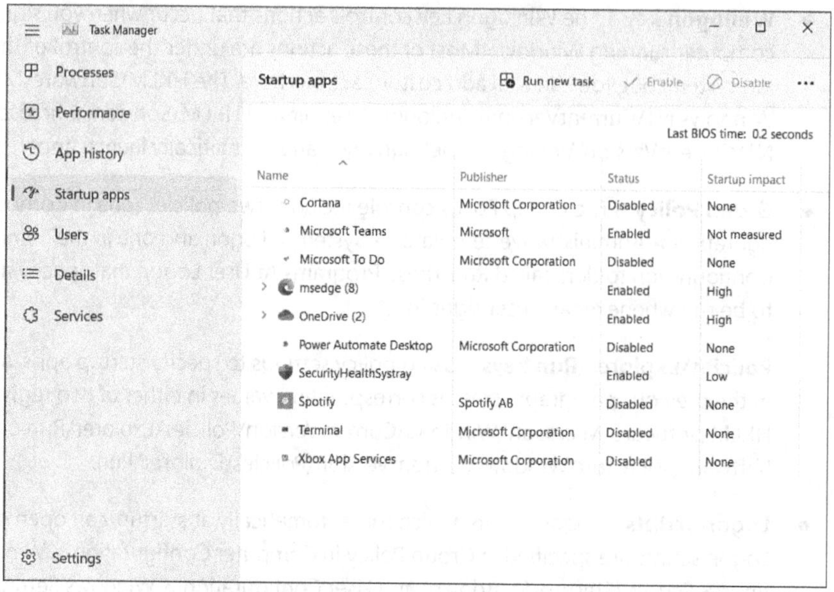

Figure 5-9   The Startup Apps tab in Task Manager shows you which startup apps are enabled and how much impact each is estimated to have on your startup time.

By default, the Startup Apps tab shows a bare minimum of information about each item on the list. For a more complete picture of each startup item, including detailed performance information, right-click any column heading on the Startup Apps tab and make one or more of the following columns visible:

- **Startup Type**   Lists where the command item is stored

- **Disk I/O At Startup**   Measures total disk activity for the selected item during the most recent startup

- **CPU At Startup**   Measures how long the CPU was active for the selected item during the most recent startup

- **Running Now**   Distinguishes between commands that continue to run and those that exit after performing a startup task

- **Disabled Time**   Displays the date and time when the item was disabled

- **Command Line**   Displays the full path, including switches, for startup items

This list is far from exhaustive. It includes items that are in one of the CurrentVersion\Run keys in the Registry as well as items that are installed as part of a packaged app and are programmed to run automatically at startup. (You can identify the latter class of startup items from the

Startup Type column, where the entry is blank; in addition, the Command Line column for this type of item shows the name of the executable but not the full path.)

If you're not sure whether an item on the Startup tab is justifying its existence there, try disabling it and restarting. Alternatively, or additionally, you can right-click the item and use the handy Search Online command to learn more about it. (For an alternative way to manage this set of startup apps, go to Settings > Apps > Startup.)

Advanced tools for managing startup items

The Startup tab in Task Manager is a fine way to disable startup behavior established by registry keys. Note, however, that Task Manager might not list every startup item; in particular, the list does not include items established by Group Policy or Task Scheduler.

To get the most comprehensive listing of items that run at startup, as well as a handy tool to prevent certain apps from starting, we recommend using Autoruns, a free utility from Microsoft's Windows Sysinternals collection. Autoruns, which you can download from *https://bit.ly/autoruns*, shows all the registry keys and startup locations listed earlier. As you can see from Figure 5-10, it also shows Explorer shell extensions, services, and many more exotic startup options.

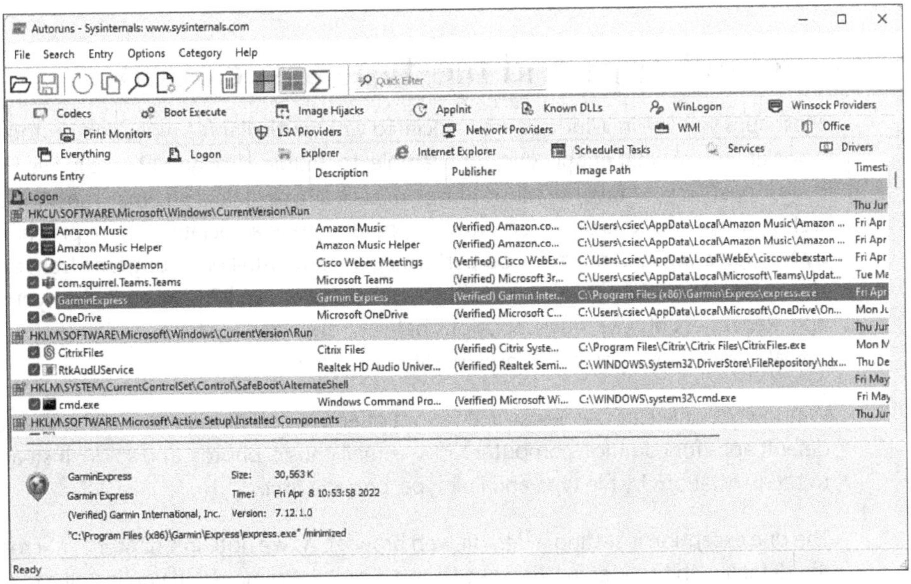

Figure 5-10   The free AutoRuns utility shows every conceivable way to automatically start a Windows process. More importantly, it offers options to remove those auto-starting programs.

Autoruns is particularly useful for finding processes that don't belong (such as a Trojan horse or other malware) or that you suspect of causing problems. You can then disable these items without removing them while you test your theory, or you can delete their autorun command altogether.

Select an item, and its details appear at the bottom of the screen, as shown in Figure 5-10. Disable an item by clearing the checkbox next to its name; you can later reenable it by selecting the checkbox. To clear an item from the autorun list, select it and click Entry > Delete. (Note that deleting an item from AutoRuns removes only the entry in the registry or other location that causes the item to run; it does not uninstall the app or delete its executable file.)

Although the tabs at the top of the Autoruns window filter the list of autorun items into various categories, the number of items can still be daunting. One nice feature of Autoruns is its ability to filter out components that are part of Windows or are digitally signed by Microsoft because these are presumably safe to run. Commands on the Options menu control the appearance of these items.

You can also use the Compare feature in Autoruns to compare before and after snapshots of the data it finds. Run Autoruns before you install a new app, save the data, run Autoruns again after you install the app, and compare the results to see what changes to autorun behavior were made during the installation process.

Setting default apps and file-type associations

Most apps you use in Windows are associated with particular file types and protocols. These associations are what enable you, for example, to double-click an MP3 file in File Explorer and have it open in your favorite music player, or click a hyperlink in an email message and have that webpage open in your preferred browser. Some of these associations were probably established by the operating system when you performed a clean install or an upgrade from an earlier version of Windows. Others were set (with or without your explicit consent) when you installed an app. Regardless of how the associations between apps and file types and protocols are currently set, Windows allows you to see and modify the settings.

Windows 11, unlike its predecessor, does not offer a consolidated page where you can choose default apps for common computer tasks—email, music, photos, and so on. Instead, you have to set associations by file type and link type, one at a time.

The one exception is setting a default web browser. As we note in Chapter 7, Microsoft Edge is the default web browser in Windows 11, and it can't be removed. If you install a third-party web browser, however, Windows 11 provides a simple mechanism for configuring the newly installed browser as the default app for handling web links.

After installing Google Chrome, for example, you can go to Settings > Apps > Default Apps and select Google Chrome from the list of installed apps. When you do, you see a new option at the top of the page, as shown in Figure 5-11. Click Make Google Chrome Your Default Browser to immediately transfer the association of most web protocols from Edge to the alternative browser.

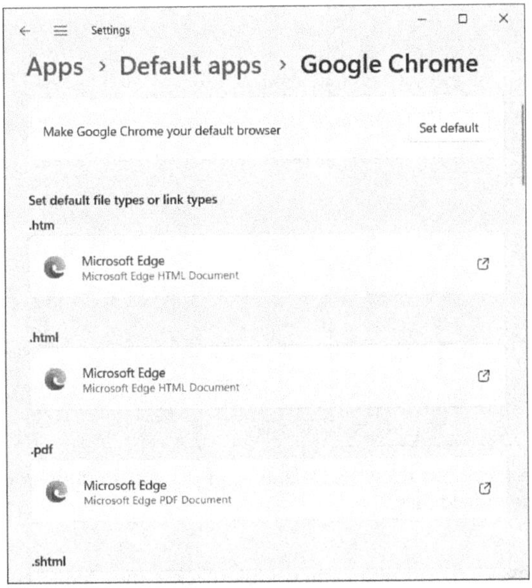

Figure 5-11   After installing a third-party web browser, use this option on the Default Apps page in Settings to specify that you want to use the new browser for opening links to webpages in email messages and documents.

The task of assigning defaults is not as easy for other app categories. After installing a new app, for example, you might discover that it has assumed the right to open a file type that you'd prefer to use with its previously assigned default app. Alternatively, you might find that a newly installed app hasn't claimed associations with file types it's capable of opening.

In those circumstances, you can reassign default app associations, but doing so requires that you have a deep understanding of file type extensions—a topic that can be bewildering even to experts.

If you start from Settings > Apps > Default Apps, you can choose an app from the list and then proceed, one by one, through the list of file types it's capable of handling. Figure 5-12, for example, shows the settings available after installing the popular VLC media player. Although it's capable of handling playback of .mov files, those file types remain associated with the built-in Windows 11 Media Player app.

CHAPTER 5

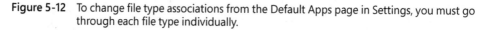

Figure 5-12   To change file type associations from the Default Apps page in Settings, you must go through each file type individually.

If you'd prefer to use the newly installed app when you double-click a .mov file, you have three choices:

- From File Explorer, find a file with the .mov extension, right-click, and choose Open With > Choose Another App. Select your preferred app and then click Always Use This App To Open .MOV Files. Click OK to save your preference.

- From Settings > Apps > Default Apps, type **mov** in the Set A Default For A File Type Or Link Type search box at the top of the page. Click the currently associated program, which appears immediately below, and then choose VLC Media Player from the How Do You Want To Open .MOV Files From Now On dialog.

- From the Default Apps page in Settings, click the entry for the newly installed VLC program, click the .mov file type, and then choose VLC Media Player from the How Do You Want To Open .MOV Files From Now On dialog.

CHAPTER 5

Inside OUT

Using a nondefault program on a case-by-case basis

If you just want to open a file occasionally in an application that's not the default for that file type, there's no need to go through all the business of changing the default application. Right-click the file in File Explorer and choose Open With. Windows displays a menu offering the various applications that can open the selected file type. It's almost certain that the app you prefer will be on this list. In the unlikely chance it's not available, click Choose Another App.

You can do two things in this menu. You can change the default for the selected file type (by selecting one of the listed apps and then clicking Always Use This App), or you can go for something altogether different by clicking More Apps. Doing this brings up a list of apps, many if not most of which are completely unsuitable for the selected file type. Select one of these if you're curious to see what happens. But don't click Always Use This App unless you're quite sure. If the program isn't what you want, it simply makes a nuisance of itself, and you have to go to the trouble of making something else the default.

Turning Windows features on or off

If you want to manage Windows features that can be installed independently of the core operating system, go to Settings > Apps > Optional Features. Under the Installed Features heading are default features that are currently installed. This list includes some important features, such as Windows Hello Facial Recognition and Internet Explorer mode functionality for Microsoft Edge; it also includes some classic system apps like WordPad and the legacy Windows Media Player app. Unless you have a compelling reason to remove them, we recommend leaving these default features installed.

Click View Features to open a list of optional features that can be installed if needed. This group includes supplemental fonts for alternate languages that aren't currently installed, as well as support for some legacy hardware not typically found on modern PCs, such as IrDA infrared devices. You'll also find some specialized management tools here, including a group of utilities required for Windows domain administrators' use with Remote Server Administration Tools. Most users have no need for any of these features.

An additional group of Windows features is available by way of a link at the bottom of the Optional Features page; click More Windows Features to open the Windows Features dialog shown in Figure 5-13.

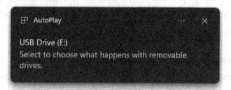

Figure 5-13   The Windows Features dialog provides a simple way to disable or enable selected features and capabilities.

Here you can enable Hyper-V Management Tools (if they're not already enabled) and Windows Sandbox (for more on these features, see Chapter 17, "Running Windows 11 in a virtual machine or in the cloud"). You can also disable features that are available by default. You might want to remove the Microsoft Print To PDF feature, for example, if you already have this capability available through a third-party app. Note that some items in the list have subentries. Those marked by a filled checkbox (rather than a check mark) have some components enabled and some not.

Setting AutoPlay options

AutoPlay is the feature that enables Windows to take appropriate action when you insert removable storage media such as a USB flash drive, audio CD, DVD, or memory card into a drive. When this feature is turned on, the operating system detects the kind of disc or media you inserted and takes the action you requested for that type of media. If you have not already made a decision about what the operating system should do, you see a window similar to the one shown in Figure 5-14.

Figure 5-14   When you insert a removable drive, AutoPlay offers to perform an action on your behalf.

If you don't want Windows to take any action, you can simply ignore the message; it disappears after a few seconds. Otherwise, clicking or tapping the message brings you to the screen shown in Figure 5-15.

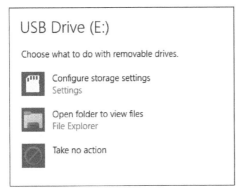

Figure 5-15   When you insert a removable drive, Windows asks what you'd like to do with similar actions in the future.

Notice that your choices here are limited to ones that are appropriate for the device type and Take No Action. (For example, if you insert an audio CD, your choices include any installed apps capable of playing audio CDs, in addition to Take No Action.) If you don't want to commit to any of the options on this menu, press Esc.

To turn this feature on or off, go to Settings > Bluetooth & Devices > AutoPlay and slide the switch at the top of the page to the Off position. When this option is on, you can change the default action for removable drives and memory cards here. To configure AutoPlay settings for DVDs, Blu-ray discs, and CDs, you need to go the corresponding page in Control Panel. To open that page, click Start, type **autoplay**, and then click Start Or Stop Using AutoPlay For All Media And Devices from the results list.

Inside OUT

You don't want a default action?

To have no default action for a given media type, choose Ask Me Every Time as the option for that media type. To suppress the AutoPlay dialog completely for a specific media type, choose Take No Action.

CHAPTER 5

Using and managing built-in Windows apps

In this chapter, we discuss the apps that are included with a default installation of Microsoft Windows 11. Windows 11 offers a whole set of modern productivity and communication apps, all designed for touch and pen as well as more traditional input methods. Our goal is to provide an overview of those productivity apps, as well as the apps you can use to manage and edit media files. We also mention (albeit briefly) a handful of legacy utility apps, including Notepad and Paint, which have been updated for Windows 11.

For the most part, we deal with system utilities, such as Registry Editor, PowerShell, and Windows Terminal, in other chapters. We reserve the bigger topic of Microsoft Edge, the default browser in Windows 11, for Chapter 7.

NOTE

Because Microsoft regularly delivers feature-enhancing cumulative updates to Windows 11 as well as updates to apps delivered through the Microsoft Store, several apps described in this chapter might have undergone changes—some minor, others significant—by the time you read this. We describe the apps as they appeared around the time that version 22H2 was released.

Some of these apps were also included with Windows 10 and are essentially identical to their predecessors. In other cases, there are substantial differences or new features that we highlight here. For example, the Clock app still offers the capability to function as a timer or stopwatch, but the Windows 11 update adds the ability to manage "focus sessions," which allow you to work uninterrupted for a specific period of time. Likewise, the built-in music app, known as Groove Music in Windows 10, is now called Media Player. (Confusingly, the legacy Windows Media Player app is also included with Windows 11; we cover the differences in this chapter.)

To make sure we're on the same page, we begin with an overview of apps included with a default installation of Windows 11.

Apps included with Windows 11

Every installation of Windows 11 includes a collection of apps that enable the core features of the operating system and add productivity functions. By design, these apps are updated through the Microsoft Store, as needed, rather than requiring a separate update mechanism. They fall into three categories: system apps, provisioned apps, and installed apps. In this section, we describe the differences between these categories and inventory the apps that are a part of current Windows 11 installations.

Note that the listing in this section does not include the dozens of legacy apps that appear in a File Explorer window when you click Start > All Apps > Windows Tools. Some of those apps are essential administrative tools (Task Manager, Event Viewer, and Registry Editor, for example), but many were originally designed for use with earlier Windows versions and are included with Windows 11 primarily for compatibility reasons.

Windows system apps

System apps are installed as part of Windows and are considered integral to the operating system. Many of them are essentially invisible, even though you use their features constantly as you work with Windows 11. For example, every time you click Start, you're launching the Microsoft Windows Start Menu Experience Host. Likewise, the Search system app goes to work whenever you use the search button on the taskbar. You regularly interact with the Accounts Control Host and Credential Dialog Host apps without ever seeing their names. In fact, the only instantly recognizable app in this category is the Settings app (also known as the Immersive Control Panel).

Most system apps are located in the Windows\SystemApps folder. The two exceptions are the Settings app, whose files are located in C:\Windows\ImmersiveControlPanel, and the Windows Print Dialog app, which is stored in C:\Windows\PrintDialog.

System apps cannot be uninstalled through the Windows user interface, and the reasons seem obvious. Frankly, we can't think of a good reason why anyone would want to do so.

To list all system apps, use this PowerShell command:

```
Get-AppxPackage -PackageTypeFilter Main | ? { $_.SignatureKind -eq "System" } | Sort
Name | Format-Table Name, InstallLocation
```

Provisioned Windows apps

Provisioned Windows apps are installed in a user account the first time you sign in with that account.

You can list all provisioned Windows apps from an elevated PowerShell window using the following command:

```
Get-AppxProvisionedPackage -Online | Format-Table DisplayName, PackageName
```

In Windows 11 version 22H2, the list of provisioned apps includes a small number of core apps that are essential to the operation of Windows but aren't installed as system apps:

- **Microsoft Store** (which still goes by its old moniker of Windows Store when you use PowerShell to list provisioned apps) is the place to acquire and update apps of all kinds; for details, see "Using and managing Store apps" in Chapter 5, "Installing and configuring apps." Also on the list of provisioned apps is one called the **Store Purchase App**, which assists with the process of paying for Store apps.

- **Desktop App Installer** provides the capability to install packaged desktop apps by double-clicking an app package without having to go through the Microsoft Store or use esoteric PowerShell commands. The command-line version of this tool, Winget, can find, install, and update packaged apps from Microsoft's official repository. (A companion provisioned app, the Visual C++ Runtime framework, is also available for packaged desktops that require it.)

- The new **Microsoft Edge** is included as a provisioned app in Windows 11. For more details, see Chapter 7, "Using Microsoft Edge."

- **Windows Security** provides the user interface for Microsoft Defender and related security features built into Windows 11. You can read more about these features in Chapter 12, "Windows security and privacy."

- The **Web Experience Client** manages the Widgets feature, which is described in more detail in Chapter 3, "Using Windows 11."

The collection of provisioned apps also includes a healthy assortment of extensions that allow Windows apps to process some relatively new media file formats: HEIF Image Extensions, VP9 Video Extensions, Web Media Extensions, a Raw Image Extension, and the WebP Image Extensions.

In addition, OEMs might include some provisioned apps, such as utilities for managing hardware, as part of their default image for PCs that ship with Windows 11 preinstalled.

In the remainder of this section, we break down the lengthy list of provisioned apps by category.

Information

- **Cortana** is installed as an app in Windows 11. It's no longer tied directly to Windows Search as it was in early versions of Windows 10; instead, it's used as a voice assistant for Microsoft 365 business accounts and requires signing in with an Azure Active Directory account. Curiously, its name in the list of provisioned apps doesn't include any hint of its true identity but only a number: Microsoft.549981C3F5F10.

- **Feedback Hub** allows anyone to create, search, share, and upvote bug reports and offer suggestions for the Windows development team.

CHAPTER 6

- **Get Help** puts you in touch with Microsoft's Virtual Agent. You can tell your troubles to the agent, who provides automated assistance; if that doesn't solve your problem, you can ask to speak to a live human.

- **Get Started** is a bare-bones tutorial for Windows 11.

- **Maps** displays maps and aerial photos along with directions between points. It also offers a supported way to provide a default location for your PC, as detailed later in this chapter.

- **News**, a news aggregator that displays results similar to those found on the Microsoft Start page and in the corresponding Windows 11 widget, is powered by Microsoft's Bing search engine.

- **Weather** displays current conditions and detailed forecasts for locations around the world, with information drawn from Microsoft's Bing search engine.

Communications and productivity

- The **Windows Communications App** package includes two apps that can be opened separately but use the same infrastructure: **Mail** allows you to send, receive, and manage email messages using a variety of industry-standard protocols. **Calendar** keeps track of appointments and other events. A separate **People** app manages contact information from connected accounts. (We cover all three apps later in this chapter.)

- **Microsoft To Do** is a relatively recent addition to the above suite of apps, delivered as a separate package but integrated with Mail and Calendar in Windows.

- **Microsoft Teams** replaces the legacy Skype app and enables audio/video conferencing capabilities. (As we explain later in this chapter, there are two separate apps that use the Microsoft Teams brand, one for enterprise communications and the other for home/personal use.)

- **Phone Link** (formerly called Your Phone) connects your Windows device to your mobile device. On compatible Android devices, it allows you to send and receive text messages and mirror your phone's screen on your PC.

- **Office**, which has also been known as My Office, Get Office, and the Office Hub in its time on Windows, is scheduled to get yet another name change in 2023, to Microsoft 365. It provides details about your Microsoft 365 subscription and lists Office files that you have recently worked with. If you don't have a Microsoft 365 subscription, the app offers access to the web-based versions of Office apps, with files stored in OneDrive.

- **Sticky Notes** provides a place to jot small notes that are reminiscent of the ubiquitous yellow Post-it Notes from 3M. These notes can sync with OneNote and with the Microsoft Launcher on Android devices.

Entertainment

- **Media Player** is the default player app for files in supported audio formats. It was previously known as Groove Music, and its app package betrays its roots as the client for the ill-fated Zune player. (For details, see "Music, photos, and movies," later in this chapter.)

- **Movies & TV** plays personal videos and allows you to purchase or rent movies and TV shows that can also be played on Xbox consoles. (For details, see "Music, photos, and movies," later in this chapter.)

- **Solitaire and Casual Games** includes an updated version of the classic Klondike time-waster, along with four other solo card games, with access to online challenges and tournaments and a paid, ad-free version.

- **Xbox** connects you to the world of computer gaming in genres ranging from card games to shoot-em-ups. (The list of provisioned apps also includes a handful of Xbox-related tools intended to perform under-the-hood tasks, including Xbox Game Bar, Xbox Game Overlay, Xbox Gaming Overlay, Xbox Identity Provider, Xbox Speech to Text Overlay, and Xbox Title-callable UI.)

Creative tools

- **Clipchamp**, which was acquired by Microsoft in 2021, is a lightweight utility for creating and editing short video clips.

- **Microsoft Photos** allows you to store, organize, and edit a collection of digital images. We cover this app later in this chapter.

- **Paint** is a Store-compatible version of the venerable Microsoft image editing utility. In Windows 10, Microsoft tried to replace it with a dramatically different app called Paint 3D, but Paint partisans protested so vociferously that Microsoft canceled its plans to deprecate the older Paint and updated the legacy app with new features.

- **Voice Recorder**, previously called Sound Recorder, uses your PC's microphone to record audio files. You can add markers to identify key moments and use the app's rudimentary editing tools to trim saved audio files.

Utilities

- **Alarms & Clock** shows world time and acts as an alarm, stopwatch, and timer. In Windows 11, it adds the ability to start and manage "focus sessions," so you can work without interruptions for a continuous block of time.

- **Calculator** includes a programmer mode (specialized for bitwise operations on binary, octal, and hexadecimal values) along with the more common standard and scientific modes. It can also serve as a handy converter for measurements of weight, volume,

CHAPTER 6

length, angles, time, and so on, and with the help of up-to-date exchange rate tables, it can also perform currency conversions.

- **Camera** captures still images and video from a webcam.

- **Notepad** is an updated version of the classic text editor, delivered as a Store app and augmented with a few new features, including support for dark themes.

- **Power Automate** is a low-code platform that allows users to automate repetitive tasks, using prebuilt actions and a recorder that captures mouse and keyboard input to save tasks as "desktop flows."

- **Quick Assist** allows Windows users to get live, hands-on help from a friend or a support professional using simple screen-sharing tools.

- **Snipping Tool** is a utility for capturing and editing screen images. This app was previously known as Snip & Sketch.

- **Windows Terminal** offers a multitabbed interface for working with the Windows Command Processor, PowerShell, and the command-line shell from the Windows Subsystem for Linux. We describe these tools in more detail in Chapter 16, "Windows Terminal, PowerShell, and other advanced management tools."

Some provisioned apps can be uninstalled using the tools in Settings > Apps > Installed Apps. If the Uninstall command is grayed out and unavailable, it may be possible to remove a provisioned app using PowerShell commands. We advise against using these options, which can have unintended consequences.

Installed apps

This last category consists of apps that are installed as part of signing in to a new account, delivered through the Windows Content Delivery Manager. These apps include some third-party products that may include a trial period followed by the requirement to pay for the full product. It also includes some apps from Microsoft.

The list of installed apps changes periodically, based on Microsoft's partnerships with third-party developers.

For PCs running Windows 11 Home or Pro where the new profile belongs to a local account or a Microsoft account, the list typically includes social media apps such as TikTok and Facebook, along with some entertainment software such as the Amazon Prime and Disney+ streaming video services.

You see a different set of installed apps, focused primarily on productivity, if you install Windows 11 Enterprise and sign in using any account type, or if you install Windows 11 Pro and sign in using either Active Directory credentials on a Windows domain or Azure Active Directory credentials, such as those associated with a Microsoft 365 Business or Enterprise subscription.

All apps in this category can be uninstalled using the tools in Settings > Apps > Installed Apps. Some of the apps in this category are added to Start as suggestions, rather than being installed. You can remove them from Start, leaving no trace of the app behind.

Mail, Calendar, People, and To Do

The Mail, Calendar, People, and To Do apps are designed to connect to cloud-based services and sync email, calendar items, contacts, and tasks from those accounts.

Mail and Calendar are the two most important apps in the group and are equal partners. In the Installed Apps list, in fact, they share a single entry, titled Mail And Calendar, but in this chapter we treat them as separate apps because they operate in separate app windows, using separate processes. They're capable of syncing with a wide assortment of online services: You can sign in using free and paid accounts from Microsoft (Outlook.com and Microsoft 365) and Google (Gmail and Google Workspace); other supported services include Apple's iCloud, Yahoo Mail, and any server that communicates using industry-standard mail and calendar protocols. If your workplace uses Microsoft Exchange on its own servers, you can connect to those accounts as well.

Using the Mail and Calendar apps, you can connect to accounts on multiple services and display their contents simultaneously. That capability makes it easy to switch between personal and business email accounts or provide a unified view of multiple accounts; it also allows you to see the contents of multiple calendars in a single overlaid view. Any additions, deletions, or changes you make to messages and calendar items in either app are saved on the server associated with that account; for cloud-based accounts that support synchronization, changes you make using another app (including those on mobile devices) are synced automatically to the Mail and Calendar app.

Although they are tightly linked, the Mail, Calendar, People, and To Do apps display their contents in separate windows. Shortcuts for the Mail and Calendar apps are pinned by default to the Start menu, and you can use icons in the lower-left corner of those apps to open or switch to any of the other apps.

The To Do app does not have the same navigation bar as Mail and Calendar. Although you can connect to multiple accounts, it displays the contents of only one account at a time.

The People app has no shortcut in All Apps and is of little use on its own. Its primary role is to organize contact information for sending email messages and calendar invitations.

CHAPTER 6

Inside OUT

What are the Mail and Calendar apps good for?

If you already have a preferred email client, you can continue using it and you can safely ignore the Windows 11 Mail and Calendar apps. But that doesn't mean you have to delete the shortcuts for those apps from your Start menu. The Mail app is an excellent option for checking in on secondary accounts, such as a free Outlook.com account that you use for newsletters, promotions, and other correspondence that you want to keep out of your primary account. You can also use Mail and Calendar as a backup client for your primary account, especially on devices that you don't use regularly.

Managing online accounts

As we noted earlier, the Mail and Calendar apps are tightly linked. When you add a new account in the Mail app, it's automatically added to Calendar and vice-versa.

Also, any accounts you add in either place are automatically added to the list of accounts available to other Windows apps, in Settings > Accounts > Email & Accounts.

The first time you open the Mail or Calendar app, you're asked to add an account, as shown in Figure 6-1.

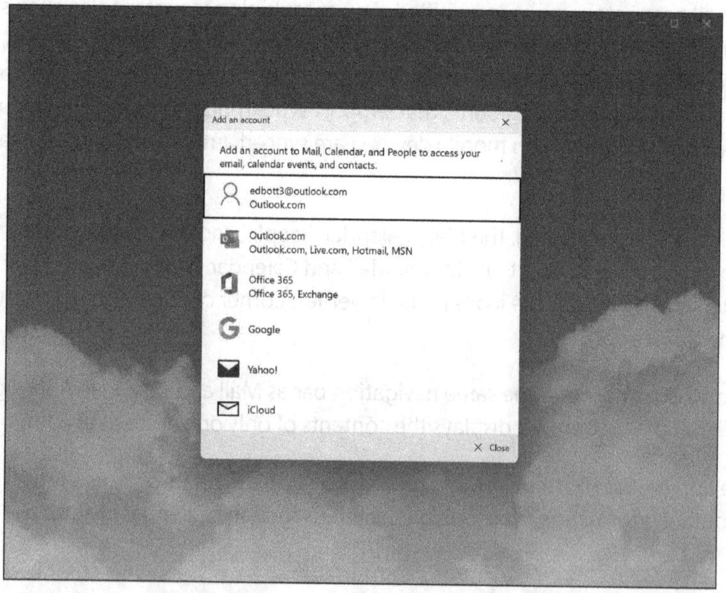

Figure 6-1   To set up an account that uses any of these well-known cloud services, you only need to enter an email address and password.

If you sign in to Windows using a Microsoft account or an Azure AD account, the email address associated with that account appears at the top of this setup page. If that's the only email account you use, you can move on by selecting that account and allowing Windows to add its account automatically.

If you log on with a local account or if you'd prefer to set up a different email account than the one associated with your Windows sign-in account, choose an account type from the Add An Account dialog box. Mail supports Outlook.com, Office 365, Microsoft Exchange, Google accounts (Gmail and Google Workspace), Yahoo! Mail, and Apple's iCloud, as well as generic accounts based on the POP and IMAP standards. The setup process is straightforward, prompting you for your email address and password.

If your account requires you to enter additional settings, such as the names of your incoming and outgoing servers, scroll to the bottom of the Add An Account list and then click Advanced Setup.

Adding, deleting, and renaming accounts

To add email and calendar accounts after completing this initial configuration, open Settings by clicking the gear icon in the lower-left corner of the Mail window, and then click Manage Accounts > Add Account. Choose an account type, enter your credentials, and follow the authentication prompts.

Each account you add gets its own entry in the navigation pane that appears on the left in both the Mail and Calendar apps. To change the display name that appears there, open the Manage Accounts menu and then click the account name to display a dialog box like the one shown in Figure 6-2.

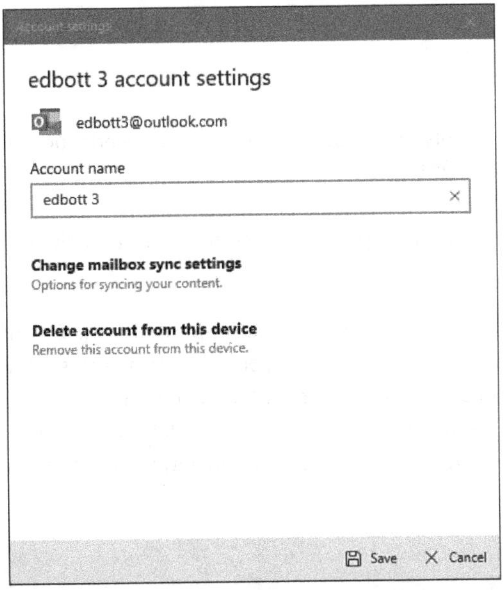

Figure 6-2   Click in the Account Name box to change the display name that appears in the navigation pane for both the Mail and Calendar apps.

CHAPTER 6

To delete an existing account, select its entry from the Manage Accounts menu and then click Delete Account From This Device. Note that doing so removes all synced copies of email messages and calendar items but does not make any changes to items stored on the server.

Setting sync options

To configure sync options for an account, open the Mail or Calendar app and go to Settings > Manage Accounts; select the account you want to configure, and then click Change Mailbox Sync Settings. That opens a dialog box like the one shown in Figure 6-3. Don't be misled by the name of that option; as the dialog box makes clear, it allows you to configure synchronization of mail, calendar, and contact items.

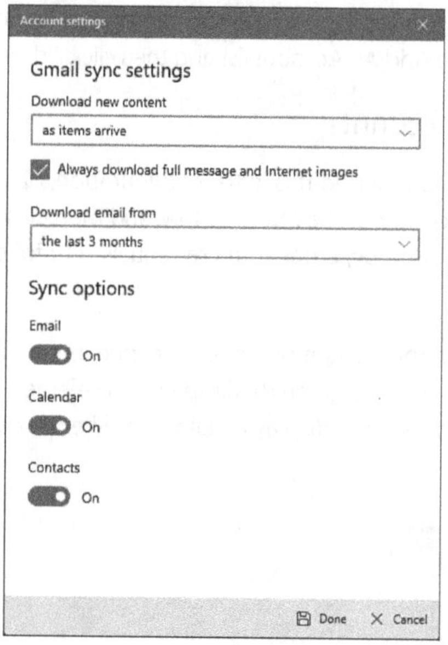

Figure 6-3   For secondary email accounts where you don't maintain a calendar or contacts, feel free to turn off the bottom two switches.

The two settings at the top allow you to manage network connections and disk space, respectively.

For your primary account, the default, As Items Arrive, is appropriate for the Download New Content setting. That option minimizes the chance that you will miss a time-sensitive message. For secondary accounts that don't contain important content, you might want to change the sync interval to something more leisurely. Options include Every 15 Minutes, Every 30 Minutes, or Hourly. Choose Manually for low-traffic accounts you are willing to update and read on demand.

The Download Email From setting is a way to save disk space by leaving old messages on the server and only syncing recent correspondence. Options here range from Past 3 Days to Past 3 Months. The default setting, Any Time, syncs the entire contents of your email account, which might require a significant amount of disk space.

The three switches under the Sync Options heading allow you to control the type of data the Mail and Calendar apps sync from your account. If you maintain a calendar and a contacts list as part of your email account, you probably want to sync all three items here. But for secondary accounts that you use to keep newsletters and promotional email messages out of your primary inbox, you probably want to turn the Calendar and Contacts switches to the Off position.

Reading, composing, and managing email messages

In the Mail app, each account you add gets its own heading in the navigation pane on the left. Clicking that heading displays the list of folders associated with that account in the bottom of the navigation pane. (If the Mail window is too narrow, you need to click the Expand/Collapse icon in the upper-left corner to see the folder list.) Figure 6-4 shows the Mail app in action with a single account.

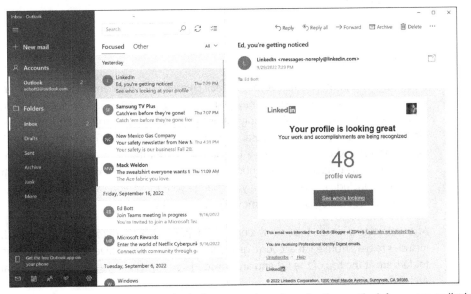

Figure 6-4   The Mail app uses a classic three-pane layout: navigation on the left, a message list in the center, and preview pane on the right.

If you've ever used a PC-based mail client, this three-pane layout should feel familiar. By default, the entries under the Folders heading show the most commonly used folders: Inbox, Drafts, Sent, and so on. Click More (at the bottom of the folder list) to slide out a pane with a list of

CHAPTER 6

additional folders that are available for that account. Select any folder to display its contents in the message pane. Click the plus sign to the right of the All Folders list to add a new folder.

Right-click any existing folder to perform basic management tasks: rename the folder, delete it, empty its contents, or create a new subfolder. Use the Add To Favorites option to add a star to the folder and pin its shortcut to the navigation pane under the Folders heading. Any folder in the Favorites list is a convenient drag-and-drop target for messages you want to move out of your Inbox.

Inside OUT

Pin a folder or an entire account to Start

Want to skip a step or two when checking your messages? If you have multiple accounts set up, you can right-click an account name and then click Pin To Start. Clicking that pinned tile takes you directly to the contents of that account. You can also right-click a folder and pin it to Start. This option is especially effective if you use rules to automatically file incoming messages into folders and you want to review the latest arrivals in that folder.

Linking inboxes

If you have two or more email accounts, Mail creates a separate entry for each one under the Accounts heading in the left-hand navigation pane. When you select an account heading, the folders list and message list show only items from that account. You might find it more convenient to consolidate incoming messages from those two accounts in a unified inbox. To do this, open Settings > Manage Accounts > Link Inboxes. Enter the name you want to see in the navigation pane (the default is Linked Inbox) and then select the check boxes next to each account you want to include in that group. If you change your mind, you can unlink the accounts by returning to this dialog box and removing check marks.

After selecting a Linked Inbox in the navigation pane, click More to see a folders list that includes folders from each account, grouped under their respective account headings. Four folders are at the top of the list and are consolidated from linked accounts: Inbox, Drafts, Archive, and Sent.

Reducing mailbox clutter with Focused Inbox

The Focused Inbox feature uses machine learning to sort your incoming messages into two groups: those that the algorithm thinks you want to read immediately and those that it believes you find less important. With Focused Inbox, two tab headings appear above the list of messages in the message header pane—Focused and Other—as shown in Figure 6-5. If the algorithm correctly categorized your incoming messages, you see only important messages on the Focused tab, with everything else on the Other tab.

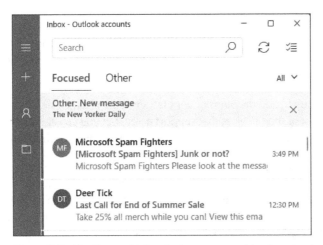

Figure 6-5 The Focused Inbox feature uses machine learning to highlight important messages and shift less valuable content to the Other tab.

The Focused Inbox algorithm makes its sorting decisions based on signals it divines from the content of incoming messages and by making notes of whom you exchange mail with most frequently. Newsletters, commercial pitches, and the like are considered less important and thus kept on the Other tab. You can train the Focused Inbox feature to work more accurately by right-clicking a message in the message list and choosing Always Move To Other or Always Move To Focused.

That same menu also includes an Ignore option, which enables you to tell Mail to stop showing you messages in a specific conversation. This option is extremely handy if you're part of a mailing list whose members can't stop adding to a long, ongoing thread.

The Focused Inbox feature works on a per-account basis; to turn it on or off for a specific account, open the Mail app's Settings menu, click Focused Inbox, choose an account, and then slide the switch to the preferred position. If Focused Inbox is turned off, all incoming messages for that account appear in a single Inbox tab.

Creating and sending email messages

To create a new message, select an account first and then click the New Mail icon at the top of the navigation pane. If you start from a linked inbox, the From field contains a drop-down list you can use to choose the correct sending account.

The message composition window contains a ribbon that provides a basic set of editing and formatting tools. On the Format tab, for example, are options for changing fonts and font sizes and adjusting the size and color of text

To attach a file to your message, click the Insert tab. You can use that part of the ribbon to insert tables, pictures, and hyperlinks as well. Alternatively, you can create an attachment by dragging a file into your new message document. Mail also provides a proofreader; click Options and then click Spelling to check your messages for typos.

Use the Draw menu option to add drawings or annotations to a message using familiar drawing tools. These options work best on devices that support a pen, but you can also insert a drawing canvas and mark up a message using a mouse or even your finger on a touchscreen

In a new Mail message or a reply, you can insert @ *mentions* into an email message. When you type @ and then begin typing a name, Mail suggests auto-completions from your address book and from previous messages; after you select the name you want to add, Mail highlights the name in the message and adds it to the To line of the message header (if it isn't already there), helping to ensure that the person you tagged sees your message.

You can then edit the name in the message body if you like; for example, you might want to keep things informal by trimming off the last name.

When people receive a message with an @ mention, it remains highlighted for good visibility. In addition, the highlighted name is a mailto: link, so when recipients click the name, it opens a new message window with the name already in the To box.

You can filter your inbox to show only messages that include an @ mention with your name. Click the arrow at the top of the message header pane and choose Mentions.

Setting up and using Calendar

Not surprisingly, the Calendar app is similar in design to its counterpart, Mail. There's a navigation pane on the left, with a one-month date picker control on top and check boxes for available calendars below. Figure 6-6 shows a calendar displaying events from three calendars over the course of one work week.

CHAPTER 6

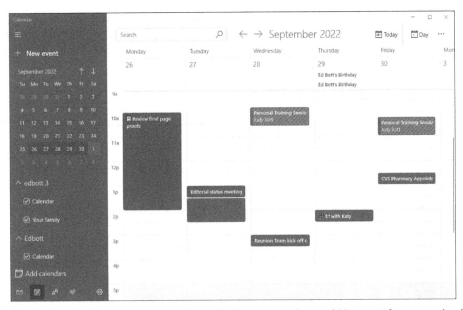

Figure 6-6   Use the check boxes in the navigation pane to show or hide events from any calendar. Each calendar applies its own color to events.

Calendar allows you to switch between views of your upcoming appointments, meetings, and events: Day, Week, Month, and Year. You can choose a particular period of time to work with using the thumbnail calendar in the navigation pane or the left/right arrows at the top of the calendar itself. To return to the current date, click Today.

As expected, clicking Day changes the display to a single column that shows only events from the currently selected day. But move the mouse pointer over that button and a small arrow appears to the right; click to display a Multi-Day Views menu, where you can show between two and six days' worth of events. In similar fashion, clicking the arrow to the right of the Week control displays the option to change the view to Work Week. The Year view displays no event information but is useful if you want to jump to a future date without scrolling one month at a time in the navigation pane.

If you've set up multiple accounts for syncing calendar items, your meetings and events are combined into a single view on the right. Use the check boxes in the navigation pane to determine which accounts can contribute to the composite calendar.

Each account's calendar items are distinguished by color, with the specific color assigned to that calendar visible when you select its check box. To change the color for a calendar, point to its entry in the navigation pane, click the down arrow that appears to its right, and select a color.

CHAPTER 6

You can also add specialty calendars that show schedules for sports teams, network television shows, and so on. To do that, click Add Calendars. (If you have multiple Microsoft-hosted accounts set up in Calendar, you specify which one displays the calendars you add by going to Settings > Calendar Settings > Interesting Calendars.)

Adding an event

To add an event to your calendar, click or tap New Event; that action opens the full Details window for the event, as shown in Figure 6-7.

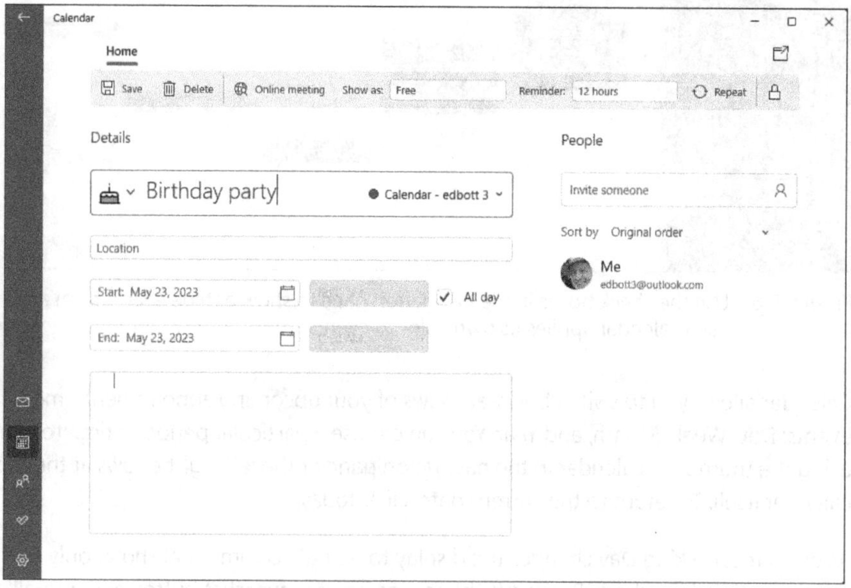

Figure 6-7   The New Event form offers all of the details you need to create an event or a meeting. Make sure to select the correct calendar from the drop-down list at the right of the event name.

If you click a specific time (in Day or Week view) or double-click a date in Month view, you get a smaller version of the New Event window, in pop-up form. It contains all the information you need to create a basic appointment on the selected day and set a reminder up to a week before the event time. If you need to change a detail that isn't in this compact form, like the event date, you can move to the full view by clicking More Details. In either case, if you have Calendar configured to use more than one account, be sure to specify which account the new event should belong to.

For events you add to a Microsoft 365 or Outlook.com calendar, typing in the Location box performs a live lookup of local addresses that match your entry. Using that data makes it possible for linked navigation apps to get you (and your guests) to the correct meeting place.

To set up an event that occurs at regular intervals, start a new event and then click the Repeat button, which is on the right of the menu bar in the New Event window. Calendar offers daily, weekly, monthly, and yearly options, with variations like Every 4 Weeks or Every Month On The Second Tuesday.

Inviting others to a meeting

To create a meeting event and invite others to join, add the email addresses of your invitees to the People section of the event; if the prospective attendees are in your Contacts list, you can click the icon to the right of the Invite Someone prompt and then choose names from the list. Use the Online Meeting button to schedule a virtual meeting using Microsoft Teams (click again to clear the online details if you're planning an in-person event).

Entering one or more email addresses changes the event form's Save button to a Send button. After you click Send, each invitee gets an email message with the option to provide a yes/no/maybe response. The Accept, Tentative, and Decline links, with associated drop-down options, make it easy for you, as an invitee, to respond to an invitation.

Setting options

To specify the days of your work week and the hours of your work day, click Settings > Calendar Settings. You can do a few other things as well on the Calendar Settings page, such as opting for week numbers and switching to alternative languages and calendars. If you stick with English, the calendar choices include Hijri, Umm al-Qura, Hebrew Lunar, and Saka Era, in addition to the default Gregorian. Many other options are available for languages other than English.

Printing from Calendar

To print, click Show (the ellipsis icon in the upper-right corner of the Calendar window) and then click Print, or use the standard Windows keyboard shortcut, Ctrl+P. There you can specify the starting date for your output as well as whether to print by day (choosing a range of one to seven days), week, work week, or month. A preview button gives you the opportunity to check the output (with the option to zoom in using a touchpad or by holding down Ctrl as you use a mouse wheel) before you commit it to paper.

Adding or editing contacts with People

Among the four apps we cover in this section, People is definitely the most limited. It's also well hidden, with no shortcut on the Start menu's All Apps list.

Microsoft had much greater expectations for this app when it debuted at the dawn of the Windows 10 era. In those days, the Windows taskbar included a special toolbar called My People, with the option to pin items from the People app for quick access to messaging apps and other details. The Pin To Taskbar option is still available when you right-click a contact item in the People app in Windows 11, but it does absolutely nothing. (The option to pin a contact to the Start menu, however, works as expected.)

The primary job of People is to serve as a repository for contacts associated with accounts you set up in Mail or Calendar. That feature is readily accessible when creating a new email message or calendar event; click the small Choose Contacts icon to display a streamlined version of the People app with a list of suggested contacts and a search box to help you pick the right contact from the full list.

To launch the full People app, click its icon at the bottom of the navigation pane in the Mail or Calendar app. That view provides a full list of contacts from multiple accounts, summarizing contact information and shared calendar events for the selected contact in a pane to the right.

Although People has an interesting feature set, it doesn't make a compelling case for using it as a standalone app. In most cases, you get better results managing your contacts in your web browser; then you can connect that contacts list to People and make those addresses available for the basic tasks of picking email addresses for new messages and meetings.

Managing tasks and lists with Microsoft To Do

Microsoft To Do, the newest member of Microsoft's group of communication-related apps, is specifically designed to make you more productive—or at least to help you see at a glance what you haven't accomplished today. The app works only with Microsoft accounts (personal and business), offering tools for managing upcoming tasks and creating lists that can become surprisingly complex.

You can open To Do from its shortcut on the Start menu or from its place at the bottom of the navigation pane in Mail or Calendar. As Figure 6-8 illustrates, the To Do app follows many of the same navigation principles as its peers, with a navigation pane on the left and a details pane on the right displaying the contents of whatever you select in the navigation pane.

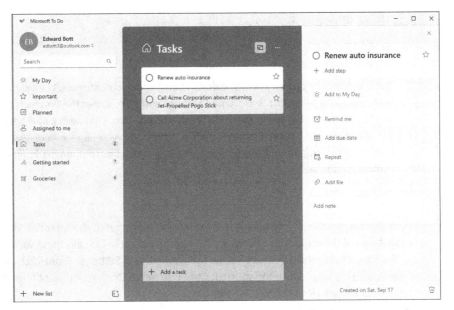

Figure 6-8   The primary focus of Microsoft To Do is this Tasks list, but you can use it to create anything from a simple grocery list to a step-by-step action plan.

To add a new task to the list, click in the box at the bottom of the Tasks pane and type a title. If you need to add details to the task, click its entry in the list to open an editing window on the right. There, you can add a reminder, specify a due date, or begin adding steps to break a big task into discrete milestones. You can also add notes and file attachments to any task and assign tasks to other people. If this is the first time you've used To Do with a Microsoft account, look for an at-a-glance tutorial in the Getting Started list. If that option's not available, try visiting *https://support.microsoft.com/todo*, which contains an assortment of tips, tricks, and troubleshooting advice.

You can create as many lists as you want using the New List button at the bottom of the navigation pane.

Although you can configure To Do for use with multiple accounts, you can only see one group of lists at a time. To configure To Do for use with an additional account, click the double-headed arrow to the right of your account name and then click Manage Accounts. A link to the app's Settings page is also available there, with options to automatically start To Do when you sign in to Windows and control whether the app automatically turns text like "next Tuesday" into deadlines.

Inside Out

Add email messages to your list of tasks

The Flag Message option in the Windows 11 Mail app and in Microsoft Outlook works seamlessly with Microsoft To Do. Open Settings and then, under the Connected Apps heading, turn the Flagged Email switch to the On position. That adds a new heading in the navigation pane called Flagged Email. Any messages you flag for follow-up show up here, with a snippet of the message text along with a link to open the full message in Outlook on the web.

Clicking the star next to any item flags it as Important, moving it to the top of its list and also making it part of the Important view in the navigation pane. (To Do calls these views "smart lists." You can control which ones are visible using switches in Settings.) Right-click any item and choose Add To My Day (or use the shortcut Ctrl+1) to tell To Do that you want to make that item a top priority and add it to the My Day view.

Using Microsoft Teams

Microsoft Teams is a unified communications app that takes over many of the functions offered in previous Windows versions by the Skype app. Confusingly, this free app, which is included with Windows 11, requires a Microsoft account and doesn't currently interoperate with the business version of Microsoft Teams, even though the feature sets overlap significantly.

When you're signed in with a personal Microsoft account, you can chat with friends and family with no limits, using the Teams app on Windows PCs, Macs, and mobile devices. You can also set up group calls and online meetings, with audio and video, with calls limited to no more than 60 minutes and 100 participants. Those limits are increased substantially if you're a Microsoft 365 subscriber.

Microsoft Teams offers a bare-bones interface, as shown in Figure 6-9, with four icons in a slim navigation bar on the left.

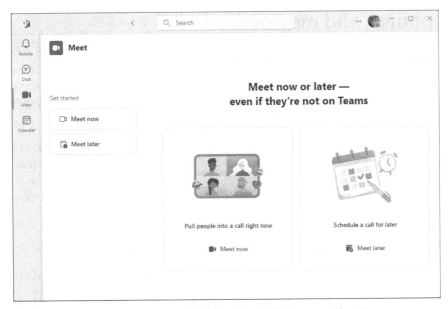

Figure 6-9   Use this tab to start or schedule a Microsoft Teams meeting. You can copy a meeting link that allows other people to join from a browser without installing the app.

The Activity page shows a feed that combines notifications from all your contacts, while the remaining icons allow you to start a chat (in text mode or with audio and video support), launch an online meeting, or schedule a meeting for later.

Inside Out

Stop Teams from running automatically

If your friends, family, and small business associates are all comfortable using Microsoft Teams, it makes sense to sync your contacts with the app so that you can quickly start a conversation. Open Settings in the Teams app, click People, and then click Manage under the Sync Contacts heading to import contact information from your Outlook.com and Skype accounts, from Google and iCloud services, and from your mobile device.

If you don't use Teams, however, you'll probably be annoyed by its insistence on starting automatically even though you have no intention of using it. That's easy enough to rectify. When the app starts up, click the Settings menu (to the left of your profile picture in the upper-right corner), click the General tab, and then clear the Auto-Start Teams check box. If you're sure you'll never use the app, go to Settings > Apps > Installed Apps, find the free Microsoft Teams app, and uninstall it.

Music, photos, and movies

The rise of the smartphone, coupled with cloud-based streaming entertainment services, means the PC is no longer the indispensable hub of digital media. PCs are still uniquely qualified for tasks that involve editing and managing a personal media collection and syncing your collection with cloud services; but you're just as likely to use a smaller mobile device or tablet to play music, watch a movie, or flip through a collection of digital pictures.

Microsoft Windows 11 includes three core media apps—Media Player, Photos, and Movies & TV. A fourth app, Clipchamp, is a relatively recent addition to Windows 11, offering tools for creating and editing short video clips. We cover all four apps in this section, with the understanding that most of our readers probably prefer third-party apps for many of the tasks these apps are designed to perform.

Using Media Player to play music and video files

No, you're not seeing double. Windows 11 includes two apps with the name Media Player:

- Media Player is the replacement for the Groove Music app introduced with Windows 10. Like its predecessor, it's a modern Windows app capable of playing music files, but updates to the Windows 11 version have added the ability to play audio CDs and video files and to rip CD tracks to digital file formats.

- Windows Media Player Legacy, as it's labeled in Windows 11 version 22H2, is virtually identical to the app that debuted more than a decade ago in Windows 7. It exists exclusively for backward compatibility, and most Windows 11 users will have no use for it.

Both apps support the same audio file formats and create indexed libraries from the contents of folders in your Music library. The newer Media Player also creates an index library of video files. (The indexes created by the two apps use different formats and are stored separately.) A recent update to the newer Media Player app allows it to play and rip tracks from audio CDs.

Media Player's role in Windows 11 is to offer native playback capability for a wide assortment of file formats. Although you can install third-party apps as an alternative, this app does a competent job of playback for just about any media file. We can't think of any good reason for anyone to use the Windows Media Player Legacy app.

Supported file formats

Windows 11 installs a collection of codecs that enable support for a wide variety of audio, video, and image file formats. All of these codecs work with the native Windows 11 apps, including Media Player and Photos. For a full list of supported formats, see *https://bit.ly/supported-codecs*.

When it comes to compression, Windows 11 supports both lossy and lossless formats. Most popular algorithms used to compress audio (and video) files are lossy, which means that they achieve compression by eliminating data. In the case of audio files in the popular MP3 and AAC formats (as well as the less popular Ogg formats), the data that's tossed out during the compression process consists mostly of frequencies that are outside the normal range of human hearing. The level of compression is determined by the *bit rate*. Higher bit rates preserve more of the original sound quality of audio tracks but result in larger files on your hard disk or portable player. Lower bit rates pack more music into limited space at a cost in fidelity.

Windows 11 supports lossless compressed formats as well, including Apple Lossless Audio Codec (ALAC) and Free Lossless Audio Codec (FLAC). These formats require more disk space than their lossy counterparts but offer better audio quality and take up dramatically less space than uncompressed Waveform Audio (WAV) files.

Windows 11 also supports playback of multiple video formats, including MPEG-4 video (.mp4 and .m4v), QuickTime (.mov), Matroska video (.mkv), WebM (.webm), and Ogg container or Theora files (.ogv).

Every installation of Windows 11 sets Media Player as the default music and video player for supported formats.

Managing music and video libraries

As with other native Windows 11 apps, the Media Player interface includes a navigation pane on the left and a contents pane on the right. The no-frills interface includes a Home page that allows you to revisit music and video tracks you've played recently, with separate links below that for your music and video libraries. Figure 6-10 shows the Music Library, sorted to show albums grouped by artist.

Figure 6-10   Media Player uses its online smarts to retrieve album art and other metadata for tracks in your music library.

The Music Library page includes grouping options that allow you to slice and dice your local collection, displaying its contents by song, album, or artist, with a variety of sort and filter options. If you have a large library, the option to display albums sorted by year is an effective way to time-travel through musical history.

The Video Library page is far less customizable. It shows every video file in your library, period.

Media Player follows the conventions of most modern player apps, so its basic look and feel should be familiar. Click the Play button to begin playing a song, album, or video immediately. Right-click any song, album, or video and then click Add To > Play Queue to build a continuous live playlist. Click Play Queue in the navigation pane to see what's playing now and what's up next.

Below those core navigation links is the Playlists option, which opens a pane where you can create custom playlists from tracks in your library and manage previously created playlists.

CHAPTER 6

TROUBLESHOOTING

You can't hear any sound from your speakers

Modern PCs often have multiple playback channels, in both digital and analog formats. Audio playback hardware can be found in various locations: on your motherboard; as an optional feature on an add-in video card, with multichannel sound typically delivered over an HDMI cable; on an add-in sound card; or through headphones connected physically or wirelessly using a Bluetooth connection. It's not unusual to find multiple audio playback options in a single PC, especially one that has been upgraded extensively.

If your hardware and drivers appear to be installed correctly, but you're unable to hear any sound, click the speaker icon in the notification area, click the arrow to the right of the volume slider, and look at the playback device listed there. Choose a different sound output device and see if your audio returns.

Playing and ripping CDs

Thanks to a July 2022 update, the Media Player app can play back audio CDs and convert ("rip") tracks from an audio CD, saving those tracks in digital formats on your local hard drive.

When Media Player detects that you've inserted an audio CD, it displays a new entry in the navigation pane for that CD, just below the Music Library and Video Library nodes. The app uses online data sources to determine the name of your disc, as well as the names of the artist and the titles of individual songs.

To choose the digital format for your ripped CD tracks, select the entry for the audio CD in the navigation bar and click the Rip Settings button to the right of the Play button. If this button isn't visible, click See More (the three dots). That displays the Rip Settings options, shown in Figure 6-11.

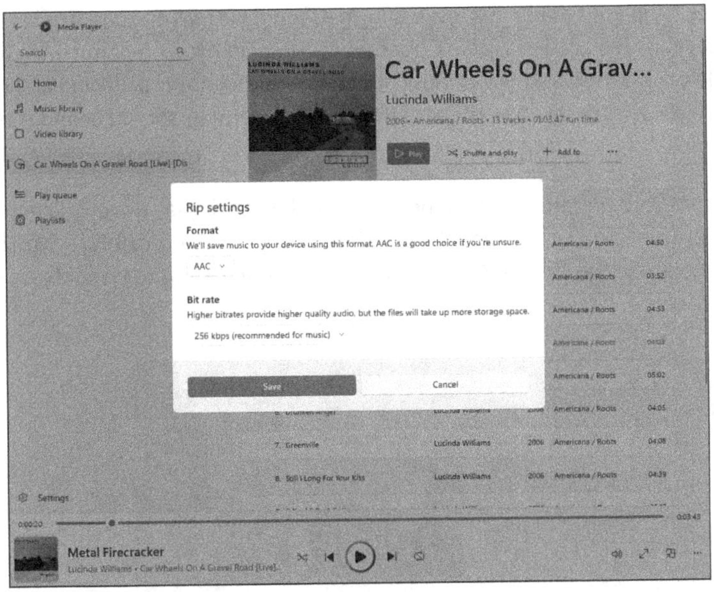

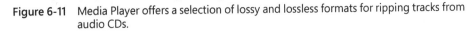

Figure 6-11   Media Player offers a selection of lossy and lossless formats for ripping tracks from audio CDs.

The Format menu offers four options. For maximum compatibility, choose AAC, which is functionally equivalent to the well-known MP3 format and should be playable in any modern media playback software. If you choose this format, use the Bit Rate menu below it to choose a quality level, where higher bit rates result in greater fidelity but also require more disk space. (We can't think of any good reason to choose the lossy WMA format.)

Inside Out

Why is there no option to rip MP3 tracks in Media Player?

Why doesn't Media Player offer the option to rip tracks in the popular MP3 format? Blame that design decision on software licensing requirements. Software developers that use the MP3 encoding algorithms have to pay a licensing fee to Fraunhofer Gesellschaft, the owner of the MP3 patents. For Microsoft, that would require paying a few pennies for every one of the 1 billion–plus Windows PCs in the world, even though only a tiny fraction of those PCs will ever encode a single MP3 track. From a compatibility standpoint, the AAC format is equally attractive, and the licensing fees are significantly smaller.

If you'd prefer to rip your tracks in a lossless format, you have two options: Apple Lossless Audio Codec (ALAC) and Free Lossless Audio Codec (FLAC). In general, we recommend choosing FLAC, which is widely supported and stores music files efficiently without sacrificing any information. In theory, at least, a track saved in either of these lossless formats should be indistinguishable from the original.

Click Save to set your preferences, and then click Edit Info to display a listing like the one shown in Figure 6-12, where you can change the details for the album—correcting a typo in a song title, for example. Use the Update Album Info Online link at the top to have Media Player check for alternative versions of the album online.

Figure 6-12   Spend some time getting this metadata right before you rip a CD to ensure that the resulting digital files are organized correctly.

Media Player uses that metadata to create a folder for the artist and a subfolder for the album being ripped as well as naming the tracks. Click Rip to begin. Media Player copies each CD track to a separate file and stores it, by default, in the Save location for the Music library of the currently signed-in user profile (by default, this location is %UserProfile%\Music).

➤ For details on how to change the default save location, see "Using libraries," in Chapter 9, "Using File Explorer."

Using Photos to view and edit image files

Microsoft Photos, which is included with every edition of Windows 11, is a lightweight but capable tool for viewing, managing, and editing a collection of digital images. Microsoft shipped a significant upgrade to this app with Windows 11 version 22H2, and we cover that version in this chapter.

NOTE

The grizzled elder of image editors, Paint, has been repackaged and updated for Windows 11 but still remains a part of the operating system primarily for compatibility's sake. We do not cover it in this chapter.

Microsoft Photos version 2022 sports a new interface more in keeping with other built-in Windows apps. It includes most of the capabilities of its predecessor, with one notable exception: It doesn't offer the video editing tools from the previous release. (If you need to edit a video clip, the designers of Windows 11 expect you to use Clipchamp, the new default video editor.)

The previous version of the Photos app updates itself automatically to the new one; if you need to install the previous version, it's available in the Microsoft Store, under the name Microsoft Photos Legacy. A shortcut to that Store listing is available in the new Photos app; go to Settings and click Get Photos Legacy, under the About heading. The Photos app gathers your digital photos (from local folders and from OneDrive) and displays them in a thumbnail view that's easy to browse. If you've installed the OneDrive app on your smartphone and configured it to automatically upload your new photos as you take them, you have easy access to the lightweight editing tools in the Photos app without having to fuss with importing photos.

Figure 6-13 shows the user interface of the new Photos app, with the entire collection available for browsing and editing.

Figure 6-13   Clicking All Photos at the top of the navigation pane displays a unified collection of digital pictures from different folders, sorted by date, with the newest photos first.

The Photos app displays a unified view of all the image files it finds in your Pictures library. It also includes the option to show photos and videos from OneDrive, even if those files are not synchronized with your PC or tablet.

The navigation pane on the left includes an All Photos link at the top. Clicking that shortcut opens a combined view of all the digital images in the Pictures folder of the linked OneDrive account and all folders in the local Pictures library. Click an individual folder heading in the navigation pane to see just image files stored in that location.

➤ For details about how libraries work, see "Using libraries," in Chapter 9.

To add or remove a folder, click the Folders heading. That actions displays all currently available folders in the contents pane. Click the Add A Folder button and choose any existing folder to add it to the Pictures library and make it available in the Photos app. Right-click any folder and choose Remove Folder to stop displaying its contents in the Photos app. (Removing a folder here does not delete the folder from local storage or from OneDrive.)

NOTE

As we were putting the finishing touches on this chapter, Microsoft announced that the latest release of Apple's iCloud app, which is available in the Microsoft Store, allows your iCloud Photo Library to integrate with the Photos app. This integration adds an iCloud Photos heading to the navigation pane in File Explorer and in the Photos app; its contents appear in the All Photos view.

The three icons in the upper right allow you to change how the contents pane appears. There, you can set the sort order (Date Taken is the default), filter the contents to show only photos or only videos, and change the way thumbnails appear. For the latter setting, choose River to see thumbnails in their actual aspect ratio and Square to show each photo as a square. With either option, you can also choose a size, from large (best when you want to quickly go through a small group of related images) to medium to small (ideal for browsing quickly through a time-line to find photos from a specific date).

As you scroll through a collection, the heading above those thumbnails changes to show the date taken (or, if you've changed the sort order, the date when the image was created or modi-fied). On the thumbnails themselves, a blue icon means the image is in OneDrive; a separate icon showing three overlapping rectangles denotes an image that has duplicate copies.

Click any thumbnail to open it full size, zooming the image to fit in the app window without any cropping and displaying small thumbnails of other images from the same point in the collec-tion using a filmstrip at the bottom of the window. Right-click the image to display additional options, as shown in Figure 6-14.

Figure 6-14   After opening an image, select one or more additional thumbnails from the filmstrip along the bottom to compare the pictures side by side.

The options at the top of that right-click menu are relatively straightforward—Save As, Print, Copy, and so on. Choose Resize Image if you're planning to use an image on a web page or as part of an email and you want to reduce the amount of file space it uses.

The View Actual Size and Fill Window options enable you to take a closer look at an image that's larger than the app window while possibly requiring that you scroll to see details that don't fit. Click Zoom To Fit to return to the default view. Use the Add To/Remove From Favorites menu below that to tag images you like so that you can retrieve them quickly using the Favorites view.

When you select multiple thumbnails from the filmstrip, Photos shows the images side by side in the app window, making it easy to compare similar shots from the same sequence to decide which one is better.

The small toolbar centered at the top of this pane includes some editing options as well as a File Info button. (If you'd prefer to keep your hands on the keyboard, press Alt+Enter.) The Info pane displays details about the image file and some of its metadata, as shown in Figure 6-15.

CHAPTER 6

Figure 6-15   Press Alt+Enter to open this info pane, where you can rename the image file, look at image metadata, and add your own description.

From the info pane, you can change the name of an image file—useful when you want to replace the default filename generated by the camera with something more descriptive. You can also add a description to the image file that you can use to find it in File Explorer. Note that much of the metadata displayed in the File Info pane, including technical details about the camera, is read-only. You can, however, modify the Date Taken and Time Taken details; this might be necessary if the clock on your camera or smartphone was still set to your home time zone, for example, even though the photo was taken on a different continent.

In the case of photos stored in a local or network folder, you can work with the file and its metadata directly; click the link under the File Path heading to open the folder containing the image in File Explorer.

Using the Photos app to crop and edit pictures

The greatest strength of the Photos app is its collection of lightweight editing tools. After opening an image, click or tap Edit Image in the toolbar at the top of the window, or press Ctrl+E.

To quickly turn a casual shot into something worth keeping and sharing, start with the tools on the Crop menu, where you can crop, flip, rotate, and straighten the image as needed. Two sets of editing tools are available beneath the image. The first, shown at the top of Figure 6-16, contains a slider you can use to straighten an image, as well as additional buttons for rotating the image or flipping it. Click the icon beneath the center of the slider to reveal the display shown at the bottom of Figure 6-16, where you can lock in a specific aspect ratio.

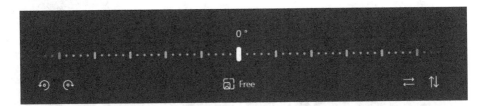

Figure 6-16   Click the icon below the straightening slider to reveal a selection of fixed aspect ratios, useful for cropping to a specific shape.

Straighten an image by moving the horizon of the image in either direction, one degree at a time. After choosing an aspect ratio, grab any of the sides or corners of the image and drag to resize the image. If you choose the Free option, you can drag the image to any rectangular shape without constraints.

Click Adjustment to switch to a different set of editing tools, as shown in Figure 6-17.

CHAPTER 6

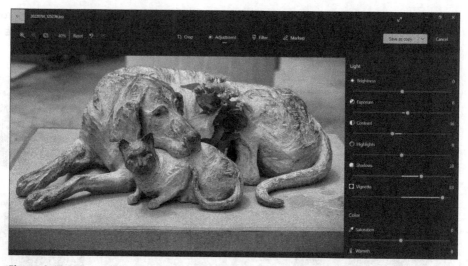

Figure 6-17 It's possible to improve a photo with judicious application of these light and color editing tools, which can compensate for poor lighting or exposure.

The Brightness and Exposure sliders at the top of the pane work in straightforward fashion. Slide to the left to make an overexposed photo darker, or to the right to brighten an image that seems a little too dark.

Use the sliders under the Color heading to change the temperature, tint, or saturation of the image—for example, to compensate for a blue tint from indoor lighting. Move the bar all the way to the left to remove all color, converting the image to monochrome, and to the right to punch up the saturation of the image. All of these effects are best used in moderation.

If you don't like the results after tinkering with these effects, click the Reset option in the top left to return the image to its original settings and start over.

The Filter heading opens a palette of 15 predefined filters that collectively give the image a distinctive look and feel. Use the Intensity slider to adjust the filter's effects. There's no penalty in trying different filters to see whether you like the result; you can always choose Original (the first item in the list of filters) to remove all effects.

After you're satisfied with your edits, use the menu in the top right to save a copy of the image under a new name or to apply all edits, using the same file name and replacing the current image.

Using Movies & TV to watch purchased media files

With Microsoft's recent enhancements making Media Player the default player for personal video files, the Movies & TV app has been demoted significantly. As of Windows 11 version 22H2, its primary role is to play movies and TV shows purchased from the Microsoft

Store—which is, not coincidentally, the same source used for buying and playing media on Xbox consoles. If you're an enthusiastic consumer of content on the Xbox platform, this app might be of interest. If not, it's mostly irrelevant.

As of late 2022, the Movies & TV app has not been updated to follow the design principles of other native Windows 11 apps. Instead of a navigation pane on the left, there's a navigation bar along the top, as shown in Figure 6-18.

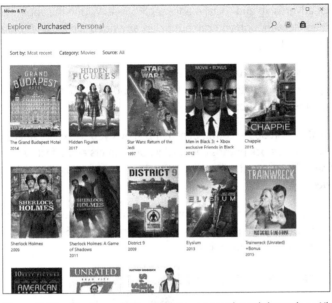

Figure 6-18   Movies and TV programs you purchased through an Xbox or from the Microsoft Store are available for playback in the Movies & TV app.

Inside OUT

Why won't the built-in apps play my DVDs?

Like its predecessor, Windows 11 doesn't include the capability to play DVDs (or MPEG-2 files ripped from DVDs). That decision is a reflection of two market realities: Most new PCs don't include optical disc drives at all, and the cost of royalties for DVD playback software is significant. On the small percentage of PCs that do ship with optical media drives, the manufacturer typically includes playback software.

Microsoft offers a DVD Player app that is available for purchase in the Store. As a no-cost alternative, we recommend the free VLC software, which contains the necessary codecs and is available in a desktop version from *https://videolan.org*. The VLC desktop app is also available in a packaged version from the Microsoft Store. An older version of the VLC app is also available in the Store, under the name VLC UWP; avoid this release, which includes a prominent warning in the Store listing that it does not support DVD playback.

CHAPTER 6

Although this app includes a Personal tab that displays files from your video library, that display duplicates what you find in the newer Media Library, and we recommend using that app for your collection of personal video files.

Using Clipchamp to edit video clips

Although the title bar calls Clipchamp a video editor, that label might be slightly misleading. This app might be more appropriately labeled a video creation tool, with a special emphasis on short-form videos for advertising and social media applications. Within the application, there's no way to open a video file, although you can right-click any video clip in File Explorer and choose to open it with Clipchamp.

Microsoft purchased Clipchamp in 2021 and rolled the app into Windows 11 the following year. Unlike most of the apps included with Windows 11, Clipchamp follows a freemium model, where advanced features require a paid subscription.

If you already have a Microsoft 365 account, Clipchamp allows you to export videos up to a resolution of 1080p, with free stock photos and a selection of filters and effects. A paid subscription adds premium stock photos and a "brand kit" that businesses can use to apply fonts, colors, and logos to any video.

The Clipchamp interface encourages you to create videos using templates for common online services, including YouTube, Instagram, and TikTok, as shown in Figure 6-19. You can record a video using your screen, your webcam, or both.

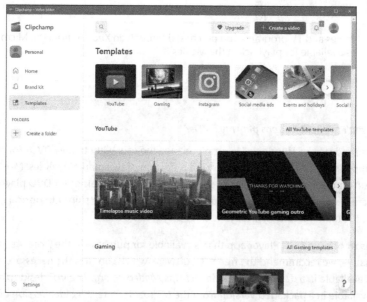

Figure 6-19   The Clipchamp interface is designed for creating social media content, ads, and other short clips.

Creating a video from one of these templates takes you to a full-featured video editor that we could probably spend many pages describing. We suspect that Clipchamp is going to go through some significant revisions as it finds its place in the Windows app landscape, so rather than document its features here, we encourage you to try it for yourself.

Performing screen captures with Snipping Tool

Pictures speak louder than words, and sometimes an image capture of the current window or screen can be the ideal way to enhance a PowerPoint presentation, explain a procedure, or remind yourself at some future time of what you were doing and how. All Windows versions, from the very first to the present, have offered two keyboard shortcuts for capturing screens:

- PrtScn captures an image of the entire screen. If you have multiple monitors, the image includes all screens.

- Alt+PrtScn captures an image of the current window.

Both capture methods post bitmaps to the Clipboard, and you can paste the results into any app that accepts graphics.

NOTE

These two screen-capture methods can also automatically save an image file (in PNG format) to your personal OneDrive account. To turn this feature on or off, right-click the OneDrive icon in the notification area and choose Settings. The setting is on the Backup tab under Screenshots.

Windows 11, like its recent predecessors, offers two additional built-in shortcuts:

- Windows key+PrtScn captures an image of all current screens (including secondary screens) and saves that image as a PNG file in the Screenshots subfolder of your Pictures folder.

- Windows key+Shift+S dims the screen and opens the Snipping Tool app, displaying a toolbar at the top border of the screen with four options that you can use to capture all or part of the current display, as shown in Figure 6-20.

Figure 6-20   The Snipping Tool app allows you to capture all or part of a Windows 11 screen.

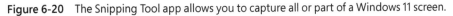

CHAPTER 6

From left to right, these options allow you to specify any of the following types of snips:

- **Rectangular Mode**   Click to define one corner of the area you want to capture and then drag diagonally, releasing the mouse when you reach the opposite corner of the rectangular area.

- **Freeform Mode**   Click and drag in any direction to define an irregular shape.

- **Window Mode**   After selecting this option, move the mouse pointer over the window you want to capture until it appears undimmed and then click.

- **Fullscreen Mode**   Click anywhere to capture the entire display.

When you finish your capture, your selection is copied to the Clipboard and a notification appears in the lower-right corner of the screen and in the notification center. Click that notification to open your saved capture in the Snipping Tool app. There, you can annotate or crop the capture and then save the results as a file, paste it into another app, or print it.

Using Maps

Mapping applications have long been one of the indispensable tools of modern life. Microsoft's modern Maps app is a competent alternative to web-based options; it allows you to explore an unfamiliar city, plot a road trip, find a restaurant or a bank, print a set of turn-by-turn directions to take with you on the road, or just enjoy aerial views of the world or your neighborhood.

On first run, Maps asks for permission to track your location information. If you consent, Maps plants a marker at your current location. Tapping Show My Location (the target-shaped button in the toolbar on the right side of the screen) at any time displays your current location, assuming the app knows where that is. (The keyboard shortcut Ctrl+Home performs the same function.)

Searching for places and services

To find a location, click the Search tool at the left of the menu bar or press Ctrl+F. You can type an address, the name of a person or business in your contacts list, or the name of a place known to Maps—an institution or a restaurant, for example. As shown in Figure 6-21, Maps displays the location on the map, one or more street-side pictures, and other interesting information.

Figure 6-21   Use the icons under the What's Nearby heading to find restaurants, hotels, parking, and useful stops near your search location.

Controls on the right of the menu bar allow you to change the display (from Road to Aerial, for example) and to save places to your Microsoft account so you can revisit them on a different device when signed in using the same account. The vertical toolbar on the right side of the map allows you to tilt the map view, change its orientation, or zoom in and out. (If you zoom in far enough in Road view, you see street numbers on the outlines of individual buildings.)

Getting directions

Even if you plan to use the navigation options in your mobile device or your car to help you get from Point A to Point B, it can be useful to look at your route before you leave. Doing so can give you a "big picture" view of where you're going.

To get directions, click the Directions button in the upper-left corner (to the right of the Search button) and then select your starting and ending points. (One of them might already be in place if you just searched for it.) Click Get Directions to display a set of route alternatives in a drop-down list. Each destination includes an estimated travel time and a color-coded route on the map. You can change the route details to show estimated time if you drive, take mass transit, or walk.

Click or tap the left side of a route listing to see step-by-step directions. Click or tap Go to see and hear turn-by-turn instructions. Note, though, that using turn-by-turn directions is only practical on a device that's equipped with a GPS.

CHAPTER 6

Downloading maps for offline use

If you're out and about without a data connection for your portable device, you can still use maps that you previously downloaded. To take advantage of this feature, go to Settings > Apps > Offline Maps. Choose a region and then click Download.

Maps are updated frequently. To ensure that you have the most recent data, go to Settings > Apps > Offline Maps > Map Updates and select Update Automatically When Plugged In And On Wi-Fi.

Using Microsoft Edge

Since the dawn of the internet era, Microsoft has included a web browser with every copy of Windows that it shipped. In the early days, that browser was Internet Explorer, which once ruled the World Wide Web, but eventually fell out of favor because of widespread security and compatibility issues.

In Windows 10, Microsoft introduced a new browser called Microsoft Edge. It was a noticeable improvement over Internet Explorer, but it had just enough compatibility issues that it failed to make a dent in the popularity of the world's undisputed browser champion, Google Chrome.

So, in 2020, Microsoft decided to reboot Microsoft Edge, building it on the same open-source Chromium codebase as Google Chrome. It also released the new browser on every major mobile and desktop platform. Because this new Edge shares its core code with Google Chrome, it's not plagued by compatibility issues. In fact, many add-ons originally written for Chrome work unmodified in Edge, and Microsoft has layered on privacy features that differentiate it from Chrome.

Every copy of Windows 11 includes Microsoft Edge as the default browser. For those who prefer a different browser, you can use Edge to download that alternative and set it as the new default. But Microsoft Edge is a good browser, and it's worth getting to know. You might even like it enough to replace your old favorite.

As for Internet Explorer, it's no longer available as a standalone app, but Windows 11 includes a novel solution to help you deal with webpages designed for that old browser.

An overview of Microsoft Edge

If you previously used Windows 10, you're probably already familiar with the Chromium-based version of Microsoft Edge, which has been the default browser in that operating system since the beginning of 2021. Type a URL or a search term in the address bar and press Enter to find a specific destination; navigation controls are to the left of the address bar and additional commands are on a toolbar to its right, as shown in Figure 7-1. More options are available on a menu that drops down when you click Settings And More—the three dots at the far right of the toolbar.

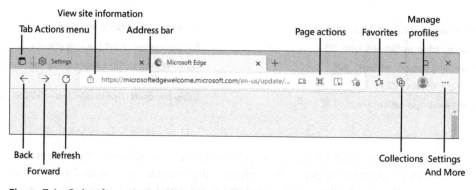

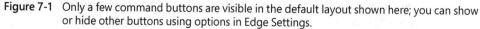

Figure 7-1   Only a few command buttons are visible in the default layout shown here; you can show or hide other buttons using options in Edge Settings.

Using the open-source Chromium engine eliminates many of the compatibility and security issues that plagued earlier Microsoft browsers. If a page works properly on Google Chrome, which is by far the most popular web browser in use today, then it should work equally well on Microsoft Edge. Likewise, security issues that affect the core browser engine can be quickly addressed thanks to the rapid update cycle for new Edge versions.

Basic design and navigation principles for Microsoft Edge should also be familiar to anyone who's used Google Chrome (or another browser based on that shared codebase). But if you look carefully, you can spot plenty of places where the designers of Microsoft Edge have added or modified features. For example, clicking the padlock at the left of the address bar in Edge shows an informational pane like the one shown in Figure 7-2. The items at the top are identical to those that appear when you perform the same action in Chrome, but the Tracking Prevention section at the bottom is unique to the new Edge.

In the remainder of this chapter, we walk through the details of using and customizing Edge to take advantage of its unique features. But first, let's talk about how to get the latest version of Edge and keep it up to date.

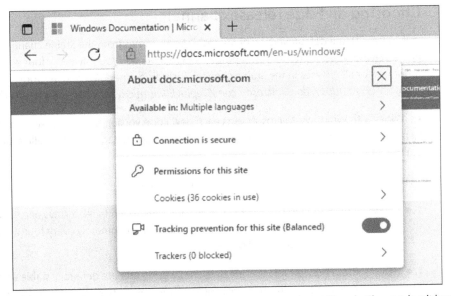

Figure 7-2   Microsoft Edge uses the same open source engine as Google Chrome, but it has some key differences, like the Tracking Prevention feature whose controls are visible at the bottom of this information pane.

CHAPTER 7

Inside OUT

Change your default browser

Microsoft Edge is Microsoft's recommended default browser, but you're free to change that default at any time. After installing a different browser, make it your default by going to Settings > Apps > Default Apps and selecting the name of your newly installed browser from the list of installed apps. On Windows 11 version 22000, you need to adjust this setting for each associated file type or link type individually, a task that's not only tedious but runs the risk that you'll remove an association that should remain with another program. In later versions of Windows 11, this process is much simpler: Select your preferred browser from the Default Apps page and then look for a Set Default button at the top of that page.

➤ For information about fine-tuning your default settings—for example, assigning particular browsers to particular web protocols—see "Setting default programs and file-type associations" in Chapter 5, "Installing and configuring apps."

Choosing an Edge release channel

In Windows 11, the default version of Microsoft Edge comes from the Stable channel. That's the public release, which automatically updates to a new version roughly every four weeks. To check the status for all releases in the Stable channel (including scheduled releases for the next several months), go to *https://docs.microsoft.com/DeployEdge/microsoft-edge-release-schedule*.

As it does with Windows, Microsoft tests each new Edge version before it's released; if you want to be a part of that testing program, you can do so by downloading and installing preview builds.

Microsoft Edge Insider builds are available in three channels:

- **Beta**   This is the most stable Microsoft Edge preview channel. It stays one version ahead of the public release and receives major updates approximately every four weeks. This release is fully supported by Microsoft.

- **Dev**   These preview releases are delivered weekly and are generally stable enough for everyday use, although you might encounter issues. As the name suggests, these unsupported releases are intended for use by developers who want to test features that will be available to the public in another month or two.

- **Canary**   Releases you install from this channel are updated daily with the latest code from the Microsoft Edge engineering team and are not officially supported. Microsoft's description of this channel pointedly calls it the "bleeding edge." Running a release from this channel results in not-so-occasional crashes and unexpected behavior.

The good news is that you can install multiple preview versions alongside one another and switch freely between them. (Microsoft Edge preview releases are distinguished by a colored stripe on the taskbar icon.) If you encounter problems while loading a page in an Edge Insider release, you can switch to the stable channel and continue on your way.

No signup is required. Just download and install a preview version (or versions) from *https://www.microsoftedgeinsider.com*.

Managing updates

Although Microsoft Edge is installed with Windows 11, it doesn't update itself through the same channels as the operating system or Store apps. Instead, Edge has its own updater, which runs as a system service. If you have versions of Edge installed from multiple release channels, each version updates independently.

When an update is ready, it downloads in the background; a green up-arrow icon on the Settings And More menu indicates that the update is available and will be applied automatically when you restart Edge. You can also check for the presence of an update by choosing Help And Feedback > About Microsoft Edge from the Settings And More menu (or go to *edge://settings/ help*, which leads to the same destination). That dialog displays the currently installed version; if an update is ready to install, you see a message like the one shown in Figure 7-3.

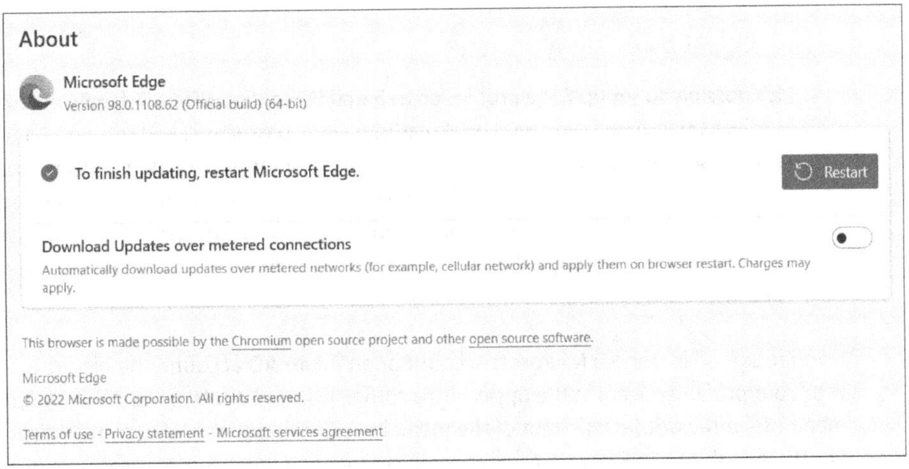

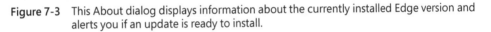

About

Microsoft Edge
Version 98.0.1108.62 (Official build) (64-bit)

✓ To finish updating, restart Microsoft Edge.   ↻ Restart

Download Updates over metered connections
Automatically download updates over metered networks (for example, cellular network) and apply them on browser restart. Charges may apply.

This browser is made possible by the Chromium open source project and other open source software.

Microsoft Edge
© 2022 Microsoft Corporation. All rights reserved.

Terms of use - Privacy statement - Microsoft services agreement

Figure 7-3   This About dialog displays information about the currently installed Edge version and alerts you if an update is ready to install.

In home and small business settings, there's no good reason to defer browser upgrades. In enterprise deployments, administrators might want to manage the timing of updates and update checks. To do so, use the update-related group policies described in this Microsoft Edge Reference document:

https://docs.microsoft.com/deployedge/microsoft-edge-update-policies

Inside OUT

Slow the Edge update pace with the Extended Stable Channel

For organizations that are put off by the prospect of managing browser updates on an every-four-weeks cycle, Microsoft offers a servicing option called the Extended Stable channel. Enterprise customers who opt into this release cadence receive new browser versions every eight weeks instead of every four weeks, skipping odd-numbered releases from the Stable channel. (Security patches and bug fixes are delivered independently.) Enabling this feature requires setting Group Policy, as explained in this article: *https://bit.ly/edge-extended-stable-release*.

Managing Edge profiles and sync

When you run Edge for the first time, the browser prompts you to create a profile, which it uses to keep track of your settings, privacy preferences, saved passwords, browsing history, and so on. You can set up multiple profiles and switch between them with relative ease. The most common use case is to separate your work-related activity from personal browsing so that you don't accidentally mix up your work and personal browsing histories, email, and services.

CAUTION

It's possible to set up Edge profiles on a shared PC so that different family members can browse using their own saved bookmarks, history, passwords, and settings. For occasional use under supervision, that configuration might be acceptable. From a security standpoint, though, you're much better off setting up a separate user account for each person who plans to use the computer regularly. It's easy to switch between accounts, and doing so avoids any risk that one person will actually use someone else's browser profile.

If you're signed in using a Microsoft account or an Azure AD account, the picture associated with your profile appears in the upper-right corner, just to the left of the Settings And More menu (the three dots at the right of the menu bar). Clicking that profile picture displays a pane like the one shown in Figure 7-4, where you can manage your existing profile, switch to a different profile, browse as a guest, or add a new profile.

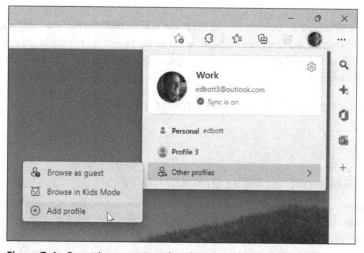

Figure 7-4   By setting up personal and work profiles in Edge, you can switch between them to keep saved settings and history separate.

Edge creates generic names for profiles you set up using the Add Profile option: Personal for those associated with Microsoft accounts, Work for those associated with Azure AD via Microsoft 365 business subscriptions, and Profile *<number>* for profiles where you don't sign in. The advantage of signing in with a Microsoft or Azure AD account, of course, is that you can sync your browsing data across multiple devices. Click Manage Profile Settings from the profiles menu to open a page like the one shown in Figure 7-5.

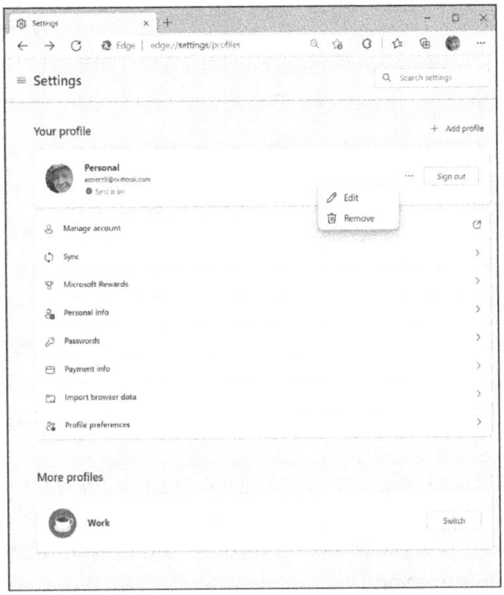

Figure 7-5   To change the name of the current profile or remove it completely, use the menu shown under the More Actions menu.

The Profile Preferences page includes some useful options. By default, if you try to sign in to a service using an account that's associated with a different profile, Edge offers to switch to that profile. You can disable this option if you prefer to switch profiles only when you choose to do so. On that same page, you find an option to specify which profile Edge uses when you click a link in an email message or a document. The default setting sends the request to the profile you used most recently. If you prefer, you can specify that you want external links to always open in a specific profile.

For a profile that's tied to an online account, click Sync to manage what kinds of browsing data are synced between browsing sessions. This sync works between different devices, including PCs and Macs as well as mobile devices running Edge on iOS or Android. Using matching profiles also makes it more convenient to use Edge Insider builds alongside the stable release on the same PC. You have the option to turn off sync completely, using the profile strictly as a way to sign in to online services and save your settings and history locally. But most people will want to adjust the settings using the controls shown in Figure 7-6.

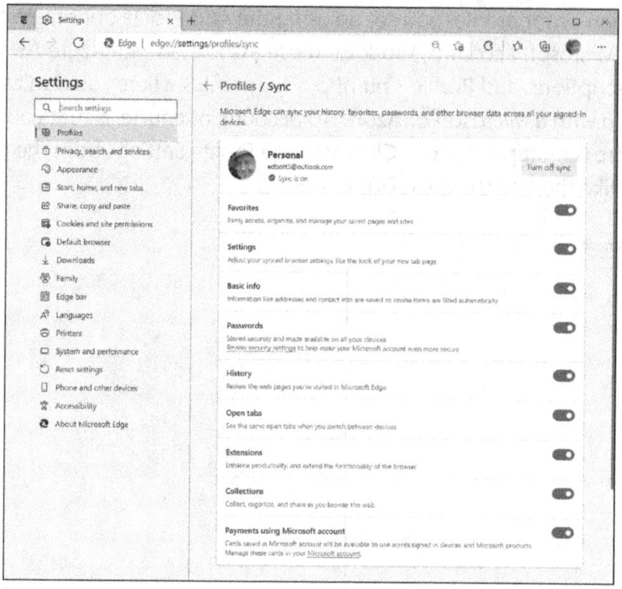

Figure 7-6   When you're signed in with a Microsoft account, you can choose which types of browsing data to sync or turn off sync completely.

We can't imagine why anyone would turn off automatic syncing of Favorites and Collections, but if you use a third-party password manager, you probably want to turn the Passwords and Basic Info switches to the Off position. (See the following section for more information about syncing and managing this type of information.)

By definition, profiles that are not signed in cannot sync browsing data across different sessions. The Sync command is grayed out and unavailable, but you can still save passwords and basic information such as addresses as part of the local profile.

To switch profiles, click the profile picture and then choose the alternative profile from the menu. Each profile opens in a separate browser window, with its own taskbar button marked by a tiny profile picture to help distinguish it from other profiles. The Browse As Guest option uses a temporary profile, separate from all other profiles on the device; it does not save history, cookies, or other site data, nor can it use extensions. Browse In Kids Mode switches the browser to a full-screen session with site access limited to sites that are on an Edge-approved list. As the device administrator, you set up Kids Mode, and you need to supply your credentials to return to a normal Edge session or to visit a site that's not on the safe list.

Using the built-in password manager

Security experts have some simple advice for creating secure online passwords: Use a random combination of numbers, symbols, and mixed-case letters that can't be guessed, and never, ever use the same password on different sites. But how do you possibly keep track of those random, unique credentials when you visit dozens of password-protected sites every month?

The solution is to use a password manager, which can keep track of those secrets and fill them in automatically when you visit a shopping site, check your email, pay bills online through your financial institution, or use a subscription service.

Like all modern browsers, Microsoft Edge includes a robust set of password management tools that can store, sync, and help you manage those credentials. It can suggest strong passwords on new websites and alert you if your saved credentials have been involved in an online data breach. It doesn't require an extra download, and it doesn't charge a subscription fee, as some third-party password management utilities do. Your saved/synced data is secured by the same encryption and two-factor authentication features you use with Microsoft's email and cloud storage services.

Inside OUT

Use Microsoft Authenticator to save and sync passwords

There's no built-in feature that allows you to sync passwords that are saved in Microsoft Edge with the corresponding features in other browsers (such as Chrome or Safari) on another Windows PC or a Mac. On mobile devices, however, including Android and iOS smartphones, you can sync passwords and other autofill information (such as addresses and payment details) using Microsoft Authenticator. After installing the Authenticator app on your smartphone, tap the Passwords button on the home page and select the Microsoft account you want to sync with. Set Authenticator as an autofill provider, and you can fill in the passwords you saved in the matching Edge profile on your Windows PC using any mobile browser or app.

Regardless of how you choose to manage your own passwords, go to *edge://settings/passwords*, as shown in Figure 7-7, and confirm that the settings for your profile match your preferences.

When the Offer To Save Passwords option is turned on, Edge watches your activity and prompts you after you enter credentials to sign in at a password-protected website. When you see a dialog like the one in Figure 7-8, click Got It to add the credentials to your profile, or click Never to add that site to a list of sites where you don't want your credentials saved.

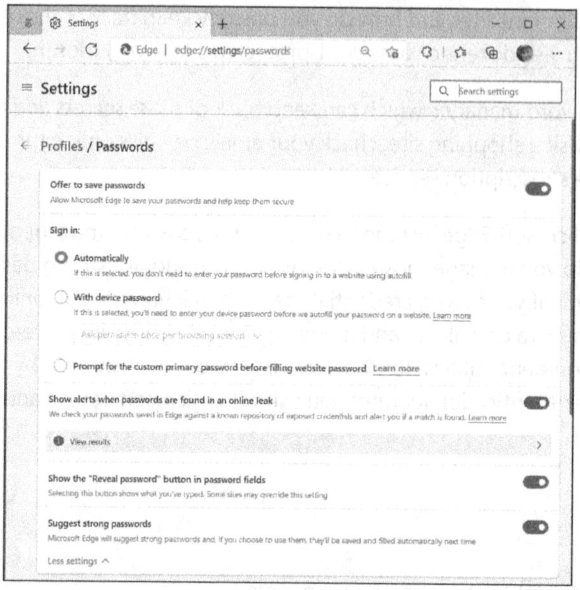

Figure 7-7   The switches on this page control the built-in password management features in Edge.

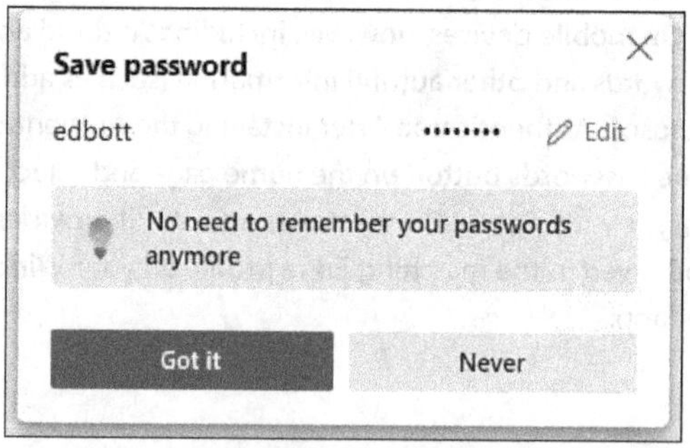

Figure 7-8   If you click Got It, Edge saves the username and password for the current site; click Never if you'd prefer not to save those credentials and don't want to be prompted again for this site.

When signing up at a website for the first time, or when changing your password, click in the password box to have Edge generate a strong password. You can save the password or click Refresh to generate a new password. You cannot change the way Edge generates passwords, but you can manually change a password that Edge generates, a task that might be required if that password doesn't meet the website's password complexity standards.

If you manually change a password that Edge automatically filled in, a similar dialog offers to update the saved password. Clicking the Edit button allows you to view and, if necessary, modify the username and password before saving it.

When filling in saved credentials on webpages, use the Sign In options on the *edge://settings/passwords* page to enforce additional security measures. Choose one of the following options:

- **Automatically**   Edge shows matching saved credentials on any page that asks you to enter a password. Click to enter the username and password without any additional steps.

- **With Device Password**   This option requires you to authenticate with the same credentials that you use for signing in to your Windows PC (including Windows Hello, if you've set that up). You can specify that you want Edge to perform this check once per browsing session; or, to avoid any chance that someone can walk up to your unlocked PC and sign in to a webpage using your credentials, insist that Edge always ask permission before filling in passwords.

- **Prompt for the custom primary password before filling website password**   When you choose this security step, Edge prompts you to create a custom password of at least four characters, which you need to enter the first time you try to autofill a saved password in a browser session. Note that the custom password is saved locally and is not synced to other devices. If you forget this password, you'll be unable to retrieve any saved passwords on that device; if you've chosen to sync passwords, you can disable and then re-enable sync to download a fresh copy of the saved passwords. If you've chosen not to sync passwords and you forget the custom password, your saved passwords will be unrecoverable.

Note that you can turn off the Offer To Save Passwords option and still fill in saved passwords for websites. You might choose this configuration if you want to save a handful of credentials for a small number of sites in a specific Edge profile, while ensuring that you don't inadvertently save any others in that profile.

At the bottom of the Passwords page in Edge Settings is a complete list of sites for which Edge has saved passwords. The list includes the website's domain or subdomain, the username, the password, and the Password Health icon, as in the example in Figure 7-9. Below that is the list of sites where you've specified that you don't want Edge to save passwords.

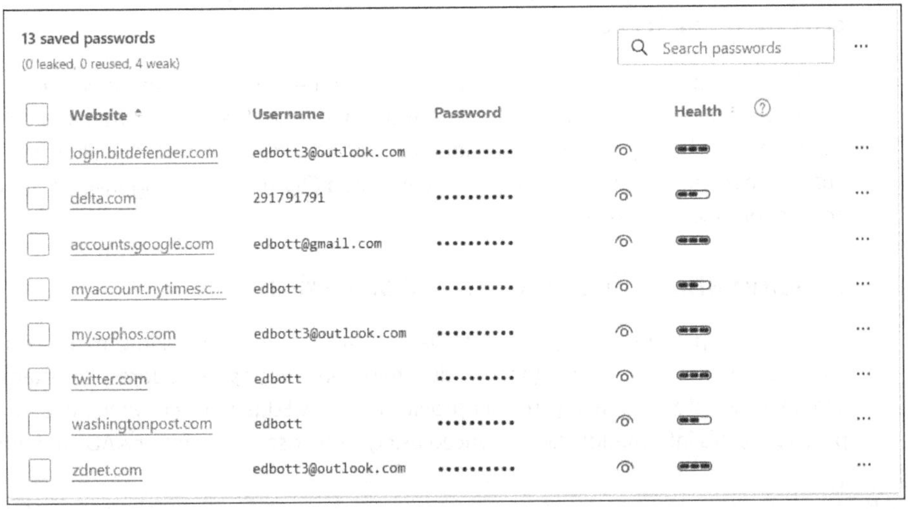

Figure 7-9   You need to authenticate your identity before you can view, edit, or copy saved passwords on this page. Use the Health option to identify weak or reused credentials.

For security reasons, saved passwords are displayed as a string of dots that doesn't reveal the contents or even the length of an individual password. To reveal a password, click the eye icon and then be prepared to establish your identity with a password, PIN, or Windows Hello biometric proof. Click the More Actions menu (the three dots at the far right) to display additional actions for any saved credential. From there, you can edit and save the username and password (but not the saved web address) for any entry, copy the password to the Clipboard, or delete an entry to remove it permanently from the list.

Inside OUT

Let Edge help you create stronger passwords

The Password Health icon uses a simple scheme to highlight passwords that are weak or used on other sites. If all three black bars are filled in, the password meets Edge's standards for strength and is not reused. If only two of three bars are filled in, the password is either weak or is used on multiple sites; one bar means the password is weak and is reused.

Click the Password Health heading to sort by that field and bring together all the credentials that need your attention. For each one, you can click the More Actions menu and choose Change to go to the website, where you can sign in with the existing credentials. Then, use the Suggest Strong Password option to create a complex, unique password and save it in Edge. Repeat that process until every saved password is up to snuff.

For large collections of saved passwords, scrolling through the list to find a specific entry can be tedious. Instead, use the search box at the top of the Passwords page in your profile to find a specific website or username. For security reasons, this tool doesn't search through the contents of the passwords themselves.

The More Actions menu at the top of the list, just to the right of the search box, allows you to export your saved passwords as a CSV file. You can use that file to move your saved Edge passwords to a third-party password manager; you can also keep it in a safe location as a backup. That same menu also includes an option to import a CSV file containing saved passwords from another browser or password manager.

Syncing and filling in other information

In addition to passwords, Edge can automatically fill in other types of information on web-based forms. Instead of typing (and possibly mistyping) your street address, for example, you can save that information in your user profile and allow Edge to use it when needed. As with passwords, this information can be synced using a Microsoft account or AAD credentials.

To save this sort of information for reuse, click Personal Info on the Profiles page, or go to *edge://settings/personalinfo*. From there, you can edit any existing entries or click Add Basic Info to open a new form. You might want to create separate entries for your home and work email and street addresses, as well as additional entries for alternate email addresses and identities. Figure 7-10 shows the Edit Basic Info form in use.

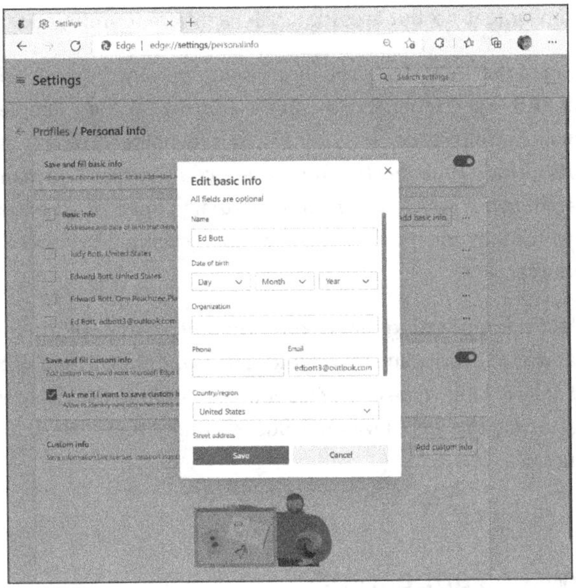

Figure 7-10   Fill out this basic profile to give Edge the information it needs to fill in web forms with addresses, birthdates, and other details.

If the Basic Info form doesn't include all the details you want to keep handy, scroll down to the Custom Info section, where you can add free-form fields with driver's license and passport details, membership numbers for organizations you belong to, and anything else that you can imagine wanting to keep handy and sync for later use.

Finally, from the Profiles page, choose Payment Info to add credit card numbers, expiration dates, and verification codes for easier entry when it comes time to pay for online purchases. As with other sensitive data, you're required to authenticate before Edge fills in a credit card number.

Customizing browser settings

For each profile you create in Microsoft Edge, you can customize the browser settings so they match your preferences. If you're using a single profile tied to the same Microsoft account with which you sign in to Windows, these settings persist as you use Edge. But if you've created additional profiles, as described in the previous section, each profile has its own settings.

Inside OUT

Use the edge:// syntax for quick shortcuts

Google's Chrome browser allows you to access a plethora of options using the chrome:// prefix, followed by specific keywords. Using the same Chromium codebase, Microsoft Edge implements a similar feature, but uses (naturally) a different prefix: edge://

You can see a sampling of these shortcuts just by choosing options from the Edge Settings And More menu (Alt+F) and then looking in the address bar. For example, clicking Settings opens the main Settings page, whose shortcut is (expectedly) *edge://settings*. Other useful shortcuts include *edge://extensions*, where you can view and manage extensions, and *edge://newtab*, which (again, quite naturally) opens the new tab page, and *edge://version*, which tells you more than you probably wanted to know about the currently installed browser.

Every option you select in Edge Settings has a corresponding custom URL in this format, which you can add as a favorite and revisit later. For a complete listing of the many edge:// options that are available, type *edge://about*. The resulting list includes dozens of options, many useful only to a web developer. But you might find a shortcut in there worth saving for future use.

Changing the browser's appearance

The Edge user experience is, by design, extremely simple, with a limited number of controls surrounding the main window that contains content from the web. But that doesn't mean the Edge interface is fixed in stone. You can adjust the following aspects using the controls available at *edge://settings/appearance*.

Under the Overall Appearance heading, as shown in Figure 7-11, you can choose between Dark and Light modes, or instruct Edge to match the mode you've chosen for Windows. Options under the Theme heading allow you to choose a pair of complementary colors for tab headings and toolbars. The final option in this section, Discover More Themes, takes you to the Edge Add-ons market, where you can download custom themes that include colors and a background image for new tab pages.

You find more practical customization options under the Customize Toolbar heading, shown in Figure 7-12. The toolbar is the region just below the tab headings; you can show or hide the Home button to the left of the address bar and curate the collection of toolbar buttons to highlight features and extensions you use regularly.

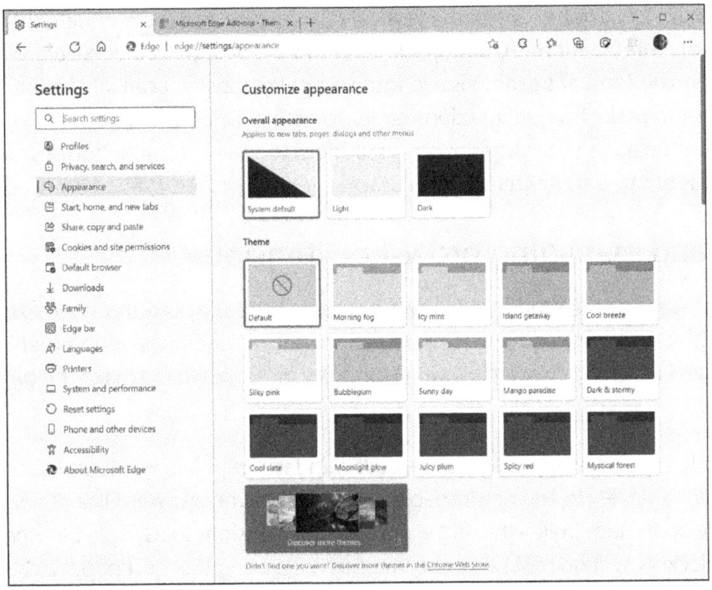

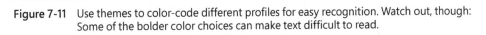

Figure 7-11   Use themes to color-code different profiles for easy recognition. Watch out, though: Some of the bolder color choices can make text difficult to read.

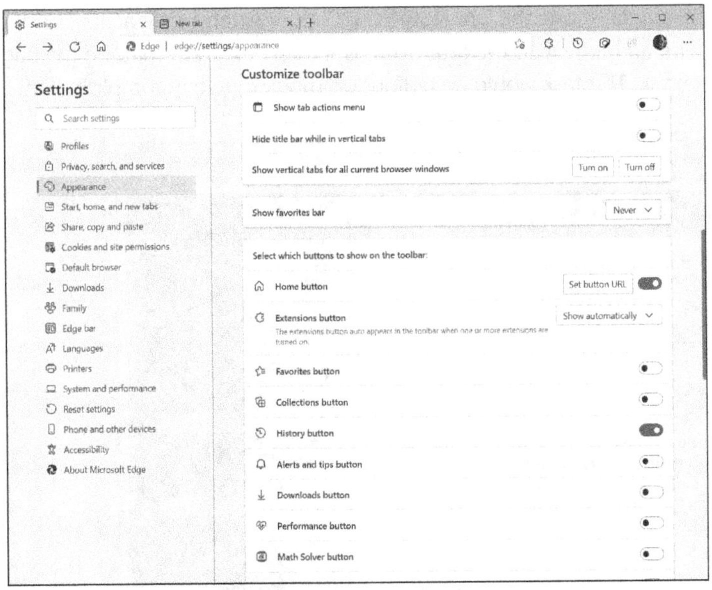

Figure 7-12   Customizations you make here can improve your productivity by making frequently used features more easily accessible while hiding those you rarely use.

CHAPTER 7

The top two groups of options control the vertical tabs feature and show or hide the favorites bar. You can read more about those features later in this chapter. Under the Select Which Buttons To Show On The Toolbar heading is a lengthy list of buttons you can add to (or remove from) the toolbar to make built-in functions easier to access. Resist the urge to make all those buttons available; on all but the largest displays, adding too many toolbar buttons can compress the address bar to a width that's barely usable.

Installing and managing browser extensions

From the earliest days of the World Wide Web, browsers have supported ways to extend their functionality with third-party add-ons. The original Windows web browser, Internet Explorer, supported ActiveX controls, a powerful but notoriously insecure way to make the browser perform new tricks.

By contrast, modern browsers use *extensions*—built with JavaScript and HTML and distributed through a managed store—to add new capabilities securely to the browser. Over the past decade, third-party developers have built a thriving ecosystem of extensions for Google Chrome. Password managers, ad blockers, writing tools, and research aids are among the most popular categories, but the sheer breadth of extensions is staggering. Almost all of those extensions work, unmodified, in Microsoft Edge (the exceptions mostly require access to a Google account or to Google services), and many of them have been adapted for distribution in Microsoft's Edge Add-ons store.

Figure 7-13, for example, shows the OneNote Web Clipper extension in action. Clicking its button on the Edge menu bar reveals the four options shown here, reformatting the page for use in a OneNote notebook. This task would be tedious or impossible to accomplish manually.

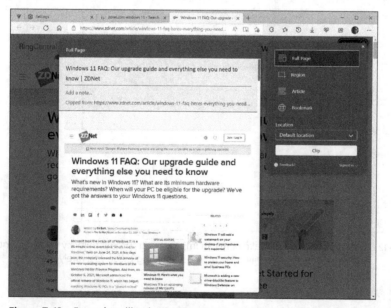

Figure 7-13   Extensions like the OneNote Web Clipper can reformat pages on the fly to make them easier to save as part of a OneNote notebook.

Developers can make a few small modifications to a Google Chrome extension and submit it to the Edge Add-ons store. You can browse through the full selection by categories or search for a specific extension at *https://microsoftedge.microsoft.com/addons*.

If the extension you need isn't available from Microsoft, chances are you can get it from Google's Chrome Web Store. To install extensions from that source, you need to enable the Allow Extensions From Other Stores setting in Edge on the Extensions page, as shown in Figure 7-14. That's also where you go to manage installed extensions.

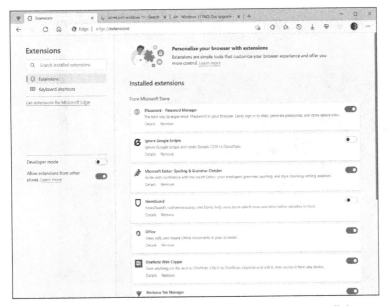

Figure 7-14   Installed extensions show up on this list. Click the Details button to see any additional settings, including the option to show the extension's button or uninstall it.

The on/off switch next to each installed extension allows you to enable or disable it on the fly. Most extensions are designed to run at all times, but you might have special-purpose add-ons that you turn on only when they're required.

By default, a button for each extension shows up on the Edge toolbar, to the right of the address bar. That's preferred for extensions that require interaction to do their magic. For extensions that work mostly in the background, consider cutting down on clutter by right-clicking the button and choosing the Hide From Toolbar option. (You can move the button back by choosing More Actions > Extensions and choosing Show In Toolbar from the More Actions menu for that extension.)

Finally, take advantage of keyboard shortcuts to expand the utility of extensions. On the Extensions page, click Keyboard Shortcuts (or go to *edge://extensions/shortcuts*). Click in the box to the right of any extension and press a shortcut that consists of either Ctrl or Alt plus a letter or number.

Customizing the new tab page

When you set up a new profile for the first time, you're prompted to choose a design for the page you see each time you open a new tab. If you're signed in with a Microsoft account or a local account, your options include a search box, with the option to add Microsoft news headlines, a fresh background image, or both. Figure 7-15 shows a Custom layout, with a search box and a background image, but no news headlines.

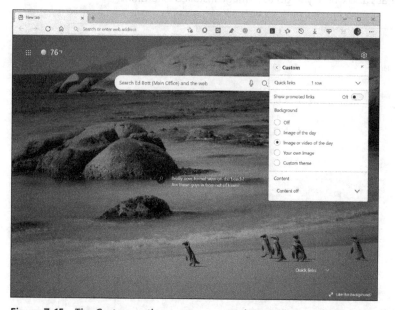

Figure 7-15   The Custom option creates a new tab page that combines a search box with an image that changes daily. Note that the Content selection, which shows MSN news headlines, is off.

If your Edge profile uses an Azure AD account associated with a Microsoft 365 business subscription, you get a few additional options that include links to online apps and documents you've worked with recently. In either case, you can change the layout any time by opening a new tab and clicking the gear icon in the upper-right corner.

In either page layout, the new tab page also includes a row of seven quick links, each shown as a tile with a name and a favicon (that's the formal name of the icon that appears alongside the page title in each browser tab). Click in the upper-right corner of any of these quick links to edit the name or remove the tile.

If none of these options meet your requirements, you need to find a browser extension that can take over the new tab page.

Customizing the startup page

If you prefer to start each new browser instance in a predictable way, go to Edge Settings > Start, Home, And New Tabs (*edge://settings/startHomeNTP*), and choose one of the alternatives there:

● Open The New Tab Page, the default setting, opens each new instance of Microsoft Edge to the new tab page, as described in the previous section.

● Open Tabs From The Previous Session restores the tabs that were open the last time you shut down Edge.

● Open These Pages starts each session by reviewing a specific group of sites.

In Figure 7-16, for example, Edge is configured to open two news sites and the local forecast from the National Weather Service at startup.

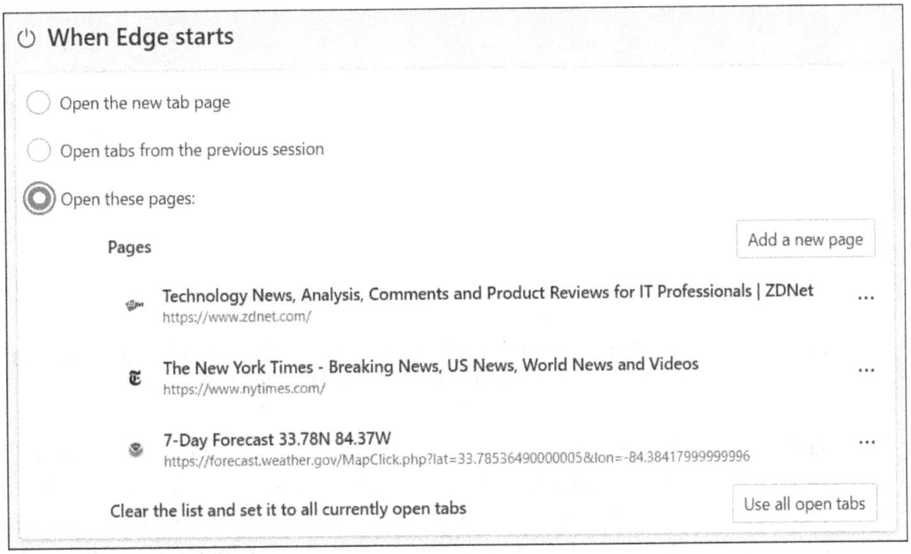

Figure 7-16 Choose this option if you want to start each day by checking your favorite news and weather pages.

The easiest way to specify that you want multiple pages to open at startup is to open those pages (and only those pages) in separate tabs in the current browser session. Then, in a new tab, go to the When Edge Starts section, choose Open These Pages, and click Use All Open Tabs. To add another page to the current selection, copy its URL, click Add A New Page, and paste the Clipboard's contents into the Enter A URL box.

Fine-tuning browser performance

Edge includes two sets of features designed to improve the web browsing experience. One set of features works by making sure Edge is always running in the background, so you never have to wait for the browser to load. The other allows Edge to put inactive tabs to sleep so they don't continue using system resources. Both sets of controls are on the System And Performance tab in Edge Settings (*edge://settings/system*), as shown in Figure 7-17.

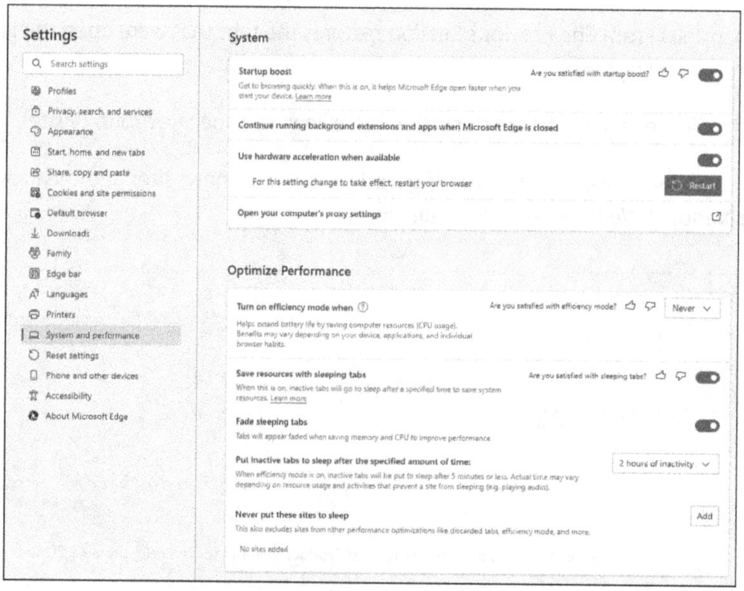

Figure 7-17   When Startup Boost is on, Edge remains running in the background when you close the browser window, allowing it to start up faster when you need it again.

At the top of this page is the Startup Boost feature, which loads the Edge browser at startup and keeps the core processes running in the background even when you close the browser. When you reopen a browser window, it should load nearly instantly thanks to those background processes. The impact on performance and resource usage is minimal, which means this feature is usable on all but the most resource-constrained systems.

On some systems, Startup Boost is disabled by default and can't be enabled because of conflicting extensions. (Ironically, one of those extensions is Microsoft's own Office add-in.) A button on the Edge Settings page allows you to shut down the conflicting extension to enable Startup Boost.

The second group of options appears under the Optimize Performance heading. One common complaint with web browsers is that activity on tabs running in the browser can use excessive amounts of power; that's especially unwelcome when using a laptop on battery power. Enabling *efficiency mode* helps minimize power usage and extend battery life. In efficiency mode, Edge puts background tabs to sleep after 5 minutes of inactivity (if the sleeping tabs feature is enabled) and also minimizes the impact of video playback and animations.

By default, efficiency mode is off. You can specify that you want to turn efficiency mode on by changing the Turn Efficiency Mode On setting. The most conservative setting is Unplugged, Low Battery, which kicks in this resource-saving mode only when the laptop battery hits the low battery setting (20%, by default).

Edge can also put tabs to sleep, leaving the tab in place but shutting down all background activity as a memory- and CPU-saving measure. This option is ideal if you like to keep large numbers of tabs open but don't want a runaway background process to slow down the rest of your system. Four options control this feature:

- **Save Resources With Sleeping Tabs**   This switch turns the feature on or off; if you set it to off, the remaining options are grayed out and unavailable.

- **Fade Sleeping Tabs**   With this feature enabled, you can tell at a glance which tabs are running in the background and which have been put to sleep.

- **Put Inactive Tabs To Sleep After The Specified Amount Of Time**   Choose an interval from the list here, ranging from extremely aggressive (30 seconds) to extremely generous (12 hours). A value of 30 minutes or 1 hour should be about right for most uses.

- **Never Put These Sites To Sleep**   Click the Add button to enter a specific address or domain whose pages are allowed to run in the background at all times.

Undoing all customizations

If Edge begins behaving unpredictably, one drastic but useful troubleshooting step is to reset all browser settings to their default values. This option is the only one on the Reset Settings page in Edge Settings. Doing so changes the startup page, the new tab page, and the default search engine to their default values; it also clears all cookies, removes any pinned tabs, and turns off (but does not remove) any extensions. Saved favorites, browsing history, and saved passwords remain intact.

Working with tabs

Like all modern browsers, Microsoft Edge allows you to keep multiple pages open at the same time, with each page occupying its own tab in the browser window. This feature is a tremendous timesaver for anyone doing research or trying to juggle multiple tasks. It's also a recipe for information overload, which is why Edge includes an assortment of features to help you switch between tabs and keep them organized.

CHAPTER 7

You can open a new tab in any of several ways. Note that most of these actions include keyboard shortcuts that are worth memorizing if you regularly juggle large numbers of tabs:

- To open a new tab, press Ctrl+T, or click the New Tab button, just to the right of the rightmost open tab.

- To open a link in a new tab without shifting focus from the current tab, right-click the link and choose Open Link In New Tab, or hold down Ctrl while you click the link.

- To open a link in a new tab and shift focus to the newly opened tab, hold down Ctrl+Shift as you click the link.

- To duplicate a tab, press Ctrl+Shift+K, or right-click the tab and choose Duplicate from the shortcut menu. Note that your new duplicate tab also includes the history associated with the original tab.

- To close any open tab, point to its tab heading and click the X at the right side. (Note that the X is hidden for all but the current tab once you open enough tabs.) To close the current tab, press Ctrl+W.

You can also use keyboard shortcuts to cycle between tabs: Press Ctrl+Tab to move from left to right or Ctrl+Shift+Tab to go from right to left. To reposition a tab within an array of tabs, drag the tab you want to move laterally. To peel a tab from the current browser window and make it appear in a new window, drag the tab away from the tab bar and release it.

You can also select multiple tabs, using the standard Windows shortcuts, Ctrl+click (to select a noncontiguous set of tabs) and Shift+click (for a contiguous set). After making a selection, right-click and choose the option to move those tabs to another window, or drag the selection out of the current window to open them in their own browser window. Right-click the selection to perform another action: Add the tabs to your favorites, add them to a collection, add them to a new tab group, or close them. Other options on the right-click menu include Close Other Tabs, which closes those you haven't selected, and Close Tabs To The Right, which lets you close sites you opened in new tabs if you tumbled innocently down a rabbit hole of browser tabs.

Inside OUT

Silence a noisy tab

There is nothing quite as frustrating as suddenly hearing sound blasting out of your PC's speakers because a webpage began automatically playing a video clip. If the sound is coming from the current page, you can press Ctrl+M to mute the audio. If you're not sure which page has decided to suddenly start screaming, yelling, or singing, scan the tab headings and look for a speaker icon, which indicates that sound is playing from that tab. Click that speaker icon to immediately mute the sound without having to open the tab itself. Click again to unmute the tab's audio stream.

Using vertical tabs

In the traditional, horizontal arrangement, browser tabs get narrower as the number of open tabs grows. Open enough tabs and they become so narrow that all you see is the page icon, with no title and no Close Tab button.

One solution to the too-many-tabs problem is a feature called Vertical Tabs, which moves the tabs from the top of the browser window to the left side. On a wide display, that arrangement allows you to see a meaningful portion of the title of each tab, with pinned tabs appearing at the top of the pane. Figure 7-18 shows the Microsoft Edge window after turning on vertical tabs.

Figure 7-18   Configuring tabs so they appear in a vertical list along the side allows you to see the full page title, even with a large number of tabs open.

To switch between horizontal and vertical tabs quickly, use the first option on the Tab Actions menu, which appears at the far left (or top) of the open tabs in Edge. If you find the appearance of that icon distracting, you can hide it by going to *edge://settings/appearance* and toggling the Show Tab Actions Menu to off. You can still switch between the two tab modes by using a keyboard shortcut: Ctrl+Shift+Comma (,).

Pinning tabs for quick access

If you want a particular tab to be available and easy to find every time you launch Microsoft Edge, the simplest solution is to pin that tab. Pinned tabs occupy a minuscule amount of visual space, with only an icon and no visible title, at the left of the row of tabs (or at the top of the column if you've turned on vertical tabs). Right-click any tab and choose Pin Tab to add it as a pinned tab. Right-click the pinned tab and choose Unpin Tab if you change your mind.

Yet another way to make a particular tab easily reusable is to pin it to the taskbar. To pin the currently open page to the taskbar, click Settings And More > More Tools > Pin To Taskbar.

Sites that can be installed as Progressive Web Apps (PWAs) can also be pinned to Start, by choosing Settings And More > Apps > Install This Site As An App. (For more details on how PWAs work, see Chapter 6.)

Making webpages easier to read

Microsoft Edge provides easy ways to make text and graphics on a webpage larger or smaller. If you're working on a touchscreen or on a device with a precision touchpad, you can zoom in and out with the standard touch gestures. Spread two fingers on a page to make the content larger; bring two fingers together to make it smaller.

The Zoom command on the Settings And More menu allows you to increase or decrease the size of the page in logical increments. With a wheel mouse, you can zoom in or out by holding down the Ctrl key as you roll the wheel forward or back. Zooming with the mouse wheel has the advantage of maintaining the position of whatever object you're pointing to when you begin zooming. Suppose, for example, that you're zooming in to get a better look at a graphical element lying near the right edge of the screen. If you use other zooming methods, the element you care about eventually drifts out of the window. However, if you zoom in by pointing to that element and then rolling the wheel, the element retains its position relative to your mouse pointer as it gets larger.

If you prefer the keyboard, you can use a pair of shortcuts to zoom in and out. Hold down Ctrl and press Plus (+, typically found to the left of the Backspace key) to increase magnification; hold down Ctrl and press Minus Sign (–) to zoom back out. Because the plus and minus keys are right next to one another, it's easy to hold down control and zoom in and out with precision. To return to normal (100%) magnification, press Ctrl+0.

Changes to display magnification are persistent on a per-site basis, so if you nearly always require a certain zoom level at a particular address, you can set it once and not have to worry about it again. Saved zoom levels for every site are saved at *edge://settings/content/zoomLevels*. To change zoom settings globally, go to *edge://settings/appearance* and choose a magnification percentage.

Zooming in is an excellent way to make small text easier on the eyes. But for more improvement in reading comfort, try the Immersive Reader in Microsoft Edge. This view removes distracting elements from a webpage and reformats the text so that you can focus on what you're trying to read. Immersive Reader is especially useful on pages that are cluttered with ads and where the designer has used type that's too small or has contrast problems with the background.

To display the current page in Immersive Reader view, click the Enter Immersive Reader icon, which resembles an open book; it's located near the right end of the address bar. An easier option is to press the keyboard shortcut, F9. To return to normal view, click the Immersive Reader icon again or click Back.

Inside OUT

Force a page into Immersive Reader view to bypass annoying pop-ups

Some website publishers try to discourage casual viewing of their pages by anyone who's not a subscriber, often by truncating the article after a few paragraphs and displaying a pop-up asking you to sign in. Sometimes these pop-ups represent a paywall for which there's no easy workaround. But for many publishers, the interruption is little more than a speed bump. In those cases, you can try clicking the Immersive Reader icon to see if the full page loads.

If the Immersive Reader icon is not available, you might be able to force the page to display in that view by typing *read://* at the front of the URL, with no space afterward. Leave the original page URL intact, including the *https://* portion.

Figure 7-19 shows the same page in normal display (left) and with Immersive Reader on (right). Note the Reader Mode icon where the Site Information icon normally appears at the left of the address bar.

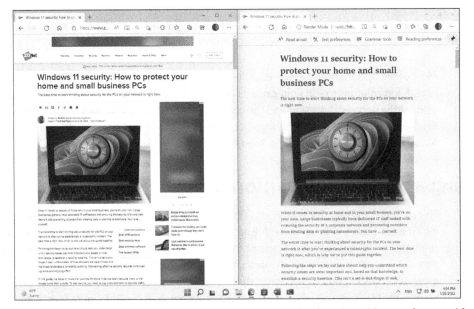

Figure 7-19   Press F9 to turn a busy webpage into a streamlined version with text reformatted for readability.

A toolbar appears at the top of the window in Reader Mode. (If the toolbar is hidden, move the mouse pointer to the top of the page until it slides down. Click the pushpin icon to pin

CHAPTER 7

the toolbar in place so it doesn't automatically hide.) Click Text Preferences to customize the appearance of the page, as shown in Figure 7-20.

Figure 7-20   In Reader Mode, you can choose a font, adjust text size and spacing, and select a color scheme for the text and background.

Most of the options here are self-explanatory. Choose a font and adjust the size and spacing of text and columns to suit your preferences. Under Page Themes are five options to adjust the color of the page background and the contrasting text. If reading is still a challenge, you can ask Reading View to read to you. Turn on your speakers or connect your headset and click the Read Aloud button on the toolbar. (The Read Aloud option is also available for PDF files.)

Finding and organizing information

This section covers the tools built into the Microsoft Edge browser that allow you to track down information on the web using the full array of online search tools and then organize, reuse, and share those results as needed. Some of these tools are familiar, like the favorites that have been part of Microsoft browsers for a quarter century. You can organize favorites into folders or use a new alternative called Collections, which is found only in Edge. But the most obvious starting point is the place you go when you don't know where to go: your favorite search engine.

Changing the default search provider

You don't need to go directly to a search engine to find information in Microsoft Edge. If you use one of Microsoft's layouts for the new tab page, you can open a tab and enter your request in the search box on that page. Even easier is to just start typing in the address bar. When you use the address bar in this fashion, the browser offers autocomplete suggestions as you type, along with trending topics and a list of matching sites from your browsing history.

On a clean installation of Windows 11, Microsoft's Bing is, unsurprisingly, the default search provider. With a few simple steps, you can change the default to one of the predefined alternatives. From Edge Settings, choose the Privacy, Search, And Services tab. Scroll to the bottom of the page and click Address Bar And Search. (If that seems like too much work, go directly to *edge:// settings/search*.) Your options are shown in Figure 7-21.

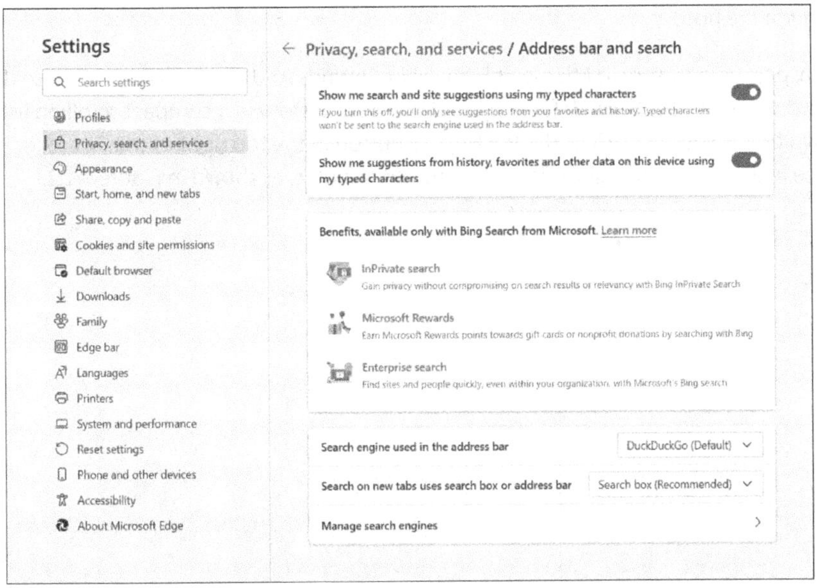

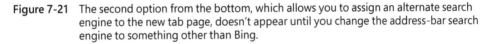

Figure 7-21   The second option from the bottom, which allows you to assign an alternate search engine to the new tab page, doesn't appear until you change the address-bar search engine to something other than Bing.

If you find the autocomplete suggestions distracting, the top two options on this page allow you to turn off search suggestions and suggestions from your history and favorites, respectively.

Your options for the Search Engine Used In The Address Bar setting include some familiar names, including Google and Yahoo as well as the privacy-focused DuckDuckGo. To add a search provider that supports the OpenSearch standard but isn't on the default list, go to the search provider's website and search for anything; that action is enough to add the new provider to the list of available search engines.

Changing the source of search results from the address bar doesn't affect the search box on Microsoft's new tab page, which continues to use Bing even after you make the change. When you select a search engine other than Bing, a second option appears: Search On New Tabs Uses

Search Box Or Address Bar. Set this option to Address Bar to make both locations match. (Note that this setting has no effect on what you type in the search box on the Windows taskbar.)

Finding previously visited pages in History

Microsoft Edge maintains a local history of the sites you visit; this history is saved separately for each profile you create in Edge. For profiles where you're signed in to a Microsoft account or an Azure Active Directory account, Edge maintains a separate history and syncs that list to all instances of Edge where you're signed in and syncing with that account. If you need to return to a site and you neglected to add it to your favorites, you should be able to find it by searching through the history.

To inspect your history in Microsoft Edge, click Settings And More > History, or use the keyboard shortcut Ctrl+H. By default, Edge shows your history in a compact scrolling list that drops down from the toolbar. Click the Pin History button in the top right of that list to lock it into place in a pane on the right side of the browser window, as shown in Figure 7-22.

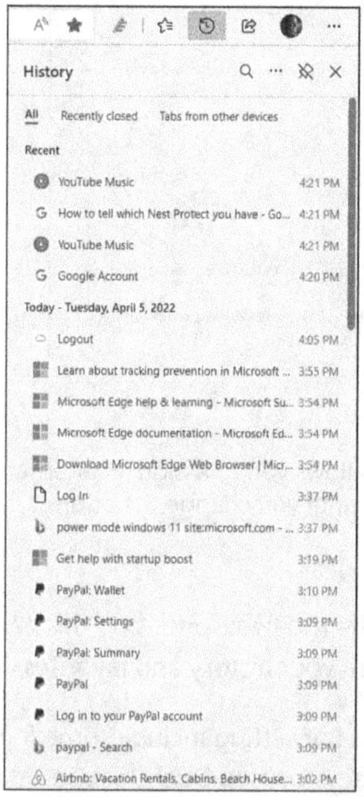

Figure 7-22   Clicking the All tab combines your local and synced browsing history and displays the results in reverse chronological order. This list is pinned to the right side of the browser window.

The list is arranged in three tabs, with the All tab shown by default; it combines local and synced history lists, presenting the joint results in descending chronological order, using relative dates and times for headings: Recent, Today, Yesterday, Last Week, and so on. The Recently Closed tab displays a short list of local pages that you can reopen if necessary, while the Tabs From Other Devices list shows your history from other synced devices, with the history arranged by device in reverse chronological order.

You might be able to find a page by scrolling through the list, especially if your visit was relatively recent. For a more targeted search, try clicking the Search History button (the magnifying glass icon) and entering a word or a snippet of text to find entries that include the search text in the page title or the URL. Enclose the search text in quotes to find a specific phrase; if you enter the words separately without quotes, Edge returns results for any page that includes all the specified words.

If you find a page of interest, right-click its entry in the list to display a shortcut menu of options that allows you to open the page in a new tab or a new window, copy the page link to the Clipboard, or delete the item from your history. The final item on the shortcut menu, More From The Same Site, allows you to filter the History list to show only pages from the same domain as the one you selected.

From the All list, you can delete any entry by hovering the mouse pointer over it until an X appears at the right of the item. Click that X to permanently remove the page from your history.

The More Options menu, indicated by three dots to the right of the Search History button, offers three interesting options. The first, Open History Page, displays your history in a full-page view that includes a search box and controls for filtering by date. The second option, Clear Browsing Data, erases your local history, completely and irrevocably. The final option, Show History Button In Toolbar, offers an additional way to quickly open and close the history list.

Saving, editing, and organizing Favorites

Like every modern browser, Microsoft Edge allows you to build a repository of favorite webpages—destinations that you know or suspect you'll want to return to now and then—and organize that collection into folders. Once a page has been designated a favorite, you can reopen it with only a few clicks instead of having to search for it again or pull it up from your browsing history.

To add a shortcut for the current page to the favorites list, click the star at the right side of the address bar in Microsoft Edge, or use the keyboard shortcut Ctrl+D. As Figure 7-23 shows, that action opens the Edit Favorite dialog, where you can change the name to something descriptive and move the link to an existing folder. (Click More to see a full list of folders and create a new folder, if necessary.) Click Done to save your changes.

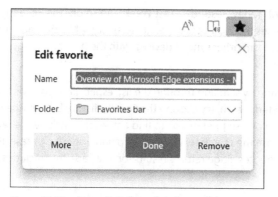

Figure 7-23   Press Ctrl+D or click the star icon at the right of the address bar to add or remove a page from your Favorites list.

Inside OUT

Always rename favorites

Get in the habit of assigning a descriptive name when you save a favorite. Make sure the name you choose contains the words your future self is likely to use as search terms. Steer clear of extra-long file names. Web designers often create outrageously long page titles, packing descriptions and keywords together with the goal of ranking higher on search engines, and that name is entered automatically as the default for a new favorite you create. Shorter, more meaningful names are easier to spot when you're scrolling through a folder full of favorites. And speaking of folders, by all means use them to categorize your favorites. The more favorites you accumulate, the happier you'll be that you have them organized.

The Favorites Bar is a special folder whose contents can be displayed below the address bar in Microsoft Edge. (Think of this location as your favorite favorites.) By default, it's hidden. To make it visible, click Settings And More > Favorites > More Options > Show Favorites Bar. Or use the keyboard shortcut Ctrl+Shift+B to show and hide the Favorites Bar.

The easiest way to access your saved favorites is to start typing in the address bar. Any matching favorites display at the top of the list. To see the entire list, click the Favorites button on the toolbar. You can also get to the favorites list by pressing Ctrl+Shift+O. From that same page, you can search for Favorites using the search box at the top of the page.

Click a favorite to launch it in the current tab. Hold down Ctrl as you click to open the link in a new tab (or right-click the link and then click Open In New Tab). Hold down Shift and click to open the link in a new window. The menu that appears when you right-click also gives you the means to rename or remove a shortcut as well as an option to edit the URL associated with each saved favorite. Right-click any empty space in the Favorites list to create a new folder on the fly or sort the list by name.

If you are switching from another browser to Microsoft Edge, you might have favorites or bookmarks that you want to import. If you've exported those bookmarks to a file, go to *edge://settings/profiles/importBrowsingData*. Click Choose What To Import, select the exported file from the dropdown at the top, choose the data you want to add to your Edge profile, and then click Import.

Saving and sharing your research as Collections

Collections are a signature feature of Microsoft Edge, offering a way to save and share research that's unlike anything in any other modern browser. Collections are an ideal solution for researching travel, purchases, projects, and school papers. Superficially, they resemble folders full of favorites, with content appearing in a pane that drops down from the toolbar and can be pinned to the right of the main browser window. Unlike a folder full of favorites, however, collections can include more than just simple links. Figure 7-24 shows a collection containing research collected ahead of a new car purchase.

Figure 7-24   Collections consist of cards that you can drag to rearrange. You can save images, snippets of text, product details, or even notes.

Collections consist of cards, each of which contains a discrete piece of data you want to collect. You can add entire pages by clicking Add Current Page from the top of the Collections pane.

CHAPTER 7

Doing so creates a card with a link and a thumbnail of the webpage. You can also drag a link or a snippet of text from a webpage to the Collections pane to save it directly, along with a link you can click to return to the source page. Right-click just about any web-based content, including images, and use the Add To Collections menu to save it as part of an existing collection or start a new one.

Clicking the Add Note icon at the top of the Collections pane opens a yellow sticky note. There, you can change the font, add bullets, or add headers using the toolbar at the top of the note. When you're ready to save the note, click Save.

To create a new collection from scratch, click the Collections button on the toolbar, and then click the Start A New Collection link at the top of the Collections pane. If you've already begun doing some research in the current Edge window, use Ctrl+click to select a group of tabs, right-click to display a menu, and then click Add All Tabs To Collections.

You can drag collections in the Collections pane to the order you prefer and drag cards in a collection to reorder them. Hover the mouse pointer over a card to display a checkbox in the upper-right corner. Select that box (and repeat the process for other cards, if necessary) to display a toolbar that allows you to copy, share, or delete the selected items.

Collections integrate well with Microsoft Office apps. When you choose the option to share a selection or an entire collection, the menu options shown in Figure 7-25 appear. You can share using Excel, OneNote, or Word. You can also open, copy, or paste the cards in your collection in just about any target, including another collection.

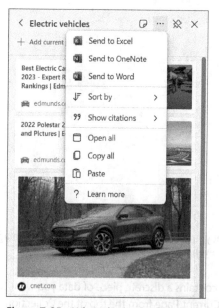

Figure 7-25   When sharing a collection, you can send selected items to key Office apps, making it possible to create a tidy report with minimal effort.

Managing privacy and tracking prevention

The beauty of the web is that you can use it to connect instantly to an almost unlimited world of information. The bad news is that some of those destinations are potentially dangerous to your PC's health and to your privacy.

There's no way to make the web perfectly safe, but Windows 11 does include features that help you minimize concerns over security and privacy.

If you care about online security, one smart practice you should adopt for everyday browsing is to prefer a secure connection (HTTPS) even on sites that don't traditionally require it. Insecure links to seemingly harmless destinations can leak information about you and can also be used to spoof sites, potentially compromising a machine using a man-in-the-middle attack. All modern browsers, including Microsoft Edge, flag the addresses of sites that are insecure as well as those that contain a mix of secure and insecure content (look for a Not Secure label where you would normally see the padlock icon in the address bar). In that spirit, we have gone out of our way in this book to use HTTPS links. In this section, we focus primarily on features that are unique to web browsing.

Unless you go to extraordinary lengths, such as using a virtual private network for every browser session, simply connecting to a webpage reveals information about your PC, your internet service provider, and your general location. When combined with other details, even a single, seemingly harmless visit to a webpage can become part of your permanent online profile, used by companies and organizations you've never heard of. Privacy advocates have demonstrated repeatedly that even anonymized data can create a profile that can identify you just as surely as if you had left a fingerprint behind.

You can't completely disappear online, but you can take some commonsense precautions to cover your tracks and avoid disclosing too much about yourself.

Preventing online tracking

Some websites use *tracking* capabilities to gather information about your browsing history, information you enter in your browser, and other details of your online life to build a profile that companies can use for targeted advertising and other purposes. If that bothers you, you can order Microsoft Edge to prevent certain types of tracking. To set your preferences, use the Tracking Prevention tools at the top of the Privacy, Search, And Services tab in Edge Settings. Figure 7-26 shows the three options available for this feature.

CHAPTER 7

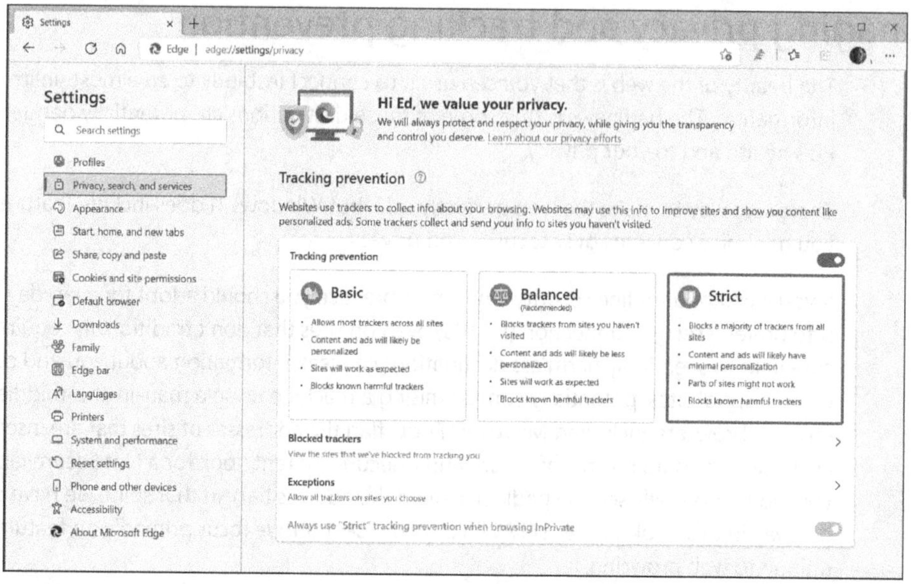

Figure 7-26   By default, Tracking Prevention is set to Balanced. Choosing the Strict option effectively turns this feature into an ad blocker and may cause problems for some sites.

The Tracking Prevention feature in Microsoft Edge uses open source tracking protection lists to classify online trackers and group them into categories. These "Trust Protection Lists" are maintained by Disconnect, a firm based in San Francisco, California. (The most recent version is available for inspection at *https://github.com/disconnectme/disconnect-tracking-protection*.) These lists are downloaded automatically and stored locally; Edge uses them to prevent resources that are defined as trackers from storing resources or accessing stored resources. (For a detailed discussion of how this feature works, see the Microsoft Docs article, "Tracking Prevention in Microsoft Edge," at *https://docs.microsoft.com/microsoft-edge/web-platform/tracking-prevention*.)

The three available Tracking Prevention levels work as follows:

- **Basic**   This is the least restrictive level, allowing almost all trackers and blocking only malicious trackers such as those that attempt to perform unauthorized cryptomining. If you use a third-party ad-blocking tool, this setting might be appropriate.

- **Balanced**   The default level blocks trackers from sites that you haven't visited directly while minimizing the risk of compatibility issues.

- **Strict**   Turning on this setting delivers the maximum privacy benefit and effectively turns the Tracking Prevention feature into an ad-blocking tool. In the process, you can expect some webpages to break.

By default, Tracking Prevention is set to the Balanced level. With that setting on, you'll still see a fair number of ads, but most third-party tracking is blocked. Turning the setting up to Strict can break some web functionality and will subject you to lots of "please disable your ad blocker" messages.

You can see which trackers have been blocked and turn this feature on or off for an individual website by clicking the padlock button and using the controls at the bottom of the information pane for that page. To see a list of all the trackers that have been blocked, go to *edge://settings/privacy/blockedTrackers*.

Inside OUT

Don't bother sending Do Not Track requests

An impressive group of web experts and privacy advocates spent years developing the Do Not Track (DNT) standard, under the auspices of a committee of the World Wide Web Consortium (W3C). The underlying concept is simple: If DNT is enabled, the browser sends a DNT=1 header with every request for a new page. That header serves as a formal request: "Do not track me."

Alas, this seemingly straightforward option was not widely accepted, and the final version of the standard is toothless, backed by no technical or legal enforcement mechanisms. You'll find a Send "Do Not Track" Requests switch on the Privacy, Search, And Services tab in Edge Settings, but because DNT is universally ignored, turning it on or off has no practical effect.

Using InPrivate browsing to suppress your history

If you want to cover your local tracks only for a particular browsing session, don't bother fussing with history settings or clearing items after the fact. Instead, open an InPrivate window. During an InPrivate session, Microsoft Edge keeps all your browsing data (including history, cookies, and cached images) in temporary storage and clears it completely when you close the last InPrivate window. An InPrivate session allows you to access favorites, saved passwords, and form data from the profile where you started. Any files you download are retained, although the download history is cleared.

To open an InPrivate window, click Settings And More > New InPrivate Window, or use the keyboard shortcut Ctrl+Shift+N. Any additional InPrivate windows you open are part of the same session. When you close the last InPrivate window, the browser ends the session and deletes browsing data it stored (session cookies and other temporary files, for example). No record of the visit is saved in history.

Be aware that browsing privately is different from browsing anonymously. Sites you visit can record your IP address, and your network administrator or internet service provider (which includes anyone in control of a public Wi-Fi hotspot) can see which sites you connect to and can capture any unencrypted information you transmit or receive.

You can allow or prohibit the use of extensions in InPrivate mode on a per-extension basis, as described in "Installing and managing browser extensions," earlier in this chapter.

Controlling site permissions

Microsoft Edge includes a dizzying array of permissions that you can configure to control how webpages interact with your PC. To see the full list, go to the Cookies And Site Permissions page at *edge://settings/content*. There, you can adjust global options for Cookies And Data Stored and Site Permissions, including access to your camera and microphone. You might decide, for example, that you don't want any websites to disturb you with notifications, ever, so you can set the Notifications permission to block all such requests.

One of the most useful settings in this group is the Media Autoplay switch, which normally is set to allow any site to start playing a video or audio clip when you arrive. Go to *edge://settings/content/mediaAutoplay* and confirm that this option is set to Limit.

To adjust settings for a specific site, click the padlock icon at the left of the address bar and then click Permissions For This Site.

Clearing your browsing history and other personal information

Your browser keeps a copy of webpages, images, and media you've viewed recently. This cached information is saved to generally inaccessible locations, but even so, it might give someone with physical access to your computer more information than you might want them to have—especially when combined with cookies, saved form data, saved passwords, and other details.

To wipe away most of your online trail in Microsoft Edge, open the Privacy, Search, And Services tab in Edge Settings. Then, under the Clear Browsing Data heading, click Choose What To Clear. These steps take you to the set of checkboxes shown in Figure 7-27.

Before specifying the types of data you want to clean and prune, you can restrict the data to be cleared by choosing one of the options on the Time Range menu: Last Hour, Last 24 Hours, Last 7 Days, Last 4 Weeks, or All Time. If you were researching possible birthday gifts for a household member who occasionally uses your computer, for example, you might want to delete all or part of your browsing data for the past week to avoid accidentally spoiling the surprise.

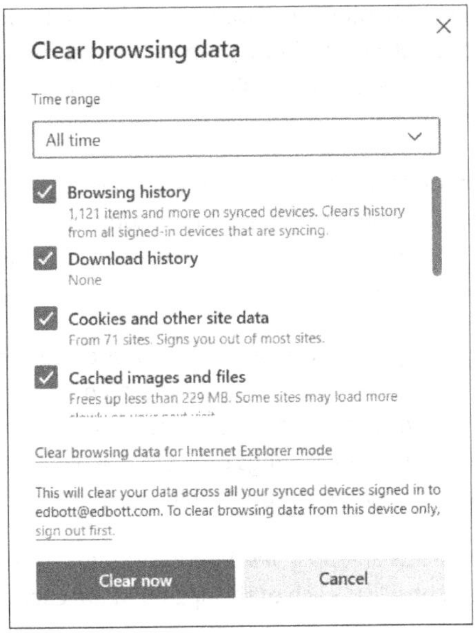

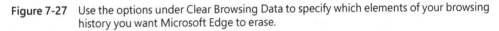

Figure 7-27   Use the options under Clear Browsing Data to specify which elements of your browsing history you want Microsoft Edge to erase.

In addition, be aware that if you're signed in and syncing data to a Microsoft account, the data you clear here may also be removed from other devices that sign in to that account. To remove only local data, sign out first.

After attending to those details, you can choose from the following types of data to clear:

- **Browsing History**   This is simply a list of sites you've been to since you last cleared your history, whether you went to them directly or followed another site's hyperlinks. You can also view this list from the History list and delete individual entries there. (For details, see "Finding previously visited pages in History," earlier in this chapter.)

- **Download History**   This is the list that appears on the Downloads page. Deleting this history here (or clicking Clear All at the top of the Downloads list) does not remove the downloads themselves, which remain where you put them.

- **Cookies And Other Site Data**   A *cookie* is a small text file that enables a website to store persistent information on your hard disk. Cookies, particularly first-party cookies, are generally benign and useful. Note that removing cookies via this option does not block their arrival in the future. (To do that, see "Managing cookies" later in this chapter.)

- **Cached Images And Files**   These are local copies of pages and media content from sites you visit. The browser saves local copies of this data to speed up its display on subsequent visits.

- **Passwords**   As discussed earlier in this chapter (see "Using the built-in password manager"), there are pros and cons associated with saving sign-in credentials for websites. If you switch to a third-party password manager after you've allowed the browser to store some credentials, you can erase the data here.

- **Autofill Form Data (Includes Forms And Cards)**   Your browser allows you to store some address information—for example, your shipping or email address—as well as credit card details. Using this saved information makes it more convenient to fill out forms. This option erases saved entries for the selected period.

- **Site Permissions**   When you visit a webpage, it can request permission to perform specific actions, such as delivering notifications, switching to full screen, or using your location for personalization. Click this checkbox to remove all saved permissions, or click Manage Permissions to review and modify these settings on a per-site basis. You can browse the full list of saved permissions by going to *edge://settings/content*.

- **Hosted App Data**   Installing a website as an app gives it permission to store some data for its own use. The text beneath this entry lists each of the apps that are capable of storing app data.

- **All Data From The Previous Version Of Microsoft Edge**   This option is available only on devices that have been updated from legacy Edge to the newer Chromium-based Edge. After clearing this data, the option is no longer available.

- **Media Foundation Data**   This data is used to authorize playback of copy-protected digital media.

After making your selections, click Clear. To automatically clear a specific type of browsing data every time you shut down the browser or sign out, go back to Edge Settings and click Choose What To Clear Every Time You Close The Browser. That leads to a page with on-off switches for the first seven data types listed above.

Managing cookies

Cookies—small bits of information that websites store on your hard disk—come in two flavors. First-party cookies are used by the site you're currently visiting, generally for such purposes as personalizing your experience with the site, storing shopping-cart information, and so on. Third-party cookies are used by a site other than the one you're visiting—such as an advertising network or social media service that has placed an ad or a sharing button on the site you're currently visiting.

Cookies do not carry executable code (they're text files), and they can't be used to spread viruses or malware. A cookie can provide a website only with information you supply while visiting the site; a cookie has no access to the Windows file system and can't read any of your personal information, including your address book or financial records. The information a cookie gathers can be read only by pages in the same domain as the one that created the cookie.

Nevertheless, privacy concerns arise when advertisers and web-analytics companies begin to correlate the information from third-party cookies to build a profile of your activities. Because it's not always obvious who's sending you a cookie and what purposes that cookie serves, some people are understandably wary about allowing cookies on their systems.

The most effective way to block this form of tracking is with the use of the Tracking Prevention feature in Microsoft Edge (described earlier in this chapter), or with third-party ad-blocking software. You can, however, set global cookie policies from the Cookies And Site Permissions page in Edge Settings. To review and allow or block cookies from the current webpage, click the padlock icon to the left of the address bar and then click Cookies. That opens a dialog like the one in Figure 7-28.

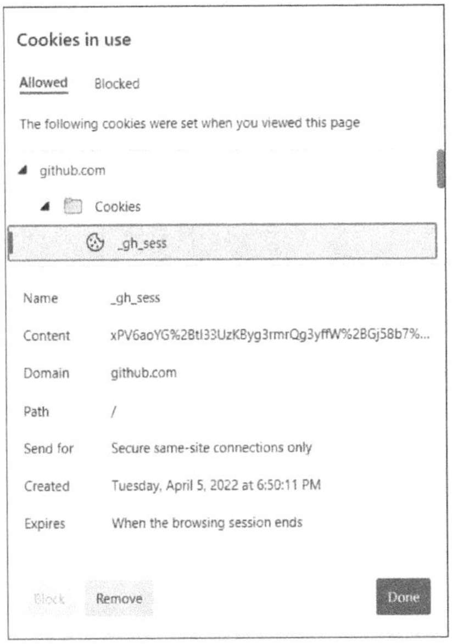

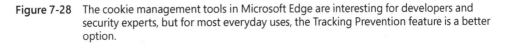

Figure 7-28   The cookie management tools in Microsoft Edge are interesting for developers and security experts, but for most everyday uses, the Tracking Prevention feature is a better option.

If you're having troubles with a specific page, you might be able to troubleshoot that page by removing cookies for that page. Open the dialog shown earlier in Figure 7-28, select one or more cookies from the list, and click Remove. Then try reloading the page.

Opening incompatible pages in Internet Explorer mode

Microsoft has officially retired the Internet Explorer 11 browser for Windows. It's not included with a clean install of Windows 11, and there's no supported way to add it.

Aside from a slight twinge of nostalgia, there's little reason for most people to care about the absence of Internet Explorer. Modern webpages are designed for modern browsers, including Microsoft Edge, and there are few sites on the open web that still require Internet Explorer.

The one place where that obsolete browser still has a role to play is on corporate networks, where web-based apps written many years ago are still used daily and are unlikely to be updated. In some cases, those apps rely on features that are unsupported by any modern browser. For those sites, Edge offers Internet Explorer (IE) mode, which opens those legacy web apps in specialized tabs that use the older Trident rendering engine and support Internet Explorer features such as ActiveX controls and Browser Helper Objects. Sites that are loaded in IE mode open in tabs within the Edge browser, distinguished only by a small logo in the address bar, as shown in Figure 7-29.

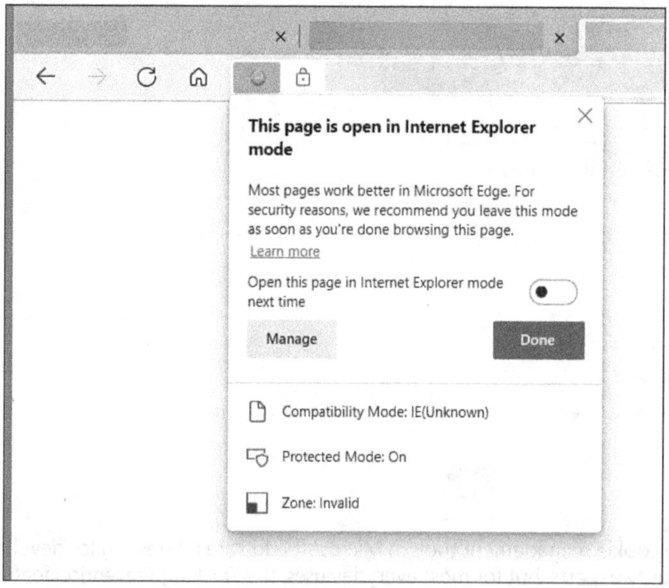

Figure 7-29   When you encounter a page that requires Internet Explorer, you can reload it in IE mode.

In a corporate setting, administrators can define a list of specific sites using group policy so that Edge automatically opens those pages using IE mode. On Windows computers installed in homes and small businesses and not managed using group policy, you can reload specific pages in IE mode if you encounter compatibility problems with Edge and suspect that the page was originally written for the older browser. The Reload In Internet Explorer Mode option is on the Settings And More menu. If you don't see this option, go to Edge Settings and look at the options on the Default Browser page, specifically the Allow Sites To Be Reloaded In Internet Explorer Mode options. Change this setting to Allow and restart the browser to make that menu option available; set it to Don't Allow if you never want to open a page in IE mode.

Using Microsoft Edge to read and edit PDFs

On a clean installation, Windows 11 sets Microsoft Edge as the default reader for PDF files. When you download a file in PDF format, it opens in the Edge window with a toolbar like the one shown in Figure 7-30. You can use those tools to rotate, zoom, print, save, and annotate the file.

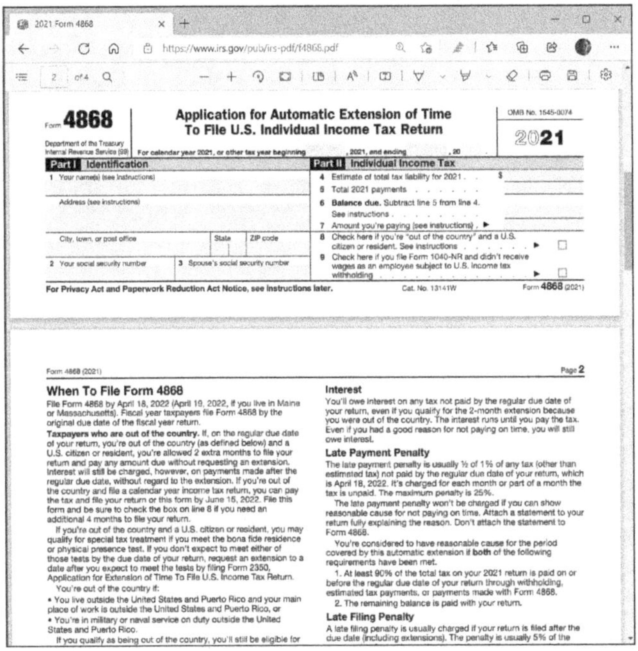

Figure 7-30   You can fill in a PDF-based form in Edge using a mouse and keyboard, but the drawing and marking tools work best on a PC with pen support.

Edge allows you to fill in forms for documents that have been created with that feature enabled and saved as a PDF file. You can also use the tools on the PDF toolbar to draw on the document (good for adding signatures) and highlight portions of the document using a digital marker in one of five colors. Use the Print and Save buttons to preserve a copy of the document after you've filled in a form or annotated it.

CHAPTER 8

Managing local and cloud storage

The late, great comic George Carlin once observed, "All you need in life is a little place for your stuff." Unless you use your computer exclusively as a game machine, learning to manage your digital "stuff"—your documents, programs, and communications—is probably the single most critical computing skill you need to acquire. The addition of cloud services adds extra flexibility as well as new organizational challenges, especially as you juggle multiple devices with different storage capacities.

In this chapter, we cover how to set up and manage the places where we put all that stuff: old-fashioned hard drives, fast solid-state drives, and removable devices that make it possible to move stuff from one device to another. (We get to the tools and techniques for managing and organizing those files in Chapter 9, "Using File Explorer.")

In the modern era, there's also the option to put your stuff in the cloud, where it's accessible from any device with an internet connection. Microsoft's cloud storage service, OneDrive, offers a generous allotment of storage with every free Microsoft account and much more with a Microsoft 365 subscription. Its sync engine, built into Windows 11, allows you to browse through your cloud storage without having to fill all of your local storage. In this chapter, we explain how to configure OneDrive so that your most important files are available when you need them, even if you're not connected to the internet.

Finally, this chapter also covers the tools and techniques for working with existing local drives—internal, external, and removable—including managing volumes and monitoring disk usage.

Setting up hard disks and other storage devices

Like its predecessors, Windows 11 includes two tools that are useful for setting up a new storage device:

- **Disk Management**   This console offers a graphical interface for initializing, partitioning, and formatting storage devices. It's accessible from the Quick Link menu, which appears when you right-click Start or press Windows key+X.

- **DiskPart**   For those who need to incorporate disk-management tasks in scripts or who simply prefer carrying out administrative tasks using a command line, Windows also provides this utility, which is in the Windows\System32 folder.

Everything you can do with Disk Management you can also do by using DiskPart; you just have to work harder and more carefully.

➤ The Windows 11 Settings app includes some additional tools for inspecting the properties of storage devices, managing disk usage by category, and cleaning up unwanted files. We cover these options later in this chapter.

Knowing when to use which tool is the secret of disk wizardry in Windows 10 and Windows 11. Disk Management, for example, is ideal for shrinking and expanding volumes, whereas the Clean command in DiskPart makes short work of preparing a disk to be formatted for a new role. That command has no counterpart in Disk Management.

In this section, we cover the commands required to prepare a new drive for use on a Windows PC and to maintain and reconfigure existing storage devices.

Running Disk Management

To run Disk Management, type **diskmgmt.msc** at a command prompt; as an alternative, you can press Windows key+X (or right-click the Start button) and then click Disk Management on the Quick Link menu. If you're signed in with a standard account, you need to supply administrative credentials. Figure 8-1 shows the Disk Management console on a typical PC, with two fixed disks and one removable drive.

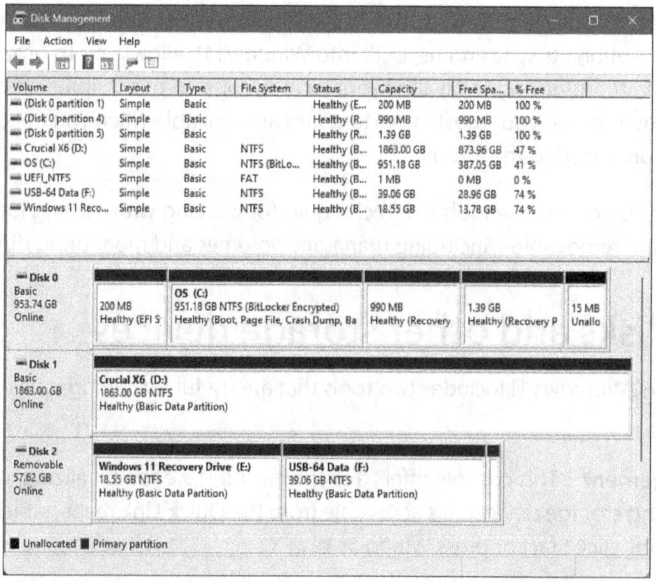

Figure 8-1   Use the Disk Management console to gather information about and manage fixed and removable disk drives.

Disk Management provides a wealth of information about physical disks and the volumes, partitions, and logical drives in place on those disks. You can use this utility to perform the following disk-related tasks:

- Check the size, file system, status, and other properties of disks and volumes.

- Create, format, and delete volumes, partitions, and logical drives.

- Assign drive letters to hard disk volumes, removable disk drives, and optical drives.

- Create mounted drives.

- Extend or shrink a volume.

UNDERSTANDING DISK-MANAGEMENT TERMINOLOGY

Most of the tasks you're likely to perform using Disk Management are fairly straightforward, but if you poke around long enough, you'll undoubtedly encounter the arcane language of disk administration. The following terms and concepts are the most important:

- **Basic disk and dynamic disk**   In modern versions of Windows, every fixed disk is set up as a basic disk. All volumes on a basic disk must be simple volumes. Older versions of Windows, especially servers, offered a second option called a dynamic disk, which can contain spanned or striped volumes that combine space from multiple disks. Although this disk type is still available for compatibility reasons in Windows 11, it is formally deprecated, and we expect that very few of our readers will ever use dynamic disks.

- **Partition style**   On devices that are set up using the Unified Extensible Firmware Interface (UEFI)—which includes all devices that meet the minimum standards for running Windows 11—the hard drive that includes the Windows partition must be formatted using a GUID Partition Table (GPT) file system. On legacy BIOS-based devices, all drives must be formatted using a Master Boot Record (MBR) file system. A GPT drive can hold up to 128 partitions; an MBR drive can hold up to four partitions, including an extended partition that uses all remaining unallocated space on the disk and can be further subdivided into as many logical partitions as the disk can hold.

- **Volume**   A volume is a disk or subdivision of a disk that is formatted with a file system and available for storage. On basic disks, primary partitions and logical drives within extended partitions are known as *basic volumes* (in Disk Management, these are known as *simple volumes*). When a volume is assigned a drive letter, it appears as a separate entity in File Explorer. A basic hard disk can have one or more basic volumes.

- **Mounted drive**   A mounted drive is an NTFS-formatted volume (which may be a single primary partition occupying an entire physical disk) that is mapped to an empty folder on a different NTFS-formatted disk. A mounted drive does not get its own drive letter and does not appear separately in File Explorer. Instead, it appears in the file system as though it were a subfolder on another drive.

CHAPTER 8

- **Spanned volume and striped volume**   On a dynamic disk, a spanned volume is a volume that combines space from physically separate disks to function as though it were a single storage medium, and a striped volume is one in which data is stored in 64-KB strips across physically separate disks to improve performance. Both types are now deprecated, and Microsoft recommends using Storage Spaces (described later in this chapter in the "Using Storage Spaces to combine disks" section) for configurations that use multiple drives to provide resiliency against drive failure.

- **System partition**   The system partition contains the bootstrap files that Windows uses to start your system and display the boot menu. On a GPT drive, this function is carried out by the EFI System Partition (ESP); it is at least 100 MB in size, formatted using the FAT32 file format, and managed by the operating system. On an MBR drive, the system partition is also at least 100 MB in size and must be set as active.

- **Windows partition**   This partition, which must be formatted as NTFS, is where the Windows operating system files are located.

- **Microsoft reserved partition (MSR)**   This partition is required on GPT drives to help with partition management. It is at least 16 MB in size but does not receive a partition ID and cannot be seen using the disk management tools in Windows 11.

- **Recovery tools partition**   On new installations, this partition is at least 300 MB in size (hardware OEMs may create a larger recovery partition to accommodate additional tools). It includes the Windows Recovery image and is always in a separate partition from the one where Windows system files are located.

Disk Management displays information in two panes. In its default arrangement, the upper pane lists each volume on your system and provides information about the volume's type, status, capacity, available free space, and so on. You can carry out commands on a volume by right-clicking any entry in the first column of this pane (the column labeled Volume) and choosing a command.

In the lower pane, each row represents one physical device. The heading at the left of each row shows the name by which that device is known to the operating system (Disk 0, Disk 1, and so on), along with its type, size, and status. To the right are areas that display information about the volumes of each device. Note that these areas are not by default drawn to scale. To change the scaling used by Disk Management, click View and then Settings. You find various options on the Scaling tab of the Settings dialog.

Right-clicking one of the headings at the left in the lower pane (labeled by a disk number) displays commands pertinent to an entire storage device. Right-clicking an area representing a volume provides a menu of actions applicable to that volume.

Managing disks from the command prompt

To use DiskPart, start by running Windows PowerShell or Command Prompt (Cmd.exe) with admin privileges.

➤ For more information about PowerShell and Cmd.exe, see Chapter 16, "Windows Terminal, PowerShell, and other advanced management tools."

When you run DiskPart, it switches to a command interpreter, identified by the DISKPART> prompt. If you type **help** and press Enter, you see a screen that lists all available commands.

Even if you prefer to avoid the command line and don't intend to write disk-management scripts, you should know about DiskPart. Consider it an essential survival skill: If you ever find yourself needing to manage hard disks from the Windows Recovery Environment (Windows RE), you will have access to DiskPart, but you won't have access to the Disk Management console. (Windows RE is a special environment you can use for system-recovery purposes if a major hardware or software problem prevents you from starting Windows.)

CAUTION

DiskPart is not for casual experimentation. Its primary purpose is for scripting rather than for interactive use. The DiskPart command-line interpreter is dense and cryptic, with a complex structure that requires you to list and select objects before you act on them. For more details about DiskPart, see "DiskPart Commands" (*https://bit.ly/diskpart-commands*). The details about the syntax and usage of DiskPart in this article are invaluable.

Setting up a new hard disk

Whether you're installing Windows on a brand-new disk or simply adding a new disk (internal or external) to an existing system, you should consider how you want to use the new storage space before you begin creating volumes. If your goal is to set up a large space for backup or media storage, for example, you might want to devote the entire disk to a single volume. On the other hand, if your plan is to establish two or more separate volumes—one for Windows system files and another for data files, for example—decide how many gigabytes you want to assign to each partition. You can change your mind later, but it's easiest to adjust the number of volumes on a disk and their relative sizes before you fill a volume with a large amount of data.

Installing Windows on a new disk

When you run the Windows 11 Setup program on a computer with a single, raw hard disk (such as a desktop computer you built yourself from new parts or any PC in which you've replaced the system drive or completely wiped its partitioning details), you're presented with a screen identifying the disk and its size. If you want to create a single volume encompassing the entire disk, you can click Next to proceed, and Setup takes care of initializing the disk, creating a new volume, and formatting it. Otherwise, you can click New, and then in the same screen, you can choose the size of the volume you want to create for your Windows installation.

If you decide not to use the entire disk capacity for the Windows system drive, you can create additional volumes from within the Setup program. But there's no particular need to do this. After you install Windows, you can use Disk Management to create one or more additional volumes in the unallocated space remaining on the disk.

➤ For more information about setting up Windows, see Chapter 2, "Setting up a new Windows 11 PC."

Adding a new disk to an existing Windows installation

When you open Disk Management for the first time after installing a new hard disk, Windows offers to initialize the disk, as shown in Figure 8-2. (If you don't see this dialog automatically, or if you dismissed it earlier, you can force it to appear by right-clicking the box to the left of the disk in Disk Management's lower pane and clicking Initialize Disk.) This action defines the partition style for the disk and is an essential first step before you can use Disk Management to perform any further actions.

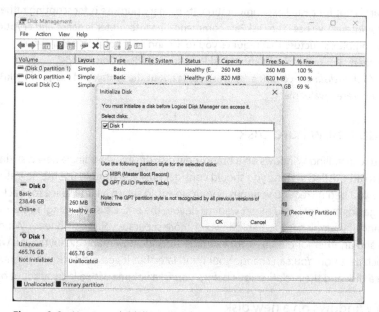

Figure 8-2   You must initialize a disk using one of these two partition styles before you can create a new volume and format it for data storage.

MBR (Master Boot Record) and GPT (GUID Partition Table) are terms describing alternative methods for maintaining the information that defines how a disk stores data. Which partition style should you choose? GPT is required on drives that contain the Windows partition on

UEFI-based systems—a description that applies to every PC that is compatible with Windows 11. Choose MBR only in those rare circumstances when compatibility with older operating systems on legacy hardware is required. GPT disks support larger volumes (up to 18 exabytes) and more partitions (as many as 128 on a basic disk).

Inside OUT

Convert an MBR disk to GPT

In earlier versions of Windows, you could convert a disk from MBR to GPT (or vice versa) only before a disk had been partitioned for the first time (or after all partitions have been removed). Both Windows 10 and Windows 11 include a utility called MBR2GPT that provides a way past this limitation.

MBR2GPT.exe does what its name implies—it converts a system disk from the Master Boot Record partition style to GUID Partition Table. The primary purpose of the tool is to facilitate the conversion of systems running in legacy BIOS mode to UEFI. (You can't use this tool on a non-system disk.) MBR2GPT is designed for administrators to run during deployment, from the Windows Preinstallation Environment (Windows PE); you can also run it from the Windows command line, using the /AllowFullOS switch. It completes its task without deleting data on the target disk.

Just as with DiskPart, which is described earlier in this chapter, using MBR2GPT requires a high level of technical competence. Full documentation is provided at *https://learn.microsoft.com/windows/deployment/mbr-to-gpt.*

After this task is complete, you need to create one or more volumes in the unallocated space, assign a drive letter to each volume, label the volumes (if you don't want them to be identified in File Explorer as simply New Volume), and format them. You can carry out all these steps with the help of a wizard. To begin, right-click anywhere in the area marked Unallocated and then click New Simple Volume. The New Simple Volume Wizard appears. Complete the following steps to create your new volume:

1. **Specify Volume Size.** This page displays the maximum and minimum amounts of space you can devote to the new volume. The wizard doesn't give you the option of designating volume space as a percentage of unallocated space, so if your goal is to create two or more volumes of equal size, you need to do a bit of arithmetic before proceeding.

2. **Assign Drive Letter Or Path.** You can assign any available drive letter to the new volume. (Note that the letters A and B, which used to be reserved for floppy disks, are no longer reserved.) You also have the option to assign no drive letter. (An additional option, Mount In The Following Empty NTFS Folder, allows you to access the volume as if it were a

subfolder on an existing volume. For details, see "Mapping a volume to an NTFS folder," later in this chapter.)

3. **Format Partition.** You don't have to format the new volume immediately, but there is rarely a good reason to wait. Your choices, as shown in Figure 8-3, are as follows:

   - **File System**   A file system is a method for organizing folders (directories) and files on a storage medium. For hard disk volumes larger than 4 GB (4,096 MB), your only options are NTFS (the default) and exFAT. If you're formatting removable media such as USB flash drives or a writable optical disc, other file systems are available. For more information, see "Choosing a file system" later in this chapter.

   - **Allocation Unit Size**   The allocation unit size (also known as the cluster size) is the smallest space that can be allocated to a file. The Default option, in which Windows selects the appropriate cluster size based on volume size, is the best choice here.

   - **Volume Label**   The volume label identifies the drive in File Explorer. The default label is New Volume. It's a good idea to replace this generic label with one that describes the volume's purpose.

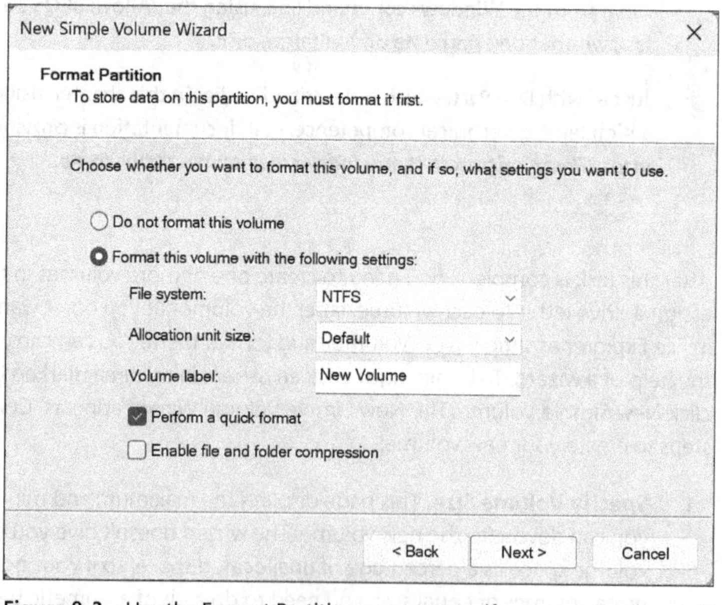

Figure 8-3   Use the Format Partition page to specify your new volume's file system, allocation unit size, and volume label.

Select the Perform A Quick Format check box if you want Disk Management to skip the sometimes lengthy process of checking the disk media. Although you might be tempted by the Enable File And Folder Compression option, we recommend leaving the check box cleared. NTFS compression is not appropriate for disks that contain Windows system files or for drives containing data files that are already compressed, such as MP3 audio files. It's most useful on secondary data volumes that contain large quantities of data files in uncompressed formats, such as audio WAV files.

After making those selections, click Next to advance to the wizard's final page, where you have one more chance to review your specifications. You should take a moment to read this display before you click Finish.

After Disk Management has done its work and disk formatting is complete, a dark blue bar appears over the new volume in the console's graphical view pane. Figure 8-4 shows the result after we added a second drive and created a partition using half of the available space for storing an archive of video files.

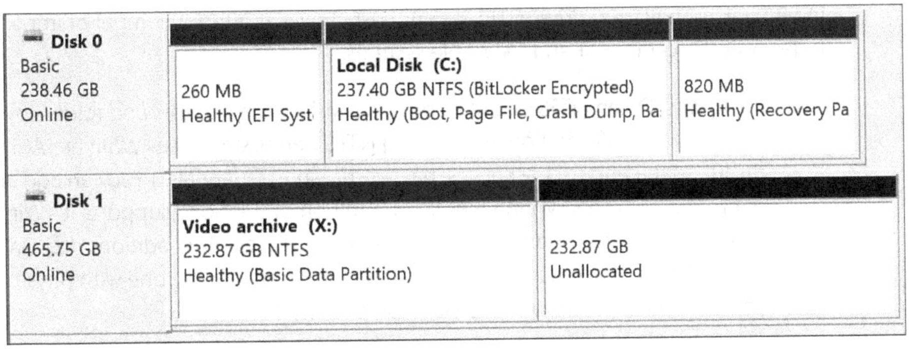

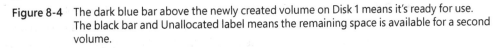

Figure 8-4   The dark blue bar above the newly created volume on Disk 1 means it's ready for use. The black bar and Unallocated label means the remaining space is available for a second volume.

If your disk still has unallocated space (as the disk in this example does), you can add another volume by right-clicking that part of the disk map, clicking New Simple Volume, and running through the wizard again.

Choosing a file system

Formatting a disk prepares it for data storage; the first step in formatting is choosing a file system. Windows 11 supports the following file systems: FAT (File Allocation Table), NTFS, exFAT (Extended File Allocation Table, optimized for use with flash drives), CDFS (Compact Disc File System, also sometimes identified as ISO-9660), and UDF (Universal Disk Format). Windows 11 provides read/write ability for the relatively new Resilient File System (ReFS), but creating and formatting a new ReFS volume requires Windows Pro for Workstations editions.

The formatting choices available for a specific volume depend on the type of media you're formatting. With hard disks, the only options made available by Disk Management are NTFS and exFAT. If you want to format a hard disk in FAT32, you need to use the Format command with the **/FS** switch at a command prompt. (Type **format /?** at the command prompt for details.) The only good reason to do this, however, is for the sake of compatibility with devices running non-Microsoft operating systems that don't natively support NTFS.

If you're formatting a USB flash drive or a MicroSD card, on the other hand, either FAT32 or exFAT is a reasonable choice. Because NTFS is a journaling file system, reading and writing files on NTFS disks involves more disk input/output than similar operations on FAT32 and exFAT disks. Flash drives can perform a finite number of reads and writes before they need to be replaced—hence, they might have a longer life expectancy under FAT32 or exFAT than under NTFS. On UEFI systems, FAT32 is required for bootable installation media. (For more information about exFAT, see the "exFAT versus FAT32" sidebar later in this section.) For a tabular comparison of file systems, see the Microsoft Docs article, "File System Functionality Comparison," at *https:// bit.ly/file-systemcomparison*.

In general, for any fixed drive, NTFS is your best choice. It offers a number of important advantages over the earlier FAT and FAT32 file systems:

- **Security**   On an NTFS volume, you can restrict access to files and folders by using permissions. (For information about using NTFS permissions, see "What are ACLs?" in Chapter 10, "Managing user accounts, passwords, and credentials.") You can add an extra layer of protection by encrypting files if your edition of Windows supports it. (Windows Home edition does not support file encryption using EFS; all other editions do.) On a FAT or FAT32 drive, native encryption options are not available; anyone with physical access to your computer can access any files stored on that drive.

- **Reliability**   Because NTFS is a journaling file system, an NTFS volume can recover from disk errors more readily than a FAT32 volume. NTFS uses log files to keep track of all disk activity. In the event of a system crash, Windows 11 can use this journal to repair file-system errors automatically when the system is restarted. In addition, NTFS can dynamically remap clusters that contain bad sectors and mark those clusters as bad so that the operating system no longer uses them. FAT and FAT32 drives are more vulnerable to disk errors.

- **Expandability**   Using NTFS-formatted volumes, you can expand storage on existing volumes without having to back up, repartition, reformat, and restore.

- **Efficiency**   On partitions greater than 8 GB, NTFS volumes manage space more efficiently than FAT32. The maximum partition size for a FAT32 drive created by Windows 10 or Windows 11 is 32 GB; by contrast, you can create a single NTFS volume of up to 16 terabytes (16,384 GB) using default settings, and by tweaking cluster sizes, you can ratchet the maximum volume size up to 256 terabytes.

- **Optimized storage of small files**   Files on the order of 100 bytes or less can be stored entirely within the Master File Table (MFT) record, rather than requiring a minimum allocation unit outside the MFT. This results in greater storage efficiency for small files.

EXFAT VERSUS FAT32

Microsoft introduced the Extended FAT (exFAT) file system first with Windows Embedded CE 6.0, an operating system designed for industrial controllers and consumer electronics devices. Subsequently, exFAT was made available in Windows Vista Service Pack 1 (SP1). Its principal advantage over FAT32 is scalability. The exFAT file system removes the 32-GB volume and 4-GB file-size limitations of FAT32. It also handles more than 1,000 files per directory. Its principal disadvantage is limited backward compatibility. Some non-PC consumer electronics devices might be able to read earlier FAT systems but not exFAT. Likewise, PCs running non-Microsoft operating systems can generally read FAT32 disks.

If you're formatting a flash drive and you expect to store large video files on it, exFAT might be a good choice for the file system. On the other hand, if you're planning to use that flash drive to share photos with a local print shop, FAT32 is definitely the way to go.

Inside OUT

Formatting does not remove a volume's data

When you use Windows utilities to format a volume, you're warned that the action of formatting a volume makes that volume's data inaccessible. That's true. Whatever data is there when you format will no longer be available to you by normal means after the format operation is complete. Unless you use the Format command with the **/P** switch, however, the data remains in some form and might be recoverable by someone who has physical access to the device and the right tools. If you're concerned about the possibility that someone might gain access to sensitive data files formerly stored on that physical disk, either use `Format /P:`*x* (where *x* represents the number of passes) or wipe the disk after you format it by using the command-line program Cipher.exe, with the **/W** switch. (Type **cipher /?** at the command prompt for details.) For information about other ways to clean a disk, see "Permanently wiping all data from a disk" later in this chapter.

Using Storage Spaces to combine disks

Storage Spaces is a technology that has been a part of Windows server and desktop editions for more than a decade. Using this technology allows you to aggregate collections of physical disks into "storage pools" and then create virtualized volumes ("storage spaces") within those pools.

For example, you could start with two external USB drives, each with a capacity of 3 TB, and use Storage Spaces to combine those physical disks into a single virtualized disk with a capacity of 6 TB.

You can also use Storage Spaces to establish resiliency for critical data. For example, using your two 3-TB disks, you could create a mirrored storage space in which each file saved on one of the physical disks is mirrored on the other; if one of the physical disks fails, your data is preserved.

Three types of resiliency are available:

- **Two-way mirror**   The system writes two copies of your data. You can lose one physical disk without data loss. A minimum of two physical disks is required. The amount of storage available is half of the total storage pool or the capacity of the smaller disk, whichever is less.

- **Three-way mirror**   The system writes three copies of your data. You can lose two physical disks without data loss. A minimum of three physical disks is required, and the amount of storage available is approximately one-third of the storage pool.

- **Parity**   The system stripes data across physical disks while also maintaining parity information that allows it to protect and recover your data more efficiently in the event of drive failure. A minimum of three drives is required.

Simple (nonresilient) storage spaces are recommended if you prefer a single large virtual disk instead of separate physical disks. You might make this choice, for example, if you have a large media collection and several older (hence smaller) disks that are not currently in service. Simple storage spaces are also a good choice for space-intensive operations (video editing, for example) that do not require resiliency. Files in a simple storage space are striped across physical disks, resulting in better performance.

Use parity for maximum resiliency, but note that write performance is degraded by the requirement for the system to calculate and store parity information. This choice might be appropriate for archival storage.

Note the following:

- You can create a storage space only on disks that contain unallocated space. The Windows 11 version of Storage Spaces does not allow you to create a storage pool using disks that you have already partitioned, even if those volumes are unformatted and empty.

- You can have multiple storage pools and multiple storage spaces on a single PC.

- Each storage pool you create appears in Disk Management as if it were a physical drive. Its properties identify it as a Microsoft Storage Space Device. Each storage space within that storage pool appears in Disk Management as a basic volume.

- Storage spaces should not be used as your only backup option. They do not protect your data against theft, fire, or other catastrophic events that affect the entire collection of physical disks.

In Windows 10, the controls for setting up and managing a storage space were buried in the old-style Control Panel; in Windows 11, those controls have been redesigned using a more modern interface. Go to Settings > System > Storage, click Advanced Storage Settings, and then click Storage Spaces.

If you don't currently have any storage spaces available, this page contains only a single control, labeled Add A New Storage Pool. Click Add to begin. That opens the dialog shown in Figure 8-5.

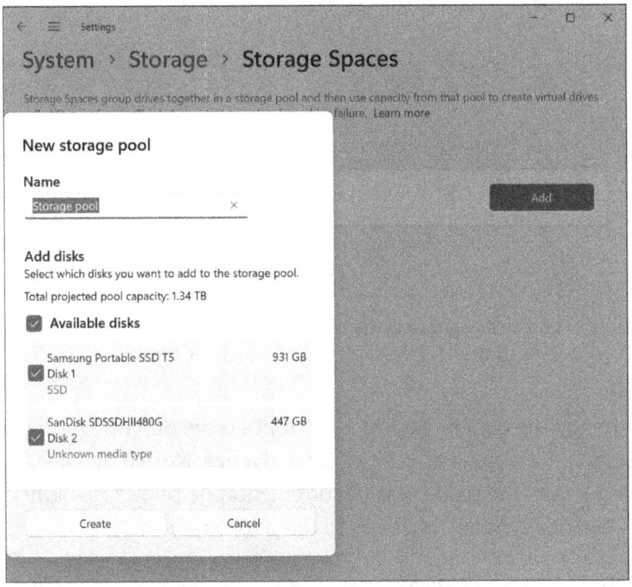

Figure 8-5   Create a new storage pool by combining two or more unallocated disks.

TROUBLESHOOTING

The drives you want to add aren't available

When using the Windows 11 controls for creating a new storage pool, Windows displays only disks that contain unallocated space. If you've attached a disk but don't see it in the Available Disks list, click Cancel and open Disk Management. Find the entry for the disk you're trying to add and delete any existing volumes (even if they're unformatted) so that the disks contain only unallocated space.

After confirming that you want to add the selected disks to your new storage pool, replace the generic name with a descriptive one and click Create. After you create a storage pool, Windows prompts you to create a new storage space. Figure 8-6 shows the New Storage Space dialog.

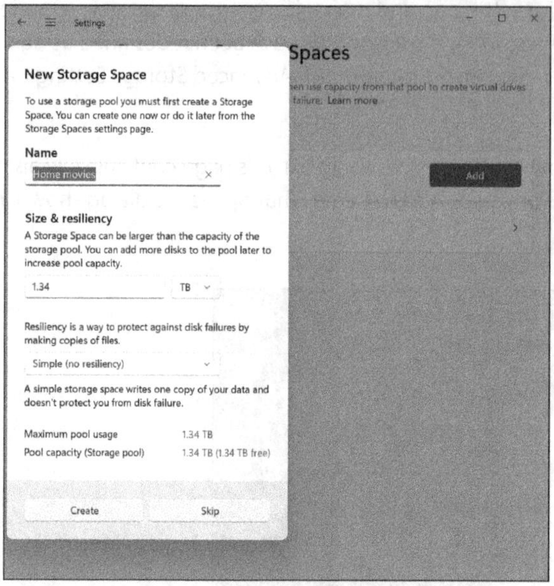

Figure 8-6   The most important setting here is the resiliency type. We've chosen to create a simple space that combines multiple drives into a single, larger drive.

Once again, you can change the generic name to one that's more descriptive. (If you skip this step, it's easy to adjust later.) Choose a resiliency type and a size. Note that you can create a storage space that's larger than the space in your current storage pool. You might choose to do this if you know you'll be adding additional disks to the pool later.

Click Create to save your changes. The dialog that appears next allows you to choose a drive letter and file system for your new space (the default of NTFS is usually appropriate). Add a drive label, if you want, and then format the new storage space.

To manage existing storage spaces, open the Storage Spaces page in Settings and expand the pane for the storage pool you want to work with. The resulting page should look like the one shown in Figure 8-7.

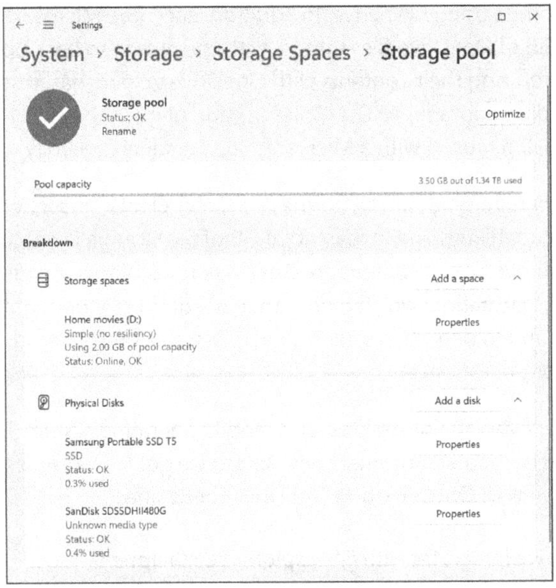

Figure 8-7   Use this page to increase the size of a storage pool by adding a new disk. If you've created multiple storage pools, use the Rename button at the top to give each one a descriptive name.

You can rename a pool or space, add a new space, and increase the capacity of an existing pool by adding a new disk.

To delete a storage space, click the Properties button to the right of the space and then click the Delete button. Note that deleting a storage space permanently deletes all data associated with it. There's no Recycle Bin for a storage space.

To remove a disk from a simple storage pool, you first need to delete any storage spaces associated with that pool. Then click the Properties button to the right of the disk you want to remove and click Prepare For Removal. After Storage Spaces completes its housekeeping, you can click Remove.

For much more information about Storage Spaces, see the support information at *https://bit.ly/storage-spaces-help*. Some architectural details about the feature are at *https://bit.ly/storage-spaces*. At the time we wrote this chapter, the latter article had not been updated for Windows 11, but the information it contains is still accurate.

Connecting OneDrive to your Windows PC

OneDrive, Microsoft's cloud-based file-storage service, is a crucial part of the Windows experience. When you sign in with a Microsoft account, Windows 11 synchronizes settings and stores recovery keys for encrypted storage using OneDrive. In addition, each free Microsoft account includes at least 5 gigabytes (GB) of OneDrive file storage, with the option to back up key data folders by automatically synchronizing their contents with OneDrive's cloud-based servers. You can expand that capacity with paid upgrades to OneDrive storage or get a massively increased cloud storage allotment (1024 GB per user) with a Microsoft 365 Personal or Family subscription.

OneDrive for Business, which shares a sync client with the consumer OneDrive service, offers enterprise-class management capabilities and at least 1024 GB of file storage for each Microsoft 365 Business and Enterprise subscription. By definition, OneDrive for Business accounts are assigned and managed by an organization, which means that an administrator might place limits on your ability to share files and folders or to access OneDrive for Business files from a device that isn't registered with your organization.

OneDrive offers a sync client for every major desktop and mobile operating system. In Windows 11, this sync client is built in and is updated automatically. Before we get to that sync client, though, let's start with an overview of OneDrive and OneDrive for Business.

➤ **For details on how OneDrive integrates with File Explorer, see Chapter 9.**

How OneDrive and OneDrive for Business work

Microsoft's two cloud-based file-storage services share a brand name and a common sync client, but there are some big differences in how the two services work.

OneDrive, the consumer service, is designed for personal use, with special views that showcase photo libraries and albums. (The OneDrive client on mobile devices offers the option to sync the device's camera roll to OneDrive.) A free OneDrive account allows anyone to create and edit documents using common Office file formats and the online versions of Word, Excel, PowerPoint, and OneNote. Microsoft 365 Family and Personal editions automatically connect to OneDrive accounts, allowing subscribers to create and edit files using the Windows versions of those Office apps.

Files stored in OneDrive are organized into folders and subfolders just as they would be on a local drive. Figure 8-8 shows the top-level folders in a OneDrive account, as viewed in a web browser. Note the range of options available in the command bar for the selected folder, as well as the additional menu choices available from the More (ellipsis) menu.

Clicking the usage graph in the lower-left corner opens a page with details about storage for that subscription. (The Premium OneDrive label indicates this account is attached to a Microsoft 365 subscription.)

OneDrive for Business offers a similar web-based view, with one crucial difference: Subscription settings aren't accessible from the navigation pane on the left. That's because a OneDrive for Business subscription is managed by a company administrator, with additional security and collaboration options appropriate for use in an organization.

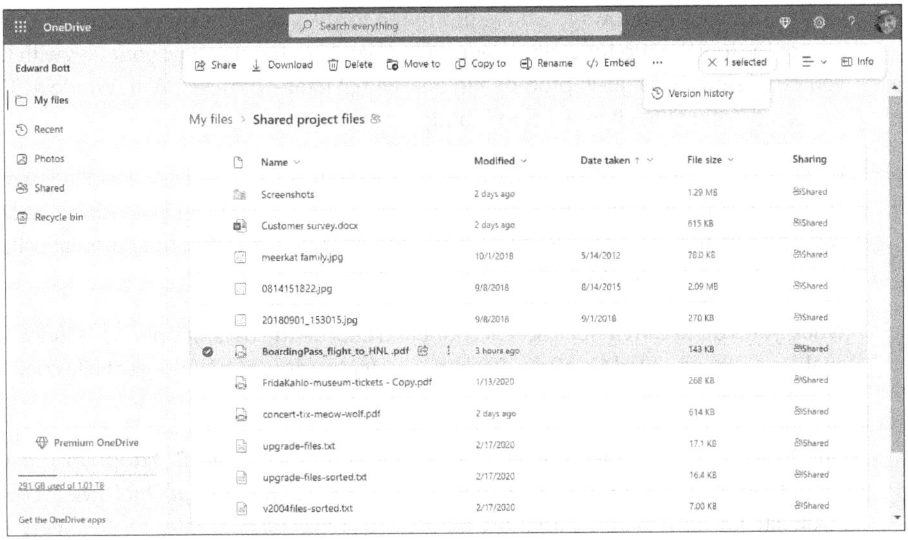

Figure 8-8   When using OneDrive in a web browser, you can perform most file-management tasks and have the ability to create, edit, and collaborate on Office documents.

Both services allow subscribers to share files and folders with other people. The consumer edition of OneDrive allows complete control of sharing: You can choose to make a file, a photo, or an entire folder public. You can also share access by using a link that doesn't require signing in with a Microsoft account.

Sharing options for OneDrive for Business are managed by a company administrator, who might apply restrictions on sharing files with other people, especially in folders that contain confidential company information.

Both OneDrive and OneDrive for Business include built-in versioning, so you can see the history of a document and download an earlier version if you want to recover a portion of an earlier draft. The Recycle Bin for both services makes it possible to retrieve deleted documents for up to 30 days.

Setting up and using OneDrive

Although you can use OneDrive on the web and on mobile devices, it is most useful when synced with a PC running Windows, especially in combination with the Office desktop apps in Microsoft 365. You can link one and only one personal OneDrive account to a Windows 11 user profile. You can also link one or more OneDrive for Business accounts to each user profile.

CHAPTER 8

On a PC running Windows 10, you're prompted to link your Windows account to OneDrive as part of the initial setup for a new user profile. If you'd rather not sync your files with OneDrive, you can dismiss the sign-in prompt and deal with it later—or never. With Windows 11, however, this setup option has changed significantly.

When you use a Microsoft account to sign in for the first time on a new installation of Windows 11, the initial setup for the user profile connects your device to OneDrive using that account. (If you sign in with a local account or an Azure AD account, your PC is not automatically linked to OneDrive; you have to make that connection manually.)

When you sign in with a Microsoft account and choose the default options, Windows also enables a feature called OneDrive Backup. This feature is useful but potentially confusing. Here's how it works.

OneDrive Backup is available for three folders in your user profile: Desktop, Documents, and Pictures. When you turn on OneDrive Backup, Windows checks your OneDrive account to see if you already have folders with those names and, if necessary, creates those folders. Next, Windows moves the files from your local folders to their OneDrive equivalents. Finally, Windows changes the location assigned to the shortcuts in your user profiles so that when you click on Documents, you open the synced location for the OneDrive\Documents folder instead of the local folder, C:\Users*username*\Documents.

Although you have the option when you first set up a profile to store files locally instead of turning on OneDrive Backup, many people will simply click Next and enable this automatic integration. That can result in an unpleasant surprise if you're not prepared for it.

If the newly configured computer is the only PC connected to this Microsoft account, the One-Drive Backup feature is probably a welcome addition. But if another PC is also backing up those folders to OneDrive, you see all of its files in the corresponding folders on your new PC, and any files you create, edit, or delete on either device are synced to both locations. That can cause problems with available space, especially if you have limited OneDrive storage. It can also cause problems with third-party programs that store configuration and data files in the Documents folder.

To confirm whether OneDrive Backup is set up, open File Explorer and click Home (on a PC running Windows 11 version 21H2, click Quick Access). If you see the OneDrive label beneath the Desktop, Documents, and Pictures folders, as in Figure 8-9, you can choose to turn the automatic backup off before proceeding any further.

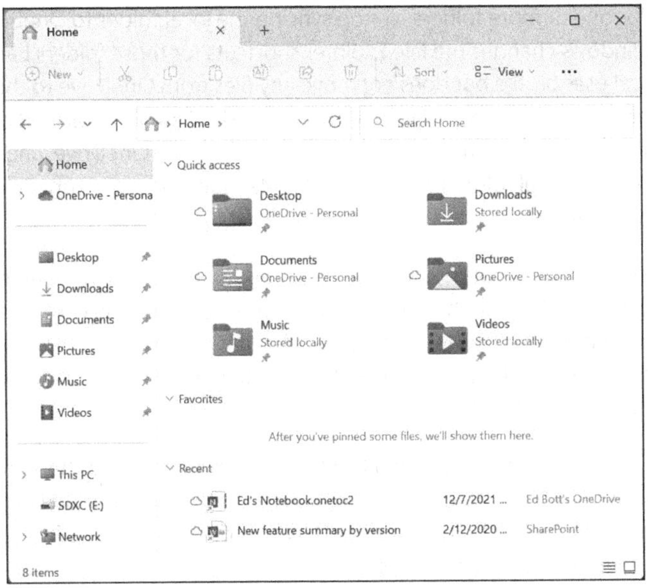

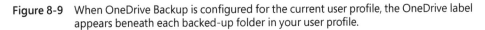

Figure 8-9   When OneDrive Backup is configured for the current user profile, the OneDrive label appears beneath each backed-up folder in your user profile.

To turn OneDrive Backup off, right-click the OneDrive node in File Explorer's navigation pane and then click OneDrive > Settings. In OneDrive Settings, click the Sync And Backup tab, and then click Manage Backup. That action opens the Manage Folder Backup dialog, shown in Figure 8-10.

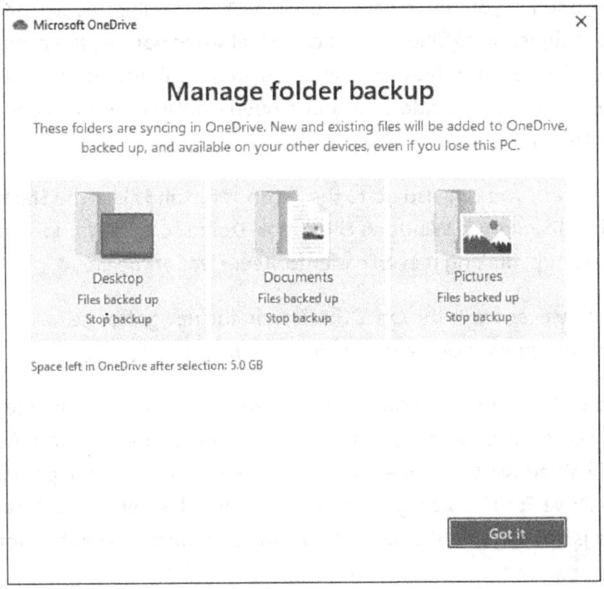

Figure 8-10   When you stop OneDrive backup, the contents of individual folders remain in their respective OneDrive folders. Changes are no longer synced to your local PC.

CHAPTER 8

Click Stop Backup for one or more folders to stop syncing the local folder to OneDrive. After you stop backup, Windows changes the File Explorer shortcuts for those folders back to the locations in your local user profile but does *not* move any files from OneDrive to the local folder. Instead, Windows adds a Where Are My Files? link to the folder. Don't be alarmed if your files appear to be missing; they're still available in the matching folder in OneDrive, and you can copy or move them to the local folder (or return to the Manage Folder Backup dialog and click Start Backup) to restore order.

Note that the Microsoft account you link in OneDrive does not have to be the same one you use to sign in to Windows, although that's the most common (and logical) configuration. If you decide, for whatever reason, that you want to use a different OneDrive personal account than the one you sign in with, you first have to unlink the default account; open OneDrive Settings and, on the Account tab, click Unlink This PC.

To add a OneDrive for Business account, open OneDrive Settings, switch to the Account tab, and click Add An Account. After entering your credentials, go through the OneDrive setup wizard, which creates a local folder to hold your synced files. Repeat this process if you want to set up additional OneDrive for Business accounts.

Inside OUT

Disable OneDrive integration with Windows 11

Maybe you're philosophically opposed to storing files in the cloud. Maybe you prefer a cloud service from another provider. Or maybe you just don't see the need for OneDrive. Regardless of the reason, if you don't want to use OneDrive, you're free to disconnect it. If you haven't yet signed in to OneDrive, click Cancel when you see the prompt to sign in to the sync client; all your files will remain on your local drive or your network. If OneDrive is connected to your Windows account, open OneDrive Settings and, on the Account tab, click Unlink This PC.

From OneDrive Settings, you can also go to the Settings tab and clear the Start OneDrive Automatically When I Sign In To Windows check box. Doing so tells Windows not to load the sync client at startup, making it even easier to steer clear of the cloud.

That option does, however, leave the OneDrive icon in the navigation pane of File Explorer. To make it disappear, you need to make a simple registry edit.

In Windows 11 Pro or Enterprise, you can use Group Policy to make this change. Open Local Group Policy Editor (Gpedit.msc) and go to Computer Configuration > Administrative Templates > Windows Components > OneDrive. Double-click the policy Prevent The Usage Of OneDrive For File Storage and set it to Enabled. After you restart your PC, the OneDrive icon is no longer in the navigation pane and the sync client no longer runs.

On devices running Windows 10 Home, where Group Policy isn't available, you must edit the registry manually. Using Registry Editor, navigate to HKLM\Software\Policies\Microsoft\Windows\OneDrive. (If that key doesn't exist, you need to create it.) Add a new DWORD value, **DisableFileSyncNGSC**, and set it to **1**. Restart the PC to make the policy setting effective.

Note that this change applies to every user of the selected device. Any previously synced files stored in the local OneDrive folder are still available but are no longer linked to their cloud counterparts.

The default location for synced files is a folder in your user profile, with the name OneDrive; if you have multiple accounts, the folder name is followed by a hyphen and either the word *Personal* or, in the case of OneDrive for Business accounts, the name of your organization. Although you can change the folder name and location, most people accept the default here.

By default, both versions of OneDrive turn on the space-saving Files On-Demand feature. A full listing of files and folders in your OneDrive account appears in File Explorer, and you can open any file by double-clicking it; if the file is currently available only online, the OneDrive sync client downloads it automatically and keeps the local copy in sync with the cloud. We discuss this feature in more detail in Chapter 9.

At any time, you can change your OneDrive configuration: Right-click the OneDrive folder in File Explorer's navigation pane and then click Settings; or, in the taskbar, click the icon associated with that account (the OneDrive account icon is white; OneDrive for Business icons are blue), click the gear icon, and then click Settings. From the resulting dialog, you can add a new account, unlink an existing account, change the selection of folders that are visible, and limit the amount of bandwidth your system uses when syncing files.

Using Personal Vault

The consumer version of OneDrive (but not OneDrive for Business) offers a feature called Personal Vault, a BitLocker-encrypted virtual folder that requires two-step authentication to access and that locks automatically after a period of inactivity (20 minutes, by default). You can use Personal Vault to store sensitive documents or images—such things as financial or insurance records, scans of drivers licenses and passports, tax and banking forms, and so on. Any time you want to view items in the vault or upload material to it, you'll be prompted for a second form of authentication; if you've set up the Microsoft Authenticator app on a mobile device, you can respond to a push notification to approve the request, or you can ask OneDrive to send a code via text message or email. A shortcut for Personal Vault is in the top-level folder tree for your personal OneDrive account—either in File Explorer or in the corresponding location in the online view of OneDrive.

CHAPTER 8

Managing disk space

Two long-term trends have converged in recent years to change the way PC makers approach data storage. The plummeting cost of fast solid-state drives (SSDs) and flash memory means that even inexpensive devices can have fast, reliable storage. In addition, dramatic increases in internet speeds have made cloud storage more practical; as a result, system drives don't need to be enormous to be useful.

On a desktop PC, you have the option to expand storage by replacing the primary drive with one that's faster, larger, or both; on most full-size desktop PCs, you can also install additional drives to make room for extra data files. Many portable devices, on the other hand, provide built-in primary storage that is soldered to the system board and can't be replaced easily. For some portable devices, the option to expand storage using inexpensive removable media is available. Some PCs, for example, include a slot that accepts removable storage in the form of a MicroSD card, which can be treated as dedicated storage and used for File History.

Managing storage on a Windows 11 device involves two separate challenges:

- Setting default file locations to make the best use of available storage

- Performing occasional maintenance to ensure that useful space (especially on the system drive) isn't being wasted with unnecessary files

For an overview of how much total storage is available and what's in use on a Windows 11 device, open Settings > System > Storage to see a page like the one shown in Figure 8-11. This example shows a high-end laptop PC with a C drive on which 557 GB of a total capacity of 951 GB is currently in use.

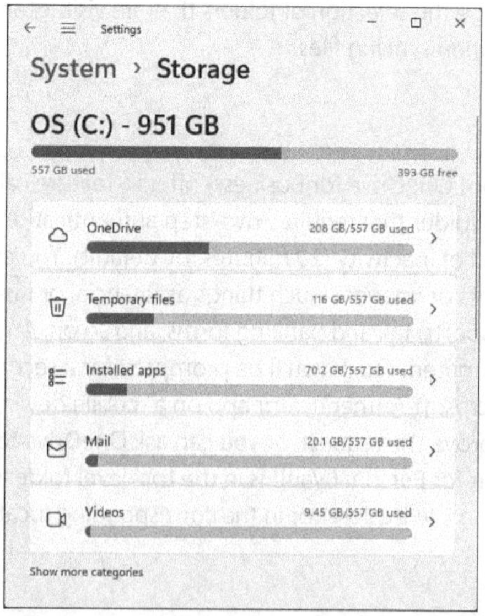

Figure 8-11   The Storage page in Settings shows how much storage is in use on each drive in the current system.

Inside OUT

Why is actual storage capacity lower than advertised disk sizes?

When you use Microsoft's built-in disk utilities to view the storage capacity of a disk, the capacity is reported by using the binary system (base 2) of measurement: 1 KB is 1,024 bytes; 1 MB is 1,024 KB; 1 GB is 1,024 MB; and so on. Thus, measured in binary terms, 1 GB is calculated as 1,073,741,824 bytes. But the makers of storage devices and the PC makers who build SSDs and hard disks into their products typically advertise storage using the convenient metric that 1 GB is equal to 1 billion bytes. That difference is why a system advertised with 1 TB of storage displays only about 951 GB when detailed in Disk Management and other Windows tools. Fortunately, those same tools are also capable of reporting the number of bytes of storage, which allows more accurate comparisons with the advertised space.

The initial view on this page shows only the top five categories, which in this example represents about 50% of total storage in use. To see the full list, click the Show More Categories link below this list. For more details about space consumption in a particular category, click the category name. Figure 8-12, for example, shows the breakdown of the System & Reserved category.

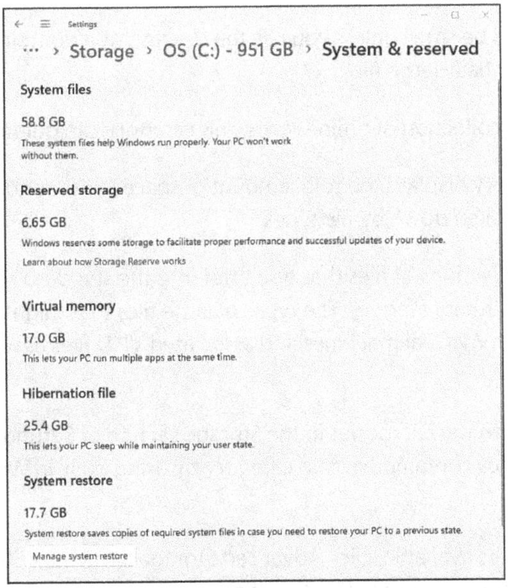

Figure 8-12   As you dig deeper into the details of storage usage, you get a clearer picture of which features and apps are using the most disk space.

Here are some examples of what's in various top-level categories:

- **System & Reserved**   This category is typically large and includes files that are essential to the operation of the system. The actual amounts of storage in use depend on the type of device and how much memory it contains. More memory means a bigger paging file, for example, which is reflected in the Virtual Memory subcategory.

- **Temporary Files** The total shown here includes files that are managed by Windows but are not typically necessary for the operation of a Windows 11 device.

- **Installed Apps**   This category includes default apps as well as legacy desktop apps and those you downloaded from the Microsoft Store.

- **Documents, Pictures, Music, Videos**   These separate categories show how much space is in use in each of the default save locations for the respective file types. Note that this value is not the total found in the libraries of the same names.

- **Mail**   This value measures the space used by local copies of messages saved using the default mail app. Clicking or tapping the Manage Mail button takes you to the default email app: Mail or Microsoft Outlook, for example.

- **OneDrive**   Check this category to see the total amount of space used by local copies of files synced from OneDrive.

- **Desktop**   This total should be small unless you use the desktop as a dumping ground for downloads and other potentially large files.

- **Maps**   If you have a large collection of offline maps, this category can get fairly large.

- **Other People**   This category displays the total amount of space in use for data files from other user accounts, not broken down by file types.

- **Other** If you have large collections of files that don't slot into the standard categories, you might see a very large Other category. The types of large files that might show up in this category include Hyper-V virtual machines and associated VHD files as well as ISO files.

As you click to navigate deeper into the categories in the Storage section of Settings, you find buttons and links for managing files contained in that category by using built-in Windows tools, including File Explorer.

If you have multiple storage devices available, click Advanced Storage Settings > Storage Used On Other Drives. The resulting display includes USB disks, flash disks, and other media. Click any drive to display a categorized list that you can navigate the same as the one available for the system drive.

Changing default save locations

On systems with multiple drives (including removable media), you can change the default location for specific file types. If you have a large music collection, for example, you might prefer to store MP3 files on a disk you dedicate for that purpose. To make that possible, go to Settings > Storage > Advanced Storage Settings > Where New Content Is Saved.

NOTE

Changing the default location for a file type affects the storage of new items. It does not move current items.

When you set the default save location for these categories to a secondary drive, Windows 11 creates folders on the secondary drive, with subfolders that correspond to the category name for each file type within a folder named after your user account name.

Note that if you are redirecting an item type that is currently stored in a library, Windows expands the library definition to include the new location.

➤ For information about libraries, see "Using libraries" in Chapter 9.

Cleaning up unneeded files

A feature called Storage Sense is designed to free up disk space automatically by deleting files that Windows determines you no longer need. Because this feature has the potential to guess wrong and remove files you really do need, it is turned off by default. To turn Storage Sense on and fine-tune its capabilities, go to Settings > System > Storage and flip the Storage Sense switch to the On position. Then click the Storage Sense pane to open a page like the one shown in Figure 8-13.

Normally, Storage Sense runs only when you're low on disk space. If you prefer to run a leaner disk operation, change the Run Storage Sense option to one of its alternatives: Every Day, Every Week, or Every Month.

In its default settings, Storage Sense empties the Recycle Bin every 30 days. You can change this value to 1, 14, or 60 days. Alternatively, if you have ample disk space and you would rather preserve the option to recover files from the Recycle Bin for as long as possible, you can set it to Never.

As we can attest from personal experience, the Downloads folder has the potential to swell to gargantuan size if left unchecked. The Delete Files In My Downloads Folder If They Haven't Been Opened For More Than option allows you to automatically purge those old files to make room for a new batch of downloads.

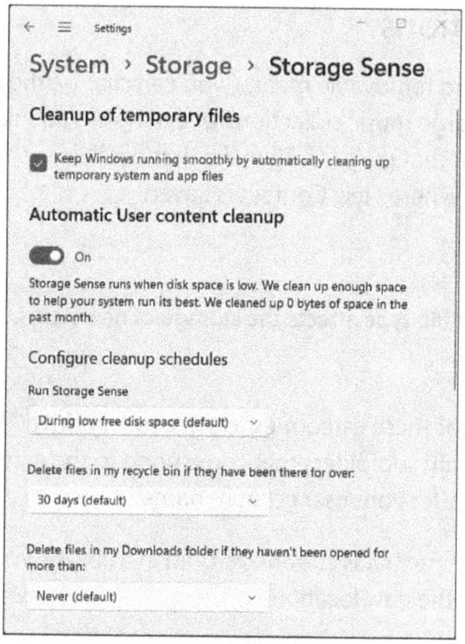

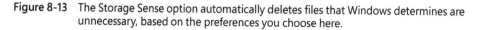

Figure 8-13   The Storage Sense option automatically deletes files that Windows determines are unnecessary, based on the preferences you choose here.

Storage Sense also offers the option to purge locally available copies of files from OneDrive, OneDrive for Business, and SharePoint accounts. For each such category, you can specify an age for files: from 1 day to 60 days, or Never.

At any time, you can perform ad-hoc deletions of temporary or download files. Scroll to the bottom of the Settings page and click Run Storage Sense Now to carry out the specified deletions.

More options for tidying up are available via the legacy Disk Cleanup utility (Cleanmgr.exe). You can use the search box to locate this tool. Note that this utility initially opens in standard user mode, allowing you to manage files available to your user account but blocking access to system files. To enable the full range of Disk Cleanup options, click Clean Up System Files, entering the credentials for an administrator account if necessary. That restarts the utility and unlocks access to the full range of cleanup options.

CAUTION

You might be tempted to obsess over disk space usage and use every trick to create as much free space as possible. That strategy might come back to haunt you, however. If you remove previous Windows installations, for example, you lose the ability to roll back to a previous version to recover from compatibility problems. As a general rule, we recommend keeping at least 20 percent of total disk capacity free. That allows enough room to process temporary files properly without affecting performance dramatically. Beyond that baseline, think long and hard before deleting what might be important files.

Managing existing disks and volumes

No matter how well you plan, your approach to deploying storage resources is likely to change over time. The Disk Management tool (Diskmgmt.msc) can help you adjust to changing requirements. You can change a volume label, assign new drive letters, and reformat a secondary volume (but not the system drive). For advanced configurations, you can shrink, extend, and delete volumes and even map a volume so that it appears as a subfolder within a separate volume. We consider these options next.

> ➤ This section assumes you are working with physical disks that have already been prepared for use with Windows and volumes that already contain data. For details on how to use Disk Management with new physical disks, see "Setting up hard disks and other storage devices" earlier in this chapter.

Assigning or changing a volume label

In Windows 11, as in previous versions of Windows, you can assign a descriptive text label to any volume. Assigning a label is purely optional, but it's a good practice, especially if you have a multiboot system or if you set up separate volumes to keep your data organized. It's especially helpful if you have a collection of removable drives (such as USB flash drives) that don't contain physical labels. You can use Data as the label for your data volume, Music for the volume that holds your collection of digital tunes, and so on.

You can enter a volume label when you format a new volume, or you can do it at any time afterward by right-clicking a volume (in Disk Management or in File Explorer), clicking Properties, and entering text in the edit field near the top of the General tab. The volume label can be no longer than 32 characters.

Assigning and changing drive letters

You can assign one and only one letter to a volume. Windows assigns the drive letter C: to the system drive when you boot to an installed instance of Windows, and changing that assignment is impossible. In addition, you are unable to assign a drive letter to the EFI System Partition, the recovery partition, or the Microsoft Reserved (MSR) partition. For all other volumes, you can change or remove the drive letter at any time.

To change a drive-letter assignment, right-click the volume in Disk Management and then click Change Drive Letter And Paths. (You can do this in either the upper or lower pane.) To replace an existing drive letter, select it and click Change. To assign a drive letter to a volume that currently has none, click Add. Select an available drive letter from the Assign The Following Drive Letter list, and then click OK twice.

If the volume whose drive letter you're changing is currently in use, you might need to restart Windows to make the change. Until you do so, both the old and new drive letters are available for the volume.

Mapping a volume to an NTFS folder

In addition to (or in place of) a drive letter, you can assign a volume so that its contents are mapped to the path for one or more NTFS folders. Assigning a drive path creates a mounted volume (also known as a mounted drive, mounted folder, or volume mount point). A mounted volume appears as a folder within another NTFS-formatted volume that has a drive letter assigned to it. Besides allowing you to sidestep the limitation of 26 drive letters, mounted volumes offer these advantages:

- You can extend storage space on an existing volume that's running low on free space. For instance, if your digital music collection has outgrown your drive C, you can create a subfolder of your Music folder and call it, say, More Music. Then you can add a new physical disk to your system, create a new volume on that disk, and assign a drive path from that new volume to the More Music folder—in effect increasing the size of your original Music folder. The More Music folder in this example appears to be part of the original Music folder but actually resides on the new volume.

- You can make commonly used files available in multiple locations. Say you have a collection of boilerplate documents that you store on a secondary drive with the drive letter X. In each user's Documents folder, you can create an empty subfolder called Boilerplate and assign that folder's path to volume X. That way, the entire collection is always available from any user's Documents folder, and no one has to worry about creating shortcuts to X or changing drive letters while they work.

Note that the volume you map to an NTFS folder path does not have to be empty, nor does it have to be formatted using NTFS. If you have a removable drive formatted as exFAT containing existing files, you can map it to an empty NTFS folder on another volume.

To create a mounted volume, follow these steps:

1. In Disk Management, right-click the volume you want to change (in either the graphical view pane or the volume list pane), and then click Change Drive Letter And Paths.

2. Click Add to open the Add Drive Letter Or Path dialog.

3. Select Mount In The Following Empty NTFS Folder. (This is the only option available if the volume already has a drive letter assigned.)

4. Click Browse. The Browse For Drive Path dialog that appears shows only NTFS volumes, and the OK button is enabled only if you select an empty folder or click New Folder to create one.

5. Click OK to add the selected location in the Add Drive Letter Or Path dialog, and then click OK to create the drive path.

You can manage files and subfolders within a mounted volume just as though they were stored in a regular folder. In File Explorer, the mounted volume appears within the list of folders, identified by a drive icon with a shortcut arrow. And as Figure 8-14 shows, when you right-click the folder icon and then click Properties, the General tab reveals that the folder is actually a mounted volume and provides more details about the drive to which the folder is mapped.

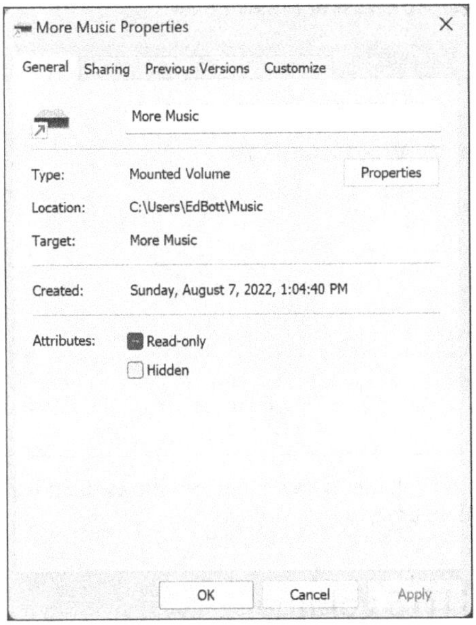

Figure 8-14   The properties dialog for a mounted volume identifies the folder that appears to hold files that are actually stored on another volume.

Click the Properties button on the General tab to see more details about the drive to which the folder is mapped.

If you use the Dir command in a Command Prompt window to display a folder directory, a mounted volume is identified as <JUNCTION> (for junction point, yet another name for a mounted volume), whereas ordinary folders are identified as <DIR> (for directory, the MS-DOS term for a folder).

CAUTION

When creating mounted volumes, avoid establishing loops in the structure of a drive—for example, by creating a drive path from drive X that points to a folder on drive D and then creating a drive path on drive D that points to a folder on drive X. Windows allows you to do this, but it's invariably a bad idea because an application that opens subfolders (such as a search) can go into an endless loop.

To see a list of all the mounted drives on your system, click View > Drive Paths in Disk Management. A dialog like the one shown in Figure 8-15 appears. Note that you can remove a drive path from this dialog; if you do so, the folder remains in the same spot it was previously located, but it reverts to being a regular, empty folder. The files and folders remain in that volume, accessible if you assign a drive letter or a different empty folder to it.

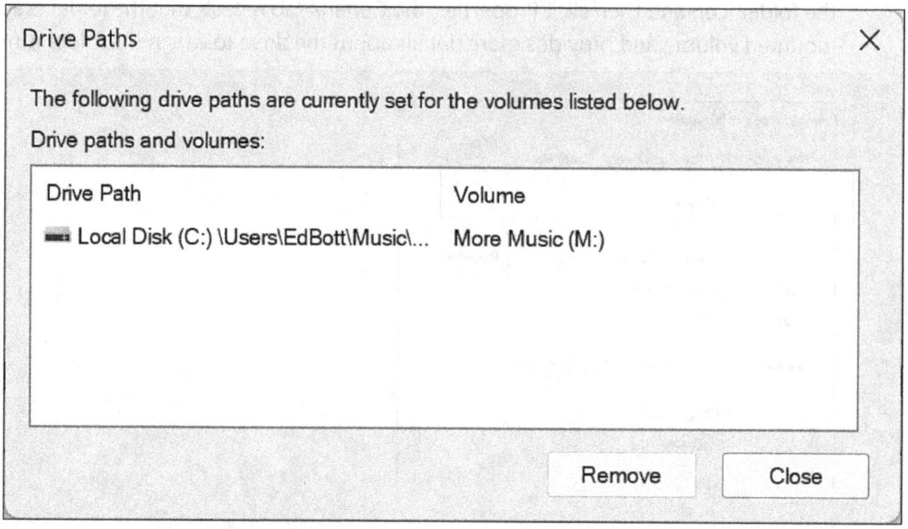

Figure 8-15   This dialog lists all the mounted volumes on a system and shows the drive path and label, if any, of each mounted volume.

Shrinking or extending an NTFS volume

Provided space is available, you can shrink an NTFS-formatted volume to make more space available for other volumes. You might want to do this on a very large physical disk, on which you want to segregate different types of data using separate drive letters. Shrinking a volume also comes in handy if you want to create a separate volume so that you can install an alternative operating system (or a second copy of Windows 11) in a dual-boot configuration.

To accomplish this task, open Disk Management, right-click the volume in either the volume list or graphical view pane, and then click Shrink Volume. Disk Management responds by analyzing the disk, and then it reports the amount of shrinkage possible, as shown in Figure 8-16.

Enter the number of megabytes by which you want to reduce your volume and then click Shrink. Disk Management defragments the disk, moving all its data to a contiguous block, and then performs the shrink.

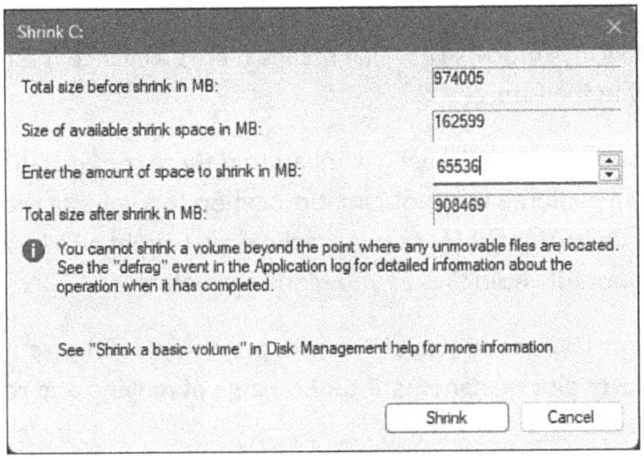

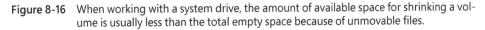

Figure 8-16   When working with a system drive, the amount of available space for shrinking a volume is usually less than the total empty space because of unmovable files.

Be aware that two types of system-managed files—paging files and volume shadow copy files—cannot be moved during the defragmentation process. This means you might not have as much room to shrink as you would like. Microsoft also advises that the amount by which you can shrink a volume is "transient" and depends on what is happening on the volume at the time. In other words, if you're trying to eliminate, say, 10 GB from the volume and Disk Management can manage only 7, take the 7 and then try for more later.

On a disk that contains a single large volume, there's no way to increase the size of a volume. But if you have a volume that uses less than the full amount of space on a disk, you might be able to extend that volume. This configuration is unusual and only likely to occur when the disk you're working with was originally partitioned into multiple volumes and you have deleted one or more volumes—for example, if you previously shrank a volume so that you could install a second copy of Windows 11 in a dual-boot configuration and then removed the added volume.

INSIDE OUT

When expanding a volume, keep it simple

Extending a volume is simple and quick if the unallocated space appears to the immediate right of the volume you want to extend. If the unallocated space is to the left of the volume to be expanded, however, or if an existing volume resides between the volume to be expanded and the unallocated space, Disk Management warns you that the action will convert your basic disk to a dynamic disk. The same is true if you choose to extend an existing volume to unallocated space on a different physical disk.

Creating a dynamic disk adds another layer of complexity to future Disk Management tasks, and we recommend avoiding this option if possible. As we noted earlier, Microsoft has deprecated dynamic disks in Windows 11, which means there's a chance the feature will be removed completely in the future.

Although it's more cumbersome, you can usually work around these configuration issues by copying the contents of the volume in a problematic location to a volume that has unallocated space available on its right. If that's not practical, you might also be able to use an external drive to temporarily hold files as you rearrange volumes.

If you regularly tinker with the layout and size of volumes on multiple disks, you should probably consider a third-party disk management tool capable of moving and resizing volumes with more flexibility.

To accomplish the expansion, right-click the volume you want to expand and then click Extend Volume. Click Next to move past the Extend Volume Wizard's welcome page. The Select Disks page, shown in Figure 8-17, appears.

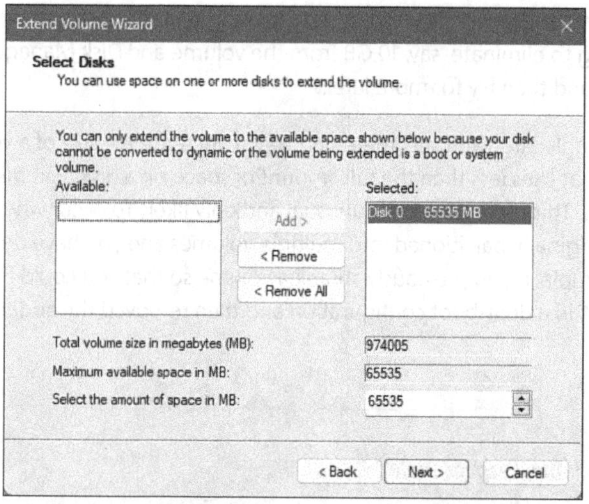

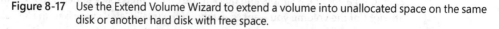

Figure 8-17   Use the Extend Volume Wizard to extend a volume into unallocated space on the same disk or another hard disk with free space.

The Selected list, on the right side of this dialog, initially shows the disk whose volume you intend to extend. The Maximum Available Space In MB box shows you how much larger you can make the volume, assuming you want to confine your expansion to the current disk. The Select The Amount Of Space In MB box, initially set to equal the maximum available space, is where you declare the number of megabytes you want to add to the volume, and the Total Volume Size In Megabytes (MB) box shows you how big your volume is about to become.

When you're ready to continue, click Next, review your orders on the ensuing page, and then click Finish. Note that no separate formatting step is required; the newly expanded volume uses the same formatting options as the original.

Converting a FAT32 volume to NTFS

To convert a FAT or FAT32 volume to NTFS, use the command-line Convert utility. The essential syntax is

```
convert d: /fs:ntfs
```

where *d* is the drive letter you want to convert. For information about optional parameters, type **convert /?** at the command prompt.

The Convert utility can do its work within Windows if the volume to be converted is not in use. If you see an error message when you run Convert, you must schedule the conversion to occur the next time you start Windows or use the /X switch to force the volume to be dismounted immediately. After you restart the computer, you see a prompt that warns you that the conversion is about to begin. You have 10 seconds to cancel the conversion. If you allow it to proceed, Windows runs the Chkdsk utility and performs the conversion, restarting automatically.

Note that the Convert utility does not work on volumes formatted using exFAT.

Deleting a volume

Deleting a volume is easy—and irreversible. All data is lost in the process, so be sure you have backed up or no longer need whatever the volume currently contains. Then right-click the volume and click Delete Volume. The volume reverts to unallocated space, and if it happens to have been the last volume on a dynamic disk, the disk itself is converted to basic.

Permanently wiping all data from a disk

Formatting a volume results in a root folder that appears to be empty. Because of the way formatting works, however, someone with data-recovery tools might be able to restore deleted files even after you format the volume. If you're discarding or recycling an old computer or hard disk, you don't want to risk the possibility of it landing in the hands of someone who might search it for recoverable data that can be used for identity theft or other nefarious purposes.

If your old disk has no salvage value and is headed for the dumpster, the best way to ensure that the data can't be recovered is to remove the disk and physically destroy it. Using tools as varied as a power saw, drill, torch, or sledgehammer, you can render the disk inoperable. (Be sure you're wearing safety goggles.) Although this method is effective, it has several disadvantages: It takes time and considerable physical effort, and it has all the usual risks associated with tools. In the case of an otherwise functional piece of hardware, you're left with a disk that can't be sold or donated to someone who can use it.

CHAPTER 8

As we discuss earlier, you can use the Format command (with the /P switch) and the Cipher command (with the /W switch) to overwrite everything on a disk, but these tools are impractical for cleaning the system volume.

Inside Out

Use BitLocker drive encryption to wipe a drive clean

One highly effective method using built-in tools is to install Windows 11 Pro or Enterprise (you don't need to activate your installation) using a local account with a long, completely random password you create by simply mashing the keyboard. Don't write that password down. Use the built-in BitLocker management tools to encrypt the entire drive, including empty space. Then restart the computer using a Windows recovery drive and use the disk management tools to remove all partitions from the system drive. Even if a would-be data thief can reconstruct the partitions, they'll be unable to gain anything useful from the encrypted system drive.

Another simple solution is to use a third-party disk-wiping tool. A free one that we like is Darik's Boot And Nuke (DBAN), which you can download from *https://dban.org*. DBAN is a bootable disk that securely wipes a computer's hard disks. If you're worried that DBAN or another utility that is allowed to access your disks might surreptitiously steal your data before destroying it, consider disconnecting your computer from your network before using the program.

If your disk contains highly sensitive material and you want to be absolutely sure its data can't be recovered, search for a utility that follows the guidelines set out in "NIST Special Publication 800-88: Guidelines for Media Sanitization" (*https://bit.ly/nist-800-88*). Software that adheres to these guidelines for clearing and sanitizing storage media can defeat even the most sensitive data-recovery tools.

Working with virtual hard disks

Using Disk Management, you can create a virtual hard disk (VHD) in the same formats used by the Windows 11 Hyper-V Manager program. A VHD file encapsulates all the characteristics of a simple disk volume in a single file. Once you've created, initialized, and formatted a VHD file, you can mount the file so that it appears as a disk drive in File Explorer and Disk Management; unlike a physical disk, however, you can back up or move the entire disk by copying the VHD file. This type of file can be a useful alternative to Zip files for archiving and sharing large amounts of information with a detailed folder hierarchy.

➤ For more information about Hyper-V Manager, see "Creating and managing virtual machines with Hyper-V Manager," in Chapter 17.

To create a virtual hard disk, open Disk Management and click Action, Create VHD. Disk Management responds with the Create And Attach Virtual Hard Disk dialog, as shown in Figure 8-18.

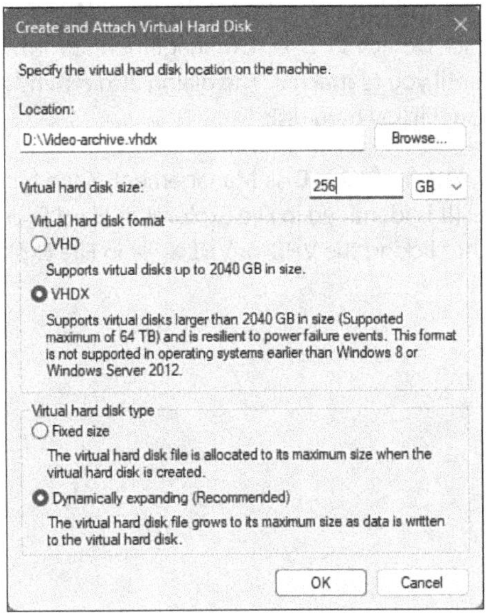

Figure 8-18   You can create a virtual hard disk using either of two formats. The Dynamically Expanding option makes the best use of existing disk space.

Specify a file name with a fully qualified path. It's easiest to do this with the help of the Browse button, but note that the file cannot be stored in your %SystemRoot% (usually C:\Windows) folder.

You can create a virtual hard disk in either of two file formats. The VHD format supports disks up to 2 TB; these can be used on systems running Windows 7 or later. The VHDX format supports much larger disks, up to 64 TB, but it's supported only by Windows 10 and Windows 11. VHDX is the default format in Windows 11, and for good reason: It's more resilient to power failures and is a better choice if you don't require interoperability with older Windows versions.

If you want the disk to expand in size as you add files to it, select Dynamically Expanding. Otherwise, select Fixed Size. (The Recommended option changes depending on which VHD format you chose.) Either way, you must also specify a size (that's a maximum size if you select Dynamically Expanding). The minimum size is 3 MB; the maximum is the amount of free space available on your (real) disk. After you finish with the Create And Attach Virtual Hard Disk dialog, Disk Management adds the new virtual disk to its graphical view pane as an unknown, uninitialized disk with unallocated space.

Right-click the area at the left side of this disk, click Initialize Disk, set it up just as if it were a newly attached physical disk, and then follow the procedures described earlier in this chapter to create one or more volumes on the new disk. After you have created a volume, formatted it, and assigned it a drive letter, the disk appears like any other in Disk Management and File Explorer.

To remove a virtual hard disk, right-click the disk-number box at the left side of Disk Management's graphical view pane, and then click Detach VHD. Disk Management informs you that deleting the disk makes it unavailable until you reattach it. The dialog also reminds you of the location of the file that encapsulated your virtual hard disk.

To reattach a virtual disk, click Action > Attach VHD in Disk Management. Then type or browse to the location of the VHD or VHDX file. (It is identified in File Explorer as Hard Disk Image File.) You can also attach a virtual disk by right-clicking the VHD or VHDX file in File Explorer and choosing Mount.

PART II
Managing Windows 11

Using File Explorer

The primary tool for managing files in Microsoft Windows 11, regardless of where they are located, is File Explorer (the direct descendant of what was known as Windows Explorer in Windows 7 and earlier versions). File Explorer is an amazingly powerful tool, filled with features that can streamline your work processes and make it easier to find files of all types, regardless of where they're stored. Most Windows users barely scratch the surface of File Explorer, which is why we devote a significant section of this chapter to a master class in its rich feature set.

In Windows 11, Microsoft has significantly streamlined the user interface of File Explorer, removing the Office-style ribbon from its immediate predecessor and replacing it with a single command bar. A much more significant change is the version 22H2 addition of a tabbed interface that allows you to organize open folders the way you manage multiple tabs in a modern web browser.

Perhaps more than any other feature in Windows, the search tools have the potential to change the way you work. If your filing philosophy involves the digital equivalent of throwing everything into a giant shoebox, you'll be startled at how easy it is to find what you're looking for. Even if you consider yourself an extremely well-organized Windows user, we predict you'll find ways to integrate File Explorer's search tools into your everyday routine.

Mastering File Explorer

You can't become a Windows expert without learning how to move quickly and confidently through File Explorer. This general-purpose tool is used throughout Windows for all sorts of file-management tasks, for opening and saving files in Windows apps, and even in parts of the Windows shell. The more you understand about how File Explorer works, the more effective you'll be at speeding through tasks without unnecessary delays. Because it's vital to know your way around, we begin this section with a short tour.

Inside OUT

Zoom through File Explorer with keyboard shortcuts

You can find File Explorer in various places in Windows 11, but if you're handy with the keyboard, don't bother hunting for it. Press Windows key+E to open a new instance of File Explorer directly. If you want to jump to an open instance of File Explorer, use the taskbar keyboard shortcut, Windows key+*number*, where *number* marks the position of the File Explorer button on the taskbar. By default, the File Explorer button is in the first position, just left of the button for Microsoft Edge, so unless you've changed the layout, Windows key+1 should switch between open File Explorer windows.

Figure 9-1 shows the default File Explorer layout.

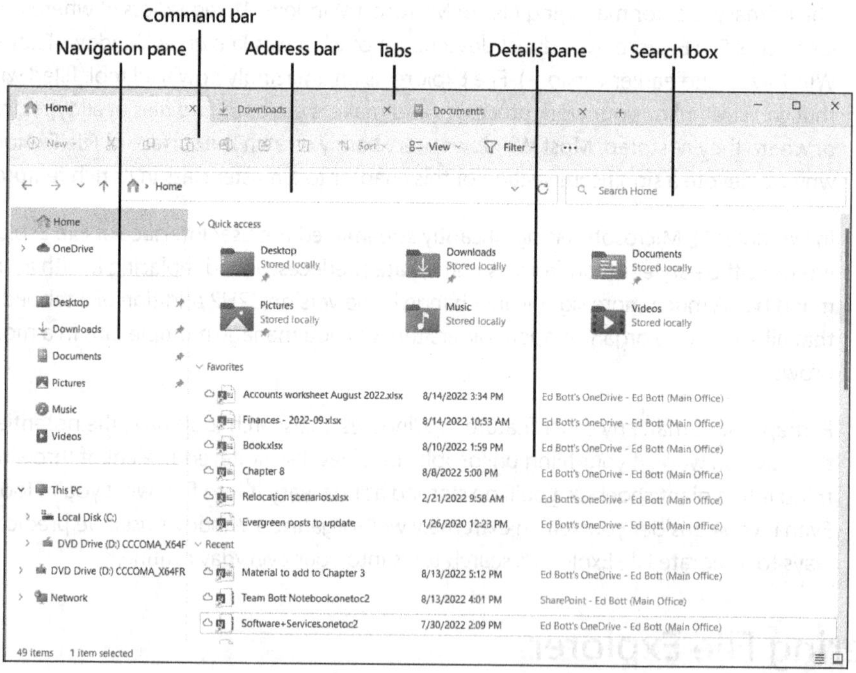

Figure 9-1   File Explorer includes the navigation and display elements shown here, some of which can be customized.

In the transition from Windows 10 to Windows 11, File Explorer received a serious makeover. The most visible change was the removal of the Office-style ribbon, which is replaced by a simpler command bar. The navigation pane adds a Home icon at the top; clicking Home displays a contents pane with three regions, holding shortcuts to pinned folders and recently used folders (Quick Access), pinned files (Favorites), and recently accessed files (Recent). Beginning with version 22H2, File Explorer also offers the option to display the contents of folders in separate tabs within a single window.

The disappearance of the File Explorer ribbon means you might have to search harder to find menu options you're looking for. If you're looking to display the details or preview panes, for example, you have to go three levels deep in the menus: View > Show > Details Pane (or Preview Pane). The Show menu is also where you find options to display item checkboxes (which make it easier to select multiple items without holding down shortcut keys) or to display file name extensions (which are normally hidden).

The See More menu, represented by the ellipsis at the right side of the command bar, contains some useful menu options: Select All, Select None, and Invert Selection, for example. (That last option is a great way to select a large number of files while leaving only a few unselected. Control+click to select the files you want to leave unselected, then click the Invert Selection option to select all the remaining files and clear the ones you previously selected.) A Copy As Path menu option is also here, which is useful when you want to work with a specific file in a Command Prompt or PowerShell window.

As is the case elsewhere in Windows, right-clicking any object (or a blank space in a window) is often the most effective way to get things done. In Windows 11, right-clicking in File Explorer reveals a simplified shortcut menu that usually, but not always, has the option you're looking for on it. If you need access to an option that isn't on this short menu, click Show More Options (or press Shift+F10) to see the full, old-style menu. Figure 9-2 shows the short menu (left) and the corresponding full menu (right).

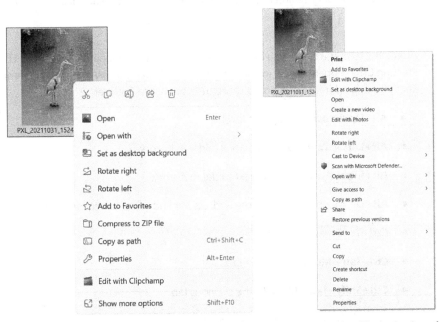

Figure 9-2 By default, right-clicking menus in File Explorer shows a simplified selection of commands (left). Click Show More Options to see the full menu (right).

If you're accustomed to seeing the most common file operations—Cut, Copy, Paste, Rename, and so on—listed as options on the shortcut menu, you're likely to be confused by the simplified shortcut menus, at least at first. As Figure 9-2 shows, those commands now appear as icons at the top or bottom of the shortcut menu.

Inside Out

Switch back to full right-click menus in File Explorer

If you've given the simplified menus a proper trial and you just can't get used to them, it's easy enough to tweak Windows so that it always shows the full menus. Right-click Start and choose Terminal (Admin). In the resulting PowerShell or Command Prompt window, enter the following command:

```
Reg.exe add "HKCU\Software\Classes\CLSID\
{86CA1AA0-34AA-4E8B-A509-50C905BAE2A2}\InprocServer32" /f /ve
```

(Note the use of curly braces around that long GUID.)

After issuing this command, restart your PC or open Task Manager, select Windows Explorer, and click Restart Task. To restore the Windows 11 simplified menus, use this command to delete the key you added previously:

```
Reg.exe delete "HKCU\Software\Classes\CLSID\{86CA1AA0-34AA-4E8B-A509-
50C905BAE2A2}"
```

After restarting Explorer.exe, everything should be back to normal.

After File Explorer is open, you have a wide assortment of keyboard shortcuts to choose from. Pressing Ctrl+N opens a new window on the same folder. Ctrl+W closes the current window. The following additional keyboard shortcuts work in File Explorer:

- **Alt+Up Arrow**   Go up one level.

- **Alt+Left Arrow**   Go to previous folder in history.

- **Alt+Right Arrow**   Go to next folder in history.

- **Alt+D**   Move the focus to the address bar and select the current path.

- **Ctrl+T**   Open a new tab.

- **Ctrl+Tab**   Move to the next tab.

- **Ctrl+Shift+Tab**   Move to the previous tab.

- **F4**   Move the insertion point to the address bar and display the contents of the drop-down menu of previous addresses.

- **Alt+Enter**   Show properties of the selected file.

- **Tab**   Cycle through the following elements: tabs, navigation controls, column headings, navigation pane, address bar, search box.

- **F11**   Switch in and out of full-screen mode.

- **Ctrl+Shift+N**   Create a new subfolder in the current folder.

- **Ctrl+Shift+E**   Expand the navigation pane to the current folder.

Using the navigation pane

In its default arrangement, the navigation pane on the left is arranged into nodes that expand and collapse on demand. As part of its redesign for Windows 11, this pane now consists of three zones:

- The top zone contains a Home icon, which displays the Home page; it also displays nodes for any OneDrive and OneDrive for Business accounts that are connected to the current user profile.

- The middle zone displays pinned and recent folders—the same as the Quick Access list on the Home page.

- The bottom zone shows This PC, which expands to show all local drives, followed by separate nodes for libraries, removable drives, for the local network, and for third-party cloud service providers.

Each of the top-level nodes in the navigation pane offers a starting point for navigating through files in its associated location. Note that you can right-click any empty space in the navigation pane to display a menu that allows you to show or hide the nodes for This PC and Network. You can also choose to show or hide the Libraries node. (For more on how Windows uses libraries to organize files, see "Using libraries" later in this chapter.)

If you prefer the older, tree-style view with a single hierarchy, right-click an empty space in the navigation pane and choose Show All Folders. With the Show All Folders option selected, the navigation pane includes your profile folders (which you can expand by clicking your username in the navigation pane), removable drives (which also appear directly under This PC), OneDrive accounts, SharePoint sites, Control Panel, Recycle Bin, and any folders you've created directly on the desktop.

If you simply want to see the files in a folder without being distracted by the navigation pane, you can make it disappear with ease: Click View > Show and clear the checkbox to the left of the

Navigation Pane menu entry. You might choose this option if you're comparing the contents of two folders in side-by-side windows and don't need the distraction of the navigation pane.

Navigating faster with favorite files and folders

In Windows 11, the Home page takes the place of Quick Access, which appeared at the top of the navigation pane in Windows 10. When Home is selected, the contents pane displays three groups of shortcuts, giving you ready access to the folders and files you use most frequently.

Quick Access is no longer a top-level node in the navigation pane; instead, it's a place where you can collect shortcuts to folders you use regularly. Windows automatically pins the Desktop, Downloads, Documents, and Pictures folders here. To add to that selection, right-click any folder and choose Pin To Quick Access. You can unpin a pinned folder by right-clicking it and then clicking Unpin From Quick Access.

In addition to pinned folders, Quick Access includes folders you've worked with recently, in a lineup that shifts depending on your work habits.

The section immediately below Quick Access, Favorites, offers similar access to individual files. Any files you tag as Favorites in Office apps (Word, Excel, and so on) are automatically included here. You can also right-click any file and choose Add To Favorites to pin it to this list. (Note that unlike the folders in Quick Access, pinned files in Favorites do not include a pin icon.) To remove a file from the Favorites list, right-click and then click Remove From Favorites.

The Recent Files section of Quick Access contains files you recently worked with, sorted with the most recently used one at the top. By right-clicking a file name and clicking Open File Location, you can go directly to the folder in which the file resides. If you find that you no longer need to see a particular file in this list and want to make room for another, you can right-click that file and then click Remove From Recent.

File Explorer's Home page is an extremely handy navigational tool, because it gathers together the stuff you're most likely to be concerned with, regardless of where that stuff is actually stored. But if you don't need it, or you're not keen on having other people see what you've been working on when they peer over your shoulder, you can tell Windows not to add files or folders unless you specifically pin them. To do this, click See More > Options. On the General tab of the Folder Options dialog, the checkboxes you need are in the Privacy section, as shown in Figure 9-3.

(If you just want to cover your immediate tracks without changing the overall behavior of File Explorer, it's probably simpler to click Clear in the Privacy section.)

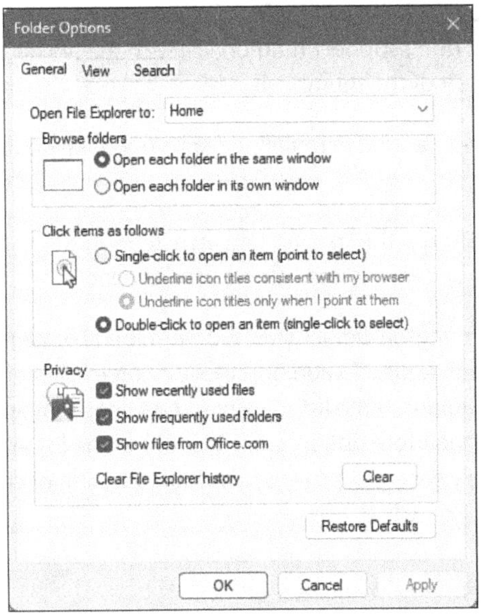

Figure 9-3   Use the checkboxes under the Privacy heading to tell Windows not to automatically display recently used files and folders on the File Explorer Home page.

Layouts, previews, and other ways to arrange files

You can adjust the display of any individual folder's contents in File Explorer by means of options on the View menu. Your choices are numerous: Icons (in four sizes), List, Details, Tiles, and Content. Display options are folder-specific and persistent.

The range of options for the various icon views is larger than it looks. Although there are four discrete choices available at the top of the View menu—Extra Large Icons, Large Icons, Medium Icons, and Small Icons—the actual number of sizes is 76. You can cycle smoothly through all 76 sizes by choosing one of the four preset sizes and then holding down the Ctrl key as you turn the wheel on your mouse or scroll up or down with two fingers on a trackpad. With each step, you see the icons grow or shrink (although at some of the smaller sizes, the change is barely perceptible).

The remaining four options work as follows:

- **List**   This view is extremely efficient, displaying file names only, arranged in columns.

- **Details**   This view is one of the most important alternatives, offering a multicolumn tabulation of your files that unlocks a wide range of sorting, filtering, and grouping options, as we discuss later in this chapter, "Sorting, filtering, and grouping in File Explorer."

- **Tiles**   Choose this view to display each file and folder in a single rectangle that displays a thumbnail (or icon, for files that don't support thumbnails) with the file name, type, and size in three lines of text to the right of the thumbnail.

- **Content**   In this view, listings are arranged in multiline bands that take up the full width of the window.

One additional option, Compact View, shrinks the spacing between items in the navigation pane and, in List and Details views only, between items in the contents pane.

The default arrangement of column headings in Details view is determined by the folder type, but you can tailor this arrangement in any folder. To add or remove a column heading, right-click anywhere in the row of column headings. If the list of column headings that appears doesn't include the one you want, click the More option at the bottom of the list. As Figure 9-4 shows, the Choose Details dialog that appears next provides you with a wealth of choices—more than 300 if you scroll through the entire list.

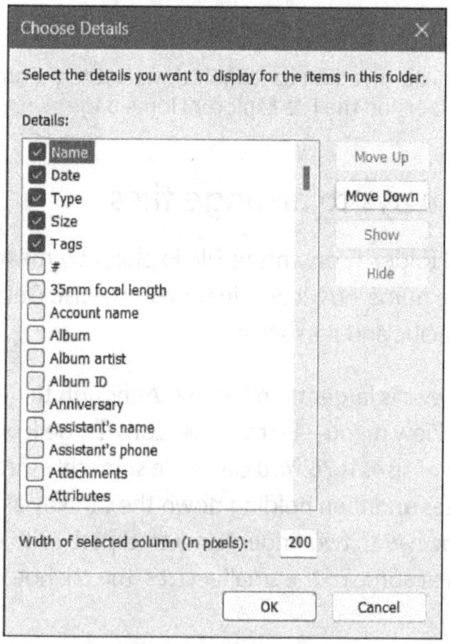

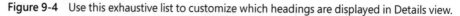

Figure 9-4   Use this exhaustive list to customize which headings are displayed in Details view.

In the Choose Details dialog, column headings that are currently visible appear at the top of the list. Use the Move Up and Move Down buttons to change the order in which headings appear. (You can also change the column order in File Explorer by dragging headings with the mouse.)

Inside OUT

Use keyboard shortcuts to change views

Each of the eight view options on the View menu has an easy-to-remember keyboard shortcut: Ctrl+Shift+*number*, where *number* corresponds to the position on the View menu. If you don't feel like memorizing the entire menu, it's worth noting that Ctrl+Shift+6 corresponds to Details view and Ctrl+Shift+2 is Large Icons. For those two views, you can also use the unobtrusive buttons in the lower-right corner of the File Explorer window. Allow the mouse pointer to hover over either of those buttons for a quick reminder of their function and the keyboard shortcut.

Initially, all folders intended for the storage of user data (including those you create) are assigned one of five folder templates that define the default headings File Explorer considers appropriate for the content type. The logic is straightforward: You probably want to sort a folder full of MP3 tracks by track number, and the Date Taken column is extremely useful for filtering digital photos, but neither column would be particularly useful in a folder full of Microsoft Word documents.

Inside OUT

Customize folder templates

Not sure what folder "type" you're in? Right-click a blank space in the folder and then click Show More Options > Customize This Folder. On the Customize tab of the Properties dialog for the selected folder, look at the selection in the Optimize This Folder For drop-down list, which shows the folder type that's currently in effect.

The final option on the View menu, Show, leads to a submenu with six additional elements of the File Explorer interface that you can show or hide. Every item on the Show menu is a toggle, allowing you to quickly show or hide file name extensions and item checkboxes, for example. The Details Pane and Preview Pane options appear to the right of the contents pane, showing either details about the current file (a topic we discuss in the next section) or a preview of the currently selected file. File formats supported in the preview pane include most image files, Microsoft Office documents, and PDF files. Click once to make the pane visible; click again to hide the pane. If you use either capability regularly, it's worth memorizing the keyboard shortcuts: Alt+P for Preview, Alt+Shift+P for Details.

CHAPTER 9

Managing file properties and metadata

Every file you view in File Explorer has a handful of properties that describe the file itself: the file name and file name extension (which is associated with the app that opens that type of file), the file's size, the date and time it was created and last modified, and any file system attributes. These properties are stored in the file system and are central to displaying the contents of a folder or other location and performing simple searches.

In addition to these basic file properties, many data-file formats can store custom metadata. These additional properties can be added by a device or by software; in some cases, the user can modify them. When you take a digital picture, your camera or smartphone might add the device make and model, exposure time, ISO speed, and other details to the file when it's saved. When you buy a digital music track or album, the individual audio files include custom properties (often referred to as *tags*, from the IDv3 tag format used in MP3 files) that identify the artist, album, track number, and other details. You can also add free-form tags to digital images saved in formats that support that additional metadata. Microsoft Word and other Microsoft Office apps automatically add your name to the Author field in documents you create; you can fill in additional properties such as keywords and comments and save them with the file.

The simplest way to view metadata for a file is to click View on the File Explorer command bar and then click Show > Details Pane. Doing so opens a pane on the right that displays a thumbnail of the selected file (if a thumbnail is available), plus metadata saved as file properties. You can click through a group of files in rapid succession, with the contents of the details pane changing with each new selection. Figure 9-5 shows these details for a photo saved in JPEG format; saved file properties include the date and time the photo was taken, the make and model of the camera (in this case, the camera is a smartphone), the dimensions of the picture, the exposure settings, and many more details.

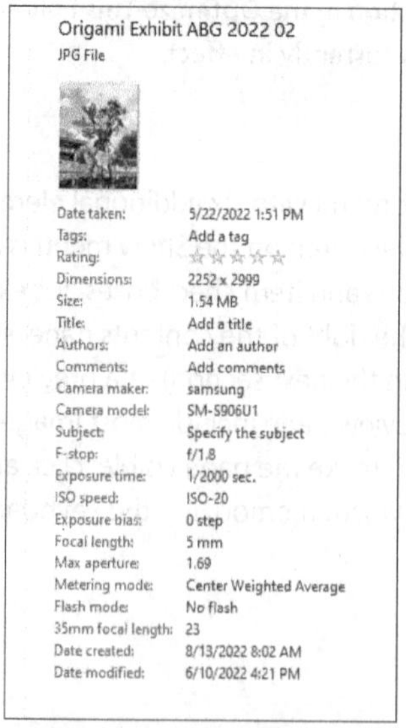

Origami Exhibit ABG 2022 02
JPG File

Date taken:	5/22/2022 1:51 PM
Tags:	Add a tag
Rating:	☆ ☆ ☆ ☆ ☆
Dimensions:	2252 x 2999
Size:	1.54 MB
Title:	Add a title
Authors:	Add an author
Comments:	Add comments
Camera maker:	samsung
Camera model:	SM-S906U1
Subject:	Specify the subject
F-stop:	f/1.8
Exposure time:	1/2000 sec.
ISO speed:	ISO-20
Exposure bias:	0 step
Focal length:	5 mm
Max aperture:	1.69
Metering mode:	Center Weighted Average
Flash mode:	No flash
35mm focal length:	23
Date created:	8/13/2022 8:02 AM
Date modified:	6/10/2022 4:21 PM

Figure 9-5   The Details Pane in File Explorer shows a selection of properties from the currently selected file. Some are directly editable; others are fixed and can't be changed.

CHAPTER 9

Saving custom information as metadata can make it easier to find that file (and others like it) using the search tools we describe later in this chapter.

The properties displayed in the details pane are an excellent starting point, but they might not represent every detail available for the selected file. To see the complete list, right-click the item and click Properties (or select the item and press Alt+Enter). Then click the Details tab in the properties dialog.

Inside OUT

Rate your favorite digital media files

For digital photos, music, and other media files, you'll notice that the Rating field is available in the details pane. Instead of providing a box to enter free-form text or a number, this field shows five stars, all displayed in gray if this value is empty. You can rate any file on a scale of one to five stars by clicking or tapping the appropriate star in the details pane. Adding ratings is a useful way to filter large media collections so that they show only the entries you previously rated highly. Ratings are also useful for assembling playlists and slide shows.

Figure 9-6 shows a side-by-side comparison of the Properties dialog and the details pane for a music track. A casual listener might not care that scrolling down through the Properties dialog reveals such exotica as Mood, Beats-Per-Minute, and Initial Key, but a professional DJ can certainly find uses for those extra details.

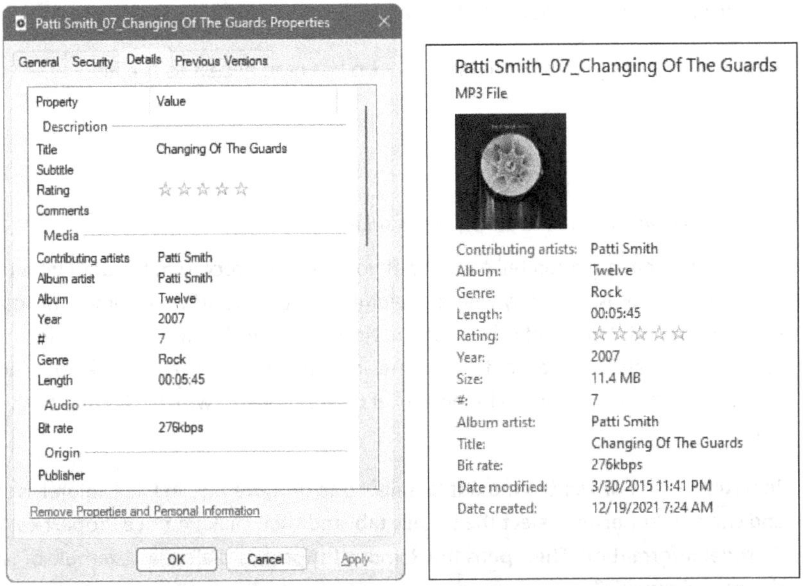

Figure 9-6 The Details tab in a file's Properties dialog (left) offers a more exhaustive set of editable properties than the simpler details pane (right).

In either place, the details pane or the Properties dialog, you can edit many (but not all) of the item's properties. Some properties, such as file size, photo dimensions, and MP3 bitrate, are calculated by the file system or are otherwise fixed and cannot be directly modified. But you can edit custom metadata if the format of the underlying file allows you to do so.

To enter or change a property's value, click the field name and type in the box containing its value. If you add two or more words or phrases to a field that accepts multiple entries (such as Tags, Composers, or Authors), use semicolons to separate them. Press Enter or click Save to add the new or changed properties to the file.

You can edit properties for multiple files at one time. This is especially useful when you're correcting an error in an album or artist name; just select all the songs in the album's folder. When more than one file is selected, note that some properties in the details pane (such as track numbers and song titles) change to indicate that the specified field contains multiple values. A change you make to any field is written to all the files in your selection.

Metadata is saved within the file itself, using industry-standard data storage formats. Software developers who need to create a custom file format can make its metadata available to Windows by using an add-in called a property handler, which opens the file format to read and write its properties. Because metadata is saved within the file itself, the properties you edit in File Explorer or a Windows program are fully portable. This opens some useful possibilities:

- You can move files to other computers, even those running other operating systems, without losing the files' tags and other metadata.

- You can edit a file in an app other than the one in which it was created without losing any of the file's properties (assuming the other app properly adheres to the file format's standard for reading and writing metadata).

- A file's properties are visible to anyone who has read access to the file.

Inside OUT

Remove personal metadata for privacy's sake

Metadata within a file can tell a lot about you. Cameras record data about when (and, with some cameras, precisely where) a picture was taken and what camera or smartphone was used. Microsoft Office automatically adds author and company information to documents and spreadsheets. With user-created tags, you can add personal and business details that might be useful on a local copy but are unwise to disclose to the wider world.

To scrub a file of unwanted metadata, select one or more files in File Explorer, right-click and choose Properties, select the Details tab, and then click Remove Properties And Personal Information. This opens the Remove Properties dialog, an example of which is shown in Figure 9-7.

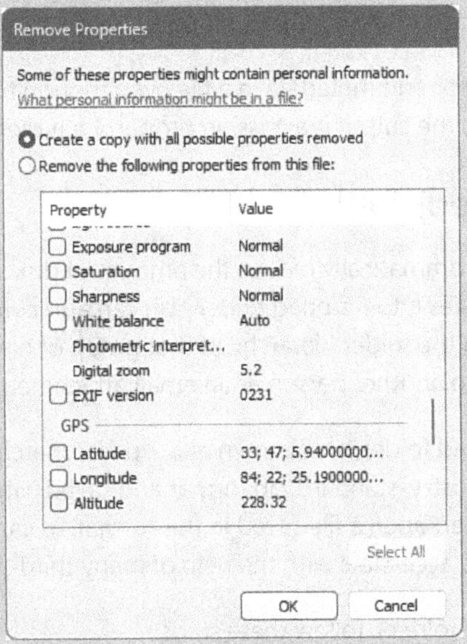

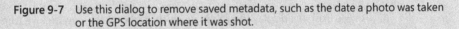

Figure 9-7   Use this dialog to remove saved metadata, such as the date a photo was taken or the GPS location where it was shot.

At this point, you have two choices. The default option creates a copy of your file (using the original file name with the word *Copy* appended to it) and removes all properties that can be changed, based on the file type. With the second option, Remove The Following Properties From This File, you select the checkboxes next to individual properties and permanently remove those properties from the file when you click OK. (If no checkbox is visible, that property is not editable.)

Of course, common sense should prevail when it comes to issues of privacy. This option zeroes out metadata, but it does nothing with the contents of the file itself. You need to be vigilant to ensure that a digital photo doesn't contain potentially revealing information in the image itself or that sensitive personal or business details aren't saved within a document's contents.

You can edit custom properties only in files saved using a format that accommodates embedded metadata. For digital image files, Windows supports the JPEG, GIF, and TIFF formats, but you cannot save metadata in bitmap images and graphics files saved in PNG format, because these formats were not developed with metadata in mind. Among music file formats, MP3, WMA, and FLAC fully support a wide range of properties designed to make it easy to manage a music collection; files saved in the uncompressed WAV (.wav) format do not support any custom tags. Plain text and Rich Text Format (.rtf) files do not support custom metadata; files saved in

Word formats expose a rich set of additional properties, as do all other native file formats from Microsoft Office programs.

In some cases, you're unable to view or edit metadata in a file even though the underlying format supports metadata. In that case, the culprit is a missing property handler.

Using compressed (zipped) folders

Depending on the file type, you can dramatically reduce the amount of disk space used by one or more files by compressing those files into a zipped folder. You can also combine multiple files into a single Zip file while preserving the folder hierarchy of that group of files, making it easier to store multiple files or send them to another person as an email attachment.

Don't be fooled by the name: A zipped folder (also known as a Zip file or archive) is actually a single file, compressed using the industry-standard Zip format and saved with the .zip file name extension. Any version of Windows can open a file saved in this format, as can other modern operating systems. The format is also accessible with the help of many third-party utilities.

To create a new archive using zipped folders, follow these steps:

1.   In File Explorer, display the folder in which you want the new archive to reside.

2.   Right-click any empty space in the folder, and then click New > Compressed (Zipped) Folder.

3.   Enter a new, descriptive name in place of the highlighted default name and press Enter.

To add files and folders to your archive, drag and drop them onto the zipped folder icon in File Explorer (or double-click to open the zipped folder in its own window and then drag items into it). You can also use the Clipboard to copy and paste items. To remove an item from the zipped folder, double-click the folder to display its contents, right-click the item, and then click Delete.

You can also create a compressed folder from the current selection in File Explorer by right-clicking any selected file or folder and clicking Compress To Zip File. Windows creates an archive file with the same name as the selected object. If you're compressing a single file, that default name might be acceptable. If you're compressing a group of files and/or folders, replace it with a more descriptive one.

To extract individual files or folders from a zipped folder, open it in File Explorer and then drag the items you want to extract to a new location, or use the Clipboard to copy and paste. To extract all items from a zipped folder to a specific location, right-click the zipped folder icon and then click Extract All, or open the zipped folder in File Explorer and click Extract All on the command bar.

Organizing personal data with user profile folders and libraries

Windows uses a logical organizational structure that helps keep data together in known system folders. As we explain in this section, you can change the location of some of these folders to make best use of your available storage. You can also create virtual storage locations called *libraries* to make searching easier.

What's what (and where) in your user profile

Your personal files and settings are stored by default in your *user profile*, which is created by copying the contents of the Default profile to a new folder when you sign in to a user account for the first time on a device. In addition to predefined folders for personal documents and digital media files, this new profile also includes the details that define the desktop environment: the user's own registry settings (HKEY_CURRENT_USER), as well as user data and settings for installed apps and desktop programs.

NOTE

Although you can customize the Default profile, doing so requires the use of enterprise deployment tools and is impractical for home and small business installations.

In addition to individual user profiles, Windows 11 creates a Public profile containing a group of folders for common document types that mirror those in your user profile. You can see the Public Documents, Public Music, Public Pictures, and Public Videos folders in their matching libraries. The advantage of these folders is that other users can save files to these locations from different user accounts on the same computer or from across the network.

Local user profiles are stored in %SystemDrive%\Users. (On most Windows 11 PCs, this address is equivalent to C:\Users.) Each user's profile is stored in a subfolder whose name is based on the user account name (for example, C:\Users\Katy). The entire path for the current user's profile is accessible via another commonly used environment variable, %UserProfile%. If you have File Explorer's navigation pane set to show all folders, you can see the subfolders of your profile by clicking your username in the navigation pane. (To turn this navigation pane option on or off, right-click a blank space in the pane and select or clear the Show All Folders menu option.)

TROUBLESHOOTING

Your user account name and user profile folder name don't match

As we mentioned earlier, Windows creates the user profile folder when you first sign in to a device. If you do so with a local or Azure AD account, the name of the profile folder matches the username (unless there's already a folder with that name from a previous installation, in which case Windows appends a dot and the name of the PC to the folder name).

This naming convention breaks down if you sign in for the first time using a Microsoft account. In that case, Windows creates a folder name using the first five characters of the username associated with the Microsoft account. If your username is six characters or longer, the folder name (which is also shown in File Explorer as the profile name) is truncated. So the profile folder for edbott@example.com becomes C:\Users\edbot.

If that folder name bothers you, we have some bad news: There's no supported way to change the user profile folder name after that first sign-in. But you can make sure it doesn't happen again. The trick is to create a local user account with the same name as what you want to use for your user profile folder. (Follow the instructions in "Creating and managing user accounts," in Chapter 10.) Then, after signing in for the first time using that local account, you can connect your Microsoft account.

To see the folders included in your user profile, open its folder directly from C:\Users or from the drop-down menu at the left of the address bar. As you can see from Figure 9-8, the list includes some familiar destinations. (Because third-party apps can add their own data folders to the user profile, your system might include some additional folders.)

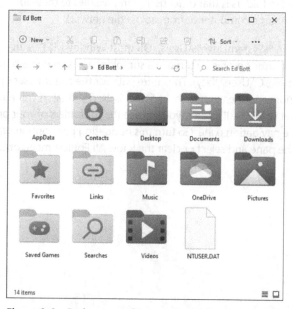

Figure 9-8   Each user profile contains folders intended for specific types of data as well as a hidden AppData folder for data that should be accessed only from within an app.

Inside OUT

What's in the AppData folder?

The hidden AppData folder, introduced in Windows Vista, is used extensively by legacy Windows programs as a way to store user data and settings in a place where they'll be protected from accidental change or deletion. This folder contains application-specific data—customized dictionaries and templates for a word processor, synchronized copies of messages stored on an email server, custom toolbar settings, and so on.

It's organized into three subfolders, named Local, LocalLow, and Roaming. The Roaming folder (which is also accessible via the environment variable %AppData%) is for data that's made available to a roaming profile (a profile stored on a network server; the server makes the profile available to any network computer where the user signs in). The Local folder (which is also accessible via the system variable %LocalAppData%) is for data that should not roam. This location includes the Temp folder (accessible with the environment variable %Temp%), where Windows and apps create files that are strictly for temporary use. The LocalLow folder is used by applications that run at a lower integrity level, including some games, pages running in Internet Explorer mode in Microsoft Edge, and Mozilla's Firefox browser in Private Mode.

The personal data folders (Documents, Downloads, Music, Pictures, and Videos) serve as the default location for applications that use those file types. You'll also find folders containing the contents of synced OneDrive and SharePoint data stores. Here's everything you need to know about the remaining folders:

- **3D Objects**   This system folder made its first appearance in Windows 10. It's used for storing data files created by apps like Paint 3D that are no longer included with Windows 11.

- **Contacts**   This folder first appeared in Windows Vista and was designed to store contact information used by Windows Mail. It is not used by any programs included in Windows 10 or Windows 11 and is maintained for compatibility purposes with older third-party personal information management programs.

- **Desktop**   This folder contains items that appear on the user's desktop, including files and shortcuts. (A Public counterpart also contributes items to the desktop.) A link to this location appears in the Quick Access section of the navigation pane.

- **Favorites**   Internet Explorer saves shortcuts to websites here. As we note in Chapter 7, Microsoft Edge handles its favorites collection differently, and because the Internet Explorer app is no longer accessible from Windows 11, the contents of this folder are not used.

- **Links**   In Windows 7, this folder contains shortcuts that appear in the Favorites list at the top of the navigation pane. Its contents are not used in Windows 11.

- **Saved Games**   This folder is the default storage location for apps that can save a game in progress.

- **Searches**   This folder stores saved search specifications, allowing you to reuse previous searches. (We explain how to use this feature later in this chapter.)

Inside OUT

Customize the Send To menu

The SendTo folder, in %AppData%\Microsoft\Windows, contains shortcuts to some folders and applications that appear on the Send To submenu when you right-click a file or folder in File Explorer (or on the desktop). The SendTo folder is not hidden. You can add your own items to the Send To menu by creating shortcuts here. Type **shell:sendto** in the File Explorer address bar or in the Run dialog (Windows key+R) to open this folder and add or delete shortcuts.

Relocating personal data folders

The organizational scheme that Windows uses for personal data folders—keeping documents, music, pictures, and so on in visible subfolders of %UserProfile%—is perfectly appropriate for most configurations. In fact, for portable devices and all-in-one PCs that have only a single storage device, it's the only option.

On PCs that include options for multiple storage devices, some users prefer to store documents and other personal data on a volume other than the one that contains system files. With this configuration, it's easier to organize large collections of data; that's especially true of digital media files, which have a way of overwhelming available space on system volumes. (It's a good idea to keep a portion of your system drive free for maintenance, such as updates, and for performance, which reduces available data storage even further.)

This option is especially attractive on desktop PCs where Windows is installed on a solid-state drive (SSD) to maximize performance. Adding a second, much larger conventional hard disk—at a cost per gigabyte that's typically a fraction of an SSD—makes it possible to store large amounts of data without compromising system performance.

The easiest, safest way to accomplish this goal is to store personal data in folders on a separate drive, and then include those folders in your libraries and set them as the default save location, a topic we cover in the next section. This approach leaves you with a default set of profile folders, which you can still use when it's convenient to do so, but it keeps the bulk of your data files on a separate drive.

Not everyone loves libraries, however, and there's no requirement to love them. You can still move some or all of your profile subfolders in Windows 11, just as you could in earlier versions. (In fact, this is the exact technique Microsoft uses with the OneDrive Backup feature, which we describe in Chapter 8.) To relocate a user profile folder by editing its properties, follow these steps:

1. Open your user profile folder by starting at This PC, navigating to C:\Users, and then double-clicking your profile name. Alternatively, enter **%UserProfile%** in the address bar.

2. Right-click a folder you want to relocate and choose Properties. (Or select the folder, and then click Properties on the Home tab.)

3. On the Location tab, enter the address you want to relocate the folder to. For example, to move the Videos folder from its default location in the user profile on drive C to D:\ Videos, type or paste the path as shown in Figure 9-9.

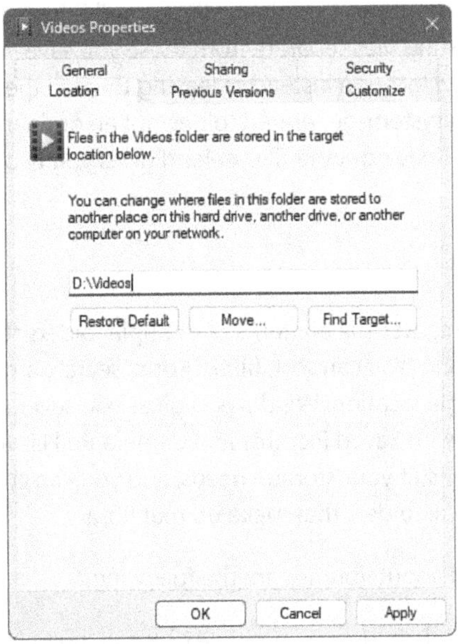

Figure 9-9 Use this dialog to change the location of system folders.

4. Click OK. Windows asks permission to create the target folder if it doesn't already exist. Click Yes. A Move Folder dialog similar to the one shown in Figure 9-10 appears.

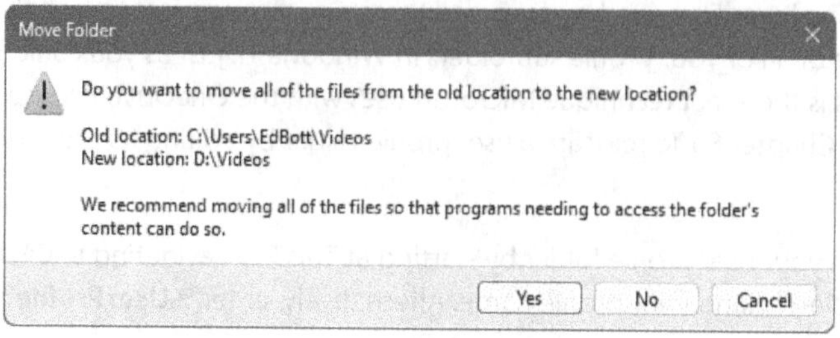

| Move Folder | × |

⚠ Do you want to move all of the files from the old location to the new location?

Old location: C:\Users\EdBott\Videos
New location: D:\Videos

We recommend moving all of the files so that programs needing to access the folder's content can do so.

| Yes | No | Cancel |

Figure 9-10   When moving the default location for a user profile folder to a new drive, it's wise to move its files as well.

5. Unless you have some good reason not to move the existing files from the original location to the new one, click Yes.

It's really not a good idea to click No in this dialog. First, it's difficult to imagine why you would want to divide your personal documents into two identically named folders on different volumes. (If you want to keep your existing files separate from those you save in the future, move the old files to a subfolder in the new location instead of leaving them in the old location.) Second, because %UserProfile% is a system-generated folder, not an ordinary data folder that corresponds to a fixed disk location, leaving some files behind gives you two subfolders with the same name in %UserProfile%.

Using libraries

A *library* is a virtual folder that aggregates the contents of multiple folders stored on your computer, on your network, or in the cloud. You can sort, filter, group, search, arrange, and share the data in a library as if it were in a single location. Windows 11 gives you several by default: Documents, Music, Pictures, and Videos, with Saved Pictures and Camera Roll libraries also available. You can create additional libraries to suit your storage needs, and you can customize any library by changing or adding to the physical folders that make up that library.

The important things to understand about libraries are the following:

- A library can encompass multiple folders on multiple disks on multiple networked devices.

- All folders in a library must be capable of being indexed, which in turn means you can perform fast searches covering the full contents of a library by entering a search term in the search box while viewing the contents of a library in File Explorer. That action quickly pulls up all matching documents, even if they're located on a networked PC or server or on an external drive. (It also means that you cannot add a shared folder to a library if it's located on a network-attached storage device that doesn't support Windows indexing.)

- Library files are automatically backed up by File History, but only if you've enabled this feature.

Libraries are useful for large collections of digital media files, where archived files are stored in a shared network folder or on an external drive, with current projects on a local drive. They're also invaluable for keeping projects organized—create a separate library for each project that includes your local project folder and the shared folders where you and your coworkers store templates, graphics, and submissions from outside contributors.

To create a new library, right-click the Libraries heading in the navigation pane, click Show More Options, and then click New > Library. (If you don't see the Libraries heading, right-click in an empty space in the navigation pane and then click Show Libraries.) Give the new library a descriptive name and then press Enter. Your newly created library appears in the navigation pane. Open it and then click the Include A Folder button to populate the library.

Using the Include Folder In dialog, select the folder you want to use as the default location for saving files in this library, and then click Include Folder. That opens the library and lists the contents of the folder you just selected.

To add more folders to the library, right-click the library name in File Explorer's navigation pane and then click Properties. That opens a dialog like the one shown in Figure 9-11, where you can manage the library's locations.

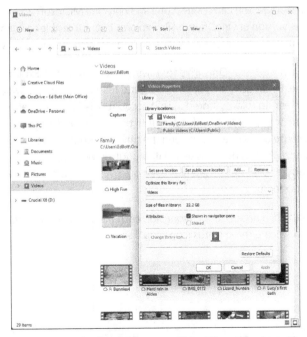

Figure 9-11   The first folder you add to a library becomes the default location for saving files within that library. Use this dialog to add more folders and change settings.

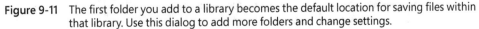

In this dialog, you can remove folders as well as add them, of course, and you can change the library's default save folder. The default save folder is important for applications that expect to save their documents in particular places—a music service, for example, that expects to save downloaded songs in a certain folder within the Music library. It's also the folder that File Explorer will use if you drag a file to the library's heading in the navigation pane.

To delete a library, right-click its entry in the navigation pane and click Delete. Doing so removes the library, but its component folders and their contents remain.

Inside OUT

Open a file or folder location from a library

Because libraries are virtual folders, it's sometimes difficult to perform operations directly on their contents. If you want to see a file or folder in its actual location in File Explorer, right-click and choose Open File Location or Open Folder Location.

Integrating OneDrive with File Explorer

As we explain in Chapter 8, every Microsoft account includes a generous allotment of free, cloud-based file storage from OneDrive. If you have a paid Microsoft 365 subscription, that allotment goes up to a full terabyte of storage. You can connect one and only one Microsoft account to Windows to access the consumer version of OneDrive in File Explorer, but you're able to connect one or more Azure AD accounts for access to multiple OneDrive for Business storage allocations.

To view the contents of any OneDrive or OneDrive for Business account in File Explorer, click its node in the navigation pane. By default, the Files On-Demand feature is enabled, which means File Explorer shows all the files and folders stored in that account. The files themselves are available on demand, but they're not actually downloaded until they're needed. Depending on the size of the file, that might cause a brief delay between the time you double-click a file and when it opens in the associated app. That trade-off is worth it, though, knowing you can have ready access to hundreds of gigabytes of cloud-based files even on a device that has only a fraction of that space available for data storage.

With Files On-Demand enabled, a green badge alongside each file or folder displays its availability status. Figure 9-12 shows the three status icons you'll see.

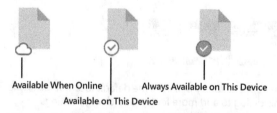

Available When Online

Available on This Device

Always Available on This Device

Figure 9-12   These badges alongside each file and folder indicate its current status. Online-only files take up no local disk space but can be downloaded on demand.

Items that are currently being synced (or are pending sync, because you have them open) are denoted by rotating arrows.

On a device with sufficient storage, you can sync your entire cloud file collection; just make sure there's enough disk space to handle all the photos, music files, video clips, and documents stored there. On devices that have limited local storage, you can selectively sync folders in the cloud to the local device so that those files are available even when you're offline.

By default, all files and folders are marked initially as Available When Online. Their status changes to Available On This Device after you double-click an item to download it. If you want one or more individual files or folders to be available at all times, right-click the item and choose Always Keep On This Device. Note that if you choose this option for a folder, any new files you save in that folder are automatically marked as Always Available On This Device.

With Files On-Demand enabled, you can selectively show or hide files and folders in File Explorer. Open the OneDrive Settings dialog for the account you want to adjust, click the Account tab, and then click Choose Folders. By default, all folders and all files are selected. From the list of folders, as shown in Figure 9-13, clear the checkbox for any you want to keep online without displaying in File Explorer.

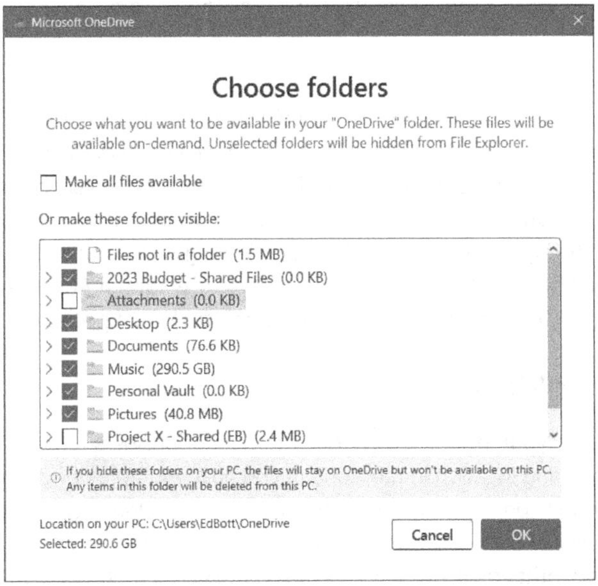

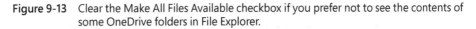

Microsoft OneDrive

Choose folders

Choose what you want to be available in your "OneDrive" folder. These files will be available on-demand. Unselected folders will be hidden from File Explorer.

☐ Make all files available

Or make these folders visible:

- ☑ 🗋 Files not in a folder (1.5 MB)
- ☑ 📁 2023 Budget - Shared Files (0.0 KB)
- ☐ 📁 Attachments (0.0 KB)
- ☑ 📁 Desktop (2.3 KB)
- ☑ 📁 Documents (76.6 KB)
- ☑ 📁 Music (290.5 GB)
- ☑ 📁 Personal Vault (0.0 KB)
- ☑ 📁 Pictures (40.8 MB)
- ☐ 📁 Project X - Shared (EB) (2.4 MB)

ⓘ If you hide these folders on your PC, the files will stay on OneDrive but won't be available on this PC. Any items in this folder will be deleted from this PC.

Location on your PC: C:\Users\EdBott\OneDrive
Selected: 290.6 GB

[Cancel]   [OK]

Figure 9-13   Clear the Make All Files Available checkbox if you prefer not to see the contents of some OneDrive folders in File Explorer.

Inside OUT

Move your local storage folder after setup is complete

Unlike many other data folders in your user profile, the OneDrive sync folders don't include a Location tab as part of the properties dialog. That's why we recommend that you make this configuration decision wisely when you first link your OneDrive account to your PC.

But if you realize after the fact (and after syncing lots of files) that you want to move the OneDrive folder, there's a relatively simple workaround.

Right-click the OneDrive icon in the notification area and then click Settings. On the Account tab of the resulting dialog, click Unlink This PC—don't worry, your local files and those in the cloud are unaffected. After OneDrive confirms that your account is unlinked, move the (now unsynced) local folder, and then go through OneDrive setup again, specifying the folder that contains your relocated data folder as the sync location. (You're asked to confirm that you want to merge the local files into your cloud storage.)

When setup is complete, OneDrive confirms that the files in the cloud match those in the new location. The process should go swiftly, with no loss of data.

You can disable the Files On-Demand feature if you prefer; in that configuration, only files and folders you choose to sync from the cloud to the local device are visible in File Explorer. To find this setting, select the OneDrive or OneDrive for Business icon in the navigation pane, just below Home. Then click the OneDrive icon in the upper-right corner of File Explorer, just above the details pane, to open the sync status menu. Finally, click the gear icon to open OneDrive Settings; on the Sync And Backup tab, click the down arrow to the right of Advanced Settings to display its options, and then turn the Files On-Demand switch to the Off position.

Syncing files and folders

Any file or folder you save in your local OneDrive or OneDrive for Business folder is automatically copied to a corresponding location in the cloud. If you have multiple devices (including PCs, Macs, tablets, and mobile phones) using the same OneDrive or OneDrive for Business account, changes, additions, and deletions you make to files and subfolders on one device are synchronized with all those other devices. So, for example, if you routinely work on the same documents on separate computers at the office and at home, saving to the OneDrive folder on each system ensures that you can retrieve the latest version from anywhere.

If you need to interrupt this normal syncing activity, right-click the OneDrive or OneDrive for Business icon in your notification area, click the gear icon, and choose Pause Syncing. You can pause for two hours, eight hours, or a complete day.

You can get a quick overview of OneDrive sync status (as well as how much of your available storage you've used) by clicking the cloud icon in the top-right corner of the File Explorer window for the OneDrive or OneDrive for Business account. Get detailed information about a sync operation in progress by clicking the OneDrive icon in your notification area, as shown in Figure 9-14.

Figure 9-14   Click the cloud icon in the notification area (white for personal, blue for a OneDrive for Business account) to display this sync status window.

The gear icon at the top of the status window opens a menu that includes a link to OneDrive Settings. The three icons in the navigation bar along the bottom of this status display are live. Click Open Folder to open the corresponding OneDrive or OneDrive for Business folder in File Explorer. Click View Online to open the OneDrive account in a browser window. Click Recycle Bin to open a browser window that shows files and folders you've deleted but are available for recovery.

Sharing OneDrive files and folders

To share a file or folder in your personal OneDrive, right-click the item in File Explorer and then click OneDrive > Share. A Share dialog like the one in Figure 9-15 appears.

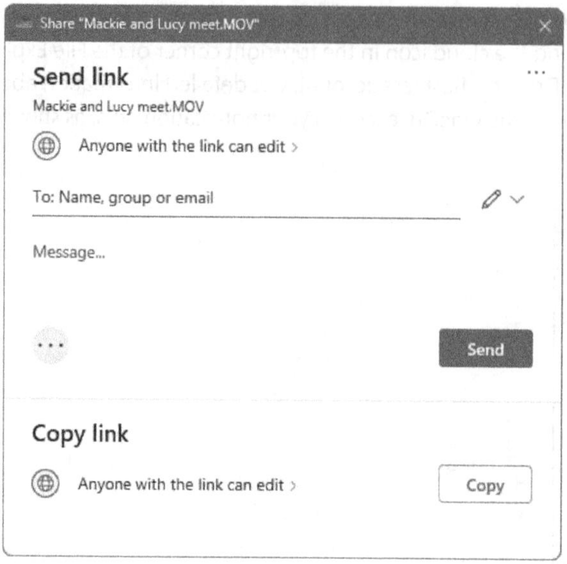

Figure 9-15   You can share any file or folder with another person using these controls or create a link that anyone can use to open that file or folder.

As Figure 9-15 shows, the share is initially set to offer full editing privileges to any recipient. Click the right-pointing arrow to reveal additional settings, including an Allow Editing checkbox that you can clear to make a shared file read-only. You can also assign a password and an expiration date to the share.

Enter an email address to share the link with a specific person, or click the Copy Link button, which copies the sharing link to the Clipboard so that you can paste it into a message yourself. Sharing options and procedures are similar in OneDrive for Business. Right-click a OneDrive for Business item in File Explorer and click Share. This opens the same Send Link dialog as in OneDrive Personal; click the arrow to the right of the link to see additional settings, such as an option to allow sharing only by members of your organization. Note that options to share outside your organization might be restricted by your administrator. You can also assign read-only or edit permissions and choose various other options.

Inside OUT

Share and sync files between accounts

One of OneDrive's best-kept secrets is the capability for friends and coworkers to work together using shared folders. (Over the years, the authors and editors who worked on this book and its predecessors have made extensive use of shared folders for their collaborative work.) The technique is simple: You mark a folder as shared, giving your colleagues access to it when they sign in with an account that has permission to read and write to that folder.

On the other end, your colleague opens OneDrive on the web and clicks Shared in the navigation pane on the left. They then open the shared folder and click Add To My OneDrive. The folder is now available in their list of folders that are eligible to be synced. Both of you now have full access to the contents of the shared folder.

For this technique to be most effective, you should name the shared folder carefully, using a descriptive name such as "Shared Files for Budget Committee," so that everyone who sees it knows immediately that it's a shared folder.

Recovering lost, damaged, and deleted files and folders

It takes only a fraction of a second to wipe out a week's worth of work. You might accidentally delete a folder full of files or, worse, overwrite an entire group of files with changes that can't be undone. Whatever the cause of your misfortune, Windows includes tools that offer hope for recovery. If a file is simply lost, try searching for it. (See "Searching from File Explorer" later in this chapter.) For accidental deletions, your first stop should be the Recycle Bin, a Windows institution since 1995.

NOTE

Like its predecessors, Windows 11 includes an alternative backup and recovery tool called File History. In Windows 11, Microsoft has removed the configuration options for this feature from the Settings app; to enable and use File History, you have to use a well-hidden option from the legacy Control Panel, as we describe in Chapter 15, "Troubleshooting, backup, and recovery." In Windows 11, the preferred method for protecting important data files is syncing them to OneDrive, which offers a Recycle Bin of its own, along with robust version history features that make it possible to recover from a simple accidental deletion or even from a ransomware attack.

The Recycle Bin provides protection against accidental erasure of files. In most cases, when you delete one or more files or folders, the deleted items go to the Recycle Bin, not into the ether. If you change your mind, you can go to the bin and recover the thrown-out items. Eventually, when the bin fills up, Windows begins emptying it, permanently deleting the files that have been there the longest.

The following kinds of deletions do not go to the Recycle Bin:

- Files stored on removable storage devices, such as USB flash drives

- Files stored on network drives, even when that volume is on a computer that has its own Recycle Bin

CHAPTER 9

- Files deleted from a command prompt

- Files deleted from compressed (zipped) folders

You can bypass the Recycle Bin yourself, permanently deleting an item, by holding down the Shift key while you delete the item. You might choose to do this if you're trying to reclaim disk space by permanently getting rid of large files and folder subtrees.

The root of each fixed drive on a Windows 11 PC has its own hidden $Recycle.Bin folder, which contains deleted files for all user accounts and whose contents are not accessible except through the virtual view afforded by the Recycle Bin shortcut. Windows ordinarily allocates up to 10 percent of each fixed disk's space for use by the Recycle Bin. To see and adjust the amount of space currently allocated to the Recycle Bin for each drive that it protects, right-click the Recycle Bin icon on your desktop and then click Properties. In the Recycle Bin Properties dialog (shown in Figure 9-16), you can select a drive and enter a different value in the Custom Size box. (When the bin is full, the oldest items give way to the newest.)

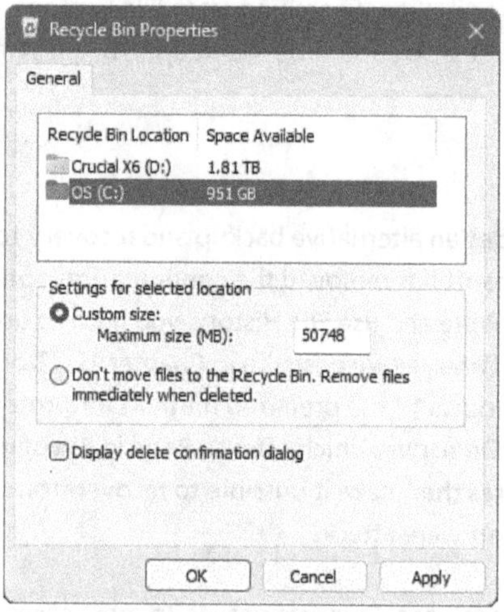

Figure 9-16   Use this dialog to fine-tune the amount of space the Recycle Bin is allowed to use—or to turn the feature off completely for selected drives.

(Note that this dialog doesn't show the amount of space currently being used by the Recycle Bin on a per-drive basis. To find those details, you need to go to Settings > System > Storage, as we describe in "Managing disk space," in Chapter 8.)

If you think that amount of space is excessive, enter a lower value. If you're certain you don't need to recover files from a particular drive, select the Don't Move Files To The Recycle Bin setting for that drive.

Windows normally moves files to the Recycle Bin silently when you delete them. If you'd prefer to see a confirmation prompt every time you delete a file or folder, select the Display Delete Confirmation Dialog checkbox.

Restoring files and folders

Opening the Recycle Bin in File Explorer displays a virtual view that contains the names and other essential details of all recently deleted items from the current user profile. In Details view, you can see when each item was deleted and which folder it was deleted from. Use the column headings to sort the folder—for example, to display items that have been deleted most recently at the top, with earlier deletions below. Alternatively, you can organize the bin by disk and folder by clicking the Original Location heading. If these methods don't help you find what you're hoping to restore, use the search box.

Note that deleted folders are shown only as folders; you don't see the names of items contained within the folders. If you restore a deleted folder, however, Windows re-creates the folder and its contents.

The Restore commands on the File Explorer command bar (Restore All Items and Restore The Selected Items) put items back in the folders from which they were deleted. If a folder doesn't currently exist, Windows asks your permission to re-create it. Note that if your Recycle Bin contains hundreds or thousands of deleted files dating back weeks or months, Restore All Items can create chaos. That command is most useful if you recently emptied the Recycle Bin and all of its current contents are visible.

If you want, you can restore a file or folder to a different location. Drag the item out of the Recycle Bin and drop it in the folder where you want to save it. To create a compressed backup copy of one or more items in the Recycle Bin, make a selection, right-click, and then choose Compress To Zip File from the shortcut menu.

Purging the Recycle Bin

A deleted file sitting in your Recycle Bin takes up as much space as it did before it was deleted. If you're deleting files to free up space for new programs and documents, transferring them to the Recycle Bin doesn't help. You need to remove them permanently. The safest way to do this is to move the items to another storage medium—a different hard disk or a removable disk, for example.

If you're sure you'll never need a particular file again, however, you can delete it in the normal way, and then purge it from the Recycle Bin. Display the Recycle Bin, select the item, and then press Delete.

To empty the Recycle Bin entirely, click Empty Recycle Bin on the File Explorer menu bar.

Sorting, filtering, and grouping in File Explorer

Regardless of the view settings you've chosen for a folder, you can adjust the way its contents are displayed at any time by changing the sort order, filtering the contents by one or more properties to include only selected items, and grouping and arranging the contents by a particular heading. In any view, the sort and group options are available by right-clicking anywhere in the contents pane and choosing a Sort By or Group By option. In most cases, however, these actions are easier to accomplish by switching to Details view and using the column headings; that's also the preferred way to filter.

Note that all these techniques also work with virtual folders, such as search results and libraries.

Sorting a folder's contents

To sort a folder in Details view, click the heading you want to use as a sort key. For example, to sort by Date Modified, click the Date Modified heading. Click again on the same heading to reverse the sort order. An up arrow or down arrow above the heading indicates whether the folder is sorted in ascending or descending order by that field.

In all other views, right-click any empty space in the contents pane and select a value from the Sort By menu. A bullet next to Ascending or Descending indicates the current sort order; choose the other option to reverse the sort order.

Filtering folder contents

In Details view only, you can use headings to filter the contents of a folder. If you rest your pointer on a heading, a drop-down arrow appears at the right. Clicking the arrow reveals a set of filter checkboxes appropriate for that heading. In most cases, the filter list is built on the fly from the contents of the current file list. If you're looking for a particular type of file—a Word or PDF document, for example, or an executable file—you can filter by type to show only those files. Figure 9-17 shows the filter list for the Type field in the Downloads folder, with the contents filtered to show only files whose type matches Application.

Select the checkbox next to any item to add it to the filter list; clear the checkbox to remove a previously selected item from the filter. After you filter the list in Details view, you can switch to any other view and the filter persists. Look in the address bar to see the specific filter applied and then click the folder name to the left of the search term in the address bar (also known as a *breadcrumb*) to remove all filtering without switching back to Details view.

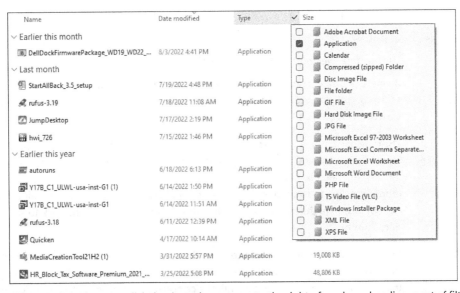

Figure 9-17   When you click the drop-down arrow to the right of a column heading, a set of filtering options appropriate for that heading appears.

If you filter by Size or Name, you get a much more limited set of choices that includes ranges rather than discrete values.

A single filter can include multiple items from each heading's filter list, which are treated as a logical OR—in other words, File Explorer displays items that match any of the selected check-boxes. A filter can also include multiple headings, which together function as a logical AND, with File Explorer displaying only items that satisfy the criteria applied to each heading. So, for example, you can filter a picture folder to show only photos where the value in the Rating column is four or five stars and the value in the Date Taken field is in this year, resulting in a list of your favorite photos of the year, suitable for a year-end newsletter or family photo album.

When a folder is filtered, check marks appear to the right of headings used for filtering. The values on which you have filtered appear in the address bar. You can perform most common file-management tasks on the items in the results list, including renaming individual files or using the Clipboard to copy or move files from their current location to a new folder.

Inside OUT

Use the date navigator to zoom through time

If you click a date heading, the filter options display a date navigator that resembles a calendar, with common date groupings available at the bottom of the list. You can also click Select A Date Or Date Range and use the calendar to filter the file list that way.

The date navigator is much more powerful than it looks at first glance. Use the calendar to zoom in or out and narrow or expand your view of the contents of a folder or a search. Initially, the calendar shows the current month, with today's date highlighted. Click the month heading to zoom out to a display showing the current year as a heading with the current month highlighted. You can then drag or hold down Ctrl and click to select multiple months.

Click the year to zoom out again to show the current decade. Click once more to show the current century. In any calendar view, you can use the arrows to the left and right of the column heading to move through the calendar a month, year, decade, or century at a time. To zoom back in, click any month, year, decade, or century on the calendar control. This technique is especially valuable with folders or search results containing hundreds or thousands of files and folders.

Grouping folder contents

If sorting and filtering don't give you enough ways to organize or locate files, try grouping. When you group items, File Explorer collects all the items that have some common property, displaying each group under a heading that can be expanded or collapsed in most views.

List view offers a particularly interesting perspective, with each group of results appearing under a column heading. The grouped arrangement is saved as part of the custom view settings for that folder; the next time you open the folder, it will still be grouped.

To group items in a File Explorer window, open the View tab, click Group By, and then click the property you want to use. File Explorer displays a bullet before the selected property. You can remove the grouping by returning to Group By and choosing None.

Inside OUT

Use checkboxes to simplify file selection

File Explorer offers two modes of file and folder selection—with and without checkboxes. You can switch between them by clicking View > Show and selecting or clearing Item Check Boxes.

With checkboxes on, you can select multiple items that are not adjacent to one another by clicking or tapping the checkbox for each one in turn; to remove an item from the selection, clear its checkbox. In either case, there's no need to hold down the Ctrl key. (This option is especially useful when you're trying to select files using a touchscreen.) In any case, though, Ctrl-selecting and Shift-selecting work as they always have, with or without checkboxes.

Searching from File Explorer

The search capabilities in Windows 11 are direct descendants of standalone tools and Windows features that date back to the turn of the 21st century. Those original search tools relied on something called Advanced Query Syntax (AQS), which survives, only slightly modified, in a mostly undocumented form today.

Windows 11 thoroughly hides most signs of AQS when you build a search using the Search Options menu. If you master the advanced query syntax, you can create your own searches and even save them for reuse, as we explain later in this section. But we start with the simplest of searches.

To use File Explorer's search tools, start by selecting a folder, a library, or a OneDrive account. That defines the *scope* of your search—the set of files from which you want to draw search results. (If you're not sure which folder contains the files you're looking for, choose Home from the navigation pane.)

Next, click in the search box in the upper-right corner of the File Explorer window. Start typing a word or phrase in the search box. As you type, File Explorer displays an abbreviated list of files and folders whose name, properties, or contents match that search term. Press Enter or click the arrow to the right of the search box, and your search results appear. At the same time, File Explorer adds a Search Options menu to the command bar; click it to display the additional options shown in Figure 9-18.

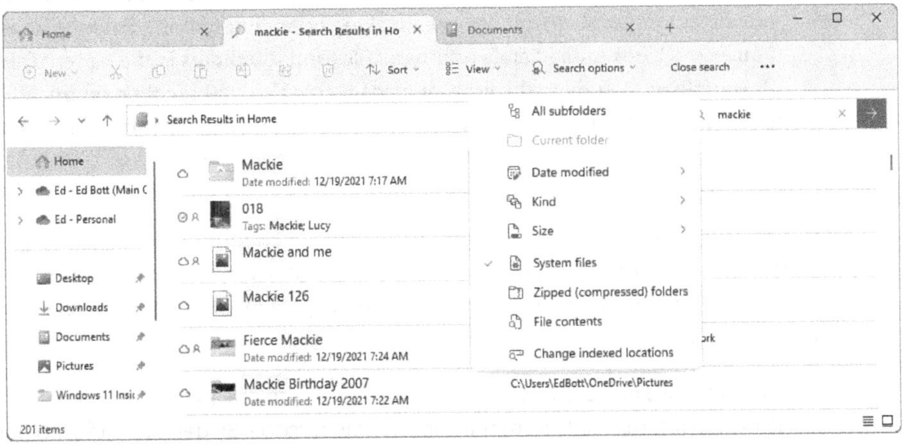

CHAPTER 9

Figure 9-18   Start a search by entering a search term or search operator in the search box; then click the Search Options menu to refine the search.

The following rules govern how searches work:

- Whatever text you type as a search term must appear at the beginning of a word, not in the middle. Thus, entering **des** returns items containing the words *des*ire, *des*tination, and *des*troy but not un*des*irable or sad*des*t. (You can override this behavior by using wildcard characters, as we explain in "Advanced search tools and techniques" later in this chapter.)

- Search terms are not case sensitive. Thus, entering **Bott** returns items with *Ed Bott* as a tag or property, but the results also include files containing the words *bott*om and *bott*le.

- By default, searches ignore accents, umlauts, and other diacritical marks. If you routinely need to be able to distinguish, say, Händel from Handel, click Search Options > Change Indexed Locations to open the Indexing Options dialog, click Advanced (for which you need administrative credentials), and then select Treat Similar Words With Diacritics As Different Words.

- To search for an exact phrase, enclose the phrase within quotation marks. If you enter two or more words without using quotes, the search results list includes items that contain all of the words individually.

Search results for indexed folders appear so quickly that you might have a substantial number of results before you type the second or third character in the search string. A complicating factor: If your search term is part of a subfolder name, your results list includes the entire contents of that subfolder.

Inside OUT

See all files in a folder and its subfolders

If you open File Explorer to a particular folder and you want to avoid the tedium of opening subfolders to view their contents, try using the wildcard character that's been around as long as Microsoft has been making operating systems. Entering an asterisk (*) in the search box immediately returns all files and subfolders in the current folder and all its subfolders. Assuming the list is of manageable size, you can then group, filter, sort, or otherwise rearrange the items within the folder to find exactly what you're looking for.

If simply entering a search term doesn't return the needed results, you have two options. The easiest is to build a new search (or refine the current one) using the point-and-click commands on the Search Options menu. The other is to use the powerful but cryptic search syntax to build a search manually.

The Search Options menu offers a wealth of options to create and refine a search. The choices you make here return results from the current search scope. By default, All Subfolders is selected on the Search Options menu. Click Current Folder to constrain results so that the contents of subfolders are not included.

Three filters get top billing on the Search Options menu:

- **Date Modified**   This property represents the most recent date a file or folder was saved. For a downloaded program file, it shows the date you saved the file locally, not the date the developer created it.

- **Kind**   This field shows predefined groups of file types, including those for some items that aren't stored in File Explorer. The most common choice to make here is Document, which includes text files, any file saved in a Microsoft Office format, and PDF files. Try Music, Movie, or Picture if you're looking for digital media files.

- **Size**   This list shows a range of sizes. If you're trying to clear space on your system drive, choosing Huge (1 – 4 GB) or Gigantic (>4 GB) is a good way to locate large files that can safely be deleted or archived on an external drive.

Any of those filters can help find a specific file. For example, if you're looking for an invoice you're certain was created last month, click Search Options > Date Modified and then select Last Month. If the set of results is still too large to scan, you can use additional choices on the Search Options menu to refine the search, or click in the search box and enter a word or phrase that you know was in the file's name or its contents.

You can also use search operators, followed by a colon, to restrict search results. For a folder optimized for General Items, the following four operators are useful:

- **Type**   Enter a file extension (pdf, xls, or docx, for example) or any part of the description in the Type field in Details view; enter **Excel**, for example, to return Excel workbooks in any format.

- **Name**   Enter a string of text here. The results list shows any file or folder that contains that exact string at the beginning of any word in its name.

- **Folder Path**   Enter a string of text here. The results list shows any file or folder that contains that exact string anywhere in its full path. If you enter **doc**, the results include all files and folders in your Documents folder and any of its subfolders (because Documents is part of the path for those subfolders), as well as the contents of any other folder whose name contains a word beginning with those three letters.

- **Tags**   Almost every data file contains this field, which is stored as metadata in the file itself. You can add one or more tags to any file using the Details pane or the Details tab in its properties dialog.

The list of available options changes slightly for other folder types. Documents folders include Authors and Title operators, and Photos folders include Date Taken and Rating, for example.

CHAPTER 9

To run the same search from a different location, click Search Again In and choose an available scope. Or just switch to a different node in the navigation pane and start again.

Configuring the Windows search index

At its heart, the Windows Search service relies on a speedy, powerful, and well-behaved indexing service that does a fine job of keeping track of files and folders by name, by properties, and (in supported formats) by contents. All those details are kept in the search index, a database that keeps track of indexed file names, properties, and the contents of files. As a rule, when you do most common types of searches, Windows checks the index first and returns whatever results it finds there.

NOTE

The search index is stored by default in %ProgramData%\Microsoft\Search\Data. Default permissions for this folder are set to allow access only to the System account and to members of the Administrators group. You can change its location using the Indexing Options dialog (available by searching from the taskbar or Control Panel). We can't, however, think of a good reason to do so. This folder contains no user-editable files, and we recommend that you leave it in its default location with its contents undisturbed.

Inside OUT

When do searches skip the index?

Although we focus mostly on indexed searches in this section, Windows 11 actually includes two search engines. The second engine is informally known as *grep* search. (The name comes from an old UNIX command derived from the full name *global | regular expression | print*.) Windows Search uses the index whenever you use the search box on the taskbar, and in libraries. In those circumstances, search looks only in the index and ignores any subfolders that are excluded from the index. (To include or exclude system files from your search results, click Search Options and then select System Files or clear its check mark.)

Windows uses the grep search engine if you begin your search from the This PC folder, from the root of any local drive (including the system drive), or from a local file folder. Grep searches include the contents of all subfolders within the search scope regardless of whether they're included in the search index.

To build the index that makes its magic possible, Windows Search uses several separate processes. The index is constructed dynamically by the Windows Search service, SearchIndexer.exe. It includes metadata for all files in all locations that are prescribed to be indexed; for documents

CHAPTER 9

in formats that support indexing of file contents, the indexer extracts the text of the files and stores it alongside the file properties for quick retrieval.

The Windows Search service begins running shortly after you start a new Windows session. From that point on, it runs in the background at all times, creating the initial index and updating it as new files are added and existing ones are changed or deleted. Protocol handlers do the work of opening different data stores to add items to the index. Property handlers allow Windows Search to extract the values of properties from items and store them properly in the index. Filters extract the contents of supported file types so that you can do full-text searches for those items.

The Search service does its best to minimize the effect of its activities on the performance of your system. The indexing process steps back or stops when the system perceives peak disk usage and under these other conditions:

- When gaming mode is on

- When power savings or a low power mode is on

- When your system switches from AC to DC or your battery charge is less than 50 percent

- When CPU usage goes above 80 percent or disk usage above 70 percent

In addition, the indexing algorithm in Windows 11 is designed to detect high disk usage and manage the indexer so that it doesn't negatively affect performance.

Which files and folders are in the index?

Indexing every 0 and 1 on your hard disk would be a time-consuming and space-consuming task—and ultimately pointless. When you search for a snippet of text, you're almost always looking for something you wrote, copied, or saved, and you don't want the results to include random program files that happen to have the same snippet embedded in the midst of a blob of code. (Yes, we know some developers might disagree, but they're the exception, and developer tools are the preferred method of dealing with those exceptions.) So the default settings for the indexer make some reasonable inclusions and exclusions.

Certain locations are specifically included. These include all user profiles (but not the AppData folder), the contents of the Start menu, and, if Microsoft 365 is installed, your OneNote and Outlook data. Locally synced files from OneDrive are automatically included in your local index. You can explicitly add other folders to the index, but Windows 11 eliminates the need to do that. Instead, just right-click the folder, click Include In Library, and select an existing library or create a new one; when you do so, Windows automatically adds that folder to the list of indexed locations and begins indexing its contents without requiring additional steps on your part.

If you understand the potential impact on performance and still want to extend Windows Search to include more folders than the default, go to Settings > Privacy & Security > Searching Windows and change the Find My Files option from Classic to Enhanced. This option changes the behavior of search, returning results from across all folders and drives, including your desktop.

To see which folders are currently being indexed, open the Indexing Options dialog. You can get there in various ways, including by typing **Indexing Options** in the search box on the taskbar.

CAUTION

We strongly recommend that you not try to manage locations manually using the Indexed Locations dialog. If you add a folder to a library and then remove it from the list of indexed locations, the folder remains in the navigation pane under the associated library, but none of its contents will be visible in the library itself.

Within that list of indexed locations, the Windows Search service records the file name and properties (size, date modified, and so on) of any file or folder. Files marked as System and Hidden are indexed but are displayed in search results only when you change File Explorer settings to show those file types. Metadata for common music, image, and video file formats is included in the index by default. The indexer also includes the contents of a file and its custom properties if the file format has an associated property handler and filter, as is the case with most popular document formats.

To see whether a particular file format supports content indexing, open the Indexing Options dialog, click Advanced, and then click the File Types tab. Find the extension associated with the file type and then look in the Filter Description column for the name of the filter that handles that extension. If you see File Properties Filter, the file type does not support content indexing. File types that are supported have a named filter, such as Microsoft Office Filter, Open Document Format ODT Filter, HTML Filter, or Reader Search Handler.

The list of formats on the File Types tab on your computer might include more file types if you installed Windows programs that include custom property handlers and filters, such as the Office Open XML Format Word Filter installed with Microsoft 365.

Windows Search does not index the content of files that are saved without a file name extension, nor does it index the contents of files that are protected by Information Rights Management (IRM) or digital rights management (DRM).

A handful of locations are specifically excluded from indexing. Even if you manually specify that you want your system drive (normally C) to be included in the index, the following files and folders will be excluded:

- The entire contents of the \Windows folder and all its subfolders. The Windows.old folder that's created by an upgrade installation of Windows 10 is also excluded.

- \$Recycle.Bin (the hidden folder that contains deleted files for all user accounts).

- \Users\Default and all of its subfolders. This is the user profile template used to create a profile for a new user.

- The entire contents of the \Program Files and \Program Files (x86) folders and all their subfolders.

- The \ProgramData folder (except the subfolder that contains shortcuts for the shared Start menu).

Monitoring the index and tuning indexer performance

The status message at the top of the Indexing Options dialog offers real-time updates on what the indexer is doing at the moment. "Indexing complete" means there are no pending tasks. The status message lists the number of items (files, folders, and so on) that are currently in the index.

"Indexing paused" means the service has temporarily stopped all indexing tasks; you see this message if you check the indexer status shortly after you start the computer because the default setting for the Windows Search service is Automatic (Delayed Start).

If indexing tasks are currently underway, the status message displays an increase or decrease in the number of items indexed as new, changed, and deleted files are processed. The indexer is designed to throttle itself whenever it detects that the system is working on other, presumably more important tasks. As a result, you'll most likely be told that "Indexing speed is reduced due to user activity" when you first check.

That message indicates the indexing service has backed off in response to your activity and is operating at a fraction of its normal speed. If the number of files to be indexed is big enough (if you copied a folder with several thousand documents, for instance), you see the indexing speed pick up dramatically after you keep your hands off the keyboard and mouse for a minute or so.

The exact speed of indexing depends on various factors, including the speed of your CPU and storage subsystem, as well as the number, size, and complexity of documents and whether their full contents are being indexed. Unfortunately, the status message in the Indexing Options dialog doesn't include a progress bar and doesn't indicate how many files are yet to be indexed, so there's no easy way to tell whether the current task is barely underway or nearly complete. If you haven't recently added any new folders to the index but have simply been changing a few files in the course of normal work, the index should stay close to complete (assuming you've ever had a complete index).

In the past, some websites for performance-obsessed Windows users complained about the performance hit that Windows Search causes; some even recommended disabling the Windows Search service to improve overall system performance. We recommend you leave it running. In our experience, the Windows Search service uses only a small percentage of available CPU resources even at its busiest. The indexing service is specifically designed to back off when you use your computer for other activities, switching to low-priority input/output (I/O) and allowing

CHAPTER 9

foreground I/O tasks, such as opening Start, to execute first. When Windows 11 first builds its index, or if you copy a large number of files to the system at once, indexing can take a long time and cause some spikes in CPU and disk activity, but you shouldn't notice a significant impact on performance. Some unusual indexing activity might be the result of maintenance activities, which the Search service performs automatically every 100,000 files. The operations typically last less than five minutes.

File Explorer accesses the index directly, so even if the indexer is busy processing new and changed files, it shouldn't affect the speed of a search operation. In normal operation, retrieving search results from even a very large index should take no more than a few seconds. You might notice a delay in opening a folder that contains a large number of compressed folders, including Zip files and ISO disk images.

TROUBLESHOOTING

You encounter problems finding files that should be in the search index

If you're certain that the files you're looking for are in an indexed location, but they don't turn up in search results, the index might have become corrupted. As with so many Windows features, there's a troubleshooter for that.

Open Settings and begin typing **Find And Fix Problems With Windows Search** in the search box. The resulting troubleshooter automatically finds and fixes any problems it can detect. If it finds none, it leads you through a series of steps to identify and resolve your problem.

Alternatively, you can manually rebuild the search index. From the Indexing Options dialog, click Advanced and then click Rebuild under the Troubleshooting heading.

We recommend you restart your system before trying to rebuild the index to ensure that no open files are interfering with the indexing process. Rebuilding the index might take a considerable amount of time, especially if you have a large number of files to index. To maximize the efficiency of the reindexing process, start the operation when you know you don't need to use your PC and you can leave it powered on—before lunch or at the end of your workday, for example.

Advanced search tools and techniques

The most basic query typically begins with a keyword (or a portion of a word) typed in the search box. Assuming you begin typing in a location that supports indexed searches (the search box in Start or, from File Explorer, your locally synced OneDrive folder, for example), the list of search results includes any item in that location containing any indexed word (in its name or properties or content) that begins with the letters you type. You can then narrow the results list by using additional search parameters.

NOTE

The advanced search syntax we describe here works in the File Explorer search box but not in searches from Start.

Advanced queries support the following types of search parameters, which can be combined using search operators:

- **File contents**   Keywords, phrases, numbers, and text strings

- **Kinds of items**   Folders, documents, pictures, music, and so on

- **Data stores**   Specific locations in the Windows file system containing indexed items

- **File properties**   Size, date, tags, and so on

In every case, these parameters consist of a word that the search query recognizes as a property or other index operator, followed by a colon and the value to search for or exclude. (When Windows Search recognizes a word followed by a colon as a valid property, it turns that operator blue.) You can combine search terms using Boolean operators and parentheses.

The value that immediately follows the colon can take several forms. If you want a loose (partial) match, just type a word or the beginning of a word. Thus, **type:Word** turns up files of the type Microsoft Word Document, Microsoft Word 97 – 2003 Document, Microsoft Word 97 – 2003 Template, Microsoft Word Macro-Enabled Document, and so on. To specify a strict (exact) match, use an equal sign and, if necessary, quotation marks, as in this example:

```
type:="Microsoft Word Document"
```

You can also use Boolean operators (AND, OR, and NOT) and parentheses to combine criteria. If you have fond memories of MS-DOS, you'll welcome using ***** and **?** as wildcards, and you can dramatically change the behavior of a search by means of the innocuous-looking tilde (~) character (which forces Windows to perform a strict character search in indexed locations, as discussed later in this section).

Of course, all these techniques become much more useful when you're able to reuse your carefully crafted search criteria, as we explain in "Saving searches" at the end of this chapter.

Searching by item type or kind

To search for files with a particular file name extension, you can simply enter the extension in the search box, substituting your file name extension for *ext*, like this:

```
*.ext
```

(Note that this method of searching does not work for .exe or .msc files.) The results include files that incorporate the extension in their contents as well as in their file names—which might or might not be what you want. You get a more focused search by using the ext: operator, including an asterisk wildcard and a period like this:

```
ext:*.txt
```

NOTE

As with many properties, you have more than one way to specify an exact file name extension. In addition to ext:, you can use fileext:, extension:, or fileextension:.

File name extensions are useful for some searches, but you get even better results using two different search properties: Type and Kind. The Type property limits your search based on the value found in the Type field for a given object. Thus, to look for files saved in any Microsoft Excel format, type this term in the search box:

```
type:excel
```

To find any music file saved in MP3 format, type this text in the search box:

```
type:mp3
```

To constrain your search to groups of related file types, use the Kind property, in the syntax kind:=*value*. Enter **kind:=doc**, for example, to return text files, Microsoft Office documents, Adobe Acrobat documents, HTML and XML files, and other document formats. This search term also accepts **folder**, **pic**, **picture**, **music**, **song**, **program**, and **video** as values to search for.

Changing the scope of a search

You can specify a folder or library location by using **folder:**, **under:**, **in:**, or **path:**. Thus, **folder:documents** restricts the scope of the search to your Documents library, and **in:videos mackie** finds all files in the Videos library that contain *Mackie* in the file name or any property.

Searching for item properties

You can search on the basis of any property recognized by the file system. (The list of available properties for files is identical to the ones we discuss in "Layouts, previews, and other ways to arrange files" earlier in this chapter.) To see the whole list of available properties, switch to Details view in File Explorer, right-click any column heading, and then click More. The Choose Details dialog that appears enumerates the available properties.

When you enter text in the search box, Windows searches file names, all properties, and indexed content, returning items where it finds a match with that value. That often generates more search results than you want. To find all documents of which Jean is the author, omitting documents that include the word Jean in their file names or content, you type **author:jean** in the search box. (To eliminate documents authored by Jeanne, Jeannette, or Jeanelle, add an equal sign and enclose jean in quotation marks: **author:="jean"**.)

When searching on the basis of dates, you can use long or short forms, as you please. For example, the search values

```
modified:9/29/22
```

and

```
modified:09/29/2022
```

are equivalent. (If you don't mind typing the extra four letters, you can use **datemodified:** and get the same results.)

To search for dates before or after a particular date, use the less-than (**<**) and greater-than (**>**) operators. For example,

```
modified:>09/30/2022
```

searches for dates later than September 30, 2022. Use the same two operators to specify file sizes less than and greater than some value.

Use two periods to search for items within a range of dates. To find files modified in September or October 2022, type this search term in the Start menu search box:

```
modified:9/1/2022..10/31/2022
```

You can also use ranges to search by file size. The search filters suggest some common ranges and even group them into neat little buckets, so you can type **size:** and then click Medium to find files in the range 1 MB to 128 MB.

Again, don't be fooled into thinking that this list represents the full selection of available sizes. You can specify an exact size range using operators such as **>**, **>=**, **<**, and **<=**. Also, you can use the **..** operator. For example, **size:0 MB..1 MB** is the same as **size:<=1 MB**. You can specify values using bytes, KB, MB, or GB.

Using multiple criteria for complex searches

You can use the Boolean operators **AND**, **OR**, and **NOT** to combine or negate criteria in the search box. These operators need to be spelled in capital letters (or they're treated as ordinary text). In place of the **AND** operator, you can use a plus sign (**+**), and in place of the **NOT** operator, you can use a minus sign (**–**). You can also use parentheses to group criteria; items in parentheses separated by a space use an implicit **AND** operator. Table 9-1 provides some examples of combined criteria.

Table 9-1   Some examples of complex search values

This search value	Returns
Mackie AND Lucy	Items in which at least one indexed element (property, file name, or an entire word within its contents) begins with or equals *Mackie* and another element in the same item begins with or equals *Lucy*
title:("report" NOT draft)	Items in which the Title property contains the word *report* (without the quote marks, this term would return any item whose title began with that word) and does not contain a word that begins with *draft*
tag:tax AND author:Edward	Items authored by Edward that include one or more tags that begin with the word *Tax*
tag:tax AND author:(Ed OR Edward) AND modified:<1/1/20	Items authored by Ed or Edward, last modified before January 1, 2020, that have an entry in the Tags field that begins with *Tax*

NOTE

When you use multiple criteria based on different properties, an AND conjunction is assumed unless you specify otherwise. The search value tag:Ed Author:Carl is equivalent to the search value tag:Ed AND Author:Carl.

Using wildcards and character-mode searches

File-search wildcards can be traced back to the dawn of Microsoft operating systems, well before the Windows era. In Windows 11, two of these venerable operators are alive and well:

- The asterisk (*****), also known as a star operator, can be placed anywhere in the search string and matches zero, one, or any other number of characters. In indexed searches, which treat your keyword as a prefix, this operator is always implied at the end; thus, a search for **voice** turns up *voice*, *voices*, and *voice-over*. Add an asterisk at the beginning of the search term (***voice**), and your search also turns up any item containing *invoice* or *invoices*. You can put an asterisk in the middle of a search term as well, which is useful for searching through folders full of data files that use a standard naming convention. If all your invoices start with **INV**, followed by an invoice number, followed by the date (**INV-0038-20220227**, for example), you can produce a quick list of all 2022 invoices by searching for **INV*2022***.

- The question mark (**?**) is a more focused wildcard. In index searches, it matches exactly one character in the exact position where it's placed. Using the naming scheme defined in the previous item, you can use the search term **filename:INV-????-2022*** to locate any file in the current location that has a 2022 date stamp and an invoice number (between hyphens) that is exactly four characters long.

To force Windows Search to use strict character matches in an indexed location, type a tilde (~) as the first character in the search box, followed immediately by your term. If you open your Documents library and type **~??v** in the search box, you find any document whose file name contains any word that has a *v* in the third position, such as *saved, level,* and, of course, *invoice.* This technique does not match on file contents.

Saving searches

After you have completed a search and displayed its results in File Explorer, you can save the search parameters for later reuse. Right-click anywhere in the pane displaying the search results and click Save Search. The saved search is stored, by default, in %UserProfile%\Searches; keep the default name or give it a more descriptive name. You can run the search again at any time, using the then-current contents of the index, by clicking that saved search in the navigation pane or Searches folder. (For easier access, try pinning the Saved Search shortcut to Quick Access or to Start.)

When you save a search, you're saving its specification (technically, a persistedQuery), not its current results. If you're interested in the XML data that defines the search, right-click the saved search in your Searches folder, choose Open With, and choose a text editor like Notepad or WordPad.

Inside OUT

Make your searches flexible

You don't need to enter a precise date as part of a search term. Instead, Windows Search recognizes "fuzzy" date qualifiers like *today, yesterday, this week,* and *last month.* This technique lets you create saved searches you can use to quickly open a window showing only the files you've worked on this week or last week, using **datemodified:(this week OR last week)** to define the search results. A search that uses dates picked from the calendar wouldn't be useful next month for identifying current projects, but one built using these relative dates is useful indefinitely.

Managing user accounts, passwords, and credentials

Before you can begin working with a device running Microsoft Windows 11, you must sign in with the credentials for a user account that is authorized to use that device. User accounts are an essential cornerstone of Windows security and are important in helping to provide a personalized user experience. As an administrator, you determine which user accounts are allowed to sign in to a specific device. In addition, you can configure user accounts on a Windows 11 device to accomplish the following goals:

- Control access to files and other resources

- Audit system events, such as sign-ins and the use of files and other resources

- Sync files and settings between different computers when signing in with the same account on those computers

- Authenticate automatically to email and other online services

- Require each user to provide additional proof of their identity (also known as multifactor authentication) when signing in for the first time on a new device

The credentials associated with a user account consist of a username and password that serve as identification and, in theory, ensure that no one can use the computer or view files, email messages, and other personal data associated with a user account unless they're authorized to do so.

If you believe your computer is in a secure location where only people you trust have physical access to it, you might be tempted to allow family members or coworkers to share your user account. We strongly caution against using that configuration and instead recommend that you create a user account for each person that uses the computer. Doing so allows each account to access its own user profile, store personal files and user preferences within that profile, and access cloud-based resources. With fast user switching, a feature described in this chapter, you can switch between user accounts with only a few clicks.

CHAPTER 10

With the right hardware and some initial setup, you can sign in and sign out without having to enter your full credentials. The Windows Hello feature allows you to sign in using biometric information, such as facial recognition or a fingerprint. In this chapter, we also explain how you can install the Microsoft Authenticator app on a trusted mobile device and use it to sign in to a Microsoft account or Azure AD account without having to enter a password.

Creating and managing user accounts

When you configure Windows 11 for the first time on a new computer (or on a PC with a clean installation of Windows), the setup program creates a profile for one user account, which is an administrator account. (An *administrator account* is one that has full control over the computer. For details, see "Administrator or standard user account?" later in this chapter.) Depending on what type of account you select during setup, that initial account can be a Microsoft account, an Azure Active Directory (Azure AD) account, or a local user account. A fourth user account type—an account on a local Active Directory domain—is available only on a managed network after this initial local account is created and you join the machine to the Windows domain. (For information about the differences between these account types, see the next section, "Choosing how you sign in.")

If you upgrade to Windows 11 from Windows 10 and you had local accounts set up in your previous operating system, Windows migrates those accounts to your Windows 11 installation. These migrated accounts maintain their group memberships and passwords.

After signing in for the first time, you can go to Settings > Accounts to create new user accounts and make routine changes to existing accounts. The Your Info page enables you to configure your account picture and access Account Settings, as shown in Figure 10-1.

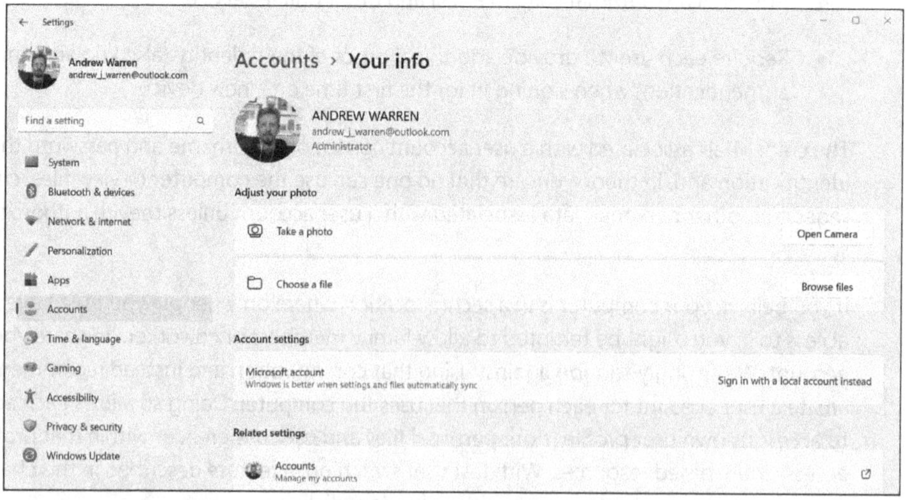

Figure 10-1   The Your Info page displays your account details.

You find different options and settings in Accounts depending on the type of account that you use (Microsoft account, Azure AD account, or local account), whether your account is a member of the Administrators group, and—if your computer is joined to a domain—whether group policies are in effect. On a computer joined to an Active Directory domain, all management of user accounts beyond basic tasks such as selecting a picture is normally handled by a domain administrator.

Some account-related settings are under the User Accounts heading in Control Panel, which is shown in Figure 10-2. Several of these settings duplicate functions that are available in Settings > Accounts.

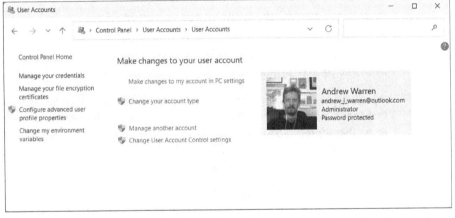

Figure 10-2   Visiting this Control Panel page is rarely necessary, as most options for creating and managing accounts are available in the Settings app.

You can add a new account only from the Accounts page in Settings. You can remove an account or change its type from that location or its Control Panel counterpart. All the esoteric options along the left side of the User Accounts page, as well as the Change User Account Control Settings option, are available only in Control Panel.

Choosing how you sign in

As we mentioned earlier, Windows 11 supports four different varieties of user accounts, each defined by how they handle authentication.

Microsoft account

When you set up a new account on a device running Windows 11, the default options strongly encourage you to sign in using a Microsoft account. You've probably used Microsoft accounts for years, perhaps without even knowing it. If you've signed up for a Microsoft service, including Outlook.com (or its predecessor, Hotmail), Microsoft 365 Family or Personal, Skype, or Xbox

Live, you already have a Microsoft account. Every email address that ends with hotmail.com, msn.com, live.com, or outlook.com is, by definition, a Microsoft account.

During setup, you can enter the email address associated with an existing Microsoft account, or you can create a new email address in the outlook.com domain. However, you do not need to sign up for a Microsoft email address to create a Microsoft account; you can set up a Microsoft account using an existing personal email address from any email provider, including Gmail and other non-Microsoft services.

Inside OUT

Avoid using a business email address as a Microsoft account

As we noted earlier in this section, you can use any personal email address as a Microsoft account. That includes free Gmail and Yahoo Mail accounts as well as accounts supplied by an internet service provider.

If you have an email address on a custom domain that is hosted on Microsoft 365 Exchange Online or Google Workspace servers, however, Microsoft no longer allows you to use that address as a Microsoft account. The new account creation process detects commercial accounts with custom domains that are hosted on either of those server types and rejects attempts to use them for a Microsoft account.

That is, frankly, a welcome change. Previously, if you used a work email address for a Microsoft account, you were inconvenienced every time you tried to sign in to either service because Windows 11 would ask whether you meant to use your Microsoft account or your work or school account. If you're saddled with this unfortunate configuration, you can set things right by assigning a new email alias to your Microsoft account, making it the primary address, and then removing the unwanted work address from the Microsoft account. We provide detailed instructions for accomplishing this task later in this section.

Signing in with a Microsoft account enables you to synchronize PC settings between multiple computers. If you use more than one PC—say, a desktop PC at work, a different desktop at home, a laptop for travel, and a tablet around the house—signing in with a Microsoft account lets you effortlessly use the same desktop background, stored passwords, account picture, accessibility configuration, and so on. The synchronization happens automatically and nearly instantly.

Some features in Windows 11, including OneDrive and family settings, require the use of a Microsoft account or an Azure AD account. It's possible to use OneDrive and other services that depend on a Microsoft account even if you sign in to Windows with a different account type. However, in this configuration, you must sign in to each service individually, and some features might be unavailable or less convenient to use.

Under normal circumstances, you associate a single personal email address with your Microsoft account and use that address to sign in to Windows. But because every Microsoft account supports up to 10 email aliases, you can use any alias associated with your primary address to sign in using your Microsoft account.

To manage Microsoft account aliases, go to *https://account.live.com/names/Manage* and sign in with your Microsoft account. Under the Account Alias heading, click Add Email Address to create a new alias or use an existing personal email address as an alias. (Click Add Phone Number to use a mobile phone number as a username.) After verifying the added email address, you can make it the primary address and, if you wish, remove the old address. (Every alias uses the same password as the original account.)

Under the Sign-In Preferences heading, you can also change the settings for email aliases so that a specific alias can't be used to sign in to your Microsoft account. That precaution allows you to use aliases to send and receive email but prevents them from being used to access your Microsoft account.

Local account

A *local account* is one that stores its sign-in credentials and other account data on your PC. A local account works only on a single computer. It doesn't require an email address as the username, nor does it communicate with an external server to verify credentials.

This type of account was the standard in Windows for decades. In Windows 11, Microsoft recommends the use of a Microsoft account rather than a local user account for PCs that aren't part of a managed business network. But using a Microsoft account is not a requirement; local accounts are still fully supported.

You might prefer a local account if your home or small business network includes computers running Windows 7 or earlier (that is, versions that do not explicitly support the use of Microsoft accounts).

> ➤ For details, see "Sharing files, printers, and other resources over a local network" in Chapter 11, "Configuring Windows networks."

In addition, some folks have privacy and data security concerns about storing personal information on the servers of a large corporation, whether that infrastructure is managed by Microsoft, Google, Apple, Amazon, or another cloud provider. Signing in with a local account minimizes the amount of information your PC exchanges with Microsoft's servers.

Inside OUT

How should you handle the password reset questions for a local account?

When you set up a new, password-protected local account using Windows 11, you're required to choose three security questions (from a list of six) and provide answers to those questions. The intent of this feature is to help you reset your password if you forget it. (You can skip this step by disconnecting from the Internet before you reach this page when you create the new account.)

The questions on offer aren't particularly robust. Some of these details, like your first pet's name or the name of the first school you attended, might be easy pickings for an attacker who knows you. A thief who steals your laptop probably won't have ready access to that information, but someone in your immediate circle might.

On a home PC in a secure location, this option might be useful, especially if you're setting up a PC for a forgetful relative. But if you find the idea of answering those questions to be too risky, here's an alternative approach: *Don't tell the truth.* Windows doesn't make even the slightest effort to check whether your answers are true or even sensible. Instead of answering the questions you're asked, think of a three-word challenge phrase and use those words in place of the actual answers. If you'd prefer to render the question-based password reset feature completely unusable, by yourself or a would-be attacker, just mash the keys randomly and enter a long stream of gibberish as the "answer" to each question.

As an alternative, consider creating a password reset disk, which you can lock away in a secure location separate from your PC. You need removable media, such as a USB flash drive, external hard drive, or memory card. After signing in to your account, open Control Panel > User Accounts and click Create A Password Reset Disk. Follow the Forgotten Password Wizard's instructions. You can have only one password reset disk for each local user account. If you make a new one, the old one is no longer usable. We explain how to reset your password using this disk later in this chapter.

You can switch between using a Microsoft account and a local account by going to Settings > Accounts > Your Info. On this page (shown earlier in Figure 10-1), click Sign In With A Local Account Instead. Windows leads you through a few simple steps to create a local account, which you then use for signing in.

If you're currently signed in using a local account, the link on that page reads Sign In With A Microsoft Account Instead. Click that link to replace your local account with a Microsoft account. As part of making the switch, you need to enter your local password one more time. A few screens later, you're connected to an existing Microsoft account or a new one you create. From that time forward, you sign in using your Microsoft account.

Azure Active Directory account

The third type of account, available during the initial setup of Windows 11 Pro, Enterprise, or Education, is a work or school account using Azure Active Directory. Azure AD offers some of the advantages of a Microsoft account, including support for two-factor authentication and single sign-on to online services, balanced by the capability of network administrators to impose restrictions using management software. These accounts are most common in medium-size and large businesses and schools.

Organizations that subscribe to Microsoft's business-focused online services—including Business or Enterprise editions of Microsoft 365 (formerly known as Office 365), Microsoft Intune, and Microsoft Dynamics CRM Online—automatically have Azure AD services as part of their subscription. Every user account in that service automatically has a corresponding Azure AD directory entry.

You can connect an Azure AD account to a new Windows 11 installation during the initial setup of Windows 11, as we explain in "Performing a clean install," in Chapter 2, "Setting up a new Windows 11 PC." You can also associate a Windows 11 device with Azure AD after it has been set up to use a local account or a Microsoft account. To accomplish this task, go to Settings > Accounts > Access Work Or School, and then click Connect. The resulting dialog, shown in Figure 10-3, gives you two options.

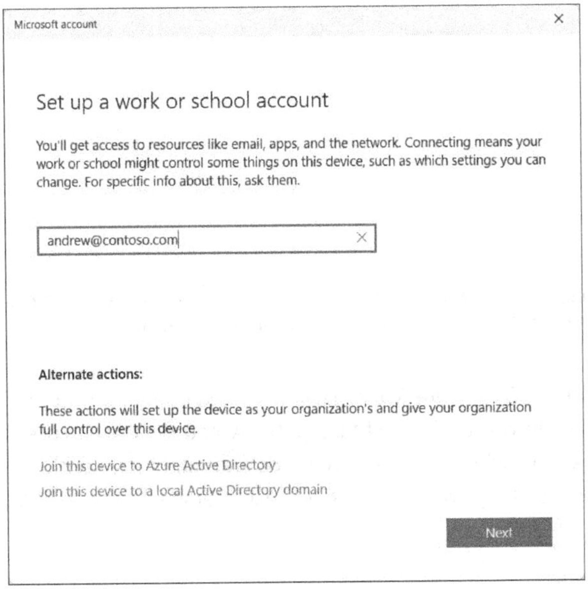

Figure 10-3   Adding a work or school account using the Settings app offers multiple options. The "Join this device" links give your organization control over the device.

The default option allows you to continue using your Microsoft account or your local account to sign in to Windows and simply adds your Azure AD account for easier access to Microsoft 365 services, including Exchange Online email and OneDrive for Business. If that's your goal, click Next and follow the prompts.

If you want to reconfigure the PC so that you sign in to Windows using your Azure AD account, don't enter an email address in the Set Up A Work Or School Account dialog; instead, click the Join This Device To Azure Active Directory link at the bottom of that dialog. That option opens the dialog shown in Figure 10-4. After you sign in using your Azure AD credentials, you have one final chance to confirm that you want to sign in with your organization's credentials and allow administrators to apply policies to your device.

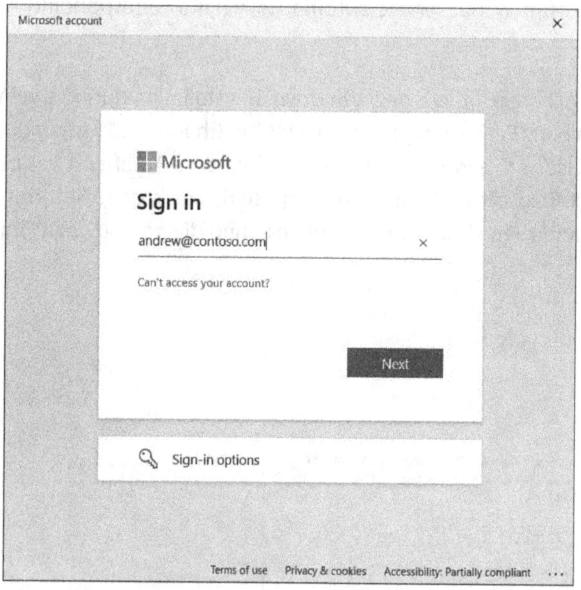

Figure 10-4   Enter credentials from an Azure Active Directory account, such as a Microsoft 365 Enterprise subscription, to join the device to that organization.

After connecting a Windows 11 PC to Azure AD, you can view and edit your user profile by going to Settings > Accounts > Your Info and clicking Manage My Accounts. You can use the tabs to manage security information, including sign-in methods and multifactor authentication. Depending on organizational settings, you might be able to reset your own password.

Active Directory domain account

In organizations with a Windows domain server running Active Directory services, administrators can join a PC to the domain, creating a domain machine account. (This option is available only with Windows 11 Pro, Enterprise, or Education editions.) After this step is complete, any user with a domain user account can sign in to the PC and access local and domain-based resources. We cover this account type more fully in Chapter 19, "Managing Windows PCs in the enterprise."

Administrator or standard user account?

The backbone of Windows security is the ability to uniquely identify each user. While setting up a computer—or at any later time—an administrator creates one or more user accounts, each of which is identified by a username and is normally secured by a password. When the user signs in to the PC using these credentials, Windows controls access to system resources on the basis of the permissions and rights associated with each user account by the resource owners and the system administrator.

Windows classifies each user account as one of two account types:

- **Administrator**   Members of the Administrators group are classified as administrator accounts. By default, the Administrators group includes the first account you create when you set up the computer and an account named Administrator that is disabled and hidden by default. Unlike other account types, administrators have full control over the system.

- **Standard user**   Members of the Users group are classified as standard user accounts. Users have limited administrative access, but can perform basic administrative functions, such as modifying the properties of their own account or managing Windows updates.

Assigning an appropriate account type to the people that use a computer is straightforward. At least one user must be an administrator; naturally, that should be the person who manages the computer's use and maintenance. As a best practice, all other regular users should have standard user accounts.

NOTE

For computers running Windows 11 that you join to Azure AD, you can specify a user within your Azure AD tenant as a device administrator; this task can be accomplished automatically during the Azure AD join process.

CHAPTER 10

WHAT HAPPENED TO THE ADMINISTRATOR ACCOUNT?

Every computer running Windows has a special account named Administrator. In versions of Windows before Windows 7, Administrator was the primary account for managing the computer. Like other administrator accounts, the Administrator account has full rights over the entire computer. But in Windows 11, the Administrator account is disabled by default.

In Windows 11, there's seldom a need to use the Administrator account instead of another administrator account. With default settings in Windows, the Administrator account does have one unique capability: It's not subject to UAC, even when UAC is turned on for all other users. All other administrator accounts (which are sometimes called Protected Administrator accounts) run with standard-user privileges unless the user consents to elevation. The Administrator account runs with full administrative privileges at all times and never needs your consent for elevation. (For this reason, of course, it's rather risky. Any app that runs as Administrator has full control of the computer—which means apps written by malicious or inexperienced programmers might do significant damage to your system.)

Inside OUT

And the Guest account?

Historically, the built-in Guest account provided a way to offer limited access to occasional users. Not so in Windows 11. Although this account still exists, it's disabled by default, and the supported tools for enabling it (the Local Users And Groups console, for example) do not work as you might expect. In our experience, trying to trick Windows 11 into enabling this capability is almost certain to end in frustration. In the cloud-centric world of Windows 11, the Guest account no longer works as it used to, and enabling it can cause a variety of problems. A better solution (if your guests don't have their own device that can connect to your wireless network) is to set up a standard account for guest use.

Changing account settings

With options in Settings and Control Panel, you can make changes to your own account or to another user's account.

To change your own account, go to Settings > Accounts > Your Info, shown earlier in Figure 10-1. Even quicker: Open Start, click or tap your account picture, and then choose Change Account Settings.

Here, you can change your account picture, either by browsing for a picture file or by using your webcam to take a picture. If you sign in with a Microsoft account, the Manage My Accounts link opens your default web browser and loads your account page at *https://account.microsoft.com*. On that page, you can change your password or edit the name associated with your Microsoft account. Click other links along the top of the page to review your services and subscriptions, security settings, and order history and payment and to review or change your payment options. You can also get information about other devices associated with your Microsoft account.

If you have added one or more users to your computer, you (as a computer administrator) can make changes to the account of each of those users. (For information about adding users, see "Adding a user to your computer" later in this chapter.)

To change a user's account type, go to Settings > Accounts > Other Users. Click the name of the account you want to change, and click Change Account Type. Your choices are Standard User or Administrator, as described in the previous section.

If the person signs in with a Microsoft account, there are no other changes you can make. (You can't make changes to someone else's Microsoft account; only the owner of that account can make changes by signing in at *https://account.microsoft.com*.) For users who sign in with a local user account, you can make a few additional changes, but you must start from User Accounts in Control Panel (shown earlier in Figure 10-2). Click Manage Another Account, and then click the name of the account you want to change. You can make the following changes:

- **Account Name**   The name you're changing here is the full name, which is the one that appears on the sign-in screen, on the Start menu, and in User Accounts.

- **Password**   You can create a password and store a hint that provides a reminder for a for- gotten password. If the account is already password protected, you can use User Accounts to change the password or remove the password. For more information about passwords, see "Setting or changing a password" later in this chapter.

- **Account Type**   Your choices here are the same as in Settings > Accounts: Administrator (which adds the account to the Administrators group) or Standard User (which adds the account to the Users group).

- **Delete**   You can also delete the account, optionally choosing to either delete the user's files or retain them.

If you sign in with a local user account, you can make the following additional changes to your own account (that is, the one with which you're currently signed in) by clicking links in the left pane:

- **Manage Your Credentials**   This link opens Credential Manager, where you can manage stored credentials that you use to access network resources and websites. Note that the new Microsoft Edge browser, based on the Chromium engine, has its own store of saved credentials and ignores this one.

CHAPTER 10

- **Create A Password Reset Disk**   This link, available only when you are signed in with a local account, launches the Forgotten Password Wizard, from which you can create a password reset tool on removable media. As an alternative, Windows 11 allows you to recover from a lost password using answers to the password reset questions you chose when setting up the account.

- **Manage Your File Encryption Certificates**   This link opens a wizard you can use to create and manage certificates that enable the use of Encrypting File System (EFS). EFS, which is available in Pro and Enterprise editions of Windows 11, is a method of encrypting folders and files so that they can be accessed only by someone who has the appropriate credentials. For more information, see "Encrypting information" in Chapter 12, "Windows security and privacy."

- **Configure Advanced User Profile Properties**   This link is used to switch your profile between a local profile (one that is stored on the local computer) and a roaming profile (one that is stored on a network server in a domain environment). With a local profile, you end up with a different profile on each computer you use, whereas a roaming profile is the same regardless of which computer you use to sign in to the network. Roaming profiles require a domain network running Windows Server Active Directory services. Microsoft accounts and Azure AD accounts use a different mechanism to sync settings.

- **Change My Environment Variables**   Of interest primarily to programmers, this link opens a dialog in which you can create and edit environment variables that are available only to your user account; in addition, you can view system environment variables, which are available to all accounts.

Deleting an account

As a local administrator, you can delete any local account or Microsoft account set up on a Windows 11 PC, unless that account is currently signed in. To delete an account, go to Settings > Accounts > Other Users and click the name of the account you want to delete. Then click Remove. Windows then warns about the consequences of deleting an account, which include removing the user's files.

NOTE

Windows won't let you delete the last local account on the computer, even if you signed in using the built-in account named Administrator. This limitation helps to enforce the sound security practice of using an account other than Administrator for your everyday computing.

After you delete an account, that user can no longer sign in. Deleting an account also has another effect you should be aware of: You cannot restore access to resources that are currently shared with the user simply by re-creating the account. This includes files shared with the user and the user's encrypted files, personal certificates, and stored passwords for websites and network resources. That's because those permissions are linked to the user's original security identifier (SID)—not the username. Even if you create a new account with the same name and password, it will have a new SID, which will not gain access to anything that was restricted to the original user account. (For more information about security identifiers, see "Introducing access control in Windows" later in this chapter.)

Inside OUT

Delete an account without deleting its data

Earlier versions of Windows included an option for preserving an account's data files—documents, photos, music, downloads, and other files and folders stored in the user's profile—when you delete the user account. Windows 11 offers that option, too, but you won't find it in Settings. Instead, open User Accounts in Control Panel. Click Manage Another Account, select the account you want to remove, and then click Delete The Account.

This option gives you a choice about what to do with the account's files:

- **Delete Files**   After you select Delete Files and confirm your intention in the next window, Windows deletes the account, its user profile, and all files in that account's user profile.

- **Keep Files**   Windows copies certain parts of the user's profile—specifically, files and folders stored on the desktop and in the Documents, Favorites, Music, Pictures, and Videos folders—to a folder on your desktop, where they become part of your profile and remain under your control. All other folders in the user profile are deleted after you confirm your intention in the next window that appears; email messages and other data stored in the AppData folder are also deleted, as are settings stored in the registry.

CHAPTER 10

Making the sign-in process more secure

As we noted in the previous section, every account on a Windows 11 PC is backed by a set of credentials, comprising a username (which might be in the form of an email address) and a password. You can use those credentials to sign in to your account on a Windows 11 PC: At the sign-in screen, select your name (if it's not already selected) and then enter a password.

NOTE

When you first turn on your computer or return to it after signing out, the *lock screen* is displayed. The lock screen normally displays a picture, the current time and date, and alerts from selected apps. (You can select your own lock screen picture and specify what information you want displayed on the lock screen. For details, see "Customizing the lock screen and sign-in screen" in Chapter 4.) To get from the lock screen to the sign-in screen, click anywhere, press any key, or (if you have a touchscreen) swipe up.

Inside OUT

Press Ctrl+Alt+Delete without a keyboard

Some network administrators enable a policy that requires you to press Ctrl+Alt+Delete to switch from the lock screen to the sign-in screen. (That keystroke combination, whose role in Windows security dates back to the earliest versions of Windows NT, is called the *secure attention sequence*.) That requirement can make it tough to sign in to your corporate network on a tablet with no keyboard—until you know the trick. On modern hybrid Windows 11 PCs such as the Surface Pro and Surface Book device families from Microsoft, the display can be detached from its keyboard; in that configuration, press the Power button and Volume Down simultaneously to send the required sequence. In the unlikely event that you're running Windows 11 on a Windows 8–era device with a dedicated Windows button (usually on the bezel along the right or bottom edge of the screen), press that button and the power button simultaneously.

Signing in with a strong password can be inconvenient, especially when it's long and consists of a mix of upper- and lowercase letters, numbers, and special characters. The degree of difficulty becomes even more extreme when you need to enter that strong password on a device where the physical keyboard is unavailable.

To make the sign-in process more convenient without sacrificing security, Windows 11 supports several options you can use in place of your account password. Figure 10-5 shows the full range of alternatives, which you can find by going to Settings > Accounts > Sign-In Options.

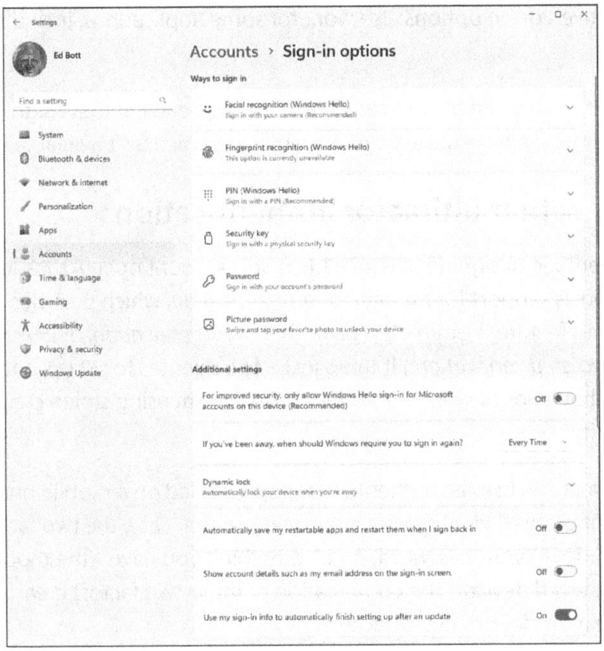

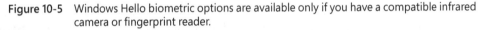

Figure 10-5   Windows Hello biometric options are available only if you have a compatible infrared camera or fingerprint reader.

The first three options on the list apply to Windows Hello, a feature that augments the Windows 11 sign-in process with a form of hardware-based security. Additional sign-in options on this page include tools for managing physical security keys, and setting up and managing Dynamic Lock.

If you set up more than one option for signing in, you can choose a method other than the default by clicking Sign-In Options on the sign-in screen. This ability might come in handy, for example, if Windows Hello fails to recognize your face or fingerprint. Icons for each of the options you set up then appear as shown in Figure 10-6; click or tap one to switch methods.

Figure 10-6   Click Sign-In Options to choose a different method for signing in. If Windows Hello biometric authentication is set up, icons for Face or Fingerprint might appear here.

Note that these alternative sign-in options also work for some applications, including the Microsoft Store.

In the following sections, we explain how to set up and manage each of these sign-in methods. We start with the most important secure sign-in option of all, which isn't available in Settings.

Adding security with multifactor authentication

The single greatest advantage of signing in with a Microsoft account or an Azure AD account, as far as we're concerned, is support for *multifactor authentication*, which provides security for your PC and its data. (This feature is often called *two-factor authentication*, or 2FA, but it can also be referred to as *two-step verification*.) It takes just a few minutes to set up, and the result is a layer of protection that helps prevent a malicious person from using stolen credentials to impersonate your identity.

The most common form of 2FA uses an authenticator app installed on a mobile phone to provide a secondary form of proof of identity when necessary. In that case, the two factors are the classic "something you know" (your password) and "something you have" (the mobile device that you've set up as a trusted device). The combination of those two factors creates a hurdle that will stop all but the most determined attackers.

To turn on this feature for a Microsoft account, go to *https://account.live.com/proofs* and sign in. On that page, you can add approved contact info for receiving security requests and turn on two-step verification.

For devices that are connected to an organization using Azure AD, an administrator must enable multifactor authentication; after that step is complete, users can manage security verification from the Azure AD My Account portal. Start at *https://myaccount.microsoft.com*, signing in with your work or school account, and then click Additional Security Verification, under the Security Info heading; you can go directly to the page from *https://mysignins.microsoft.com/security-info*.

For Windows 11, the identity verification process works best with the Microsoft Authenticator app, which is available on both Android and iOS smartphones from each platform's store or from *https://www.microsoft.com/authenticator*. This app handles authentication for Azure AD and Microsoft accounts; it also supports most third-party accounts, including those from Google, Facebook, and Amazon. The Authenticator app supports fingerprint- and face-based approvals on compatible hardware and works with several types of smart watches.

When 2FA is turned on, you need to use that additional factor to prove your identity in situations that Microsoft defines as requiring extra security, such as when signing in on a new device for the first time or making changes to account settings; typically, this involves approving a prompt on a previously verified device, such as the Microsoft Authenticator app on a smartphone.

Using Windows Hello

The Windows Hello feature enables you to configure your Windows 11 PC as a trusted device that you can unlock using biometric hardware or a device-specific PIN. In this configuration, your credentials are stored in encrypted form on the device; to sign in, you unlock those credentials with a PIN or biometric identification (using your fingerprint or face).

To set up Windows Hello, you first have to confirm your identity by correctly entering your credentials. After passing that test, you can add a PIN and, with the right hardware support, register your biometric information. When this enrollment process is complete, you can skip the password and sign in to Windows 11 by entering your PIN or supplying what Microsoft engineers call your "biometric gesture," using facial recognition or a fingerprint reader.

The device you sign in on acts as an authentication component because you established your identity when you set up the device; your additional information (the PIN or your biometric data) is associated with the enrolled device and is not stored on a remote server. This arrangement prevents so-called shoulder surfing attacks, where someone tries to steal your password by watching your keystrokes as you sign in. Because Windows Hello uses a device-specific PIN, other people can't sign in to your account unless they also steal your computer.

If you want, you can also configure a device so that the only available options use the Windows Hello PIN or biometric information; in this configuration, the Password and Picture Password sign-in options are not available. To enable this option, go to Settings > Accounts > Sign-In Options and enable the For Improved Security, Only Allow Windows Hello Sign-In For Microsoft Accounts On This Device (Recommended) setting.

Inside Out

Configure Windows Hello for Business

For PCs running Windows 11 in unmanaged environments, Windows Hello uses what it calls a "convenience PIN" to unlock encrypted credentials on the device. In managed deployments, administrators can configure Windows Hello for Business settings using Group Policy or mobile device management software such as Microsoft Intune. When these policies are enabled, device credentials are backed by a certificate or encryption key that in turn is bound to the Trusted Platform Module (TPM) on the device; unlocking the device provides an authentication token based on the certificate or key. This architecture makes network-based authentication less susceptible to "replay" attacks. For more details about Windows Hello for Business, see https://bit.ly/WindowsHelloForBusiness.

CHAPTER 10

Setting up a Windows Hello PIN

Windows 11 encourages you to set up a PIN when you create a new user account for the first time. If you skipped this step during Setup, go to the Sign-In Options page and click PIN (Windows Hello). Then click Set Up and follow the on-screen instructions. You need to confirm your identity by entering your account password first. Then enter and confirm your new PIN, as shown in Figure 10-7. The minimum length is four digits (0–9 only), but your PIN can be as long as you want. If you prefer something more complex and harder to guess, select the Include Letters And Symbols option.

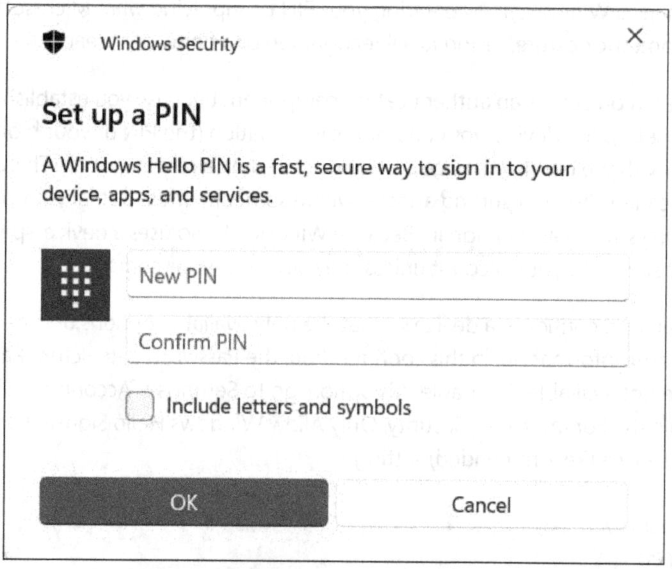

Figure 10-7   A PIN serves as a convenient alternative for signing in to Windows and verifying your identity in apps and services. You can choose a PIN that's longer than the minimum of four characters.

If you want to change your PIN, from the Sign-in Options page, select PIN (Windows Hello) and then click Change Your PIN. Follow the on-screen instructions to complete the process.

To sign in using a PIN, enter the numbers on your keyboard. Note that keypresses in the numeric keypad area of the keyboard register as numbers while you type in the PIN box on the sign-in screen, regardless of whether Num Lock is set. If your computer doesn't have a keyboard, a numeric pad appears on the screen so that you can tap your PIN. (If the numeric pad does not appear, tap in the PIN-entry box.)

Inside OUT

Make your PIN even stronger

You might be worried that a four-digit numeric PIN, presenting 10,000 possible combinations from 0000 to 9999, is too easy to guess. You'll probably rest a little easier knowing that Windows 11 offers only five incorrect tries before locking you out. After four incorrect attempts, you're required to enter a challenge phrase (which incidentally confirms that your keyboard is working correctly). After the fifth incorrect attempt, a would-be intruder is locked out. At that point, Windows requires you to restart your device and try signing in again. After a handful of failed tries, Windows stops accepting new guesses and requires you to enter your password.

And imagine an intruder's surprise when they learn that a PIN can be more than four digits long. When you set up your PIN, we recommend that you make it six digits instead of four, allowing up to a million possible numeric combinations and trying the patience of even the most persistent attacker. Even an eight-digit PIN (100 million numeric combinations) is still easier to enter than a complex password.

As an even more secure alternative, you can select the Include Letters And Symbols check box and set up a complex PIN consisting of eight characters representing more than a trillion possible combinations of numbers, letters, and symbols.

If you sign in to an Active Directory domain or Azure AD, a network administrator can use Group Policy on Windows 11 Pro or Enterprise to mandate a minimum PIN length and to force the use of letters and numbers, making the PIN practically unguessable. These settings are in the Group Policy Editor under Computer Configuration > Administrative Templates > Windows Components > Windows Hello For Business.

Using Windows Hello for biometric sign-ins

With the proper hardware, you can sign in simply by swiping your fingerprint or, even easier, showing your face in front of your computer's camera. You might also be able to verify your identity with Windows Hello when making a purchase or accessing a secure service.

To use Windows Hello for biometric sign-ins on a PC, you need one of the following:

- A fingerprint reader that supports the Windows Biometric Framework; if this hardware isn't built in to your computer, you can add a USB-based fingerprint reader.

- An illuminated 3-D infrared camera such as those found on Surface laptops and tablets from Microsoft, as well as other advanced devices; note that a standard webcam does not work.

NOTE

You must add a PIN as described earlier in this chapter before you can use Windows Hello biometric features. This PIN becomes a backup sign-in option in the event your biometric hardware malfunctions or isn't able to recognize you.

To set up Windows Hello, go to Settings > Accounts > Sign-In Options. Under Windows Hello, expand either Facial Recognition (Windows Hello) or Fingerprint Recognition (Windows Hello) as appropriate. Then click Set Up for the biometric device you want to use.

Windows asks you to enter your PIN to verify your identity. After that, you need to enter your biometric data. With face recognition, that involves looking into the camera (as shown in Figure 10-8); to set up a fingerprint reader, follow the prompts to swipe your fingerprint several times, until Windows Hello has recorded the data it needs.

If you're setting up fingerprint scanning, you can enroll additional fingers so that you have an alternative if the finger you normally use is, for example, covered with a bandage. Click Add Another after you complete registration for a fingerprint. To add another fingerprint later, return to Settings > Accounts > Sign-In Options and click Add Another. You can also associate an additional fingerprint with a different user account on the same device. Sign in to the alternate account, and set up the second fingerprint there. When you restart, you can choose your account by choosing the fingerprint associated with that account.

Figure 10-8   Setup for Windows Hello guides you through the brief process of scanning and storing your biometric data.

Using a picture password

This option is a bit of a misfit on the list of sign-in options. It doesn't offer the same level of security as Windows Hello (which is the main reason we don't recommend using it), but the option survives for users who like the idea of personalizing the sign-in process.

NOTE

If you have enabled the For Improved Security, Only Allow Windows Hello Sign-In For Microsoft Accounts On This Device (Recommended) setting, Picture Password is not displayed on the Sign-in Options page.

With a picture password, you can sign in on a touchscreen using a combination of gestures (specifically, circles, straight lines, and taps) that you make on a picture displayed on the sign-in screen. The easiest way to get comfortable with a picture password is to go ahead and create one.

To get started, go to Settings > Accounts > Sign-In Options. Under Picture Password, click Add. Verify your identity by entering your password to display an introductory screen where you can choose a picture. You then get to select one of your own pictures to appear on the sign-in screen. When you're satisfied with your selection, click Use This Picture.

On the next screen that appears, you specify the three gestures you'll use to sign in. These gestures can consist of circles, straight lines, and taps. After repeating the series of gestures to confirm your new "password," click Finish.

To sign in with a picture password, you must perform the same three gestures on the sign-in screen, in the same order, using the same locations, and in the same direction. You don't need to be *that* precise; Windows allows minor variations in location.

Setting or changing a password

When you set up a Microsoft account, you're required to create a password. Similarly, if you add a local user account to your computer, Windows 11 prompts you to specify a password.

NOTE

If you sign in with a local account, you must add a password before you can use a PIN, picture password, or Windows Hello.

To set or change your Microsoft account password, go to Settings > Accounts > Sign-In Options. Click or tap Change under Password. If Windows Hello is set up, you first need to enter your PIN or supply biometric authentication. Next, you must enter your existing password to confirm your identity. Windows then asks you to enter your new password.

CHAPTER 10

NOTE

If you have enabled the For Improved Security, Only Allow Windows Hello Sign-In For Microsoft Accounts On This Device (Recommended) setting, Password is not displayed on the Sign-in Options page.

Changing the password for a local account requires an extra step: You must specify a password hint. The password hint appears after you click your name on the sign-in screen and type your password incorrectly. Be sure your hint is only a subtle reminder because any user can click your name and then view the hint. (Windows won't allow you to create a password hint that contains your password.)

NOTE

If you sign in with a local account, you can use a quicker alternative: Press Ctrl+Alt+Delete, and click Change A Password. This method does not include the option to enter a password hint.

You can also set or change the password for the local account of another user on your computer. To do so, open User Accounts in Control Panel, click Manage Another Account, and click the name of the user whose password you want to change. Then click Change The Password or (if the account doesn't currently have a password) Create A Password.

CAUTION

If another user has files encrypted with EFS, do not create or change a password for that user; instead, show the user how to accomplish the task from his or her own account. Similarly, do not remove or change another user's password unless the user has forgotten the password and has exhausted all other options to access the account. (For more information, see the sidebar "Recovering from a lost password.") If you create, change, or remove another user's password, that user loses all personal certificates and stored passwords for websites and network resources. Without the personal certificates, the user loses access to all encrypted files and all email messages encrypted with the user's private key. Windows deletes the certificates and passwords to prevent the administrator who makes a password change from gaining access to them—but this security comes at a cost!

RECOVERING FROM A LOST PASSWORD

It's bound to happen someday: You try to sign in to your computer and are faced with the password prompt, and you can't remember the password. This is perhaps more likely when you usually sign in using facial recognition or a PIN because you're seldom entering your password.

For a Microsoft account or an Azure Active Directory account, clicking a link on the sign-in screen (either I Forgot My Password or I Forgot My PIN) connects to Microsoft's servers and leads you through the steps to verify your identity and reset your password or PIN. During this process, an alternative method is offered: Use Microsoft Authenticator—an app you install on your mobile device—to verify your identity and sign in.

Another alternative for a Microsoft account is to use another computer or a mobile device to go to *https://account.live.com/password/reset*. Answer a series of questions there, and you can send a code to one of the alternative verification methods on your account—a text message to your mobile device or an email message to an account you control. Enter the code to prove your identity, and you can reset your password.

For a local account, if the password hint doesn't jog your memory, you have two supported options. The first asks you to correctly answer the three password reset questions you chose when you set up the local account initially. The second option is to use a password reset disk, if you previously created one before you needed it and then stored it in a safe place.

When password amnesia sets in, take your best guess at a password. If you're wrong, Windows informs you that the password is incorrect and offers both a hint and a Reset Password link. For Windows 11, that option offers blanks to fill in answers to the three password reset questions; if you have a password reset disk, scroll down and click Use A Password Reset Disk Instead. That opens the Password Reset Wizard, which in turn asks for the location of the password reset disk, reads the encrypted key, and then asks you to set a new password. After you sign in using the new credentials, your password reset disk remains usable in case you forget the new password; you don't need to make a new one.

If you can't remember the password and neither of the above options works, you're out of luck. A local administrator can sign in and change or remove your password for you, but you'll lose access to your encrypted files and email messages and your stored credentials. If that prospect gives you chills, perhaps you should consider switching to a Microsoft account.

CHAPTER 10

Managing a physical security key

A security key is a physical device built around encryption hardware that supports the Fast Identity Online (FIDO2) standard. These keys, which typically plug into a USB port or connect via Bluetooth or NFC, can be used as a second identity factor to sign in to a Microsoft account or reset a password. Security keys also work with password manager apps and are supported by every major browser that runs on Windows 11, which in turn allows you to use one of these devices for 2FA support on popular web services. In this scenario, you're typically prompted to tap the security key after entering your credentials. With the addition of a PIN, you can use a security key for passwordless sign in.

Windows 11 doesn't directly support security keys for signing in, but you can use it to manage a hardware key. Go to Settings > Accounts > Sign-In Options, click Security Key, and then click Manage. Tap the hardware key to select it and then use the options shown in Figure 10-9 to add or change the security key PIN or remove saved credentials from the key and get a fresh start.

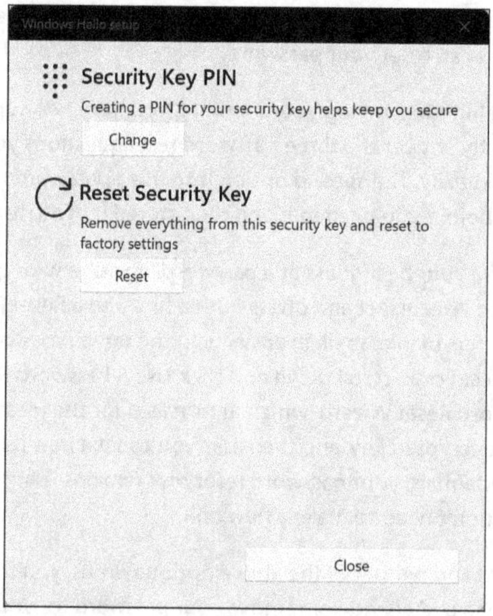

Figure 10-9   You can use a physical security key as a second factor for signing in to web services, including Microsoft accounts. Use these controls to change the PIN or remove stored credentials.

Signing out, switching accounts, or locking your computer

When you step away from your computer, you want to be sure you don't leave it in a state in which others can use your credentials to access your files, sign in to websites or services using saved passwords, read and reply to email messages, or otherwise interfere with your digital identity. For security's sake, you need to sign out, switch accounts, or lock your computer:

- **Sign Out**   With this option, all your running apps close, and the lock screen appears.

- **Switch Account**   With this option, also known as fast user switching, your apps continue to run. The sign-in screen appears, ready for the sign-in credentials of the alternative account you select. Your account is still signed in, but only you can return to your own session, which you can do when the user who is currently signed in chooses to sign out, switch accounts, or lock the computer.

- **Lock**   With this option, your apps continue to run, but the lock screen appears so that no one can see your desktop or use the computer. Only you can unlock the computer to return to your session; however, other users can sign in to their own sessions without disturbing yours.

To sign out, switch accounts, or lock your computer, click Start and click or tap your picture (in the lower left of Start). That displays a menu with Lock and Sign Out options; on a device with more than one user account set up, it also includes a profile picture and username for other available accounts. On a computer that's joined to a domain, Switch Account appears instead of individual account names. You can then enter an account name on the sign-in screen.

CHAPTER 10

Inside OUT

Use keyboard shortcuts

To lock your computer, press Windows key+L. (You might also find it more convenient to use this shortcut for switching accounts; the only difference is that it takes you to the lock screen instead of to the sign-in screen.)

For any of these actions—sign out, switch accounts, or lock—you can start by pressing Ctrl+Alt+Delete, which displays a menu that includes all three options.

Using Dynamic Lock

Windows 11 provides another way to lock a computer called Dynamic Lock. With Dynamic Lock, your computer automatically locks when it becomes separated from your phone, such as when you step away from your desk with your phone in your pocket or purse. To use Dynamic Lock, follow these steps:

If you haven't already done so, pair your Bluetooth-enabled phone to your computer. For more information, see "Setting up Bluetooth devices" in Chapter 13, "Managing hardware and devices." Open Settings > Accounts > Sign-In Options. Under the Additional Settings heading, select Dynamic Lock and then select the Allow Windows To Lock Your Device Automatically When You're Away checkbox.

After following these steps, Windows polls your phone several times each minute. (This does place a small hit on your phone's battery life.) When it discovers that the phone is no longer in range, the computer locks. Be aware, however, that locking doesn't occur instantly; Windows polls your phone only periodically, and it takes some time for you to get far enough away so that your phone is out of range.

How far is "out of range"? That sensitivity depends on several factors, including the signal strength of your two devices and the number of walls and other obstructions between the devices. A registry value sets the threshold, but calibrating it takes some experimentation. Rafael Rivera has created a tool for working with Dynamic Lock threshold values; you can read about it at *https://bit.ly/DynLock*.

For security reasons, Windows 11 does not offer a corresponding dynamic unlock feature. When you return to your computer, even with phone in hand, you need to sign in using one of the usual methods: Windows Hello, password, or PIN.

Sharing your PC with other users

Personal computers are usually just that—personal. But there are situations in which it makes sense for a single PC to be shared by multiple users. In those circumstances, it's prudent to configure the shared device securely. Doing so helps to protect each user's data from inadvertent deletions and changes as well as malicious damage and theft.

NOTE

In this section, we offer advice for configuring a PC with Microsoft accounts and local accounts. Azure AD and domain accounts are administered centrally.

When you set up your computer, consider these suggestions:

- **Control who can sign in.** Create accounts only for users who need to use your computer's resources, either by signing in locally or over a network. If an account you created is no longer needed, delete or disable it.

- **Use standard accounts for additional users.** During setup, Windows sets up one local administrative account for installing apps, creating and managing accounts, and so on. All other accounts can and should run with standard privileges.

- **Be sure that all accounts are protected by a strong password and 2FA.** This is especially important for administrator accounts and for other accounts whose profiles contain important or sensitive documents.

- **Restrict sign-in times.** You might want to limit the computing hours for some users, especially children. The easiest way for home users to do this is by setting up family accounts; for details, see "Controlling your family's computer access," later in this chapter.

- **Restrict access to certain files.** You'll want to be sure that some files are available to all users, whereas other files are available only to the person who created them. The Public folder and a user's personal folders provide a general framework for this protection. You can further refine your file-protection scheme by selectively applying permissions to varying combinations of files, folders, and users.

Adding a user to your computer

To allow another person to sign in on your computer and access their own files and settings, you must add a user account for that person. How you choose to set up that account depends on how you as an administrator want to manage the other person's access. You can add a secondary account by specifying the other person's Microsoft account email (or creating a local user account with a username and password of your choosing); your only management option in that case is choosing whether the account type is Administrator or Standard. If you're adding accounts for other family members (especially children), you can choose from a different set of options that allow you much more granular control over when and how they access the PC.

To create a conventional secondary account without using family settings, start by signing in as an administrator and then go to Settings > Accounts. Then select Other Users. (On Windows 11 version 21H2, this option is under the Family & Other Users heading.)

NOTE

The option to set up accounts for other family members is not available on PCs that are joined to a Windows domain or Azure Active Directory.

Other Users, shown in Figure 10-10, enables you to add additional accounts, either local accounts or Microsoft accounts. To add a user with a Microsoft account, click Add Account and then enter the email address (or phone number) for the account they currently use and complete the wizard to create the user's account.

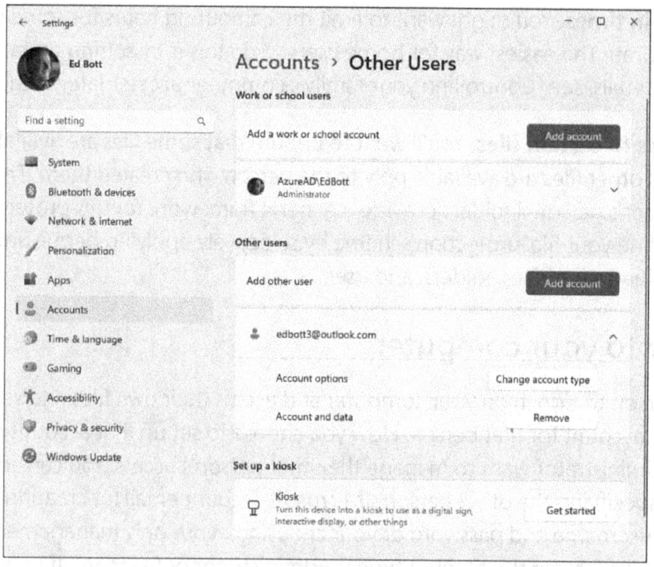

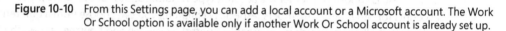

Figure 10-10   From this Settings page, you can add a local account or a Microsoft account. The Work Or School option is available only if another Work Or School account is already set up.

If you want to create a local account, click Add Account and then click I Don't Have This Person's Sign-In Information. Then, on the Create Account page, select Add A User Without A Microsoft Account.

The Create A User For This PC page displays, shown in Figure 10-11, and you can enter the username and password for the other person.

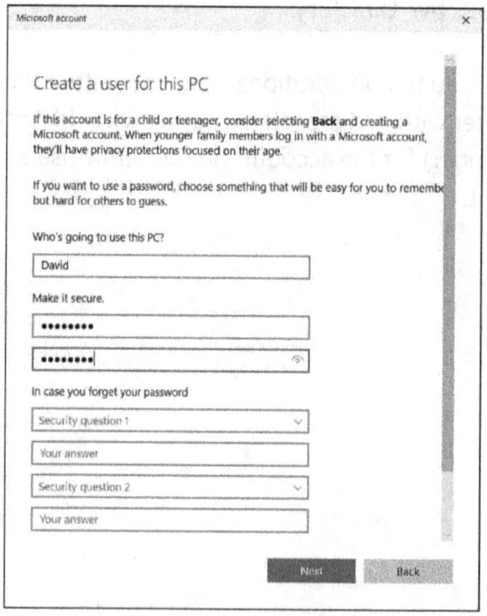

Figure 10-11   It takes some persistence, but you can resist the entreaties to use a Microsoft account and instead set up a local user account; eventually, you get to this dialog.

You're also required to choose and answer three security questions for the local account. (If your computer has only local accounts set up, you go directly to this final dialog, skipping the two that guide you toward a Microsoft account.) Click Next, and your work is done.

To add an account for a family member, go to Settings > Accounts, select Family, and then select Add Someone from the Your Family section. Enter the email address of the Microsoft account used by the family member and then complete the wizard to add the account.

You're asked to define the role that the new user has: An Organizer can edit family and safety settings; a Member can edit their own settings, using options based on their age. When you've defined the role, click Invite to send an invitation to the user's configured email account; they can then use that invitation to complete the process of adding their account to the computer.

NOTE

The invitation email has as a subject line "Microsoft Family Safety" and provides a link labeled Accept Invitation. Selecting this link opens the Family Safety online app, and enables the user to join the family group using the specified email account.

The user account is displayed with a status of Pending until the user accepts the invite.

NOTE

After you add the account, modify account type, choosing between Standard User and Administrator.

If you're adding an account for a child, select Create One For A Child on the Add Someone page. After you've created their account in the usual way, the account is added to the computer.

Controlling your family's computer access

Previous versions of Windows had a feature called Parental Controls (Windows Vista and Windows 7) or Family Safety (Windows 8), which allowed parents to restrict and monitor their children's computer use. Both Windows 10 and Windows 11 offer similar capabilities, but the implementation is completely different. Those earlier Windows versions stored their settings on your PC, but in Windows 11, family settings are now stored and managed as part of your Microsoft account.

NOTE

Rather than classifying each person as Child or Adult, you act as Organizer for your family; when you add an account to your family, you can assign that person as a Member, whose activities can be managed, or as an Organizer, who can view and change the settings online.

This approach has some benefits:

- You don't need to make settings for each member of your family on each computer. After you add a family member on one PC, you manage their settings in the cloud, and those settings apply to all the family PCs where they sign in.

- You can manage each family member's computer use from any computer that's connected to the internet.

Family settings have one requirement that some might perceive as a disadvantage: Each family member must have a Microsoft account and sign in with that account.

You use the Family Safety webpage, the Windows Family app (on a Windows 10 or Windows 11 PC), or the Family Safety app on iOS or Android to manage family settings.

NOTE

The Windows 11 Family app is typically installed automatically with Windows 11 version 22H2; on a PC running version 21H2, you might need to visit the Microsoft Store to download this useful app.

What can you do with Family Safety?

- **Set screen time.** Define limits for your children's devices, apps, and games.

- **Find your family.** Enables you to locate family members by retrieving location data from their mobile devices.

- **Monitor driving safety.** Enables you to gain insights into your family members' driving habits, including speed, phone use, and sudden braking. This is a premium feature.

- **Review reports.** Track and review family members' device and app use.

- **Define content filters.** Control what type of content members can access online.

- **Manage family email, calendar, and OneNote.** Enables you to schedule events, share notes, and set up group email.

NOTE

Family members must sign in and grant permission for organizers to view their activity and see their location on an Android device.

As the organizer, you perform all management tasks online (at *https://family.microsoft.com*) or in the Family app. Sign in with your Microsoft account to get started. Figure 10-12 shows a portion of the interface for setting up both daily limits and the times during which a family member can use a Windows 11 PC or an Xbox One console.

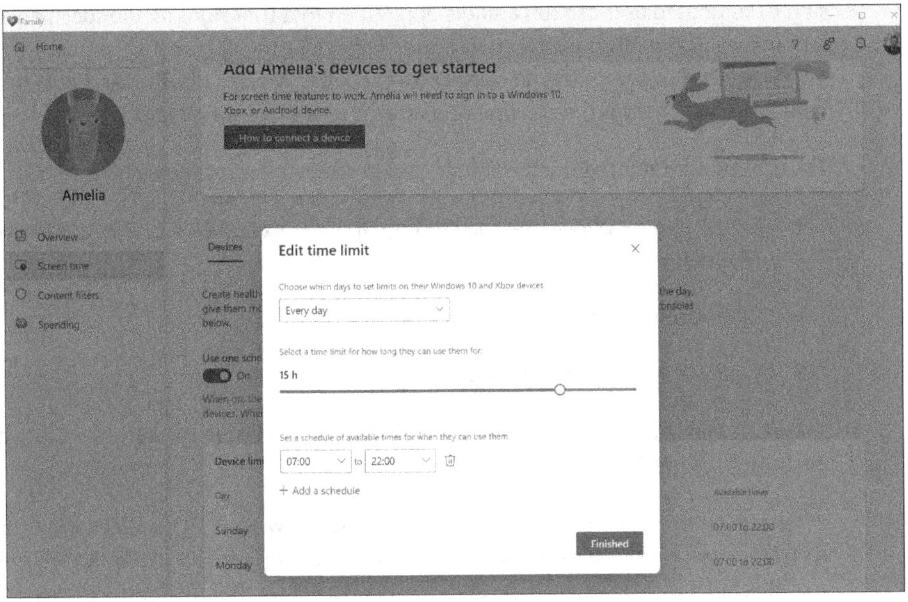

Figure 10-12   With Screen Time settings, you specify an allowable range of times for a child's daily use of Windows 11 PCs and an Xbox One console.

TROUBLESHOOTING

The email invitation never arrives

Despite repeated attempts on your part to set up a new family member, sometimes the invitation isn't sent. To get around this, browse to *https://family.microsoft.com*. On the webpage that appears, click the Add A Family Member button (the plus sign under the Your Family heading), and follow the instructions.

Note that when you sign in to one of your other computers, your family's accounts are already in place; you don't need to add family members on each device. However, by default, the other family members cannot sign in to these other devices. To enable access, return to the Family page in Settings, click the name of the family member, and then click Allow Sign In. To disable access for a family member on a specific device, click Block Sign In.

Restricting use with assigned access

Assigned access is a rather odd feature that you can use to configure your computer so that a single designated user can run a single app. When that user signs in, the specified app starts automatically and runs full-screen. The user can't close the app or start any others. In fact, the only way out is to press Ctrl+Alt+Delete (or press the Windows button and power button simultaneously), which signs out the user and returns to the sign-in screen.

The use cases for this feature are limited, but here are a few examples:

- A kiosk app for public use (see "Setting up a kiosk device" in Chapter 19 for more information)

- A point-of-sale app for your business

- A game for a very young child

If you can think of a use for this feature, click Get Started under the Set Up A Kiosk heading at the bottom of the Other Users page.

When you launch this wizard, you must either add a new account or select an existing account and designate a Windows app (not a legacy desktop program) for use with the kiosk account. If you selected a web browser as the app, you need to enter the URL for the browser to open.

Introducing access control in Windows

We've saved this fairly technical section for last. Most Windows users never need to deal with the nuts and bolts of the Windows security model. But developers, network administrators, and anyone who aspires to the label "power user" should have at least a basic understanding of what happens when you create accounts, share files, install software drivers, and perform other tasks that have security implications.

The Windows approach to security is discretionary: Each securable system resource—each file or printer, for example—has an owner. That owner, in turn, has discretion over who can and cannot access the resource. Usually, a resource is owned by the user who creates it. If you create a file, for example, you are the file's owner under ordinary circumstances. (Computer administrators, however, can take ownership of resources they didn't create.)

NOTE

To exercise full discretionary control over individual files, you must store those files on an NTFS volume (this feature is also available on PCs running Windows 11 Pro for Workstations with ReFS-formatted volumes). For the sake of compatibility, Windows 11 supports the FAT file systems (FAT, FAT32) used by early Windows versions and many USB flash drives, as well as the exFAT file system used on some removable drives. However, none of the FAT-based file systems support file permissions. To enjoy the full benefits of Windows security, you must use NTFS or ReFS. For more information about file systems, see "Choosing a file system" in Chapter 8, "Managing local and cloud storage."

WHAT ARE SECURITY IDENTIFIERS?

Windows security relies on the use of a security identifier (SID) to manage access controls and permissions for a user account. When you create a user account on your computer, Windows assigns a unique SID to that account. The SID remains uniquely associated with that user account until the account is deleted, whereupon the SID is never used again—for that user or any other user. Even if you re-create an account with identical information, a new SID is created.

A SID is a variable-length value that contains a revision level, a 48-bit identifier authority value, and a number of 32-bit subauthority values. The SID takes the form S-1-x-y1-y2- . . . . S-1 identifies it as a revision 1 SID; x is the value for the identifier authority; and y1, y2, and so on are values for subauthorities.

You sometimes see a SID in a security dialog (for example, on the Security tab of a file's properties dialog) before Windows has had time to look up the user account name. You also spot SIDs in the hidden and protected $RECYCLE.BIN folder (each SID you see in this folder represents the Recycle Bin for a particular user) and in the registry (the HKEY_USERS hive contains a key, identified by SID, for each user account on the computer), among other places. The easiest way to determine your own SID is with the Whoami command-line utility. For details, see the following Inside Out sidebar.

Not all SIDs are unique (although the SID assigned to your user account is always unique). A number of commonly used SIDs are constant among all Windows installations. For example, S-1-5-18 is the SID for the built-in Local System account, a hidden member of the Administrators group that is used by the operating system and by services that sign in using the Local System account. You can find a complete list of such SIDs under the heading "Well-known SIDS" in the document at *https://support.microsoft.com/kb/243330*.

To control which users have access to a resource, Windows uses the SID assigned to each user account. Your SID (a gigantic number guaranteed to be unique) follows you around wherever you go in Windows. When you sign in, the operating system first validates your username and password. Then it creates a security access token. You can think of this as the electronic equivalent of an ID badge. It includes your username and SID, plus information about any security groups to which your account belongs. (Security groups are described later in this chapter.) Any app you start gets a copy of your security access token.

Inside OUT

Learn about your own account with Whoami

Windows includes a command-line utility called Whoami (Who Am I?). You can use Whoami to find out the name of the account that's currently signed in, its SID, the names of the security groups of which it's a member, and its privileges. To use Whoami, start by opening a Command Prompt window. (You don't need elevated privileges.)

Then, to learn the name of the signed-in user, type **whoami**. (This is particularly useful if you're signed in as a standard user but running an elevated Command Prompt window—when it might not be obvious which account is currently "you.") If you're curious about your SID, type **whoami /user**. For a complete list of Whoami parameters, type **whoami /?**.

With User Account Control (UAC) turned on, administrators who sign in get two security access tokens—one that has the privileges of a standard user and one that has the full privileges of an administrator.

Whenever you attempt to walk through a controlled "door" in Windows (for example, when you connect to a shared printer), or any time an app attempts to do so on your behalf, the operating system examines your security access token and decides whether to let you pass. If access is permitted, you notice nothing. If access is denied, you get to hear a beep and read a refusal message.

In determining whom to let pass and whom to block, Windows consults the resource's access control list (ACL). This is simply a list of SIDs and the access privileges associated with each one. Every resource subject to access control has an ACL. This manner of allowing and blocking access to resources such as files and printers has remained essentially unchanged since Windows NT.

WHAT ARE ACLS?

Each folder and each file on an NTFS-formatted volume has an ACL (also known as DACL, for discretionary access control list, and commonly called NTFS permissions). An ACL comprises an access control entry (ACE) for each user who is allowed access to the folder or file. With NTFS permissions, you can control access to any file or folder, allowing different types of access for different users or groups of users.

To view and edit NTFS permissions for a file or folder, right-click its icon and choose Properties. The Security tab lists all the groups and users with permissions set for the selected object, as shown in Figure 10-13. Different permissions can be set for each user, as you can see by selecting each one.

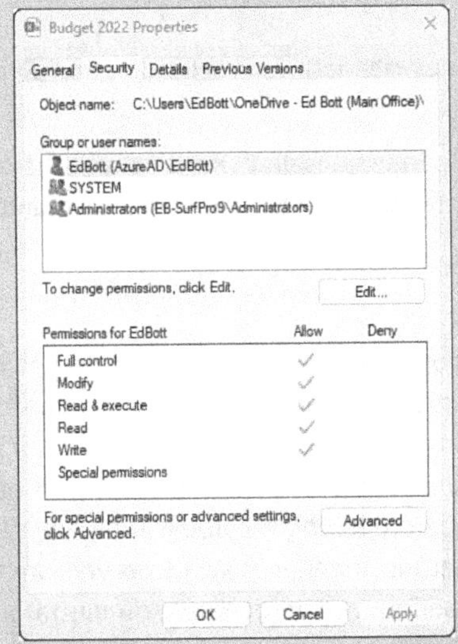

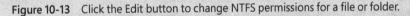

Figure 10-13   Click the Edit button to change NTFS permissions for a file or folder.

To make changes to the settings for any user or group in the list, or to add or remove a user or group in the list, click Edit. Use caution. Setting NTFS permissions without understanding the full consequences can lead to unexpected and unwelcome results, including a complete loss of access to files and folders. Above all, avoid delving into the inner workings of NTFS permissions when your goal is to manage network sharing, which is governed by a separate set of options. For details, see Chapter 11, "Configuring Windows networks."

The access granted by each permission type is as follows:

- **Full Control**   Users with Full Control can list contents of a folder, read and open files, create new files, delete files and subfolders, change permissions on files and subfolders, and take ownership of files.

- **Modify**   Allows the user to read, change, create, and delete files but not to change permissions or take ownership of files.

- **Read & Execute**   Allows the user to view files and launch executable files.

- **List Folder Contents**   Provides the same permissions as Read & Execute, but can be applied only to folders.

- **Read**   Allows the user to list the contents of a folder, read file attributes, read permissions, and synchronize files.

- **Write**   Allows the user to create files, write data, read attributes and permissions, and synchronize files.

- **Special Permissions**   The assigned permissions don't match any of the preceding permission descriptions. To see precisely which permissions are granted, click Advanced.

UAC adds another layer of restrictions based on user accounts. With UAC turned on, applications are normally launched using an administrator's standard user token. (Standard users, of course, have only a standard user token.) If an application requires administrator privileges, UAC asks for your consent (if you're signed in as an administrator) or the credentials of an administrator (if you're signed in as a standard user) before letting the application run. With UAC turned off, Windows works in the same (rather dangerous) manner as Windows versions from more than two decades ago, before Microsoft got serious about security: Administrator accounts can do just about anything (sometimes getting those users in trouble), and standard accounts don't have the privileges needed to run many older desktop apps.

➤ For more information about UAC, see "Preventing unsafe actions with User Account Control" in Chapter 12.

Configuring Windows networks

Modern computing is defined by our ability to communicate, share, and collaborate with one another by using devices of all shapes and sizes. These days, most of that activity happens over the world's largest global network, the internet, using a variety of widely accepted hardware and software standards. The internet is also the driving force behind cloud-based services, which are transforming the way we work and play.

The same network standards that allow connections to the internet can also be used to create a local area network (LAN), which makes it possible to share files, printers, and other resources in a home or an office.

In the past, setting up a network connection could be a painful process, one that often required professional help. Today, network hardware is ubiquitous, and setting up a network connection in Microsoft Windows 11 requires little or no technical knowledge. That doesn't mean the process is entirely pain-free; troubleshooting network problems can be frustrating, and understanding the basics of networking is tremendously helpful in isolating and fixing problems.

In this chapter, we cover the essentials of connecting a Windows 11 device to wired and wireless networks in a home or small office. We also discuss how to connect your Windows 11 computers to cloud apps and resources, such as Microsoft 365.

In addition, we explain how to share resources securely and how to check the status of your network connection to confirm that it's working properly. When you want access to an *entire computer* rather than just its shared resources, a feature called Remote Desktop enables you to do exactly that, and a section of this chapter is devoted to explaining how.

In earlier versions of Windows, a feature that facilitated easy resource sharing over a home network was available. Known as HomeGroup, it first appeared in Windows 7, but it was removed from Windows 10 in 2018, and Windows 11 no longer supports this feature. That doesn't mean the end of easy sharing, of course. Later in this chapter, we discuss alternatives to HomeGroup, including Nearby Sharing.

Windows 11 networking essentials

Before you can connect to the internet or a local area network, your Windows 11 device needs a network adapter, properly installed with working drivers.

Since the release of Windows 7, Microsoft's hardware certification requirements have mandated that every desktop PC, laptop, all-in-one, and portable device include a certified Ethernet or Wi-Fi adapter. Some portable devices also include modems that connect to mobile broadband networks, and Bluetooth adapters support limited types of direct connections between PCs.

You'll typically find wired Ethernet adapters in desktop PCs and all-in-ones, where a permanent wired network connection is appropriate. These adapters can be integrated into the motherboard or installed in an expansion slot and accept RJ45 plugs at either end of shielded network cables. (Most such devices also include a wireless network adapter.)

Most modern wired adapters support the Gigabit Ethernet standard, which allows data transfers at up to 1 gigabit (1,000 megabits) per second. In an office or a home that is wired for Ethernet, you can plug your network adapter into a wall jack, which in turn connects to a router, hub, or switch at a central location called a *patch panel*. In a home or an office without structured wiring, you need to plug directly into a network device.

Inside OUT

Connect to a wired network using a USB port

If you crave the consistent connection speed and reliability of a wired network but have a portable PC or mobile device that lacks a built-in Ethernet connection, consider investing in a USB network adapter. A USB 2.0 port supports Fast Ethernet speeds (up to 100 megabits per second), whereas a modern device with a USB 3.0 or USB 3.1 port should be capable of Gigabit Ethernet speeds. Some network docking stations and USB hubs include an Ethernet adapter that allows you to use a single USB Type-C connection for instant access to a wired network and other expansion devices while you're at your desk.

CHAPTER 11

In recent years, wireless networking technology has enjoyed an explosion in popularity. Wireless access points are a standard feature in most home routers and cable modems, and Wi-Fi connections are practically ubiquitous. You can connect to Wi-Fi, often for free, in hotels, trains, buses, ferries, airplanes, and even public parks in addition to the more traditional hotspot locations such as cafés and libraries.

All laptops and mobile devices designed for Windows 11 include a Wi-Fi adapter, which consists of a transceiver and an antenna capable of communicating with a wireless access point. Wireless adapters are also increasingly common in desktop and all-in-one computer designs, allowing them to be used in homes and offices where it is impractical to run network cables.

Ethernet and Wi-Fi are the dominant networking technologies in homes and offices. In lieu of the twisted-pair wiring typically used to connect endpoints on wired networks, you can use existing coaxial cable installations, such as those used by cable TV systems, with adapters at each endpoint that support MoCA technology (the acronym stands for Multimedia over Coax Alliance, the organization that defines the standard). Each adapter includes a connector for the coaxial cable and a separate RJ45 connector for an Ethernet cable. This configuration enables you to connect PCs using Ethernet adapters at Gigabit Ethernet and higher speeds.

Alternatives include phone-line networks, which plug into telephone jacks in older homes, and powerline technology, which communicates using adapters that plug into the same AC receptacles you use for power. The availability of inexpensive wireless network gear has relegated phone-line and power-line technologies to niche status; they're most attractive in older homes and offices, where adding network cable is impractical and where wireless networks are unreliable because of distance, building materials, or interference. (A hybrid approach, useful in some environments, allows you to plug a Wi-Fi extender into an existing power line to increase signal strength in a remote location or to create a so-called mesh network.)

You don't need to rely exclusively on one type of network. If your cable modem includes a router and a wireless access point, you can plug network cables into it and use its wireless signal for mobile devices or for computers located in areas where a network port isn't available.

Windows 11 detects and configures network hardware automatically, installing drivers from its built-in collection. A wired internet connection should be detected automatically; you're typically prompted to enter the access key for a wireless connection during the setup process.

NOTE

In this chapter, we assume you have an always-on broadband connection in your home or office or that you're connecting to the internet through a public or private Wi-Fi connection with internet access.

CHAPTER 11

Checking the status of your network

As we noted earlier, most network connections in Windows 11 configure themselves automatically during setup, although you might be prompted to enter security information to connect to a wireless access point. Tools included with Windows 11 allow you to inspect the status of the current connection and either make changes or troubleshoot problems.

The most easily accessible network tool is the status icon that appears by default in the system tray area at the right side of the taskbar.

This icon indicates the current network type (wired or wireless) and the status of the network. Click that icon to display the Quick Settings menu, which presents options relevant to your type of network connection, in addition to other Windows settings.

Figure 11-1 shows the system tray icon and Quick Settings menu for a desktop computer with an active wired Ethernet connection and a Wi-Fi adapter that currently has no active connection. Both networks appear to be operating properly.

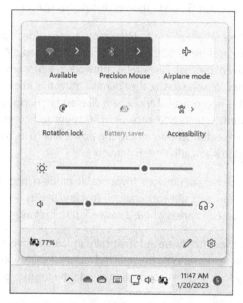

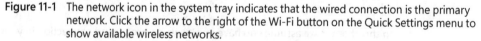

Figure 11-1   The network icon in the system tray indicates that the wired connection is the primary network. Click the arrow to the right of the Wi-Fi button on the Quick Settings menu to show available wireless networks.

In Windows 11 version 22H2, clicking or tapping Airplane Mode enables you to shut down all wireless communications, including Wi-Fi, Bluetooth, cellular, GPS, and near field communication (NFC). If you enable Bluetooth or Wi-Fi after turning on airplane mode, Windows

CHAPTER 11

remembers your choice and leaves that wireless connection enabled the next time you turn on airplane mode.

On any device with a Wi-Fi adapter, a button labeled Mobile Hotspot activates the system as a mobile hotspot. For information about using your device as a mobile hotspot, see "Mobile hotspots and other metered connections," later in this chapter.

NOTE

A portable computer with no physical Ethernet adapter sometimes shows the icon for a wired connection rather than wireless. That can occur when you have a virtual network adapter set up for virtual machines. (For details about virtual network adapters and virtual switches, see Chapter 17, "Running Windows 11 in a virtual machine or in the cloud.")

To view wireless networks, click the arrow to the right of the Wi-Fi button to display a list of available wireless networks that are advertising their SSID, along with their relative signal strengths. Figure 11-2 shows three networks, all protected.

Figure 11-2   Select any available network, click Connect, and provide the required security details. The padlock icon indicates that the connection is secured and requires a passcode. Use the Wi-Fi switch to turn the wireless adapter off or on.

To disable Wi-Fi, slide the switch at the top of the dialog to the Off position. You are then prompted to choose when to turn Wi-Fi back on. You can opt to do this manually, which is the default, or schedule this for one hour, four hours, or one day from now.

NOTE

The option to disable Wi-Fi temporarily comes in handy when you're traveling and have access only to a weak wireless signal (which might drain your PC's battery as it repeatedly tries to make a connection), or a paid Wi-Fi option that you've decided is too expensive. Setting a timer allows you to reconnect without having to remember to turn Wi-Fi back on manually.

At the bottom of the dialog, you can select the More Wi-Fi Settings link. This opens the Settings app, and navigates automatically to the Network & Internet > Wi-Fi page, as shown in Figure 11-3.

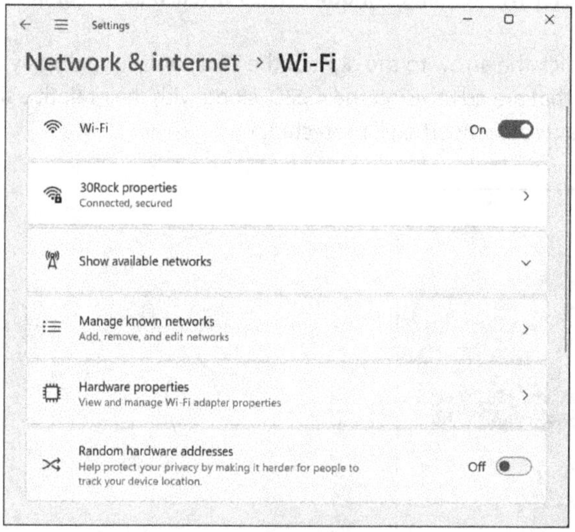

Figure 11-3   From Settings, you can configure additional Wi-Fi options.

The Wi-Fi switch at the top of this page allows you to disable or enable the wireless adapter. If you're connected to a wireless network, the entry below that switch shows the current network name; click that entry to see detailed properties for the Wi-Fi connection. You can configure the following additional settings from this page:

- Show Available Networks displays a list of nearby Wi-Fi networks that are available for connection.

- Manage Known Networks allows you to examine networks to which you've connected this device before and review or modify the settings for those networks. You can also choose to forget a network or to manually add a connection to an unadvertised Wi-Fi network.

Inside OUT

Manage known networks

If you synchronize your Windows settings between devices, then your Wi-Fi network settings are also synchronized. That option makes it easier to connect to familiar networks with a new device after signing in with the Microsoft account you used to sync those settings.

- Hardware Properties enables you to review or reconfigure the IP Assignment and DNS Server Assignment settings. These default to automatic via Dynamic Host Configuration Protocol (DHCP).

- Random Hardware Addresses provides a method to make your computer, and hence you, more difficult to track.

Inside OUT

Random Hardware Addresses

Windows helps protect you from some forms of tracking when you use this setting. It does this by generating a random media access control (MAC) address for your Wi-Fi adapter instead of using its actual physical address. That prevents nearby wireless access points from keeping track of your MAC address and using it to track your movements. With this setting on, Windows generates a new random MAC address each time you connect to that network. You can specify that you want Windows to use random hardware addresses for a specific network or for all networks.

If you have no network connectivity, or no access to the internet, the network icon displays as a globe with a superimposed no entry sign.

Network management tools

As with so many other parts of Windows 11, the knobs and dials and switches that control networking have steadily migrated from Control Panel to the Settings app. In fact, there's no longer any reason (except perhaps nostalgia) to use the old Control Panel Network And Internet page. You can find every network setting you need by going to Settings > Network & Internet, as shown in Figure 11-4. From here, you can access the following:

- Wi-Fi and Ethernet settings
- Virtual Private Network (VPN) and dial-up options

- Mobile hotspot settings

- Airplane mode

- Proxy settings

- Advanced network settings, including a list of individual network adapters, advanced sharing settings, and an option to perform network reset.

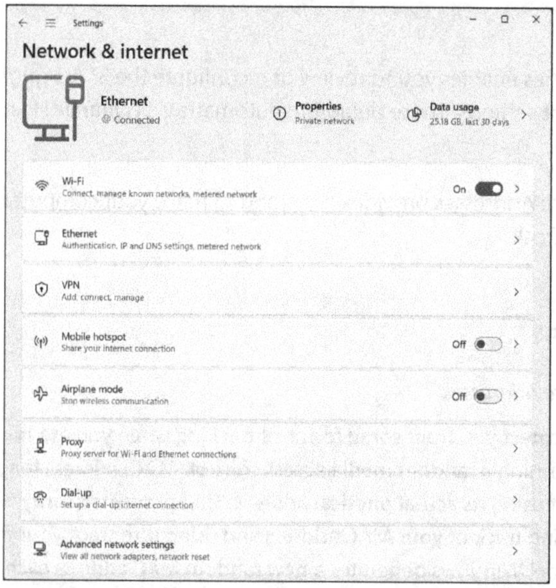

Figure 11-4   You can accomplish just about any network-related task from this starting point in Settings.

NOTE

For slightly faster access to network settings, right-click the network icon in the system tray and click Network And Internet Settings.

You can still use the Control Panel interface if you prefer. In Control Panel, select Network And Internet, and then select Network And Sharing.

You can review the available network connections in Settings by selecting Advanced Network Settings from the Network & Internet page, as shown in Figure 11-5. That action displays a list of available adapters along with the controls you need to reconfigure their settings.

NOTE

Network adapter names that begin with vEthernet are virtual adapters created when you set up a virtual switch with Hyper-V. Various diagnostic tools might display other virtual adapters used for specialized functions, such as Wi-Fi Direct connections. In general, we recommend that you avoid trying to manage these adapters manually.

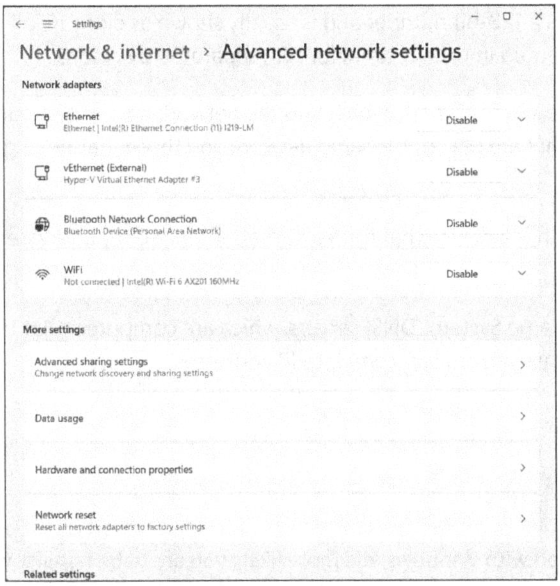

Figure 11-5   The Advanced Network Settings page displays a list of available adapters. You can disable any adapter or reconfigure an adapter's settings, including the TCP/IP settings.

TCP/IP configuration

Transmission Control Protocol/Internet Protocol (TCP/IP) is the default communications protocol of the internet and for modern local area networks; in Windows 11, it's installed and configured automatically and cannot be removed. Most of the time, your TCP/IP connection should just work, without requiring any manual configuration. (We cover some troubleshooting techniques at the end of this chapter.)

Networks that use the TCP/IP protocol rely on *IP addresses* as they route packets of data from point to point. On a TCP/IP network, every computer has a unique IP address for each protocol (that is, TCP/IPv4 and TCP/IPv6) in use on each network adapter.

A computer's TCP/IP configuration has the following elements:

- An IP address, in a format that's defined by the protocol:

    - An IPv4 address is a 32-bit number that is normally expressed as four 8-bit numbers, known as *octets* (each one represented in decimal format by a number from 0 through 255), separated by periods.

    - An IPv6 address is a 128-bit number and is usually shown as eight 16-bit numbers (each one represented in hexadecimal format) separated by colons.

- For IPv4 addresses only, a subnet mask, which tells the network how to distinguish between IP addresses that are part of the same network and those that belong to other networks

- A default gateway, which is a device that routes packets intended for addresses outside the local network.

- One or more Domain Name System (DNS) servers, which are computers that translate domain names (such as *www.microsoft.com*) into IP addresses

Inside OUT

IPv6 and Windows 11

The longer you've worked with Windows, the more likely you are to be familiar with the granddaddy of Windows networking, Internet Protocol version 4, also known as IPv4. A default network connection in Windows 11, wired or wireless, uses IPv4 but also enables the newer IP version 6. IPv6 is on by default and has been the preferred protocol in all desktop and server versions of Windows for nearly two decades, since the release of Windows Vista.

Without getting into the minutiae of network addressing, suffice it to say that IPv4, with its addresses based on four groups of numbers from 0 to 255, has a big problem. When the internet was young, that address space, consisting of 4.3 billion unique combinations of dotted addresses, like 192.168.1.108 or 10.0.0.242, seemed huge. Unfortunately, nobody anticipated just how big the internet would become, and the authorities who assign IP addresses on the internet have literally run out of IPv4 addresses.

The solution is IPv6, which uses 128-bit addresses and therefore has a maximum address space of 3.4×10^{38} addresses, which we are confident is enough to last for the next few generations of internet users. Most internet service providers support IPv6, as do the largest content services, including Microsoft, Google, Facebook, Netflix, and...well, you get the idea.

Windows veterans might be tempted to shy away from IPv6, preferring the more familiar IPv4. Some go so far as to disable IPv6. In our experience, that's a mistake. IPv6 is here to stay. Learn about it and embrace it.

Windows provides several methods for assigning IP addresses to networked computers:

- **DHCP**   This is the default configuration for Windows 11, and in fact, most other devices. A DHCP server maintains a pool of IP addresses for use by network devices. When you connect to a network, the DHCP server assigns an IP configuration from this pool, including subnet masks and other configuration details. Almost all corporate networks use DHCP to avoid the hassle of managing fixed addresses for constantly changing resources; all versions of Windows Server include this capability. Most routers and residential gateways also incorporate DHCP servers that automatically configure computers connected to those devices.

- **Automatic Private IP Addressing (APIPA)**   When no DHCP server is available, Windows automatically assigns an IPv4 address in a specific private IP range. (For an explanation of how private IP addresses work, see the sidebar "Public and private IP addresses" later in the chapter.) If all computers on a subnet are using APIPA addresses, they can communicate with one another without requiring additional configuration. IPv6 uses a link-local IPv6 address to perform a similar function.

- **Static IP Addressing**   By specifying an IPv4/IPv6 address along with its related details (subnet mask for an IPv4 address or an IPv6 prefix, for example), you can manually configure a Windows workstation so that its address is always the same. This method takes more time and can cause some configuration headaches, but it allows a high degree of control over network addresses.

- **Alternate IP Configuration**   Use this feature to specify multiple IPv4 addresses for a single network connection (although only one address can be used at a time). This feature is most useful with portable computers that regularly connect to different networks. You can configure the connection to automatically acquire an IP address from an available DHCP server, and you can then assign a static backup address for use if the first configuration isn't successful.

CHAPTER 11

NOTE

IPv6 supports a feature called stateless autoconfiguration. An IPv6 device, such as a Windows 11 computer, "listens" to network packets on the local network interface and is able to determine the configuration details for the local subnet based on router announcements. The device then configures a valid IPv6 configuration based on the router configuration.

To see details of your current IP configuration, open Settings > Network & Internet, and then expand the relevant network adapter. As shown in Figure 11-6, you can review the current IPv4 and IPv6 settings and, where necessary, select Edit to change those settings.

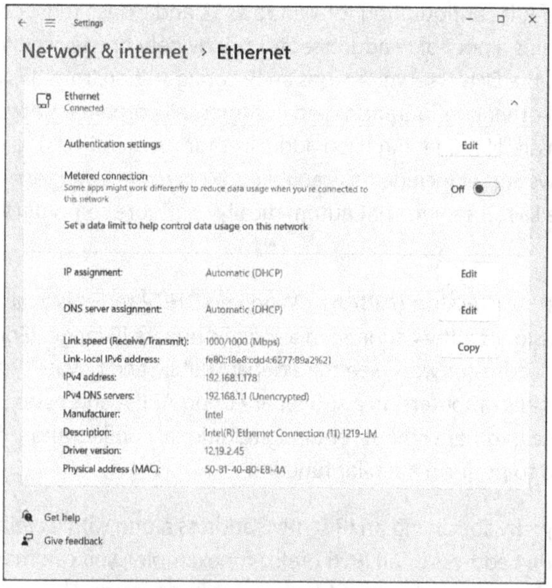

Figure 11-6   You can review the network settings for both IPv4 and IPv6. Click the Edit buttons to change the IP Assignment and DNS Server Assignment settings.

NOTE

For most Windows 11 devices, you don't need to configure IPv4 or IPv6 manually. Most devices obtain an IPv4 configuration via a DHCP server or a wireless access point with embedded DHCP functionality. For IPv6, most devices typically only have a link-local address, which begins with fe80; this is similar to an APIPA address in IPv4. Where an IPv6 router is present, the device determines additional IPv6 configuration data automatically.

It can be useful for some computers to have static IP addresses; for example, if you've set up your router to forward external packets to a specific computer running a server app, it can be convenient to have the internal address defined as static.

To set a static IP address in Windows 11, use the following procedure:

1. Open Settings and select Network & Internet.

2. Select the appropriate network adapter; for example, click Ethernet. On the Ethernet page, displayed in Figure 11-6, next to IP Assignment, click Edit.

3. In the Edit IP Settings dialog, click the dropdown and select Manual.

4. For IPv4, select the IPv4 radio button, and then enter some or all of the following details. (Note that you don't have to fill in every setting. If you just want to specify a preferred DNS server, for example, fill in the Preferred DNS box and leave the rest blank; Windows uses DHCP for the remaining IP assignments.)

    -   IP Address

    -   Subnet Mask

    -   Gateway

    -   Preferred DNS

    -   Alternate DNS

5. Click Save to apply the configuration changes. Figure 11-7 shows the dialog with all fields filled in.

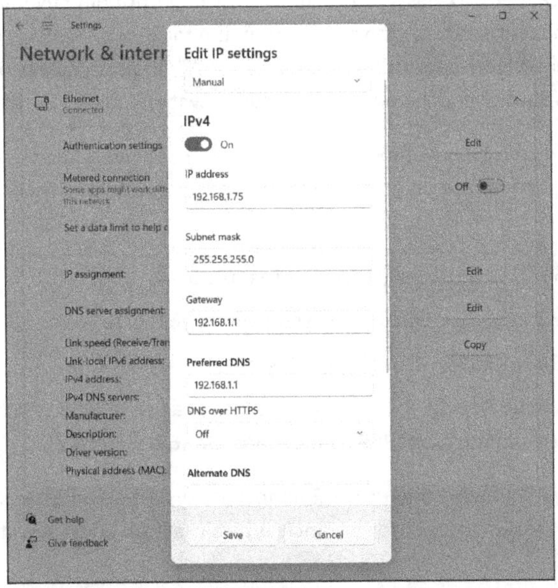

Figure 11-7   When assigning static IP addresses, you must fill in all fields correctly or leave them blank.

PUBLIC AND PRIVATE IP ADDRESSES

Any computer that's directly connected to the internet needs a public IP address—one that can be reached by other computers on the internet—so that information you request (webpages and email, for instance) can be routed back to your computer properly. When you connect to an internet service provider, you're assigned a public IP address from a block of addresses registered to that ISP. If you have a persistent connection to your ISP using a DSL, ADSL, or fiber cable connection, your IP address might be permanent—or semipermanent, changing only if you reset your router.

How do you find your public IP address? That information should be available on the web-based management interface for your internet connection. But if you aren't sure where to look, the easier alternative is to use any of several websites dedicated to this task:

- *https://whatismyip.com*
- *https://myexternalip.com* (IPv4 only)
- *https://whatismypublicip.com* (IPv4 only)
- *https://icanhazip.com* (IPv6 only)

On a home or small office network, you don't need to have a public IP address for each computer on the network. In fact, configuring a network with multiple public addresses can increase security risks and often requires an extra fee from your ISP. A safer, less costly solution is to assign a single public IP address to your router or residential gateway. All other computers on the network connect to the internet through that single address. Each of the computers on the local network has a private IP address that's not directly reachable from the outside world. To communicate with the internet, the router on the edge of the network uses a technology called Network Address Translation (NAT) to pass packets back and forth between the single public IP address and the multiple private IP addresses on the network.

The Internet Assigned Numbers Authority (IANA) has reserved the following three blocks of the IPv4 address space for use on private networks that are not directly connected to the internet:

- 10.0.0.0 – 10.255.255.255, usually expressed as 10.0.0.0/8
- 172.16.0.0 – 172.31.255.255, usually expressed as 172.16.0.0/12
- 192.168.0.0 – 192.168.255.255, usually expressed as 192.168.0.0/16

In addition, the Automatic Private IP Addressing feature in all post-1998 Windows versions uses private IP addresses in the range 169.254.0.0 through 169.254.255.255.

Routers and residential gateways that use NAT almost always assign addresses from these private ranges. Linksys routers, for instance, typically assign addresses starting with 192.168.1.*x*.

NOTE

When an IPv4 subnet or IPv4 address is expressed in the format 172.16.16.1/20, it's referred to as a classless inter-domain routing (CIDR) address, or sometimes as a variable length subnet mask (VLSM) address. This format, which is used in Microsoft Azure subnets and elsewhere, expresses the subnet mask as a prefix in a number of bits—in this example, 20. What it means is that 20 bits, in this case, are network or subnetwork bits, and the remaining 12 bits are host bits. That enables you to determine what subnet this host resides in (172.16.16.0/20, in this example).

Mobile hotspots and other metered connections

Some devices with data connections on a cellular network allow you to turn the device into a mobile Wi-Fi hotspot—a feature sometimes referred to as *tethering*. This capability is invaluable when you need to get some work done on a portable PC, and an affordable, reliable, and secure Wi-Fi connection isn't available. Most modern smartphones, including iPhones and Android devices, can act as a hotspot, although the cellular data provider must allow this capability.

When using a mobile hotspot with a plan that requires you to pay by the megabyte or gigabyte, you risk incurring potentially higher costs (especially if you're roaming outside your home network) or hitting your data limit and having your connection throttled or stopped completely. To minimize that possibility, Windows 11 identifies mobile hotspots as metered connections and automatically limits certain types of background activity. By default, the list of restricted activities includes downloads from Windows Update, syncing with OneDrive, and always-on connections to an Exchange Server in Microsoft Outlook.

To ensure that Windows 11 treats a specific network as a metered connection, open Settings > Network & Internet > Wi-Fi > Manage Known Networks. Expand the desired Wi-Fi connection, and then turn the Metered Connection switch to On, as shown in Figure 11-8.

You can set a cap on the amount of data Windows is allowed to send or receive over any currently available network by going to Settings > Network & Internet > Advanced Network Settings > Data Usage. As shown in Figure 11-9, select the appropriate network connection (if not already selected) and then click Enter Limit. You can also review the amount of data usage from the last 30 days for the selected connection. Limits can be monthly, one time, or set to unlimited. If monthly, you can set the day of the month to reset the counters. You can specify limits in MB or GB.

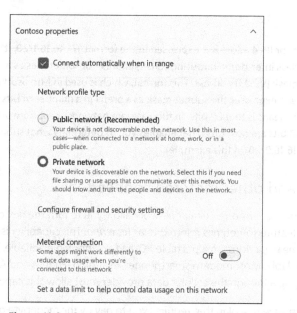

Figure 11-8 On pay-as-you-go networks, or on those with data caps, you can reduce the amount of data used by telling Windows 11 to treat the connection as metered.

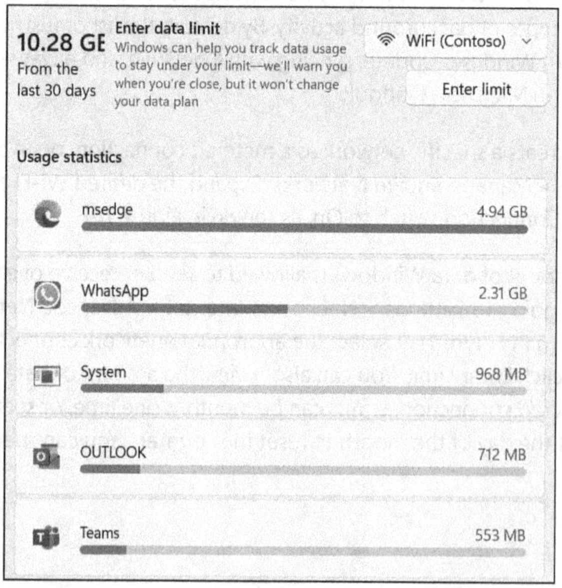

Figure 11-9 You can review data usage and also set limits for any available network connection.

Recent versions of Windows 11 have expanded the Mobile Hotspot feature to support sharing of any network connection on a Windows 11 PC. If you've paid for Wi-Fi on an airplane, for example, you can share that connection securely with up to eight other devices.

All the options you need are in Settings > Network & Internet > Mobile Hotspot. There are four settings to pay attention to here:

1. To begin sharing your network connection, flip the Mobile Hotspot switch to the On position.

2. Choose which connection you want to share. In the screenshot shown in Figure 11-10, Wi-Fi is the only option, but you can share any available connection: wired, Wi-Fi, or even mobile data.

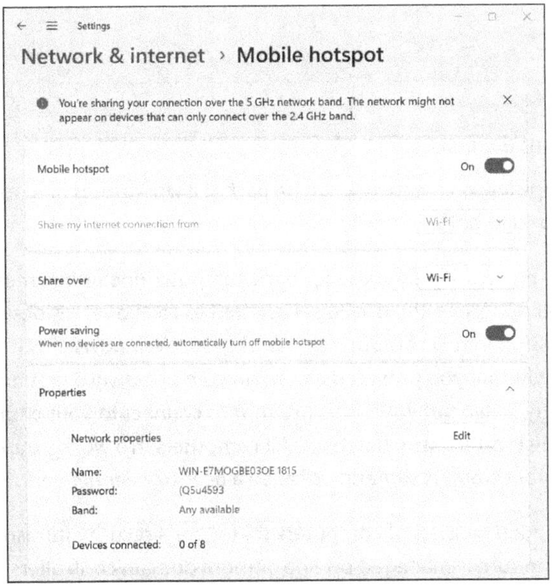

Figure 11-10   Turn on the Mobile Hotspot switch to share your internet connection with other devices. If you have multiple networks available (Ethernet and Wi-Fi, for example), you can select which one to share.

3. Choose how to share your connection: over Wi-Fi or Bluetooth.

4. Click Edit to change the connection name, replace the default random password with one of your own choosing, and customize the type of connection.

With that setup complete, you can turn on your mobile hotspot from the Quick Settings menu or from Settings and use the shared connection with any device (including a mobile phone).

CHAPTER 11

Enabling network discovery

For a local network to work properly, your computer must be able to locate other resources, including other computers. Likewise, other resources need a way to locate your computer.

In Windows 11, this feature is known as *network discovery*. By default, network discovery is disabled. To enable it, open Settings > Network & Internet > Advanced Network Settings, and then select Advanced Sharing Settings. You can enable the Network Discovery option for private networks, public networks, or both.

When you enable network discovery, a number of Windows services start, if they're not already running: DNS Client (dnscache); Function Discovery Resource Publication Services (fdrespub); Simple Service Discovery Protocol (ssdpsrv); and UPnP Device Host (upnphost). In addition, a Windows Defender Firewall exception for network discovery is created.

Inside OUT

Workgroups versus domains

Windows 11 computers on a network can be part of a workgroup or a domain. However, they cannot belong to both.

In a workgroup, the security database for each computer (including, most significantly, the list of user accounts and the privileges granted to each one) resides on that computer. When you sign in to a computer in a workgroup, Windows checks its local security database to see whether you provided a username and password that matches one in the database. Similarly, when network users attempt to connect to your computer, Windows again consults the local security database. All computers in a workgroup must be on the same subnet. A workgroup is sometimes called a *peer-to-peer network*.

By contrast, a domain consists of computers that share a security infrastructure, Active Directory, which in turn is managed on one or more domain controllers running Windows Server. Microsoft's cloud-based alternative, Azure Active Directory, provides a subset of this infrastructure without requiring IT departments to manage local servers. Active Directory and Azure Active Directory can be combined to create effective hybrid environments. When you sign in using a domain account, Windows authenticates your credentials against the security database defined by your network administrator.

In this chapter (and throughout this book), we focus primarily on unmanaged workgroup networks.

Setting the network location

Network location is closely related to network discovery. On a public network, you generally want network discovery disabled, to reduce the risk that an unknown host on the same network will access shared resources. By contrast, setting a network location to private signals that you trust other resources on the local network and want them to be available. That's especially important on mobile devices that can connect to different types of networks—a corporate domain, a wireless hotspot at a coffee shop, or a private home network.

Each type of network has its own security requirements. Windows uses network location profiles to categorize each network and then applies appropriate security settings. When you connect to a new network, Windows applies one of three security settings:

- **Public** This is the default setting for any new, untrusted network connection. Network discovery is turned off for public networks, and unsolicited incoming connections are blocked, making it more difficult for other people on the same access point to try to connect to your computer. This option is appropriate for networks in public places, such as wireless hotspots in coffee shops, hotels, airports, and libraries. It's also the correct choice if your desktop or laptop PC is directly connected to a cable modem or other broadband connection without the protection of a router and hardware firewall.

- **Private** This option is appropriate when you're connecting to a trusted network, such as your own network at home—if and only if that network is protected by a router (which may be incorporated in a cable modem or similar network access device) or comparable internet defense. When you make this choice, Windows enables network discovery for sharing with other users on the network.

- **Domain** This option is applied automatically when you sign in to Windows using a computer that's joined to a Windows domain, such as your company network. In this scenario, network discovery is enabled, allowing you to see other computers and servers on the network by using accounts and permissions controlled by a network administrator.

> ➤ If you have a mobile computer that connects to multiple networks, keep in mind that the Windows Defender Firewall maintains separate network security profiles for private (home or work), public, and domain-based networks. For more information about Windows Firewall, see "Blocking intruders with Windows Defender Firewall" in Chapter 12, "Windows security and privacy."

The location profile of the current network is shown on the details page for a selected network connection, as shown in Figure 11-8 earlier in this chapter.

To change the profile of the current network from Public to Private, or vice versa, go to Settings > Network & Internet. Look to the network name at the top of the page for a link labeled Properties, which should include the current network location. Click that Properties link and then, under the Network Profile Type heading, select Private Network or Public Network (Recommended) as appropriate.

You can also use the PowerShell **Get-NetConnectionProfile** and **Set-NetConnectionProfile** cmdlets to review and modify the NetworkCategory values for your network connections. As displayed in Figure 11-11, the administrator has retrieved the properties for the current network profile on the local computer. These cmdlets are documented at *https://learn.microsoft.com/powershell/module/netconnection.*

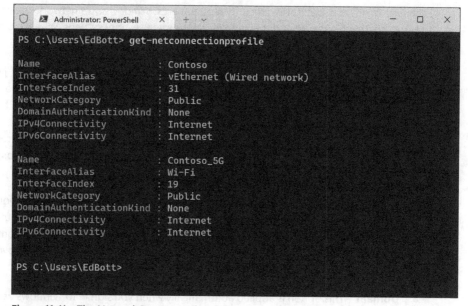

```
PS C:\Users\EdBott> get-netconnectionprofile

Name                      : Contoso
InterfaceAlias            : vEthernet (Wired network)
InterfaceIndex            : 31
NetworkCategory           : Public
DomainAuthenticationKind  : None
IPv4Connectivity          : Internet
IPv6Connectivity          : Internet

Name                      : Contoso_5G
InterfaceAlias            : Wi-Fi
InterfaceIndex            : 19
NetworkCategory           : Public
DomainAuthenticationKind  : None
IPv4Connectivity          : Internet
IPv6Connectivity          : Internet


PS C:\Users\EdBott>
```

Figure 11-11 The NetworkCategory value determines whether the network location profile is public or private.

Connecting to a wireless network

In this section, we assume you have already configured a wireless access point (often included as a feature in cable modems, internet-facing routers, and other network access devices supplied by your broadband provider) and confirmed that it is working correctly, or that you are in a location with a public or private wireless access point managed by someone else. Whenever your computer's wireless network adapter is installed and turned on, Windows scans for available wireless access points.

When you click the Network icon in the system tray and then click the arrow to the right of the Wi-Fi button, you're likely to see lots of access points available for connection, most of them owned by your neighbors or nearby visitors. Assuming those networks are adequately secured with a network security key that you don't know and can't guess, you'd have no luck connecting to them.

When you select an available wireless connection, assuming it's known, then you have the option to select the Connect Automatically checkbox, as displayed in Figure 11-12. When you get within range of the network in the future, your computer automatically enters the saved password and connects to the network.

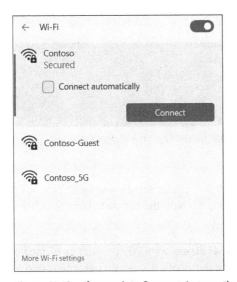

Figure 11-12   If you select Connect Automatically, your Wi-Fi connection will establish automatically the next time you're in range of the network.

NOTE

Note that saved Wi-Fi network passwords are synced between devices when you sign in with a Microsoft account, so you might find that a brand-new device, one you've never used before, automatically connects to your home or office Wi-Fi without having to ask you.

Clicking the Connect button for a secure wireless access point reveals a box in which you're expected to enter a network password, as in Figure 11-13. If what you enter matches what's stored in the access point's configuration, you're in. Getting in is easy on a network you control, where you set the network security key. For a secured access point controlled by someone else—a doctor's waiting room, a coffee shop, a friend's office—you need to ask someone, typically the network owner, for the password.

Figure 11-13   Connecting to a secure network for the first time requires that you correctly enter a passphrase or security key.

To disconnect from a Wi-Fi access point, click or tap its entry in the Quick Settings menu and then tap Disconnect. Doing so automatically turns off the option to connect automatically to that network in the future.

Windows 11 saves credentials for every Wi-Fi access point you connect to, giving you the option to connect with a tap when you revisit. If that thought makes you uncomfortable, you can see and manage the full list of networks by opening Settings > Network & Internet > Wi-Fi and clicking Manage Known Networks.

That list can be startlingly long, especially if you're a frequent traveler. To review the properties for a connection, select it from the list. If you want to abandon a network connection, click the Forget button to the right of the network name, as displayed in Figure 11-14.

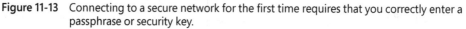
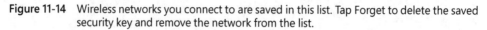

Figure 11-14   Wireless networks you connect to are saved in this list. Tap Forget to delete the saved security key and remove the network from the list.

Inside OUT

Decoding Wi-Fi standards

The most popular wireless networks use one of several variants of the IEEE (Institute of Electrical and Electronics Engineers) 802.11 standard, also known as Wi-Fi. On modern Wi-Fi networks, you're likely to encounter one of the following four standards (going from oldest to newest):

- **802.11g** This standard was current up until 2009, just before the release of Windows 7. It's still in use on some older PCs and wireless access points. It can transfer data at a maximum rate of 54 megabits per second using radio frequencies in the 2.4-GHz range. 802.11g-based networks largely supplanted those based on an earlier standard, 802.11b, which offers a maximum speed of 11 megabits per second.

- **802.11n** Using this standard, adopted in 2009, you can expect to see dramatic improvements in speed (600 megabits per second) as well as significantly greater range. Unlike the earlier standards, the 802.11n standard allows use of the 5-Ghz frequency range as well as 2.4 GHz. However, not all 802.11n hardware supports both bands.

- **802.11ac** Also known as Wi-Fi 5, this standard was finalized in 2014 and builds on the 802.11n specification. It allows multiple links at both ends of the wireless connection, advertising throughput rates of 500 megabits per second per link, with a theoretical maximum speed of up to 2,600 megabits per second.

- **802.11ax** Known as Wi-Fi 6, this is the latest Wi-Fi standard and expands on the capabilities of Wi-Fi 5. It supports switching between 2.4 Ghz and 5 Ghz, and enables higher bandwidths than with Wi-Fi 5 (potentially up to 9.6 gigabits). Most modern computers are equipped with a Wi-Fi 6 compatible network adapter. A relatively new extension to this standard called Wi-Fi 6E uses a 6 GHz band that is reserved exclusively for compatible hardware.

For the maximum throughput on networks that are not compatible with Wi-Fi 6E, use 5-Ghz 802.11ax devices throughout your network. The 5-Ghz band is subject to less radio interference than 2.4 Ghz and is capable of a higher maximum theoretical data rate. If you must maintain compatibility with older 2.4-Ghz devices, the ideal solution is to use a dual-band wireless access point.

Connecting to a hidden network

Every wireless network has a name, formally known as a *service set identifier* but typically referred to as an *SSID*. In an effort to enforce security through obscurity, some wireless networks are set up so that they don't broadcast their SSID. Connecting to such a hidden network is a bit more challenging because its name doesn't appear in the list of available networks on the network flyout Quick Settings Menu or in Network & Internet Settings. Making such a connection is possible, however, as long as you know the network name and its security settings.

NOTE

Configuring a router so that it doesn't advertise its name has been incorrectly promoted by some as a security measure. Although it does make the network less accessible to casual snoops, lack of a broadcast SSID is no deterrent to a knowledgeable attacker. Furthermore, attackers can learn the SSID even when they're not near your wireless access point, because it's periodically broadcast from your computer, wherever it happens to be. We provide these steps to help you connect to a hidden network managed by someone else; we don't recommend that you configure your home or office network in this fashion without a good reason.

To connect to a hidden network, open Settings > Network & Internet > Wi-Fi > Manage Known Networks and then click Add Network. As shown in Figure 11-15, you must enter the network name, select the security type, enter relevant security information, and then click Save.

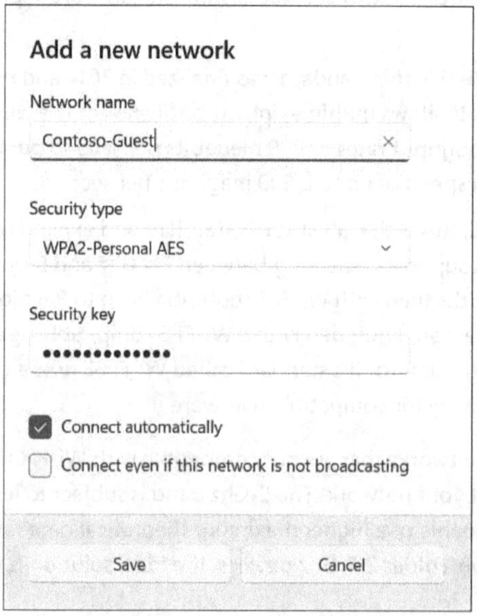

Figure 11-15   Enter the required information to connect to an unadvertised network.

If you select certain security types, the Add A New Network dialog expands to list new options. Figure 11-16 shows the settings for an enterprise network that requires the user to authenticate with credentials rather than enter a simple password.

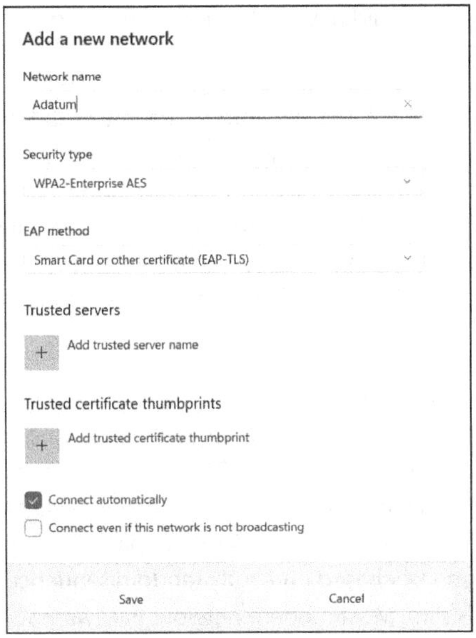

Add a new network

Network name

Adatum

Security type

WPA2-Enterprise AES

EAP method

Smart Card or other certificate (EAP-TLS)

Trusted servers

+ Add trusted server name

Trusted certificate thumbprints

+ Add trusted certificate thumbprint

☑ Connect automatically
☐ Connect even if this network is not broadcasting

Save   Cancel

Figure 11-16   On enterprise networks, some security options require additional configuration.

Wireless security

On a conventional wired network, especially in a private home or office, physical security is rea-sonably easy to maintain: If someone plugs a computer into a network jack or a switch, you can trace the physical wire back to the intruder's computer. On wireless networks, however, anyone who comes into range of your wireless access point can tap into your network and intercept signals from it.

If you run a small business, you might want to allow internet access to your customers by using an open internet connection. Some internet service providers create secure guest accounts on their customers' cable modems (or similar access devices) that allow other customers of that service to connect using their network credentials. Many modern Wi-Fi routers include the option to create a secure guest network, separate from the one you use in your home or office. That option allows customers to securely access the internet without having access to local net-work resources.

Other than those scenarios, however, you probably want to secure your network so that the only people who can connect to it are those you specifically authorize. Doing that means configuring security settings on your wireless access point or router. When you connect to a network, known or unknown, the level of security is determined by the encryption standard chosen by the net-work owner and supported by network hardware on both sides of the connection.

CHAPTER 11

Depending on the age of your hardware, you should have a choice of one or more of the following options, from least to most secure:

- **Wired Equivalent Privacy (WEP)** WEP is a first-generation scheme that dates back before the turn of the century. It suffers from serious security flaws that make it inappropriate for use on any network that contains sensitive data. Most modern Wi-Fi equipment supports WEP for backward compatibility with older hardware, but we strongly advise against using it unless no other options are available. If you have an older device that supports only WEP (and it can't be upgraded with a firmware update), consider retiring or replacing that device.

- **Wi-Fi Protected Access (WPA)** WPA is an early version of the encryption scheme that has since been replaced by both WPA2 and WPA3. It was specifically designed to overcome weaknesses of WEP. On a small network that uses WPA, clients and access points use a shared network password (called a *preshared key*, or *PSK*) that consists of a 256-bit number or a passphrase that is from 8 to 63 bytes long. (A longer passphrase produces a stronger key.) With a sufficiently strong key based on a truly random sequence, the likelihood of a successful outside attack is slim. Most modern network hardware supports WPA only for backward compatibility.

- **Wi-Fi Protected Access 2 (WPA2)** Based on the 802.11i standard, WPA2 provides a strong protection for consumer-grade wireless networks. It uses 802.1x-based authentication and Advanced Encryption Standard (AES) encryption; combined, these technologies ensure that only authorized users can access the network and that any intercepted data cannot be deciphered. WPA2 comes in two flavors: WPA2-Personal and WPA2-Enterprise. *WPA2-Personal* uses a passphrase to create its encryption keys and is a good choice for the security of wireless networks in homes and small offices. WPA2-Enterprise requires a server to verify network users. All wireless products sold since early 2006 must support WPA2 to bear the Wi-Fi CERTIFIED label.

- **Wi-Fi Protected Access 3 (WPA3)** Also based on the 802.11i standard, WPA3 extends the security of WPA2. Like WPA2, it uses 802.1x-based authentication and Advanced Encryption Standard (AES) encryption; it also implements a technology called Simultaneous Authentication of Equals (SAE) to improve security over WPA2. Similarly, WPA3 comes in two flavors: WPA3-Personal and WPA3-Enterprise. As with WPA2, WPA3-Enterprise requires a server for user verification. WPA3-Enterprise also provides a 192-bit mode for additional protection.

You might see other encryption options, including the 802.11x standard, which allows corporate networks to enforce access through user credentials such as Active Directory. Those configurations are typically designed for use on large enterprise networks and are beyond the scope of this book.

Inside OUT

Beef up security at the access point

If your data is sensitive and your network is in an apartment building or an office complex where you can reasonably expect other people to wander into range with wireless adapters, you should take extra security precautions in addition to enabling WPA. Consider any or all the following measures to protect your wireless access point from intruders:

- Change the network name (SSID) of your access point to one that doesn't match the hardware defaults and doesn't give away any information about you or your business.

- Disable remote administration of the access point; if you need to change settings, you can do so directly, using a wired connection.

- Whether you decide to allow remote administration of the access point or not, set a strong password so that a visitor can't tamper with your network settings.

- Check the firmware and drivers for wireless hardware (access points and adapters) at regular intervals and install the most recent versions, which might incorporate security fixes.

- Consider using a virtual private network (VPN) for wireless connections. A VPN sends all wireless traffic over an encrypted connection, making it impossible for others to snoop on your wireless communications. Corporate network administrators can help set up a VPN using your company's security infrastructure. For unmanaged Windows 11 devices, VPN software and services are available.

When setting up a wireless access point for a home or small office, choose a strong passphrase. A passphrase for WPA2 or WPA3 can be up to 63 characters long and can contain letters (case-sensitive), numbers, and spaces (no spaces at the beginning or end, however). Many devices generate a random alphanumeric key, but you might prefer to use a memorable phrase instead of random characters. If you do, choose a phrase that's not easily guessed, and make it long. Also, consider incorporating letter substitution or misspellings to thwart attackers. Because the phrase can be saved and synced between devices, you shouldn't need to enter it often.

CHAPTER 11

You must use the same encryption option on all wireless devices on your network—access points, routers, network adapters, print servers, cameras, and so on—so choose the best option that's supported by all your devices.

Connecting to another computer with Remote Desktop

Sharing computer resources over a properly configured network gives you access to all the files you might need, wherever they're stored. But sometimes even that's not enough. You might need to run an app that's installed only on another computer, or you might need to configure and manage another computer's files and settings in ways that can be done only by sitting down in front of that computer. For those occasions, a Remote Desktop session is the perfect solution.

With Remote Desktop, applications run on the remote computer; your computer is effectively used as a terminal. You can use a low-powered computer or even a mobile device to connect to a remote computer directly. Remote Desktop connections are encrypted, so your information is secure.

NOTE

The computer that you want to control—the one at the remote location—is called the *remote computer*. The computer you want to use to control the remote computer is called the *client computer*. By default, Remote Desktop traffic is sent and received using Remote Desktop Protocol (RDP) over TCP port 3389.

In this section, we focus on the most common scenario: configuring a PC running Windows 11 Pro, Enterprise, or Education or any supported version of Windows Server to allow incoming Remote Desktop connections and using a second PC running any edition of Windows 11 as the remote client over a local network. (PCs running Windows Home edition can be used as a Remote Desktop client but do not allow hosting Remote Desktop sessions.)

Inside OUT

Configuring Remote Desktop connections from outside your local network

Remote Desktop connections are relatively easy over a local network, especially when no third-party security software is installed. But trying to connect to Remote Desktop over the internet is far more problematic. To make that long-distance connection through the internet, you must be able to reach the remote computer by using a known public IP address, and you have to get through a router and past any security software between the two computers.

The solutions to these issues depend on your specific hardware configuration. In broad strokes, they require configuring your Remote Desktop client to connect to the external

IP address on your router and then configuring your router to pass traffic on port 3389 to the internal IP address of the Remote Desktop server. Then, of course, you have to worry about whether your broadband provider will change your external IP address. If you're a networking expert, those general guidelines should give you all the information you need to set up your remote session over the internet.

If, on the other hand, you're not a networking expert, that probably sounds like more trouble than it's worth. We agree, which is why we suggest instead using any of several third-party programs that can securely provide remote access without the hassles or security risks of allowing direct connections through your network boundary. We recommend Splashtop Business Access (*https://www.splashtop.com/business*), which offers an excellent feature set at a fraction of the cost of some better-known commercial packages.

Installing Remote Desktop client software

Windows 11 includes a desktop app for remote access called Remote Desktop Connection. Although this program's main feature set and its overall appearance have remained largely unchanged since its debut nearly 20 years ago, it's still perfectly suitable for remote connections. If you're sitting in front of a PC running any version of Windows, you can use this app to connect to a Windows 11 PC configured as a Remote Desktop server.

A slightly newer alternative, called Microsoft Remote Desktop, is available in the Microsoft Store. (To see its listing, go to *https://bit.ly/ms-rdc-store*.) This app works on any Windows 11 device, and it includes some capabilities not available in Remote Desktop Connection. In this section, we describe how to use both programs.

Even if you don't have a PC available, you might still be able to configure your Windows 11 device as a Remote Desktop server and connect to it using a non-Windows device. Microsoft has Remote Desktop clients for mobile devices running iOS and Android as well as Apple-branded PCs running macOS. For download links and installation instructions, see *https://aka.ms/rdapps*.

Enabling inbound Remote Desktop connections

For security reasons, incoming Remote Desktop sessions are not allowed without your explicit permission. To grant access on a computer running Windows 11 Pro, Enterprise, or Education, go to Settings > System > Remote Desktop and slide the Remote Desktop switch to the On position.

You must be signed in using an administrator account to make this change, and you must click Confirm in a separate step to verify the configuration change.

Enabling Remote Desktop starts a service that listens for incoming connections on port 3389. It also creates an exception in Windows Firewall that allows authenticated traffic on this port. (If you're using third-party security software that includes a firewall, it should make this configuration change for you; if it doesn't, you need to adjust that software's settings so it allows incoming access to TCP port 3389.)

After Remote Desktop is enabled, you can configure additional settings. The first of these is that you can configure Network Level Authentication (NLA) for any Remote Desktop connections; this setting is enabled by default and is recommended. You would normally only change this if you were intending to allow connections from older versions of Windows operating systems that don't support NLA.

Next, you can define which user accounts are able to connect using Remote Desktop to your computer. To do this, click Remote Desktop Users on the Remote Desktop page, as shown in Figure 11-17.

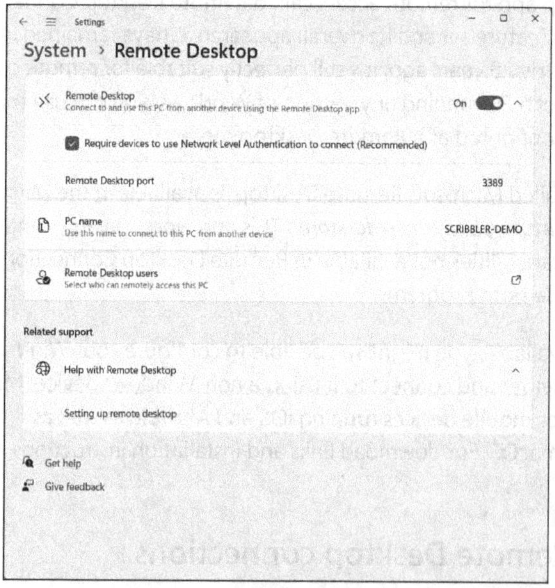

Figure 11-17   You can disable the requirement for NLA and define which users can access your computer using Remote Desktop. The TCP port used, 3389, cannot be changed using Settings.

The current user account and any user account that's a member of the local Administrators group can connect remotely to the computer. To allow access for other user accounts that are not members of the local Administrators group, click Remote Desktop Users and then select which users you want to authorize.

Using the Microsoft Remote Desktop app

As we noted earlier, the Microsoft Remote Desktop app is not included with Windows; it is, however, available as a free download from the Microsoft Store. Remote Desktop offers a simplified user experience compared to the legacy Remote Desktop Connection client. Its visual approach shows all your remote connections on the home screen, allowing you to open one with a single click or tap. In addition, Microsoft Remote Desktop includes several performance enhancements that optimize your connection quality. It supports multiple instances, so you can operate two or more Remote Desktop sessions simultaneously, each in its own window. And, of course, as a Store app, it's touch friendly.

Note that if you're planning to connect to Azure Virtual Desktop devices or to devices that are Azure AD-joined, this app will not work. Instead, use the 64-bit Windows app available from *https://bit.ly/AVC-remote-client*.

The Microsoft Remote Desktop app window is downright Spartan until you've saved a desktop or two. Adding a desktop takes minimal effort: Click the Add (+) button and then click PCs. The Add A PC page appears, as shown in Figure 11-18.

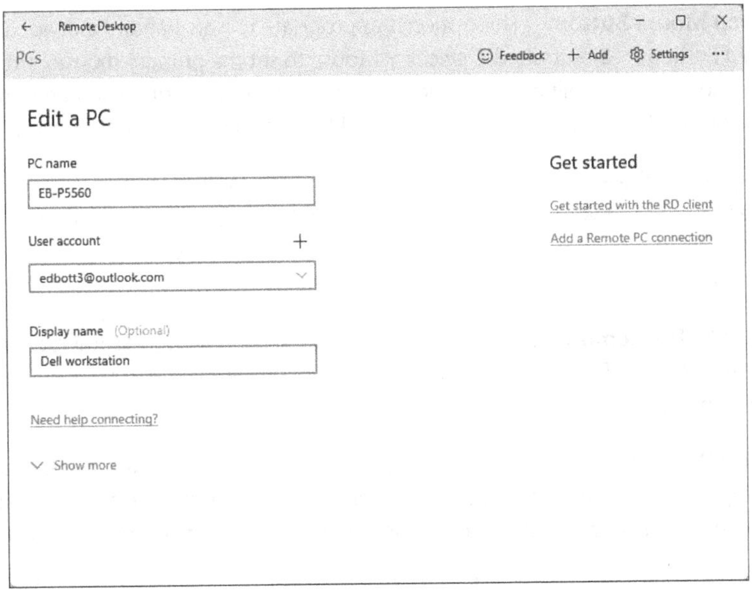

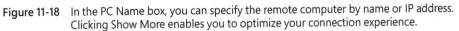

Figure 11-18   In the PC Name box, you can specify the remote computer by name or IP address. Clicking Show More enables you to optimize your connection experience.

Enter the name or IP address of the PC to which you want to connect. All the other fields in the Add A PC pane are optional.

By default, the User Account field is set to Ask Me Every Time. In this configuration, you're prompted for your username and password each time you connect to the desktop. If you know you'll always want to use the same account, you can add its credentials here, and Remote Desktop will sign you in every time without prompting. Click the arrow at the right side to select a previously configured user account. If the account you want to use doesn't appear in the list, click the plus sign above the User Account box and add the necessary details. Optionally, enter a connection Display Name and then click Save. The connection appears as a tile in the app window.

Before you save the settings, on the Add A PC pane, you can also click Show More. This displays the following additional settings:

- **Group**   If you have multiple saved connections, you can group them by adding a group name and then selecting a group for each connection.

- **Gateway**   To reach a remote PC through a gateway server on a corporate network, specify its name or IP address, along with the name of a user account with access permission.

- **Connect To Admin Session**   For connecting to a computer running Windows 11, this option has no effect, and you can safely ignore it. It enables administrative access on some older Windows Server configurations.

- **Swap Mouse Buttons**   This option is appropriate for left-handed individuals who have used Settings > Bluetooth & Devices > Mouse to set the primary mouse button as Right instead of Left. Enabling this setting swaps the functionality of the left and right mouse buttons while you work in the Remote Desktop session to match the local settings.

- **Display Settings**   These settings let you specify a screen resolution and display size for the remote PC. If you don't specify a resolution here, Remote Desktop uses the resolution of the client computer, displayed full screen, by default. After selecting a custom resolution, you can also choose a custom scaling factor.

- **Update The Remote Session Resolution On Resize**   With this setting on, you can resize a Remote Desktop session in a window and have the display resolution adjust to your changes.

- **Local Resources**   The three settings under this heading allow you to share the client computer's Clipboard contents and microphone with the remote computer and choose whether audio plays on the remote computer, on the client computer, or on neither.

Working in a Remote Desktop session

After you save a connection in the Add A Desktop pane, an icon for that connection appears in Remote Desktop. Click the icon to open a connection to the remote computer. Along the way, you might encounter a couple of obstacles:

- If you specified Ask Me Every Time in the User Account box, Remote Desktop asks for the username and password of an account authorized on the remote computer to make a connection. Select Remember Me, and you won't need to enter this information in future sessions.

- By default, Remote Desktop sessions you create on your local network use self-hosted digital certificates that aren't recognized as trusted by the client computer. If you're certain that you're connecting to the right computer, select the Don't Ask About This Certificate Again checkbox (so you won't be bothered in future sessions) and click Connect.

After bounding past those hurdles, Remote Desktop attempts to open a connection. If the account you use for the remote connection is already signed in to the remote computer—or if no one is signed in to the remote computer—the remote computer's desktop then appears on your computer.

If a different user account is signed in to the remote computer, Windows lets you know that you'll be forcing that person to sign out and gives you a chance to cancel the connection. On the other end, the signed-in user sees a similar notification that offers a short time to reject the remote connection before it takes over. Note that only one user at a time can control the desktop of a computer running Windows. Whoever is currently signed in has the final say on whether someone else can sign in.

While you're connected to the remote computer, the local display on that computer (if it's turned on) does not show what you see on the client computer but instead shows the lock screen. A person who has physical access to the remote computer can't see what you're doing (other than the fact that you're signed in remotely).

When you connect to a remote computer using the Microsoft Remote Desktop app without specifying a custom resolution, the remote computer takes over your entire screen using the resolution of the client computer. At the top of the screen, in the center, a tiny toolbar with two controls appears. Click the magnifying glass icon to zoom the remote display; click the ellipsis (three dots) icon to reveal two buttons in the upper-right corner, as shown in Figure 11-19.

Figure 11-19   Use these large buttons to disconnect from a session or expand it to full screen in the Store version of the Remote Desktop client.

Click Disconnect to end your remote session. The remote computer remains locked, ready for someone to sign in locally. Click Full Screen to toggle between full-screen and windowed views of the remote PC.

While the display is in full-screen mode, you can move the mouse pointer to the top edge of the screen to display the Remote Desktop title bar. It includes the usual window controls (minimize, resize, and close). Move the mouse pointer to the bottom edge of the screen to display the task-bar for your local computer. Clicking any icon on the local taskbar shifts the focus away from the remote session and back to your local computer. If you're running the Remote Desktop app on a touchscreen-equipped PC, you can reveal either of these controls by swiping in from the top or bottom edge of the screen.

Ending a remote session

When you're through with a Remote Desktop session, you can lock, sign out, or disconnect. If the remote computer is running Windows 11, these options are in the usual places where com-parable options appear on your local computer: Lock and Sign Out appear when you click the user avatar on Start on the remote computer, and Disconnect appears when you click Power on Start. For remote machines running earlier Windows versions, these options appear in the lower-right corner of the remote session's Start menu. (You must click the arrow to see all the options.)

Locking the computer keeps the remote session connected and all programs running, but it hides everything behind a sign-in screen that requests a password; this is comparable to press-ing Windows key + L to lock your computer.

Signing out closes all your programs, exits your user session, and disconnects.

If you disconnect without signing out, your programs continue to run on the remote computer, but the connection is ended. The sign-in screen is visible on the remote computer, and it's avail-able for another user. If you sign in later—either locally or through a remote connection—you can pick up right where you left off. As an alternative to the Start commands, you can discon-nect by clicking the Disconnect button, displaying the Remote Desktop title bar and clicking the Back button, or simply closing the Remote Desktop window.

Adjusting Microsoft Remote Desktop app settings

At the top of the Microsoft Remote Desktop app window, to the right of the Add button, is a Settings button that exposes a pane filled with options to customize the app experience. Here, you can edit credentials for saved user accounts, for example; to remove a user account, choose a username from the list, click the pen icon above the name, and then click the faint Remove This Account link at the bottom of the Edit An Account pane.

Other settings on this list that are potentially useful include a Start Connections In Full Screen switch, which you should turn off if you prefer to run remote sessions in a window, as well as a Prevent The Screen From Timing Out switch that can reduce the annoyance of having to sign back in if you leave an open session to work on other tasks.

Using Remote Desktop Connection

Remote Desktop Connection is a desktop app that should be familiar to longtime Windows users accustomed to remote administration tasks. To start it, in the search box, type **remote** and then click Remote Desktop Connection, or enter its command directly: Mstsc.exe. A dialog like the one shown in Figure 11-20 appears. In the Computer box, type the name of the remote computer or its IP address.

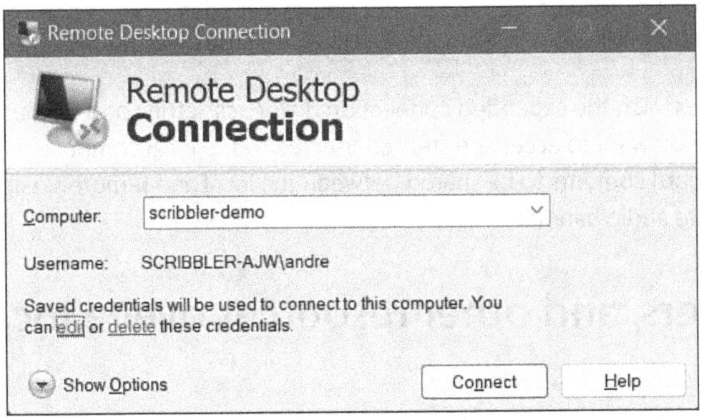

Figure 11-20   You can specify the remote computer by name or IP address.

NOTE

Both the Microsoft Remote Desktop app and Remote Desktop Connection support the use of Jump Lists. If you pin either icon to the taskbar and save credentials, you can right-click to choose saved PCs from the Jump List to go straight to a remote session.

CHAPTER 11

After entering the PC name, you can click Connect and begin the process of connecting to the remote PC immediately.

When you make a default connection, the display from the remote computer fills your entire screen, using the resolution of the client computer. Along the top of the screen, in the center, a small title bar appears. This title bar lets you switch between your own desktop and the remote PC. The pushpin button locks the connection bar in place.

> ## Inside OUT
>
> ### Move the connection bar
>
> If the connection bar covers a part of the screen you need to see, you can slide it left or right to reveal whatever's hidden underneath.

The Remote Desktop Connection client software offers a wide range of additional configuration options. We won't go through every tab, but here are two options that you might find useful:

- **Saved credentials**   On the General tab, you can enter a username and then select the Allow Me To Save Credentials checkbox. After you save credentials (in encrypted form, of course), they're entered automatically, allowing you to connect without extra steps.

- **Local Resources**   On the expanded connection dialog, click the Local Resources tab to select whether you want to access printers connected to the local computer, whether you want the Clipboard contents to be shared between the local and remote session, and how you want remote audio handled.

Sharing files, printers, and other resources over a local network

Much of the networking infrastructure of Windows 11 is a refinement of features that were developed decades ago, when the internet was still an interesting experiment. Today, the simplest way to share files, digital media, and other resources, even between computers in the same home or office, is through a cloud-based service like OneDrive. If you're a Microsoft 365 Business or Enterprise subscriber, in addition to OneDrive for Business, you can use Teams and SharePoint to easily collaborate with colleagues, customers, and suppliers.

There are, however, still valid reasons for Windows PCs to connect and share resources across a local area network. These traditional networking tools and techniques are fully supported in Windows 11, and you can use them alongside OneDrive sharing or Microsoft 365 collaboration features if you want to.

The underlying system of share permissions and NTFS permissions for controlling access to objects remains in Windows 11, working much like it has in previous versions of Windows going all the way back to Windows NT in the early 1990s. That's our starting point for this section.

Inside Out

What happened to HomeGroup?

The HomeGroup feature, originally introduced as part of Windows 7 and maintained through earlier versions of Windows 10, allowed Windows devices to share resources on a home network. In current versions of Windows 10 and in Windows 11, the HomeGroup feature is gone.

You need not shed any tears, however. HomeGroup was developed at a time when sharing files stored on a network computer was a major computing challenge, particularly for users of small home networks. In the years since, services such as OneDrive have become a convenient, safe way to store your files, photos, and videos in the cloud; doing so allows you to access those files from any device on any platform and also allows you to share them with other people—whether they're in the next room or across the country. (For details, see "Connecting OneDrive to your Windows PC" in Chapter 8, "Managing local and cloud storage.")

If you don't want to use OneDrive or a similar service, you can still use the network sharing capabilities built in to Windows to share files. The difference now—and the reason HomeGroup is no longer needed—is that Windows networking supports the use of Microsoft accounts. It's no longer necessary to create identical local user accounts on each computer in order to share.

Another benefit of HomeGroup was the ability to share a printer with other network users. Here, too, time and technological progress have made that feature irrelevant. Today, you have a choice of feature-packed home printers that can connect directly to any PC via Wi-Fi, with no network fussiness required. And even for USB-connected printers, the availability of standard credentials means shared printing is no longer painful.

Understanding sharing and security models in Windows

Much like Windows 10, Windows 11 offers two ways to share file resources, whether you're doing so locally or over the network:

- **Public folder sharing**   When you place files and folders in your Public folder or its subfolders, those files are available to anyone who has a user account on your computer. Each person who signs in has access to their own profile folders (Documents, Music, and so on), and *everyone* who signs in has access to the Public folder. (You need to dig a bit to find the Public folder, which—unlike other profiles—doesn't appear under Desktop in the left pane of File Explorer. Navigate to C:\Users\Public. If you use the Public folder often, pin it to the Quick Access list in File Explorer.)

By default, all users with an account on your computer can sign in and create, view, modify, and delete files in the Public folders. The person who creates a file in a Public folder (or copies an item to a Public folder) is the file's owner and has Full Control access. All others who sign in locally have Modify access.

Settings in Advanced Sharing Settings (accessible from Settings > Network & Internet > Advanced Network Settings, discussed in the next section) determine whether the contents of your Public folder are made available on your network and whether entering a username and password is required for access. If you turn on password-protected sharing, only network users who have a user account on your computer (or those who know the username and password for an account on your computer) can access files in the Public folder. Without password-protected sharing, everyone on your network has access to your Public folder files if you enable network sharing of the Public folder.

You can't select which network users get access, nor can you specify different access levels for different users. Sharing via the Public folder is quick and easy—but it's inflexible.

- **Advanced sharing**   By choosing to share folders or files outside the Public folder, you can specify precisely which user accounts are able to access your shared data, and you can specify the types of privileges those accounts enjoy. You can grant different access privileges to different users. For example, you might enable some users to modify shared files and create new ones, enable other users to read files without changing them, and lock out still other users altogether.

You don't need to decide between sharing the Public folder and sharing specific folders because you can use both methods simultaneously. You might find that a mix of sharing styles works best for you; each has its benefits:

- Sharing specific folders is best for files you want to share with some users but not with others—or if you want to grant different levels of access to different users.

- Public folder sharing provides a convenient, logical way to designate a collection of documents, pictures, music, and other files that you want to share with everyone who uses your computer or your network. (Presumably, those other users are trusted family members or coworkers.)

Configuring your network for sharing

If you plan to share folders and files with other users on your network, you must take a few preparatory steps. (If you plan to share only with others who use your computer by signing in locally, you can skip these steps. And if your computer is part of a domain, some of these steps—or their equivalent in the domain world—must be done by an administrator on the domain controller. We don't cover those details in this book.)

1. **Be sure that all computers use the same workgroup name.** With modern versions of Windows, this step isn't absolutely necessary, although it does improve network discovery performance.

2. **Set your network's location to Private.** This setting makes it possible for other users to discover shared resources and provides appropriate security for a network in a home or an office. (Setting the location to Public tightens network security and breaks most local networking features.) For details, see "Setting the network location," earlier in this chapter.

3. **Confirm that network discovery is turned on.** This should happen automatically when you set the network location to Private, but you can double-check the setting— and change it if necessary—in Advanced Sharing Settings. To open Advanced Sharing Settings, go to Settings > Network & Internet > Advanced Network Settings. Then click Advanced Sharing Settings to open the page shown in Figure 11-21.

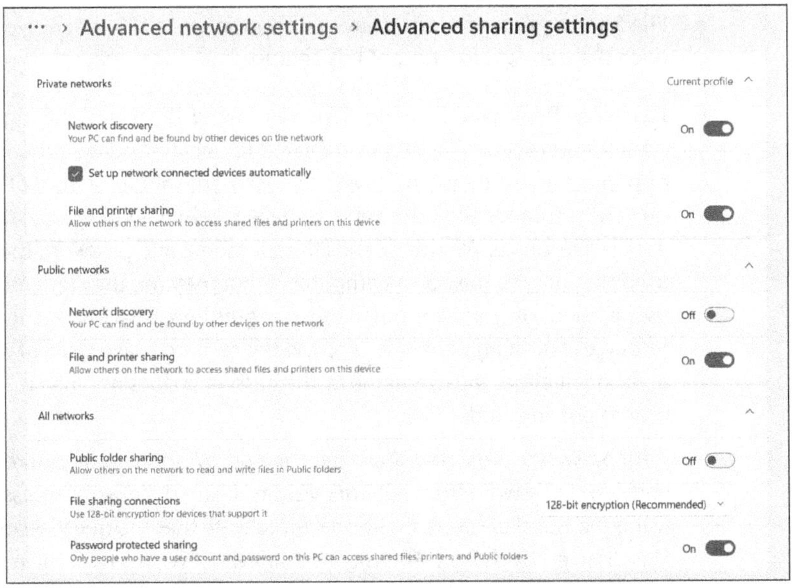

Figure 11-21   After you review settings for the Private profile, click the arrow by Public Networks and All Networks to see additional options.

4. **Select your sharing options.** In Advanced Sharing Settings, make a selection for each of the following network options. The first option is under the Private profile; to view the remaining settings, expand All Networks.

- **File And Printer Sharing** Turn on this option if you want to share specific files or folders, the Public folder, or printers; it must be turned on if you plan to share any files (other than media streaming) over your network.

  The mere act of turning on file and printer sharing does not expose any of your computer's files or printers to other network users; that occurs only after you make additional sharing settings.

- **Public Folder Sharing** If you want to share items in your Public folder with all network users (or, if you enable password-protected sharing, all users who have a user account and password on your computer), turn on Public folder sharing. If you do so, network users will have read/write access to Public folders. With Public folder sharing turned off, anyone who signs in to your computer locally has access to Public folders, but network users do not.

- **File Sharing Connections** Leave this option set to 128-bit encryption, which has been the standard for most of this century.

- **Password Protected Sharing** When password-protected sharing is turned on, network users cannot access your shared folders (including Public folders, if shared) or printers unless they can provide the username and password of a user account on your computer. With this setting enabled, when another user attempts to access a shared resource, Windows sends the username and password that the person used to sign in to their own computer. If that matches the credentials for a local user account on your computer, the user gets immediate access to the shared resource (assuming permissions to use the resource have been granted to that user account). If either the username or the password does not match, Windows asks the user to provide credentials.

  With password-protected sharing turned off, Windows does not require a username and password from network visitors. Instead, network access is provided by using the Guest account. It's important to note that the guest account in Windows 11 is disabled by default. This means that even if you turn off the requirement for password-protected sharing, a user still requires a valid user account to connect to your shared resources. You can, of course, enable the Guest account on your computer, but we strongly urge you to reconsider as this represents a significant security issue.

5. **Configure user accounts.** If you use password-protected sharing, each person who accesses a shared resource on your computer must have a user account on your computer. If you use a Microsoft account, make sure that the account is added to both

computers; for a local account, the username and password must be identical on both machines. If you've configured accounts correctly, network users will be able to access shared resources without having to enter their credentials after they've signed in to their own computer.

Sharing files and folders

Whether you plan to share files and folders with other people who share your computer or those who connect to your computer over the network (or both), the process for setting up shared resources is the same as long as the Sharing Wizard is enabled. We recommend you use the Sharing Wizard even if you normally disdain wizards. It's quick, easy, and certain to make all the correct settings for network shares and NTFS permissions—a sometimes-daunting task if undertaken manually. After you configure shares with the wizard, you can always dive in and make changes manually if you need to. (Although it's possible to use the Advanced Sharing options to configure network sharing independently of NTFS permissions, we don't recommend that technique and do not cover it in this book.)

To be sure the Sharing Wizard is enabled, open File Explorer Options. (In File Explorer, click See More > Options.) In the dialog that appears, shown in Figure 11-22, click the View tab. Near the bottom of the Advanced Settings list, verify that Use Sharing Wizard (Recommended) is selected.

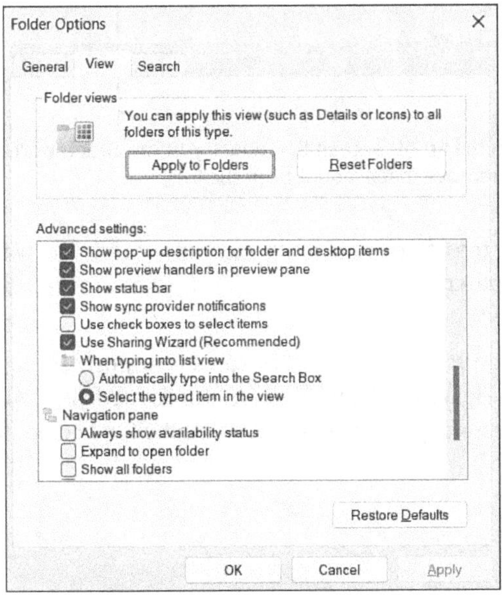

Figure 11-22   On the View tab of the Folder Options dialog, verify that the option to use the Sharing Wizard is enabled in Advanced Settings.

With the Sharing Wizard at the ready, follow these steps to share a folder or files:

1. In File Explorer, select the folders or files you want to share. (You can select multiple objects.)

2. Right-click the folder(s) and click Show More Options. Then choose Give Access To > Specific People. The Network Access dialog appears, as shown in Figure 11-23.

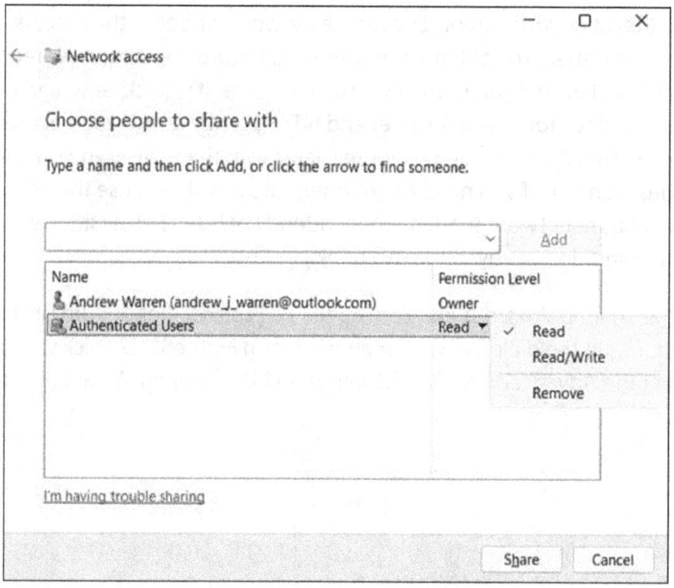

Figure 11-23   For each name in the list other than the owner, you can click the arrow to set the access level—or remove that account from the list.

3. Click in the text box and enter the name or Microsoft account for each user with whom you want to share. You can type a name in the box or click the arrow to display a list of available names; then click Add.

    Repeat this step for each person you want to add. You can add any user accounts on your computer, and also groups. In Figure 11-23, the administrator has added the Authenticated Users group—which means any user that has an account on this computer can access the shared item.

4. For each user, select a permission level. Your choices are

    ▪ **Read** Users with this permission level can view shared files and run shared pro-
    grams, but they cannot change or delete files. Selecting Read in the Sharing Wizard
    is equivalent to setting NTFS permissions to Read & Execute.

    ▪ **Read/Write** Users assigned the Read/Write permission have the same privileges
    you do as owner: They can view, change, add, and delete files in a shared folder.
    Selecting Read/Write sets NTFS permissions to Full Control for this user.

    # NOTE

    **You might see other permission levels if you return to the Sharing Wizard after you set
    up sharing. Contribute indicates Modify permission. Custom indicates NTFS permissions
    other than Read & Execute, Modify, or Full Control. Mixed appears if you select multiple
    items and they have different sharing settings. Owner, of course, identifies the owner of
    the item.**

5. Click Share. After a few moments, the wizard displays a page like the one shown in Figure
    11-24.

6. In the final step of the wizard, you can do any of the following:

    ▪ Send an email message to the people with whom you're sharing. The message
    includes a link to the shared items.

    ▪ Copy the network path to the Clipboard. This is handy if you want to send a link via
    another application, such as a messaging app. (To copy the link for a single item in
    a list, right-click the share name and choose Copy Link.)

    ▪ Double-click a share name to open the shared item.

    ▪ Open File Explorer with your computer selected in the Network folder, showing
    each network share on your computer.

    When you're finished with these tasks, click Done.

Creating a share requires privilege elevation, but after a folder has been shared, the share is
available to network users no matter who is signed in to your computer—or even when nobody
is signed in.

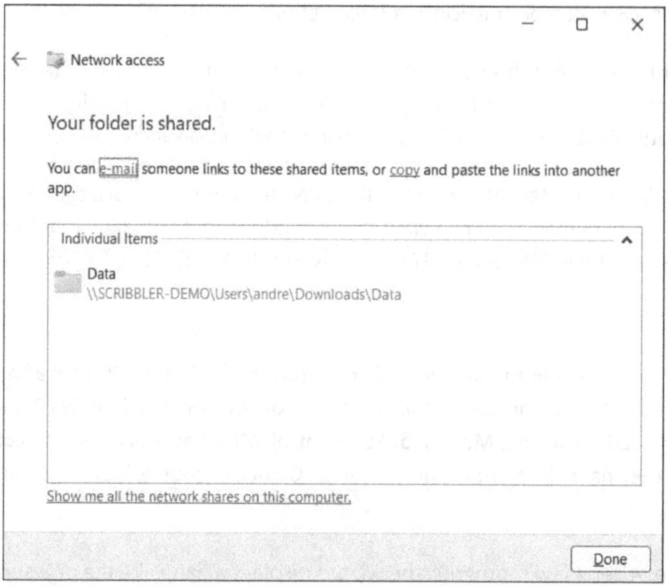

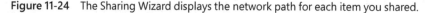

Figure 11-24   The Sharing Wizard displays the network path for each item you shared.

Inside OUT

Use advanced sharing to create shorter network paths

Confusingly, when you share one of your profile folders (or any other subfolder of %SystemDrive%\Users), Windows creates a network share for the Users folder—not for the folder you shared. This behavior isn't a security problem; NTFS permissions prevent network users from seeing any folders or files except the ones explicitly shared. But it does lead to some long Universal Naming Convention (UNC) paths to network shares. For example, sharing the Data subfolder of Downloads (as shown in Figure 11-24) creates the network path \\SCRIBBLER-DEMO\Users\andre\Downloads\Data. If this same folder had been anywhere on your computer outside the Users folder, no matter how deeply nested, the network path would instead be \\SCRIBBLER-DEMO\Data. Other people to whom you granted access wouldn't need to click through a series of folders to find the files in the intended target folder.

Network users, of course, can map a network drive or save a shortcut to your target folder to avoid this problem. But you can work around it from the sharing side, too: Use advanced sharing to share the folder directly. (Do this after you've used the Sharing Wizard to set up permissions.) And while you're doing that, be sure the share name you create doesn't have spaces. Eliminating them makes it easier to type a share path that works as a link.

Stopping or changing sharing of a file or folder

If you want to stop sharing a particular shared file or folder, select it in File Explorer. Right-click the folder, click Show More Options, select Give Access To and then click Remove Access. Doing so removes access control entries that are not inherited. In addition, the network share is removed; the folder is no longer visible in another user's Network folder.

To change share permissions, right-click the folder, click Show More Options, select Give Access To and then select Specific People. In the File Sharing dialog, you can add users, change permissions, or remove users. (To stop sharing with a user, click the permission level by the user's name and choose Remove.)

Sharing a printer

Although Windows doesn't have a wizard for sharing a printer over the network, the process is fairly simple. You configure all options for a printer—shared or not—by using the printer's properties dialog, which you access from Settings > Bluetooth & Devices > Printers & Scanners.

To make a printer available to other network users, select a printer, and then click Printer Properties. On the Sharing tab, select Share This Printer and provide a share name, as shown in Figure 11-25.

Unlike for shared folders, which maintain separate share permissions and NTFS permissions, a single set of permissions controls access to printers, whether by local users or by network users. (Of course, only printers that have been shared are accessible to network users.)

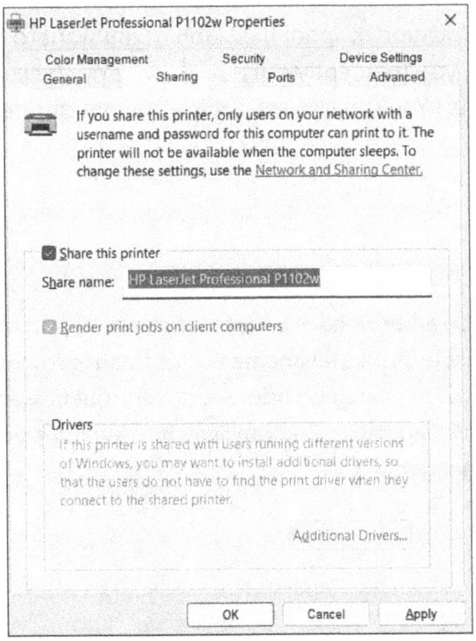

Figure 11-25   The share name for a printer can include spaces.

When you set up a printer, initially all users in the Everyone group have Print permission for documents they create, which provides users access to the printer and the ability to manage their own documents in the print queue. By default, members of the Administrators group also have Manage Printers permission—which allows them to share a printer, change its properties, remove a printer, and change its permissions—and Manage Documents permission, which lets them pause, restart, move, and remove all queued documents. As an administrator, you can view or modify permissions on the Security tab of the printer properties dialog.

Setting print server properties

In addition to setting properties for individual printers by using their properties dialogs, you can set other properties by visiting the Print Server Properties dialog. To get there, open Settings > Bluetooth & Devices > Printers & Scanners. Then, under Related Settings, click Print Server Properties.

The first three tabs control the list of items you see in the properties dialog for a printer:

- The Forms tab controls the list of forms you can assign to trays using the Device Settings tab in a printer's properties dialog. You can create new form definitions and delete any you create, but you can't delete any of the predefined forms.

- On the Ports tab, you can configure the ports that appear on the Ports tab in a printer's properties dialog.

- The Drivers tab offers a list of all the installed printer drivers and provides a centralized location where you can add, remove, or update drivers.

On the Advanced tab, you can specify the location of spool files. (You might want to change to a folder on a different drive if, for example, you frequently run out of space on the current drive when you attempt to print large documents.) You can also set notification options on this tab.

Inside OUT

Use the Print Management console

Users of Windows 11 Pro and Enterprise editions have a tool that places all print management tasks in one convenient console. Print Management (Printmanagement.msc), shown in Figure 11-26, provides a place for managing printers, drivers, queues, and shares. If your edition includes Print Management, you can start it by typing **print** in the search box and then clicking Print Management.

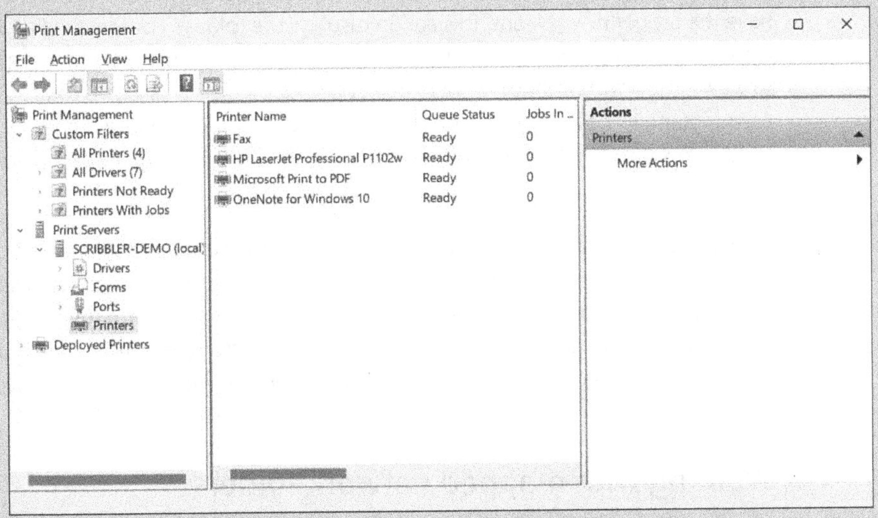

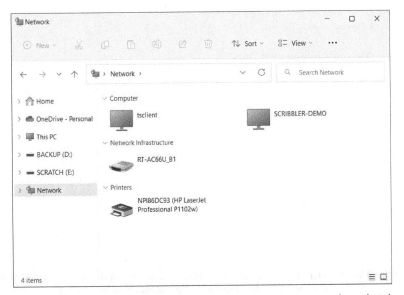

Figure 11-26   The Print Management console is useful on larger networks where you might have multiple printers to administer.

CHAPTER 11

Finding and using shared resources on a Windows network

The Network folder is your primary gateway to available network resources, just as This PC is the gateway to resources stored on your own system. The Network folder (shown in Figure 11-27) contains an icon for each computer that Windows discovers on your network; double-click a computer icon to see that computer's shared resources, if any.

Figure 11-27   The Network folder shows all computers on your network, not just those in your workgroup.

To open a shared folder on another computer, double-click its icon in the Network folder. If you have the proper permissions, this action displays the folder's contents in File Explorer. It's not always that easy, however. If the user account with which you signed in doesn't have permission to view a network computer or resource you select, a dialog asks you to provide the name of an account (and its password, of course) that has permission. Don't be fooled by the Domain reference below the User Name and Password boxes; in a workgroup, that value refers to the local computer.

Perhaps the trickiest part of using shared folders is fully understanding what permissions have been applied to a folder and which credentials are in use by each network user. It's important to recognize that *all network access is controlled by the computer with the shared resources*; regardless of what operating system runs on the computer attempting to connect to a network share, it must meet the security requirements of the computer where the shared resource is actually located.

Working with mapped network folders

Mapping a network folder makes it appear to applications as though the folder is part of your own computer. Windows assigns a drive letter to the mapped folder, making the folder appear like an additional hard drive. You can still access a mapped folder in the conventional manner by navigating to it through the Network folder. But mapping gives the folder an alias—the assigned drive letter—that provides an alternative means of access.

To map a network folder to a drive letter, follow these steps:

1. Open File Explorer, right-click Network, and then click Map Network Drive to open the dialog shown in Figure 11-28.

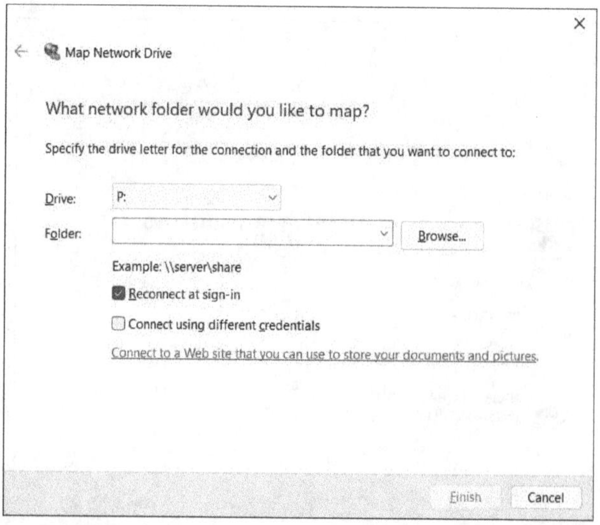

Figure 11-28 Mapping a network drive letter to a folder is a straightforward process. Enter the shared folder address in UNC format (\\server\share).

2.   Select a drive letter from the Drive list. You can choose any letter that's not already in use.

3.   In the Folder box, type the path to the folder you want or, more easily, click Browse and navigate to the folder.

4.   Select Reconnect At Sign-In if you want Windows to connect to this shared folder automatically at the start of each session.

5.   If your regular sign-in account doesn't have permission to connect to the resource, select Connect Using Different Credentials. (After you click Finish, Windows asks for the username and password you want to use for this connection.)

6.   Click Finish.

In File Explorer, the "drive" appears under This PC.

If you change your mind about mapping a network folder, right-click the folder's icon in your This PC folder. Choose Disconnect on the resulting shortcut menu to sever the connection.

Connecting to a network printer

To use a printer that has been shared, open the Network folder in File Explorer and double-click the name of the server to which the printer is attached. If the shared printers on that server are not visible, return to the Network folder, click to select the server, and then, on the ribbon's Network tab, click View Printers. Right-click the printer and choose Connect. Alternatively, from Settings > Bluetooth & Devices > Printers & Scanners, click Add Device. If the shared printer you want doesn't appear, click Add Manually and use the Add Printer Wizard to add a network printer.

Connecting to and using cloud-based apps and resources

Organizations that once maintained on-premises servers are increasingly moving those resources to the cloud, giving the cloud provider responsibility for ensuring security and reliability without having to worry about hardware failures. Small businesses and even individuals can benefit from using cloud-hosted storage and Software as a Service (SaaS) subscriptions.

Microsoft offers two main cloud services that are of interest to businesses running Windows 11:

- **Microsoft 365 Enterprise or Business**   These subscriptions can include Microsoft 365 cloud apps (such as Exchange Online, OneDrive for Business, Teams, and SharePoint Online), and mobile device management using Microsoft Intune. Some plans also include Microsoft 365 (formerly Microsoft Office) apps, including Excel, Word, and PowerPoint. The most advanced plans also include licensing for Windows 11 Enterprise or Education editions.

- **Microsoft Azure**   Microsoft's flagship cloud service supports a wide range of services that are mostly of use to enterprise customers and developers. Individual users and small businesses can create virtual devices in the Azure cloud to run server and desktop operating system and to create special-purpose cloud folders that can be used for backup and as an alternative to OneDrive.

Both Microsoft 365 and Azure are pay-as-you-go subscription-based services, and are not part of Windows 11. To access these cloud services, a user must sign in using a cloud user account (in Windows 11, these are usually called Work or School accounts). These are stored in Azure AD, which is provided as part of your Microsoft 365 or Azure subscriptions. For details on setting up and using this type of account, see "Azure Active Directory account," in Chapter 10, "Managing user accounts, passwords, and credentials."

Troubleshooting network problems

Network connectivity problems can be a source of great frustration. Fortunately, Windows 11 includes several tools that can help you identify and solve problems. Even better, Windows has built-in network diagnostic capabilities, so in many cases, if there is a problem with your network connection, Windows knows about it before you do, displays a message, and often solves the problem.

When a network-dependent activity (for example, browsing to a website) fails, Windows works to address the most common network-related issues, such as problems with file sharing, website access, newly installed network hardware, connecting to a wireless network, and using a third-party firewall.

If you encounter network problems that don't trigger an automatic response from Windows, you should first try to detect and resolve the problem with one of the built-in troubleshooters. Open Settings > System > Troubleshoot and then click Other Troubleshooters. You can then review a list of common troubleshooting tools, including

- Internet Connections

- Incoming Connections

- Network Adapter

- Shared Folders

Each of the troubleshooting wizards performs several diagnostic tests, corrects some conditions, suggests actions you can take, and ultimately displays a report that explains the wizard's findings. Sometimes, the problem is as simple as a loose connection.

If the diagnostic capabilities leave you at a dead end, restarting the affected network hardware often resolves the problem because the hardware is forced to rediscover the network. Here's a good general troubleshooting procedure:

1. Isolate the problem. Does it affect all computers on your network, a subset of your network, or only one computer?

2. If it affects all computers, try restarting the internet device (that is, the fiber router, or cable/DSL modem). If the device doesn't have a power switch, unplug it for a few moments and plug it back in.

3. If the problem affects a group of computers, try restarting the router to which those computers are connected.

4. If the problem affects only a single computer, try repairing the network connection for that computer. Open Settings > Network & Internet > Advanced Network Settings and then click More Network Adapter Options. Control Panel opens. In Network Connections, right-click the suspect network connection and choose Disable. Then right-click and choose Enable. This reinitializes the adapter and its configuration.

Inside OUT

As a last resort, use Network Reset

The Settings > Network & Internet > Advanced Network Settings page offers detailed information about the current connections. It also includes a Network Reset command. If you're unable to resolve networking problems by using the network troubleshooter, click Network Reset to remove your network adapters, reinstall them, set other networking components to their default settings, and restart your computer.

Network troubleshooting tools

The following list includes some of the command-line utilities you can use to perform these troubleshooting procedures. To learn more about each utility, including its proper syntax, open a Command Prompt window and type the executable name followed by /?.

- **IP Configuration Utility (Ipconfig.exe)**   Enables you to check the current IP configuration for your installed network adapters.

- **Name Server Lookup (Nslookup.exe)**   Provides a great way to test name resolution.

- **Net services commands (Net.exe)**   Performs a broad range of network tasks. Type **net** with no parameters to see a full list of available command-line options.

CHAPTER 11

- **Network Command Shell (Netsh.exe)**   Displays or modifies the network configuration of a local or remote computer that's currently running. This command-line scripting utility has a huge number of options, which are fully detailed in Help.

- **TCP/IP Ping (Ping.exe)**   Verifies IP-level connectivity to another internet address (or hostname) by sending Internet Control Message Protocol (ICMP) packets and measuring the response time in milliseconds.

- **TCP/IP Traceroute (Tracert.exe)**   Determines the path to an internet address (or hostname) and lists the time required to reach each hop. It's useful for troubleshooting connectivity problems on specific network segments.

As is the case with other command-line utilities, the Windows PowerShell environment includes cmdlets that offer much of the same functionality along with the scripting capability of PowerShell. You can get a list that includes many of the more commonly used network-related cmdlets by entering the following at a PowerShell prompt:

```
get-command -module nettcpip, netadapter
```

➤ For more information about PowerShell, see "An introduction to PowerShell" in Chapter 16, "Windows Terminal, PowerShell, and other advanced management tools." For details about the Net TCP/IP cmdlets, go to *https://bit.ly/NetTCPIP*. On that page, you'll also find (using the navigation pane on the left) details about other network-related cmdlets, including those for Network Adapter, Network Connection, and Network Connectivity Status.

Troubleshooting TCP/IP problems

When you encounter problems with TCP/IP-based networks, such as an inability to connect with other computers on the same network or difficulty connecting to external websites, the problems might be TCP/IP related. You need at least a basic understanding of how this protocol works before you can figure out which tool to use to uncover the root of the problem.

Checking for connection problems

Any time your network refuses to send and receive data properly, your first troubleshooting step should be to check for problems with the physical connection between the local computer and the rest of the network. Assuming your network connection uses the TCP/IP protocol, the first tool to reach for is the Ping utility. When you use the Ping command with no parameters, Windows sends four echo datagrams—small Internet Control Message Protocol (ICMP) packets—to the address you specify. If the machine at the other end of the connection replies, you know that the network connection between the two points is alive.

To use the Ping command, open a Command Prompt window (Cmd.exe) and type the command **ping *target_name*** (where *target_name* is an IP address or the name of another host machine). The return output looks something like this:

```
C:\>ping www.example.com
Pinging www.example.com [93.184.216.34] with 32 bytes of data:
Reply from 93.184.216.34: bytes=32 time=54ms TTL=51
Reply from 93.184.216.34: bytes=32 time=40ms TTL=51
Reply from 93.184.216.34: bytes=32 time=41ms TTL=51
Reply from 93.184.216.34: bytes=32 time=54ms TTL=51

Ping statistics for 93.184.216.34:
    Packets: Sent = 4, Received = 4, Lost = 0 (0% loss),
Approximate round trip times in milli-seconds:
    Minimum = 40ms, Maximum = 54ms, Average = 47ms
```

If all the packets you send come back and the time values are roughly equal, your TCP/IP connection is fine, and you can focus your troubleshooting efforts elsewhere. If some packets time out, a "Request timed out" message appears, indicating your network connection is working, but one or more hops between your computer and the target machine are experiencing problems. In that case, repeat the Ping test using the **-n** switch to send a larger number of packets; ping -n 30 192.168.1.1, for example, sends 30 packets to the computer or router at 192.168.1.1.

NOTE

The -n switch is case-sensitive; don't capitalize it.

A high rate of timeouts, also known as *packet loss*, usually means the problems are elsewhere on the network and not on the local machine. (To see the full assortment of switches available for the Ping command, type **ping** with no target specified.)

If every one of your packets returns with the message "Request timed out," the problem might be the TCP/IP connection on your computer or a glitch with another computer on that network. To narrow down the problem, follow these steps, in order, stopping at any point where you encounter an error:

1. Ping your own machine by using any of the following commands:

   ```
   ping ::1
   ping 127.0.0.1
   ping localhost
   ```

   These are standard addresses. The first line is the IPv6 address for your own computer; the second line is the IPv4 address; the third line shows the standard host name. If your local network components are configured correctly, each of these three commands should allow the PC on which the command is run to talk to itself. If you receive an error, TCP/IP is not configured properly on your system. For fix-it details, see "Repairing your TCP/IP configuration" later in this chapter.

2.   Ping your computer's IP address.

3.   Ping the IP address of another computer on your network.

4.   Ping the IP address of your router or the default gateway on your network.

5.   Ping the address of each DNS server on your network. (If you don't know these addresses, see the next section for details on how to discover them.)

6.   Ping a known host outside your network. Well-known, high-traffic websites are ideal for this step, assuming that they respond to ICMP packets.

7.   Use the PathPing command to contact the same host you specified in step 6. This command combines the functionality of the Ping command with the Traceroute utility to identify intermediate destinations on the internet between your computer and the specified host or server.

Inside OUT

Choose your test site carefully

In some cases, pinging an external website results in a string of "Request timed out" messages, even when you have no trouble reaching those sites. Don't be misled. Some popular sites block all ICMP traffic, including Ping packets, as a routine security measure. Some routers and residential gateways are also configured to block certain types of ICMP traffic. Try pinging several sites before concluding that your internet connection is broken.

If either of the two final steps in this process fails, your problem might be caused by DNS problems, as described later in this section. (For details, see "Resolving DNS issues.") To eliminate this possibility, ping the numeric IP address of a computer outside your network instead. (Of course, if you're having DNS problems, you might have a hard time finding an IP address to ping!) If you can reach a website by using its IP address but not by using its name, DNS problems are indicated.

If you suspect that there's a problem on the internet between your computer and a distant host or server, use the Traceroute utility (Tracert.exe) to pinpoint the problem. Like the Ping command, this utility works from a command line. You specify the target (a host name or IP address) by using the syntax **tracert** *target_name*, and the utility sends out a series of packets, measuring the time it takes to reach each hop along the route. Timeouts or unusually slow performance indicate a connectivity problem. If the response time from your network to the first hop is much higher than the other hops, you might have a problem with the connection to your internet service provider; in that case, a call to your ISP's support line is in order. Problems further along in the traceroute might indicate congestion or hardware problems in distant parts of the internet that are out of your ISP's hands. These symptoms might disappear when you check another URL that follows a different path through the internet.

If your testing produces inconsistent results, rule out the possibility that a firewall program or NAT device (such as a router or residential gateway) is to blame. If you're using Windows Defender Firewall or a third-party firewall program, disable it temporarily. Try bypassing your router and connecting directly to a broadband connection such as a cable modem. (Use this configuration only for testing and only very briefly, because it exposes your computer to various attacks.)

If the Ping test works with the firewall or NAT device out of the picture, you can rule out network problems and conclude that the firewall software or router is misconfigured. After you complete your testing, be sure to enable the firewall and router again.

Diagnosing IP address problems

You can also get useful details of your IP configuration by using the IP Configuration utility, Ipconfig.exe, in a Command Prompt window. Used without parameters, typing **ipconfig** at a command prompt displays the DNS suffix; IPv6 address, IPv4 address, or both; subnet mask; and default gateway for each network connection. To see exhaustive details about every available network connection, type **ipconfig /all**.

The actual IPv4 address you see might help you solve connection problems:

- If the address is in the format 169.254.*x.y*, your computer is using Automatic Private IP Addressing (APIPA). This means your computer's DHCP client was unable to reach a DHCP server to be assigned an IP address. Check the connection to your network.

- If the address is in one of the blocks of IP addresses reserved for use on private networks (for details, see the sidebar "Public and private IP addresses" earlier in this chapter), make sure that a router or residential gateway is routing your internet requests to a properly configured public IP address.

- If the address of your computer appears as 0.0.0.0, the network is either disconnected or the static IP address for the connection duplicates an address that already exists on the network.

- Make sure you're using the correct subnet mask for computers on your local network. Compare IP settings on the machine that's having problems with those on other computers on the network. The default gateway and subnet mask should be identical for all network computers. The first one, two, or three sets of numbers in the IP address for each machine should also be identical, depending on the subnet mask. A subnet mask of 255.255.255.0 means the first three IP address numbers of computers on your network must be identical—192.168.0.83 and 192.168.0.223, for instance, can communicate on a network using this subnet mask, but 192.168.1.101 will not be recognized as belonging to the network. The gateway machine must also be a member of the same subnet. (If you use a router, switch, or residential gateway for internet access, the local address on that device must be part of the same subnet as the machines on your network.)

NOTE

Are you baffled by subnets and other related technical terms? For an excellent overview of these sometimes confusing topics, read "Understanding TCP/IP addressing and sub-netting basics" (*https://bit.ly/ipv4-overview*), which offers information about IPv4. For comparable details about IPv6, see the "Internet Protocol version 6 (IPv6) overview" at *https://bit.ly/ipv6-overview*.

Repairing your TCP/IP configuration

If you suspect a problem with your TCP/IP configuration, try either of the following repair options:

- **Use the automated repair option**   Right-click the connection icon in Network Connections in Control Panel and click Diagnose.

- **Release and renew your IP address**   Use the **ipconfig /release** command to let go of the DHCP-assigned IPv4 address. Then use **ipconfig /renew** to obtain a new IP address from the DHCP server. To renew an IPv6 address, use **ipconfig /release6** and **ipconfig / renew6**.

Inside OUT

Translate names to IP addresses and vice versa

The Nslookup command is a buried treasure in Windows. Use this command-line utility to quickly convert a fully qualified domain name to its IP address. You can tack on a host name to the end of the command line to identify a single address; for instance, you can type **nslookup github** to look up the IP address of Microsoft's open source developer platform, GitHub. Or type **nslookup** to switch into interactive mode. From this prompt, you can enter any domain name to find its IP address.

If you need more sophisticated lookup tools, a good starting point is MXToolBox (*https://mxtoolbox.com/DNSLookup.aspx*), which offers a form-based utility that can provide an extensive collection of details about a domain name, IP address, or host name.

Resolving DNS issues

The Domain Name System (DNS) is a crucial part of the internet. DNS servers translate host names (*www.microsoft.com*, for instance) into numeric IP addresses so that packets can be routed properly over the internet. If you can use the Ping command to reach a numeric address outside your network but are unable to browse websites by name, the problem is almost certainly related to your DNS configuration.

Here are some questions to ask when you suspect DNS problems:

- **Do your TCP/IP settings point to the right DNS servers?**   Inspect the details of your IP configuration, and compare the DNS servers listed there with those recommended by your internet service provider. (You might need to call your ISP to get these details.)

- **Is your ISP experiencing DNS problems?**   A misconfigured DNS server (or one that's offline) can wreak havoc with your attempts to use the internet. Try pinging each DNS server to see whether it's available. If your ISP has multiple DNS servers and you encounter problems accessing one server, remove that server from your TCP/IP configuration temporarily and use another one instead.

Temporary DNS problems can also be caused by the DNS cache, which Windows maintains for performance reasons. If you suddenly have trouble reaching a specific site on the internet and you're convinced there's nothing wrong with the site, type this command to clear the DNS cache: **ipconfig /flushdns**.

A more thorough solution is offered by **ipconfig /registerdns**, which renews all DHCP leases (as described in the previous section) *and* reregisters all DNS names.

CHAPTER 11

Windows security and privacy

We don't mean to be scaremongers, but they *are* out to get you. Computer attacks continue to increase in number and severity each year. And while the big data breaches—the loss of millions of credit card numbers from a major retailer or the loss of millions of personnel records from the U.S. government—command the most media attention, don't think that the bad guys wouldn't like to get into your computer, too. Whether it's to steal your valuable personal data or hold it for ransom, appropriate your computing resources and bandwidth, or use your PC as a pathway into a bigger target with whom you do business, there are plenty of actors with bad intent.

In this chapter, we examine the types of threats you're likely to face at home and at your office and then introduce the security tools and technologies in Windows 11—many of which are in layers you can't see, such as hardware-based protection that operates before Windows loads.

All currently supported retail and OEM versions of Windows 11 include the Windows Security app, which functions as a dashboard for common security functions. It also offers access to other visible security features, including Windows Defender Firewall, Microsoft Defender Antivirus, and Microsoft Defender SmartScreen. This chapter covers all of these tools as well as other, related security features, including Windows Update, User Account Control, and BitLocker Drive Encryption.

Understanding security threats

A decade ago, the threat landscape for Windows users was dominated by viruses and worms. Ah, for the good old days! The modern threat landscape is much more complex and, unfortunately, more insidious. Today, an attacker is likely to be part of an organized crime ring or even acting on behalf of a state-sponsored organization, and attacks are typically designed to go unnoticed for as long as possible.

CHAPTER 12

A rogue program, installed without your knowledge and running without your awareness, can perform malicious tasks and transfer data without your consent. This category of software is often referred to as *malware*.

The goal of the bad guys is to get you to run their software. They might, for example, convince you to install a *Trojan*—a program that appears legitimate but actually performs malicious actions when it's installed. This category of malware doesn't spread on its own but instead uses social engineering (often using popular social networking sites such as Facebook and Twitter) to convince its victims to cooperate in the installation process. As part of its payload, a Trojan can include a downloader that installs additional malicious and unwanted programs. Some Trojans install a "back door" that allows an outside attacker to remotely control the infected computer.

What's in it for the bad guys? Money, mostly, gathered in various ways, depending on how the attackers got through your defenses. Here are just a few examples:

- A *password stealer* runs in the background, gathers usernames and passwords, and forwards them to an outside attacker. The stolen credentials can then be used to make purchases, clean out bank accounts, or commit identity theft.

- Bad guys prey on fear with rogue security software (also known as *scareware*), which mimics the actions and appearance of legitimate antivirus software. If you install their program, it inevitably reports the presence of a (nonexistent) virus and offers to remove the alleged malware—for a fee, of course. A related category includes tech-support scams, in which a Windows user receives a phone call from a scammer masquerading as a Microsoft support professional.

- The fastest rising star in the malware hall of shame continues to be *ransomware*, a form of digital extortion in which a program encrypts all your data files and offers to unlock them only upon payment of a ransom.

- *Phishing attacks*, which use social engineering to convince visitors to give away their sign-in credentials, are a separate but potentially devastating avenue to identity theft that can strike in any browser using any operating system.

You can review lists of current malware threats, along with links to details about each one, at the Microsoft Security Intelligence site, *https://bit.ly/malware-encyclopedia*. For a more comprehensive view of the changing threat landscape, Microsoft Security issues occasional reports, using data from hundreds of millions of Windows users and other sources. The most recent Microsoft Digital Defense Report (November 2022) is available at *https://bit.ly/digital-defense-report*.

SECURING YOUR COMPUTER: A DEFENSE-IN-DEPTH STRATEGY

A multidimensional threat landscape requires a multilayered approach to protecting your PC and your network. The big-picture goal is to secure your device, secure your data, secure your identity, and block malware. On a home or small business network, those layers of security include the following:

- **Keep Windows and vulnerable programs up to date.** Windows Update handles this chore for Windows, Office, and other Microsoft programs. This chapter includes a detailed discussion of how to monitor and manage security updates delivered through this channel.

- **Use a hardware router to protect your broadband connection.** This is an essential part of physical security, even if your network consists of a single PC. Most gateway devices from internet providers include this functionality.

- **Enable a software firewall, and keep it turned on.** You can use Windows Defender Firewall, which is included with Windows 11, or a third-party firewall such as those included with security suites. To learn more, see "Blocking intruders with Windows Defender Firewall" later in this chapter.

- **Strengthen the sign-in process.** Biometric sign-in using a fingerprint reader or facial recognition with Windows Hello offers much more than convenience. Because biometric sign-in is linked to a specific device, it provides effective two-factor authentication. If you sign in using a Microsoft account or Azure AD, turn on two-factor authentication to prevent your credentials from being used if they're stolen. For more information, see "Making the sign-in process more secure" in Chapter 10, "Managing user accounts, passwords, and credentials."

- **Set up standard user accounts, and keep User Account Control enabled.** Standard accounts help to prevent (or at least minimize) the damage that an unwitting user can do by installing untrusted programs. User Account Control (UAC) helps in this regard by restricting access to administrative tasks and virtualizing registry and file-system changes. For details, see "Choosing how you sign in" in Chapter 10 and "Preventing unsafe actions with User Account Control" later in this chapter.

- **Use an antimalware program, and keep it up to date.** Microsoft Defender Antivirus, which is included with Windows 11, provides effective antimalware protection, but many third-party solutions are also available. For details, see "Using Microsoft Defender Antivirus" later in this chapter.

- **Protect yourself from threats in email messages.** At a minimum, your email solution should block or quarantine executable files and other potentially dangerous attachments. In addition, effective antispam features can block scripts and prevent phishing attempts.

- **Use parental controls to keep kids safe.** If you have children who use your computer, family safety features in Windows can help you keep them away from security threats and keep them from wandering into unsafe territory online by restricting their computer activities in other ways. For details, see "Controlling your family's computer access" in Chapter 10.

The most important protective layer—and the one that's most easily overlooked—is user education. Everyone who uses a computer must have the awareness and knowledge to read and evaluate security warnings when they're presented and to allow the installation only of software that is known to be safe. (Although users with standard accounts can't install or run a program that wipes out the entire computer, they can still inflict enough damage on their own user profile to cause considerable inconvenience.) Countless successful malware attacks worldwide have proven that many users do not have adequate awareness of safe computing basics.

Monitoring your computer's security

You can open Windows Security directly from its place on the Start menu's app list, or use the slightly unconventional navigation options in Settings > Privacy & Security > Windows Security. That Settings page includes a prominent Open Windows Security button and seven headings, each of which opens or switches to the corresponding page in the Windows Security app. Figure 12-1 shows the Windows Security home page, displaying the status of those seven groups of security-related settings, plus an additional Protection History option.

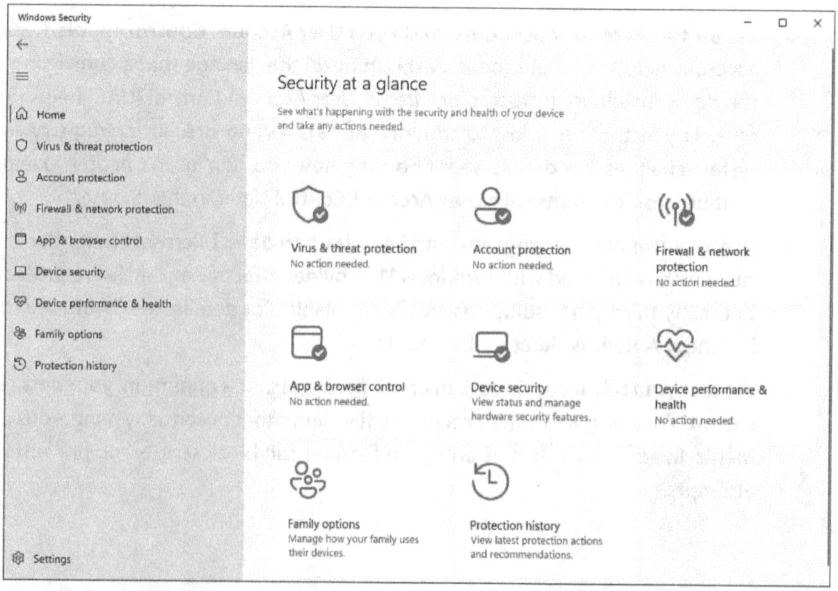

Figure 12-1   The Windows Security dashboard offers a consolidated view of security status. Clicking any item provides access to settings for that group of features.

Windows Security provides status information even when it's not open. A badge over the app's icon in the system tray shows the current security status with a green check mark, a yellow exclamation point, or a red X and, if necessary, options for resolving problems. Additional notifications of activity (results of recent virus scans, for example) appear in the notification center. Click the gear icon in the lower-left corner of the Windows Security app window to configure these options, as shown in Figure 12-2. (Note that making changes here requires that you provide an administrator's credentials.)

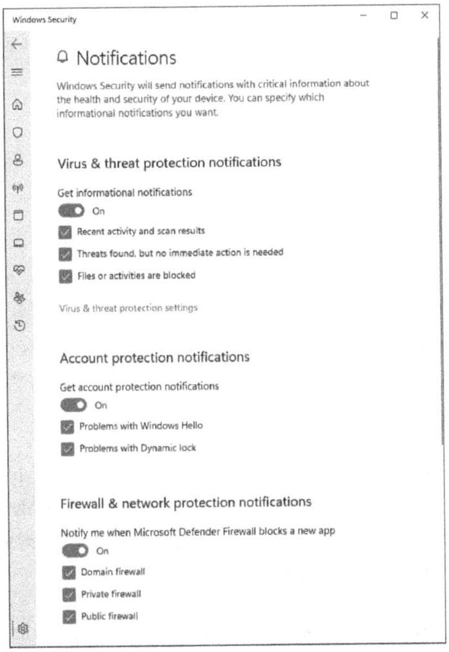

Figure 12-2   If you don't want to be bothered with noncritical notifications from Microsoft Defender Antivirus, such as successful scans that detect no threats, clear the Recent Activity And Scan Results check box.

We cover individual settings available via Windows Security later in this chapter. But first, we discuss the most important security feature of all—Windows Update.

Keeping Windows up to date

Windows Update runs as a service that is set to start as needed; its associated services, including the Background Intelligent Transfer Service (BITS), also run automatically, with little or no attention required from you other than an occasional restart. We strongly suggest checking in at regular intervals to confirm that updates are being delivered as expected and that the various Windows Update services are working properly. To do this, go to Settings > Windows Update. Figure 12-3 shows what you see if Windows has pending updates available.

CHAPTER 12

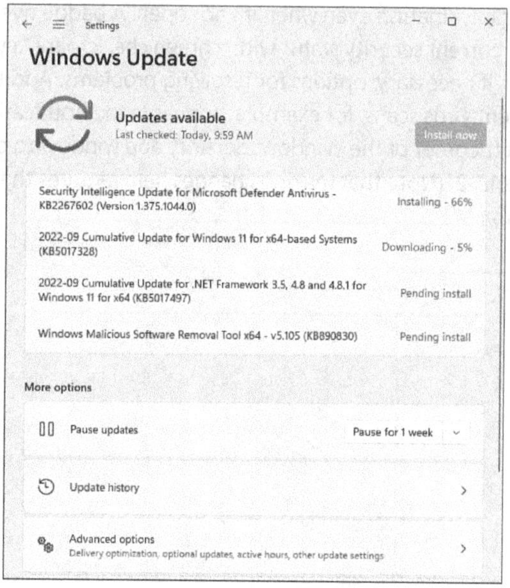

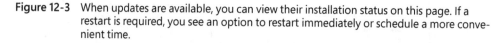

Figure 12-3   When updates are available, you can view their installation status on this page. If a restart is required, you see an option to restart immediately or schedule a more convenient time.

The text below the Windows Update heading tells you whether your system was up to date as of the most recent check. If updates are ready to install, you can do so immediately. For updates that require a restart, you can take advantage of the scheduling options we describe later in this chapter. (See "Choosing when and how updates are installed.")

Windows Update checks daily to see whether new updates are available, so you don't ordinarily need to use the Check For Updates button. If you're preparing for travel, you might want to make a manual check before your departure to avoid having to deal with pending updates while on the road.

Inside OUT

Don't fear automatic updates—manage them

As the global internet has become more pervasive, Microsoft and other software companies, large and small, have ratcheted up the speed at which they deliver updates. Occasionally, those updates end up causing new problems of their own. Among conservative IT pros, it has become practically dogma to stand out of the line of fire when updates are first released. Historically, problematic updates are usually identified within the first week and either pulled or fixed, making it safe to deploy them after a suitable delay.

So, are things different this time around? Are monthly cumulative updates in Windows 11 more trustworthy than their predecessors? Is it safe to dive into a new feature update on the day it's released?

There's no right or wrong answer to those questions. But two crucial differences in the modern Windows development process are worth noting. One is Microsoft's use of telemetry, the diagnostic feedback loop that allows it to identify problems in real time before customers begin lighting up support lines. The other is the maturation of the Windows Insider Program, which allows a large group of early adopters to test feature updates before they are released to the general population.

Yes, seemingly innocuous updates can and do cause problems on some PCs. But after more than seven years' experience with Windows 10 and Windows 11, we can testify that those problems are resolved far more quickly than before. On devices running business editions of Windows—Pro, Enterprise, and Education—administrators can avoid the occasional flawed update that sneaks into circulation by delaying quality updates, managing the installation of feature updates after a suitable deferral period, and instituting pilot programs in their organizations to evaluate updates firsthand. (We discuss all these options at length in this chapter.) For truly mission-critical systems, where any downtime could be disastrous and a conservative approach is imperative, the Windows Enterprise Long Term Servicing Channel is an essential option.

What you get from Windows Update

When you check for new updates in Windows 11, even on a device that hasn't been updated in many months, you are likely to see, at most, only a handful of updates. These updates fall into the following categories.

Quality updates

Windows 11 receives so-called *quality updates*, which fix security and reliability issues, in cumulative packages targeted at each supported version. (This category includes the fixes delivered like clockwork on the second Tuesday of each month, also known colloquially as Patch Tuesday or, more formally, Update Tuesday.) Each newly released cumulative update supersedes all previous updates for that version. When you install the latest cumulative update, it applies the most recent revision of all quality updates that apply to your Windows version.

Feature updates

Feature updates are the equivalent of major version upgrades. For Windows 11, they are released annually in the second half of the calendar year. Because these updates are much larger than quality updates and take significantly longer to install, they have their own set of management options, which we describe later in this chapter.

Servicing stack updates

The *servicing stack* is the code that installs operating system updates to Windows. It also includes the *component-based servicing stack (CBS)*, which powers several Windows-based deployment and management features, including the Deployment Image Servicing and Management command-line tool (DISM.exe); the System Integrity Check and Repair tool (Sfc.exe), a direct descendant of the Windows XP-era System File Checker tool; and the Windows Features tool (OptionalFeatures.exe).

Servicing stack updates are delivered on an as-needed basis (typically not every month) and include reliability and security fixes. They are version-specific, with separate servicing stack updates available depending on the currently installed Windows version. They are typically delivered along with, but separate from, the cumulative quality updates in a given month.

If you are manually installing updates from the Microsoft Update Catalog as part of setting up a new Windows installation, Microsoft recommends installing the most recent servicing stack update before downloading the latest cumulative update. Manually installing the most recent servicing stack update is also a recommended step for troubleshooting Windows Update problems.

Driver updates

Microsoft delivers some device drivers and firmware updates through Windows Update. All Microsoft Surface devices, for example, receive hardware-related updates through this channel. Windows Update provides some third-party drivers to complete setup for devices that are not available in the Windows installation package, as well as occasional replacements for installed device drivers that have been deemed to be the source of significant reliability issues.

Microsoft Defender Antivirus security intelligence updates

Microsoft Defender Antivirus has its own update mechanism that regularly downloads security intelligence updates—typically several times each day. If you manually check Windows Update, it downloads and installs any available security intelligence updates that have been released since the most recent check by Microsoft Defender Antivirus.

Malicious Software Removal Tool

The Malicious Software Removal Tool (MSRT) is typically delivered monthly, on Update Tuesday. Its purpose is to detect and remove prevalent malware from Windows computers; it is not a substitute for the comprehensive antimalware code included as part of Microsoft Defender Antivirus. MSRT runs automatically in the background; it generates a log file automatically and saves it as %windir%\debug\mrt.log.

For additional details about MSRT, including download links and deployment instructions for IT administrators, see *https://www.microsoft.com/download/details.aspx?id=9905*.

Choosing when and how updates are installed

All editions of Windows 11 include a group of settings that give you control over how Windows Update works. Click Advanced Options to see these settings, as shown in Figure 12-4.

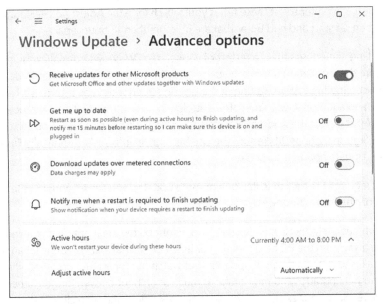

Figure 12-4   The options shown here are available in all editions of Windows 11.

If you turn the Receive Updates For Other Microsoft Products switch to On, Windows Update expands its scope to include other products developed by Microsoft, such as perpetual-license versions of Microsoft Office. (Microsoft 365 installations use a separate update mechanism.)

The Get Me Up To Date switch bypasses some of the normal precautions against unexpected restarts when updates are ready to install. It's an appropriate option when you're working with a PC that hasn't been used in several months and is well behind on updates.

The third option, Download Updates Over Metered Connections, applies only if you have configured a metered data network connection, such as an embedded LTE modem or a mobile phone configured as a Wi-Fi hotspot. In those circumstances, Windows normally refrains from downloading updates to avoid racking up unexpected charges for what is often a pay-as-you-go data plan. Turn this switch to On if you're comfortable that updates won't overrun your data budget. (For details, see "Mobile hotspots and other metered connections" in Chapter 11, "Configuring Windows networks.")

The final switch, Notify Me When A Restart Is Required To Finish Updating, provides one extra confirmation before Windows automatically restarts to install updates. Use this option to minimize the possibility of losing any work when a restart is required.

If Windows needs to restart your system to complete the installation of an update, you have the option to restart immediately or specify a time when you want the system to restart. If you do neither of these things, Windows Update restarts at a time outside your active hours. By default, Windows automatically adjusts the allowable update times based on its observations of your activity. If you prefer to set these times yourself, change the Adjust Active Hours setting to Manually; then set start and end times that are no more than 18 hours apart.

When installing an update entails a restart of your system, Windows normally requires you to sign in before the installation finishes. If you're away from your PC while an upgrade is in progress, you might find the system waiting at the sign-in screen when you return, with additional setup tasks (and additional wait time) after you sign in. You can streamline the process by clicking Restart Apps (under the Additional Options heading); that action takes you to Settings > Accounts > Sign-in Options. Make sure the Use My Sign-In Info To Automatically Finish Setting Up After An Update option is turned on.

If Windows requires a restart to install one or more updates, you see a banner in the notification center and on the main Windows Update page.

Restarting immediately, by clicking Restart Now, might be the ideal option if you know you're going to be away from the PC for a meeting or lunch break that will last longer than the few minutes it takes to install a batch of updates. (But watch out for feature updates, which are equivalent to full upgrades and might take as much as an hour or even longer, depending on your hardware.) Save your existing work, close any open files, and then click Restart Now. Be sure to wait for all open apps to close before you head out the door. It's annoying (and a big drag on productivity) to come back from a meeting and discover that the restart hasn't taken place because a dialog was open, waiting for your approval.

If instead you want to specify a restart time, click Schedule The Restart. Pick the exact date and time (up to one week from the current day) when you want your PC to restart and begin installing the updates.

Inside Out

Stop updates from installing after they've been downloaded

What if you check Windows Update and see that updates are waiting to be installed even though you're not ready? You might have read reports that a pending update has issues with your PC, or perhaps you just would prefer not to go through the update-and-restart cycle. Can you interrupt the process?

Indeed you can. If you have pending updates waiting to be installed, you can cancel that process and forestall any further updates by going to the main Windows Update page and clicking Pause For 1 Week. Need more time? Use the drop-down menu to choose a longer pause, up to five weeks. If you're already paused, click Extend For 1 Week, or use the drop-down menu to choose more time, up to five weeks total. Windows Update remains paused for the time you specify, unless you manually click the Resume Updates button on the Windows Update page.

Deferring and delaying updates

The level of control that administrators have over how and when updates are installed on a device depends on which edition of Windows is installed on that device. Note that the following rules apply to public releases of Windows 11 and are not applicable to Insider Preview builds.

On devices running Windows 11 Home, all updates are delivered automatically on a schedule defined by Microsoft's update servers. No options to defer updates are available on this edition, although you can pause updates for up to five weeks, one week at a time, as described in the previous section. You don't need to take any additional action aside from observing the occasional reminders to restart your computer and, if you choose, to schedule a restart.

On devices running Windows 11 Pro, Enterprise, and Education, the default settings are the same as those in Windows 11 Home. As an administrator, however, you can take advantage of additional options, available as part of Group Policy; these settings allow you to delay installation of quality updates by up to 30 days after they are initially available from Microsoft and to defer installation of feature updates by up to 365 additional days.

To apply these Windows Update settings, you must use Group Policy, either as part of a Windows domain using Active Directory or using the Local Group Policy Editor, Gpedit.msc. These policy settings are available in Computer Configuration > Administrative Templates > Windows Components > Windows Update > Manage Updates Offered From Windows Update. Figure 12-5 shows an example of these policies.

CHAPTER 12

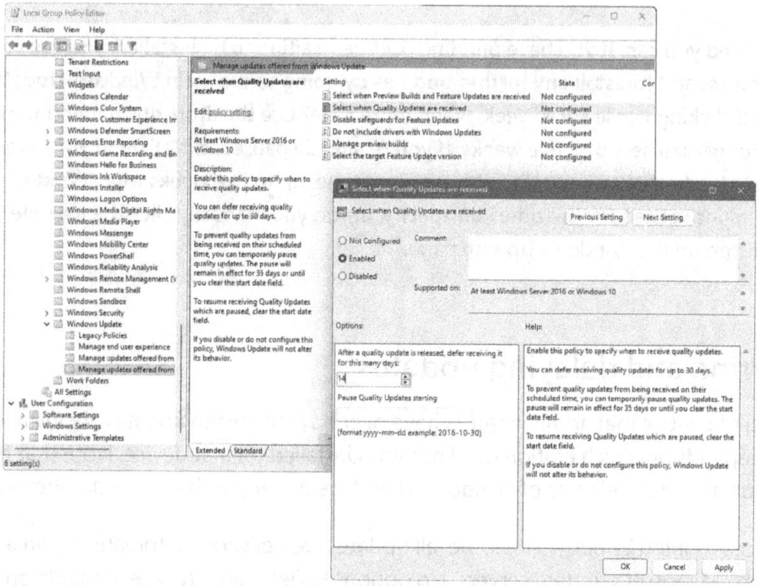

Figure 12-5   Using Group Policy, you can adjust Windows Update settings to defer quality and feature updates. The options shown here defer a quality update until 14 days after Microsoft releases it to Windows Update.

The policies available for configuration are as follows:

- **Select When Preview Builds And Feature Updates Are Received**   Configure this policy to defer feature updates and, for devices enrolled in the Windows Insider Program, preview builds. You can then specify an amount of time to defer the update after it's released. This value is entered in days, with deferral periods up to 365 days allowed for feature updates in the General Availability channel and 14 days for all prerelease channels.

- **Select When Quality Updates Are Received**   With this policy, you can defer the regular cumulative updates (which include security, reliability, and driver updates) for up to 30 days. Deferring quality updates requires a balancing act: Configuring this policy gives you an opportunity to test the latest update on a subset of PCs in your organization before deploying the update widely; that delay can also put your other machines at risk because they haven't received potentially important security fixes.

- **Disable Safeguards For Feature Updates**   Normally, Microsoft blocks installation of a feature update on devices that are known to have compatibility issues. This policy is for administrators and developers who want to evaluate a feature update on such a device, perhaps because they've deployed a workaround or other form of mitigation for the issue.

- **Do Not Include Drivers With Windows Updates**   Turn this policy on to ensure that Windows Update doesn't deliver any driver updates to the device.

- **Manage Preview Builds**   This policy includes the options to choose one of the three Windows Insider Program prerelease channels. A fourth option allows you to specify that you want to receive only quality updates from the Release Preview channel.

- **Select The Target Feature Update Version**   Use this policy to define a specific feature update that you want Windows Update to offer to a device or a group of devices; use the version information as it appears under the Windows 11 Release Information heading at *https://aka.ms/WindowsTargetVersionInfo*. Note that Windows Update overrides this policy if the specified version has reached its end-of-service date.

An additional group of policies under the Manage End User Experience heading are roughly equivalent to those in Settings > Windows Update. In addition, administrators who want to keep a fleet of machines up to date can remove user access to the Pause Updates feature.

Inside Out

The Windows Update calendar includes more than one Tuesday

Microsoft delivers most scheduled updates on the second Tuesday of each month. Update Tuesday (more commonly known as Patch Tuesday) is the primary day for delivering monthly updates, and it is the only regular release that includes new security fixes.

Additional nonsecurity updates are released on the third and fourth weeks of the month, respectively. (Microsoft refers to these as the "C" and "D" releases, in contrast to the "B" releases on Update Tuesday. Scheduled updates are never released on the first Tuesday of the month, the "A" week.) These are preview releases that are not installed automatically but instead appear under the Optional Updates heading; they are intended to allow administrators to test the nonsecurity fixes that will be shipped as part of the following month's "B" release.

On rare occasions, an *out-of-band release* appears on Windows Update to fix an urgent security vulnerability (typically one that is being actively exploited) or to resolve a quality issue that has widespread impact. Because out-of-band updates are both urgent and rare, they are issued without respect to the calendar.

Finding technical information about updates

The information that appears in the list of available updates and in your update history is brief and often less than informative. Why, exactly, are you being offered a particular update? Which reliability and security issues, exactly, are addressed in the latest quality update?

For the answers, prepare to do some clicking. Start with Settings > Windows Update > Update History. That opens a categorized list of all updates installed on the current system, similar to the one shown in Figure 12-6.

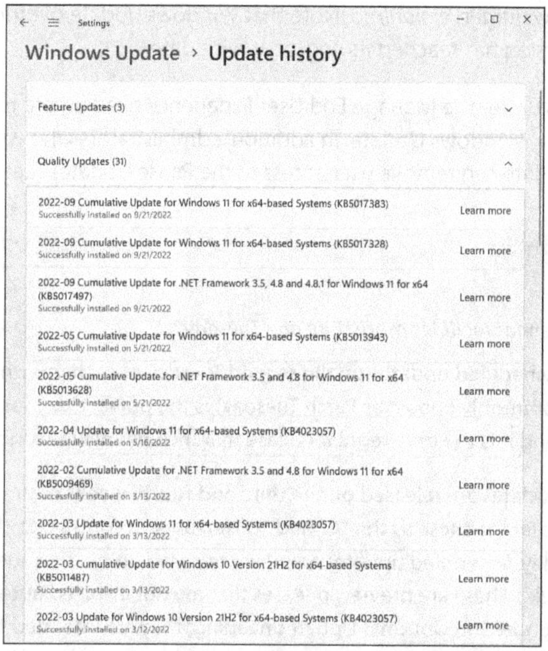

Figure 12-6   Click the Learn More link alongside any entry in the Update History list to see additional details about a quality update.

Each cumulative update listed under the Quality Updates heading includes a descriptive title and the number associated with a related Knowledge Base (KB) article. For releases in the General Availability channel, clicking the Learn More link opens that KB article, which in turn typically contains a list of key changes—security updates and quality improvements that are new in that cumulative update, along with a listing of any known issues for the update. It also includes a link to the Microsoft Update Catalog, where you can download a standalone package that allows you to install the updates manually. A File Information section provides a link to a list of files and version information associated with the update (in CSV format). (Note that much of this information is unavailable if you're running a Windows Insider Program preview release.)

Inside OUT

Open any KB article directly

If you're reading about a Knowledge Base article and don't have access to a hyperlink, your best bet is to visit Microsoft's Bing search engine (*https://bing.com*) and search for the article using the seven-digit number following "KB." Note that one of the most common updates in this list, KB2267602, Security Intelligence Update for Microsoft Defender Antivirus, does not have an associated support article.

For cumulative updates that include security content, the associated KB article typically does not include detailed information about those fixes. Instead, the KB article includes a link to release notes that are part of the Microsoft Security Update Guide, which includes listings for all Microsoft products. These release notes are not associated with a KB number.

Every cumulative update, complete with KB number and minor build number, is also listed on the Windows 11 Update History page. That index is categorized by version; the most recent updates are listed at *https://aka.ms/Windows11UpdateHistory*, with specific versions (21H2 and 22H2) available for selection in the navigation pane on the left of the page.

Security updates include a rating of the threat's severity. These are the four ratings that are used, listed in order of severity (with the most severe first):

- **Critical**   A critical vulnerability can lead to code execution with no user interaction.

- **Important**   An important vulnerability is one that can be exploited to compromise the confidentiality or integrity of your data or to cause a denial-of-service attack.

- **Moderate**   A moderate vulnerability is one that's usually mitigated by default settings and authentication requirements. In other words, you'd have to go a bit out of your way for one of these to damage your system or your data.

- **Low**   A vulnerability identified as low usually requires extensive interaction or an unusual configuration to cause damage.

For vulnerabilities with a rating of Critical or Important, Microsoft provides an Exploitability Index that estimates the likelihood that a vulnerability addressed in a security update will be exploited. This information is intended to help Windows administrators prioritize their deployment of updates.

CHAPTER 12

The Exploitability Index includes four values:

- **0 – Exploitation Detected**   The vulnerability is actively being exploited.

- **1 – Exploitation More Likely**   There is a strong likelihood that attackers could consistently exploit this vulnerability, making it an attractive target.

- **2 – Exploitation Less Likely**   Attackers would have difficulty creating exploit code, making it a less attractive target.

- **3 – Exploitation Unlikely**   Successfully functioning exploit code is unlikely to be utilized in real attacks, and the full impact of exploitation is likely to be limited.

For more information about the Security Update Severity Rating System, see *https://www.microsoft.com/msrc/security-update-severity-rating-system*. For more information about the Microsoft Exploitability Index, see *https://www.microsoft.com/msrc/exploitability-index*.

Troubleshooting update problems

In our experience, Windows Update is generally reliable, but problems can and do occur. These problems fall into a handful of categories: updates that cause stability problems; updates that fail to install properly; and general problems with Windows Update.

For updates that cause problems, the first step is to remove the offending update. (For particularly nettlesome problems, this might require booting into Safe Mode.) Go to Settings > Windows Update > Update History to display the list of installed updates (as described in the previous section) and then click the unobtrusive Uninstall Updates link at the bottom of that page.

Doing so takes you to an Uninstall Updates page that lists recent updates that can safely be uninstalled. Click the Uninstall link to the right of the update you want to remove.

> ➤ For information about uninstalling a problematic device driver, see "Uninstalling a driver," in Chapter 13, "Managing hardware and devices."

That action (after a restart) removes the immediate problem. But because of the way Windows Update works, the unwanted item will reappear the next time Windows checks for updates. You can interrupt this cycle by pausing updates (as described earlier in this chapter) while you troubleshoot the issue. For serious problems, you might need to contact Microsoft Support.

TROUBLESHOOTING

Windows Update is stuck in a reboot loop

In some cases, Windows Update can get stuck in a loop, failing to complete the installation of one or more updates and continually repeating the unsuccessful update process each time you restart.

The solution? Reset Windows Update completely, removing content from the update cache and starting with fresh downloads. In most cases, that's enough to get things unstuck.

Microsoft created a help resource for diagnosing and fixing Windows Update problems, which is available at *https://support.microsoft.com/help/971058*. The process involves stopping several services, removing the folder containing updates in progress, and reregistering a list of system files. You can download a troubleshooter that performs these steps automatically from *https://aka.ms/wudiag*. (Don't be alarmed if Microsoft Edge complains that the file is unsafe and blocks the download. It's a valid, signed file from Microsoft, and you can override that block by clicking the three dots to the right of the error message and then clicking Keep.)

Configuring privacy options

You don't need to be a conspiracy theorist to be concerned about privacy. Some companies abuse your trust by taking your information—often without your knowledge or consent—and sharing it with others who hope to profit from that information. Even a trustworthy third party can slip up and allow your private information to be stolen from its servers in a security breach. In the European Union, the General Data Protection Regulation (GDPR) requires organizations (including Microsoft) to follow strict privacy controls when collecting, processing, and storing personal data within the EU. In the United States, the State of California recently passed a similarly comprehensive privacy law. Some privacy advocates have argued that these protections should be extended worldwide.

Because Windows 11 is tightly integrated with cloud services, some of your information is stored, with your permission, on Microsoft-owned servers. Likewise, Microsoft requests permission when you first set up a user account to use some of your information to provide personalized suggestions. In addition, Windows 11 shares what Microsoft calls *diagnostic data* (sometimes called *telemetry* data) for the purpose of improving the reliability of the operating system.

Diagnostic data, which is collected by the Connected User Experiences And Telemetry service, includes information about the device and how it's configured, including hardware attributes such as CPU, installed memory, and storage. This data also includes details about quality-related events and metrics, such as uptime and sleep details and the number of crashes or hangs. Additional required information includes a list of installed apps and drivers. For systems that are set to send optional diagnostic data in addition to required data, the information collected includes events that analyze the interaction between the user and the operating system and apps.

Microsoft insists that its diagnostic-data system is designed to prevent any privacy issues. "We collect a limited amount of information to help us provide a secure and reliable experience," the company says. "This includes data like an anonymous device ID and device type. ... This doesn't include any of your content or files, and we take several steps to avoid collecting any information that directly identifies you, such as your name, email address or account ID."

NOTE

For a full discussion of how Windows diagnostic data works, with an emphasis on how to manage settings for collecting diagnostic data in an organization, see *https://bit.ly/configure-telemetry*.

Some of your personal information is used to provide more relevant advertising in apps. If you opt to turn off that personalization, you'll still see ads, but those ads will not be based on your browsing history or other information about you. Regardless of your privacy settings, Microsoft does not use the contents of your email, chat, files, or other personal content to target ads.

A single privacy statement covers most of Microsoft's consumer products and services, including Windows 11 and related services. For information about the privacy policy and to make choices about how Microsoft uses your data, visit *https://privacy.microsoft.com*. (A direct link to the Windows section of the Microsoft privacy statement is also available at Settings > Privacy & Security > General page.)

More important still, Windows includes a raft of options for controlling your privacy. You'll find them under the Privacy & Security heading in Settings, where you can specify which apps are allowed to use each of your computer's many devices, whether to disclose your location, whether to allow Windows to use cloud-based speech recognition, and so on.

For each privacy option, you'll find a link to the Microsoft privacy statement and links to additional information as well as the controls for viewing and changing settings. The privacy statement is detailed yet clearly written, and it's an important aid for deciding which options to enable. You should examine each of these options carefully and decide for yourself where the proper balance is between your personal privacy and convenience.

To minimize the collection of diagnostic data, for example, go to Settings > Privacy & Security > Diagnostics & Feedback. Under the Diagnostic Data heading, shown in Figure 12-7, set the Send Optional Diagnostic Data switch to Off. (Note that on PCs that are configured as part of the Windows Insider Program, turning this setting off prevents the PC from receiving Insider preview builds; a message at the top of the section appears if you choose this configuration.)

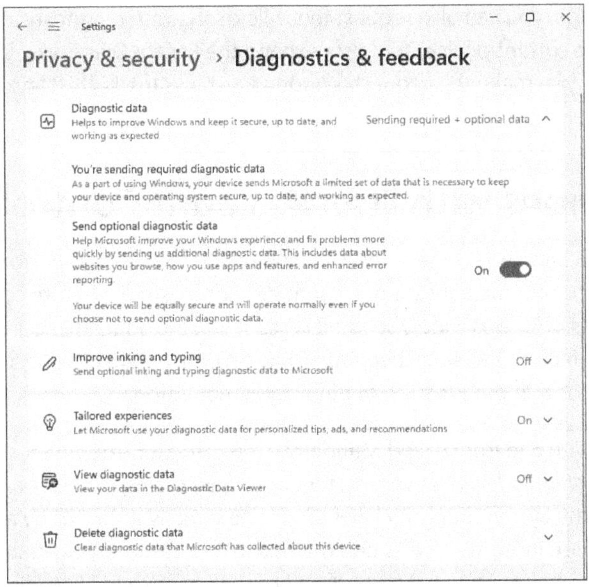

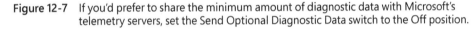

Figure 12-7   If you'd prefer to share the minimum amount of diagnostic data with Microsoft's telemetry servers, set the Send Optional Diagnostic Data switch to the Off position.

Using Group Policy and device management software, it's possible to disable diagnostic data collection. Note that this setting applies only to devices running Windows Enterprise and Education editions; if you select it on a device running Windows 11 Pro, Windows ignores the policy and uses the Send Required Diagnostic Data setting. Because this policy setting also disables Windows Update, it is not recommended and should be used only when an alternative update mechanism such as Windows Server Update Services is available.

To view and configure these settings, open the Local Group Policy Editor, Gpedit.exe, and navigate to Computer Configuration > Administrative Templates > Windows Components > Data Collection And Preview Builds. Double-click Allow Diagnostic Data and set its value to Enabled to see all three levels under Options.

Two advanced tools allow you to inspect and manage diagnostic data on your computer. These tools are available on all currently supported Windows 11 editions.

The first is Diagnostic Data Viewer, an app that displays the collected data so you can see for yourself exactly what is going to Microsoft. To use Diagnostic Data Viewer, go to Settings > Privacy & Security > Diagnostics & Feedback, expand the View Diagnostic Data section, and set the associated switch to On. Then click the Open Diagnostic Data Viewer button. The Diagnostic Data Viewer app includes search and filtering capabilities to help you narrow the display of diagnostic information.

From that same Settings page, you can also request that Microsoft erase diagnostic data that has been collected from the current device. To do so, expand the Delete Diagnostic Data section and then click Delete. After you make this request, Windows displays the Last Delete Request date to the right of the Delete button.

Preventing unsafe actions with User Account Control

User Account Control (UAC) intercedes whenever a user or an app attempts to perform a system administrative task, requiring the consent of a computer administrator before commencing what could be risky business. UAC was widely scorned when it was introduced as part of Windows Vista in 2006, but the feature has since been tuned to become an effective security aid—without the annoyance factor that plagued the original implementation.

UAC works in conjunction with a feature called Mandatory Integrity Control, which assigns a measure of trust called an *integrity level* to every system object, including processes and registry keys. Processes that run at the System integrity level cannot be directly accessed by any user account. A process with a High integrity level is one that is capable of modifying system data and requires an administrator access token. Most normal processes run with a Medium integrity level and require a standard user access token. (Store apps run with the AppContainer integrity level, and web browsers run at Low or Untrusted integrity levels. A standard user account can run either type of app, but the lower integrity level effectively creates a "sandbox" that prevents those apps from modifying objects with higher integrity levels.)

In Windows 11, standard user accounts can carry out all the usual daily computing tasks but are prevented from running any process with a High integrity level. These restrictions apply not just to the user; more importantly, they also apply to any programs launched by the user.

At sign-in, Windows creates a token that's used to identify the privilege levels of your account. Standard users get a standard token, but administrators get two: a standard token and an administrator token. (This dual-token configuration is called Admin Approval Mode.) The standard token is used to open Explorer.exe (the Windows shell), from which all subsequent programs are launched. Child processes inherit the token of the process that launches them, so by default, all applications run as a standard user—even when you're signed in with an administrator account. Any activity that runs a process with a High integrity level requires an administrator token; if your account provides that token, the program runs. This process is called *elevation*. Note that an elevated process can, in turn, run additional processes as an administrator.

> ➤ For information about user accounts, see Chapter 11. For a detailed technical discussion of UAC, see "How User Account Control Works," at *https://bit.ly/how-UAC-works*.

Most modern Windows desktop programs and all Store apps are written so that they don't require administrator privileges for performing everyday tasks. Programs that truly need administrative access (such as utility programs that change computer settings) request elevation—and that's where UAC comes in.

What triggers UAC prompts

The types of actions that require elevation to administrator status (and therefore display a UAC elevation prompt) include those that make changes to systemwide settings or to files in %SystemRoot% or %ProgramFiles%. (On a default Windows installation, these environment variables represent C:\Windows and C:\Program Files, respectively.) Among the actions that require elevation are the following:

- Installing and uninstalling most desktop applications (except those converted into app packages and delivered through the Microsoft Store, or those that install completely into the user profile)

- Installing device drivers that are not included in Windows or provided through Windows Update

- Installing ActiveX controls (which are still supported in Windows 11 in Microsoft Edge Internet Explorer mode)

- Changing settings for Windows Defender Firewall

- Changing UAC settings

- Configuring Windows Update

- Adding or removing user accounts

- Changing a user's account type

- Running Task Scheduler

- Editing the registry

- Restoring backed-up system files

- Viewing or changing another user's folders and files

Within the classic Windows desktop interface (including the remnants of Control Panel that have yet to migrate to Settings), you can identify in advance many actions that require elevation. A shield icon next to a button or link indicates that a UAC prompt will appear if you're using a standard account.

If you sign in with an administrator account (and if you don't change the default UAC settings), you'll see fewer consent prompts than if you use a standard account. That's because the default setting uses Admin Approval Mode, which prompts only when a program tries to install software or make other changes to the computer, but not when you make changes to Windows settings—even those that would trigger a prompt for a standard user with default UAC settings. Windows uses this automatic elevation, without the expected UAC prompt, for certain

CHAPTER 12

programs that are part of Windows. Programs that are elevated automatically are from a pre-defined list; they must be digitally signed by the Windows publisher, and they must be stored in certain secure folders.

LIMITATIONS OF USER ACCOUNT CONTROL

User Account Control isn't a security silver bullet. It's one layer of a defense-in-depth strategy.

Some Windows users assume that UAC consent dialogs represent a security boundary. They don't. They simply represent a place for an administrator to make a trust decision. If a bad guy uses social engineering to convince you that you need a program, you've already made a trust decision. You'll click at least a half-dozen times to download, save, and launch the bad guy's program. A UAC consent request is perfectly normal in this sequence, so why wouldn't you click one more time?

If this scenario bothers you, the obvious solution is to adjust UAC to its highest level. Among other changes, this setting disables the autoelevation behavior. (For details on how to do this, see "Modifying UAC settings" later in this chapter.) If a program tries to use this subterfuge to sneak system changes past you, you'll see an unexpected consent dialog from the system. But as soon as you provide those elevated credentials, the code can do anything it wants.

A better alternative is to sign in using a standard account, which provides a real security boundary. A standard user who does not have the administrator password can make changes only in their own user profile, protecting the system from unintended tampering.

Even running as a standard user doesn't provide complete protection. Malware can be installed in your user profile without triggering any system alarms. It can log your keystrokes, steal your passwords, encrypt your personal data files and hold them for ransom, and send out email using your identity. Even if you reset UAC to its highest level, you could fall victim to malware that lies in wait for you to elevate your privileges and then does its own dirty work alongside you.

As we said, enabling UAC is only one part of a multilayered security strategy. It works best when supplemented by a healthy skepticism, good training, and up-to-date antimalware software.

Dealing with UAC prompts

When you attempt to run a process that requires elevation, UAC evaluates the request and then displays an appropriate prompt. If you signed in to the current session with an administrator account, the most common prompt you're likely to see is the consent prompt, which is shown in

Figure 12-8. Check the name of the program and the publisher, and click Yes if you're confident that it's safe to proceed. (Note that the default action is No; if you absentmindedly press Enter, Windows cancels the elevation request.)

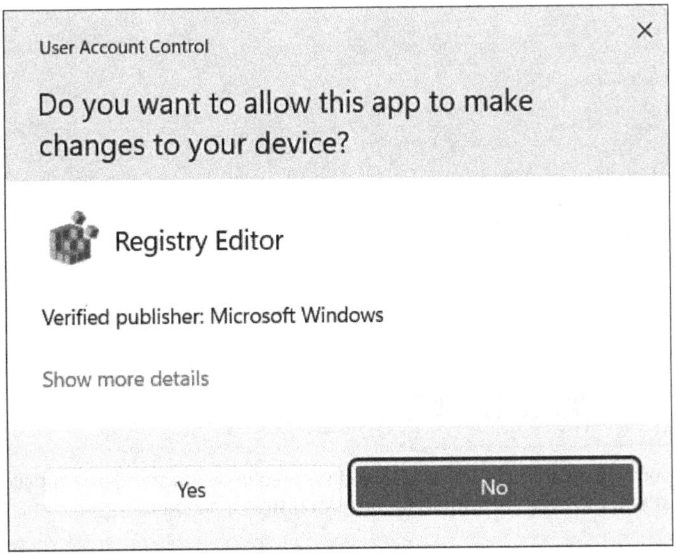

User Account Control

Do you want to allow this app to make changes to your device?

Registry Editor

Verified publisher: Microsoft Windows

Show more details

Yes   No

Figure 12-8   For a program that's digitally signed, clicking Show More Details displays a link to the associated certificate.

If, on the other hand, you signed in to the current session with a standard account, any attempt to run a program that requires elevation displays the credentials prompt, which is shown in Figure 12-9. The user must provide the credentials of an administrator (that is, username and password, smart card, or biometric authentication, depending on how sign-in options are configured on the computer); after entering those credentials, the application opens using the administrator's access token.

By default, the UAC dialog sits atop the secure desktop, which runs in a separate session that requires a trusted process running with System privileges. (If the UAC prompt were to run in the same session as other processes, a malicious program could disguise the UAC dialog, perhaps with a message encouraging you to let the program proceed. Or a malicious program could grab your keystrokes, thereby learning your administrator sign-in password.) When the secure desktop is displayed, you can't switch tasks or click any open window on the desktop. (In fact, in Windows 11, you can't even see the taskbar or any other open windows. When UAC invokes the secure desktop, it displays only a dimmed copy of the current desktop background behind the UAC dialog.)

Figure 12-9   To perform an administrative task when signed in with a standard user account, you must enter the full credentials for an administrator account.

NOTE

If an application other than the foreground application requests elevation, instead of interrupting your work (the foreground task) with a prompt, UAC signals its request with a flashing taskbar button. Click the taskbar button to see the prompt.

It becomes natural to click through dialogs without reading them or giving them a second thought. But it's important to recognize that security risks to your computer are real and that actions that trigger a UAC prompt are potentially dangerous. Clearly, if you know what you're doing, and you click a button to open Registry Editor or run a desktop program you just down-loaded from a trusted location, you can blow past that security dialog with no more than a quick glance to be sure it was raised by the expected application. But if a UAC prompt appears when you're not expecting it—stop, read it carefully, and think before you click.

Modifying UAC settings

To review your User Account Control options and make changes to the way it works, type **uac** in the search box in Start or in Settings, and then click Change User Account Control Settings. A window similar to the one shown in Figure 12-10 appears.

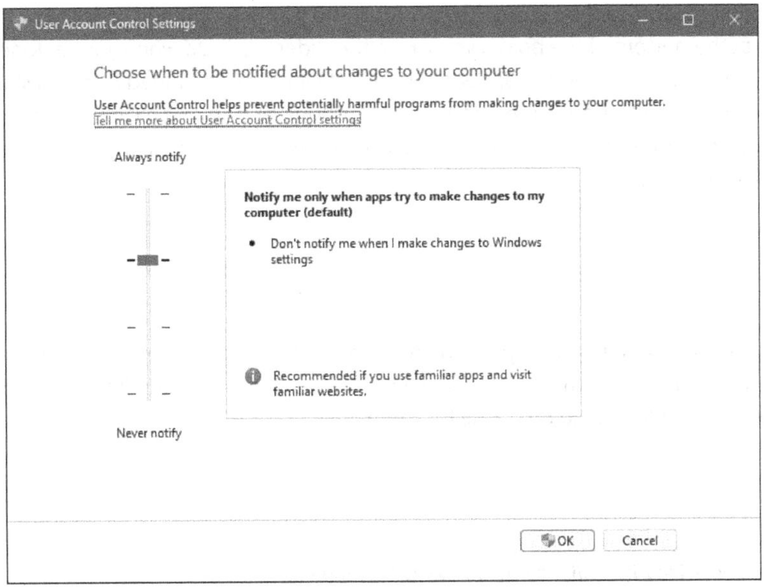

Figure 12-10 We don't recommend changing the default UAC settings unless you fully understand the consequences.

Your choices in this window vary slightly depending on whether you started the current session using an administrator account or a standard user account. For standard user accounts, the top setting is the default; for administrator accounts, the second setting from the top is the default. Table 12-1 summarizes the available options.

Table 12-1 User Account Control settings

Slider position	Prompts when a program tries to install software or make changes to the computer	Prompts when you make changes to Windows settings	Displays prompts on a secure desktop
Standard user account			
Top (default)	✓	✓	✓
Second	✓	✓	
Third	✓		
Bottom (off)			
Administrator account			
Top	✓	✓	✓
Second (default)	✓		✓
Third	✓		
Bottom (off)			

To make changes, move the slider to the position you want. Be sure to take note of the advisory message at the bottom of the box as you move the slider. Click OK when you're done—and then respond to the UAC prompt that appears. Note that when you're signed in with a standard user account, you can't select one of the bottom two options, even if you have the password for an administrator account. To select one of those options, you must sign in as an administrator and then make the change.

TROUBLESHOOTING

User Account Control settings don't stick

If you find that nothing happens when you make a change to User Account Control settings, be sure you're the only one signed in to your computer. Simultaneous sign-ins that use Fast User Switching can cause this problem.

Inside OUT

Use Local Security Policy to customize UAC behavior

On PCs running Windows 11 Pro, Enterprise, or Education, an administrator can use the Local Security Policy console to modify the behavior of UAC. Start Local Security Policy (Secpol.msc), and open Security Settings > Local Policies > Security Options. In the details pane, scroll down to the policies whose names begin with "User Account Control." For each policy, double-click it and then click the Explain tab for information before you decide on a setting. With these policies, you can make several refinements in the way UAC works—including some that are not possible in the User Account Control Settings window. (Administrators on Windows-based enterprise networks can also configure these options using Group Policy management tools.) For details about each of these policies, see "User Account Control Group Policy and registry key settings" at *https://bit.ly/10uac-gpo*.

Regardless of your UAC setting, the shield icons still appear throughout Control Panel, but you don't see UAC prompts if you've lowered the UAC protection level. Clicking a button or link identified with a shield immediately begins the action. Administrators run with full administrator privileges; standard users, of course, still have only standard privileges.

CAUTION

Don't forget that UAC is more than annoying prompts. Only when UAC is enabled does an administrator run with a standard token. Only when UAC is enabled do web browsers run at Low or Untrusted integrity levels to thwart web-based attacks. Only when UAC is enabled does Windows warn you when a rogue application attempts to perform a task with system-wide impact. And, crucially, disabling UAC also disables file and registry virtualization, which can cause compatibility problems with applications that use fixes provided by the UAC feature. For all these reasons, we urge you not to select the bottom option in User Account Control Settings, which turns off UAC completely.

Blocking malware

The best way to fight unwanted and malicious software is to keep it from being installed on any PC that's part of your network. You can install third-party software for this task, or you can use Microsoft Defender Antivirus, which is included with every edition of Windows 11.

Microsoft Defender Antivirus runs as a system service (two services, to be precise: Microsoft Defender Antivirus Service and Microsoft Defender Antivirus Network Inspection Service); it uses a scanning engine to compare files against a database of virus and spyware definitions. It also uses heuristic analysis of the behavior of programs to flag suspicious activity from a file that isn't included in the list of known threats. It scans each file you access in any way, including downloads from the internet and email attachments you receive. (This feature is called *real-time protection*—not to be confused with scheduled *scans*, which periodically inspect all files stored on your computer to root out malware.)

Using Microsoft Defender Antivirus

In general, you don't need to "use" Microsoft Defender Antivirus at all. As a system service, it works quietly in the background. The only time you'll know it's there is if it finds what it believes to be an infected file; one or more notifications will pop up to alert you to the fact.

Nonetheless, there are a few settings you can tweak and a few tasks you can perform manually. In the Windows Security app, open the Virus & Threat Protection page to see details about the most recent scan (manual or automatic). Under normal circumstances, this number should be zero; if Microsoft Defender Antivirus detected a threat, it displays the details and offers options for dealing with the threat.

Click Manage Settings, under the Virus & Threat Protection Settings heading, to open a page containing a group of switches for adjusting the behavior of Microsoft Defender Antivirus.

Slide the Real-Time Protection switch to Off to temporarily disable protection (an option you should use only for short periods and only if you're absolutely certain you're not allowing malware to sneak onto your PC as a result of actions that would otherwise be blocked). The Cloud-Delivered Protection and Automatic Sample Submission options work together to help block threats that have not yet been identified in the latest security intelligence update. Most people should keep these options turned on. Tamper Protection prevents malicious apps from changing Microsoft Defender Antivirus settings.

Finally, in the Exclusions section, you can specify files, folders, file types (by extension), or processes you want Microsoft Defender Antivirus to ignore. This option is especially useful for developers working with files that might otherwise trigger alarms.

Manually scanning for malware

The combination of real-time protection and periodic scheduled scanning is normally sufficient for identifying and resolving problems with malware and spyware. However, if you suspect that a PC you manage has been compromised by malware, you can initiate a scan on demand. To immediately scan for problems, open the Virus & Threat Protection tab in Windows Security and click Quick Scan. This option kicks off a scan that checks only the places on your computer that malware and spyware are most likely to infect, and it's the recommended setting for frequent regular scans.

For a more intensive (or more focused) inspection, click Scan Options, which leads to a page containing three additional options. Choose Full Scan if you suspect infection (or you just want reassurance that your system is clean) and want to inspect all running programs and the complete contents of all local volumes. Click Custom Scan if you want to restrict the scan to any combination of drives, folders, and files. The Microsoft Defender Offline Scan option is useful for removing persistent infections that are able to successfully block normal operation of Microsoft Defender Antivirus. It requires a restart and can take a significant amount of time.

Inside OUT

Run a scan from a script or a scheduled task

Microsoft Defender Antivirus includes a command-line utility you can use to automate scans with a script or a scheduled task. MpCmdRun.exe is in %ProgramFiles%\Windows Defender. For details about using the utility, open an elevated Command Prompt window and run the program with no parameters.

CHAPTER 12

Dealing with detected threats

If Microsoft Defender Antivirus detects the presence of malware or spyware as part of its real-time protection, it displays a banner and a notification and, in most cases, resolves the problem without requiring you to lift a finger.

To learn more about its findings, open Windows Security and, on the Virus & Threat Protection tab, click Protection History. Windows Security shows the name, severity level, and detection date of each blocked or quarantined item. Click an entry for additional information about detected threats and a list of actions you can take.

Blocking ransomware with controlled folder access

One of the pernicious threats in recent times is *ransomware*. Typically, this type of malware works in the background to encrypt all your documents and other files. Upon completion, the program displays a digital ransom note that says, in effect: *If you ever want to see your files again, send us money.* Supposedly, after you pay up (usually via untraceable digital currency), the hijacker sends you a decryption key and instructions for recovering your files.

The Controlled Folder Access feature is designed to stop ransomware attacks by preventing malicious and suspicious apps from making changes to any files stored in designated folders—typically, all your document folders. To enable this feature, open the Virus & Threat Protection page in Windows Security and then click or tap Manage Ransomware Protection. Turn on Controlled Folder Access to enable this feature and its two configurable settings. The Protected Folders link allows you to view and modify the list of folders monitored by this feature. A second link, Allow An App Through Controlled Folder Access, leads to a page where you can allow an app that you know to be safe. You need to do this only if Controlled Folder Access blocks an app you trust; most legitimate apps are on a known-good list and need no further clearance to go about their work.

On this same page are details about file recovery options for OneDrive and OneDrive for Business accounts.

Protecting Windows from exploits

One group of settings in Windows Security deserves special mention here, primarily so that we can encourage you to leave them alone.

If you go to the App & Browser Control page and click Exploit Protection Settings (under the Exploit Protection heading), there is a group of advanced settings. Here, you can adjust features that control how program code is allowed to execute in memory. Data Execution Prevention (DEP), for example, is a hardware feature that marks blocks of memory so that they can store data but not execute program instructions. Address Space Layout Randomization (ASLR)

randomizes the location of program code and other data in memory, making it difficult for malware to carry out attacks that write directly to system memory because the malware can't find
the memory location it needs.

These settings were previously available only as part of a separate download called the
Enhanced Mitigation Experience Toolkit, intended for use by administrators in enterprise
deployments. Although it's possible to change each of these settings on a systemwide basis or
on a per-application basis, we suggest that you avoid experimenting with these settings unless
you understand exactly what the effects are likely to be. For full documentation, see *https://
bit.ly/win10-exploit-protection*. (Be sure to use the navigation pane on the left to view more
detailed pages in this topic.)

Stopping unknown or malicious programs with Microsoft Defender SmartScreen

Microsoft Defender SmartScreen, which has been a part of Windows for more than a decade,
puts up a roadblock whenever you try to run a program that is unknown or has a questionable
reputation based on the experience of other users. It does so by comparing a hash of a downloaded program with Microsoft's application-reputation database. (It also checks web content
used by Microsoft Store apps.)

This reputation check occurs when you download a program using Microsoft Edge. Smart-
Screen also kicks in when you attempt to run a program you downloaded from the internet—
regardless of what browser you use.

Programs with a positive reputation run without fuss. Programs that are known to be bad or
that have not yet developed a reputation are blocked. In Microsoft Edge, the notice that a
potentially dangerous program has been blocked might appear in the details for the download
that appear at the bottom of the screen. If you download a file using another browser and then
try to run it, you might see a message that tells you "Windows protected your PC."

Ironically, you might see this sort of block even when running code written and distributed by
Microsoft, if the code is too new to have earned a positive reputation. If you're certain that a
program is safe, you can override the block by clicking the Run Anyway button. With default
settings in place, you then need the approval of someone with an administrator account before
the program runs. Don't say you weren't warned.

To configure Microsoft Defender SmartScreen settings, including those for Microsoft Edge and
for app content in Microsoft Store apps, open Windows Security, click App & Browser Control,
and then click Reputation-Based Protection Settings.

A related feature called Smart App Control is new in Windows 11 version 22H2. It uses a similar cloud-based reputation feature to predict whether an app is safe to run. This feature can only be enabled on a clean install of Windows 11. For more details, see *https://bit.ly/smart-app-control*.

Encrypting information

The increased mobility of PCs also increases the risk of theft. Losing a computer is bad enough, but handing over all the data you've stored on the computer is potentially a much greater loss. Windows 11 includes a variety of data protection features to ensure that a thief can't access your data:

- **Device encryption** On devices that support InstantGo, data on the operating system volume is encrypted by default. (Formerly called Connected Standby, InstantGo is a Microsoft hardware specification that enables advanced power-management capabilities. Among other requirements, InstantGo devices must boot from a solid-state drive.) The encryption initially uses a clear key, but when a local administrator first signs in with a Microsoft account, the volume is automatically encrypted. A recovery key is available when you sign in using that Microsoft account at *https://onedrive.com/recoverykey*; you need the key if you reinstall the operating system or move the drive to a new PC.

- **BitLocker Drive Encryption** This feature protects data by encrypting the entire contents of any hard-disk volume, not just the system drive, and on corporate networks, it allows centralized management. By linking this encryption to a key stored in a Trusted Platform Module (TPM), BitLocker reduces the risk of data being lost when a computer is stolen or when a hard disk is stolen and placed in another computer. A thief's standard approach in these situations is to boot into an alternate operating system and then try to retrieve data from the stolen computer or drive. With BitLocker, that type of offline attack is effectively neutered.

- **BitLocker To Go** This feature extends BitLocker encryption to removable media, such as USB flash drives.

- **Encrypting File System (EFS)** This technology, which predates BitLocker, encrypts the contents of files and folders rather than entire volumes. The files are readable only when you sign in to the computer or network with a user account that has access to the certificate used to encrypt them. If you lose that certificate, the data cannot be recovered.

NOTE

The BitLocker Drive Encryption and Encrypting File System features are not available in Windows Home edition. Using BitLocker To Go to encrypt a removable drive requires Windows Pro, Enterprise, or Education; the resulting encrypted drive can be unlocked and used to read and write files on a device running any edition of Windows 7 or later.

Encrypting with BitLocker and BitLocker To Go

BitLocker Drive Encryption can encrypt entire NTFS volumes, which provides excellent protection against data theft. BitLocker can secure a drive against attacks that involve circumventing the operating system or removing the drive and placing it in another computer. Because Windows 11 requires a Trusted Platform Module (TPM), BitLocker can use the TPM to store the encryption key and ensure that a computer has not been tampered with while offline.

To apply BitLocker Drive Encryption to the system drive, right-click the drive in File Explorer and then click Turn On BitLocker. (If you see the menu option Manage BitLocker instead, the drive is already encrypted.) Before proceeding, the software prompts you to back up your recovery key, as shown in Figure 12-11. (Note that the PC in this example is connected to an Azure AD account; if you've signed in using a Microsoft account, the first option offers to save the encryption key to that account.)

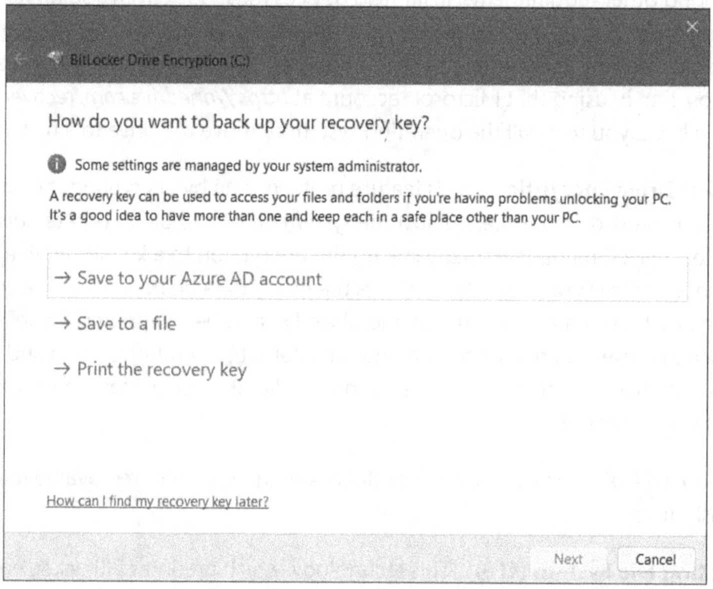

Figure 12-11 The option of saving the recovery key to an Azure AD or Microsoft account makes it much easier to find this key when you need it.

Your recovery key is a system-generated, 48-character, numeric backup password. You need that recovery key if you lose the ability to log in to your PC and need to reinstall Windows or access the drive's encrypted data from another PC. BitLocker offers to save that key in a plain text file or cloud storage; you should accept the offer and store the file in a secure location. We recommend also printing the recovery key, labeling it with a descriptive name, and storing it in a secure location (such as a locked file cabinet) alongside the recovery keys for secure websites that are protected with multifactor authentication.

Inside OUT

Store your recovery keys on OneDrive or in Azure AD

If you're signed in with a Microsoft account, the Save To Your Microsoft Account option saves the recovery key on OneDrive, making it possible to recover quickly from an encryption problem, provided that you have another Internet-connected device (even a smartphone) from which to recover the key. The recovery keys for every device associated with your Microsoft account are at *https://onedrive.com/recoverykey*.

When you're signed in with an Azure AD account, the Save To Your Azure AD Account option saves the recovery key in your organization's Azure AD portal. To find the Bit-Locker recovery keys for a device, go to *https://myprofile.microsoft.com*, sign in with your Azure AD account, and click Devices in the navigation pane on the left. That results in a list of all the devices associated with that account. Click a device name to expand its entry; if any BitLocker recovery keys are associated with that device, you can retrieve them from here.

Because Azure AD accounts are associated with a managed domain, a Global Administrator can sign in at *https://portal.azure.com* and retrieve the recovery key from the Devices tab for an individual user account.

CHAPTER 12

With all preliminaries out of the way, BitLocker begins encrypting your media. This process takes a few minutes, even if the disk is freshly formatted. However, if you're in a hurry, you can opt to encrypt only the used space on the drive. This choice can save you a considerable amount of time if your disk contains only a small number of files. The security risk, of course, is that any old data in the erased portion of the drive might still be recoverable by an attacker with physical access to the device.

To remove BitLocker encryption from a disk, use the Manage BitLocker option, select the encrypted drive, and click Turn Off BitLocker. The software decrypts the disk; allow some time for this process.

➤ For more information about BitLocker, see *https://bit.ly/BitLocker-win10*.

Using BitLocker To Go

With BitLocker To Go, you can encrypt the entire contents of a USB flash drive, SD card, or other removable storage device, assigning a strong password to unlock its contents. If the drive is lost or stolen, the thief will be unable to access the data without the password.

To encrypt a removable drive using BitLocker To Go, hold down the Shift key as you right-click the drive in File Explorer, click Turn On BitLocker, and then follow the prompts. The procedure is similar to the one you follow when encrypting the system drive on a Windows 11 PC, with one noteworthy exception: Instead of unlocking the drive's contents by signing in with your

Windows credentials, you assign a password that's used as the decryption key. (There's also an option to use a smart card, but that technology is used primarily in enterprise deployments.)

After encryption is complete, make sure to back up the recovery key to a safe place; then use the drive as you normally would.

To read a BitLocker-encrypted removable disk, you need to unlock it by entering your password. The drive icon in File Explorer has a padlock to indicate it's encrypted. Double-click that icon to display the dialog shown in Figure 12-12. Enter your password and click Unlock to decrypt the drive and work with it as normal.

BitLocker (E:)

Enter password to unlock this drive.

Fewer options

Enter recovery key

☐ Automatically unlock on this PC

Unlock

Figure 12-12 When you insert an encrypted removable drive into a Windows PC, you must supply a password to unlock it.

On a trusted PC, you can avoid the hassle of entering your password every time you want to use that removable drive by clicking Automatically Unlock On This PC before clicking the Unlock button. With that option set, you no longer have to enter your password on that PC. If you change your mind and want to turn this feature off, right-click the removable drive's icon in File Explorer, choose Manage BitLocker, and then click Turn Off Auto-Unlock for that drive.

If you plug in an encrypted drive and discover that you have lost or forgotten the password, click More Options and then click Enter Recovery Key. Find your recovery key backup and enter the 48-digit key here. In case you have several recovery-key text files, BitLocker To Go gives you an eight-character Key ID that can help you locate the right one.

If you signed in to Windows with a Microsoft account, your recovery key might be available online. Look for the entry on OneDrive (*https://onedrive.com/recoverykey*); if you saved the recovery key as a text file or printout, look for that key ID, and then enter the recovery key in the BitLocker dialog. You're granted temporary access to the files, which is good until you remove the disk or restart the computer. Before going any further, change the password; right-click the drive in File Explorer and click Manage BitLocker. Select the encrypted removable drive and then click Change Password.

Using the Encrypting File System

As we mention at the beginning of this section, EFS is a legacy technology that provides a secure way to store sensitive data in files, folders, or entire drives on PCs running Windows 11 Pro, Enterprise, or Education. Windows creates a randomly generated file encryption key (FEK) and then uses the FEK to encrypt the data transparently, as the data is being written to disk. Windows then encrypts the FEK using your public key. (Windows creates a personal encryption certificate with a public/private key pair for you the first time you use EFS.) The FEK, and therefore the data it encrypts, can be decrypted only with your certificate and its associated private key, which are available only when you sign in with your user account. (Designated data-recovery agents can also decrypt your data.) Other users who attempt to use your encrypted files receive an "access denied" message. Even administrators and others who have permission to take ownership of files are unable to open your encrypted files.

You can encrypt individual files, folders, or entire drives. (You cannot, however, use EFS to encrypt the boot volume—the one with the Windows operating system files. For that, you must use BitLocker.) We recommend you encrypt folders or drives instead of individual files. When you encrypt a folder or drive, you can choose to encrypt the files it already contains, and new files you create in or copy to that folder or drive are encrypted automatically.

To encrypt a folder, follow these steps:

1. In File Explorer, right-click the folder, choose Properties, click the General tab, and then click Advanced, which displays the dialog shown in Figure 12-13. (If the properties dialog doesn't have an Advanced button, the folder is not on an NTFS-formatted volume, and you can't use EFS.)

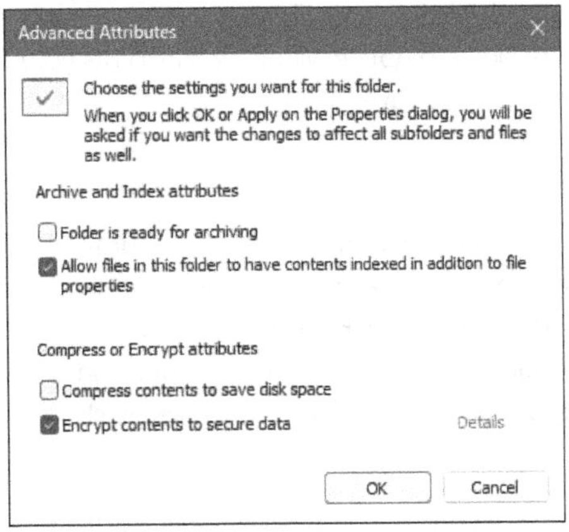

Figure 12-13   Click the Encrypt Contents To Secure Data check box to encrypt a folder using EFS.

2. Select Encrypt Contents To Secure Data. (Note that you can't encrypt compressed files. If the files are already compressed, Windows clears the compressed attribute.)

3. Click OK twice. If the folder contains any files or subfolders, Windows then displays the confirmation message shown in Figure 12-14.

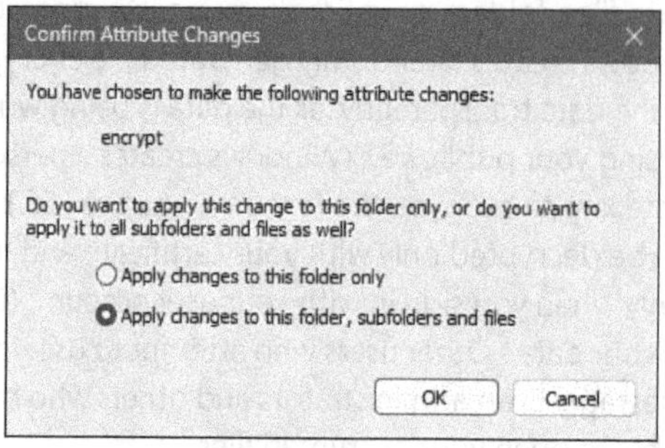

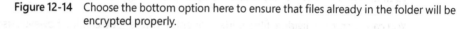

Figure 12-14 Choose the bottom option here to ensure that files already in the folder will be encrypted properly.

NOTE

If you select Apply Changes To This Folder Only, Windows doesn't encrypt any of the files currently in the folder. Any new files you create in the folder, however, including files you copy or move to the folder, will be encrypted. We don't recommend this option, which is needlessly confusing.

4. Click OK to finish encrypting the folder and its files. A Windows notification urges you to back up your FEK. Click the notification to launch a wizard that helps you create a copy of the certificate and save it in a safe place (in cloud storage or on removable media).

After a file or folder has been encrypted, File Explorer displays its name in green. This minor cosmetic detail is the only change you're likely to notice. Windows decrypts your files on the fly as you use them and reencrypts them when you save.

CAUTION

Before you encrypt anything important, you should back up your file-recovery certificate and your personal encryption certificate (with their associated private keys), as well as the data-recovery-agent certificate, to a USB flash drive or to your OneDrive. Store the flash drive in a secure location. To do this, open User Accounts in Control Panel, click User Accounts to make changes to your own account, and then click Manage Your File Encryption Certificates.

If you ever lose the certificate stored on your hard drive (because of a disk failure, for example), you can restore the backup copy and regain access to your files. If you lose all copies of your certificate (and no data-recovery-agent certificates exist), you won't be able to use your encrypted files. To the best of our knowledge, there's no practical way for anyone to access these encrypted files without the certificate. (If there were, it wouldn't be very good encryption.)

To encrypt one or more files, follow the same procedure as for folders. You see a different confirmation message to remind you that the file's folder is not encrypted and to give you an opportunity to encrypt it. You generally don't want to encrypt individual files because the information you intend to protect can too easily become decrypted without your knowledge. For example, with some applications, when you open a document for editing, the application creates a copy of the original document. When you save the document after editing, the application saves the copy—which is not encrypted—and deletes the original encrypted document. Static files that you use for reference only—but never for editing—can safely be encrypted without encrypting the parent folder. Even in that situation, however, you'll probably find it simpler to encrypt the whole folder.

Blocking intruders with Windows Defender Firewall

Typically, the first line of defense in securing your computer is to protect it from attacks by outsiders. Once your computer is connected to the internet, it becomes just another node on a huge global network. A firewall provides a barrier between your computer and the network to which it's connected by preventing the entry of unwanted traffic while allowing transparent passage to authorized connections.

Using a firewall is simple, essential, and often overlooked. You want to be sure that all network connections are protected by a firewall. You might be comforted by the knowledge that your portable computer is protected by a corporate firewall when you're at work and that you use a firewalled broadband connection at home. But what about the public hotspots you use when you travel?

And it makes sense to run a software-based firewall on your computer even when you're behind a residential router or corporate firewall. Other people on your network might not be as vigilant as you are about defending against viruses, so if someone brings in a portable computer infected with a worm and connects it to the network, you're toast—unless your network connection has its own firewall protection.

Windows includes a two-way, stateful-inspection, packet-filtering firewall called, cleverly enough, Windows Defender Firewall. (This product is labeled Microsoft Defender Firewall if you dig deep enough in the Windows Security app, but Microsoft has not extended that rebranding consistently.) This protection is enabled by default for all connections, and it begins protecting your computer as it boots. The following actions take place by default:

- The firewall blocks all inbound traffic, with the exception of traffic sent in response to a request by your computer and unsolicited traffic that has been explicitly allowed by creating a rule.

- All outgoing traffic is allowed unless it matches a configured rule.

You notice nothing if a packet is dropped, but you can (at your option) create a log of all such events.

CHAPTER 12

Inside Out

Dig deep into firewall settings

Windows 11 includes an advanced user interface for Windows Firewall that allows you to create rules to cover specific ports and protocols. You can open Windows Defender Firewall with Advanced Security using its executable file, Wf.exe. It's a dense and nearly impenetrable interface that even the most advanced users will probably never need. If you want to explore its inner workings, we recommend reading the documentation at *https://bit.ly/WF-Advanced.*

Using Windows Defender Firewall with different network types

Windows Defender Firewall maintains a separate profile (that is, a complete collection of settings, including rules for various programs, services, and ports) for each of three network types:

- **Domain**   Used when your computer is joined to an Active Directory domain. In this environment, firewall settings are typically (but not necessarily) controlled by a network administrator.

- **Private**   Used when your computer is connected to a home or work network in a workgroup configuration.

- **Public**   Used when your computer is connected to a network in a public location, such as an airport or a library. It's common—indeed, recommended—to have fewer allowed programs and more restrictions when you use a public network.

If you're simultaneously connected to more than one network (for example, if you have a Wi-Fi connection to your home network while you're connected to your work domain through a virtual private network, or VPN, connection), Windows uses the appropriate profile for each connection with a feature called multiple active firewall profiles (MAFP).

You make settings in Windows Defender Firewall independently for each network profile. The settings in a profile apply to all networks of the particular type to which you connect. (For example, if you allow a program through the firewall while connected to a public network, that program rule is then enabled whenever you connect to any other public network. It's not enabled when you're connected to a domain or private network unless you allow the program in those profiles.)

➤ For more information about network types, see "Setting the network location" in Chapter 11.

Managing Windows Defender Firewall

Earlier in this chapter, we describe the Windows Security app, which includes Firewall & Network Protection as one of the categories it monitors. The icon on that app's home page displays the current status of Windows Defender Firewall; a green check mark means that Windows Defender Firewall is on and protecting the current network connection.

Clicking the Firewall & Network Protection icon offers access to additional status information as well as links to advanced configuration options. Click any of the three network entries to see a status page for that connection, with a simple on/off switch for the firewall for that network type, as shown in Figure 12-15.

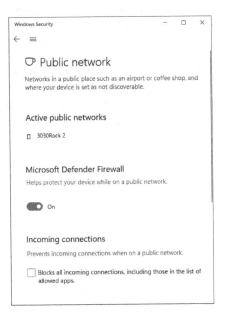

CHAPTER 12

Figure 12-15   Each network profile—Public, Private, and Domain—has its own control page.

In general, the only reason to turn off Windows Defender Firewall is for brief (and extremely cautious) troubleshooting purposes, or if you have installed a third-party firewall that you plan to use instead of Windows Defender Firewall. Most compatible third-party programs perform this task as part of their installation.

The Blocks All Incoming Connections check box provides additional protection from would-be intruders. When it's selected, the firewall rejects all unsolicited incoming traffic—even traffic from allowed programs that would ordinarily be permitted by a rule. Invoke this mode when extra security against outside attack is needed. For example, you might block all connections when you're using a suspicious public wireless hotspot or when you know that your computer is actively under attack by others.

NOTE

Selecting Blocks All Incoming Connections does not disconnect your computer from the internet. Even in this mode, you can still use your browser to connect to the internet. Similarly, other outbound connections—whether they're legitimate services or some sort of spyware—continue unabated. If you really want to sever your ties to the outside world, open Settings > Network & Internet and disable each network connection. Alternatively, use brute force: physically disconnect wired network connections and turn off wireless adapters or access points.

As you'll discover throughout Windows Defender Firewall, domain network settings are available only on computers that are joined to a domain. You can make settings for all network types—even those to which you're not currently connected. Settings for the domain profile, however, are often locked down by the network administrator using Group Policy.

The traditional alternative for monitoring the status of Windows Defender Firewall is the Control Panel application of the same name. That dashboard is still available, but its primary tasks—allowing a program through the firewall or blocking all incoming connections—are now accessible directly from links at the bottom of the Firewall & Network Protection page in Windows Security. Click Allow An App Through Firewall, for example, to display a list of allowed apps and features like the one shown in Figure 12-16.

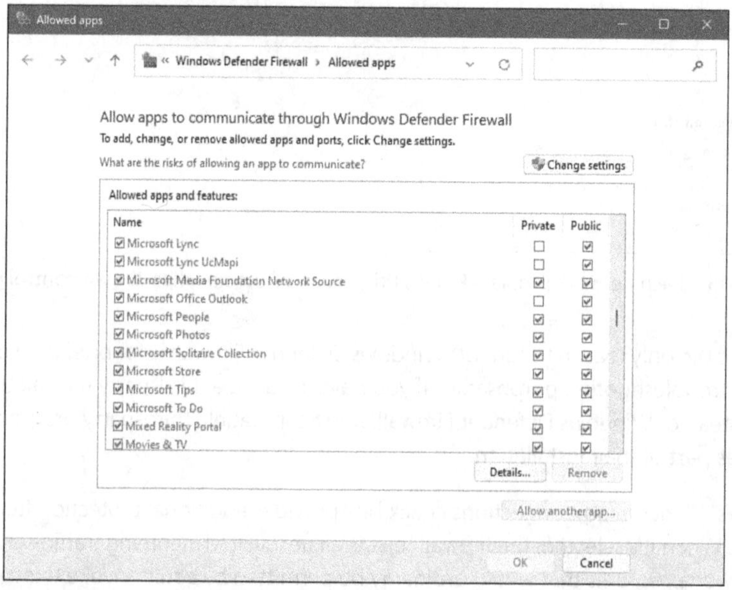

Figure 12-16   Click Change Settings, and then select or clear a check box to control connections over each network type by a specific app or feature.

The Allowed Apps And Features list includes programs and services that are installed on your computer; you can add others, as described in the following section. In addition, program rules are created (but not enabled) when a program tries to set up an incoming connection. To allow connections for a program or service that has already been defined, simply select its check box for each network type on which you want to allow the program. (You need to click Change Settings and approve a UAC consent request before you can make changes.)

In each of these cases, you enable a rule in Windows Defender Firewall that opens a pathway in the firewall and allows a certain type of traffic to pass through it. Each rule of this type increases your security risk to some degree, so you should clear the check box for all programs you don't need. If you're confident you won't ever need a particular program, you can select it and then click Remove. (Many items on this list represent apps or services included with Windows and don't allow deletion, but as long as their check boxes are not selected, these apps present no danger.)

The first time you run a program that tries to set up an incoming connection, Windows Defender Firewall asks for your permission by displaying a dialog. You can add the program to the allowed programs list by clicking Allow Access.

When such a dialog appears, read it carefully:

- Is the program one that you knowingly installed and ran?

- Is it reasonable for the program to require acceptance of incoming connections?

- Are you currently using a network type where it's okay for this program to accept incoming connections?

If the answer to any of these questions is no—or if you're unsure—click Cancel. If you later find that a needed program isn't working properly, you can open the allowed apps list in Windows Defender Firewall and enable the rule.

Restoring default settings

If you've played around a bit with Windows Defender Firewall and perhaps allowed connections that you should not have, you can get back to a known secure state by opening the Firewall & Network Protection page in Windows Security and clicking Restore Firewalls To Default. Be aware that doing so removes all rules you've added for all programs. Although this gives you a secure setup, you might find that some of your network-connected programs no longer work properly. As that occurs, you can re-create the Allow rules for each legitimate program, as described on the previous pages.

CHAPTER 12

Managing hardware and devices

It's probably only a slight exaggeration to say that no two computers are alike. Motherboards, storage devices and controllers, video and network adapters, and peripherals of all shapes and sizes combine to create a nearly infinite number of possible computer configurations.

The good news for anyone using Windows 11 is that most of these devices should just work. For most common hardware upgrades, Windows detects the device automatically and installs a driver so that you can use the device and its full array of features. This chapter covers those installations as well as devices that need to be added manually and those that have optional configuration steps.

This chapter covers a feature called Swift Pair, which simplifies the experience of setting up some Bluetooth devices. It also offers advice on how to work with display-related improvements such as support for high-DPI hardware configurations, typically found in high-end, business-class notebooks, and the Night Light feature that makes portable computing easier on the eyes.

In this chapter, we cover the traditional nerve center of hardware, Device Manager, as well as the newer hardware configuration options in Settings. We explain how drivers work (and how to work with drivers). We also offer hints on the best ways to set up specific device configurations, including multiple monitors, Bluetooth adapters, and printers.

Adding, configuring, and removing hardware devices

Since its introduction in Windows 95, Plug and Play technology has evolved tremendously. Early implementations of this technology were somewhat unreliable, leading some users to dismiss the feature as "plug and pray." As this now-mature technology passes the quarter-century mark, however, hardware and software standards have converged to make most device configuration tasks completely automatic.

Any computer that was certified as compatible with Windows 7 or later supports the Plug and Play device standard, which handles virtually all the work of configuring computer hardware and attached devices. A Plug and Play device sends a unique identifier to Windows; that identifier helps Windows discover its required resources (including drivers) and allows software to configure it.

Plug and Play devices can interact with the operating system, with both sides of the conversation responding to device notification and power management events. A Plug and Play driver can load automatically when Windows detects that a device has been plugged in, and it can suspend operations when the system sleeps and resume smoothly when the system wakes.

NOTE

Although you still can find older devices that require non–Plug and Play inputs—such as scanners, plotters, and similar peripherals that connect to serial and parallel ports—these legacy devices are becoming increasingly rare. If you own this type of device, we recommend retiring it if possible and replacing it with a supported modern alternative. If you have no choice but to keep it around, look for a community of fellow owners of that device; they're the most likely to be able to help you with configuration issues.

Installing a new Plug and Play device

When you install a Plug and Play device for the first time, the Plug and Play manager queries the device to determine its hardware ID and any compatible IDs. It then compares the hardware ID with a master list of corresponding tags drawn from all the Setup Information files in the %SystemRoot%\Inf folder. If it finds a signed driver with a matching tag, it installs that driver package and makes other necessary system modifications with no intervention required from you. If everything goes as expected, the only subtle indication you might see is a progress dialog (typically minimized) that displays a green bar over its taskbar button and then vanishes when its work is complete.

NOTE

Any user can plug in a new device and begin using it if a driver for that device is included with Windows 11 or is available via Windows Update. Installing a new driver that is downloaded from a third-party site and is digitally signed by a third party rather than by Microsoft requires an administrator's credentials.

If Windows detects a Plug and Play device (after you've plugged it into a USB port, for instance) but cannot locate a digitally signed driver that matches the device ID, it looks for generic driver packages that match any compatible IDs reported by the device. If that search still doesn't turn up a suitable driver, the Plug and Play manager installs a stub for the device and awaits the arrival of a proper driver. These partially installed devices appear in Device Manager, under the Other Devices heading, with a yellow exclamation point over the device name.

TROUBLESHOOTING

Drivers for built-in devices are missing

Device Manager might show some devices in the Other Devices category, with a yellow exclamation point indicating that the correct drivers are missing, after a clean installation of Windows 11. This usually occurs on a PC where some low-level devices built into the motherboard aren't recognized during Windows 11 setup. (This is most likely to be an issue when installing Windows 11 on hardware that doesn't meet the minimum requirements for the operating system.) Try checking Windows Update manually to see whether the correct drivers turn up; if that search doesn't retrieve the desired drivers, check with the device manufacturer to see whether drivers are available for download. Pay special attention to chipset drivers, which add the necessary entries to the Windows Plug and Play database to allow the correct built-in drivers to be installed.

When Windows Update can't find a signed driver (and, thankfully, those occasions are becoming rarer as the Windows ecosystem matures), you might need to manually download and install a device driver.

The built-in Windows drivers are perfectly adequate for many device classes. Some devices, especially complex ones like scanners and all-in-one printers, might require utility software and additional drivers to enable the full range of features for that device.

How device drivers and hardware work together

Before Windows can work with any piece of hardware, it requires a compatible, properly configured device driver. Drivers are compact control programs that hook directly into Windows and handle the essential tasks of communicating your instructions to a hardware device and then relaying data back to you. After you set up a hardware device, its driver loads automatically and runs as part of the operating system, without requiring any further intervention on your part.

Many individual technologies used in Windows 11 devices use minidriver models, where the device driver is made up of two parts. Typically, Microsoft writes a general class driver that handles tasks that are common to devices in that category. The device manufacturer can then write device-specific code to enable custom features.

Windows 11 includes a comprehensive library of class drivers that allow most devices to function properly without requiring any additional software. There are class drivers for pieces of hardware that are, these days, typically integrated into a larger system: audio devices, network adapters, webcams, and display adapters, for example. Windows 11 also includes drivers for external add-ons (wired and wireless) including printers, monitors, keyboards, scanners, mice and other pointing devices, smartphones, and removable storage devices.

This core library is copied during Windows setup to a protected system folder, %SystemRoot%\System32\DriverStore. (Driver files and associated elements are stored in the FileRepository

CHAPTER 13

subfolder.) Anyone who signs in to the computer has Read & Execute permissions for files that are saved in that location, but only an installation program working with authorization from a member of the Administrators group can create or modify files and folders there.

You can add new drivers to the driver store in a variety of ways, including the following:

- Windows Update offers drivers when it detects that you're running a device that's compatible with that driver but is currently using an older version. (You can also search for the most recent driver via Windows Update when installing a new device.)

- A Windows quality or feature update can refresh the driver store with new and updated drivers.

- As an administrator, you can add signed third-party drivers to the driver store by running an installer app. All drivers added to the driver store in this fashion are saved in their own subfolder (with a cryptic folder name that ends in a 16-character unique identification string) within the FileRepository folder, along with some supporting files created by Windows that allow the drivers to be reinstalled if necessary.

Any driver that has been added to this store is considered to be trusted and can be installed without prompts or administrator credentials. All drivers, new or updated, that are downloaded from the Windows Update service are certified to be fully compatible with Windows 11 and are digitally signed by Microsoft.

Inside OUT

Copy the FileRepository folder before a clean reinstall

If you're planning a clean reinstall of Windows 11 using bootable installation media rather than using the Reset function, consider copying the FileRepository folder from %SystemRoot%\System32\DriverStore to removable media, such as a USB flash drive. After your clean install is complete, you can quickly reinstall any custom drivers by using the Update Driver option from Device Manager and specifying that saved folder as the location for the new driver files.

A Windows hardware driver package must include a Setup Information file (with the extension .inf). This is a text file that contains detailed information about the device to be installed, including the names of its driver files, the locations where they are to be installed, any required registry settings, and version information. All devices with drivers in the DriverStore folder include Setup Information files in the %SystemRoot%\Inf folder.

Although the Setup Information file is a crucial part of the driver installation process, you don't work with it directly. Instead, this file supplies instructions that the operating system uses during

Plug and Play detection, when you use an installer app to set up a device or when you manually install a driver update.

CAUTION

The syntax of Setup Information files is complex, and the intricacies of .inf files can trip up even experienced software developers. If you find that a driver setup routine isn't working properly, you might be tempted to try editing the Setup Information file to work around the hang-up. Trust us: That approach is almost certain to fail. In fact, by tinkering with .inf files to install a driver that's not certified to be compatible with your hardware, you run the risk of corrupting registry settings and making your system unstable.

When Windows completes installation of a driver package, it performs the tasks specified by the Setup Information file and copies the driver files to %SystemRoot%\System32\Drivers.

Inside OUT

For Windows 11, signed drivers only

For all editions of Windows 11, all kernel-mode drivers must be submitted to Microsoft and digitally signed by the Windows Hardware Dev Center Dashboard portal. (Kernel-mode drivers run at the same level of privilege as Windows itself, as opposed to user-mode drivers, which run in the context of the currently signed-in user and cannot cause the system to crash.) In addition, any drivers submitted to Microsoft must be signed by a valid Extended Validation Code Signing Certificate—a higher-cost option that provides extra assurance about the identity of a software publisher.

The net effect of these requirements is to make it extremely difficult for malware to be delivered as part of a driver update.

Driver signing establishes an initial threshold of trust, but by itself it's not necessarily an indicator of quality. For that, you need to look at the signature a little more closely.

The highest level of quality is found with drivers that have passed compatibility and reliability tests for that category of device, as defined in Microsoft's Hardware Lab Kit. Those devices earn the right to use the Windows logo and can be included on Microsoft's Certified Products List.

Hardware developers who simply want to deliver a signed driver to their customers can submit the driver to Microsoft and "attest" to its quality rather than submitting actual test results. The Attested Signing Service signature is different from the one for a logo-certified device, but Windows 11 treats them the same, allowing either type of signed driver to be installed by any user with no prompts.

Getting useful information from Device Manager

The more you know about individual hardware devices and their associated driver software, the more likely you are to make short work of troubleshooting problems or configuring advanced features for a device. In every case, your starting point is Device Manager, a graphical utility that provides detailed information about all installed hardware, along with controls you can use to configure devices, assign resources, and set advanced options.

> **NOTE**
>
> In Windows 11, Device Manager also includes categories that don't represent actual hardware—print queues, for example, or anything under the Software Devices heading. In this section, we focus only on physical hardware devices and their associated drivers.

The easiest way to open Device Manager (Devmgmt.msc) is to right-click the Start button (or press Windows key + X) and then click the Device Manager shortcut on the Quick Link menu. Alternatively, type **device** in the search box and then click the Device Manager entry from the top of the results list. (Device Manager is also available as a snap-in under the System Tools heading in the fully stocked Computer Management console.)

As Figure 13-1 shows, Device Manager is organized as a hierarchical list that inventories every piece of hardware within or connected to your computer. The default view shows devices by type.

Figure 13-1   Click the arrow to the left of any category in Device Manager to expand or collapse the list of individual devices within that category.

To view information about a specific device, double-click its entry in Device Manager's list of installed devices. Each device has its own multitabbed properties dialog. Most hardware devices include a selection of tabs, including General and Driver. The General tab lists basic facts about the device, including the device name and type, the name of its manufacturer, and its current status, as in the example in Figure 13-2.

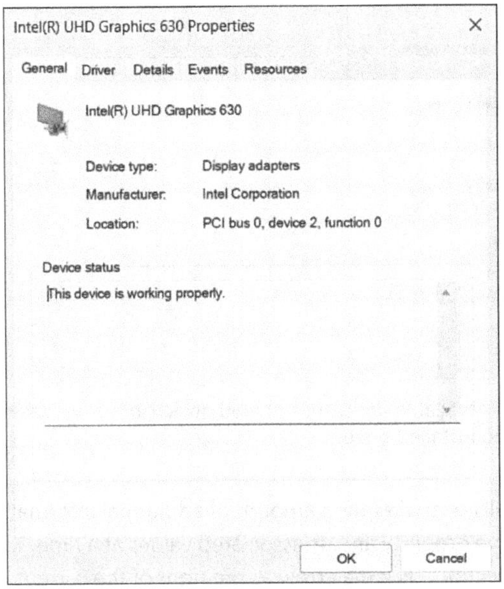

Figure 13-2   The General tab supplies basic information about a device and indicates whether it's currently functioning properly.

The Driver tab, shown in Figure 13-3, lists version information about the currently installed driver for the selected device. Although the information shown here is sparse, it covers the essentials. You can tell at a glance who supplied the driver, and you can see who digitally signed it; you can also determine the date and version number of the driver, which is important when considering whether you should download and install an available update.

Clicking the Driver Details button on the Driver tab leads to another dialog that lists the names and locations of all files associated with that device and its drivers. Selecting any file name from this list displays details for that file in the lower portion of the dialog. (We get to the other buttons in the next section.)

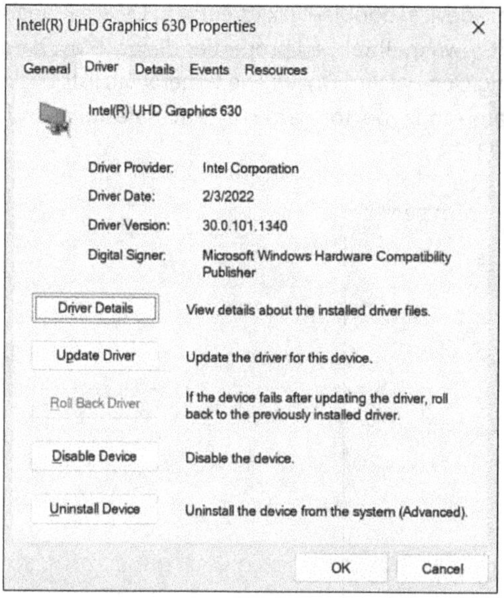

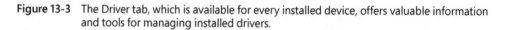

Figure 13-3   The Driver tab, which is available for every installed device, offers valuable information and tools for managing installed drivers.

Click the Details tab for a potentially overwhelming amount of additional information, arranged in a dialog in which you can see one property and its associated values at a time. To see the full list of properties available for inspection, click the arrow to the right of the current entry in the Property box; Figure 13-4 shows the typically dense result.

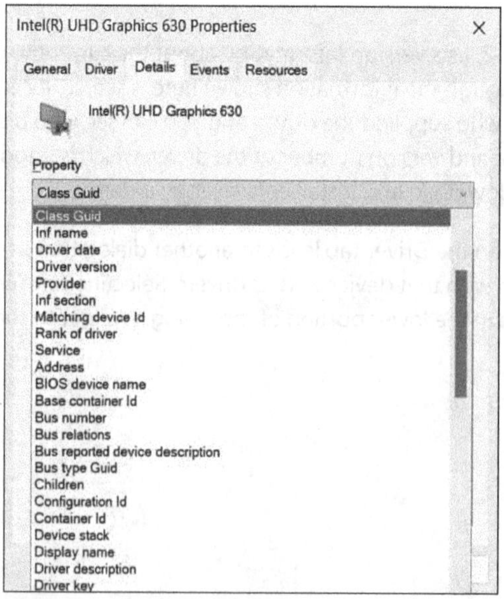

Figure 13-4   Most device properties you can select from this list return obscure details, but a few are useful for troubleshooting purposes.

Choosing a property tucks the list away and displays the value or values associated with that property, as in the example shown in Figure 13-5, which lists the Plug and Play Hardware IDs associated with the selected device.

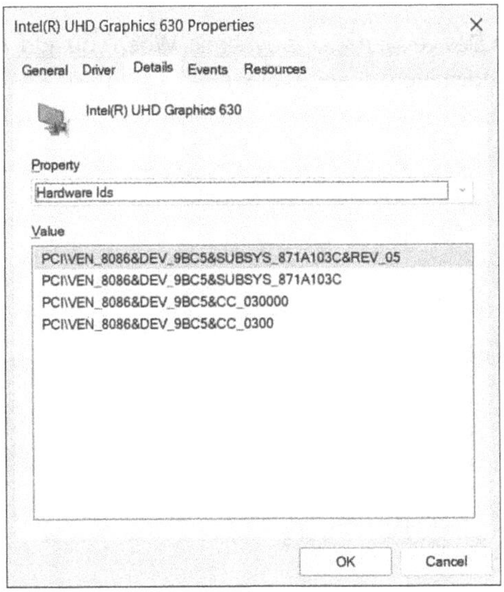

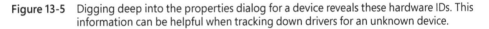

Figure 13-5   Digging deep into the properties dialog for a device reveals these hardware IDs. This information can be helpful when tracking down drivers for an unknown device.

TROUBLESHOOTING

Device Manager shows an unknown device

Most modern hardware built for Windows 7 or later just works with Windows 11. But occasionally you might find mysterious entries under the Other Devices heading in Device Manager, with few or no details, no associated drivers, and no clue about what to do next. This problem is most likely to appear after you perform a clean install of Windows 11 on a device originally designed for an earlier Windows version, but the issue can also occur with older external hardware.

You can often get important clues by opening the properties dialog for the device and looking on the Details tab. The Hardware IDs property, in particular, can be invaluable. The first three characters, followed by a backslash, identify the bus to which the device is connected: USB or PCI, for example. The string VID_ followed by a number is a Vendor ID code; PID_ is a Product ID code; REV_ is the revision code. Use your favorite search engine, entering the first value as a search term, to identify the vendor that made the device, which might help to narrow your search; search for a combination of the first two values to identify a specific device.

In addition to this basic information, the Properties dialog for a given device can include any number of custom tabs. The wireless network adapter in the laptop PC shown in Figure 13-6, for example, adds a custom tab (Advanced) that you can use to configure the device at the hardware level—such as setting allowed wireless modes.

By design, the information displayed in Device Manager is dynamic. When you add, remove, or reconfigure a device, the information shown here changes as well.

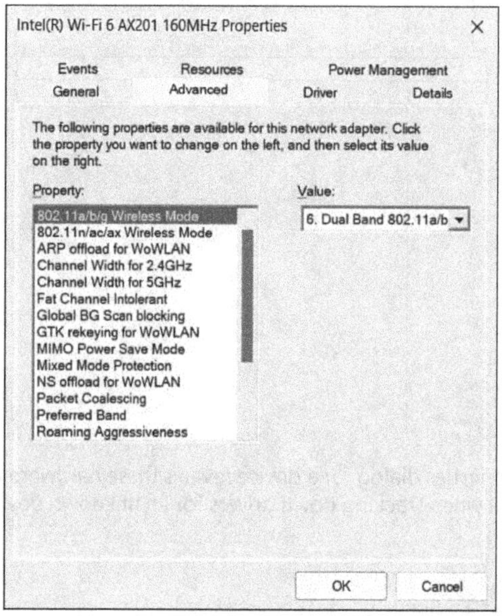

Figure 13-6   You can configure advanced properties for some devices, such as the allowed wireless modes for this network adapter, using Device Manager.

Enabling and disabling devices

You can temporarily disable any device listed in Device Manager. You might choose this option if you're certain you won't need an installed device under normal conditions, but you want to keep it available just in case. On a desktop PC with a permanent wired Ethernet connection, for example, you can keep a Wi-Fi adapter installed but disabled. That configuration gives you the option to enable the device and use the wireless adapter to connect to a hotspot on a mobile device if the wired network is temporarily unavailable.

Right-click any active entry in Device Manager to see a shortcut menu with a Disable Device command. To identify any device that's currently disabled, look for the black, downward-pointing arrow over its icon in Device Manager, as shown in Figure 13-7. To turn a disabled device back on, right-click its entry in Device Manager and then click Enable Device.

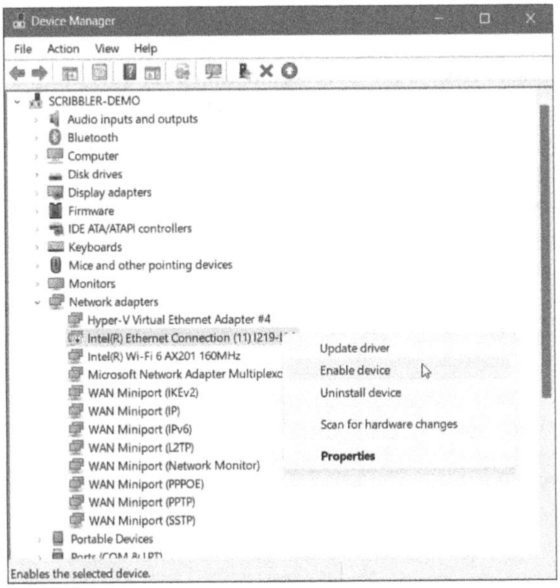

Figure 13-7   Use this shortcut menu in Device Manager to temporarily disable a device and then enable it the next time it's needed.

Adjusting advanced device settings

As we mentioned earlier, some devices include specialized tabs in the properties dialog available from Device Manager. You use the controls on these additional tabs to change advanced settings and properties for devices. For example:

- Network cards, modems, input devices, and USB hubs often include a Power Management tab you can use to control whether the device can force the computer to wake up from Sleep mode. This option is useful if you have fax capabilities enabled for a modem (yes, some businesses still use faxes and modems) or if you use the Remote Desktop feature over the internet on a machine that isn't always running at full power. On both portable and desktop computers, you can also use this option to allow Windows to turn off a device to save power.

- The Volumes tab for a disk drive contains no information when you first display the properties dialog for that device. Click the Populate button to read the volume information for the selected disk, as shown in Figure 13-8, and click the Properties button to check the disk for errors, run the Defrag utility, or perform other maintenance tasks. Although you can perform these same tasks by right-clicking a drive icon in File Explorer, this option might be useful in situations where you have multiple hard disks installed and you suspect that one of those disks is having mechanical problems. Using this option, you can quickly see which physical disk a given volume is stored on.

CHAPTER 13

CAUTION

DVD drives offer an option to change the DVD region, which controls which discs can be played on that drive. The DVD Region setting actually increments a counter on the physical drive itself, and that counter can be changed only a limited number of times. Be extremely careful with this setting, or you might end up losing the capability to play any regionally encoded DVDs in your collection on that device.

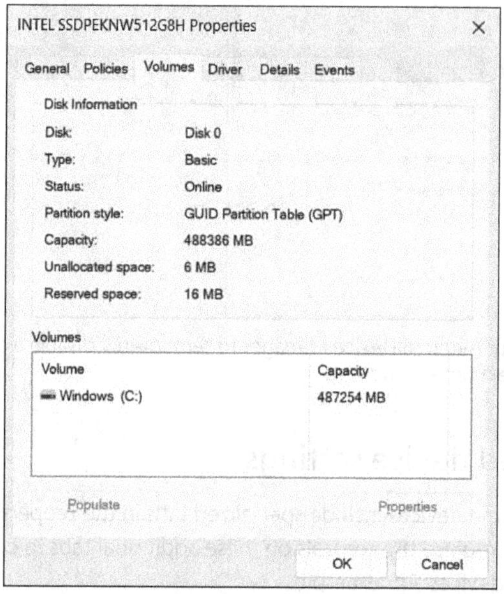

Figure 13-8   After you click the Populate button, the Volumes tab lists volumes on the selected drive. Select any volume and click Properties for full access to trouble-shooting and maintenance tools.

- When working with network cards, you can often choose from multiple performance-related settings on an Advanced tab. Randomly tinkering with these settings is almost always counterproductive; however, you might be able to solve specific performance or connectivity problems by adjusting settings as directed by the device manufacturer or a Microsoft Support article.

Setting up Bluetooth devices

Bluetooth is one of those rare standards that passes the "it just works" test consistently. These days, virtually every portable device supports Bluetooth for wirelessly connecting headsets and pairing fitness devices.

Most desktop PCs include Bluetooth support, making it possible to connect wireless keyboards and mice. Bluetooth technology also works with the Phone Link app on Windows 11, which enables you to make and receive calls through an Android smartphone using your PC's audio hardware.

Recent feature updates have added a bevy of new features designed to make Windows 11 devices work better with Bluetooth LE devices such as fitness monitors. In Settings, the Bluetooth & Devices page provides a single interface, from which you can manage Bluetooth accessories, wireless docks, Xbox wireless controllers, and media devices.

You use the Bluetooth & Devices page in Settings to manage your Bluetooth devices, as displayed in Figure 13-9.

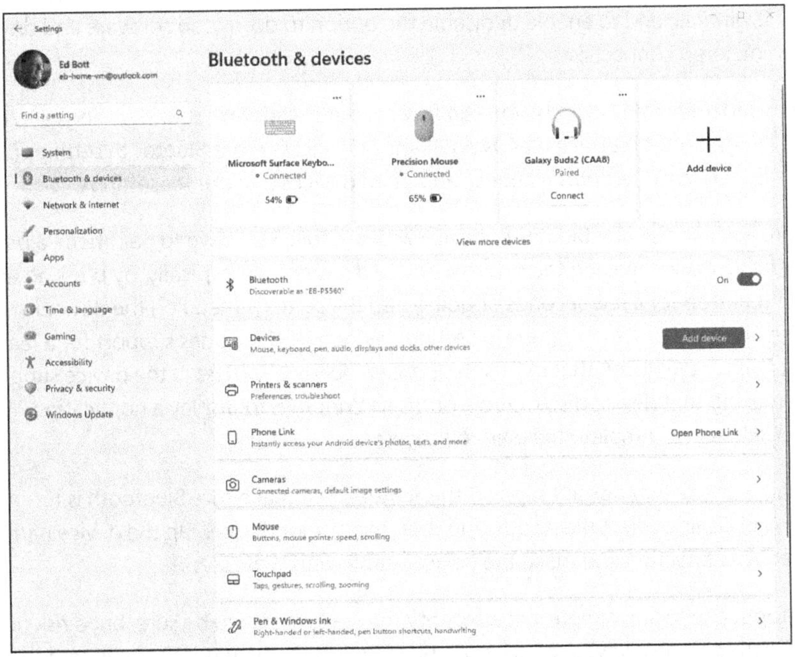

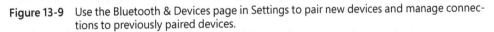

Figure 13-9   Use the Bluetooth & Devices page in Settings to pair new devices and manage connections to previously paired devices.

The Bluetooth & Devices page provides a good deal of information about your devices. For example, you can check the current battery charge of powered devices, as shown in Figure 13-9. From this page, you can perform the following tasks:

- Review paired devices and their current status

- Add or remove devices

- Enable or disable the Bluetooth adapter

- Access links for connected peripherals, such as printers and scanners, cameras, touchpad, mice, and other devices

- Access and configure Phone Link for your Android phone

- Select the View More Devices link

When you select View More Devices, Windows displays all your paired and connected devices by category: Input, Audio, and Other Devices. There are also sections for Device Settings and Related Settings:

- Device Settings provides options to enable or disable notifications for connections using Swift Pair, and to enable or disable the option to download software and drivers over metered connections.

- Under Related Settings, you can access your computer's sound settings and display settings, send or receive files using Bluetooth, access more Bluetooth settings (such as discovery and alert notifications), and open devices and printer settings.

Before you can use one Bluetooth device with another, you have to pair them, a process that generally involves making the external device discoverable (typically, by pressing and holding a pairing button for a few seconds or going into the settings menu on the device) and switching to the Bluetooth & Devices page in Settings. Windows 11 includes support for a feature called Swift Pair for Bluetooth that makes this process nearly effortless. If the device supports Swift Pair, making that device discoverable prompts Windows to display a notification. You can then click Connect to complete the pairing process.

To pair a device that doesn't support this feature, first make sure Bluetooth is turned on; then click Add Device, select Bluetooth, and then select your device. Tap the device name to complete the connection and make the device usable with Windows 11.

Bluetooth connections represent a security risk—a low one, to be sure, but a risk nonetheless. That's why pairing a keyboard, for example, requires that you use the keyboard to enter a code from the PC's screen. Without that precaution, an attacker might be able to connect a wireless keyboard to your computer without your knowledge and then use it to steal data or run unauthorized and potentially dangerous software.

As mentioned earlier, the Bluetooth & Devices page in Settings contains an on/off switch for the Bluetooth adapter. On mobile PCs, this is a power-saving feature. On a desktop PC without a touchscreen, be careful before disabling Bluetooth, because doing so could render your wireless keyboard and mouse—and thus the entire PC—unusable. The only cure, in that case, is to plug in a wired keyboard or mouse and turn the setting back on.

Managing USB devices

Universal serial bus, more commonly known as USB, is one of the oldest and most reliable Plug and Play standards in the world. Through the years, the USB standard has progressed from version 1.1 to 2.0 to 3.2 to USB4, with the jump to USB 3.1 and beyond making a monumental difference in the speed of data transfer between USB-connected devices (up to 20 Gb/sec for USB 3.2 Gen 2x2 devices).

In an unfortunate bit of timing that has inspired some confusion, a new USB Type-C connector arrived at the same time as USB 3.1 began to appear in high-end computing equipment, including Microsoft's Surface Laptop, Surface Pro, and Surface Go models. With the help of so-called alternate modes (and appropriate adapters), you can use a USB Type-C port to connect to devices using HDMI, DisplayPort, Thunderbolt, and Mobile High-Definition Link (MHL) connections.

One popular USB Type-C category is the multiport hub, which accepts HDMI and DisplayPort cables, RJ-45 plugs from wired networks, traditional USB Type-A cables, and even laptop-grade power supplies, transforming a portable PC into a fully connected desktop PC through a single USB Type-C input. The USB Type-C connector is reversible (no more flipping the USB plug three times until you find the right orientation). These new connectors are compatible with older USB devices but require an adapter.

NOTE

USB Type-C connectors and cables typically support at least USB 3.1 and can connect to older USB devices using adapters. However, because the USB Type-C specification mandates support only for the older, slower USB 2.0 standard, you have no guarantee of USB 3.1 compatibility. This is most likely to be a problem with off-brand devices that were released as part of the first wave of USB Type-C support.

All USB devices are Plug and Play compatible. Knowing the types of connectors and the highest standard supported on your device can help ensure that you avoid compatibility hassles and carry the right cables.

Updating and uninstalling drivers

If you're having a hardware problem that you suspect is caused by a device driver, your first stop should be Device Manager. Open the Properties dialog for the device, and use the following buttons on the Driver tab to perform maintenance tasks:

- **Update Driver** This choice opens the Update Drivers dialog, which we describe in the next section.

- **Roll Back Driver**   This option uninstalls the most recent manually updated driver and rolls back your system configuration to the previously installed driver. This option is available from Safe Mode if you need to remove a driver that's causing blue-screen (Stop) errors. Unlike System Restore, this option affects only the selected device. If you have never updated the selected driver or if you updated it through Windows Update, this option is unavailable.

- **Uninstall Device**   This button completely removes driver files and registry settings for the selected device. For driver packages you downloaded and installed separately, it also offers the option to completely remove the associated driver files. Use this capability to remove a driver that you suspect was incorrectly installed, and then reinstall the original driver or install an updated driver.

Inside OUT

Create a safety net before tinkering with drivers

When you install a new hardware driver, Windows automatically attempts to create a new System Restore checkpoint. That doesn't mean it will be successful, especially if System Restore is turned off or if a problem with your System Restore settings has caused this utility to suspend operations temporarily. To make certain you can roll back your changes if necessary, set a new System Restore checkpoint manually before making any kind of hardware configuration change. (For more details, see "Rolling back to a previous restore point" in Chapter 15, "Troubleshooting, backup, and recovery.")

Managing automatic driver updates

Microsoft uses the Windows Update mechanism to deliver drivers for many devices. Using this feature, you can plug in a new device with relative confidence it will work without extra effort on your part. You also can use it to automatically receive updated drivers, which typically fix reliability, stability, and compatibility problems.

In earlier versions of Windows, it was important that you considered the impact of automatically installing driver updates as part of your Windows update strategy. In fact, the recommendation was to avoid doing so, and instead, to manually update drivers only when needed.

However, updating drivers through Windows Update is now recommended. The process has become significantly more reliable, and it's highly unlikely that you'll experience problems with updated drivers that are installed from Windows Update.

NOTE

Many driver updates are marked as optional and can be reviewed in Settings > Windows Update > Advanced Options > Optional Updates> Driver Updates. In some cases, these drivers are older than the ones you currently have installed and should only be installed if the newer versions are causing problems. If you don't want to install optional driver updates, you don't have to. If you do, select the updates you want to install and click Download & Install.

Updating a device driver manually

Microsoft and third-party device manufacturers frequently issue upgrades to device drivers. In some cases, the updates enable new features; in other cases, the newer version swats a bug that might or might not affect you. New Microsoft-signed drivers are often (but not always) delivered through Windows Update. Other drivers are available only by downloading them from the device manufacturer's website. Kernel-mode drivers must still be digitally signed before they can be installed.

If the new driver includes an installer, run that app to copy the necessary files to your system's driver repository. Then start the update process by opening Device Manager, selecting the entry for the device you want to upgrade, and clicking the Update Driver button on the toolbar or the Update Driver option on the right-click shortcut menu. (You can also click Update Driver on the Driver tab of the Properties dialog for the device.)

That action opens the dialog shown in Figure 13-10.

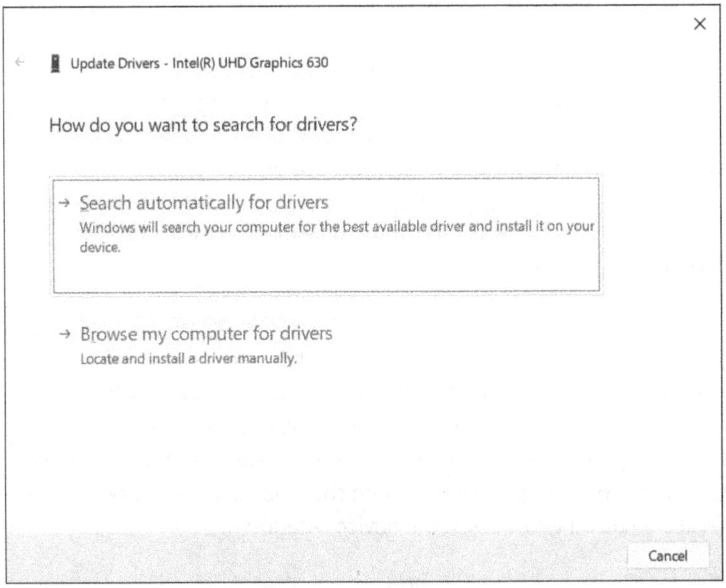

CHAPTER 13

Figure 13-10   When manually updating a driver, try the automatic option first unless you want to select a specific driver you previously downloaded.

Click Search Automatically For Drivers if you know that the driver file is available on a removable media device. Click Browse My Computer For Drivers to enter the location of a downloaded driver package or choose from a list of available drivers in the driver store folder. Clicking the Browse My Computer For Drivers option opens a dialog like the one shown in Figure 13-11, with two options for manually selecting a driver.

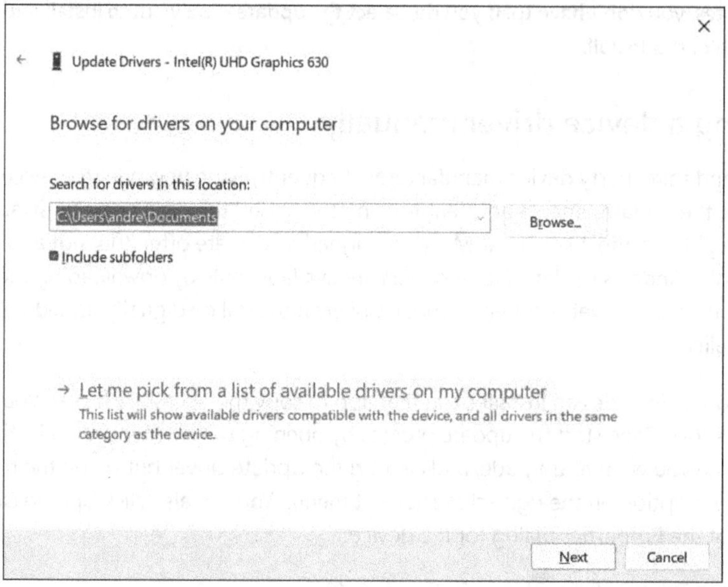

Figure 13-11   If you've downloaded a driver package that doesn't include an installer, select its location here to allow the update to proceed.

If you've downloaded the driver files to a known location or copied them to removable storage, click Browse to select that location, and then click Next to continue. (If you have a copy of the FileRepository folder from a previous Windows installation on the same hardware, you can choose that location.) With the Include Subfolders option selected, as it is by default, the driver update software will do a thorough search of the specified location, looking for a Setup Information file that matches the hardware ID for the selected device; if it finds a match, it installs the specified driver software automatically.

Use the second option, Let Me Pick From A List Of Available Drivers On My Computer, if you know that the driver software you need is already in the local driver store. In general, choosing this option presents a single driver for you to choose. In some cases, as in the example in Figure 13-12, you can see previous versions of a driver, with the option to replace a new driver with an older one for troubleshooting purposes. If you need to install an alternative driver version that isn't listed, clear the Show Compatible Hardware checkbox and then choose a driver from an expanded list of all matching devices in the device category.

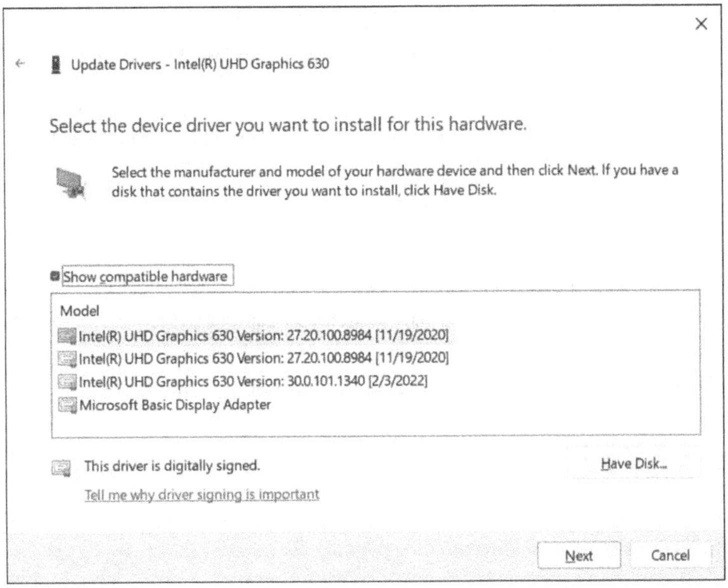

Figure 13-12 Clear the Show Compatible Hardware checkbox only if you're absolutely certain that Plug and Play has selected the wrong driver and you want to manually install a different driver.

Inside OUT

Make sure that update is really an update

How do you know whether a downloaded version is newer than the currently installed driver on your system? A good set of release notes should provide this information and is the preferred option for determining version information. In the absence of documentation, file dates offer some clues, but they're not always reliable. A better indicator is to inspect the properties of the driver files themselves. After unzipping the downloaded driver files to a folder on a local or network drive, right-click any file with a .dll or .sys extension and choose Properties. On the Version tab, you should be able to find version details about the proposed driver replacement, which you can compare with the version details shown in Device Manager for the current driver.

Rolling back to a previous driver version

Unfortunately, manually updated drivers can sometimes cause new problems that are worse than the woes they were intended to fix. This is especially true if you're experimenting with prerelease versions of new drivers. If your troubleshooting leads you to suspect that a newly installed driver is the cause of recent crashes or system instability, consider removing that driver and rolling your system configuration back to the previously installed driver.

To do this, open Device Manager and double-click the entry for the device you want to roll back. Then go to the Driver tab and click Roll Back Driver. The procedure that follows is straightforward and self-explanatory.

NOTE

You can also roll back a driver indirectly by performing a System Restore. Assuming system protection is enabled on your computer, you can use System Restore to apply a complete computer configuration from an earlier time. Keep in mind, though, that this rolls back the entire computer configuration rather than just the driver.

Uninstalling a driver

There are at least three circumstances under which you might want to completely remove a device driver from your system:

- You're no longer using the device, and you want to prevent the previously installed drivers from loading or using any resources.

- You've determined that the drivers available for the device are not stable enough to use on your system.

- The currently installed driver is not working correctly, and you want to reinstall it from scratch.

Inside OUT

Manage Plug and Play drivers

Removing and reinstalling the driver for a removable Plug and Play device requires a little extra effort. Because these drivers are loaded and unloaded dynamically, you can remove the driver only if the device in question is plugged in. Use the Uninstall button to remove the driver before unplugging the device. To reinstall the device driver without unplugging the device, open Device Manager and choose Action, Scan For Hardware Changes.

To remove a driver permanently, open Device Manager, right-click the entry for the device, and click Uninstall Device. (If the entry for the device in question is already open, click the Driver tab and click Uninstall Device.) Click OK when prompted to confirm that you want to remove the driver, and Windows removes the files and registry settings completely. You can now unplug the device.

If you installed the driver files from a downloaded file, the Uninstall Device dialog includes a checkbox (shown in Figure 13-13) that you can select to attempt to remove the files from the driver store as well. This prevents a troublesome driver from being inadvertently reinstalled when you reinsert the device or restart the computer.

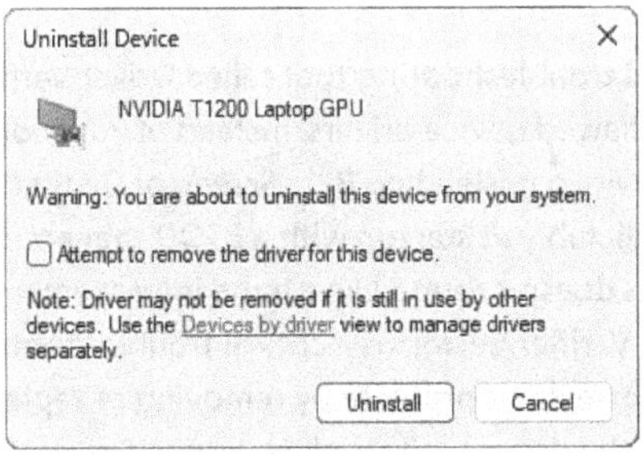

Figure 13-13 Be sure to select this checkbox to attempt to remove a troublesome driver so that it doesn't reinstall itself automatically.

Note that you can't delete driver software that's included with Windows 11.

Inside OUT

What happened to the Windows Show/Hide Updates tool?

If Windows Update delivers a problematic device driver, removing it is only a temporary fix. The next time Windows checks for new updates, it downloads and installs that same driver.

Longtime Windows administrators might remember the Windows Show/Hide Updates Tool, which was designed to work around this dilemma. Delivered as a Troubleshooting Pack file with the name Wushowhide.diagcab, this utility allowed Windows administrators to explicitly exclude drivers and other updates from downloading again.

Unfortunately, this tool is no longer available on the Microsoft download website, and support articles that reference it also contain links that no longer work. Although it's possible to discover alternative download sites for this utility, we don't recommend looking for them.

CHAPTER 13

TROUBLESHOOTING

Sporadic hardware errors

When your computer acts unpredictably, chances are good that defective hardware or a buggy device driver is at fault.

In those circumstances, using a powerful troubleshooting tool called Driver Verifier (Verifier.exe) is a terrific way to identify flawed device drivers. Instead of your computer locking up at a most inopportune time with a misleading Blue Screen of Death (BSOD), Driver Verifier stops your computer predictably at startup with a BSOD that accurately explains the true problem. Although this doesn't sound like a huge improvement (your system still won't work, after all), Driver Verifier performs a critical troubleshooting step: identifying the problem. You can then correct the problem by removing or replacing the offending driver. (If you're satisfied that the driver really is okay despite Driver Verifier Manager's warning, you can turn off Driver Verifier for all drivers or for a specific driver. Any driver that Driver Verifier chokes on should be regarded with suspicion, but some legitimate drivers bend the rules without causing problems.)

Driver Verifier works at startup to thoroughly exercise each driver. It performs many of the same tests that are run as part of the Windows certification and signing process, such as checking for the way the driver accesses memory.

Beware: If Driver Verifier finds a nonconforming driver—even one that doesn't seem to be causing any problems—it will prevent your system from starting. Use Driver Verifier only if you're having problems. In other words, if it ain't broke...

To begin working with Driver Verifier, open an elevated Command Prompt window and type **verifier**. In the Driver Verifier Manager dialog, shown in Figure 13-14, select Create Standard Settings. (If you want to assess current conditions before proceeding, select the last option: Display Information About The Currently Verified Drivers.)

When you click Next, the Driver Verifier Manager displays a list of all currently installed drivers that match the conditions you specified. Note that the list might contain a mix of hardware drivers and some file-system filter drivers, such as those used by antivirus programs, backup utilities, CD- and DVD-burning apps, and other low-level system software.

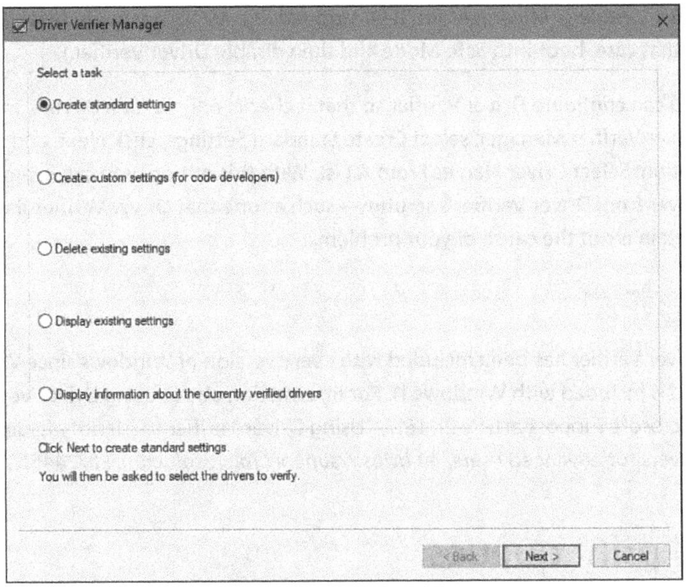

Figure 13-14   The top choice in Driver Verifier Manager creates a list of all currently installed drivers, which you can use for troubleshooting.

At this point, you have two choices:

- Go through the list, make a note of all drivers identified, and then click Cancel. No changes are made to your system configuration; all you've done is gather a list of suspicious drivers, which you can then try to remove or disable manually.

- Click Finish to complete the wizard and restart your computer. Don't choose this option unless you're prepared to deal with the consequences, as explained in the remainder of this sidebar.

If you choose the second option and your computer stops with a blue screen when you next sign in, you've identified a problem driver. The error message includes the name of the offending driver and an error code.

To resolve the problem, boot into Safe Mode using Windows 11's Recovery Environment and disable or uninstall the problem driver. Then check with the device vendor to get a working driver that you can install.

To disable Driver Verifier so that it no longer performs verification checks at startup, run Driver Verifier Manager again and select Delete Existing Settings in the initial dialog. Alternatively, at a command prompt, type **verifier /reset**. (If you haven't yet solved the driver problem, of course, you'll be stopped at a BSOD, unable to disable Driver Verifier. In that case, boot into Safe Mode and then disable Driver Verifier.)

You can configure Driver Verifier so that it checks only certain drivers. To do that, open Driver Verifier Manager, select Create Standard Settings, click Next, and select the last option: Select Driver Names From A List. With this option, you can exempt a particular driver from Driver Verifier's scrutiny—such as one that Driver Verifier flags but you're certain is not the cause of your problem.

NOTE

Driver Verifier has been included with every version of Windows since Windows 2000 and is included with Windows 11. For information about using Driver Verifier, see the Microsoft Support article 244617, "Using Driver Verifier to identify issues with Windows drivers for advanced users," at *https://support.microsoft.com/kb/244617*.

Printers and print queues

To install a modern printer that plugs into a USB port on the PC where you plan to use it, just connect the device. Plug and Play does the rest of the work. (See "Installing a new Plug and Play device" earlier in this chapter.)

NOTE

Although it's nearly certain there are still some non–Plug and Play printers out there, we don't cover manual connection options for legacy devices in this book.

Wireless printers that connect over Wi-Fi or by using Bluetooth also support Plug and Play. Follow the manufacturer's instructions to complete the wireless connection, or skip ahead a few pages to our explanation of the Add A Printer option.

> ➤ You can share a printer for use by other users on the same local network. Follow the instructions in "Sharing files, printers, and other resources over a local network" in Chapter 11, "Windows networking."

To configure a printer or work with documents in a print queue, go to Settings > Bluetooth & Devices > Printers & Scanners. You can then review the available devices, as shown in Figure 13-15.

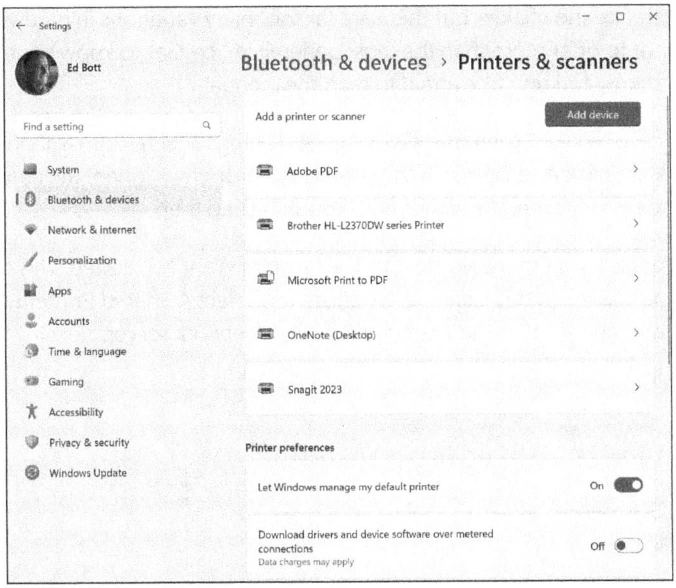

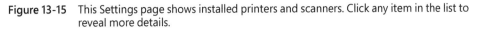

Figure 13-15   This Settings page shows installed printers and scanners. Click any item in the list to reveal more details.

To review printer options, select a printer. You can then use the following options to manage the printer:

- Open Print Queue takes you to a list of pages waiting to print.

- Print Test Page enables you to send a test page to the selected printer.

- Run The Troubleshooter forces Windows to check the printer for issues and to suggest solutions to any detected problems.

- Printer Properties enables you to review the detailed configuration of the printer, including Sharing, Ports, Device Settings, Color Management, Security, and Advanced.

- Printing Preferences lets you review or change orientation, page order, pages per sheet, and paper source—plus many other settings.

- Hardware Properties displays access to Details and Events about the printer.

- Device Information displays additional information about the selected printer, including manufacturer, model, serial number, and if network connected, useful data such as MAC address and IP address.

Printers aren't exactly like snowflakes, but there are far too many variations in hardware and software design for us to offer more than the most general advice: Get to know your printer by inspecting these settings, and don't be afraid to read the manual.

To make a wireless or networked printer available, go to Settings > Bluetooth & Devices > Printers & Scanners and click Add Device. If the planets are properly aligned, the autodiscovery software might locate your printer and walk you through setting it up.

If you're not so lucky, click Add Manually next to The Printer I Want Isn't Listed. This opens the dialog shown in Figure 13-16. In this example, we chose the Select A Shared Printer By Name option, clicked Browse, and located the shared printer on a network server.

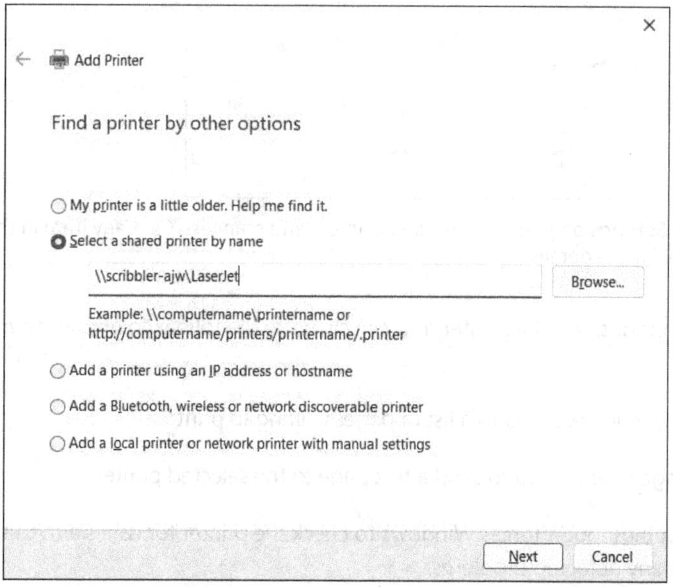

Figure 13-16   The Add Printer Wizard offers numerous paths to connect to a printer, especially those that are available over a network.

Among the "other options" available on this page in the Add Printer Wizard is one that you can use to connect to a network printer using its Universal Naming Convention (UNC) name. The device shown in Figure 13-16, for example, is connected to a printer named Laserjet on a server named scribbler-ajw, making its UNC address \\scribbler-ajw\Laserjet. You can also use an IP address for a device that has a permanently assigned address, and you can enlist the help of a wizard to connect a wireless or Bluetooth printer.

Inside OUT

Find a printer's TCP/IP address or host name

Often the easiest way to determine the TCP/IP address or host name for a printer is to use the printer's control panel to print a configuration page, which usually includes this information.

One of the simplest ways to connect to a shared network printer doesn't involve any wizards at all. Just use File Explorer to browse to the network computer (entering and saving credentials for the share, if necessary), where you should see an entry for any shared printer available to you. Double-click that icon to begin the process of connecting to that printer. Because Windows requires a local copy of the network printer's driver, you may need an administrator's credentials.

Inside OUT

Use a compatible driver

If you can't find a driver that's specifically designed for your printer, you might be able to get away with using another driver. Check the hardware documentation to find out whether the printer emulates a more popular model, such as a Hewlett-Packard LaserJet. If so, choose that printer driver, and then print some test documents after completing setup. You might lose access to some advanced features available with your model of printer, but this strategy should allow you to perform basic printing tasks.

Configuring displays and graphics adapters

On a desktop or portable PC with a single screen (and, when connecting to an external monitor, the proper cable), you shouldn't need to do anything to configure your display. All modern display adapters deliver up-to-date drivers via Windows Update, and the display is capable of configuring itself as soon as it's connected. In this chapter, we cover a handful of scenarios when you might need to review and adjust these settings manually.

Changing display settings

As we noted earlier, Windows typically does a good job of configuring display settings. To review them, go to Settings > System > Display. Figure 13-17 shows this Settings page, with display options for a Surface Laptop.

The Brightness settings at the top of this dialog are typically available only on a laptop PC. We discuss the Night Light settings a bit later in this section. Pay particular attention to the settings under the Scale & Layout heading:

- **Scale**   On high-resolution monitors, you can increase or decrease the apparent size of apps and text, a process known technically as *scaling*. Here, too, Windows recommends a scaling factor based on the size of the display and the resolution. You might choose a larger or smaller scaling factor for your personal comfort. On a system with a single display, you can adjust the scaling by using a slider below the thumbnail of the current monitor on the Display page in Settings.

➤ We cover scaling in "Making text easier to read" in Chapter 4, "Personalizing Windows 11."

- **Display Resolution**   Every display has a native resolution, one in which the number of physical pixels matches the number of pixels Windows shows. Configuring the display at something other than native resolution generally results in a subpar viewing experience, often with a blurry, stretched display. Figure 13-17 shows a Surface Laptop running at its native resolution of 2256 × 1504 pixels, as indicated by the word "Recommended" in the label. Click that value to open a full list of other supported resolutions. Why would you choose a non-native resolution? One common scenario is projecting to a large display—in a conference room, for example, or to an adapter connected to the HDMI input on a TV. If you choose the option to duplicate displays, you need to set the resolution to match the large monitor or TV, even if it looks distorted on your laptop screen.

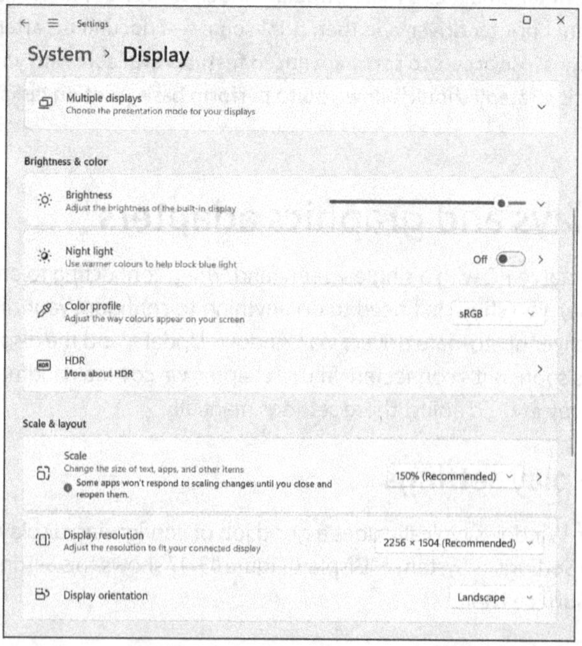

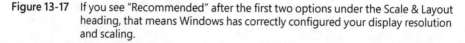

Figure 13-17   If you see "Recommended" after the first two options under the Scale & Layout heading, that means Windows has correctly configured your display resolution and scaling.

TROUBLESHOOTING

Display options stop at 1920 by 1080 even though your monitor supports higher resolutions

The most likely cause of this problem is an HDMI connection that's incapable of handling the desired resolution. If either the display adapter or the monitor supports only the HDMI 1.3 standard, you're limited to Full HD (1920 by 1080) resolution. If both ends of the connection support HDMI 1.4 or later, you need to use a High Speed HDMI cable (a standard HDMI cable is limited to Full HD resolution). In most cases, the best workaround is to switch to a different connection, if one is available. The DisplayPort 1.2a standard, which uses mini and full-sized connectors and also works with USB-C adapters using alternative modes, supports 4K (3840 by 2160 or 4096 by 2160) resolutions, and the HDMI 1.4 standard supports 5K displays (5120 by 2880).

- **Display Orientation**   This setting is available on portable devices that can be used as tablets and on external displays that can be rotated 90 degrees for use in portrait mode. For a laptop or desktop computer where the orientation of the display is fixed, changing orientation would result in an odd, mostly unreadable display; thus, this setting is typically unavailable.

An increasingly popular configuration for high-powered portable PCs is the inclusion of two GPUs. Some laptop models, for example, can switch between the power-saving but still capable built-in graphics and a more powerful discrete GPU based on an Nvidia or AMD chipset. If you own a PC that includes two GPUs, Windows 11 allows you to associate a GPU with a specific app.

To configure custom per-GPU options, go to Settings > System > Display and click Graphics. That opens the Graphics page shown in Figure 13-18. As you can see, we've already customized this device to give an extra GPU boost to the Clipchamp video editor app.

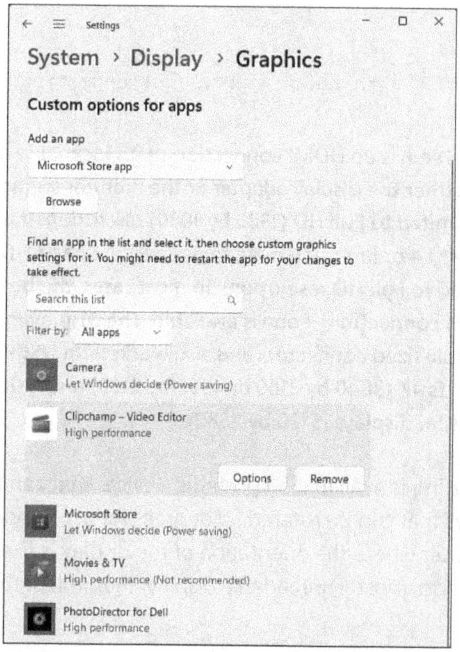

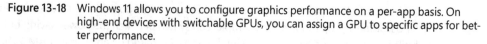

Figure 13-18   Windows 11 allows you to configure graphics performance on a per-app basis. On high-end devices with switchable GPUs, you can assign a GPU to specific apps for better performance.

The technique to add an app to this list varies. For a legacy desktop app, choose Desktop App, and then click Browse and locate the executable file for that program. For a Windows app delivered through the Store, choose Microsoft Store App and then select the app from the resulting drop-down list.

Click Add to create a new entry on the list for your selected app, and then click Options to open the Graphics Preference dialog shown in Figure 13-19. On systems with multiple GPUs, the discrete adapter is for high performance, and the onboard graphics are for power saving. Regardless of the graphics hardware, Windows offers three options:

- Let Windows Decide

- Power Saving

- High Performance

The Don't Use Optimizations For Windowed Games checkbox allows you to keep games running at top speed. For older games, you might need to experiment with this option to see its effect.

If you have multiple GPUs, the GPU name appears beneath these options. In Figure 13-19, the computer, a Dell workstation, has a discrete Nvidia graphics adapter assigned for High Performance work with apps like Microsoft's Clipchamp video editor.

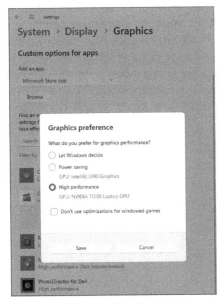

Figure 13-19   Normally, Windows chooses the appropriate GPU settings for an app. To override that choice, choose Power Saving or High Performance from this dialog.

At any time, you can see which GPU is in use for a given app by opening Task Manager and looking at the GPU Engine column on the Performance tab. Click the GPU Engine column heading to sort the list so that all apps currently using either GPU appear at the top of the list.

Controlling scaling on high-DPI displays

So-called high-DPI displays are typically found today on high-end portable PCs. The Microsoft Surface Pro 9, for example, has a screen size of 13 inches (measured diagonally) and a native resolution of 2880 × 1920 pixels. That translates to 267 pixels per inch (a measure sometimes referred to in casual usage as dots per inch, or DPI).

That density is far greater than (typically more than double) the density of a high-resolution desktop display or a budget-priced laptop PC with a similar display size running at a lower native resolution. If you use a high-DPI system at normal (100 percent) scaling, the icons and text will be so small as to be unreadable. That's why, by default, the Surface Pro 9 is configured to run Windows 11 at 200 percent scaling. The result is an impressively sharp display. Everything in the Windows interface and in Windows apps is magnified at twice its normal size, using multiple physical pixels to create each effective pixel (at 200 percent scaling, each effective pixel is made from four physical pixels). The most popular classic desktop apps look great on primary high-DPI displays, as does any desktop app that was built using Windows Presentation Foundation (WPF).

Windows 11 includes display code that improves rendering for some older desktop apps that previously looked a little blurry on high-DPI displays. If you notice that a desktop app isn't scaling properly, you can use another option to change its behavior. Find the app's executable file, right-click to open its properties dialog, click Change High DPI Settings on the Compatibility tab, select the Override High DPI Scaling Behavior setting shown in Figure 13-20, and change it to System (Enhanced). This setting overrides the way the selected app handles DPI scaling, eliminating the use of bitmap stretching and forcing the app to be scaled by Windows:

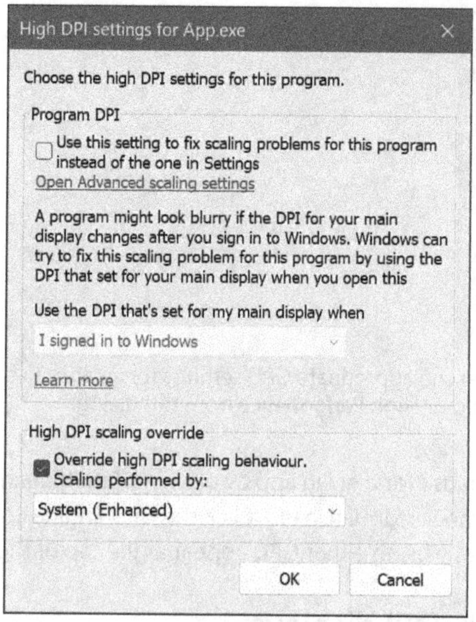

Figure 13-20   Most Windows apps should work just fine on high DPI displays. You might need to adjust the settings shown here for software that was originally written for much older Windows versions.

Windows 11 supports scaling factors from 100 percent all the way to 450 percent, with most elements of the user interface looking crystal-clear even at the highest scaling levels. That includes Start, File Explorer, and the Windows taskbar.

In general, scaling produces a display that looks perfectly natural. In some scenarios, however, scaling issues can cause problems, including blurry text, desktop apps that appear too large or too small, or interface elements such as menus and toolbars that are clipped or overlap.

These types of scaling problems are most likely to occur when you try to change the display scaling dynamically. This can happen in a variety of scenarios: connecting a portable PC with a high-DPI internal display to a larger external monitor, for example, using a video output or a laptop dock; projecting that high-DPI display to a large TV screen; or making a Remote Desktop connection. Any of those scenarios can result in some unfortunate scaling combinations, especially when using desktop apps that weren't written to handle scaling changes gracefully.

When that happens, the only sure cure is to close all running apps, sign out of Windows, and then sign back in. Ironically, the same problem occurs in reverse when you disconnect from the docking station. Microsoft has dedicated some serious engineering resources to solving this annoyance in Windows 11, thankfully.

Using multiple displays

When you attach a second (or third or fourth) display to your computer, the Display page in Settings changes. Thumbnails, one for each attached display, appear in a preview pane like the one shown in Figure 13-21. You can drag the displays to either side of one another (or even move one above the other), adjusting the alignment of displays to match their actual physical alignment, with the goal of having your mouse pointer move naturally between displays without a jarring shift when crossing the bezels.

It's worth noting that the thumbnails have only a casual relationship to the size of the physical displays they represent. In Figure 13-21, for example, display 1 is a Surface Laptop 3 with a 13-inch screen, with a display resolution of 2256 × 1504 and scaling set to 175 percent. Display 2 and display 3 are both external 24-inch monitors. They each have a resolution of 1920 × 1080 and a scaling factor of 125 percent.

If you're working with two or more displays and you're not sure which is which, click the Identify button, which temporarily positions a large number on each display that corresponds to the number on its thumbnail. Note that you can drag the thumbnail for the appropriate display to represent their physical layout on your desk.

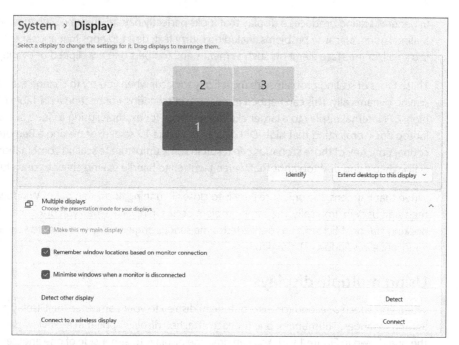

Figure 13-21   With multiple monitors, you can arrange each so that it matches the physical layout. Drag the monitor thumbnail up, down, or to either side of another display's thumbnail.

If you want to duplicate your internal display to an external display, select the dropdown adjacent to Identify, and then choose Duplicate These Displays; other options might be available, depending on how many monitors you have. Select the Multiple Displays tile to display more options. These include the following:

- **Make This My Main Display**   Provides access to the taskbar (although you can configure the taskbar to appear on all displays) and notifications. Even if the taskbar appears on all displays, the system tray area only appears on your main display.

  ## NOTE

  You can configure this taskbar behavior by accessing Settings > Personalization > Taskbar > Taskbar Behaviors. Select Show My Taskbar On All Displays.

- **Remember Window Locations Based On Monitor Connection**   Ensures that when you redock your computer and external monitors are reenabled, your open windows and apps are directed back to their previous displays.

- **Minimize Windows When A Monitor Is Disconnected**   Ensures that any apps on a disconnected display are minimized, rather than being left in a space that might be inaccessible.

You can also select the Detect button to search for other attached displays, or click Connect to locate and connect to wireless displays.

Night Light

The Night Light feature is based on a relatively recent scientific discovery: Blue light suppresses the secretion of melatonin, disrupting circadian rhythms and negatively affecting your sleep. To adjust for this effect, you can turn on the Night Light feature, which favors warm colors and reduces the amount of blue light on a display.

To enable this feature, go to Settings > System > Display and, under the Brightness & Color heading, slide the Night Light switch to On. To make fine-grained adjustments in how this feature works, click Night Light, which opens the page shown in Figure 13-22.

The Strength slider allows you to fine-tune how the display looks by adjusting the values of red and yellow. Use the Schedule Night Light settings to automatically turn on Night Light at sunset and turn it off after sunrise, based on the current location; as an alternative, you can assign specific hours based on your sleep schedule or use the button at the top of the dialog to turn the feature on or off manually. (You might choose to ignore the schedule if you're on a transcontinental flight in a darkened airplane cabin, for example.)

And one major caveat: Obviously, turning on the Night Light feature severely distorts the color of your display; if you're editing photos or videos or doing any other kind of work that depends on accurate color fidelity, don't use this feature.

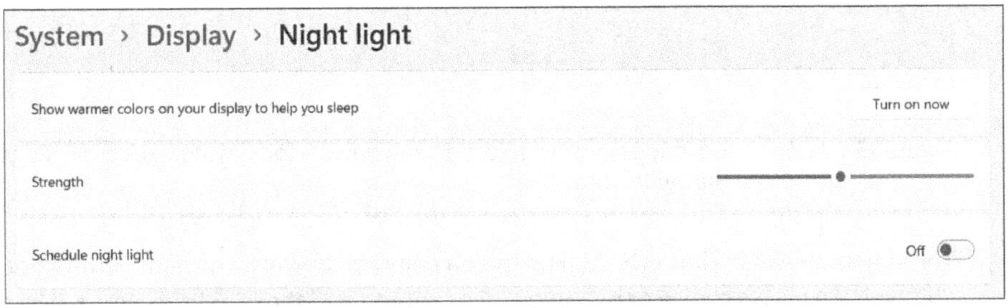

System › Display › **Night light**

Show warmer colors on your display to help you sleep   Turn on now

Strength

Schedule night light   Off

Figure 13-22   If you regularly check your email and perform work-related tasks right before bedtime, consider scheduling Windows 11 to reduce the amount of blue light in the display at night.

Speakers, microphones, and headsets

Windows 11 supports a broad array of high-quality audio outputs that are capable of delivering multichannel surround sound to sophisticated home theater setups or just driving the tiny speakers on a laptop. That audio support also encompasses input devices, in the form of internal microphones (often designed to work with webcams) as well as external devices integrated

CHAPTER 13

into headphones that connect via USB and Bluetooth. As with other hardware subsystems, most of this capability is built into the Windows core drivers and doesn't require custom drivers from hardware manufacturers. (That, of course, doesn't prevent OEMs from including custom drivers and audio control software with their Windows 11 PCs.)

To manage audio devices, open Settings > System > Sound, which displays a list of output and input devices available on the current PC, as shown in Figure 13-23.

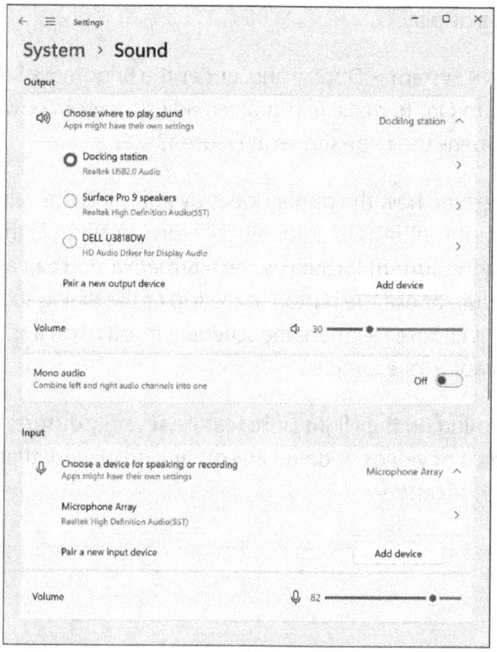

Figure 13-23   Use this Settings page to select default devices for playing back audio as well as for communication apps.

The system shown in Figure 13-23 illustrates a common dilemma with modern Windows PCs: You typically have a choice of multiple audio outputs, and those outputs aren't always labeled in a way that makes it obvious what each one does. On this PC, a Surface Pro 9 laptop, available audio outputs include external speakers plugged into the headphone jack on a docking station, the internal speakers on the laptop itself, and speakers built into a large external monitor connected to that same docking station.

By default, the top two output devices are labeled with generic names: Headphones and Speakers, respectively. To change those names so that they're more descriptive, click the entry for any device, which opens a Properties page like the one shown in Figure 13-24.

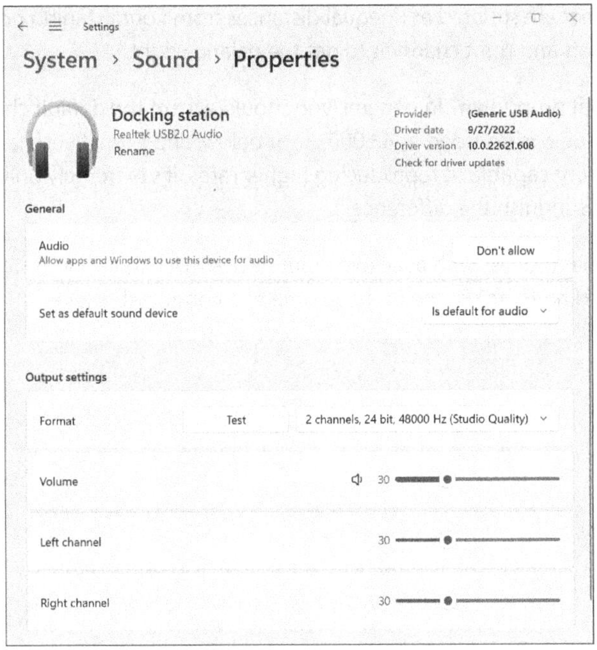

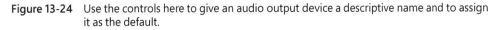

Figure 13-24   Use the controls here to give an audio output device a descriptive name and to assign it as the default.

The information block at the top of this page shows the name and icon assigned to the device, along with information about the installed driver. Click Rename to change the device name. (There's no way to change the icon.)

The dropdown in the Set As Default Sound Device box enables you to choose which device you want to be the default audio playback device and which one you want to use as the default communication device for apps like Microsoft Teams and Zoom. You might, for example, want to use a set of high-quality external speakers for playing back music, but use the internal speakers for online meetings, so that the sound comes from the same screen where your fellow meeting participants are visible.

If Windows automatically sets up an audio output device that you never want to use, such as a pair of low-quality speakers in an external monitor, click Don't Allow in the first box under the General heading. That removes it from the list of available output devices on the previous page and also removes it from the Quick Settings menu.

The Volume slider under the Output Settings heading does exactly the same thing as the similar control on the Quick Settings menu, which is generally more convenient to use. If you're using external stereo speakers that are situated at unequal distances from your listening position, you might want to adjust the left and right channels to get the balance right.

And what about the Format dropdown? In general, you should accept the default choice Windows offers. Most digital audio is encoded at 48,000 Hz or below, and even if you have media files and playback equipment capable of reproducing higher rates, it's extremely unlikely that your ears will be able to distinguish the difference.

You can go through a similar process with available input devices. Use the options under the Test Your Microphone heading to adjust the input volume to a comfortable level.

Performance and power management

"I feel the need, the need for speed." That was the memorable line uttered by Tom Cruise's character, Lieutenant Pete "Maverick" Mitchell, in the movie *Top Gun*. It's also the guiding principle for many longtime Windows aficionados.

It's true that raw speed can improve your productivity, especially for activities like editing and converting massive video files, which can take minutes on a high-powered workstation but can drag on for an hour or more on a low-end laptop. A speedy PC can even make life a bit more fun after the workday is over. Just ask any serious gamer how much time they've spent obsessing over frame rates.

But here's the reality: Most of the time, Windows is an innocent bystander when it comes to making things go fast. The out-of-the-box performance of a PC running Windows 11 should be acceptable, assuming that the hardware you're using is capable of the work you're asking it to perform. A budget laptop with a low-power mobile processor will almost certainly struggle at a CPU-intensive task like video rendering, for example. But even a workstation-class PC can perform poorly if you have a problem with a major subsystem or if Windows is configured incorrectly.

Like its predecessors, Windows 11 offers two valuable tools for monitoring the performance of your system in real time: Task Manager and Resource Monitor. Task Manager has been a mainstay of Windows through many versions. As discussed in Chapter 5, "Installing and configuring apps," you can use it for terminating recalcitrant processes and disabling unwanted startup programs. Task Manager also includes valuable performance-monitoring tools (more on that later in this chapter). To help zero in on performance issues with even more detail, you can use an advanced tool called Resource Monitor. In combination, these tools help you to keep an eye on CPU, memory, disk activity, and network usage.

What causes performance problems?

When people complain that their Windows PC is sluggish, they're usually expressing frustration over having to wait unexpectedly. If a task is taking an unusually long time to complete, the cause of that poor performance is most likely one of the following factors (in no particular order):

- **Inadequate hardware resources**   Microsoft's high compatibility requirements for Windows 11 PCs should ensure that baseline performance is acceptable. But more demanding tasks, such as digital media encoding, can push some systems to the breaking point. The performance-monitoring tools described in this chapter should help you identify areas where hardware resources are being overstressed.

- **Defective hardware**   Memory and disk errors are most obvious when they cause system crashes, but hardware-related problems can also cause performance to drag. Check with your hardware manufacturer to see what diagnostic tools are available.

- **Outdated or flawed device drivers**   PC and device makers are responsible for supplying drivers for the individual hardware components that go into their hardware. If you do a clean install, Windows might install a generic driver instead of one written specifically for that device. Many performance problems vanish immediately after a simple driver upgrade. (Don't assume that a newer driver is automatically better than an older one, however; any driver update has the potential to cause new problems.)

- **Out-of-control processes or services**   Sometimes, a program or background task that normally runs just fine will spin out of control, consuming up to 100 percent of CPU time or grabbing increasing amounts of memory or other system resources. Of course, performance of all other tasks slows down or grinds to a halt. Knowing how to identify and kill this sort of process or service and prevent it from recurring is a valuable troubleshooting skill.

- **Malware**   Viruses, Trojan-horse programs, spyware, and other forms of unwanted software can wreak havoc on system performance. Be sure to check for the possibility that malware is present on a system that exhibits otherwise unexplained performance problems.

It would be wonderful if one could simply open Registry Editor, create a new DWORD value called MakeEverythingGoFaster, set its value to 1, and automatically send a system into overdrive. Alas, the most reliable strategy for optimal performance is far less magical: Use quality hardware, make sure all devices have correct and up-to-date drivers, have plenty of memory on board, maintain enough free disk space to allow for a large paging file, have a speedy internet connection, and keep your system abreast of enhancements and security fixes delivered via Windows Update.

Several of these measures are discussed elsewhere in this book. See, for example, Chapter 13, "Managing hardware and devices." This chapter focuses on diagnosis, introducing tools that you can use to gather information about your system and identify any performance bottlenecks that might be present. It concludes with the subject of power management.

Viewing details about your system

For answers to basic questions about your operating system and computer, there's no better place to start than the built-in system information tools, which display basic system details: the current Windows edition; processor type and installed memory; details about the computer name and network membership (domain or workgroup); and the current activation status.

Windows 11 offers multiple versions of this information. On a tablet or touchscreen-enabled system, you'll probably use the Settings app. Open Settings > System > About to display details like those shown in Figure 14-1.

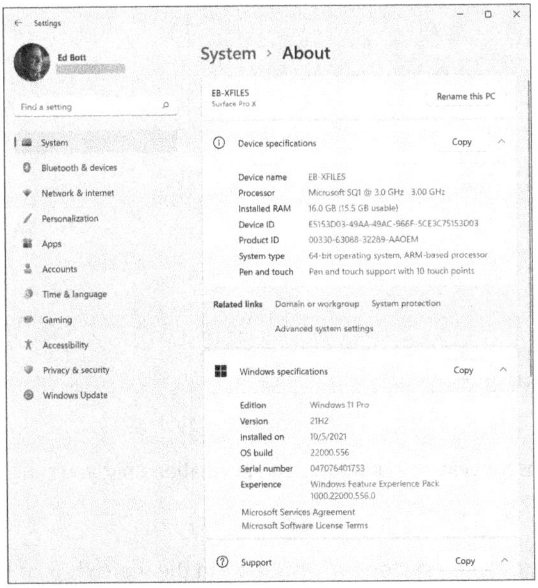

Figure 14-1   Go to Settings > System > About to display a page like this one, which includes basic details about the local PC along with the option to change its name.

A (slightly) faster way to get to the About page in Settings is via the Quick Link menu: Right-click Start (or press Windows key+X) and then click System. If File Explorer is open, you can reach the same destination by right-clicking This PC and clicking Properties. Regardless of how you get there, you'll find useful information about the device and the current Windows installation. A copy button alongside either heading allows you to capture those details and paste them into an email or messaging app for support purposes.

For the most exhaustive inventory of system configuration details in a no-frills text format, Windows offers three tools that provide varying levels of technical information: System Information, Systeminfo, and a collection of PowerShell commandlets for Windows Management Instrumentation. We describe these tools in the following sections.

System Information

System Information—often called by the name of its executable, Msinfo32.exe—is a techie's paradise. It displays a wealth of configuration information in a simple tree-and-details arrangement, as shown in Figure 14-2. You can search for specific information, save information, view information about other computers, and even view a list of changes to your system.

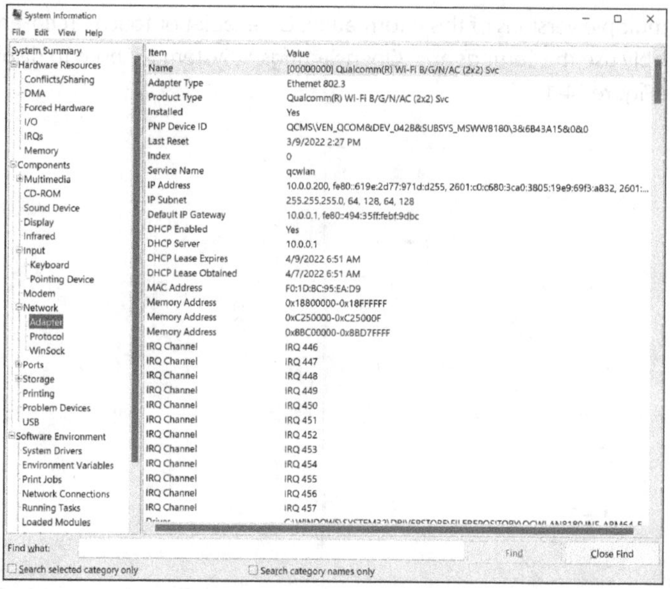

Figure 14-2   System Information is for viewing configuration information only; you can't use it to configure settings.

To start System Information, begin typing **system information** in the search box or type **msinfo32** at a command prompt.

You navigate through System Information much as you would through File Explorer: Click a category in the left pane to view its contents in the right pane. To search for specific information, use the Find What box at the bottom of the System Information window. (If the Find bar is not visible, press Ctrl+F, or click Edit and then clear the check box next to Hide Find.)

The Find feature is basic but effective. Here are a couple of things you should know:

- Whenever you type in the Find What box to start a new search, Find begins its search at the top of the search range (which is the entire namespace unless you select Search Selected Category Only)—not at the current highlight.

- Selecting Search Category Names Only causes the Find feature to look only in the left pane. When this check box is cleared, the text in both panes is searched.

Using the System Information tool, you can preserve your configuration information—which can be helpful when reconstructing a system—in several ways:

- **Save the details as a System Information (.nfo) file.** You can view your saved information by opening the file using System Information on the same computer or on a different computer. To save information in this format, click File, Save. Saving this way always saves the entire collection of information.

- **Save all or part of the information as a plain-text file.** To save information as a text file, select the category of interest and click File, Export. To save all the information as a text file, select System Summary before you export it.

- **You can print all or part of the information.** Select the category of interest; click File, Print; and be sure that Selection is selected under Page Range. To print everything, select All under Page Range—and be sure to have lots of paper on hand. Depending on your system configuration and the number of installed applications, your report could top 100 pages. (Even better, consider "printing" to PDF and saving the results.)

Regardless of how you save your information, System Information refreshes (updates) the information immediately before processing the command.

CHAPTER 14

Inside Out

Save your system information periodically

Saving system configuration information when your computer is working properly can be useful if you encounter problems at a later date. Comparing your computer's current configuration with a known good baseline configuration can help you spot possible problem areas. You can open multiple instances of System Information to display the current configuration in one window and a baseline configuration in another. Save the configuration in OneDrive, and you can retrieve the information even after a hard-disk replacement.

Systeminfo

Systeminfo.exe is a command-line utility that displays information about your Windows version, BIOS, processor, memory, network configuration, and a few more esoteric items. Figure 14-3 shows sample output.

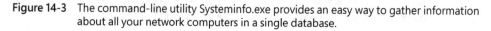

```
PS C:\Users\EdBott> systeminfo

Host Name:                 EB-XFILES
OS Name:                   Microsoft Windows 11 Pro
OS Version:                10.0.22000 N/A Build 22000
OS Manufacturer:           Microsoft Corporation
OS Configuration:          Standalone Workstation
OS Build Type:             Multiprocessor Free
Registered Owner:          edbott3@outlook.com
Registered Organization:   N/A
Product ID:                00330-63088-32289-AAOEM
Original Install Date:     10/5/2021, 4:20:23 PM
System Boot Time:          3/9/2022, 2:27:09 PM
System Manufacturer:       Microsoft Corporation
System Model:              Surface Pro X
System Type:               ARM64-based PC
Processor(s):              1 Processor(s) Installed.
                           [01]: ARMv8 (64-bit) Family 8 Model 805 Revision D0E Qualcomm Technologies Inc ~1766 Mhz
BIOS Version:              Microsoft Corporation 3.590.140, 1/7/2022
Windows Directory:         C:\WINDOWS
System Directory:          C:\WINDOWS\system32
Boot Device:               \Device\HarddiskVolume1
System Locale:             en-us;English (United States)
Input Locale:              en-us;English (United States)
Time Zone:                 (UTC-05:00) Eastern Time (US & Canada)
Total Physical Memory:     15,842 MB
Available Physical Memory: 7,887 MB
Virtual Memory: Max Size:  18,274 MB
Virtual Memory: Available: 7,995 MB
Virtual Memory: In Use:    10,279 MB
Page File Location(s):     C:\pagefile.sys
Domain:                    WORKGROUP
Logon Server:              \\EB-XFILES
Hotfix(s):                 5 Hotfix(s) Installed.
                           [01]: KB5010474
                           [02]: KB5004567
                           [03]: KB5008295
                           [04]: KB5011493
                           [05]: KB5009641
Network Card(s):           3 NIC(s) Installed.
                           [01]: Qualcomm(R) Wi-Fi B/G/N/AC (2x2) Svc
                                 Connection Name: Wi-Fi
                                 DHCP Enabled:    Yes
                                 DHCP Server:     10.0.0.1
```

Figure 14-3   The command-line utility Systeminfo.exe provides an easy way to gather information about all your network computers in a single database.

To run Systeminfo, open a Command Prompt or PowerShell window, type **systeminfo**, and then press Enter. In addition to the list format shown in Figure 14-3, Systeminfo offers two formats that are useful if you want to work with the information in another program: Table (fixed-width columns) and CSV (comma-separated values). To use one of these formats, append the **/fo** switch to the command, along with the Table or Csv parameter. You also need to redirect the output to a file. For example, to store comma-delimited information in a file named Info.csv, enter the following command:

```
systeminfo /fo csv > info.csv
```

Using the **/S** switch, you can get system information about another computer on your network. (If your username and password don't match that of an account on the target computer, you also need to use the **/U** and **/P** switches to provide the username and password of an authorized account.) When you've gathered information about all the computers on your network, you can import the file you created into a spreadsheet or database program for tracking and analysis. The following command appends information about a computer named Bates to the original file you created:

```
systeminfo /s Bates /fo csv >> info.csv
```

Windows Management Instrumentation tools

Windows Management Instrumentation (WMI) is Microsoft's comprehensive infrastructure for automating administrative tasks on servers and desktop computers running Windows. WMI uses the Common Information Model (CIM), an industry standard developed and maintained by the Distributed Management Task Force (DMTF), to help gather details about hardware, system configuration details, user accounts, and other management information on enterprise networks.

WMI commands can be scripted and are commonly used to collect information for use by enterprise management utilities, including System Center Operations Manager and Windows Remote Management. But WMI can also be used for basic management tasks on a single PC.

IT pros who've worked with Windows for long enough are probably familiar with the WMI Command-Line Utility, better known by the name of its executable, Wmic.exe. That utility is still available in Windows 11, although it's officially deprecated in favor of native WMI cmdlets for use with PowerShell.

Type **wmic** at a command prompt, and the utility runs in console mode, wherein you can enter commands and view output interactively. Alternatively, you can add global switches or aliases, which constrain the type of output you're looking for, and see the output in a Command Prompt window or redirect it to a file. For example, use the following command to produce a neatly formatted HTML file:

```
wmic qfe list brief /format:htable > %temp%\hotfix.html
```

(Note that this command won't work in a PowerShell session because PowerShell doesn't recognize the %temp% variable.)

You can then open that file in a web browser to see a list of all installed updates on the current system. To see the full syntax for Wmic, open a Command Prompt window and type **wmic /?**. Official documentation for how to use this tool, including a list of aliases, verbs, switches, and commands, is at *https://bit.ly/wmic-syntax*.

For more information on PowerShell WMI cmdlets, see *https://bit.ly/powershell-wmi*.

Monitoring performance with Task Manager

When you need to analyze system performance, Task Manager's Performance page is without peer. It gives you a quick overview of your system's performance in real time, measured in multiple dimensions. The details and charts shown on the Performance page offer a continuously updated snapshot of CPU, GPU, memory, disk, and network usage, while the Processes page displays details about resource usage on a per-process basis. Together, these two displays can help you very quickly figure out why your system is performing more slowly than it should.

> ➤ For details about Task Manager's other essential functions, see "Managing programs and processes with Task Manager," in Chapter 5, "Installing and configuring apps."

To open Task Manager, use any of the following techniques:

- Press Ctrl+Shift+Esc.

- Right-click Start (or press Windows key+X) and then click Task Manager on the Quick Link menu.

- Press Ctrl+Alt+Delete and then click Task Manager.

Figure 14-4 shows Task Manager's Performance page as it appears on a PC running Windows 11 version 22H2, with icons that provide access to different pages running in a vertical column along the left side and a Settings menu option in the lower-left corner. (In Windows 11 version 21H2 and all versions of Windows 10, this information is arranged using tabs that run across the top of the Task Manager window, although the display of performance information is essentially identical in both versions.)

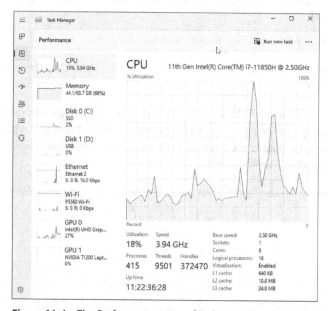

Figure 14-4   The Performance page of Task Manager gives you a big-picture view of resource usage.

It's worth noting that the display shown here is from a fairly powerful Windows workstation: Each disk, network connection, and GPU gets its own page, complete with thumbnail graph; this arrangement allows you to monitor disk speeds on internal and external drives, for example, and to distinguish the performance of a discrete GPU from that of an integrated graphics processor.

The small thumbnail graphs at the left report current data in real time; clicking any of these thumbnails displays a more detailed page to its right, with a much larger version of the same graph and additional information below the graph.

Each graph shows 60 seconds' worth of data, with updates at one-second intervals. In Figure 14-4, shown earlier, for example, the CPU graph shows a large spike caused by opening a graphics-intensive app, followed by several smaller spikes as other activities make demands on the CPU.

If that once-per-second sampling rate doesn't provide the information you need, feel free to change it. Click the Settings icon in the lower-left corner of Task Manager and change the value under the Real Time Update Speed setting from its default, Normal, to High (updates every half-second) or Low (every four seconds). You can also click Paused if you want to study the most recent data without having it scroll off the graph to the left.

Here are some additional tweaks you can make to Task Manager when viewing the Performance page:

- Double-click any thumbnail (or right-click a thumbnail and choose Summary View) to hide the full page and just show the pane of thumbnails. To return to normal view, double-click any thumbnail again, or use the right-click menu to clear the check box next to Summary View.

- From that same right-click menu, choose Hide Graphs to show a data-only summary; right-click and choose Show Graphs to restore the performance thumbnails.

- Double-click the large graph on the current page to display it in the Graph Summary View, which uses the full Task Manager window while hiding the thumbnail charts and additional data. Double-click the graph again to return to the normal display of performance data.

- Click the See More menu (the three dots in the upper-right corner) and choose Copy to make a summary of data from the current page available on the Windows Clipboard.

As we discuss shortly, each page on the Performance page offers specific information about resource usage by the selected device or subsystem. But before we get to those details, let's switch to the Processes page for a slightly different take on overall system performance.

The default view of the Processes page groups all running processes into three types: Apps, Background Processes, and Windows Processes. Figure 14-5 shows this page in action.

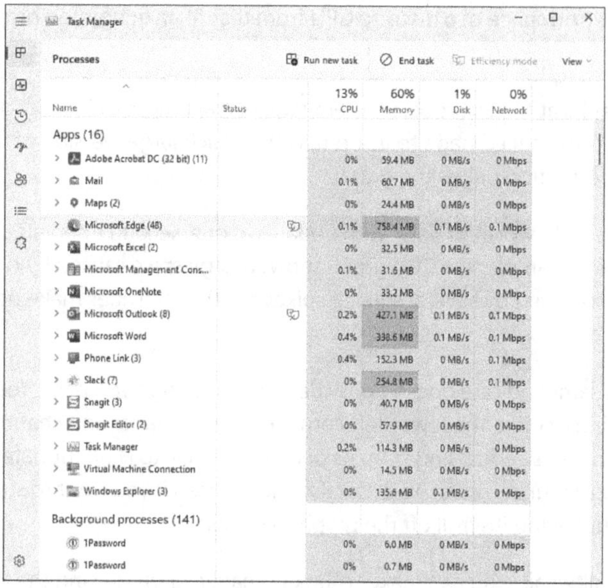

Figure 14-5   The Processes page of Task Manager allows you to look more closely at resource usage on a per-app basis.

In this default view, every process has its own entry; some apps group multiple processes under a single entry that can be expanded or collapsed. To the right of each entry, you can view resource usage for that process or group of processes, with values organized under four columns by default: CPU, Memory, Disk, and Network. Color coding highlights values that are using a higher-than-average share of the resource in that column.

Inside Out

See more details on the Processes page

The four performance-related columns visible by default on the Processes page cover the information most people will find most useful, most of the time. But additional columns are available if you need them. Right-click any column heading to display a menu of columns that can be added to the default display. For performance monitoring, the most interesting entries in this category are GPU and Power Usage; the latter can highlight apps that are making heavier than normal demands on a portable PC's battery.

The column headings on the Processes page summarize what percentage of that resource is in use by the system as a whole. To discover which apps or processes are using the most resources in that category, click the column heading. That action ungroups the processes and then sorts them in descending order by usage.

One feature that's new in Windows 11 version 22H2 is an indicator for apps that are running in Efficiency Mode, which is Microsoft's feature for tuning apps so that they're power efficient and use fewer resources when running in the background. A leaf icon under the Status column means one or more processes in a group are running in Efficiency Mode; expand the group to see details for each process.

You can manually turn on Efficiency Mode for some apps (but not for core Windows processes) by selecting the app in the Processes pane and then clicking the Efficiency Mode button in the upper-right corner. Doing so reduces the base priority of the process to Low and sets the Quality of Service (QoS) mode to EcoQoS. Collectively, these settings reduce power usage and prevent background apps from interfering with higher-priority processes, such as an app you're currently using in the foreground.

The remainder of this section examines individual pages on the Performance page, with details about what you can learn from each one.

CPU

Displaying the CPU details on the Performance page in Task Manager shows some basic information about your CPU. In the upper-right corner, above the performance graph, you can see the full name of the processor and its base speed. In the lower right, below the graph, are technical details about the processor, including the number of cores and logical processors, whether virtualization is enabled, and how much memory on the CPU is devoted to various caches (L1, L2, and L3).

Below the CPU graph, on the left, you can see total CPU utilization as well as the current CPU speed, which might be higher than the base speed shown elsewhere. This region also enumerates the number of processes, threads, and handles currently in use. Larger numbers mean a greater workload for the system; whether a given load is too much is something you can judge only after long-term monitoring.

By keeping this pane open as you work, you can see what the impact of a given activity is. For example, you might monitor CPU usage when encoding a video file to see whether the operation pins CPU usage at 100 percent; if so, that might be evidence that you need to consider upgrading your PC to one with a more powerful CPU and/or GPU that's capable of doing the same work faster, generating less heat and allowing you to do other things while the task completes in the background.

Inside OUT

How long has your PC been running?

When you display the CPU details in Task Manager, much of the information below the performance graph is obscure and only of use to developers or engineers. You probably don't need to know how many handles are in use by your current workload, for example. But one detail here is interesting as a benchmark of stability. The Up Time measure shows the amount of time that has elapsed—in days, hours, minutes, and seconds—since the machine was last restarted. Thanks to monthly updates that invariably include mandatory restarts, it's unlikely you'll ever see this number go beyond 30 days.

Memory

Clicking the Memory thumbnail on Task Manager's Performance page displays a snapshot of memory usage, as shown in Figure 14-6. Note that the total amount of memory available to this system—64 GB—is visible in the upper-right corner above the graph. Details about the physical memory itself (number of sticks and slots, for example) are shown below, alongside the amount of RAM in use and the amount available.

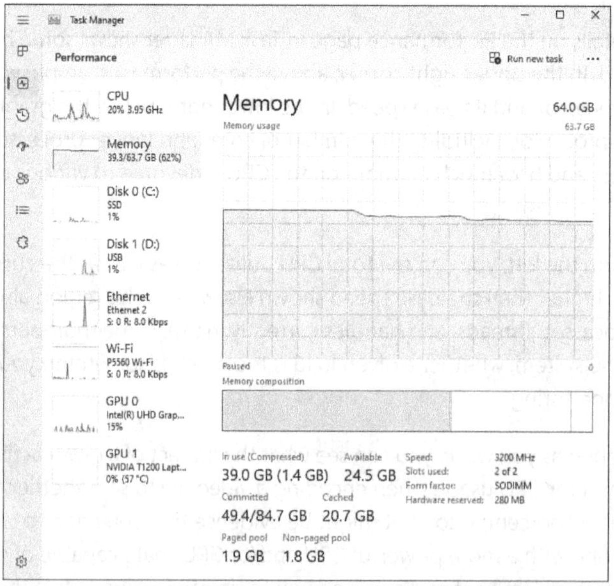

Figure 14-6   Use the Memory option on the Performance page to see how much of your system's RAM is in use. If the value is at 100 percent, it's time to close some apps to improve performance.

On this page, a detailed Memory Composition bar chart appears below the main graph. At first glance, it appears to be just an alternative view of the main Memory Usage chart, but hover the mouse pointer over any segment to see its real purpose. The ScreenTips that appear over each segment explain what each one represents, as shown in Figure 14-7.

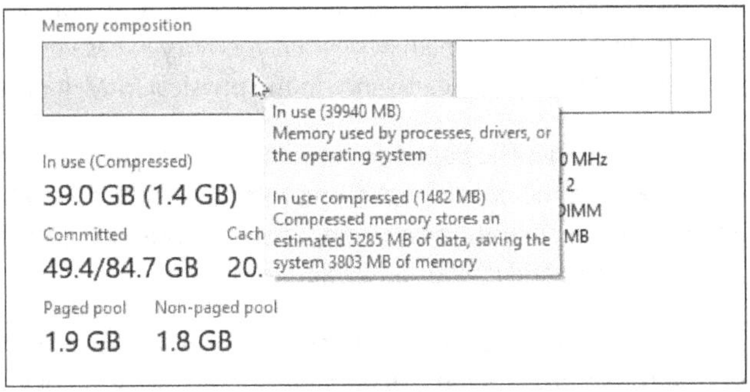

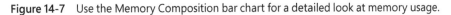

Memory composition

In use (39940 MB)
Memory used by processes, drivers, or
the operating system

In use (Compressed)

39.0 GB (1.4 GB)   In use compressed (1482 MB)
Compressed memory stores an
Committed   Cach estimated 5285 MB of data, saving the
49.4/84.7 GB   20. system 3803 MB of memory

Paged pool   Non-paged pool
1.9 GB   1.8 GB

Figure 14-7   Use the Memory Composition bar chart for a detailed look at memory usage.

CHAPTER 14

There's a fair amount of technical detail on the Memory page. Collectively, it offers a detailed picture of the total virtual address space, which includes physical memory and the *paging file*, which is one of the most misunderstood subsystems in Windows.

The paging file allows Windows to commit more memory for use by processes than is physi-cally available. That magic happens via the Windows memory management subsystem, which maps memory into pages (each page is 4 KB in size on an x86 PC) and then maps those pages to physical memory while backing them up to the paging file, which is stored by default on the system disk.

The detailed information that appears at the bottom of the page when you choose the Memory option on Task Manager's Performance page help explain how the paging file works:

- **In Use (Compressed)**   This value represents the amount of physical memory that is cur-rently allocated to running processes, including Windows itself, drivers, and apps. Some of the code in those pages is compressed, allowing Windows to make more efficient use of scarce physical memory.

- **Available**   This value is the amount of physical RAM minus the amount currently in use.

- **Committed**   When a new Windows process starts, it reserves a block of memory for its own use. Committed RAM represents pages that have been allocated for that process. Those pages might be in physical RAM or in the paging file. The first number represents the total of all memory in use; the second is the Commit Size Limit, which is the sum of physical RAM and virtual memory available in the paging file.

- **Hardware reserved**   This total, which appears in the lower-right corner, includes hardware drivers that must remain in physical memory at all times and are not available to the memory manager. If you see two values in the upper right, above the Memory graph, the small total is calculated by subtracting this amount from the total physical RAM.

- **Cached**   This group represents pages that were previously used by an app or system process but are no longer in use. They remain in physical memory in case they are needed again, but can be moved to the paging file, freeing up the physical RAM, if necessary.

Two other values are shown on this page. The *paged pool* and *non-paged pool* represent memory used by the Windows kernel; the paged pool represents pages of memory that can be written to disk (paged) when no longer in use. The non-paged pool represents data that must remain in physical memory at all times and cannot be written to disk.

(For a full discussion of Windows memory management, see the documentation in the Windows Dev Center at *https://bit.ly/windows-memory-management*. Its discussion of virtual versus physical memory is especially useful. In addition, this long article by a community member, Sushovon Sinha, includes details that apply to both Windows 10 and Windows 11 memory management: *https://bit.ly/physical-virtual-memory*.)

Inside OUT

Should you change the size of the paging file?

One common misconception about the paging file is that it somehow adversely affects performance and should be reduced in size, converted to a fixed size, or even eliminated. This advice might have been relevant in a bygone era, when running a much older version of Windows. It is not good advice for Windows 11.

You'll find the controls for managing virtual memory (the paging file) buried beneath several layers of advanced options on the System Properties dialog. To open that dialog, type *systempropertiesadvanced* in the search box and press Enter; then, under the Performance heading, click Settings; click the Advanced tab; finally, click Change under the Virtual Memory heading.

By default, the Automatically Manage Paging File Size For All Drives option is selected here and all other options are grayed out and unavailable. Clearing that check box allows you to change the size of the paging file, move it to a separate drive, or delete the paging file completely. Doing so can have undesirable side effects.

The paging file is used to back up pages in memory, but it also has a crucial secondary function, which is to save crash dump reports when Windows encounters an error. The default settings for the paging file allow Windows to manage its size and location, making sure it has enough space to perform all its functions. On a modern PC that meets the hardware requirements for Windows 11, moving the paging file to a different drive is not likely to produce any noticeable performance gains, nor will manually changing the size of the paging file improve performance except in extremely specialized configurations.

Disk

The Disk details display, in graphic terms, the performance of all disks on the current system that are marked as nonremovable. (That excludes USB flash drives and SD cards but includes external hard drives and SSDs connected to a high-speed USB or Thunderbolt port, which are technically removable but are treated as if they're fixed.)

Each disk gets its own entry on the left side of the Performance page, with details about the selected disk's performance on the right, as shown in Figure 14-8. The top graph depicts the percentage of time the disk is busy processing read or write requests; the bottom graph shows the disk transfer rate.

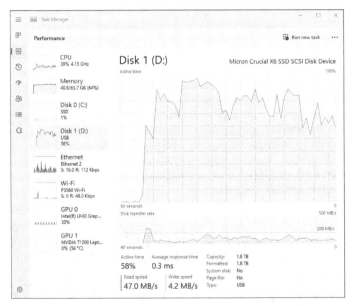

Figure 14-8   The Disk options in Task Manager let you see the throughput of a fixed disk and determine whether a particular activity is causing a bottleneck.

The information below the Disk graph provides some details about the physical disk it represents, including the total capacity and formatted capacity, whether the disk is in use as a system disk, and whether it contains a paging file. The Read Speed and Write Speed measurements, in conjunction with the data on the smaller Disk Transfer chart, can help you determine the actual transfer speed of a disk and spot any issues with disk throughput.

Network

Each active network connection gets its own graph on Task Manager's Performance page, showing network throughput for that connection. Figure 14-9 shows an example of a wired network connection in action.

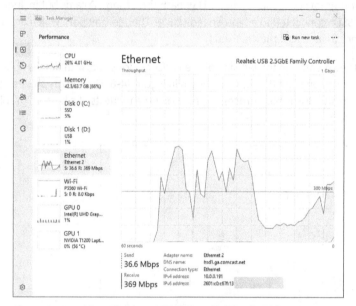

Figure 14-9   This sort of variability in network performance is common and reflects the complexity of managing network connections.

This graph illustrates the performance of a wired network connection while downloading several large files from OneDrive. Although it's not obvious at first glance, there are actually two separate lines: one for the speed at which data is being received from the other end of the network connection, and the other for the speed at which data is being sent. In the example shown here, the Send activity is working at a tiny fraction of the speed of the download, making its line so small as to be nearly invisible.

The Send and Receive values are displayed below the graph and change in real time with each sampling interval. It's also worth noting that the scale of the graph changes with network activity, making it possible to see performance data even when network activity is using less than its full bandwidth.

Data below the graph shows some useful details of the current connection, including IPv4 and IPv6 addresses; for wireless connections, this block also shows the SSID name, signal strength, and which Wi-Fi standard is in use.

One well-hidden summary of networking activity is also available from this page. Right-click the graph and choose View Network Details to open a dialog that shows a table with cumulative data for all available network connections in the current session.

GPU

Performance details for graphics processing units (GPUs) are displayed in a collection of graphs that are noticeably more complex than the other subsystems on the Performance page. Figure 14-10 illustrates the full set for a discrete graphics adapter on a Windows 11 notebook.

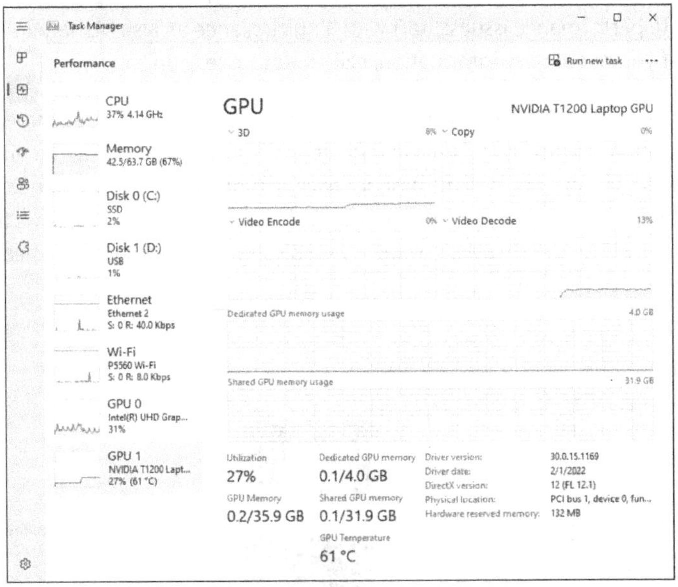

Figure 14-10   Performance details for a GPU are mostly of interest to gamers and video professsionals trying to squeeze maximum performance out of a discrete graphics adapter.

The four graphs at the top measure the speed of rendering 3D graphics, copying data between video buffers, and encoding and decoding compressed video. The two lower graphs measure usage of dedicated GPU memory, which is installed on the video hardware itself, and shared video memory, which is allocated by Windows from the main pool of RAM used by Windows and apps.

As with the other details on the Performance page, this one includes information below the graph showing details about the video hardware in use, the driver version, and (particularly important when gaming or performing GPU-intensive rendering activities) the temperature of the GPU.

Using Resource Monitor to pinpoint performance problems

Like the Performance page in Task Manager, Resource Monitor gives you both instantaneous and recent-history readouts of key performance metrics. Also like Task Manager, Resource Monitor can show you, in excruciating detail, what each process is doing.

To open Resource Monitor, you can search for it from the Start menu or use its command line, **perfmon /res**, from a Command Prompt window. But the fastest way is to click its link on Task Manager's Performance page. (In the original release of Windows 11, version 21H2, that link is at the bottom of the tab; in version 22H2, it's hidden under the See More menu—the three dots to the right of the Run New Task button in the upper-right corner.) This option offers a natural way to investigate performance issues: Start with a quick glance at Task Manager's Performance page and then, if you need more information, call on Resource Monitor.

Resource Monitor organizes information using tabs. The Overview tab provides charts that offer a visual snapshot of performance in real time in four areas: CPU, disk, network, and memory. Matching tables display details on a per-process basis for each of these four areas. (Unlike Task Manager, Resource Monitor doesn't provide performance details for GPUs.) Figure 14-11 shows this tab in action, with two of the four detail tables collapsed and displaying only a summary heading.

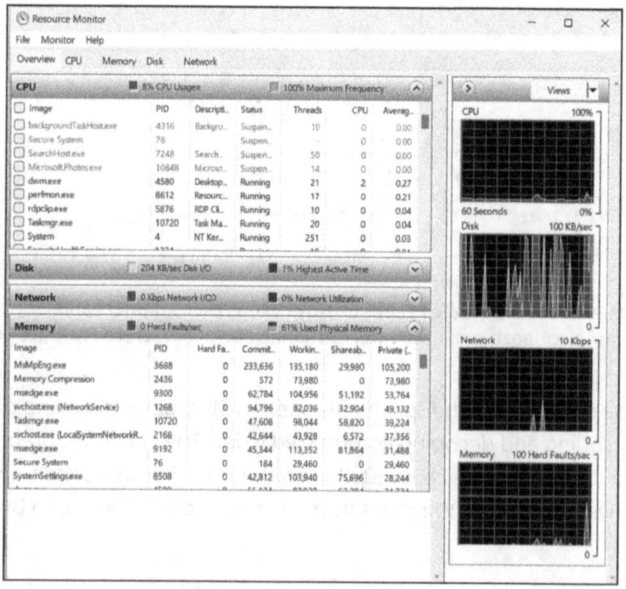

Figure 14-11   The default view in Resource Monitor shows results for all processes. If any details are truncated, hover the mouse pointer over the item to see a ScreenTip showing its details.

CHAPTER 14

Using the tabs along the top of the Resource Monitor window, you can switch to a different context and focus on a specific type of resource usage. The basic layout of each tab is similar and consists of a handful of common elements.

One or more tables contain details about the resource featured on that tab. The first table on each tab is called the *key table*; it contains a list of all processes currently using the selected resource, with a check box to the left of each process. The key table at the top of the Overview tab lists all running processes in a display that is similar to the Processes page in Task Manager.

Selecting one or more processes from the key table filters the data displayed in the tables that appear below it, showing only activity associated with that process. An orange heading appears at the top of each detail table, noting that the data display is filtered, and an additional orange line appears in the graphs on the right to show how much of that resource is in use by the selected process. Figure 14-12 shows the Resource Monitor Disk tab with the Windows Defender process (Msmpeng.exe) selected.

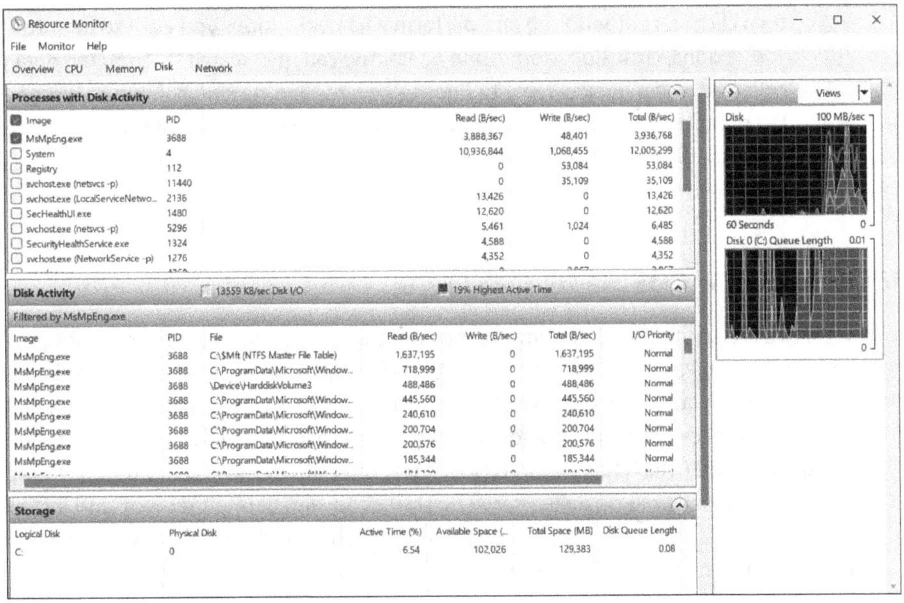

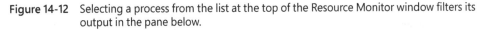

Figure 14-12   Selecting a process from the list at the top of the Resource Monitor window filters its output in the pane below.

The CPU, Disk, and Network tabs work in similar fashion, offering additional details mainly of use to programmers. (The Memory tab shows a map of current memory usage, without regard to the processes selected in the key table.)

Resource Monitor is overkill for most performance troubleshooting tasks. But it shines when you want to see exactly which process or file is responsible for an unexplained burst of activity.

It's also invaluable for tracking down the name and location of a specific file that Windows is using with a particular process and action.

Inside Out

Use the Monitor menu to keep Resource Monitor focused

When Resource Monitor is active, its display can be frustrating to follow. Even if you're not working directly with a program, Windows is constantly busy with its own house-keeping and maintenance duties, writing information to log files and to the page file, reading and writing data to the registry, and calling on all sorts of Windows system pro-cesses for managing memory and the file system.

If you're simply trying to figure out what's happening when you perform a specific task, use the two options on the Monitor menu to limit the display of data and keep it from jumping around after you've finished. Click Stop Monitoring to end the current session; then click Start Monitoring and perform whatever actions you want to monitor. When you're done, click Stop Monitoring again. You can now search through the data you collected, using the key table to filter by process and clicking column headings to sort the data and find out which processes and files were involved with the activity you just performed.

Managing services

A *service* is a specialized program that performs a function to support other programs. Many services operate at a low level (by interacting directly with hardware, for example) and need to run even when no user is signed in. Windows manages services using a special system process called the Service Control Manager (Services.exe, also known as SCM). The SCM is run by the System account (which has elevated privileges) rather than by ordinary user accounts. This sec-tion covers how to view installed services; start, stop, and configure them; and install or remove them. We also take a closer look at some services used in Windows 11 and show you how to configure them to your advantage.

For the most complete view of services running on your computer, use the Services console. You can also view running services and perform limited management functions by using Task Man-ager. This section covers both tools.

Using the Services console

You manage services with the Services snap-in (Services.msc) for Microsoft Management Con-sole, shown in Figure 14-13. To view this snap-in, type **services** in the search box and then click the Services app at the top of the results list. (You must have administrator privileges to gain full functionality in the Services console. Running it as a standard user, you can view service settings, but you can't start or stop most services, change the startup type, or make any other configuration changes.)

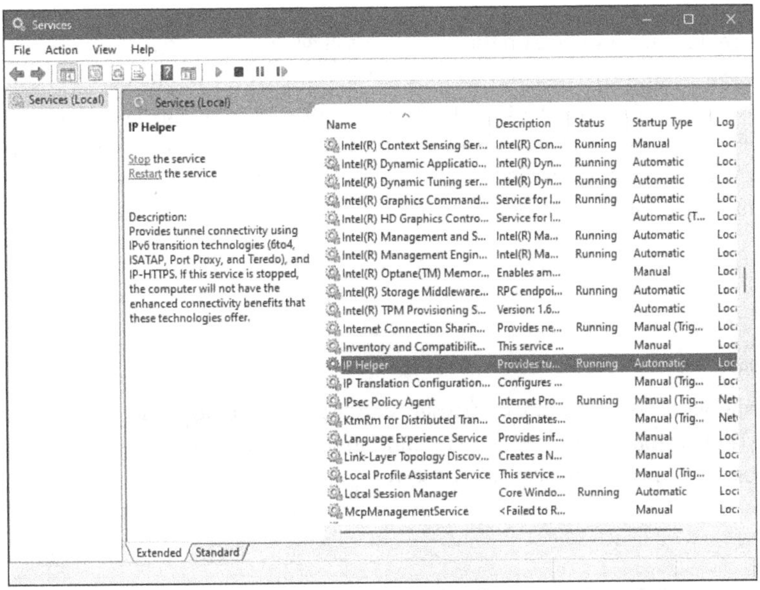

Figure 14-13 Use the Services console to start, stop, and configure services.

The Extended and Standard views in the Services console (selectable by clicking a tab near the bottom of the window) have a single difference: The Extended view provides descriptive information of the selected service in the space at the left edge of the details pane. This space also sometimes includes links for starting, stopping, or pausing the selected service. Unless you need to constrain the console display to a small area of your screen, you'll probably find the Extended view preferable to the Standard view.

The Services console offers plenty of information in its clean display. You can sort the contents of any column by clicking the column title, as you can with similar lists. To sort in reverse order, click the column title again. In addition, you can do the following:

- Start, stop, pause, resume, or restart the selected service, as described in the following section.

- Display the properties dialog for the selected service, in which you can configure the service and learn more about it.

Most essential services are set to start automatically when your computer starts, and the operating system stops them as part of its shutdown process. A handful of services that aren't typically used at startup are set with the Automatic (Delayed Start) option, which starts the associated service after the rest of startup completes, making the startup process smoother. The Trigger Start option allows Windows to run or stop a service as needed in response to specific events; the File History service, for example, doesn't run unless you enable the File History feature.

But sometimes you might need to manually start or stop a service. For example, you might want to start a seldom-used service on the rare occasion when you need it. (Because running services requires system resources such as memory, running them only when necessary can improve performance.) On the other hand, you might want to stop a service because you're no longer using it. A more common reason for stopping a service is because it isn't working properly. For example, if print jobs get stuck in the print queue, sometimes the best remedy is to stop and then restart the Print Spooler service.

Inside OUT

Pause instead of stopping

If a service allows pausing, try pausing and then continuing the service as your first step instead of stopping the service. Pausing can solve certain problems without canceling jobs in process or resetting connections.

Starting and stopping services

Not all services allow you to change their status. Some prevent stopping and starting altogether, whereas others permit stopping and starting but not pausing and resuming. Some services allow these permissions to only certain users or groups. For example, most services allow only members of the Administrators group to start or stop them. Which status changes are allowed and who has permission to make them are controlled by each service's discretionary access control list (DACL), which is established when the service is created on a computer.

To change a service's status, select it in the Services console. Then click the appropriate link in the area to the left of the service list (if you're using the Extended view and the link you need appears there). Alternatively, you can use the Start/Stop/Pause/Restart controls on the toolbar or right-click and use the corresponding command.

You can also change a service's status by opening its properties dialog and then clicking one of the buttons on the General tab. Taking the extra step of opening the properties dialog to set the status has only one advantage: You can specify start parameters when you start a service by using this method. This is a rare requirement.

Configuring services

To review or modify the way a service starts up or what happens when it doesn't start properly, view its properties dialog. To do that, double-click the service in the Services console. Figure 14-14 shows an example.

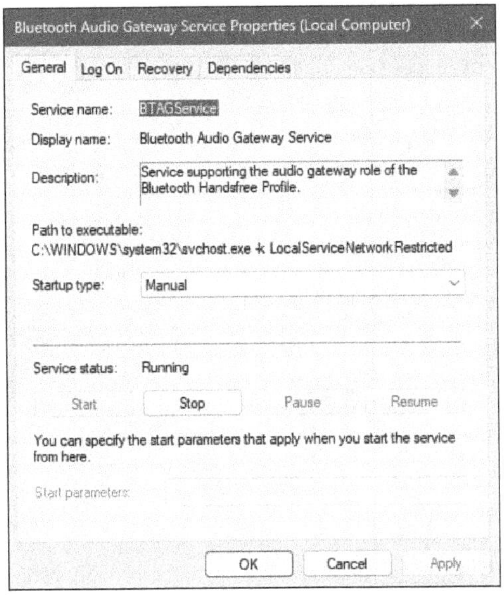

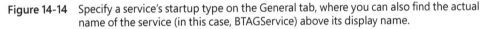

Figure 14-14   Specify a service's startup type on the General tab, where you can also find the actual name of the service (in this case, BTAGService) above its display name.

Setting startup options

On the General tab of the properties dialog (shown earlier in Figure 14-14), you specify the startup type:

- **Automatic**   The service starts when the computer starts.

- **Automatic (Delayed Start)**   The service starts after other auto-start services (plus a short delay) to improve startup performance and user experience. The SCM starts services configured using this option one at a time, honoring dependencies.

- **Manual**   The service doesn't start automatically at startup, but it can be started by a user, program, or dependent service.

- **Disabled**   The service can't be started.

The Trigger Start option cannot be configured manually from the Services console. Instead, you have to use SC (Sc.exe), a command-line program that communicates with the SCM. If you'd rather not tinker with the arcane syntax of this command, try the free Service Trigger Editor, available from Core Technologies Consulting, at *https://bit.ly/servicetriggereditor.*

Other startup options are on the Log On tab of the properties dialog, as shown in Figure 14-15. In general, there's no reason to modify the settings shown here.

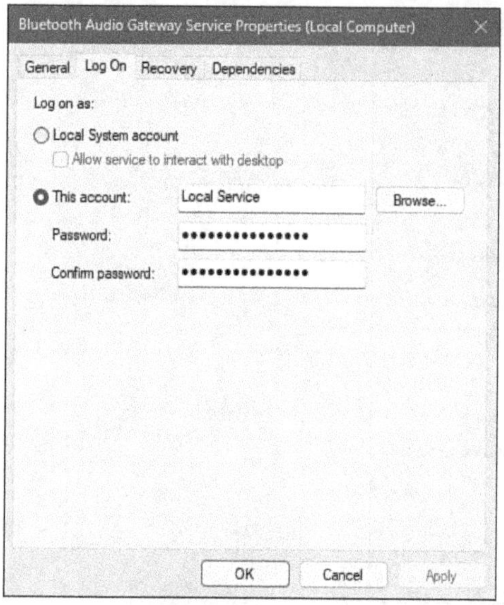

Figure 14-15 Settings shown on the Log On tab specify which user account runs the service.

> # NOTE
>
> If you specify a sign-in account other than the Local System account, be sure that account has the requisite rights. Go to the Local Security Policy console (at a command prompt, type **secpol.msc**), and then go to Security Settings\Local Policies\User Rights Assignment and assign the Log On As A Service right to the account. This option is rarely necessary for services that are part of Windows, and a third-party app that requires this type of configuration typically does so as part of the installation process.

Specifying recovery actions

For various reasons—hardware not operating properly or a network connection being down, for example—a service that's running smoothly might suddenly stop. By using settings on the Recovery tab of the properties dialog, you can specify what happens if a service fails. Figure 14-16, for example, shows the default settings for the Bluetooth Audio Gateway service.

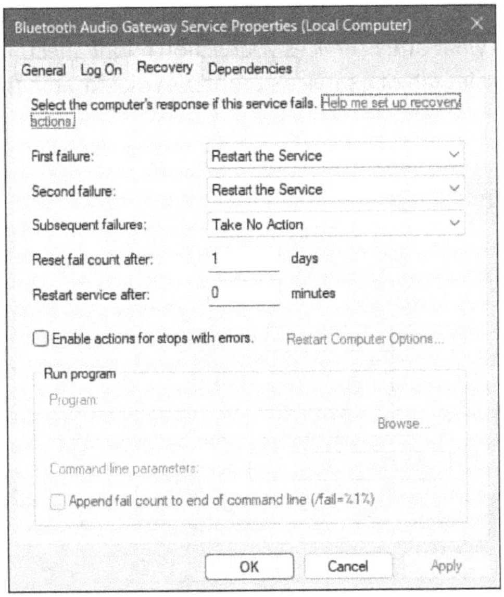

Figure 14-16   Use the Recovery tab to specify what happens if a service fails.

You might want to attempt one recovery action the first time a service fails and then perform a different action on the second or subsequent failures. The Recovery tab enables you to assign a particular response to the first failure, the second failure, and all subsequent failures, from among these options:

- **Take No Action**   The service gives up trying. In most cases, the service places a message in the event log. (Use of the event log depends on how the service was programmed by its developers.)

- **Restart The Service**   The computer waits for the time specified in the Restart Service After box to elapse and then tries to start the service.

- **Run A Program**   The computer runs the program you specify in the Run Program box. For example, you could specify a program that attempts to resolve the problem or one that alerts you to the situation.

- **Restart The Computer**   Drastic but effective, this option restarts the computer after the time specified in the Restart Computer Options dialog elapses. In that dialog, you can also specify a message to be broadcast to other users on your network, warning them of the impending shutdown.

Viewing dependencies

Many services rely on the functions of another service. If you attempt to start a service that depends on other services, Windows first starts the others. If you stop a service upon which others are dependent, Windows also stops those services. Before you either start or stop a service, therefore, it's helpful to know what other services your action might affect. To obtain that information, go to the Dependencies tab of a service's properties dialog, as in the example shown in Figure 14-17.

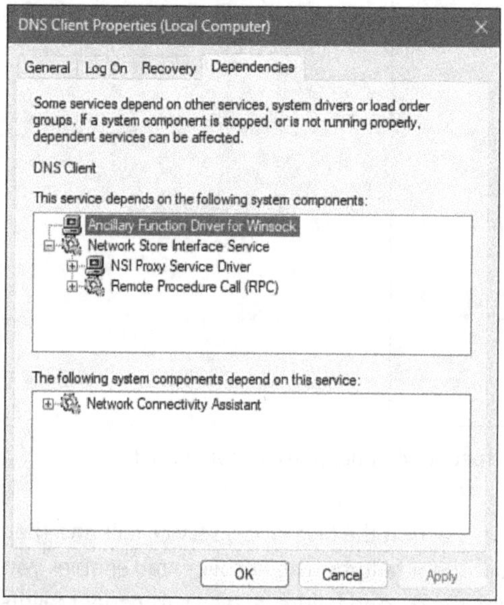

Figure 14-17   The Dependencies tab shows which services depend on other services or drivers.

The outline controls in the Dependencies tab can be expanded to show dependents of the dependents.

Managing services from Task Manager

Using the Services page in Task Manager, you can start and stop services and view several important aspects of the services, both running and available, on your computer. You can also use this page as a shortcut to the Services console.

The Services page is shown in Figure 14-18.

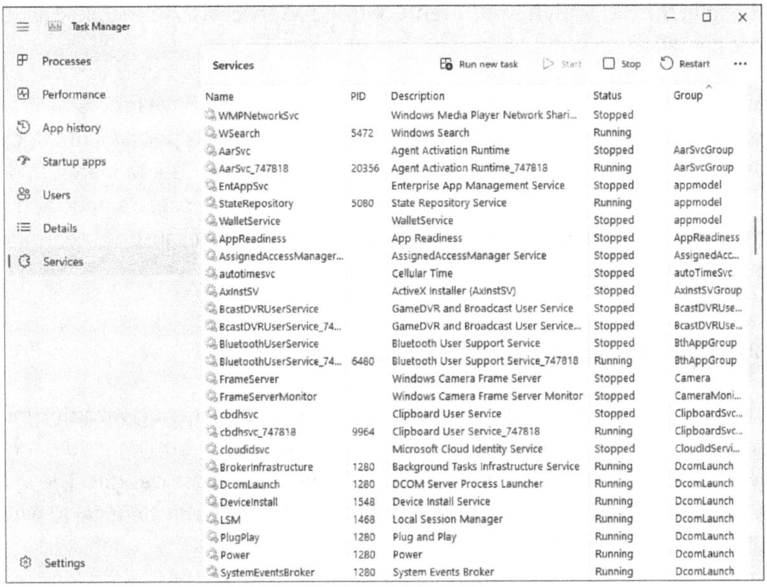

Figure 14-18   By sorting on the Group column, you can see groups of related services together.

To start, stop, or restart a service, right-click its name on the Services page and then click Start, Stop, or Restart.

Using the Services page, you can also associate a running service with its process identifier (PID) and then further associate that PID with other programs and services being run under that PID. For example, the list of services in Figure 14-18, shown earlier, includes multiple services running with PID 1280. Right-clicking any of those services and then clicking Go To Details opens the Details page in Task Manager with the particular process (typically, Svchost.exe) highlighted.

Determining the name of a service

As you view the properties dialog for different services, you might notice that the service name (shown at the top of the General tab) is often different from the name that appears in the Services console (the display name) and that neither name matches the name of the service's executable file. (Many services run as part of a service group, typically under a Host Process for Windows Services, Svchost.exe.) The General tab (shown earlier in Figure 14-14) shows all three names.

So how does this affect you? When you work in the Services console, you don't need to know anything other than a service's display name to find it and work with it. But if you use the Net or Sc command to start and stop services from a Command Prompt window, you might find using the actual service name more convenient; it's often much shorter than the display name. You also need the service name if you're ever forced to work with a service's registry entries, which can be found in the HKLM\System\CurrentControlSet\Services*service* subkey (where *service* is the service name).

And what about the executable name? You might need it if you have problems running a service; in such a case, you need to find the executable and check its permissions. Knowing the executable name can also be useful, for example, if you're using Task Manager to determine why your computer seems to be running slowly. Although the Processes page and the Services page show the display name (under the Description heading), because of the window size, it's sometimes easier to find the more succinct executable name.

Managing battery life on portable PCs

The modern portable PC is packed with feats of hardware engineering wizardry, miniaturizing powerful components to previously unheard-of sizes. On the software side, similar efforts have been successful in coaxing ever more battery life out of those designs. The upshot is you can now take a Windows PC on the road and do work that is nearly identical to what you can accomplish back at the office.

All that computing power comes at a price in battery life, however. And finding the right balance depends on what you're trying to accomplish. Sometimes you want the full power of your PC, especially if you're trying to accomplish a resource-intensive task on a tight schedule and you know that you'll be back within range of AC power well before your battery is in danger of running out of juice. Under other circumstances, when the workload is light and you know it will be many hours before you'll be able to recharge your device, you want to make that battery last as long as possible. Anything you do to extend the battery life of a portable device helps you avoid having to quit working because your battery gave up the ghost.

Being able to accomplish either goal requires mastering one essential skill first: the ability to quickly assess how much power capacity remains in the current session.

For a quick estimate of remaining battery life, hover the mouse pointer over the battery icon in the notification area. After a second or two, you should see a message with the remaining battery life, expressed as a percentage. (On a portable PC with more than one battery, such as the Surface Book line from Microsoft, each battery gets its own percentage, beneath an overall percentage that estimates the remaining battery life overall.)

If Windows has enough data to take a guess at how much time you'll be able to continue working on the remaining battery power, you see that estimate as well. When the laptop is plugged into a charger, this display shows an estimate of the amount of time before the battery is fully charged.

In Windows 10, clicking the battery icon opens a flyout menu with detailed information about remaining power. In Windows 11, clicking the battery icon opens the Quick Settings menu, with the percentage of remaining battery at the bottom left. Click that value to open the Power & Battery page in Settings, where you see a much more detailed report, similar to the one shown in Figure 14-19.

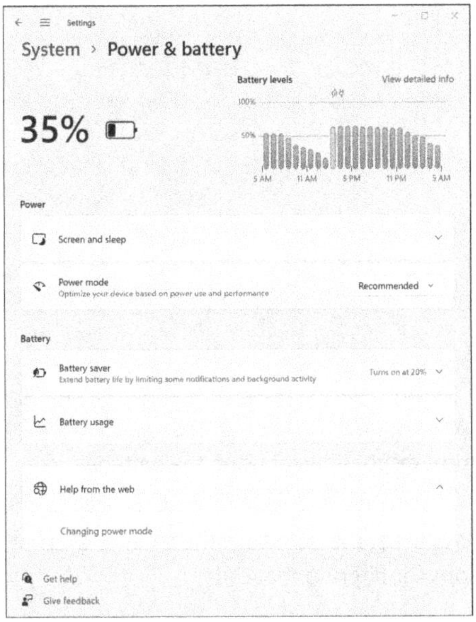

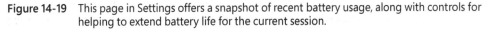

Figure 14-19   This page in Settings offers a snapshot of recent battery usage, along with controls for helping to extend battery life for the current session.

The abbreviated bar chart to the right of the current battery status gives a snapshot of power usage over the past 24 hours, with each bar representing one hour's power consumption (or charging). A yellow leaf icon over a bar means the device was in Battery Saver mode during that period. A green power plug icon means it was plugged in.

For much more detail about battery usage, click View Detailed Info, which takes you to the Battery Levels section at the bottom of the page. After running your portable PC on battery power for at least 24 hours, this section contains details similar to those shown in Figure 14-20.

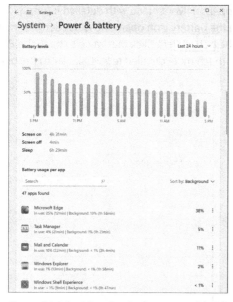

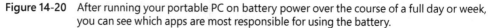

Figure 14-20   After running your portable PC on battery power over the course of a full day or week, you can see which apps are most responsible for using the battery.

By default, the bar chart shown here displays the same data as in the smaller chart at the top of the page, but it gives you two crucial options for filtering that data.

Use the options on the menu to the right of the Battery Levels heading to toggle the scale of activity between 24 Hours and 1 Week; the values returned show activity on a per-app basis for all times during the selected period when your device was running on battery power.

In addition to that filter, you can use the Sort By menu to change the display of per-app usage information from Overall Usage (the default) to show only apps that are currently in use or those that are running in the background. You can also sort the list by name.

No matter how you slice it, that's pretty powerful diagnostic information. Used properly, it can help you diagnose which apps are most responsible for draining your PC's battery. Armed with that information, you can either choose not to use those apps when power saving is high on the agenda, or you can look for configuration changes in the apps at the top of the list (such as restricting background usage) to help reduce their hunger for power.

Inside OUT

Don't forget to check the batteries on your peripheral devices

If you carry essential add-on devices when you travel, be sure to check their battery level before you leave, unless you want to experience the frustration of having your noise-canceling Bluetooth headphones stop working one hour into a trans-Atlantic flight. Go to Settings > Bluetooth & Devices to check battery life at a glance for modern Bluetooth devices.

Battery Saver and other power management options

The Power & Battery page also includes some additional controls that allow you to change the way in which Windows uses the battery during the current session. From the Power & Battery page in Settings, you can use the Power Mode menu to choose one of three options: On systems running the original release of Windows 11, Balanced is the default; if you want to shift the performance-battery ratio, select Best Performance or Best Power Efficiency.

In Windows 10, this option was implemented as a slider control accessible from the taskbar. On PCs running Windows 11, the option moves to Settings. (On some PCs, these options appear in a slightly different fashion: Recommended, Better Performance, and Best Performance.)

What's the difference? The most important change is the way the operating system throttles background apps, reducing their performance (and preserving battery life) at a slight cost to overall system performance.

Windows 11 also offers a Battery Saver feature, whose settings are available on the same page in Settings. While Battery Saver is on, Windows automatically adjusts the following settings:

- The Mail, People, and Calendar apps no longer sync automatically.

- Most apps that normally run in the background are blocked from doing so. OneDrive, for example, sends a notification that it has temporarily stopped syncing local changes to the cloud. You can override this action by clicking the Sync Anyway button.

- Display brightness (one of the biggest factors in battery usage) is reduced by 30 percent. Hardware manufacturers can change this default setting, and you can override it using the Lower Screen Brightness While In Battery Saver check box.

- All noncritical telemetry uploads are blocked.

- All noncritical downloads from Windows Update are blocked.

While Battery Saver is enabled, Windows displays an overlay of a leaf on the battery icon in the taskbar, in Settings, and in the Battery flyout menu.

By default, Windows 11 automatically turns on Battery Saver when remaining battery life falls below 20 percent. Use the Battery Saver options on the Power & Battery page in Settings to change that threshold to a round percentage between 10 and 50; choose Always to make Battery Saver mode the default, or choose Never to continue running at your chosen power mode until you reach the Low or Critical battery level.

To adjust those settings, you need to use the old-style Power Options in Control Panel. In Settings, type Edit Power Plan in the search box. Click the resulting option and then click Change Advanced Power Settings; finally, expand the Battery heading to see the options to specify the Low and Critical battery levels. At those two settings, you can ask Windows to show a notification or perform an action. For example, you might ask to see a notification when remaining battery level drops to 10 percent and have Windows automatically hibernate when it reaches 5 percent.

Inside Out

What happened to power plans?

In older versions of Windows that were written for previous generations of hardware, Windows included multiple power plans, with the option to create custom power plans using a dizzying variety of power settings.

The tools to manage custom power plans are still available in the old Control Panel, in the Power Options category, under the Advanced Settings tab. On modern hardware, there's little need to resort to this level of granularity. On a clean installation of Windows, you'll find one and only one power plan, Balanced. PC makers have the option to customize this plan.

Although it's possible to create a custom power plan using the Powercfg command, there's little reason to do so. Instead, we recommend that you start with the Balanced plan and modify it to your preferences. Doing so allows the built-in Windows power settings to continue working as designed.

Monitoring long-term battery life and capacity

Over time, if you're paying attention, you develop an instinctive sense for how long your battery will last and when you should begin looking in earnest for a power outlet. Windows 11 allows you to generate a battery report that gives you a more precise measurement of your battery's history. The report also allows you to observe the decline in battery capacity that inevitably occurs over time. To generate a battery report, open a Command Prompt or PowerShell window and run the command **powercfg /batteryreport**. That action generates a file in the current folder called Battery-report.html; double-click that file to view the report in a browser window.

That report provides a wealth of information about the current system and its battery health. The Installed Batteries section, for example, lists the manufacturer's name and serial number of the battery; it also displays how many power cycles the battery has undergone and lists its current Full Charge Capacity compared to its Design Charge Capacity. Calculating the ratio of those two numbers tells you how much battery life your system has lost over time.

The Battery Life Estimates section shows how much Windows estimates your battery life to be for each recent session, based on observed battery use measurements; an average value appears at the bottom of the list.

Configuring power options from the command line

If your work entails managing power settings for multiple systems and users, you'll find the powercfg command-line utility invaluable. With powercfg, you can query and set power schemes and parameters, export power settings to a file, import the file on remote systems, and more. (Many powercfg actions work only in an elevated Command Prompt or PowerShell window.) Even if your concerns are only with your own systems, you might find powercfg /batteryreport, powercfg /energy, and powercfg /sleepstudy useful. These commands generate reports that are not available via the interactive power-management features described earlier in this section.

To generate a list of commands available with powercfg, open a Command Prompt or PowerShell window and type **powercfg /?**. For syntax details and usage examples of any powercfg command, type **powercfg /? *command***.

Power management on desktop systems

Even when your PC isn't dependent on a battery, paying attention to power management has benefits. Allowing a PC or tablet to sleep or hibernate cuts the amount of power it consumes, which translates into monetary savings for you and a benefit for society at large.

The most obvious of these settings are available in Settings > System > Power & Battery, under the Screen And Sleep heading. The options here specify the amount of idle time before the screen goes dark and the amount of time before the system goes to a lower-power setting called sleep. On a portable computer, there are separate settings that apply when running on battery power and when plugged in, as shown in Figure 14-21. (On desktop PCs, there are only two options to choose from.)

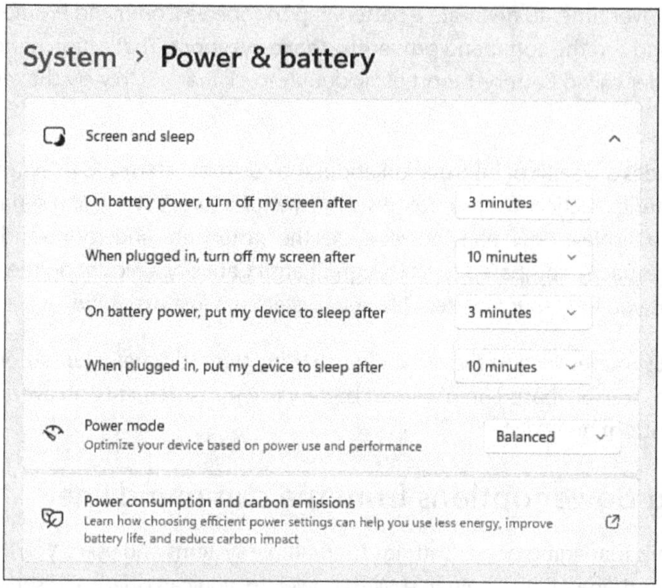

Figure 14-21   On this page, you can minimize the amount of power a computer uses even when it's plugged into AC power full time.

For each option, the choices in the drop-down menu range from 1 minute (probably more annoying than most people will accept) to 5 hours (useful if you want the computer to sleep only when you're away for a long time). To disable either option, choose Never from the drop-down menu.

Troubleshooting, backup, and recovery

As they say, stuff happens. You might remember a more colorful form of that expression, but in any case, it certainly applies whenever hardware and software are involved.

Although Microsoft Windows generally has become more stable and reliable over time, your computing experience will never be perfect. Apps stop responding or crash (shut down unexpectedly). Once in a while, a feature of Windows walks off the set without warning. And on rare occasions, the grim BSOD ("Blue Screen of Death," more formally known as a *Stop error* or *bugcheck*) arrives, bringing your whole system to a halt.

In a fully debugged, perfect world, such occurrences would never darken your computer screen. But you don't live there, and neither do we. So the prudent course is to learn to use the many tools Windows provides for diagnosing errors and recovering from problems. We examine these essential tools in this chapter.

And while those troubleshooting tools can help you understand what happened and maybe help you prevent it from happening again, they can't help you recover, which is why this chapter also explains how to use the backup tools included with Windows 11. Our goal is to help you prepare for the inevitable day when you need to restore a lost file (or an entire drive's worth of files). We also explain your options for resetting Windows when the operating system becomes damaged, for whatever reason.

Getting to know your troubleshooting toolkit

As any detective will tell you, solving a mystery requires evidence. If your mystery involves inexplicably slow performance or crashes, you have several places to look for clues.

Built-in troubleshooters

The most obvious first step on the road to resolving performance issues (including features that mysteriously stop working) is the set of troubleshooters at Settings > System > Troubleshoot > Other Troubleshooters. Here you will find a categorized roster of tools to deal with a wide assortment of common problems.

There's nothing magical about any of these troubleshooters. Their purpose is to ensure that you check the most common causes of problems, including some that might seem obvious. (Is the network cable plugged in? Is the printer turned on?) Running a troubleshooter is an obvious first step when confronting most common problems: The troubleshooter can fix some issues and, more importantly, establishes a baseline for further troubleshooting.

A troubleshooter might lead you through several steps and ask you to check settings or connections. At the end, it displays its results in a troubleshooting report similar to the one shown in Figure 15-1. The report includes links for additional information.

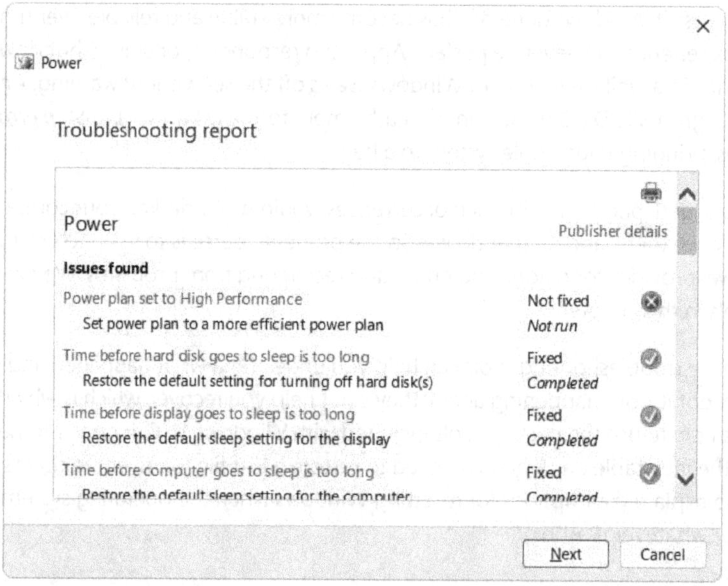

Figure 15-1   The troubleshooting report lists issues and indicates whether they were fixed. For any issues that are detected, you can click a link to see more granular information about that item.

Windows Error Reporting

The Windows Error Reporting service runs continuously in the background, keeping track of software and driver installations (successful and otherwise) as well as crashes, hangs, and other system events that indicate a possible problem with Windows. (In fact, although the service and app that enable the feature are called Windows Error Reporting, the term you're more likely to see in Windows is *problem reporting*.) If you've authorized Windows 11 to send these reports as part of its diagnostics tracking, Microsoft provides these details to the developers of the app that caused the error (including Microsoft developers when the issue occurs with a feature in Windows, Office, or another Microsoft app). The goal, of course, is to improve quality by identifying problems and delivering fixes through Windows Update and Office Update.

In previous versions, Windows was downright chatty about reporting crashes, successful updates, and minor speed bumps. In Windows 11, most of these problem reports (including diagnostic reports sent after successful upgrades) are completely silent, but each report is logged. You can use the history of problem reports on a system to review events and to see whether any patterns demand additional troubleshooting.

To view the Problem Reports log, open Settings, click in the Find A Setting search box, type **problem reports**, and then click View All Problem Reports. Figure 15-2 shows a portion of the error history for a computer running Windows 11 Pro.

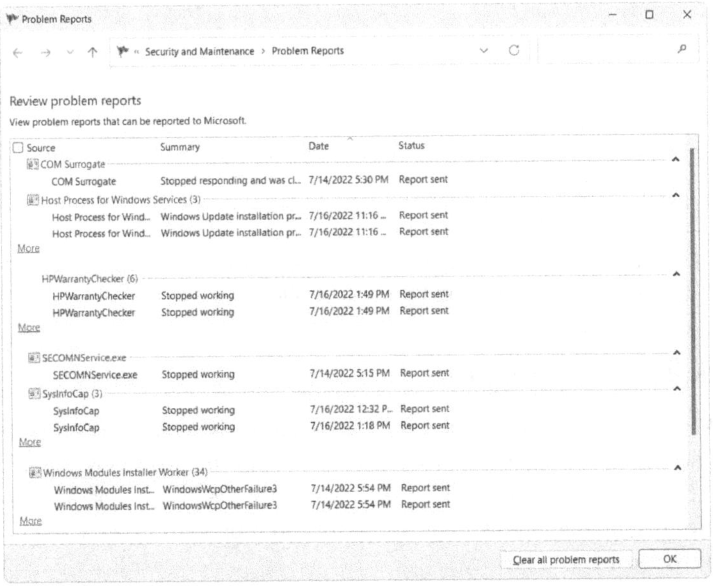

Figure 15-2   The list of saved problem reports displays the two most recent reports in each group.

If the words *Solution Available* appear in the Status column for an item, right-click that item and then click View Solution. That shortcut menu also includes commands to group the entries in the list of problem reports by source, summary, date, or status—or you can choose Ungroup to see the entire uncategorized list. Regardless of whether the list is grouped, you can sort by any field by clicking the field's column heading.

You can see a more detailed report about any event in this log by double-clicking the event. (See Figure 15-3.) The Description field usually is written clearly enough to provide potentially useful information. The rest of the details might not be meaningful to you, but they could be helpful to a support technician. Some reports include additional details sent in a text file you can inspect for yourself.

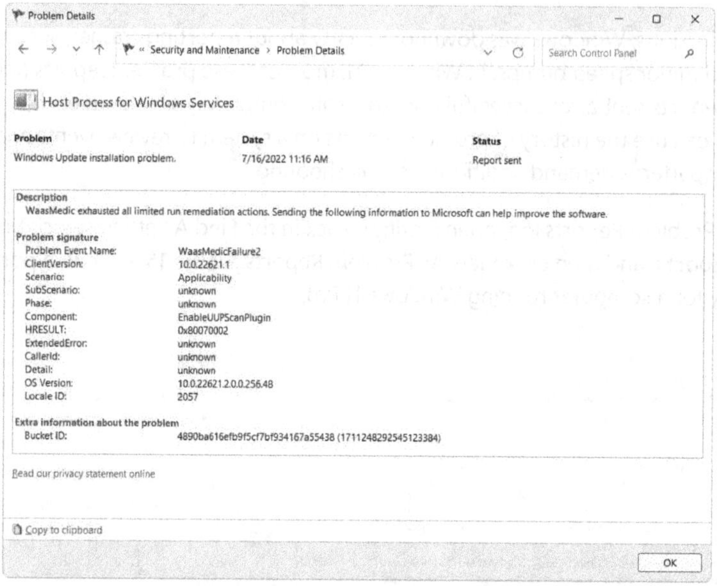

Figure 15-3   Double-clicking an entry in the problem reports list displays details about the problem that might be useful to a support technician.

Feedback and diagnostics

By default, Windows 11 configures your system so that it sends a generous amount of diagnostic and feedback information, including error reports that could inadvertently contain personal information. If you're concerned about data use or privacy, you can dial back the amount of diagnostic information using the settings we describe in "Configuring privacy options," in Chapter 12, "Windows security and privacy."

In addition to this automated feedback, Windows 11 enables you to send problem reports and feature suggestions to Microsoft. In some cases, the operating system will directly ask for your feedback on features. If you prefer not to be asked for feedback, go to Settings > Privacy & Security> Diagnostics & Feedback. The Feedback Frequency setting near the bottom of this page controls how often Microsoft asks you about your use of features. (And yes, "Never" is an option.)

Windows 11 also includes the Feedback Hub app, which you can use to send problem reports and suggestions to Microsoft. (This app was previously available only to registered members of the Windows Insider Program.) We recommend that you search for existing feedback before filling out your own problem report. You can filter and sort the list of search results to see if your specific issue has already been reported; in some cases, Microsoft engineers respond with a note the issue has been fixed (or is on the list for repair in a future update).

If you find an existing feedback entry that describes your issue, you can add a comment and an upvote. If you discover a new issue, feel free to create your own feedback item by clicking Report A Problem or Suggest A Feature. In the spirit of setting expectations, we are compelled to add that items you submit here are different from support tickets. You probably won't get personal support from a Microsoft engineer or support tech, although your feedback will be considered, especially if the number of upvotes hits double or triple digits.

Reliability Monitor

Windows 11 keeps track of an enormous range of system events, which you can monitor using Event Viewer, as we describe in the following section. For a day-by-day inventory of specific events (successful and unsuccessful) that affect your system's overall stability, open Reliability Monitor, shown in Figure 15-4. (Type **reliability** in the search box, and then click the top result, View Reliability History.)

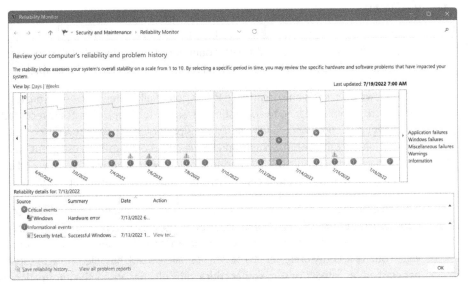

Figure 15-4   Reliability Monitor keeps a daily tally of significant events affecting system stability. Select any day to see details in the pane on the bottom.

Each column in the graphical display represents events of a particular day (or week, if you click that option in the upper-left corner). Each red X along the first three lines below the graph (the various Failures lines) indicates a day on which problems occurred. The Warnings line describes minor problems unrelated to system reliability, such as an app whose installation process didn't complete properly. The last line below the graph—the line marked Information—identifies days on which an app or an update was installed or removed. You can see the details about the events of any day by clicking on the graph for that day. Reliability Monitor retains its system stability records for up to one year but clears the history with the installation of each new feature update.

This history is most useful when you begin experiencing a new problem and are trying to track down its cause. Examine the critical events for the period when you first began to experience the problem, and see whether they correspond with an informational item, such as an app installation. The alignment of these events could be mere coincidence, but it could also represent the first appearance of a long-term problem. Conjunctions of this sort are worth examining. If you think a new app has destabilized your system, you can try uninstalling it.

Double-clicking any problem report exposes its contents, which are filled with technical details that are potentially useful, confusing, or both. Note that these reports are identical to those you can find in the listing of problem reports we discussed earlier in this chapter.

Event Viewer

Technically, we probably should have included Event Viewer (Eventvwr.msc) in the previous section. It is, after all, just another troubleshooting tool. But we think that this, the most powerful of all the diagnostic tools in Windows 11, deserves special attention in this chapter.

In Windows, an *event* is any occurrence that is potentially noteworthy—to you, to a system or network administrator, to the operating system, or to an app. Events are recorded by the Windows Event Log service, and their history is preserved in one of several log files, including Application, Security, Setup, System, and Forwarded Events. You can use Event Viewer, a Microsoft Management Console (MMC) snap-in supplied with Windows, to review and archive these event logs, as well as other logs created by the installation of certain apps and services.

You can examine the history of errors on your system by creating a filtered view of the Application log in Event Viewer. Why would you want to do this? The most likely reasons are to troubleshoot problems that have occurred, to keep an eye on your system to forestall problems, and to watch out for security breaches. If a device has failed, a disk has filled close to capacity, an app has crashed repeatedly, or some other critical difficulty has arisen, the information recorded in the event logs can help you—or a technical support specialist—figure out what's wrong and what corrective steps are required.

To start Event Viewer, find it by searching for **event** and then click Event Viewer or View Event Logs in the search results. (Alternatively, right-click Start and then click Event Viewer.)

NOTE

Event Viewer requires administrator privileges for full functionality. If you start Event Viewer while signed in as a standard user, it starts without requesting that you sign in by elevating to an administrator's credentials. However, the Security log is unavailable, along with some other features. To get access to all logs, right-click and choose Run As Administrator.

Figure 15-5 offers an overview of Event Viewer, which uses the basic three-pane Microsoft Management Console to organize and displays a truly massive amount of data from event logs.

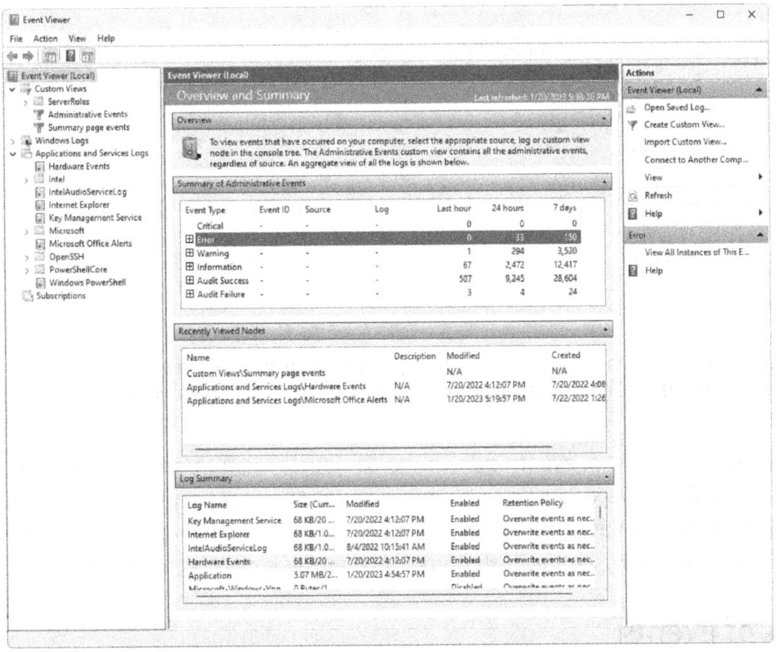

Figure 15-5   Event Viewer's console tree (left) lists available logs and views; the details pane (center) displays information from the selected log or view; the Actions pane (right) provides a menu of tasks relevant to the current selection.

When you select the top-level node in Event Viewer's console tree, the details pane displays summary information, organized into groups, in decreasing order of severity. With this view, you can see at a glance whether any significant events that might require your attention have occurred in the past hour, day, or week. You can expand each category to see the sources of events of that event type. This simple count can flag potential problems easily. If, for example,

CHAPTER 15

you see an unusually large number of recent errors from a particular source, you might want to dig deeper into that list to determine whether a particular error is a sign of a reliability or performance problem. To do that, you can right-click an event type or an event source under Summary Of Administrative Events, and then click View All Instances Of This Event, as shown in Figure 15-6.

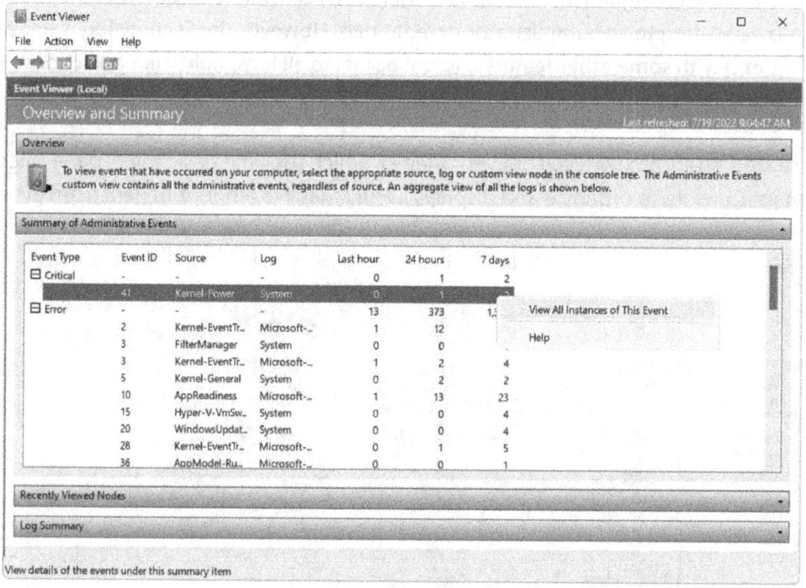

Figure 15-6   The summary view is organized by event type, in order of severity. Expand any category and then right-click a source to view all instances of that event.

The resulting filtered list of events is drawn from multiple log files, sparing you from having to search in multiple places. Armed with this information, you can quickly scroll through and examine the details of each one, perhaps identifying a pattern or a common factor that will help you find the cause and, eventually, the cure for whatever is causing the event.

Types of events

As a glance at the console tree confirms, events are recorded in one of several logs. Logs are organized in the console tree in folders, and you can expand or collapse the folder tree using the customary outline controls. The following default logs are visible under the Windows Logs heading:

- **Application**   Events are generated by applications, including apps you install, apps that are preinstalled with Windows, apps from the Microsoft Store, and operating system services. App developers decide which events to record in the Application log and which to record in a custom log under Applications And Services Logs.

- **Security**   Events that include sign-in attempts (successful and failed) and attempts to use secured resources, such as an attempt to create, modify, or delete a file.

- **Setup**   Events that are generated by app installations.

- **System**   Events that are generated by Windows itself and by installed features, such as device drivers. If a driver fails to load when you start a Windows session, for example, that event is recorded in the System log.

- **Forwarded Events**   Events gathered from other computers.

Under the Applications And Services Logs heading are logs for individual apps and services. The difference between this heading and the Windows Logs heading is that logs under Applications And Services record events related only to a particular app or feature, whereas the logs that appear under Windows Logs generally record events that are systemwide.

If you expand the Microsoft entry under Applications And Services Logs, you'll find a Windows subfolder, which in turn contains a folder for each of hundreds of features that are part of Windows 11. Each of these folders contains one or more logs.

Viewing logs and events

When you select a log or a custom view from the console tree, the details pane shows a list of associated events, sorted (by default) in reverse chronological order, with each event occupying a single line. A preview pane below the list displays the contents of the saved event record. Figure 15-7 shows one such listing from the System log.

NOTE

The Windows Event Log service records the date and time each event occurred in Coordinated Universal Time (UTC). Event Viewer translates those time values into dates and times appropriate for the currently configured time zone.

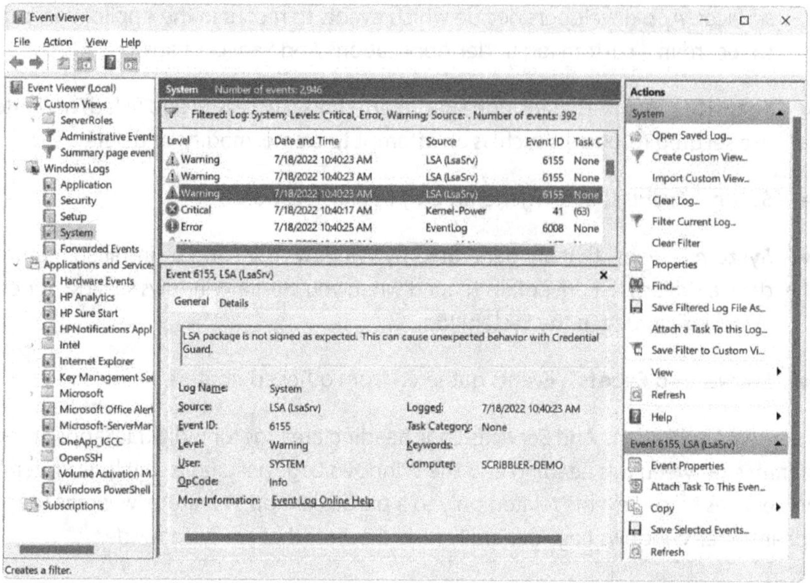

Figure 15-7   All the details you need for an individual event are visible in this preview pane. Double-click an event to see those same details in a separate window.

Events in most log files are classified by severity, with one of four entries in the Level field:

- **Critical events**   The most severe category, which includes Stop errors and other events that have the potential to damage data.

- **Error events**   The category that represents a possible loss of data or functionality. Examples of errors include events related to a malfunctioning network adapter and loss of functionality caused by a device or service that doesn't load at startup.

- **Warning events**   Less significant or less immediate problems than error events. Examples of warning events include a nearly full disk, a timeout by the network redirector, and data errors on local storage.

- **Information events**   Other events logged by Windows. This category includes any Windows Update that is successfully installed, for example, as well as events documenting startup and shutdown times.

The Security log file uses two different icons to classify events: A key icon identifies Audit Success events, and a lock icon identifies Audit Failure events. Both types of events are classified as Information-level events; "Audit Success" and "Audit Failure" are stored in the Keywords field of the Security log file.

The preview pane shows information about the currently selected event. (Drag the split bar between the list and preview pane up to make the preview pane larger so that you can see more details, or double-click the event to open it in a separate dialog that includes Next and Previous buttons and an option to copy the event to the Clipboard.)

The information you find in Event Viewer is evidence of things that happened in the past. Like any good detective, you have the task of using those clues to help identify possible issues. One hidden helper, located near the bottom of the Event Properties dialog, is a link to more information online. Clicking this link opens a webpage that might provide more specific and detailed information about this particular combination of event source and event ID, including further action you might want to take in response to the event.

Inside OUT

Export data from Event Viewer

You can save selected events, all events in the current view, or all events in a particular log to a file for archival purposes, for further analysis in a different program, or to share with a technical support specialist. (To select events for exporting, hold down the Ctrl key and click each event you want to include.) The command to export events is on the Action menu, but the command name varies depending on the current view and selection: Save Selected Events, Save Filtered Log File As, Save Events In Custom View As, or Save Events As.

Saving event data in Event Viewer's native (.evtx) format creates a file you can view only in Event Viewer (or a third-party application capable of reading native event logs). However, Event Viewer can export log data to XML and to tab-delimited or comma-delimited text files, and you can import these easily into database, spreadsheet, or even word-processing programs.

CHAPTER 15

Customizing the presentation of tabular data in Event Viewer

If you have a passing familiarity with Details view in File Explorer, you'll feel right at home with the many tabular reports in Event Viewer. You can change a column's width by dragging its heading left or right. You can sort on any column by clicking its heading; click a second time to reverse the sort order. Right-click a column heading and choose Add/Remove Columns to make more or fewer columns appear.

As with files and folders in File Explorer, you also have the option to group events in Event Viewer. To do that, right-click the column heading by which you want to group and then click Group Events By This Column. Figure 15-8, for example, shows the System log with events grouped by Source and sorted by Date And Time in descending order. Note that you can expand or collapse each grouping using the tiny arrows at the end of each group heading.

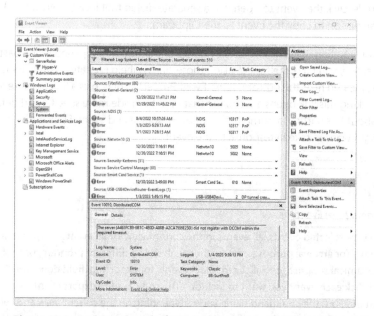

Figure 15-8   In this view, we right-clicked the Source heading and chose the option to group events, and then we clicked the Date And Time heading to bring the most recent events to the top of each group.

Filtering the log display

As you can see from a cursory look at your System log, events can pile up quickly, obscuring those generated by a particular source or those that occurred at a particular date and time. Sorting and grouping can help you find relevant events, but filtering is even more effective, especially when using multiple criteria. With a filter applied, all other events are hidden from view, making it much easier to focus on the items you currently care about.

To filter the currently displayed log or custom view, click Filter Current Log or Filter Current Custom View in the Action pane on the right. A dialog like the one shown in Figure 15-9 appears. To fully appreciate the flexibility of filtering, click the arrow by each filter. You can, for example, filter events from the past hour, 12 hours, day, week, month, or any custom time period you specify. In the Event Sources, Task Category, and Keywords boxes, you can type text to filter on (separating multiple items with commas), but you'll probably find it easier to click the down arrow and then select each item you want to include in your filtered view. In the Includes/Excludes Event IDs box, you can enter multiple ID numbers and number ranges, separated by commas; to exclude particular event IDs, precede their number with a minus sign.

Click OK to see the filtered list. If you think you'll use the same filter criteria again, click Save Filter To Custom View in the Action pane on the right. To restore the unfiltered list, in the Action pane, click Clear Filter.

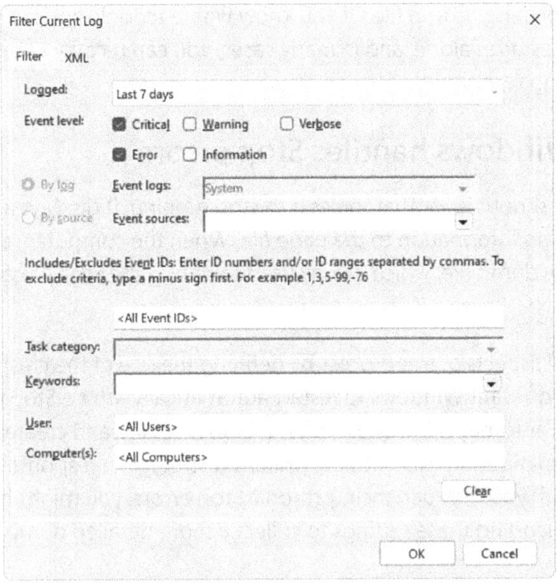

Figure 15-9   If you don't select any Event Level checkboxes, Event Viewer includes all levels in the filtered results. Similarly, any other field you leave blank includes all events without regard to the value of that property.

> ## NOTE
>
> **Event Viewer also includes a basic search capability, which you access by clicking Action, Find. You can perform more precise searches by filtering.**

Dealing with Stop errors

If Windows has ever suddenly shut down, you've probably experienced that sinking feeling in the pit of your stomach. When Windows 11 encounters a serious problem that makes it impossible for the operating system to continue running, it does the only thing it can do, just as every one of its predecessors has done in the same circumstances. It shuts down immediately and displays an ominous text message whose technical details begin with the word *STOP*. Because a Stop error typically appears in white letters on a blue background, this type of message is often referred to as a *blue-screen error* or the *Blue Screen of Death (BSOD)*. (If you're running an Insider Preview release of Windows 11, this screen is green.) When a Stop error appears, it means there is a serious problem that demands your immediate attention.

Windows 11 collects and saves a variety of information in logs and dump files, which a support engineer or developer armed with debugging tools can use to identify the cause of Stop errors. You don't have to be a developer to use these tools, which are available to anyone via download from *https://learn.microsoft.com/windows-hardware/drivers/debugger*. (Don't worry; you can't break anything by simply inspecting a .dmp file.) If you know where to look, however, you can learn a lot from these error messages alone, and in many cases, you can recover completely by using standard troubleshooting techniques.

Customizing how Windows handles Stop errors

When Windows encounters a serious error that forces it to stop running, it displays a Stop message and then writes debugging information to the page file. When the computer restarts, this information is saved as a crash dump file, which can be used to debug the specific cause of the error.

You can customize two crucial aspects of this process by defining the size of the crash dump files and specifying whether you want Windows to restart automatically after a Stop message appears. By default, Windows automatically restarts after a Stop message and creates a crash dump file optimized for automatic analysis. That's the preferred strategy in response to random, isolated Stop errors. But if you're experiencing chronic Stop errors, you might have more troubleshooting success by changing these settings to collect a more detailed dump file and to stop after a crash.

To make this change, open Settings, type **advanced system** in the search box, and then click View Advanced System Settings.

On the Advanced tab of the System Properties dialog, under Startup And Recovery, click Settings. Adjust the settings under the System Failure heading, as shown in Figure 15-10.

If you want Windows to pause at the Stop error message page, clear the Automatically Restart checkbox and click OK.

From the same dialog, you can also define the settings for crash dump files. By default, Windows sets this value to Automatic Memory Dump, which contains the same information as a kernel memory dump. Either option includes memory allocated to kernel-mode drivers and programs, which are most likely to cause Stop errors.

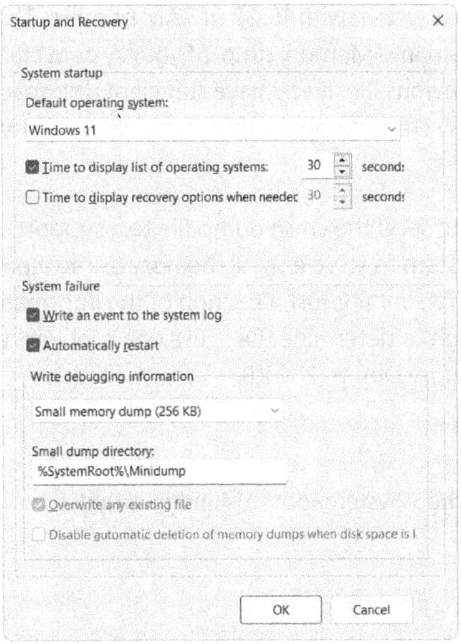

Figure 15-10 By default, Windows manages the size of the memory dump file and restarts automatically after a Stop error. You can pick a larger or smaller dump file here.

TROUBLESHOOTING

Available storage drops dramatically after a stop error

If the paging file size is set to System Managed Size and the Automatic Memory Dump option is selected, Windows can automatically increase the size of the paging file if it needs the space to save a kernel dump file. The increased paging file size is at least equal to the amount of installed RAM. Windows records the time of this event in the registry, using the LastCrashTime value in HKLM\SYSTEM\CurrentControlSet\Control\CrashControl. It reverts to the normal, smaller paging file size in four weeks.

On a PC with a large amount of RAM and a relatively full system drive, this increase in the size of the paging file can noticeably reduce the amount of available storage. If you've resolved the underlying issue that caused the crash, you can safely delete the LastCrashTime registry value, which immediately reverts your paging file to its normal, smaller size.

Because this file does not include unallocated memory or memory allocated to user-mode programs, it usually will be smaller in size than the amount of RAM on your system. The exact size varies, but in general, you can expect the file to be no larger than one-third the size of installed physical RAM, and much less than that on a system with 16 GB of RAM or more. The crash files are stored in %SystemRoot% using the file name Memory.dmp. (If your system crashes multiple times, each new dump file replaces the previous file. If you have sufficient disk space, you can change these default settings so that a new crash dump file does not overwrite any previous dump files.)

If disk space is limited or you're planning to send the crash dump file to a support technician, you might want to consider setting the system to store a small memory dump (commonly called a *mini dump*). A small memory dump contains just a fraction of the information in a kernel memory dump, but it's often enough to determine the cause of a problem. Under Write Debugging Information, select Small Memory Dump (256 KB).

NOTE

Small memory dumps are stored in the %SystemRoot%\Minidump folder.

What's in a Stop error

The exact text of a Stop error varies according to what caused the error. But the format is predictable. Don't bother copying down the error code from the blue screen itself. Instead, look through Event Viewer for an event with the source BugCheck, as shown in the example in Figure 15-11.

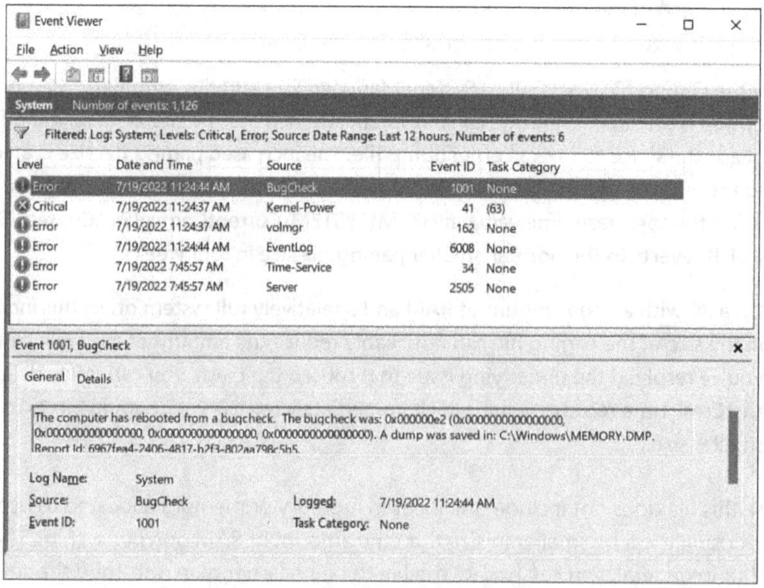

Figure 15-11   Decoding the information in a Stop error can help you find the underlying problem and fix it. Start with the error code—0x000000e2, in this example.

CHAPTER 15

You can gather important details from the bugcheck information, which consists of the error number (in hexadecimal notation, as indicated by the *0x* at the beginning of the code) and up to four parameters that are specific to the error type.

Windows 11 also displays the information in Reliability Monitor, under the heading Critical Events. Select the day on which the error occurred, and then double-click the "Shut down unexpectedly" entry for an event with Windows as the source. That displays the bugcheck information in a slightly more readable format than in Event Viewer, using the term *BlueScreen* as the Problem Event Name.

For a comprehensive and official list of what each error code means, see the Microsoft Hardware Dev Center "Bug Check Code Reference" at *https://bit.ly/bug-check-codes*. A code of 0x00000144, for example, points to problems with a USB 3 controller, whereas 0x0000009F is a driver power state failure. (Our favorite is 0xDEADDEAD, which indicates a manually initiated crash.) In general, you need a debugger or a dedicated analytic tool to get any additional useful information from a memory dump file.

Inside OUT

Create your own Stop error

If for any reason—curiosity, a desire to test debugging procedures, or whatever—you want to generate a Stop error on demand, Windows 11 will accommodate you. As outlined at *https://bit.ly/force-Stop*, the steps involve making a small registry edit and then pressing a multi-keystroke sequence on your USB, PS/2, or Hyper-V keyboard.

Inside OUT

Troubleshoot Stop errors with more powerful tools

Microsoft Windows Volume Licensing customers who have purchased a Software Assurance subscription have access to a powerful Crash Analyzer tool, which is included with the Microsoft Diagnostics and Recovery Toolset, otherwise known as DaRT. Crash Analyzer can examine the memory dump file created by a Stop error and, usually, pinpoint the cause of the problem. For details about DaRT, visit the following page:

https://learn.microsoft.com/microsoft-desktop-optimization-pack/dart-v10/

If you're troubleshooting a PC with a retail or OEM Windows license, consider using the free NirSoft BlueScreenView utility, which does a good job of reading the memory dump file and identifying the most probable cause of the Stop error. Download the tool from *https://www.nirsoft.net/utils/blue_screen_view.html*.

CHAPTER 15

Isolating the cause of a Stop error

If you experience a Stop error, don't panic. Instead, run through the following troubleshooting checklist to isolate the problem and find a solution:

- **Don't forget to rule out hardware problems.** In many cases, software is the victim and not the cause of blue-screen errors. Common hardware failures such as a damaged hard disk drive or a corrupted solid state drive (SSD), defective physical RAM, an overheated CPU chip, or even a bad cable or poorly seated memory module can result in Stop errors. If the errors seem to happen at random and the message details vary each time, there's a good chance you're experiencing hardware problems.

- **Check your memory.** Windows 11 includes a memory diagnostic tool you can use if you suspect a faulty or failing memory chip. To run this diagnostic procedure, type **memory** in the search box and click Windows Memory Diagnostic in the search results. This tool requires a restart to run its full suite of tests, which you can perform immediately or defer until your next restart.

- **Look for a driver name in the error details.** If the error message identifies a specific file name and you can trace that file to a driver for a specific hardware device, you might be able to solve the problem by disabling, removing, or rolling back that driver to an earlier version. The most likely offenders are network interface cards, video adapters, and disk controllers. For more details about managing driver files, see "Updating and uninstalling drivers" in Chapter 13, "Managing hardware and devices."

- **Ask yourself, "What's new?"** Be suspicious of newly installed hardware and software. If you added a device recently, remove it temporarily and see whether the problem goes away. Take an especially close look at software in the categories that install services or file-system filter drivers; these hook into the core operating system files that manage the file system to perform tasks such as scanning for viruses. This category includes backup programs, multimedia applications, networking tools, security software, and DVD-burning utilities. You might need to uninstall the program to resolve the problem; check with the program's developer to see if the issue has been fixed in an updated version that's newer than the one you're running.

- **Search Microsoft Support.** Make a note of the error code and all parameters. Search Microsoft Support using both the full and the short formats. For instance, if you're experiencing a KMODE_EXCEPTION_NOT_HANDLED error, use **0x1E** and **0x0000001E** as your search keywords.

- **Check your system firmware.** Is an update available from the manufacturer of the system or motherboard? Check the firmware documentation carefully; resetting all firmware options to their defaults can sometimes resolve an issue caused by overtweaking.

- **Are you low on system resources?**   Stop errors are sometimes the result of a critical shortage of RAM or disk space. If you can start in Safe Mode, check the amount of physical RAM installed, and look at the system and boot drives to see how much free disk space is available.

- **Is a crucial system file damaged?** To reinstall a driver, restart your computer in Safe Mode. (See the following section.) If your system starts in Safe Mode but not normally, you very likely have a problem driver. Try running Device Manager in Safe Mode and uninstalling the most likely suspect. Or run System Restore in Safe Mode. If restoring to a particular day cures the problem, use Reliability Monitor to determine what changes occurred on or shortly after that day.

Troubleshooting in Safe Mode

In earlier Windows versions, holding down the F8 key while restarting gave you the opportunity to start your system in Safe Mode, with only core drivers and services activated. On modern hardware, with UEFI firmware, that's no longer possible. Safe Mode is still available, but you have to work a little harder to get there.

If you can start Windows and get to the sign-in screen, you can then click the Power button in the lower-right corner of that screen. Hold down Shift as you click Restart to go to the Windows Recovery Environment; there, you can start in Safe Mode and take various other actions, including restoring Windows from an image backup, running System Restore to revert to a saved restore point, and resetting your PC. (We discuss all three topics later in this chapter.)

If you can't start Windows, use the power button on your PC to shut down and restart three times. On the third unsuccessful startup attempt, Windows will start in the Windows Recovery Environment.

When you first arrive in the Windows Recovery Environment, a menu similar to the one in Figure 15-12 appears. Your menu might look slightly different, with a custom option supplied by the OEM. The Use Another Operating System option appears only on a PC that has been configured to boot into multiple operating systems.

CHAPTER 15

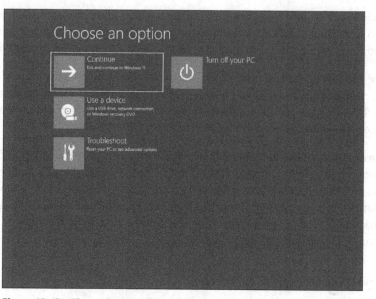

Figure 15-12   The main menu for the Windows Recovery Environment offers a range of troubleshooting options.

To get to Safe Mode, you need to navigate through several menus. Click Troubleshoot in this menu, and then click Advanced Options. On the Advanced Options menu, click Startup Settings; if BitLocker Drive Encryption is enabled on the system drive, enter the 48-digit BitLocker recovery key and then (finally!) click Restart. You then see the Startup Settings menu, as shown in Figure 15-13. You can then choose between Safe Mode, Safe Mode With Networking, or Safe Mode With Command Prompt.

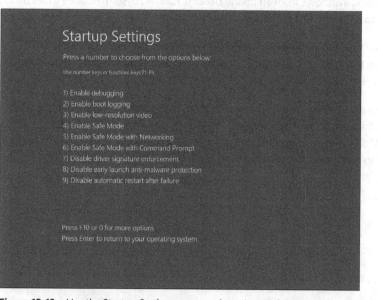

Figure 15-13   Use the Startup Settings menu to boot into Safe Mode, where you can perform tasks such as removing a troublesome program or driver that prevents you from starting normally.

In Safe Mode, you can access certain essential configuration tools, including Device Manager, System Restore, and Registry Editor. If Windows appears to work properly in Safe Mode, you can safely assume there's no problem with the basic services. Use Device Manager, Driver Verifier, and Event Viewer to try to figure out where the trouble lies. If you suspect that a newly installed device or program is the cause of the problem, you can remove the offending software while you're running in Safe Mode. Use Device Manager to uninstall or roll back a hardware driver; use Control Panel to remove a desktop program or utility. Then try restarting the system normally to see whether your changes have resolved the problem.

> ➤ For more information about Device Manager, see "Getting useful information from Device Manager" in Chapter 13. We explain how to use Driver Verifier in the "Sporadic hardware errors" troubleshooting sidebar in "Uninstalling a driver," also in Chapter 13. You can find a detailed discussion of Event Viewer earlier in this chapter.

If you need access to network connections, choose the Safe Mode With Networking option, which loads the base set of Safe Mode files and adds drivers and services required to start Windows networking.

The third Safe Mode option, Safe Mode With Command Prompt, loads the same stripped-down set of services as Safe Mode, but it uses the Windows command interpreter (Cmd.exe) as a shell instead of the graphical Windows Explorer (Explorer.exe, which also serves as the host for File Explorer). This option is unnecessary unless you're having a problem with the Windows graphical interface. The default Safe Mode also provides access to the command line. (Press Windows key+R, and then type **cmd.exe** in the Run dialog.)

The six additional choices on the Startup Settings menu are of use in specialized circumstances:

- **Enable Debugging**   Use this option if you've installed debugging tools and want to switch into a special mode that is compatible with those tools.

- **Enable Boot Logging**   With this option enabled, Windows creates a log file that lists the names and status of all drivers loaded into memory. To view the contents of this file, look for Ntbtlog.txt in the %SystemRoot% folder. If your system is hanging because of a faulty driver, the last entry in this log file might identify the culprit.

- **Enable Low-Resolution Video**   This option starts the computer in 640-by-480 resolution using the current video driver. Use this option to recover from video problems that are caused not by a faulty driver but by incorrect settings, such as an improper resolution or refresh rate.

- **Disable Driver Signature Enforcement**   Use this option if Windows is refusing to start because you installed an unsigned user-mode driver. Windows will start normally, not in Safe Mode. (Note that you cannot disable the requirement for signed kernel-mode drivers.)

CHAPTER 15

- **Disable Early Launch Anti-malware Protection**   This is one of the core security measures of Windows 11 on a UEFI-equipped machine. Unless you're a security researcher or a driver developer, we can't think of any reason to disable this important security check.

- **Disable Automatic Restart After Failure**   Use this option if you're getting Stop errors (blue-screen crashes) and you want the opportunity to see the crash details on the Stop error screen instead of simply pausing there before restarting.

A final option, Launch Recovery Environment, isn't on the main menu but is on a second page that you reach by pressing F10 or 0. Use this command to return to the recovery environment.

Checking disks for errors

Errors in disk media and in the file system can cause a wide range of problems, from an inability to open or save files to blue-screen errors and widespread data corruption. Windows can recover automatically from many disk errors, especially on drives formatted with NTFS.

Inside Out

Check the status of a disk or volume

You can check the properties of any drive—including the volume label, file system, and amount of free space available—by right-clicking the drive in File Explorer's This PC folder and then clicking Properties. You can see the same details and more in Disk Management (Diskmgmt.msc). Of particular interest are details about the status of a disk or volume.

Under normal circumstances, the status information displayed here should report that each disk is Online and each volume is Healthy. A disk status message of Not Initialized means the disk does not contain a valid signature. It might have been prepared on a system running a non-Microsoft operating system, such as Unix or Linux, or the drive might be brand new. If the disk is used by another operating system, do nothing. To prepare a new disk for use with Windows 11, right-click the disk and click Initialize Disk.

A volume status message of Healthy (Unknown Partition) indicates that Windows does not recognize the partition; this occurs with some partitions created by another operating system or by a computer manufacturer that uses a special partition to store system files. You cannot format or access data on an unknown partition using Windows 11's built-in tools. If you're certain the partition is unnecessary, use Disk Management (or a third-party tool) to delete it and create a new partition in the free space created.

To perform a thorough inspection for data errors, run the Windows Check Disk utility (Chkdsk.exe). Two versions of this utility are available—a graphical version that performs basic disk-checking functions, and a command-line version that provides a much more extensive set of customization options.

To check for errors on a local disk, follow these steps:

1. In File Explorer, open This PC, right-click the icon belonging to the drive you want to check, and then click Properties.

2. On the Tools tab, click Check. (If you're using a standard account, you need to supply credentials for an account in the Administrators group to execute this utility.) Unless Windows is already aware of problems with the selected disk, you're likely to see a message that says you don't need to scan the drive.

3. If you want to go ahead and check the disk, click Scan Drive. Windows performs an exhaustive check of the entire disk. If there are bad sectors, Windows locates them and recovers readable information where it can.

The command-line version of Check Disk gives you considerably more options. You can also use it to set up regular disk-checking operations using Task Scheduler (as described in "Task Scheduler" in Chapter 16, "Windows Terminal, PowerShell, and other advanced management tools"). To run this command in its simplest form, right-click Start, click Terminal (Admin), and then type **chkdsk** at the prompt. This command runs Chkdsk in read-only mode, displaying the status of the current drive but not making any changes. If you add a drive letter after the command (*chkdsk d:*, for instance), the report applies to that drive.

To see descriptions of the command-line switches available with the Chkdsk command, type **chkdsk /?**. Here is a partial list of the available switches:

- **/F**   Instructs Chkdsk to fix any errors it detects. This is the most commonly used switch. The disk must be locked. If Chkdsk cannot lock the drive, it offers to check the drive the next time you restart the computer or to dismount the volume you want to check before proceeding. Dismounting is a drastic step; it invalidates all current file handles on the affected volume and can result in loss of data. You should decline the offer. When you do, Chkdsk makes you a second offer—to check the disk the next time you restart your system. You should accept this option. (If you're trying to check the system drive, the only option you're given is to schedule a check at the next startup.)

- **/V**   On FAT32 volumes, /V displays verbose output, listing the name of every file in every directory as the disk check proceeds. On NTFS volumes, this switch displays cleanup messages (if any).

- **/R** Identifies bad sectors and recovers information from those sectors if possible. The disk must be locked. Be aware that this is a time-consuming and uninterruptible process.

- **/X** Forces the volume to dismount, if necessary, and invalidates all open file handles. This option is intended for server administrators. Because of the potential for data loss, it should be avoided.

The following switches are valid only on NTFS volumes:

- **/I** Performs a simpler check of index entries (stage 2 in the Chkdsk process), reducing the amount of time required.

- **/C** Skips the checking of cycles within the folder structure, reducing the amount of time required.

- **/L[:*size*]** Changes the size of the file (in kilobytes) that logs NTFS transactions. If you omit the size parameter, this switch displays the current size. This option is intended for server administrators. Because of the potential for data loss, it also should be avoided in normal use.

- **/B** Reevaluates bad clusters and recovers readable information.

Offering remote support with Quick Assist

Quick Assist offers a new name and a streamlined interface to the Windows Remote Assistance tool available in earlier Windows versions. After making a Quick Assist connection as the helper, you can see the other computer's screen on your system, run diagnostic tools such as Task Manager, edit the remote system's registry, and even use a stylus to annotate the remote display.

One ground rule applies: The computer giving assistance must be able to sign in with a Microsoft account (Quick Assist prompts for one if the user is signed in using a different account type).

The simplest way to run the Quick Assist executable (Quickassist.exe) is to start typing **quick assist** in the search box. The program should quickly appear at the top of the search results. After running the program, the party asking for help chooses Get Assistance, and the party offering support chooses Give Assistance.

The helper sees a six-digit security code and has 10 minutes to supply that code to the person asking for assistance, who enters the code to complete the connection. (You can use the Send Email link to do this, but it's probably simpler to use the phone. The two of you are likely to want to be in touch via phone in any case.) After both parties successfully enter the matching code, the Quick Assist connection is complete.

As the helper, you can choose to view the screen or ask for permission to take control, with the explicit permission of the person receiving assistance. From that point forward, the helper can see the remote screen in the Quick Assist window, with a toolbar that offers the ability to open Task Manager, annotate the screen, and send messages via a chat window. At any time, the person receiving assistance can pause screen sharing or end the Quick Assist session.

Windows 11 backup and recovery options

Through the years, the backup and recovery tools in Windows have evolved, but their fundamental purpose has not changed. How well you execute your backup strategy determines how easily you're able to get back to where you were after something goes wrong—or to start over with an absolutely clean slate. When you reach into the recovery toolkit, you're hoping to perform one of the following three operations:

- **Full reset**   If you're selling or giving away a PC or other device running Windows 11, you can reset it to a clean configuration, wiping personal files in preparation for the new owner. Some Windows users prefer this sort of clean install when they just want to get a fresh start, minus any cruft from previous installations.

- **Recovery**   The "stuff happens" category includes catastrophic hardware failure, malware infection, and system corruption, as well as performance or reliability problems that can't easily be identified with normal troubleshooting. The recovery process involves reinstalling Windows from a backup image or a recovery drive.

- **File restore**   When (not if) you accidentally delete or overwrite an important data file or (ouch) an entire folder, library, or drive, you can call on a built-in Windows 11 tool to bring back the missing data. You can also use this same feature to find and restore earlier versions of a saved file—an original, uncompressed digital photo, for example, or a Microsoft Word document that contains a section you deleted and now want to revisit.

In Windows 11, the primary built-in tool for backing up files is called File History. Its job is to save copies of your local data files—every hour is the default frequency—so that you can find and restore your personal documents, pictures, and other data files when you need them.

Inside OUT

Integrating the cloud into your backup strategy

It's tempting to think of Microsoft OneDrive and other cloud-based storage services as a primary backup. But that strategy is potentially dangerous as well. Cloud services are generally reliable, but it's not out of the question that one might fail or be temporarily unavailable. Moreover, online accounts can be compromised. There are risks associated with using the cloud as your only backup medium. And even when you think you have a backup, it might not be what you expect. On some services, for example, cloud backups of photos might be converted to a lower resolution than the original images, meaning that your only copy of a priceless photo is an inferior compressed version.

Having a complete archive of files backed up to the cloud does offer the reassurance that you can recover any or all those saved files in the event of an accident or natural disaster, such as a fire or flood, that wipes out your primary device and its separate local backup. Given the ubiquity and relatively low cost of online storage services, a truly conscientious approach might be to keep copies of important files in two separate cloud-based services. Just remember that those distant archives are not a replacement for comprehensive local backups on an external storage device or a networked PC.

Windows 11 also includes the old-style Windows 7 Backup And Restore tool. The simplest way to run it is by entering the name of its executable file, Sdclt.exe, in a Terminal window or in the search box. If you can't remember that name, you can find both backup solutions by opening Control Panel and typing **backup** in the search box, as shown in Figure 15-14. (Searching for Backup from the Start menu turns up a pointer to the Settings page Accounts > Windows Backup, which offers tools for backing up apps and preferences but not data.)

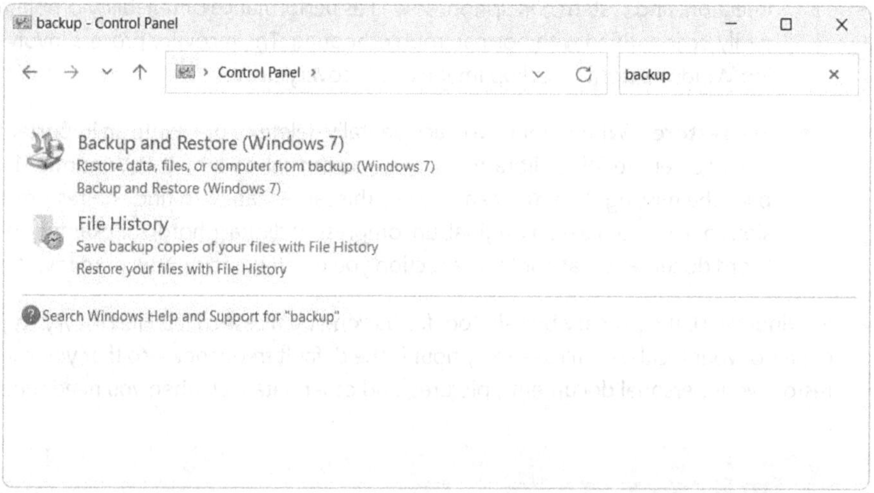

Figure 15-14   The File History feature is the preferred backup solution for Windows 11, but the older Windows 7 Backup and Restore program is still around.

Despite its advanced age, the Windows 7 backup tool can still do one impressive digital magic trick that its newer rivals can't: It can create an image of the system drive that can be restored to an exact copy of the original saved volume, complete with Windows, drivers and utilities, desktop programs, settings, and data files. System image backups were once the gold standard of backup and are still the best way to capture a known good state for quick recovery.

The disadvantage of a full image backup is that it's fixed at a moment in time and doesn't capture files created, changed, or deleted since the image was created. If your primary data files are located in the cloud or on a separate volume from the system drive, that might not be a problem.

The final backup and recovery option in Windows 11 is the "push-button reset" feature, which allows you to reinstall Windows, with the option to keep or discard personal data files. Using this option, you can reset a misbehaving system on the fly, rolling back with relative ease to a clean, fully updated Windows 11 installation. The Reset This PC option is on the Settings > System > Recovery page. (See Figure 15-15.)

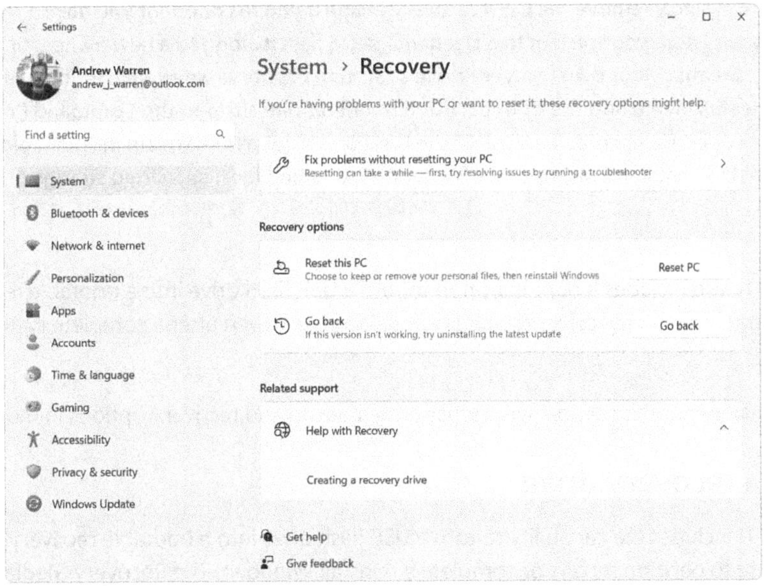

Figure 15-15   The Reset This PC option gives you a fresh start by rolling your system back to a clean Windows 11 installation.

CHAPTER 15

Inside OUT

Do you need the OEM recovery image?

The Windows 11 Reset feature is capable of reinstalling Windows without requiring a recovery partition or any external media. Instead, it uses the existing Windows system files to create a new, clean, side-by-side copy. The result, at least in theory, allows you to recover the sometimes significant disk space used by original equipment manufacturer (OEM) recovery images.

The OEM image restores the device to its original, factory-installed configuration, complete with custom drivers and utilities as well as bundled (and potentially unwanted) software. Depending on when the machine left the factory, this option is likely to be significantly out of date. Despite those shortcomings, we recommend keeping this partition on any device that's still under the manufacturer's warranty; delete it only if you're running short of space for storing data.

You can safely remove the OEM recovery image if you're confident you have a reliable way to restore your system to a clean image (to pass it along to a new owner, for example). Creating your own recovery drive or system image, as we explain in this chapter, fills either bill. Removing the OEM partition might require a trip to the Command Prompt window and some judicious use of the DiskPart utility, as we explain in "Managing disks from the command prompt" in Chapter 8, "Managing local and cloud storage."

Windows 11 also includes a built-in option to turn a USB flash drive into a bootable recovery drive. Using this recovery drive, you can restore Windows, even after a complete system drive failure.

In the remainder of this section, we discuss these backup and recovery options in more detail.

Using a recovery drive

Windows 11 includes the capability to turn a USB flash drive into a bootable recovery drive that you can use to perform repairs or completely reinstall Windows. The Recovery Media Creator (Recoverydrive.exe) creates a bootable drive that contains the Windows Recovery Environment.

➤ For instructions on how to create a recovery drive, with or without Windows installation media, see "Downloading and creating installation media," in Chapter 2, "Setting up a new Windows 11 PC."

To use the recovery drive, configure your PC so that you can boot from the USB flash drive. (That process, which is unique for many machines, might involve tapping a key or pressing a combination of buttons such as Power+Volume Up when restarting.)

If you see the Recover From A Drive option when you restart, congratulations—the system has recognized your recovery drive, and you are (fingers crossed) a few minutes away from being back in business.

Inside OUT

Download a recovery image

If your system won't start, but you can get to the internet on another machine, you might be able to download a recovery image from your hardware vendor and then copy that to a USB flash drive. Microsoft, for example, offers this service for its Surface models. (Go to *https://support.microsoft.com/surfacerecoveryimage* and provide the serial number of your device.) For other vendors, check support offerings to see whether an image is available. If a custom recovery image is not available, you can use Microsoft's Media Creation Tool to download the latest version of Windows 11 and copy it to a USB flash drive or save it as an ISO file. For details, see "Downloading and creating installation media," in Chapter 2.

The menu that appears when you start from a recovery drive allows you to repair a PC that has startup issues. Choose Troubleshoot to get to the Advanced Options menu, where you can choose to perform a startup repair, use System Restore to undo a problematic change, or open a Command Prompt window to use system tools such as DiskPart from the command line.

Using File History to protect files and folders

File History is designed as a "set it and forget it" feature. After you enable this backup application, it first copies all personal data files in your personal profile to a secondary drive, usually an external device or a network location. File History then scans the file system at regular intervals (hourly, by default), looking for newly created files and changes to existing files, and adds those files to the backup store.

NOTE

File history is not available on Windows 11 devices that run on an Arm processor.

You can browse the backed-up files by date and time or search the entire history, and then restore one or more of those backed-up files to their original location or to a different folder.

But first, you have to go through a simple setup process.

Setting up File History

Although the File History feature is installed by default, it's not enabled until you designate a drive to serve as the backup destination. This drive is typically an external storage device, such as a USB-attached hard drive, or a network location. On desktop PCs with multiple internal hard disks, you can choose a second internal hard disk as the File History location. Removable drives, such as USB flash drives, may not be eligible. (We have seen inconsistent behavior from Windows in this regard. In any case, using a small removable drive for backup purposes is not a stellar idea.) The File History setup wizard shows you only eligible drives when you set up File History for the first time.

CAUTION

Be sure you specify a File History volume that is on a separate physical drive from the one that contains the files you're backing up. Windows warns you, sternly, if you try to designate a separate volume on the same physical drive as your system drive. The problem? One sadly common cause of data loss is the failure of the drive itself. If the backups and original files are stored on the same drive, a hardware failure wipes everything out. Having backups on a separate physical drive allows them to remain independent.

To turn on File History for the first time, open Control Panel and search for and then select File History. Click Add A Drive to scan for available File History drives. The File History Wizard responds by showing you all drives that are eligible for use as a File History destination. Figure 15-16 shows a system that has a two external USB hard drives attached. Selecting one of the available locations turns on the File History service and begins the backup process, with the backup frequency set to one hour.

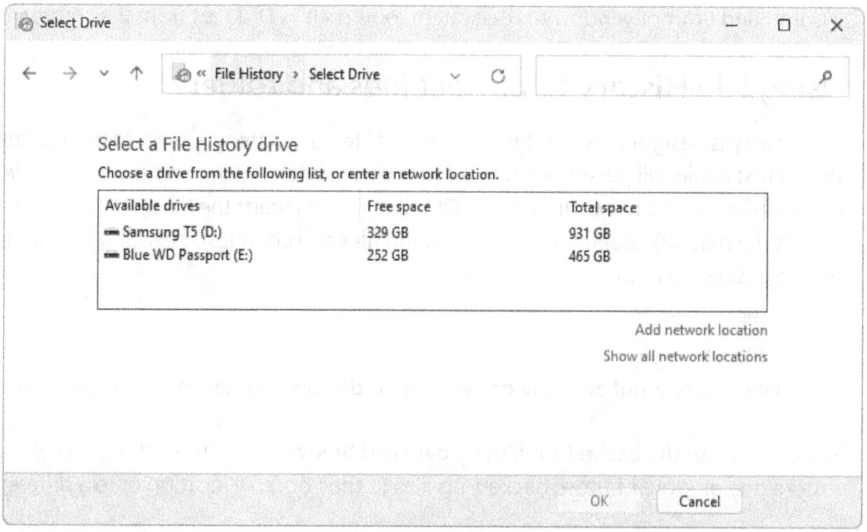

Figure 15-16   Before you can enable File History, you must specify a location (preferably an external USB drive) to hold the backed-up files.

You can also choose to back up your files to a network shared folder, presuming you have the necessary shared folder and NTFS permissions. To add a network share for which you have read/write permission, in File History, click Select Drive. Click the Add Network Location link. Browse for or enter the full path of a shared folder to which you have the necessary access. If required, enter and save alternative network credentials. Select the newly added drive and click OK.

By default, File History checks your drives and folders that are included in libraries once an hour, saving copies of any new or changed files as part of the operation. You can adjust this setting in either direction, choosing from nine intervals that range from every 10 minutes (if you really hate the idea of ever losing a saved file) to once daily.

➤ For details on how to add folders to libraries so they're automatically included in File History, see "Using libraries," in Chapter 9, "Using File Explorer."

File History backups are saved by default forever. (You receive a warning when your File History drive is full.) However, you can alter the Keep Saved Versions setting to 1, 3, 6, or 9 months or 1 or 2 years. The "set it and forget it" Until Space Is Needed setting allows File History to automatically jettison old backups to make way for new ones when the drive is full.

You can change the backup interval and time period for saving backups by selecting Advanced Settings, as shown in Figure 15-17.

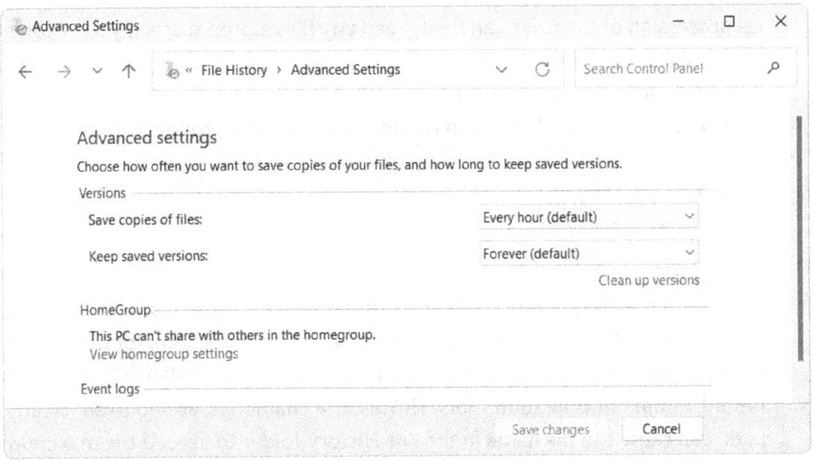

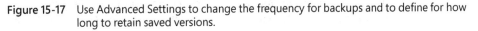

Figure 15-17 Use Advanced Settings to change the frequency for backups and to define for how long to retain saved versions.

When you first enable and run File History, it creates a full copy of all files in the locations configured for backup.

CHAPTER 15

There's nothing complicated or proprietary about File History volumes. The following rules apply to external drives and shared network folders:

- Windows creates a FileHistory folder on the destination drive, with a separate private subfolder for each user. Thus, on a device that includes multiple user accounts, each user's files can be backed up separately.

- Within each user's private subfolder are one or more additional subfolders, one for each device backed up. This folder arrangement allows you to use a single external drive to record File History backups from different devices.

- Each backup set includes two folders. The Configuration folder contains XML files and, if necessary, index files to allow speedier searches. The Data folder contains backed-up files, which are stored in a hierarchy that matches their original location.

- Backed-up files are not compressed. File names are the same as the original, with a date and time stamp appended (in parentheses) to distinguish different versions. As a result, you can browse a File History drive in File Explorer and use search tools to locate a file or folder without using the File History app.

CAUTION

Files stored on a File History drive are not encrypted by default. Anyone who has physical possession of the drive can freely read any files stored there. If you're concerned about confidential information contained in an external File History drive, we recommend you encrypt the drive. When you enable File History, you are warned to encrypt your backup drive. Click the Turn On BitLocker link to complete this task.

TROUBLESHOOTING

Some files are missing from file history backups

Because of the unique way File History organizes and names backed-up files, you might find that some files aren't backed up properly. This can happen, for example, if you append a version date and time to the name of a file, particularly if the file is deeply nested within multiple subfolders. Those extra characters, added to an already long path, can cause the file name in the File History folder to exceed the maximum path limit of 260 characters. You can spot these errors easily in the File History event logs. In Control Panel, click Advanced Settings and then click Open File History Event Logs To View Recent Events Or Errors. Resolve any issues by moving the original files or subfolders to a location with a path name that's sufficiently shorter.

What does File History back up?

By default, File History backs up all folders in the current user profile (including those created by third-party apps) as well as the contents of local folders that have been added to custom libraries.

➤ For an overview of what's in a default user profile and instructions on how to work with libraries, see "Organizing personal data with user profile folders and libraries," in Chapter 9.

To manage the list of folders backed up by File History, in Control Panel in File History, select Exclude Folders. Then select Add and define those folders you want to exclude. When you've defined all the folders you want to exclude, click Save Changes.

NOTE

It's worth noting that the configurable options for managing which folders are or are not backed up is more limited in Windows 11 than in Windows 10.

It's useful to exclude certain folders when you want to avoid filling your File History drive with large files that don't require backing up. If you routinely put interesting but ephemeral video files into a subfolder in your Downloads folder, for example, you might choose to exclude that Videos subfolder completely from File History, while leaving the rest of the Downloads folder to be backed up.

When a File History drive fills up, you can either change the settings to remove old backed-up files and make room for new ones or swap in a new drive. If you choose the latter option, on the File History page in Control Panel, click or tap Select Drive, and then browse and select a new drive.

When you select a new drive, Windows prompts you to move your existing files to the new location. This is useful if you are specifying a replacement drive that is larger than your original drive. The copy process can take an extended time depending on how much space your existing files use.

Restoring files and folders

File History backups give you multiple ways to recover files that are lost, damaged, or accidentally deleted. You can restore the entire contents of a folder or drive as part of the recovery from a hard drive crash, for example. You can even resuscitate an earlier version of a document so that you can recover content you changed or deleted in a later draft.

The simplest way to recover an earlier version of an existing file or folder is to start from File Explorer. If you know which version you want, right-click the file in File Explorer, click Show More Options and then choose Restore Previous Versions. That opens the file's Properties dialog with the Previous Versions tab selected, displaying a list of available backed-up versions sorted by date, as shown in Figure 15-18.

The arrow to the right of the Open button at the bottom of the Previous Versions list gives you a choice of how to open the selected item. Clicking Open works especially well for Office documents; you get a read-only copy of the document in the app that created it. That way, you won't accidentally overwrite the current version of the document with the older one you just opened.

Click Open In File History to use the File History application instead. (We say more about the File History application in a moment.)

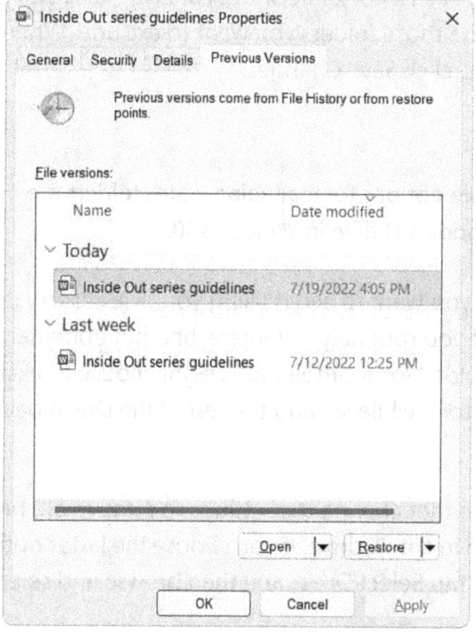

Figure 15-18 When you know exactly which file you want to restore, it's often quickest to get it from the Previous Versions tab in File Explorer.

The second button beneath the File Versions list also provides a pair of choices: Click Restore to overwrite the current version, or click Restore To and save a copy to a different location. If you attempt to restore a previous version of a file to the original location and the original file still exists, you see the Replace Or Skip Files dialog, which gives you an opportunity to change your mind or save the new file as a copy in the same location. If you want to restore a copy without deleting the original, click Compare Info For Both Files and then select the checkbox for both the original file and the restored previous version, as shown in Figure 15-19. The restored copy has a number appended to the name to distinguish it from the original.

Not sure which version you want? Select a version and click Open In File History to preview that version. Or select a document and then, on the Home tab in File Explorer, click History. That option opens a preview of the most recent saved version in the File History app. Use the left-arrow button in the group of controls at the bottom of the main window to go back in time until you find the right version. Right-click the big green button for Restore and Restore To options.

The File History app offers a distinctly different take on browsing backed-up files. Although it resembles File Explorer in some respects, it adds a unique dimension—the ability to choose a set of saved files from a specific date and time, and then scan, scroll through, or search that entire set of files.

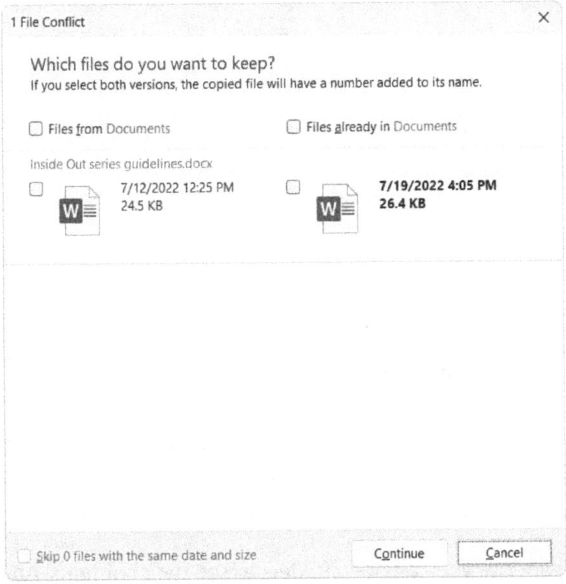

Figure 15-19   To restore a previous version of a file without replacing the original, click the Compare Info For Both Files option and then select both versions in the File Conflict dialog.

You're most likely to use the File History app in one of the following two ways:

- To restore some or all files from a backup, open File History in Control Panel and click Restore Personal Files. In the File History app, shown in Figure 15-20, you can then select the files or folders you want to restore.

- To restore one or more files or folders, open File Explorer, select the file or folder you're interested in recovering, right-click, select Show More Options, and then click Restore Previous Versions.

Figure 15-20 shows the File History app, which has an address bar, navigation controls, and a search box along the top, very much like File Explorer. What's different are the time stamp (above the file browsing pane) and the three controls below the pane that allow time travel without the need for flux capacitors or other imaginary time-machine components.

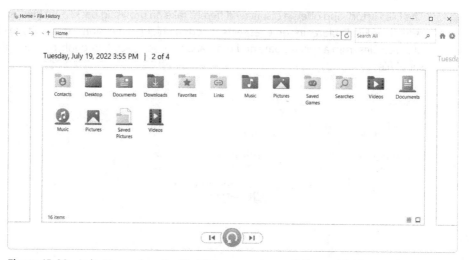

Figure 15-20   In its Home view, the File History app shows all files and folders set for regular backup. Scroll left for older backups, right for more recent ones.

The legend at the top of the window tells you the date and time of the currently displayed backup. Use the Previous Version and Next Version controls at the bottom of the window to move between backups. (You can also use the keyboard shortcuts Ctrl+Left/Right Arrow.)

Within the File History app window, you can open folders to see their contents. An address bar at the top, along with the invaluable up arrow beside it, allows you to navigate as you might in File Explorer. As with File Explorer, you can use the search box in the upper right to narrow the results by file type, keyword, or file contents. Because file names rarely provide enough detail to determine whether a specific file is the one you're looking for, File History has a preview function. Double-click a file to show its contents in the File History window.

To restore a file or folder you deleted or overwrote, move backward through the backups until you reach the desired date. Double-click to open a folder; use Ctrl+click to select multiple items. When you've made your selections, click the big green button to restore the selected items to their original location. If you'd prefer to restore the items to a separate location, right-click the green button and click Restore To.

The option to restore entire folders is especially useful when you're switching to a new PC. After you complete one last backup on your old PC, plug the File History drive into your new PC, and then use the big green Restore button to copy your backed-up files to corresponding locations on the new PC.

As with File Explorer, you can change the view of files in the File History browsing window. By using the two shortcuts in the lower-right corner, you can quickly switch between Details and Large Icons view. (The latter is particularly useful when looking through folders full of digital photos.)

Inside OUT

Transfer your File Explorer smarts to File History

There's no need to open a menu or click a tiny icon to change the view in File History. Any of the eight predefined views, from Content through Extra Large Icons, can be invoked with its keyboard shortcut, Ctrl+Shift+*number*. Any number between 1 and 8 works, with Ctrl+Shift+2 switching to Large Icons view and Ctrl+Shift+6 to Details view. These same shortcuts work in File Explorer as well.

Using the Reset option to recover from serious problems

One of the signature features of Windows 8 turned out to be quietly revolutionary: an easy way for anyone to reset Windows to its original configuration using a Refresh or Reset command, with no technical skills required.

Windows 11 significantly refines that capability under a single Reset command. The most important change eliminates the need to have a disk-hogging OEM recovery image in a dedicated partition at the end of the hard drive. In Windows 11, that recovery image and its associated partition are no longer the primary recovery option. Instead, Windows 11 accomplishes recovery operations by rebuilding the operating system to a clean state using existing system files.

This push-button reset option has the same effect as a clean install, without the hassles of finding drivers and without wiping out potentially valuable data.

The Reset This PC option is near the top of the list on the System > Recovery page in Settings, as shown earlier in Figure 15-15. It's also the featured choice on the Troubleshoot menu when you restart in the Windows Recovery Environment, as shown in Figure 15-21.

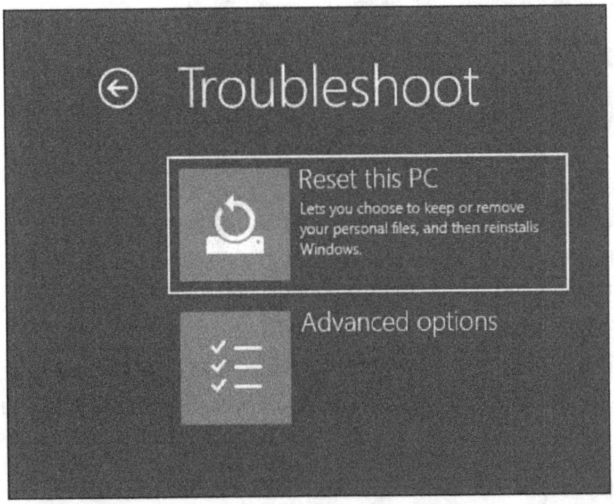

Figure 15-21   You can reset your Windows 11 PC by starting the Windows Recovery Environment and choosing the top option shown here.

CHAPTER 15

When you reset a PC, Windows 11 and its drivers are restored to the most recent rollup state. After the reset is complete, the PC includes all updates except those installed in the past 28 days, a design that allows recovery to succeed when a freshly installed update is part of the problem.

For PCs sold with Windows 11 already installed, any customized settings and desktop programs installed by the manufacturer might be restored with the Windows 11 reset. These customizations are saved in a separate container, which is created as part of the OEM setup process.

All of the default preinstalled Windows apps (Photos, Mail, and Calendar, for example) are restored, along with any Windows apps that were added to the system by the OEM or as part of an enterprise deployment. App updates are downloaded and reinstalled via the Store automatically after recovery.

Windows desktop programs are not restored and must be manually reinstalled. Likewise, any previously purchased Store apps are discarded and must be reinstalled from the Store.

Resetting a PC isn't something you do accidentally. The process involves multiple confirmations, with many opportunities to bail out if you get cold feet or realize that you need to do just *one* more backup before you irrevocably wipe the disk. The first step offers you the option to keep your personal files or remove everything, as shown in Figure 15-22.

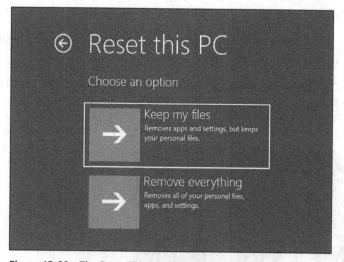

Figure 15-22   The Reset This PC option lets you choose whether to keep your personal files or remove everything and start with a completely clean slate.

If you're performing the reset operation in preparation for selling or donating your computer, you probably want to use the second option. Otherwise, choose the first option to retain your personal files.

If you're removing everything on a system with more than one drive, you can choose to remove files from only the drive where Windows is installed or from all drives.

Next, you're prompted to reinstall Windows from local files, or from a cloud download. Consider that around 4 GB of files are downloaded to reinstall from the cloud, and unless you have a reasonable internet bandwidth, that might take an extended time.

You're now asked whether you want to Just Remove My Files or Fully Clean The Drive. The Fully Clean The Drive option can add hours to the process. Note that this option, while thorough, is not certified to meet any government or industry standards for data removal.

If you made it this far through the process, you have only one more confirmation to get through. That confirmation, shown in Figure 15-23, displays the choices you made, with one last Cancel option. To plunge irreversibly ahead, click Reset.

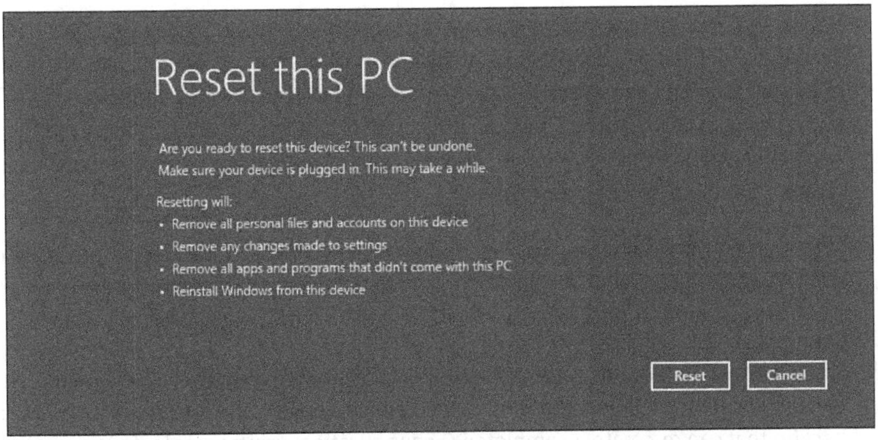

Figure 15-23   This is your last chance to back out when resetting a PC.

The reset option can be a tremendous time-saver, but it's not all-powerful. Your attempts to reset Windows can be thwarted by a handful of scenarios:

- If operating system files have been heavily corrupted or infected by malware, the reset process might not work—although the cloud download option might work better.

- If the problem is caused by a cumulative update that is more than 28 days old, the reset might not be able to resolve that problem.

- If a user chooses the wrong language during the out-of-box-experience (OOBE) phase on a single-language Windows version (typically sold in developing countries and regions), a complete reinstallation might be required.

NOTE

For workplace computers that are domain-joined, it's likely that a network administrator can reimage a problematic computer, perhaps by using Endpoint Configuration Manager desktop images. This can achieve very much the same end-result—a computer that is reset to an earlier point in time. For workplaces that manage their computers using Endpoint Manager (Microsoft Intune), administrators can choose between performing a remote Fresh Start (which is similar to Reset This PC) or, where applicable, an Autopilot Reset, which returns a device to a fully configured and managed state.

If the reset option doesn't work, the best option is reinstalling with the assistance of a recovery drive, as we describe in "Working with ISO files directly," in Chapter 2.

Using the Windows 7 Backup program

Windows 11 includes the Windows Backup program, which was originally released as part of Windows 7. Its feature set is basically the same as its distant predecessor, and it's included primarily for compatibility with backups created using that older operating system. (In fact, the name of the executable file, Sdclt.exe, is an inadvertent giveaway of just how old this program is. It's short for SafeDocs Client, the original name of this feature when it debuted as part of a very early Windows Vista beta release.)

If you have a working backup routine based on the Windows 7 Backup program, we don't want to stand in your way. The version included with Windows 11 does all the familiar tasks you depend on, and we suggest you carry on. After all, the best backup program is the one you use.

For Windows 11, there are better backup utilities, but we continue to recommend the Windows Backup program for the one task it does exceptionally well: Use it to make a system image backup that can re-create a complete PC configuration, using a single drive or multiple drives. Restoring that system image creates a perfect copy of the system configuration as it existed on the day that system image was captured, without the need to reinstall and reconfigure applications.

To restore an image backup, boot into the Windows Recovery Environment, choose an image file to restore, and complete the process by restoring from your latest file backup, which is likely to be more recent than the image. (Depending on the age of the backup image, you might also need to install the latest feature update for Windows, followed by the latest cumulative quality update.) The image files that Windows Backup creates are largely hardware independent, which means that—with some limitations—you can restore your backup image to a new computer of a different brand and type.

Inside OUT

Use a system image to save your custom configuration

The single greatest use for a system image backup is to clean up an OEM configuration, leaving Windows intact, removing unwanted software, and installing your favorite apps. Being able to return to a baseline configuration quickly is a trick that IT pros learned long ago as a way of deploying Windows in large organizations. By mastering the system image backup feature, you can accomplish the same result even in an environment with a few PCs instead of a thousand.

Creating a system image backup

To create a system image, open Control Panel and search for Backup; then click Backup And Restore (Windows 7). You can skip a few clicks by typing **sdclt** in the search box or the Run box. That opens the tool shown in Figure 15-24.

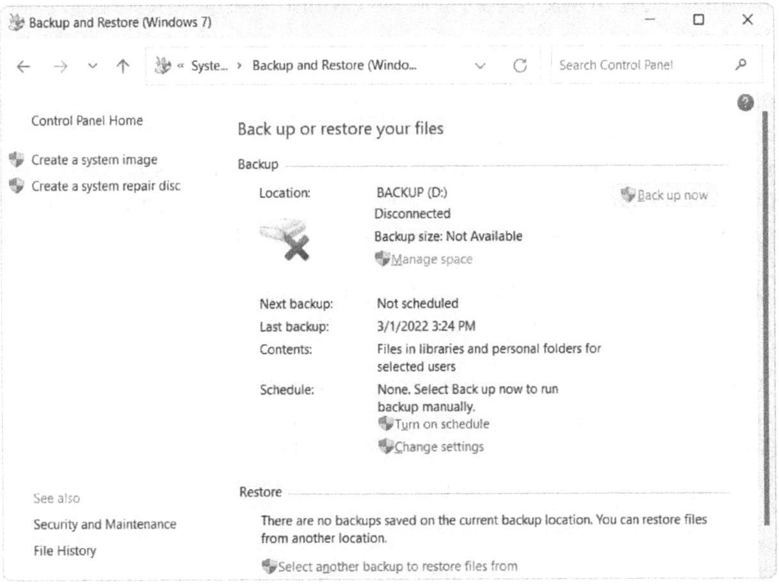

Figure 15-24   The vintage Windows 7 Backup tool isn't necessary for file backup tasks, but it's ideal for capturing a complete image of a Windows installation for disaster recovery.

When you first open Windows Backup, a message alerts you that the program has not been set up. You can ignore that message and the options in the center of that window, and instead click the Create A System Image link at the left side of the window. That opens the efficient Create A System Image Wizard. The first step asks you to define a destination for your system image.

The ideal destination for a system image backup is a local hard disk, internal or external. If the Windows Backup program detects a drive that qualifies, it suggests that destination in the list of hard disks at the top of the dialog. The second option lets you choose a DVD writer as the target for the backup operation; although this option might have made sense a decade ago, we do not recommend it today.

TROUBLESHOOTING

Windows Backup says your drive is not a valid backup location

If you try to choose a removable drive that is not a hard drive, such as a USB flash drive or SD card, Windows Backup returns this error message: "The drive is not a valid backup location." In its conventional backup role, Windows Backup can save data files on just about any storage medium. System image backups, however, must be saved on a fixed or removable hard disk (not portable media) formatted using NTFS or in a network location.

When you create a system image backup, the resulting image file stores the complete contents of all selected drives during its first backup. If the backup target is a local (internal or external) hard drive, subsequent backup operations store only new and changed data. Therefore, the subsequent, incremental backup operation typically runs much faster, depending on how much data has been changed or added since the previous image backup operation.

If you choose a shared network folder as the backup destination, you can save only one image backup. Any subsequent image backup wipes out the previous image backup.

If you have multiple hard drives, Windows displays a dialog in which you choose the volumes you want to include in the backup. By default, all volumes that contain Windows system files (including the EFI System Partition and the Windows Recovery Environment) are selected. If other volumes are available, you can optionally choose to include them in the image backup as well.

The disk space requirements for an image-based backup can be substantial, especially on a well-used system that includes lots of user data files. Windows Backup estimates the amount of disk space the image will use, as in the example in Figure 15-25, and warns you if the destination you choose doesn't have sufficient free disk space.

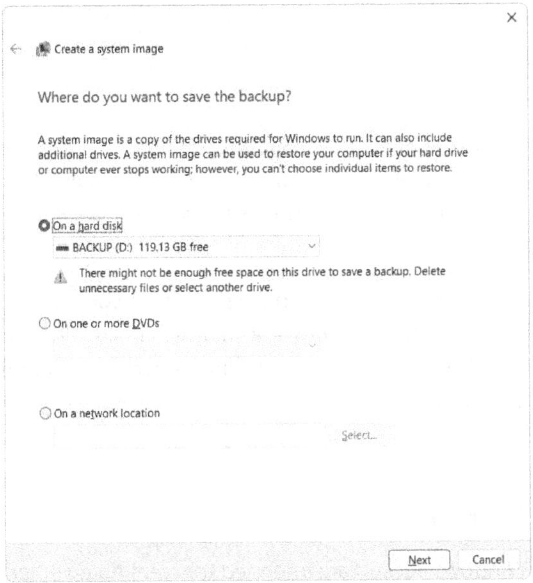

Figure 15-25 The Windows Backup program warns you if the destination drive lacks enough space to hold the image you plan to create.

After you confirm your settings, click Start Backup to begin the process of building and saving your image.

System images are stored in virtual hard disk (VHD) format. Although the data is not compressed, it is compact because the image file does not include the hard drive's unused space and some other unnecessary files, such as hibernation files, page files, and restore points. Incremental system image backups on a local drive are not written to a separate folder. Instead, new and updated files (actually, the changed blocks in those files) are written to the same VHD file. The older blocks are stored as shadow copies in the VHD file, allowing you to restore any previous version.

The final step of the image backup process offers to help you create a system repair disc on a writable CD or DVD. This option might be useful for an older PC, but it's redundant if you already created a recovery drive as described in "Downloading and creating installation media," in Chapter 2.

CHAPTER 15

Inside OUT

Save multiple image backups on a network

If you specify a shared network folder as the destination for an image backup, beware of the consequences if you try to reuse that location for a subsequent backup of the same computer. If the backup operation fails for any reason, the older backup will be overwritten, but the newer backup will not be usable. In other words, you'll have no backup.

You can avoid this risk by creating a new subfolder in the shared network folder to hold each new image backup. The disadvantage, of course, is that each image file will occupy as much space as the original disk, unlike an incremental image backup on an external hard drive, which stores only the changed data.

Restoring a system image backup

The system image capabilities in Windows Backup are intended for creating an emergency recovery kit for a single PC. In that role, they function exceptionally well. If your hard drive fails catastrophically, or if you want to wipe your existing Windows installation and start with a clean custom image you created a few weeks or months ago, you've come to the right place.

Your options (and potential gotchas) become more complex if you want to use these basic tools to work with a complex set of physical disks and partitions. That's especially true if the disk layout to which you want to restore an image has changed from the time you created the original image—if you replaced the original system disk with one that has a larger capacity, for example.

In this section, we assume you created an image backup of your system disk and want to restore it to a system that is essentially the same (in terms of hardware and disk layout) as the one you started with. In that case, you can restart your computer using a recovery drive or bootable Windows 11 installation media and then choose the Repair Your Computer option.

Choose Advanced Options, See More Recovery Options, and then select System Image Recovery. If you're restoring the image backup to the same system on which it was originally created, and the external drive containing the backup file is available, you should see a dialog proposing that option. Verify that the date and time and other details of the image match the one you want to restore, and then click Next to continue.

If the image file you're planning to restore from is on a network share or if you want to use a different image, choose Select A System Image and then click Next. You see a dialog that lists additional image files available on local drives. Select the correct file, and then click Next to select a specific image backup. If the image file you're looking for is in a shared network folder, click the Advanced button and then click Search For A System Image On The Network. Enter the network location that contains your saved image, along with credentials (a username and password) that have authorized access to that location.

Restoring an image backup completely replaces the current contents of each volume in the image file. The restore program offers to format the disk or disks to which it is restoring files before it begins the restore process; if you have multiple drives or volumes and you're nervous about wiping out valuable data files, it offers an option to exclude certain disks from formatting.

The important point to recognize about restoring a system image is that it replaces the current contents of system volumes with the exact contents that existed at the time of the image backup you select. That means your Windows system files and registry will be returned to healthy (provided the system was in good shape when you performed your most recent backup and that no hardware-related issues have cropped up since then). Whatever programs were installed when you backed up your system will be restored entirely. All other files on the restored disk, including your documents, will also be returned to their prior states, and any changes made after your most recent backup will be lost.

CAUTION

If you keep your documents on the same volume as your system files, restoring a system image is likely to entail the loss of recent work—unless, of course, you have an up-to-date file backup, or you have the good fortune to have made an image backup almost immediately before your current troubles began. The same is true if you save documents on a volume separate from your system files but have included that data volume in your image backup. If you have documents that have not been backed up, you can avoid losing recent work by first copying them to a disk that will not be affected by the restore process—a USB flash drive, for example, or some other form of removable media. You can use the Command Prompt option in the Windows Recovery Environment to copy these documents. (For details about using the Command Prompt option, see "Working in a Command Prompt session" in Chapter 16.) If you do have a recent file backup, first restore the image backup and then restore your backed-up datafiles.

The main hardware limitation for restoring a system image backup is that the target computer must have at least as many hard drives as the source system, and each drive must be at least as big as its corresponding drive in the source system. This means, for example, that you can't restore a system image from a system that has a 500 GB hard drive to a system with a 256 GB SSD, even if the original system used far less than 256 GB of drive space. Keep in mind also that on a system with multiple physical disks, you might have to adjust firmware settings to ensure that Windows restores the image of your system volume to the correct drive.

If your new computer meets the space requirements, restoring a system image should work. This is true even when the source and target computers use different disk controllers. Similarly, other differences—such as different graphics cards, audio cards, processors, and so on—shouldn't prevent you from restoring a system image to a different computer because hardware drivers are isolated from the rest of the image information and are rebuilt as part of the restore process. (You might need to reactivate Windows because of hardware changes.)

> **TROUBLESHOOTING**
>
> **Your backup folders are "empty"**
>
> If you use File Explorer to browse to the folder containing your system image backup, when you rest the mouse pointer over a folder name, the pop-up tip might identify it as an "Empty folder." Alarmed, you right-click the folder and choose Properties, only to find that the folder apparently contains 0 bytes, 0 files, and 0 folders. Don't worry. This is the normal condition when your backups are stored on an NTFS volume because, by default, only the System user account has permission to view the files. (That's a reasonable security and reliability precaution, which prevents you or another user from inadvertently deleting a key backup file.) If you're confident in your ability to work safely with backup files in their native format, the solution is simple: Double-click the folder name. Follow the prompts, including a User Account Control (UAC) consent dialog, to permanently add your user account to the folder's permissions list, giving you Full Control access to the folder.

Configuring and using System Restore

The System Restore feature is a relatively minor part of the recovery toolkit in Windows 11, but it can be useful for quickly undoing recent changes that introduced instability. When System Restore is enabled, the Volume Shadow Copy service takes occasional snapshots of designated local storage volumes. These snapshots occur before Windows Update installs new updates and when supported software installers run. You can also create snapshots manually—a sensible precaution before you make system-level changes.

System Restore snapshots take note of differences in the details of your system configuration—registry settings, driver files, third-party applications, and so on—allowing you to undo changes and roll back a system configuration to a time when it was known to work correctly.

> **NOTE**
>
> In Windows 7, the volume snapshots created by System Restore also included a record of changes to data files on designated drives, allowing you to restore previous versions of those data files. In Windows 11, this capability is part of the File History feature, which we described in detail earlier in this chapter.

Note that System Restore monitors all files it considers system-related, which includes executable files and installers. If you download the latest version of a favorite utility and store it in your Downloads folder, it is removed if you roll back to a System Restore checkpoint from before it was downloaded.

Inside OUT

What's in a restore point?

Restore points in Windows 11 include a full copy of the registry at the time of the snapshot as well as information about changes made to specific files on that volume since the previous snapshot was created. Historically, files are monitored if they include any of 570+ file name extensions specifically designated for monitoring. This list (which cannot be modified) contains many file types that are clearly programs and system files, with extensions such as .exe, .dll, and .vbs. But it also includes other files you might not think of as system files, including .inf and .ini. You can see the entire list at *https://bit.ly/ monitored-extensions*. The information there is most useful for programmers and system administrators, but you might want to browse the extension list if you're curious why System Restore deleted a file.

To check the status of the System Restore feature, in Settings, search for and select Recovery; then, in Advanced Recovery Tools, click Configure System Restore. Under Protection Settings is a list of internal and external NTFS-formatted drives. (See Figure 15-26.) A value of On indicates that restore points are being created automatically for the associated drive.

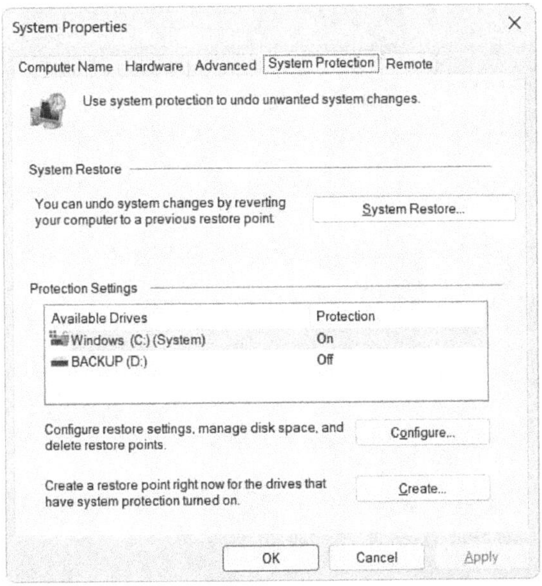

Figure 15-26   The System Protection tab shows available disks and their current protection settings (on or off). To enable protection for a drive that's off, select it and click Configure.

CHAPTER 15

Using the System Properties dialog, you can enable or disable automatic monitoring for any local drive. On previous versions of Windows, system protection is fully enabled for the system drive by default and is disabled for all other local drives. In our experience, Windows 11 typically disables system protection; we're not aware of any documentation that explains how or why Windows 11 chooses to enable or disable this feature, but the obvious reason is to save disk space. After a successful upgrade, we recommend that you check these settings and, if you find this feature important, re-enable system protection for the system drive at least.

You can manually create a restore point at any time for all drives that have system protection enabled. Click the Create button at the bottom of the System Protection tab to open the Create A Restore Point dialog. Enter a meaningful description and then click Create to enter the descriptive text.

To turn system protection on or off, or to adjust the amount of space it uses, select a drive from the Available Drives list and then click Configure. That opens the dialog shown in Figure 15-27.

The information under the Disk Space Usage heading shows both the current usage and the maximum amount of space that will be used for snapshots before System Protection begins deleting old restore points to make room for new ones. Move the Max Usage slider to change the amount of disk space reserved for restore points. We recommend using no more than 5 percent of the disk, up to a maximum of 10 GB, on volumes that are larger than 64 GB.

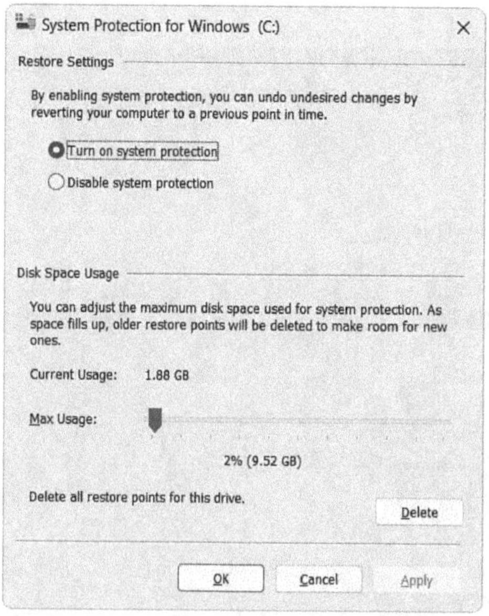

Figure 15-27   Use the Max Usage slider to adjust the amount of disk space used by System Restore snapshots.

If you're concerned about disk space usage and you're confident you won't need to use any of your currently saved restore points, you can click the Delete button in the lower-right corner under the Disk Space Usage heading to remove all existing restore points without changing other System Protection settings.

Rolling back to a previous restore point

The most common reason to roll back to a previously saved restore point is to undo the de-stabilizing effect of a freshly installed app or driver that conflicts with other software or drivers on your system. First, if possible, uninstall the offending app or driver and then apply the restore point captured before the installation. That should remove any problematic system files and registry settings that were left behind by the uninstaller.

To see a list of recent restore points, type **rstrui** at a command prompt or click System Restore on the System Protection tab of the System Properties dialog. (If you're running under a stan-dard user account, you need to enter an administrator's credentials in a UAC dialog to con-tinue.) That opens the System Restore Wizard. Select the restore point you want, then confirm your choice in the ensuing dialog.

To choose a restore point other than the most recent one, click Choose A Different Restore Point and then click Next.

What impact does your choice of restore points have? To see a full list of programs and drivers that will be deleted or restored, select the restore point you're planning to use, and then click Scan For Affected Programs. That displays a dialog that lists every change you made since that restore point was created. (Note that this list does not warn you about any executable files that might be deleted from your Desktop, Downloads, or other folders.)

After selecting a restore point, click Next to display a series of confirmation dialogs. After you successfully convince the system that, yes, you really want to do this, the System Restore wizard creates a new restore point, labeled Undo: Restore Operation, which makes it possible to restore the current configuration if this troubleshooting operation doesn't solve the underlying prob-lem. Then, after a restart, it replaces current system files and registry settings with those in the restore point you selected.

When System Restore reinstates a previously saved configuration using a restore point, your data files—documents, pictures, music files, and the like—are not tampered with in any way. (The only exception is if you or an app created or saved a file using one of the file name exten-sions from the list of monitored extensions, as described in the previous section.)

Inside Out

Watch out for System Restore gotchas

Using System Restore can have unintended interactions with other features of Windows 11. Here are a few to watch out for:

- If you create a new user account and then use System Restore to roll back your system configuration to a point before the new account was created, the new user is no longer able to sign in, and you receive no warning. (The good news is that the new user's unencrypted documents are intact.)

- System Restore does not uninstall programs, although it does remove executable files, dynamic-link libraries (DLLs), and registry entries created by the installer. To avoid having orphaned program shortcuts and files, view the list of programs and drivers that will be affected when you return to the restore point and uninstall them before running the restore operation. You can reinstall the program after the restore operation is complete.

- Any changes made to your system configuration using the Windows Recovery Environment are not monitored by System Protection. This can produce unintended consequences if you make major changes to system files and then roll back your system configuration with System Restore.

Although you can restore your system to a previously saved restore point from the Windows Recovery Environment, neither you nor Windows can create a new restore point from that location. As a result, you cannot undo a restore operation that you perform by starting from the Windows Recovery Environment. You should use System Restore in this mode only as a last resort if you are unable to start Windows normally to perform a restore operation.

Windows Terminal, PowerShell, and other advanced management tools

The simplest, most straightforward way to accomplish most tasks in Windows 11 is with the help of the graphical user interface—the dialogs and Settings pages where you can define preferences and change settings.

But just because that's usually the most direct way doesn't mean it's the only way. Many of those tasks have an alternative that you can exercise via the command line or by making changes to the Windows registry. If you're a system administrator or help desk technician, using command-line tools can save time, especially when you incorporate them into scripts. For some tasks, in fact, using a command-line tool is the only way to get a specific job done.

You have the option of performing command-line tasks in Windows 11 using the venerable Command Prompt (Cmd.exe) or the newer PowerShell. PowerShell, a .NET-based command-line shell and scripting language capable of working with every facet of Windows, is now the default shell in all currently supported Windows releases, desktop and server. You don't have to choose sides, however. Windows 11 offers Windows Terminal as a host for both shells, with the option to use additional command-line environments such as Azure Cloud Shell and the Windows Subsystem for Linux; using this modern console, you can readily switch between any of those shells just by changing to a different tab.

We begin this chapter with a brief look at Windows Terminal and its customization options. We follow that with a more extensive introduction to the PowerShell language, with pointers to additional learning resources. Because of the ongoing importance of Command Prompt (Cmd.exe), this chapter also includes an overview of its most salient features. We also cover the powerful Registry Editor utility (Regedit.exe), starting with an explanation of how the Windows registry works, and we finish with a quick overview of the many advanced management tools based on the Microsoft Management Console.

Using and configuring Windows Terminal

It is possible to run Cmd.exe in its own window (technically, it runs in the Windows Console Host, Conhost.exe). You can also run the legacy Windows PowerShell app in its own window. But it's easier and more productive to allow those command-line shells to run in the Windows Terminal application. This free, open-source application is installed by default in Windows 11 and available on the Quick Link menu. (For documentation on what's in the latest Windows Terminal builds, see the releases page at Microsoft's GitHub repository: *https://github.com/microsoft/terminal/releases*.)

One of the most appealing features of Windows Terminal is its support for multiple tabs, each of which can host a different command-line shell. To open a new tab using the default shell, click the plus sign to the right of the rightmost tab; to open a tab using a different shell, click the downward-pointing arrow at the right edge of the tab bar and choose an entry from the resulting dropdown.

Figure 16-1 shows Terminal in action, with three tabs open: one instance of Command Prompt, another of Ubuntu Linux, and a third running PowerShell.

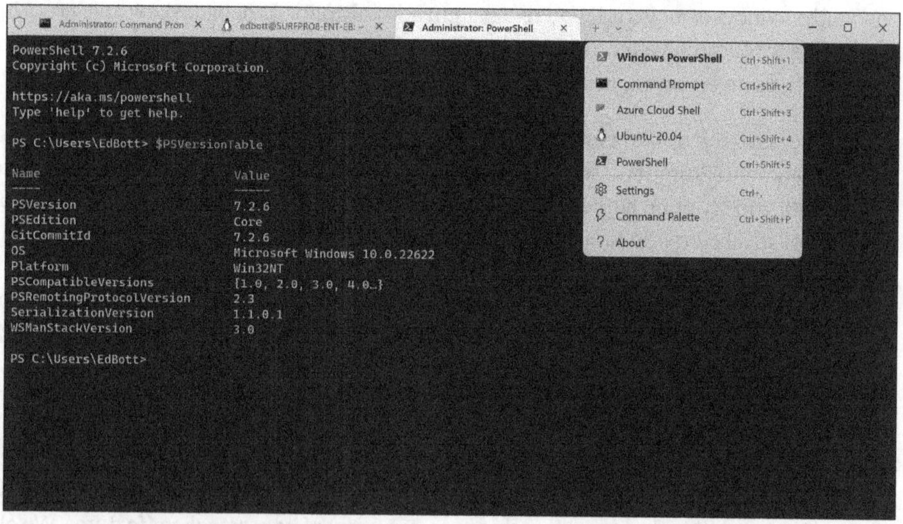

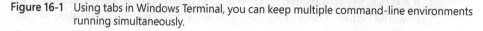

Figure 16-1   Using tabs in Windows Terminal, you can keep multiple command-line environments running simultaneously.

Windows Terminal includes a profile for each command shell installed on your system. By default, this list includes Windows PowerShell (the legacy version), Command Prompt, and Azure Cloud Shell. When you install the newer, open source PowerShell 7, the installer automatically adds a profile for that shell; likewise, installing the Windows Subsystem for Linux adds a profile for your distribution.

Note the keyboard shortcuts at the right of each new-tab option on the menu. You can use these to open a new tab using the selected profile. To move forward and backward through your current collection of open tabs, press Ctrl+Tab or Ctrl+Shift+Tab.

To modify the way Windows Terminal works, choose Settings from the new-tab menu (or use the Ctrl+Comma [,] keyboard shortcut). Figure 16-2 shows the options available on the Startup tab.

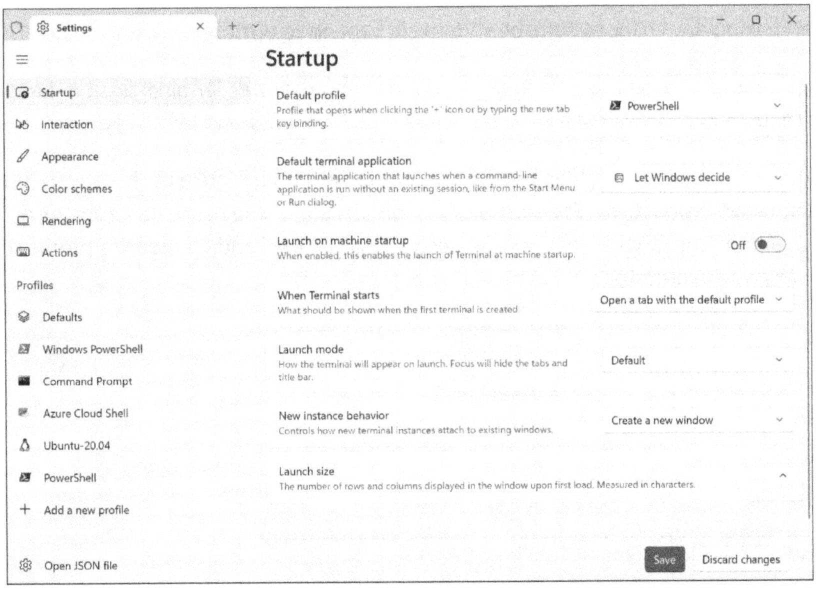

Figure 16-2   Use these menu options to tell Windows Terminal which command-line shell you prefer.

The settings on the Startup page are probably the most useful and are worth a visit if you use Windows Terminal regularly:

- **Default Profile**   Select which profile you want to use when you launch Windows Terminal or when you click the plus sign to open a new tab.

- **Default Terminal Application**   This setting determines whether command-line apps that you launch using the Run command or the Start menu open in Windows Terminal or in an old-school Windows Console Host window.

- **Launch On Machine Startup**   Developers and administrators who use the command line regularly can invoke this option to ensure that a Windows Terminal session is always available.

- **When Terminal Starts**   The default setting opens a single tab with your default profile; if you prefer, you can opt to restore your previously open tabs.

- **Launch Mode**   The Default option will suffice for most casual users; the options that include the word *Focus* hide other tabs and suppress the title bar.

- **New Instance Behavior**   By default, opening a new Terminal session spawns a new window. Choose either alternative if you want new sessions to appear in the currently open window.

- **Launch Size**   The standard column and row assignments are adequate for casual users, but experienced developers might want to create a larger workspace.

After making any changes here, be sure to click the Save button!

Other pages on the Settings menu allow you to change the way Terminal sessions handle keyboard and mouse input, adjust the appearance of Terminal windows, and tweak keyboard shortcuts.

The options under the Profiles heading, shown in Figure 16-3, are a useful way to reduce clutter and improve productivity. For each profile, you can adjust the name that appears on the drop-down and on the tab title text. You can also adjust the icon and configure a profile so it always runs as an administrator.

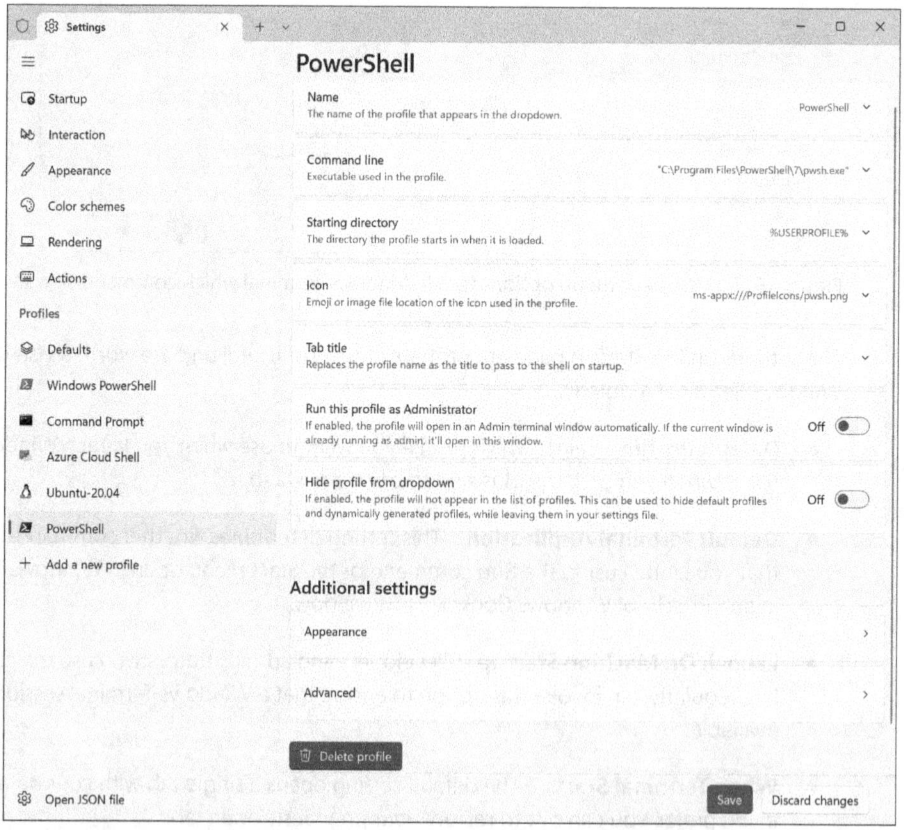

Figure 16-3   Each available command-line shell has its own profile in Windows Terminal. Use the options here to customize, hide, or delete a profile.

If you've installed the newer PowerShell 7 and have no need for the legacy Windows Power-Shell app, several options here are useful. You can hide the Windows PowerShell profile from the dropdown new-tab menu if you want to keep its settings available just in case, or choose its profile and click the big red Delete Profile button to remove its option from the dropdown. (Note that doing so does not delete the executable files for that legacy app.)

Inside Out

Use the mouse to change text size

You can certainly use the Settings file to configure text characteristics for a profile in Terminal. If you just want to magnify text temporarily to get a closer look without having to squint or move your monitor, an easy-to-remember mouse maneuver does the trick. Hold down the Ctrl key and roll the mouse wheel. This simple text manipulation comes courtesy of Terminal's GDI-based rendering engine. Other text improvements attributable to this architecture include the ability to display glyphs, symbols, ideograms, emojis, and programming ligatures.

An introduction to PowerShell

Microsoft describes PowerShell as a "cross-platform task automation solution made up of a command-line shell, a scripting language, and a configuration management framework." Long-time Windows users and administrators can use PowerShell for the same kinds of chores they previously tackled with Command Prompt, and you can use its scripting power to automate routine management tasks. If you're accustomed to using batch programs, VBScript, or JScript to automate administrative tasks, you can retain your current scripting investment but take advantage of the additional capabilities afforded by PowerShell's object orientation and .NET support as your scripting needs grow.

NOTE

As we noted earlier, Windows 11 supports two versions of PowerShell. Windows PowerShell version 5.1 is the older product, designed for use exclusively with Windows and built on the .NET Framework v4.5. PowerShell version 7 is built on .NET Core and is a cross-platform solution. PowerShell can load many traditional Windows PowerShell modules without modification; for the rare instances where this option isn't available, PowerShell 7 includes a Windows PowerShell Compatibility feature, which allows use of Windows PowerShell modules that require the full .NET framework. In this chapter, we assume that you're using the newer, cross-platform PowerShell.

To download and install PowerShell 7, go to *https://aka.ms/PSWindows*. An even simpler option is to open Windows Terminal, open a Windows PowerShell session, and issue the command **winget install Microsoft.PowerShell**.

Among the advantages PowerShell offers over previous shells and scripting platforms are the following:

- **Integration with the Microsoft .NET Framework**   Like more traditional development languages, such as C#, PowerShell commands and scripts have access to the vast resources of the .NET Framework.

- **Object orientation and an object-based pipeline**   All PowerShell commands that generate output return .NET Framework objects rather than plain text, eliminating the need for text parsing when the output of one command provides input to a second.

- **A consistent, discoverable command model**   All of PowerShell's commands (or "cmdlets," as they are called) use a verb-noun syntax, with a hyphen separating the two components. All cmdlets that read information from the system begin with Get; all those that write information begin with Set. These and other similar consistencies make the language easy to learn and understand. Each cmdlet has a help topic that can be retrieved by typing **get-help *cmdletname*** (where *cmdletname* is the name of a cmdlet). You can use a **-Whatif** parameter to test the effect of a cmdlet before you execute it.

- **Universal scripting capability**   A PowerShell script is a text file, with the extension .ps1, containing PowerShell commands. Any commands that can be used interactively can be incorporated into a script. Scripting structures, such as looping, branching, and variables, can also be used interactively—that is, outside the context of a script.

- **A focus on administrators**   PowerShell includes features of particular interest to system administrators, such as the ability to work with remote computers; access to system resources such as files, folders, registry keys, events, and logs; and the ability to start and stop services.

- **Extensibility**   Developers and administrators can extend the PowerShell language by importing modules—packages of PowerShell cmdlets and other items. Modules exist for a variety of Microsoft products, including Azure, Windows Server, and Microsoft 365. Administrators can also find PowerShell modules that work with cloud services from providers other than Microsoft, including Amazon Web Services, VMware, and Google Cloud.

The following pages introduce PowerShell. Our discussion focuses primarily on the use of PowerShell as an interactive command shell, because PowerShell scripting is itself a book-length subject. For more sources of information, see "Finding additional PowerShell resources" later in this chapter.

Interacting with PowerShell

PowerShell's default appearance offers a minimal command-line interface similar to that of Command Prompt. The *PowerShell* label and logo in the tab title, along with the copyright notice and the letters *PS* at the beginning of the command line, also help to distinguish its appearance.

If you're an old hand at the command line but new to PowerShell, the first thing you might want to try is using some of Command Prompt's familiar internal commands. Most such items—for example, *dir, cd, md, rd, pushd,* and *popd*—still work in PowerShell. Redirection symbols, such as > to send output to a file and >> to append output to a file, work as well, and you can pipe lengthy output to More, just as you're accustomed to doing in Command Prompt. PowerShell uses aliases to map Command Prompt commands to its own cmdlets. Thus, *dir* is an alias for the PowerShell cmdlet *Get-Childitem; cd* is an alias for PowerShell's *Set-Location*. You can create your own aliases to simplify the typing of PowerShell commands that you use often; for details, see "Using and creating aliases" later in this chapter.

You can use PowerShell to launch executables, just as you would use any other command-line shell. Typing **regedit**, for example, launches Registry Editor; typing **taskschd** launches Task Scheduler. (Note that with PowerShell, you also can view and edit keys and values in the registry without the use of Registry Editor; for details, see "Working with the registry" later in this section.)

Using cmdlets

The core of PowerShell's native vocabulary is a set of cmdlets, each consisting of a verb, followed by a hyphen, followed by a noun—for example, *Start-Service*. A cmdlet can be followed by one or more parameters; each parameter is preceded by a space and consists of a hyphen connected to the parameter's name followed by a space and the parameter's value. So, for example,

```
Get-Process -Name explorer
```

returns information about any currently running processes named explorer.

With parameters that accept multiple values, you can use a comma to separate the values. For example,

```
Get-Process -Name explorer, winword, excel
```

generates information about Microsoft Word and Excel as well as Windows Explorer.

Many cmdlets use positional parameters. For example, the **-Name** parameter for *Get-Process* is positional. PowerShell expects it to come first, so you can omit **-Name** and simply specify the names of the processes in which you're interested.

If you omit both the first positional parameter and its value, PowerShell typically assumes a value of *. So, for example,

```
Get-Process
```

returns information about all running processes, as shown in Figure 16-4.

CHAPTER 16

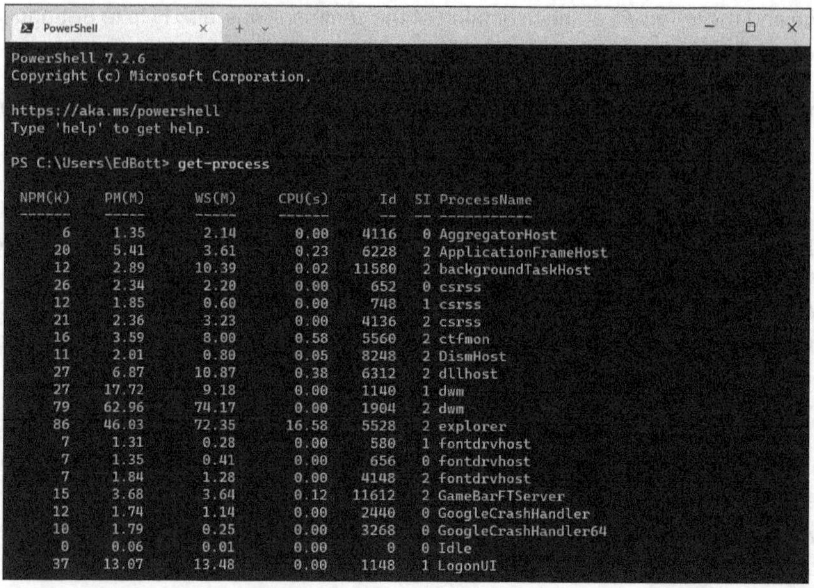

```
PowerShell                    ×    +  ˅                                          —    □    ×

PowerShell 7.2.6
Copyright (c) Microsoft Corporation.

https://aka.ms/powershell
Type 'help' to get help.

PS C:\Users\EdBott> get-process

 NPM(K)      PM(M)      WS(M)     CPU(s)       Id   SI ProcessName
 ------      -----      -----     ------       --   -- -----------
      6       1.35       2.14       0.00     4116    0 AggregatorHost
     20       5.41       3.61       0.23     6228    2 ApplicationFrameHost
     12       2.89      10.39       0.02    11580    2 backgroundTaskHost
     26       2.34       2.20       0.00      652    0 csrss
     12       1.85       0.60       0.00      748    1 csrss
     21       2.36       3.23       0.00     4136    2 csrss
     16       3.59       8.00       0.58     5560    2 ctfmon
     11       2.01       0.80       0.05     8248    2 DismHost
     27       6.87      10.87       0.38     6312    2 dllhost
     27      17.72       9.18       0.00     1140    1 dwm
     79      62.96      74.17       0.00     1904    2 dwm
     86      46.03      72.35      16.58     5528    2 explorer
      7       1.31       0.28       0.00      580    1 fontdrvhost
      7       1.35       0.41       0.00      656    0 fontdrvhost
      7       1.84       1.28       0.00     4148    2 fontdrvhost
     15       3.68       3.64       0.12    11612    2 GameBarFTServer
     12       1.74       1.14       0.00     2440    0 GoogleCrashHandler
     10       1.79       0.25       0.00     3268    0 GoogleCrashHandler64
      0       0.06       0.01       0.00        0    0 Idle
     37      13.07      13.48       0.00     1148    1 LogonUI
```

Figure 16-4   Entering the cmdlet **Get-Process** without parameters displays details about all running processes.

In some cases, if you omit values for an initial positional parameter, PowerShell prompts you to supply the parameter. For example, in response to

Get-Eventlog

PowerShell does you the courtesy of prompting for the name of an event log. (Event logs are large; it wouldn't be reasonable to ask for all of them at once.)

For information about any particular cmdlet, type **get-help** followed by the cmdlet name.

Using the pipeline

You can use the pipe operator (|) to supply the output of one cmdlet as input to another. You can connect multiple cmdlets using the PowerShell pipeline, as long as each cmdlet to the right of a pipe operator understands the output of the cmdlet to its left. Because PowerShell cmdlets return full-fidelity .NET objects rather than text, a cmdlet to the right of a pipe operator can operate directly on properties or methods of the preceding cmdlet's output.

The following paragraphs provide examples of the use of piping to format, filter, and sort the output from various Get- cmdlets.

Formatting output as a list

The default output from many Get- cmdlets is a table that presents only some of the resultant object's properties (about as many as the width of your display is likely to accommodate). For example, the cmdlet

```
Get-Service
```

generates a three-column display that includes only the Status, Name, and DisplayName properties.

If you pipe the same output to *Format-List*,

```
Get-Service | Format-List
```

PowerShell, which is no longer constrained by display width, can display more of the object's properties (as shown in Figure 16-5), including in this case such useful items as the dependencies of each service and whether the service can be paused or stopped.

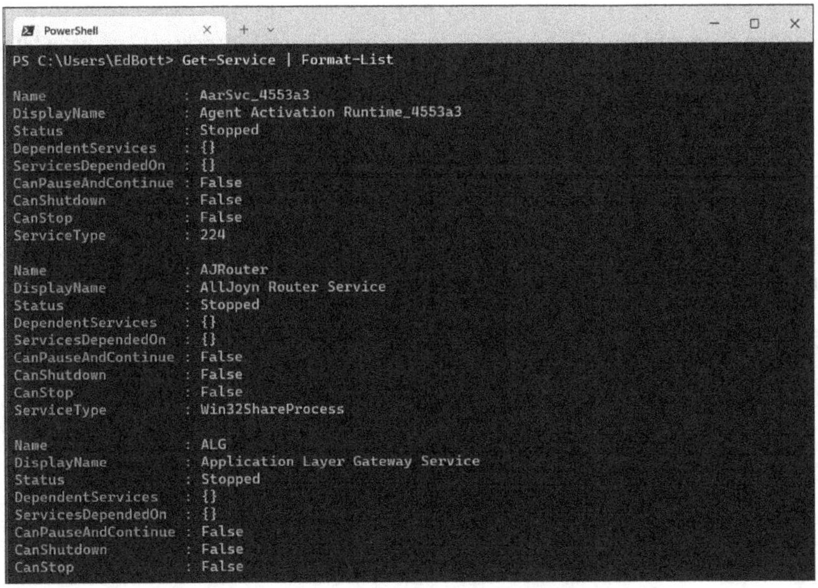

Figure 16-5   By piping a cmdlet to *Format-List*, you can see more of each resultant object's properties.

In some cases, you'll find the *Format-List* cmdlet, with no parameters, is equivalent to *Format-List -Property* *. But this is by no means always the case. For example,

```
Get-Process | Format-List
```

returns five properties for each process: ID, Handles, CPU, SI, and Name. Asking for all properties produces a wealth of additional information.

CHAPTER 16

To generate a list of particular properties, add the **-Property** parameter to *Format-List* and supply a comma-separated list of the properties you want to see. To see what properties are available for the object returned by a cmdlet, pipe that cmdlet to *Get-Member*:

```
Get-Process | Get-Member -Membertype property
```

Formatting output as a table

Perhaps you want tabular output but with different properties from those that your cmdlet gives you by default. *Format-Table* does the trick. For example,

```
Get-Service | Format-Table -Property name, dependentservices, servicesdependedon
```

generates a table consisting of these three enumerated properties. Note that PowerShell's console output is constrained by your console width, no matter how many properties you ask to see. For results that are too wide to display, redirect output to a file (using the **>** operator) or try the *Out-Gridview* cmdlet, described next.

Generating an interactive graphical table

Piping the output to *Out-Gridview* generates a graphical tabular display you can filter, sort, and copy easily into other programs, such as Excel, that accommodate tabular data. For example,

```
Get-Process | Select-Object * | Out-Gridview
```

produces output comparable to that shown in Figure 16-6. Note that in this example, *Get-Process* is piped first to *Select-Object* * because *Out-Gridview*, unlike *Format-Table*, does not include a **-Property** parameter. *Select-Object* * passes all properties of the object returned by *Get-Process* along the pipeline to *Out-Gridview*.

Name	Id	PriorityClass	FileVersion	HandleCount	WorkingSet	PagedMemorySize	PrivateMemorySize	VirtualMemorySize	TotalProcessorTime	SI	Handles
AggregatorHost	4,116			93	2,195,456	1,454,080	1,454,080	58,032,128		0	93
ApplicationFra...	6,228	Normal	10.0.220...	315	3,547,136	5,640,192	5,640,192	227,876,864	00:00:00.2343750	2	315
audiodg	9,164			271	14,282,752	7,004,160	7,004,160	112,263,168	00:00:00.0625000	0	271
csrss	652			526	2,195,456	2,457,600	2,457,600	100,884,480		0	526
csrss	748			150	630,784	1,941,504	1,941,504	88,252,416		1	150
csrss	4,136			407	3,248,128	2,404,352	2,404,352	103,088,128		2	407
ctfmon	5,560			409	9,687,040	3,813,376	3,813,376	139,538,432	00:00:00.7187500	2	409
DismHost	8,248			138	724,992	2,109,440	2,109,440	98,045,952	00:00:00.0468750	2	138
dllhost	6,312	Normal	10.0.220...	345	10,788,864	7,090,176	7,090,176	151,891,968	00:00:00.3750000	2	345
dwm	1,140			688	8,704,000	18,583,552	18,583,552	247,250,944		1	688
dwm	1,904			901	84,463,616	71,880,704	71,880,704	378,736,640		2	901
explorer	5,528	Normal	10.0.220...	2,328	75,620,352	46,698,496	46,698,496	607,522,816	00:00:17.1406250	2	2,328
fontdrvhost	580			37	294,912	1,372,160	1,372,160	71,643,136		1	37
fontdrvhost	656			37	430,080	1,413,120	1,413,120	72,171,520		0	37
fontdrvhost	4,148			37	1,585,152	1,929,216	1,929,216	76,304,384		2	37
GameBarFTSe...	11,...	Normal	5.822.06...	309	3,792,896	3,858,432	3,858,432	154,066,944	00:00:00.1250000	2	309
GoogleCrashH...	2,440			187	266,240	1,822,720	1,822,720	55,300,096		0	187
GoogleCrashH...	3,268			169	217,088	1,871,872	1,871,872	97,288,192		0	169
Idle	0			0	8,192	61,440	61,440	8,192		0	0

Figure 16-6   The *Out-Gridview* cmdlet produces a graphical tabular display you can sort, filter, and copy into a spreadsheet.

You can manipulate the contents of the *Out-Gridview* window with techniques comparable to those used by many other programs:

- To sort the display, click a column heading; click a second time to reverse the sort.

- To change the position of a column, drag its heading. You can also rearrange columns by right-clicking any column head, choosing Select Columns, and then using the Move Down and Move Up buttons in the Select Columns dialog.

- To remove columns from the display, right-click any column heading, click Select Columns, and then use the << button in the Select Columns dialog.

- To perform a quick filter, enter text in the line labeled Filter. For example, to limit the display shown previously in Figure 16-6 to processes with properties containing the word *beta*, type **beta** on the Filter line.

- To filter on one or more specific columns, click the Add Criteria button. In the drop-down list that appears, select check boxes for the columns on which you want to filter and then click Add.

Filtering output

To filter output from a cmdlet, pipe it to the *Where-Object* cmdlet. With *Where-Object*, you encapsulate filtering criteria in a script block, between curly braces. The following example filters output from *Get-Service* so that only services whose status is Stopped are displayed:

```
Get-Service | Where-Object {$_.Status -eq "Stopped"}
```

Sorting output

You can use the *Sort-Object* cmdlet to sort the output from a cmdlet on one or more of the resultant object's properties in a variety of useful ways. If you omit the **-Property** parameter, *Sort-Object* sorts on the default property. For example,

```
Get-Childitem | Sort-Object
```

sorts the contents of the current directory by Name, the default property in this case. To sort on multiple properties, follow **-Property** with a comma-separated list. *Sort-Object* sorts on the first named property first, sorting items with identical values for the first property by the second property, and so on. Sorts are ascending by default; to sort in descending order, add the parameter *-Descending*.

By piping *Sort-Object* to *Select-Object*, you can do such things as return the largest or smallest *n* items in a resultant object. For example,

```
Get-Process | Sort-Object -Property WS | Select-Object -Last 10
```

returns the processes with the 10 largest values of the working set (WS) property. Using **-First 10** instead of **-Last 10** gives you the items with the smallest values.

Piping output to the printer

To redirect output to the default printer, pipe it to *Out-Printer*. To use a nondefault printer, specify its name, in quotation marks, after *Out-Printer*. For example,

```
Get-Content C:\Users\EdBott\Documents\Inventory.txt | Out-Printer "Microsoft Print To
PDF"
```

sends the content of C:\Users\EdBott\Documents\Inventory.txt to the device named Microsoft Print To PDF.

Using PowerShell features to simplify keyboard entry

PowerShell is a wordy language and doesn't take kindly to misspellings. Fortunately, it includes many features to streamline and simplify the task of formulating acceptable commands.

Using and creating aliases

An alias is an alternative formulation for a cmdlet. As mentioned earlier, PowerShell uses aliases to translate Command Prompt commands to its own native tongue—for example, *cd* to *Set-Location*. But it includes a great many more simply for your typing convenience; *gsv*, for example, is an alias for *Get-Service*. And you can create aliases of your own.

To see what aliases are currently available (including any you created yourself during the current session), type **get-alias**. (Or just type **gal**, which is the alias for *get-alias*.) To see whether an alias is available for a particular cmdlet, pipe *Get-Alias* to *Where-Object*, like this:

```
Get-Alias | Where-Object { $_.definition -eq "Set-Variable" }
```

This particular command string inquires whether an alias is available for the *Set-Variable* cmdlet. If you type this, you discover that PowerShell offers two: *sv* and *set*. And if you think that *Where-Object* is too many characters to type, try replacing it with its alias, *?*.

To create a new alias, type **set-alias *name value***, where *name* is the alias and *value* is a cmdlet, function, executable program, or script. If *name* already exists as an alias, *Set-Alias* redefines it. If *value* is not valid, PowerShell doesn't bother you with an error message—until you try to use the alias.

Aliases you create are valid for the current session only. To make them available permanently, include them in your profile. See "Using your profile to customize PowerShell" later in this chapter.

Abbreviating parameter names

Aliases are useful for cmdlets, but they're no help for parameter names. Fortunately, with PowerShell, you can abbreviate such names. The commands *Get-Process -name explorer* and *Get-Process -n explorer* are equivalent. As soon as you've typed enough of a parameter name to let PowerShell recognize it unambiguously, you can give your fingers a rest. And, of course, you can combine aliases with parameter abbreviations to further lighten your load.

Using Tab expansion

As a further convenience, you can complete the names of files, cmdlets, or parameters by pressing Tab. Type part of a name, press Tab, and PowerShell presents the first potential completion. Continue pressing Tab to cycle through all the possibilities. Tab expansion works with all portions of a cmdlet, including verbs, nouns, and parameters.

Using wildcards and regular expressions

Like all its Windows-shell predecessors, PowerShell supports the ***** and **?** wildcards—the former standing in for any combination of zero or more characters, the latter for any single character. PowerShell also provides a vast panoply of "regular expressions" for matching character strings. For more details, go to *https://learn.microsoft.com/search/?scope=PowerShell*. Then search for **regular_expressions**. In general, you can use this method to get additional information about and documentation for any PowerShell topic.

Recalling commands from the command history

PowerShell maintains a history of your recent commands, which makes it easy to reuse (or edit and reuse) a command you already entered. To see the history, type **get-history**. Each item in the history is identified by an ID number. Type **invoke-history** *ID* (where *ID* is the ID number) to bring an item to the command line. On the command line, you can edit an item before executing it. PowerShell maintains a history of commands that you can recall using shortcut keys that are identical to those available in a Command Prompt session. (For details, see "Editing the Command Line," later in this chapter.)

The number of history items retained in a PowerShell session is defined by the automatic variable $MaximumHistoryCount. By default, that variable is set to 4096, which should be more than enough for anyone. If you find you need more, you can assign a larger number to the variable. For example, to double the default for the current session, type **$MaximumHistoryCount = 8192**. To change the history size for all sessions, add a variable assignment to your profile. For more information, see "Using your profile to customize PowerShell" later in this chapter.

Using PowerShell providers for access to file-system and registry data

PowerShell includes a set of built-in providers that give you access to various kinds of data stores. Providers are .NET Framework–based programs, and their data is exposed in the form of drives, comparable to familiar file-system drives. Thus, you can access a key in the HKLM registry hive with a path structure similar to that of a file-system folder; for example, the path HKLM:\Hardware\ACPI specifies the ACPI key of the Hardware key of the HKEY_LOCAL_MACHINE hive. Or, to use a quite different example, you can use the command *Get-Childitem env:* to get a list of current environment variables and their values.

Table 16-1 lists PowerShell's built-in providers.

Table 16-1   Built-in providers

Provider	Drive	Data store
Alias	Alias:	Currently defined aliases
Certificate	Cert:	X509 certificates for digital signatures
Environment	Env:	Windows environment variables
FileSystem	(varies)	File-system drives, directories, and files
Function	Function:	PowerShell functions
Registry	HKLM:, HKCU:	HKLM and HKCU registry hives
Variable	Variable:	PowerShell variables
WSMan	WSMan:	WS-Management configuration information

The following paragraphs provide some basic information about working with the file system and registry.

Working with the file system

For very simple file-system operations, you might find that familiar Command Prompt commands are adequate and easier to use than PowerShell cmdlets. The built-in aliases listed in Table 16-2 let you stick with time-honored methods. PowerShell supports the familiar single period (**.**) and double period (**..**) symbols for the current and parent directories, and it includes a built-in variable, $Home, that represents your home directory (by default, equivalent to the %UserProfile% environment variable).

Table 16-2   File-system aliases

Alias	PowerShell cmdlet
cd, chdir	Set-Location
copy	Copy-Item
del	Remove-Item
dir	Get-Childitem
move	Move-Item
md, mkdir	New-Item
rd, rmdir	Remove-Item
type	Get-Content

The PowerShell cmdlets, however, include valuable optional parameters:

- **-Confirm and -Whatif** The -Confirm parameter, used with *Copy-Item, Move-Item, Remove-Item*, or *Clear-Content*, causes PowerShell to display a confirmation prompt before executing the command. (*Clear-Content* can be used to erase the contents of a file.) If you use the -Whatif parameter, PowerShell shows you the result of a command without executing it.

- **-Credential** Use the -Credential parameter to supply security credentials for a command that requires them. Follow -Credential with the name of a user, within double quotation marks. PowerShell will prompt for a password.

- **-Exclude** You can use the -Exclude parameter to make exceptions. For example, *Copy-Item directory1*.* directory2 -Exclude *.log* copies everything, excluding all .log files, from Directory1 to Directory2.

- **-Recurse** The -Recurse parameter causes a command to operate on subfolders of a specified path. For example, *Remove-Item x:\garbagefolder*.* -Recurse* deletes everything from X:\Garbagefolder, including files contained within that folder's subfolders.

- **-Include** By using the -Include parameter in conjunction with -Recurse, you can restrict the scope of a command. For example, *Get-Childitem c:\users\edbott\documents* -Recurse -Include *.xlsx* restricts a recursive listing of C:\Users\EdBott\Documents to files with the extension .xlsx.

- **-Force** The -Force parameter causes a command to operate on items that are not ordinarily accessible, such as hidden and system files.

For detailed information about using these parameters with *Set-Location, Get-Childitem, Move-Item, Copy-Item, Get-Content, New-Item, Remove-Item*, or *Get-Acl*, type **get-help cmdletname**, substituting the cmdlet name for the final argument. The results include the full syntax as well as any aliases for the specified cmdlet.

Working with the registry

The built-in registry provider provides drives for two registry hives: HKEY_LOCAL_MACHINE and HKEY_CURRENT_USER. To change the working location to either of these, type **set-location hklm:** or **set-location hkcu:**, respectively. Use standard path notation to navigate to particular subkeys but enclose paths that include spaces in quotation marks—for example, *set-location "hkcu:\control panel\accessibility"*.

To display information about all subkeys of a key, use *Get-Childitem*. For example,

```
Get-Childitem -Path hkcu:\software\microsoft
```

returns information about all the subkeys of HKCU:\Software\Microsoft.

CHAPTER 16

To add a key to the registry, use *New-Item*. For example,

```
New-Item -Path hkcu:\software\mynewkey
```

adds the key *mynewkey* to HKCU:\Software. To remove this key, type **remove-item -path hkcu:\software\mynewkey**.

To copy a key, use *Copy-Item* and specify the source and destination paths; for example:

```
Copy-Item -Path hkcu:\software\mykey hkcu:\software\copyofmykey
```

To move a key, use *Move-Item*. The command

```
Move-Item -Path hkcu:\software\mykey -Destination hkcu:\software\myrelocatedkey
```

copies all properties and subkeys associated with HKCU:\Software\Mykey to HKCU:\Software\Myrelocatedkey and deletes HKCU:\Software\Mykey.

To display the security descriptor associated with a key, use *Get-Acl*. To see all the properties of the security descriptor, pipe this to *Format-List -Property **. For example,

```
Get-Acl -Path hkcu:\software\microsoft | Format-List -Property *
```

generates a display comparable to the one shown in Figure 16-7.

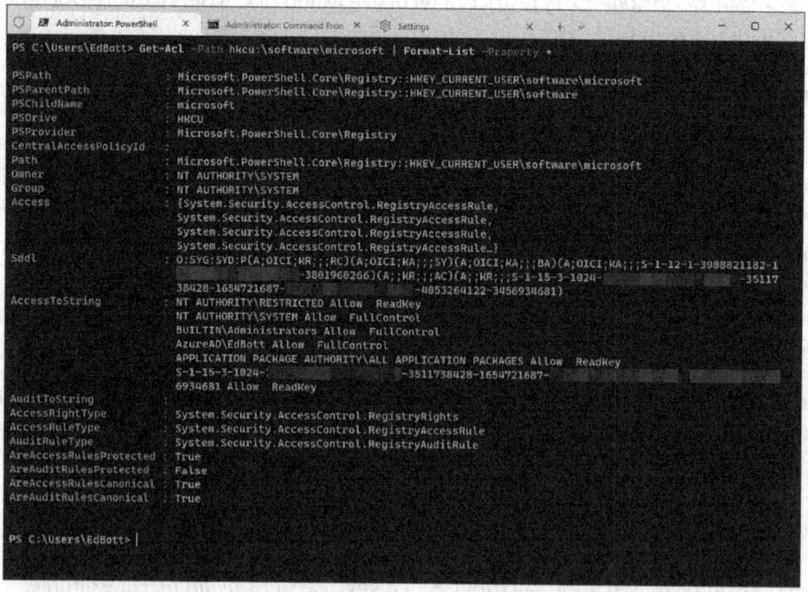

Figure 16-7   You can work with values from the registry by using one of the two predefined providers for registry hives, in this case hkcu:.

Go to *https://learn.microsoft.com/search/?scope=PowerShell* and type **registry** for more information about working with the registry.

Discovering PowerShell

PowerShell provides plenty of resources to help you learn as you go. Type **help** for a quick overview of the PowerShell Help System and its key cmdlets, *Get-Help* and *Update-Help*.

You can display help information about any cmdlet by typing **get-help *cmdletname***. If you do so on a fresh installation, *Get-Help* generates basic help information automatically for cmdlets, functions, and scripts. Type **update-help** to download the most recent help files for PowerShell modules and install them locally. (Note that that command requires that you be signed in as an administrator on Windows PowerShell but not in PowerShell 7.) After the help files are available locally, *Get-Help* returns a much more expansive set of results.

For example, to read help about *Get-Process*, type **get-help get-process**.

Among the useful parameters for *Get-Help* are the following:

- **-Examples**   To display only the name, synopsis, and examples associated with a particular help text, add the -Examples parameter.

- **-Parameter**   To get help for a particular parameter associated with a cmdlet, include -Parameter. Specify the parameter name in quotation marks.

- **-Detailed**   To get the description, syntax, and parameter details for a cmdlet, as well as a set of examples, use the -Detailed parameter. (Without this parameter, the examples are omitted; with -Examples, the syntax information is omitted.)

- **-Full**   For the works, including information about input and output object types and additional notes, specify -Full.

- **-Online**   For the latest information that Microsoft has, including additions or corrections to the native output of *Get-Help*, specify -Online. That parameter opens a browser window and displays relevant information from Microsoft's online PowerShell documentation.

Using the *Help* command instead of *Get-Help* produces the full display of help information, with the help text pausing after each screenful.

Finding the right cmdlet to use

The *Get-Command* cmdlet can help you figure out which cmdlet is the right one to use for a given task. Type **get-command** with no arguments to get the names and definitions of all available cmdlets, functions, and aliases. *Get-Command* can also give you information about non-PowerShell executables. If you type **get-command ***, for example, you get a huge list including all program files in all folders included in your current %Path% environment variable.

Either global list (with or without the non-PowerShell executables) is likely to be less than useful when you just want to know which cmdlets are available for use with a particular object. To get such a focused list, add the -Noun parameter. For example, type **get-command -noun eventlog** to get a list of the cmdlets that use that noun; you're rewarded with the names and definitions of *Clear-Eventlog*, *Get-Eventlog*, *Limit-Eventlog*, *New-Eventlog*, *Remove-Eventlog*, *Show-Eventlog*, and *Write-Eventlog*. You can get a list focused similarly on a particular verb by using the -Verb parameter.

Scripting with PowerShell

A PowerShell script is a text file with the extension .ps1. You can create a script in any plain text editor (Notepad will do fine), or you can use the Integrated Scripting Environment (ISE).

Anything you do interactively with PowerShell you can also do in a script. The reverse is true as well; you can take lines from a script, including those that involve looping or branching structures, and execute them individually outside the context of a script. For example, if you type

```
For ($i=1; $i -le 5; $i++) { "Hello, World" }
```

at the PowerShell command prompt, PowerShell performs the familiar greeting five times.

Using PowerShell's history feature, you can transfer commands you have used interactively into a script. That way you can test to see what works and how it works before committing text to a .ps1 file.

For example, the command

```
Get-History | Foreach-Object { $_.commandline } >> c:\scripts\mynewscript.ps1
```

appends the CommandLine property from each item in your current history to the file C:\Scripts\Mynewscript.ps1. (If the path doesn't exist, the command returns an error.) Once you have transferred your history to Mynewscript.ps1 in this manner, you can edit it in Notepad by typing **notepad c:\scripts\mynewscript.ps1**.

Running PowerShell scripts

Although files with the extension .ps1 are executable PowerShell scripts, running one is not quite as straightforward as double-clicking a .bat file. In the first place, if you double-click a .ps1 file in File Explorer, it opens in Notepad because the default action for a PowerShell script in File Explorer is Edit.

Second, the first time you try to run a script by typing its name at the PowerShell command prompt, you might see a distressing message displayed in red letters and with possibly unwelcome detail. This means that PowerShell has declined to run your script "because running scripts is disabled on this system." You need to change PowerShell's execution policy, as described next.

Third, even after you've cleared the execution-policy hurdle, you might still be rebuffed if you try to run a script stored in the current directory. That's because PowerShell requires a full path specification, even when the item you're running is stored in the current directory. For example, to run a script named Displayprocessor.ps1 from the current directory, you must type **.\displayprocessor**.

Getting and setting the execution policy

PowerShell's power can be used for evil ends. The majority of Windows users will never run PowerShell, but many will have .ps1 files lying about on their system or will download them inadvertently. To protect you from malware delivered in this fashion, PowerShell disables script execution until you explicitly enable it. Enabling execution requires a change to the execution policy.

Note that your profile script (if you have one) is subject to the same execution policy as any other script. (See "Using your profile to customize PowerShell" later in this chapter.) Therefore, it's pointless to set an execution policy by means of a profile script; that script itself will not run until you've enabled script execution elsewhere.

The following execution policies, listed here from least permissive to most, are available:

- **Restricted**   The default policy. No scripts are allowed to run.

- **AllSigned**   Any script signed by a trusted publisher is allowed to run. PowerShell presents a confirmation prompt before running a script signed by a publisher that you have not designated as "trusted."

- **RemoteSigned**   Scripts from local sources can run. Scripts downloaded from the internet (including scripts that originated as email or instant-messaging attachments) can run if signed by a trusted publisher.

- **Unrestricted**   All scripts can run, but PowerShell presents a confirmation prompt before running a script from a remote source.

- **Bypass**   All scripts are allowed to run.

Execution policies can be set separately for the following scopes:

- **Process**   Affects the current PowerShell session only. The execution policy is stored in memory and expires at the end of the session.

- **CurrentUser**   The execution policy is stored in a subkey of HKCU and applies to the current user only. The setting is retained between PowerShell sessions.

- **LocalMachine**   The execution policy is stored in a subkey of HKLM and applies to all users at this computer. The setting is retained between PowerShell sessions.

If policies are set at two or more of these scopes, the Process policy takes precedence over the CurrentUser policy, which takes precedence over the LocalMachine policy. Execution policy can also be set via Group Policy, however, and settings made in that manner trump any of the foregoing scopes. (Group Policy settings can be made in either the Computer Configuration or User Configuration node; a Computer Configuration setting trumps any other.)

To see the execution policies in effect at all scopes, type **get-executionpolicy -list**.

To set an execution policy, use *Set-ExecutionPolicy*. To set a policy at the LocalMachine scope, you need to be running PowerShell with administrative privileges.

The default scope for *Set-ExecutionPolicy* is LocalMachine, so if you're planning to apply a policy to all users at your computer, you can omit the -Scope parameter. For example, if you're comfortable disabling all of PowerShell's script-execution security measures, including warning prompts, you can type **set-executionpolicy bypass**. For a slightly more protective environment, type **set-executionpolicy unrestricted**.

To set an execution policy at the CurrentUser or Process scope, add -Scope followed by CurrentUser or Process. Note that you can also set an execution policy at the Process scope by adding an **-Executionpolicy** argument to a command that launches PowerShell. For example, from a command prompt in Command Prompt, in PowerShell, or on the Start menu, you can type **powershell -executionpolicy unrestricted** to launch PowerShell with the Unrestricted execution policy at the Process scope.

To remove an execution policy from a particular scope, set that scope's policy to Undefined. For example, if you set a Process policy to, say, Bypass, and you would like PowerShell to revert to the policy at the next level of precedence (CurrentUser, if a policy is set there, or LocalMachine, if not), type **set-executionpolicy undefined -scope process**.

Using your profile to customize PowerShell

Your profile is a script that PowerShell executes at the beginning of each session. You can use it to tailor your PowerShell environment to your preferences. Your profile must have the following path and file name:

`$Home\Documents\WindowsPowerShell\Microsoft.PowerShell_profile.ps1`

where $Home is a system-generated *PowerShell* variable corresponding to the environment variable %UserProfile%. You can see where this is on your system by typing **$profile**, and you can edit an existing profile by typing **notepad $profile**. If you have not yet created a profile, you can type the following:

```
if (!(test-path $profile)){New-Item -Type file -Path $profile -Force}
```

PowerShell creates the file for you in the appropriate folder. Then you can type **notepad $profile** to edit the blank file.

You can use your profile to customize PowerShell in a variety of ways. Possibilities to consider include changing the default prompt and creating new aliases.

PowerShell's prompt is derived from a built-in function called Prompt. You can overwrite that function with your own. For example, the function

```
Function prompt {"PS [$env:computername] $(Get-Date) > "}
```

replaces the built-in PowerShell prompt with the letters PS, followed by your computer name, followed by the current date and time.

To add new aliases to the ones PowerShell already offers, include *Set-Alias* statements in your profile. (See "Using and creating aliases" earlier in this chapter.)

Using the Windows PowerShell ISE

A feature introduced with Windows PowerShell 2.0 allows you to issue commands and work with scripts in a graphical environment. This ISE includes a command pane, a script pane, and an output pane. The output pane displays the results of any commands you issue in the command pane or any scripts you run in the script pane. (Note that this app uses the legacy Windows PowerShell, not PowerShell 7.)

Windows PowerShell ISE is a desktop app that you can launch from Start. Alternatively, at a PowerShell prompt or in a Command Prompt window, type **powershell_ise**.

The ISE supports multiple tabs, so you can open several scripts at once. Click File > New to open a new blank tab (for example, to write a new script) or File > Open to open an existing script in a new tab. To run the current script, click Debug > Run/Continue, press F5, or click the green arrow in the middle of the toolbar. You can use other commands on the Debug menu to set and remove breakpoints and step through execution.

The ISE offers all the usual amenities of a graphical environment. You can resize and rearrange the panes, for example. You can use the View menu's Zoom commands (or adjust the slider in the lower-right corner of the window) to make the text display larger or smaller. And you can easily select and copy text from one pane to another or from the ISE to another application.

The ISE uses its own profile, separate from the one you use to customize PowerShell itself. The path and file name are as follows:

$Home\Documents\WindowsPowerShell\Microsoft.PowerShellISE_profile.ps1

and you create the file by typing:

```
if(!(Test-Path $profile)){New-Item -Type file -Path $profile -Force}
```

Finding additional PowerShell resources

This chapter's discussion of PowerShell has barely nicked the surface. You'll find complete documentation for PowerShell at *https://learn.microsoft.com/powershell/*. For more about getting started in PowerShell, visit *https://learn.microsoft.com/powershell/scripting/*.

Working in a Command Prompt session

To open a Command Prompt session, run Cmd.exe (or double-click any shortcut for Cmd.exe). To open a separate Command Prompt window when one is already open, you can type **start** in the session that's already running. The new session opens in a separate window of your default terminal app.

Running with elevated privileges

Your activities in a Command Prompt session are subject to the same User Account Control (UAC) restrictions as anything else you do in Windows. If you use Command Prompt to launch an app (for example, Registry Editor) that requires an administrative token, you're asked to confirm a UAC prompt before moving on. If you plan to run several such tasks from Command Prompt, you might prefer to run Command Prompt itself with elevated privileges. To do this, use any of the following techniques:

- Type **cmd** in the search box and press Ctrl+Shift+Enter.

- Right-click any shortcut for Command Prompt and then click Run As Administrator, or press Ctrl+Shift as you click the shortcut or press Enter.

- Open a Terminal session from the Quick Link menu, click the arrow to the right of the rightmost tab, point to Command Prompt on the dropdown, and hold down Ctrl as you click the command.

- Open a Terminal (Admin) session from the Quick Link menu, click the arrow to the right of the rightmost tab, and choose Command Prompt from the dropdown, or use the Terminal shortcut Ctrl+Shift+2.

Windows displays the word *Administrator* in the title bar or tab title of any Command Prompt window running with elevated privileges.

Starting Command Prompt at a particular folder

If you open a Command Prompt session from Windows Terminal, your session opens in the folder specified in your Windows Terminal profile. By default, this location is the root of your user profile. (To adjust those settings, see the instructions earlier in this chapter, in "Using and configuring Windows Terminal.")

If you run Command Prompt by typing **cmd** in the Start menu search box and then pressing Enter, Windows uses the default location: %HOMEDRIVE%%HOMEPATH%.

To run a Command Prompt session at a different folder, hold down the Shift key while you right-click the folder in File Explorer. On the shortcut menu, click Open In Terminal or Open PowerShell Window Here, and then enter **cmd**.

Starting Command Prompt and running a command

By using the /C and /K command-line arguments, you can start a Command Prompt session and immediately run a command or start an app, which we refer to as *commandstring* in this section. The difference between the two is that cmd /C *commandstring* terminates the Command Prompt session as soon as *commandstring* has finished, whereas cmd /K *commandstring* keeps the Command Prompt session open after *commandstring* has finished. Note the following:

- You must include either /C or /K if you want to specify a command string as an argument to Cmd. If you type **cmd *commandstring***, the command processor simply ignores *commandstring*.

- While *commandstring* is executing, you can't interact with the command processor. To run a command or start an app and keep the Command Prompt window interface, use the Start command. For example, to run Mybatch.bat and continue issuing commands while the batch program is running, type

```
cmd /k start mybatch.bat
```

- If you include other command-line arguments along with /C or /K, /C or /K must be the last argument before *commandstring*.

Using AutoRun to execute commands when Command Prompt starts

By default, Command Prompt executes on startup whatever it finds in the following two registry values:

- The AutoRun value in HKLM\Software\Microsoft\Command Processor

- The AutoRun value in HKCU\Software\Microsoft\Command Processor

The AutoRun value in HKLM affects all user accounts on the current machine. The AutoRun value in HKCU affects only the current user account. If both values are present, both are executed—HKLM before HKCU. Both AutoRun values are of data type REG_SZ, which means they can contain a single string. To execute a sequence of separate Command Prompt statements, therefore, you must use command symbols or store the sequence as a batch program and then use AutoRun to call the batch program.

You can also use Group Policy objects to specify startup tasks for Command Prompt.

Editing the command line

When working in a Command Prompt (Cmd.exe) session, you often enter the same command multiple times or enter several similar commands. To assist you with repetitive or corrective tasks, Windows includes a feature that recalls commands you previously issued in a Command Prompt window and allows you to edit them on the current command line. Table 16-3 lists these editing keys and what they do. (Many of these keys work in a PowerShell window as well.)

Table 16-3   Command-line editing keys

Key	Function
Up Arrow or F3	Recalls the previous command in the command history
Down Arrow	Recalls the next command in the command history
Page Up	Recalls the earliest command used in the session
Page Down	Recalls the most recently used command
Left Arrow	Moves left one character
Right Arrow	Moves right one character
Ctrl+Left Arrow	Moves left one word
Ctrl+Right Arrow	Moves right one word
Home	Moves to the beginning of the line
End	Moves to the end of the line
Esc	Clears the current command
F7	Displays the command history in a scrollable pop-up box
F8	Displays commands that start with the characters currently on the command line
Alt+F7	Clears the command history

Using command symbols

Old-fashioned programs that take all their input from a command line and then run unaided can be useful in a multitasking environment. You can turn them loose to perform complicated processing in the background while you continue to work with other programs in the foreground.

To work better with other programs, many command-line programs follow a set of conventions that control their interaction:

- By default, programs take all their input as lines of text typed at the keyboard. But input in the same format also can be redirected from a file or any device capable of sending lines of text.

- By default, programs send all their output to the screen as lines of text. But output in the same format also can be redirected to a file or another line-oriented device, such as a printer.

- Programs set a number (called a *return value*) when they terminate to indicate the results of the program.

When programs are written according to these rules, you can use the symbols listed in Table 16-4 to control a program's input and output or chain programs together.

Table 16-4   Command symbols

Symbol	Function
<	Redirects input
>	Redirects output
> >	Appends redirected output to existing data
|	Pipes output
&	Separates multiple commands in a command line
&&	Runs the command after && only if the command before && is successful
||	Runs the command after || only if the command before || fails
^	Treats the next symbol as a character
(and)	Groups commands

The redirection symbols

Command Prompt sessions in Windows allow you to override the default source for input (the keyboard) or the default destination for output (the screen).

Redirecting output

To redirect output to a file, type the command followed by a greater-than sign (>) and the name of the file.

Using two greater-than signs (>>) redirects output and appends it to an existing file.

Redirecting input

To redirect input from a file, type the command followed by a less-than sign (<) and the name of the file.

Redirecting input and output

You can redirect both input and output in a command line. For example, to use Batch.lst as input to the Sort command and send its output to a file named Sorted.lst, type the following:

```
Sort < batch.lst > sorted.lst
```

Standard output and standard error

Programs can be written to send their output either to the standard output device or to the standard error device. Sometimes programs are written to send different types of output to each device. You can't always tell which is which because, by default, both devices are the screen.

The Type command illustrates the difference. When used with wildcards, the **Type** command sends the name of each matching file to the standard error device and sends the contents of the file to the standard output device. Because they both go to the screen, you see a nice display with each file name followed by its contents.

However, if you try to redirect output to a file by typing something like this:

```
type *.bat > std.out
```

the file names still appear on your screen because standard error is still directed to the screen. Only the file contents are redirected to Std.out.

With Windows, you can qualify the redirection symbol by preceding it with a number. Use **1>** (or simply >) for standard output and **2>** for standard error. For example:

```
type *.bat 2> err.out
```

This time, the file contents go to the screen and the names are redirected to Err.out.

The pipe symbol

The pipe symbol (|) is used to send, or pipe, the output of one app to a second app as the second app's input. Piping is commonly used with the More command, which displays multiple screenfuls of output one screenful at a time. For example:

```
help dir | more
```

This command line uses the output of Help as the input for More. The More command filters out the first screenful of Help output, sends it to the screen as its own output, and then waits for a keystroke before sending more filtered output.

Inside OUT

Pipe command-line output to the clipboard

Using the Clip utility, you can pipe the output of a command to the Windows Clipboard; from there, you can paste it into any app that accepts Clipboard text. Typing **dir | clip**, for example, puts a listing of the current directory's files on the Clipboard. You can also redirect the contents of a file to the Clipboard by using the < symbol. Typing **clip < myfile.txt**, for example, transfers the contents of myfile.txt to the Clipboard.

Editing the Windows registry

The Windows registry is the central storage location that contains configuration details for hardware, system settings, services, user customizations, applications, and every detail—large and small—that makes Windows work.

NOTE

The registry is the work of many hands, over many years, and capitalization and word spacing are not consistent. With readability as our goal, we made our own capitalization decisions for this book, and our treatment of names frequently differs from what you see in Registry Editor. No matter. Capitalization is irrelevant. Spelling and spacing must be correct, however.

Although it's convenient to think of the registry as a monolithic database, its contents are actually stored in multiple locations as separate *hive* files, alongside logs and other support files. Some of those hive files are read into memory when the operating system starts; hive files that contain user-specific settings are stored in the user profile and are loaded when a new user signs in. (You can't open a hive file directly except using Registry Editor.)

The Boot Configuration Data (BCD) store has its own file on the boot drive. The core hives for Windows—the Security Account Manager (SAM), Security, Software, and System—are securely stored in %SystemRoot%\System32\Config. Two hives that contain settings for local and network services are located in %SystemRoot%\ServiceProfiles\LocalService and %SystemRoot%\ServiceProfiles\NetworkService, respectively. User-specific hives are stored as part of the user profile folder.

CHAPTER 16

The Hardware hive is unique in that it has no associated disk file. This hive, which contains details about your hardware configuration, is completely volatile; that is, Windows creates it anew each time you turn your system on.

NOTE

You can see where the hives of your system physically live by examining the values associated with HKLM\System\CurrentControlSet\Control\HiveList. Windows assigns drive letters after assembling the registry, so these paths do not specify drive letters.

Windows 11 is designed in such a way that direct registry edits by end users are generally unnecessary. When you change your configuration by using the Settings app or Control Panel, for example, Windows writes the necessary updates to the registry for you. Likewise, when you install a new piece of hardware or a new app, the app's installer makes the required registry changes; you don't need to know the details.

On the other hand, because the designers of Windows couldn't provide a user interface for every conceivable customization you might want to make, sometimes working directly with the registry is the only way to make a change. Even when it's not the only way, it might be the fastest way. Removing or modifying registry entries is occasionally a crucial part of troubleshooting and repair as well. Windows includes a registry editor you should know how to use—safely. This section tells you how.

CAUTION

Most Microsoft support articles contain a dire warning about the risks associated with editing the registry. We echo those warnings here. An incorrect registry modification can render your system unbootable and, in some cases, might require a complete reinstall of the operating system. Use Registry Editor at your own risk.

Understanding the Registry Editor hierarchy

Registry Editor (Regedit.exe) offers a unified view of the registry's contents as well as tools for modifying those contents. In Windows 11, Microsoft has removed this and other administrative tools from the All Apps list, but you can still find it using the search box. Alternatively, you can type **regedit** at a command prompt or in the Run dialog. Registry Editor has been virtually unchanged since the last century, with the exception of a few small improvements that debuted in the Windows 10 era: an address bar, new keyboard shortcuts for traversing the registry, options to save favorite registry locations for easier access, and the addition of a View > Font menu option that allows you to customize the font used when viewing or editing the contents of the registry.

Figure 16-8 shows a (mostly) collapsed view of the Windows 11 registry, as seen through Registry Editor.

CHAPTER 16

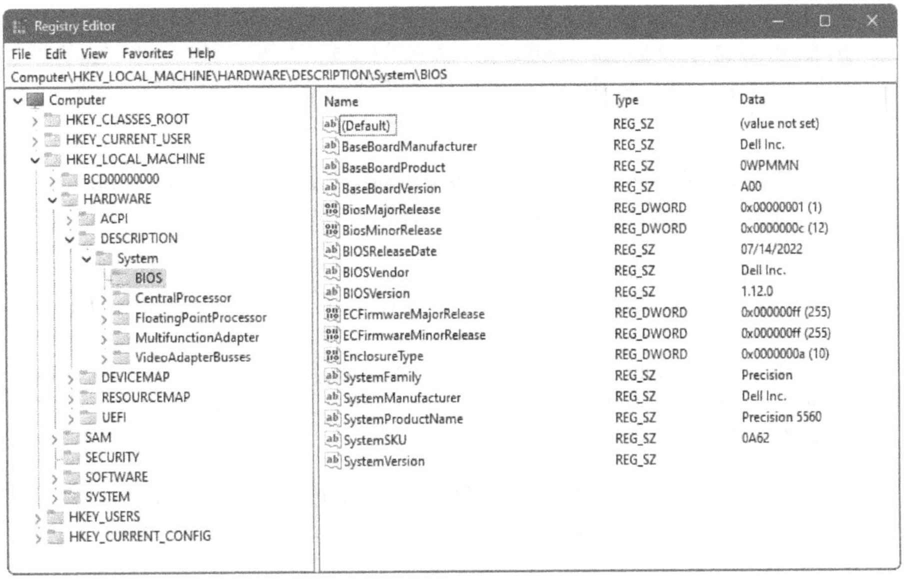

Figure 16-8 The registry consists of five root keys, each of which contains many subkeys.

The Computer node appears at the top of the Registry Editor tree listing. Beneath it, as shown here, are five root keys: HKEY_CLASSES_ROOT, HKEY_CURRENT_USER, HKEY_LOCAL_MACHINE, HKEY_USERS, and HKEY_CURRENT_CONFIG. For simplicity's sake and typographical convenience, this book, like many others, abbreviates the root key names as HKCR, HKCU, HKLM, HKU, and HKCC, respectively.

Root keys, sometimes called *predefined keys,* contain subkeys. Registry Editor displays this structure in a hierarchical tree in the left pane. In the previous Figure 16-8, for example, HKLM is open, showing its top-level subkeys.

Subkeys, which we call *keys* for short, can contain subkeys of their own, which in turn can be expanded as necessary to display additional subkeys. The address bar near the top of the Registry Editor window in the previous figure shows the full path of the currently selected key: Computer\HKLM\HARDWARE\DESCRIPTION\System\BIOS.

NOTE

One of the Registry Editor changes introduced in the Windows 10 era is the address bar. In it, you can type a registry path and press Enter to jump directly to that key, much as you can for jumping to a folder in File Explorer. For the root keys, you can type the full name or the commonly used abbreviations described earlier.

To go to the address bar and select its current content, press Alt+D or Ctrl+L, the same keyboard shortcuts that work in File Explorer as well as most web browsers.

The contents of HKEY_LOCAL_MACHINE define the workings of Windows itself, and its subkeys map neatly to several hives we mentioned at the start of this section. HKEY_USERS contains an entry for every existing user account (including system accounts), each of which uses the security identifier, or SID, for that account.

➤ For a detailed discussion of the relationship between user accounts and SIDs, see the "What are security identifiers?" sidebar in Chapter 10, "Managing user accounts, passwords, and credentials."

The remaining three predefined keys don't exist, technically. Like the file system in Windows—which uses junctions, symlinks, and other trickery to display a virtual namespace—the registry uses a bit of misdirection (implemented with the REG_LINK data type) to create these convenient representations of keys that are actually stored within HKEY_LOCAL_MACHINE and HKEY_USERS:

- HKEY_CLASSES_ROOT is merged from keys within HKLM\Software\Classes and HKEY_USERS*sid*_Classes (where *sid* is the security identifier of the currently signed-in user).

- HKEY_CURRENT_USER is a view into the settings for the currently signed-in user account, as stored in HKEY_USERS*sid* (where *sid* is the security identifier of the currently signed-in user).

- HKEY_CURRENT_CONFIG displays the contents of the Hardware Profiles\Current subkey in HKLM\SYSTEM\CurrentControlSet\Hardware Profiles.

Any changes you make to keys and values in these virtual keys have the same effect as if you had edited the actual locations. The HKCR and HKCU keys are generally more convenient to use.

Registry values and data types

Every key contains at least one value. In Registry Editor, that obligatory value is known as the default value. Many keys have additional values. The names, data types, and data associated with values appear in the right pane.

The default value for many keys is not defined. You can think of an empty default value as a placeholder—a slot that could hold data but currently does not.

All values other than the default always include the following three components: name, data type, and data. Figure 16-9, for example, shows customized settings for the current user's Cloud Clipboard. (Note the full path to this key in the address bar at the top of the Registry Editor window.)

CHAPTER 16

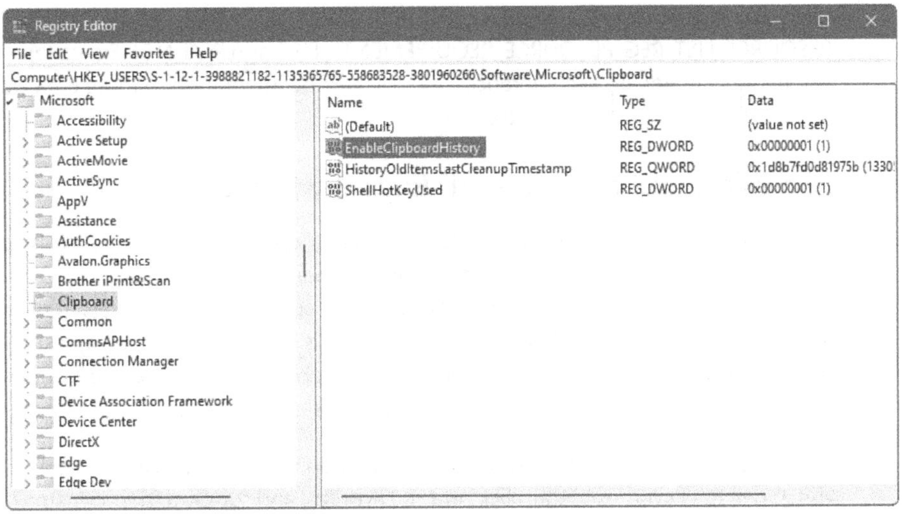

Figure 16-9   Selecting a key on the left displays all its values on the right.

The EnableClipboardHistory value is of data type REG_DWORD. The data associated with this value (on the system used for this figure) is 0x00000001. The prefix 0x denotes a hexadecimal value. Registry Editor displays the decimal equivalent of hexadecimal values in parentheses after the value.

The registry uses the following data types:

- **REG_SZ**   The SZ indicates a zero-terminated string. This variable-length string can contain Unicode as well as ANSI characters. When you enter or edit a REG_SZ value, Registry Editor terminates the value with a 00 byte for you.

- **REG_BINARY**   The REG_BINARY type contains binary data—0s and 1s.

- **REG_DWORD**   This data type is a "double word"—that is, a 32-bit numeric value. Although it can hold any integer from 0 to 2^{32}, the registry often uses it for simple Boolean values (0 or 1) because the registry lacks a Boolean data type.

- **REG_QWORD**   This data type is a "quadruple word"—a 64-bit numeric value.

- **REG_MULTI_SZ**   This data type contains a group of zero-terminated strings assigned to a single value.

- **REG_EXPAND_SZ**   This data type is a zero-terminated string containing an unexpanded reference to an environment variable, such as %SystemRoot%. (For information about environment variables, see "Interacting with PowerShell" earlier in this chapter.) If you need to create a key containing a variable name, use this data type, not REG_SZ.

CHAPTER 16

Internally, the registry also uses REG_LINK, REG_FULL_RESOURCE_DESCRIPTOR, REG_RESOURCE_LIST, REG_RESOURCE_REQUIREMENTS_LIST, and REG_NONE data types. Although you might occasionally see references in technical documentation to these data types, they're not visible or accessible in Registry Editor.

Browsing and editing with Registry Editor

Because of the registry's size, looking for a particular key, value, or data item can be daunting. In Registry Editor, the Find command (on the Edit menu and also available by pressing Ctrl+F) works in the forward direction only and does not wrap around when it gets to the end of the registry. If you're not sure where the item you need is located, select the highest level in the left pane before issuing the command. If you have an approximate idea where the item you want is located, you can save time by starting at a node closer to (but still above) the target.

After you locate an item of interest, you can put it on the Favorites list to simplify a return visit. Open the Favorites menu, click Add To Favorites, and supply a friendly name (or accept the default). If you're about to close Registry Editor and know you'll be returning to the same key the next time you open the editor, you can skip the Favorites step because Registry Editor always remembers your last position and returns to that position in the next session.

Registry Editor includes a number of time-saving keyboard shortcuts for navigating the registry:

- To move to the next subkey that starts with a particular letter, simply type that letter when the focus is in the left pane; in the right pane, use the same trick to jump to the next value that begins with that letter.

- To open a key (revealing its subkeys), press Right Arrow or Alt+Right Arrow.

- To collapse the subkeys of the current key, press Left Arrow or Alt+Left Arrow. With all subkeys collapsed, either action moves up one level in the subkey hierarchy. To move up a level without closing the subkeys as you move up, press Alt+Up Arrow.

- To move to the top of the hierarchy, press Home.

- To quickly move between the left and right panes, use the Tab key.

- In the right pane, press F2 to rename a value, and press Enter to open that value and edit its data.

Some of these shortcuts match the behavior of File Explorer shortcuts, allowing you to apply your knowledge of that app to Registry Editor.

Once you are comfortable using these keyboard shortcuts, you'll find it's usually easier to zip through the subkey hierarchy with a combination of arrow keys and letter keys than it is to open outline controls with the mouse.

You can change the data associated with a value by selecting a value in the right pane and pressing Enter or by double-clicking the value. Registry Editor pops up an edit window appropriate for the value's data type.

Adding or deleting keys and values

To add a key, select the new key's parent in the left pane, open the Edit menu, point to New, and click Key. The new key arrives as a generically named outline entry, exactly the way a new folder does in File Explorer. Type a new name.

To add a value, select the parent key, open the Edit menu, and point to New. On the submenu that appears, click the type of value you want to add. A value of the type you select appears in the right pane with a generic name. Type over the generic name, press Enter twice, enter your data, and press Enter once more.

To delete a key or value, select it and then press Delete. Note that deleting a key also deletes every value and subkey associated with it.

Using the Reg command

One expert-level option is to use the Reg command in a Command Prompt window or in a batch file or script. It's not uncommon, in fact, to see sites for Windows enthusiasts share commands using this syntax to make tweaks in the Windows user interface. Type **reg /?** to see the full list of eligible arguments for the reg command (query, add, export, import, and so on). Each of those variants has its own syntax help. Try **reg add /?** to see the correct syntax for adding a value.

Similarly, you can manipulate the registry using PowerShell commands. For more information, see "Working with the registry" earlier in this chapter.

Backing up and restoring parts of the registry

Before you make any changes to the registry, consider using System Restore to set a restore point, which includes a snapshot of the registry as it currently exists. Taking this precaution allows you to roll back any ill-advised changes.

> ➤ **For information about using System Restore, see "Rolling back to a previous restore point" in Chapter 15, "Troubleshooting, backup, and recovery."**

In addition, or as an alternative, you can use the Export command in Registry Editor to back up the portion of the registry where you plan to work. Registry Editor can save all or portions of your registry in any of four different formats, but only one is relevant in the modern era.

The Registration Files option creates a .reg file, which is a text file that can be read and edited in Notepad or a similar app. A .reg file can be merged into the registry of a system running any version of Windows. When you merge a .reg file, its keys and values replace the corresponding keys and values in the registry. By using .reg files, you can edit your registry "offline" and add your changes to the registry without even opening Registry Editor. You can also use .reg files as an easy way to share registry settings and copy them to other computers.

To export a portion of the registry before you work on it, select a key in the left pane, and then click File > Export. (Easier still, right-click a key and click Export.) In the Save As Type list in the Export Registry File dialog, select Registration Files (*.reg). Under Export Range, choose Selected Branch and then click Save. The resulting file includes the selected key and all its subkeys and values.

CAUTION

Exporting a registry hive file using the Registry Hive Files format saves the entire hive; importing the saved file replaces the entire contents of the selected key with the contents of the file—regardless of its original source. That is, it wipes out everything in the selected key and then adds the keys and values from the file. The potential for chaos is obvious, and the benefits are not worth the risk, in our estimation.

If you saved your backup as a .reg file, you use the same process to import it. (As an alternative, you can double-click the .reg file in File Explorer without opening Registry Editor.) The complete path to each key and value is stored as part of the file, and it always restores to the same location. This approach for recovering from registry editing mishaps is fine if you did not add new values or subkeys to the section of the registry you're working with; it returns existing data to its former state but doesn't alter the data you added.

> **TROUBLESHOOTING**
>
> **You used a registry cleaner and your system is no longer working properly**
>
> The registry is often inscrutable and can appear messy. Misguided attempts at cleanup can cause unexpected problems that are nearly impossible to troubleshoot, which explains why Microsoft is so insistent with its warnings that improper changes to the registry can prevent your computer from operating properly or even booting. We've never found a so-called registry cleaner that justifies the risk it inevitably entails. If you find yourself with a misbehaving system after using a registry cleaner, use the Reset option to recover your system and start over. And this time, don't bother to install that unnecessary utility.

Automating registry changes with .reg files

The .reg files created by the Export command in Registry Editor are plain text, suitable for reading and editing in Notepad or any similar editor. Therefore, they provide an alternative method for editing your registry. You can export a section of the registry, change it offline, and then merge it back into the registry. Or you can add new keys, values, and data to the registry by creating a .reg file from scratch and merging it. A .reg file is particularly useful if you need to make the same changes to the registry of several computers. You can make and test your changes on one machine, save the relevant part of the registry as a .reg file, and then import the saved file to the registry on other machines that require it.

Every .reg file includes the following elements:

- **Header line**   The file begins with the line "Windows Registry Editor Version 5.00." When you merge a .reg file into the registry, Registry Editor uses this line to verify that the file contains registry data. Version 5 (the version used with Windows 7 and later versions, up to and including Windows 11) generates Unicode text files, which can be used with all supported versions of Windows as well as the now-unsupported Windows XP and Windows 2000.

- **Key names**   Key names are delimited by brackets and must include the full path from the root key to the current subkey. The root key name must not be abbreviated. (Don't use HKCU, for example.)

- **The default value**   Undefined default values do not appear in .reg files. Defined default values are identified by the special character @. Thus, a key whose default REG_SZ value was defined as MyApp would appear in a .reg file this way:

    `"@"="MyApp"`

- **Value names**   Value names must be enclosed in quotation marks, regardless of whether they include space characters. Follow the value name with an equal sign.

- **Data types**   REG_SZ values don't get a data type identifier or a colon. The data directly follows the equal sign. Other data types are identified as shown in Table 16-5.

Table 16-5   Data types identified in .reg files

Data type	Identifier
REG_BINARY	hex
REG_DWORD	dword
REG_QWORD	hex(b)
REG_MULTI_SZ	hex(7)
REG_EXPAND_SZ	hex(2)

A colon separates the identifier from the data. Thus, for example, a REG_DWORD value named "Keyname" with value data of 00000000 looks like this:

`"Keyname"=dword:00000000`

- **REG_SZ values**   Ordinary string values must be enclosed in quotation marks. A backslash character within a string must be written as two backslashes. Thus, for example, the path C:\Program Files\Microsoft Office\ is written like this:

```
"C:\\Program Files\\Microsoft Office\\"
```

- **REG_DWORD values**   DWORD values are written as eight hexadecimal digits, without spaces or commas. Do not use the 0x prefix.

- **All other data types**   Other data types—including REG_EXPAND_SZ, REG_MULTI_SZ, and REG_QWORD—appear as comma-delimited lists of hexadecimal bytes (two hex digits, a comma, two more hex digits, and so on). The following is an example of a REG_MULTI_SZ value:

```
"Addins"=hex(7):64,00,3a,00,5c,00,6c,00,6f,00,74,00,00,75,00,73,00,5c,00,\
31,00,32,00,33,00,5c,00,61,00,64,00,64,00,64,00,69,00,6e,00,73,00,5c,00,\
64,00,71,00,61,00,75,00,69,00,2e,00,31,00,32,00,61,00,00,00,00,00,00,00,00
```

- **Line-continuation characters**   You can use the backslash as a line-continuation character. The REG_MULTI_SZ value just shown, for example, is all one stream of bytes. We added backslashes and broke the lines for readability, and you can do the same in your .reg files.

- **Line spacing**   You can add blank lines for readability. Registry Editor ignores them.

- **Comments**   To add a comment line to a .reg file, begin the line with a semicolon.

Using a .reg file to delete registry data

.Reg files are most commonly used to modify existing registry data or add new data. But you can also use them to delete existing values and keys.

To delete an existing value, specify a hyphen character (minus sign) as the value's data. For example, to use a .reg file to remove the value ShellState from the key HKCU\Software\Microsoft\Windows\CurrentVersion\Explorer, add the following line to the .reg file:

```
[HKEY_CURRENT_USER\Software\Microsoft\Windows\CurrentVersion\Explorer]"ShellState"=-
```

To delete an existing key with all its values and data, insert a hyphen in front of the key name (inside the left bracket). For example, to use a .reg file to remove the key HKCR\.xyz\shell and all its values, add the following to the .reg file:

```
[-HKEY_CLASSES_ROOT\.xyz\shell]
```

Merging a .reg file into the registry

To merge a .reg file into the registry from within Registry Editor, open the File menu and click Import. Registry Editor adds the imported data under the appropriate key names, overwriting existing values where necessary.

The default action for a .reg file is Merge—meaning merge with the registry. Therefore, you can merge a file into the registry by simply double-clicking it in File Explorer and answering the confirmation prompt.

Registry virtualization

One of the longstanding fundamental principles of security in Windows is that it prevents apps running under a standard user's token from writing to system folders in the file system and to machine-wide keys in the registry. Windows 11 respects that principle while still enabling users with a standard account to run apps without running into "access denied" roadblocks.

That's a particular challenge with older applications that require administrator-level access. Those apps are usable in Windows 11, even by standard users. The secret? User Account Control uses registry virtualization to redirect attempts to write to subkeys of HKLM\Software. (Settings in HKLM apply to all users of the computer; therefore, only administrators have write permission.) When an application attempts to write to this hive, Windows writes instead to a per-user location, HKCR\VirtualStore\Machine\Software. Like file virtualization, this is done transparently; the application (and all but the most curious users) never know this is going on behind the scenes.

CHAPTER 16

NOTE

When an app requests information from HKLM\Software, Windows looks first in the virtualized key if it exists. Therefore, if a value exists in both the VirtualStore hive and in HKLM, the app sees only the one in VirtualStore.

Note that because the virtualized data is stored in a per-user section of the registry, settings made by one user do not affect other users.

For more information about registry virtualization, see *https://bit.ly/registry-virtualization*.

Automating tasks

Windows 11 provides several ways to automate tasks. The built-in Task Scheduler tool allows you to create tasks using a point-and-click interface; batch commands and scripts, especially those using Windows PowerShell, represent the most common automation alternative.

Task Scheduler

Task Scheduler is a Microsoft Management Console (MMC) snap-in that supports an extensive set of triggering and scheduling options. Scheduled tasks can run programs or scripts at specified times, launch actions when a computer has been idle for a specified period of time, run tasks when particular users sign in or out, and so on. Task Scheduler is also tightly integrated with the Event Viewer snap-in, making it possible to use events (an application crash or a disk-full error, for example) as triggers for tasks.

Windows and third-party apps make extensive use of Task Scheduler to set up maintenance activities that run on various schedules. You can also create custom tasks. To see the full library of tasks, click Start, type **task**, and open the Task Scheduler app. To create a task, open Task Scheduler and click Action > Create Basic Task. For full documentation on this tool, see *https://learn.microsoft.com/windows/win32/taskschd/using-the-task-scheduler*.

Automating command sequences with batch programs

For automating administrative tasks on a business network, PowerShell scripts are the preferred solution. (We discuss these useful resources earlier in this chapter, in "Scripting with Power-Shell.") But for file management and other simple tasks, old-fashioned batch programs are still useful.

A batch program (also commonly called a *batch file*) is a text file with a .bat filename extension (.cmd is also a valid filename extension) that contains a sequence of commands to be executed. You execute the commands by entering the file name at a command prompt. Any action you can take by typing a command at a command prompt can be encapsulated in a batch program.

When you type the name of your batch program at the command prompt (or when you specify it as a task to be executed by Task Scheduler and the appropriate trigger occurs), the command interpreter opens the file and starts reading the statements. It reads the first line, executes the command, and then goes on to the next line. On the surface, this seems to operate just as though you were typing each line yourself at the command prompt. In fact, however, the batch program can be more complicated because the language includes replaceable parameters, conditional and branching statements, the ability to call subroutines, and so on. Batch programs can also respond to values returned by programs and to the values of environment variables.

Automating tasks with Windows Script Host

Microsoft Windows Script Host (WSH) provides a way to perform more sophisticated tasks than the simple jobs that batch programs are able to handle. You can control virtually any component of Windows and of many Windows-based programs with WSH scripts.

Run a script by typing a script name at a command prompt or double-click the script's icon in File Explorer. WSH has two nearly equivalent programs—Wscript.exe and Cscript.exe—that, with the help of a language interpreter dynamic-link library such as Vbscript.dll, execute scripts written in VBScript or another scripting language. (Cscript.exe is a command-line program; Wscript. exe is its graphical counterpart.)

With WSH, the files can be written in several languages, including VBScript (a scripting language similar to Microsoft Visual Basic) and JScript (a form of JavaScript). All the objects are available to any language, and in most situations, you can choose the language with which you are most comfortable. WSH doesn't care what language you use, provided the appropriate interpreter dynamic-link library is available. VBScript and JScript interpreters come with Windows 10 and Windows 11; interpreters for Perl, KiXtart (KixKIXE), Python, RexxHex, and other languages are available elsewhere.

Using Microsoft Management Console

Microsoft Management Console (MMC) is an application that hosts tools for administering computers, networks, and other system components. By itself, MMC performs no administrative services. Rather, it acts as the host for one or more modules, called *snap-ins*, which do the useful work. MMC provides user-interface consistency so that you or the users you support see more or less the same style of application each time you need to carry out some kind of computer management task. A combination of one or more snap-ins can be saved in a file called a Microsoft Common Console Document or, more commonly, an MMC console.

Creating snap-ins requires expertise in programming. You don't have to be a programmer, however, to make your own custom MMC consoles. All you need to do is run MMC, start with a blank console, and add one or more of the snap-ins available on your system. Alternatively, you can customize some of the MMC consoles supplied by Microsoft or other vendors simply by adding or removing snap-ins. You might, for example, want to combine the Services console with the Event Viewer console, the latter filtered to show only events generated by services. You might also want to include a link to a website that offers details about services and service-related errors. Or perhaps you would like to simplify some of the existing consoles by removing snap-ins you seldom use.

MMC consoles use, by default, the file name extension .msc, and .msc files are associated by default with MMC. Thus, you can run any MMC console by double-clicking its file name in a File Explorer window or by entering the file name at a command prompt. Windows 11 includes several predefined consoles; the most commonly used ones, described in Table 16-6, can be easily found by typing their name in the search box.

CHAPTER 16

Table 16-6   Useful predefined consoles

Console name (file name)	Description
Certificate Manager (Certmgr.msc)	Uses the Certificates snap-in to view and manage security certificates for the current user. A similar console, Certlm.msc, manages certificates on the local machine.
Computer Management (Compmgmt.msc)	Includes the functionality of the Task Scheduler, Event Viewer, Shared Folders, Local Users And Groups, Performance, Device Manager, Disk Management, Services, and WMI Control snap-ins, providing control over a wide range of computer tasks.
Device Manager (Devmgmt.msc)	Uses the Device Manager snap-in to enable administration of all attached hardware devices and their drivers. See Chapter 13 for more information on configuring hardware.
Disk Management (Diskmgmt.msc)	Uses the Disk Management snap-in for configuring disk volumes and partitions. For details, see "Setting up hard disks and other storage devices," in Chapter 8.
Event Viewer (Eventvwr.msc)	Uses the Event Viewer snap-in to display all types of logged information. See "Event Viewer" in Chapter 15.
Hyper-V Manager (Virtmgmt.msc)	Uses the Hyper-V Manager snap-in to provide an environment for creating, modifying, and running virtual machines. See Chapter 17, "Running Windows 11 in a virtual machine or in the cloud," for details.
Local Group Policy Editor (Gpedit.msc)	Uses the Local Computer Policy snap-in to configure policies that can be applied to a local machine or to a user account. See "Managing computers with Group Policy" in Chapter 19.
Local Users and Groups (Lusrmgr.msc)	Uses the Local Users and Groups snap-in to manage local user accounts and security groups. For more information, see "Creating and managing user accounts" in Chapter 10.
Performance Monitor (Perfmon.msc)	Uses the Performance Monitor snap-in to provide a set of monitoring tools. See Chapter 14, "Performance and power management," for details.
Print Management (Printmanagement.msc)	Uses the Print Management snap-in for managing printers and print jobs.
Services (Services.msc)	Uses the Services snap-in to manage services in Windows. For details, see "Managing services" in Chapter 14.
Task Scheduler (Taskschd.msc)	Uses the Task Scheduler snap-in for managing tasks that run automatically.

CHAPTER 16

Trusted Platform Module (TPM) Management (Tpm.msc)	Displays information about and enables configuration of a computer's TPM chip.
Windows Firewall With Advanced Security (Wf.msc)	Uses the Windows Firewall With Advanced Security snap-in to configure rules and make other firewall settings. For details, see "Managing Windows Defender Firewall" in Chapter 12, "Windows security and privacy."

Inside OUT

Avoiding User Account Control problems with MMC consoles

Consoles can be used to manage all sorts of computer hardware and Windows features: With a console, you can modify hard-drive partitions, start and stop services, and install device drivers, for example. In other words, MMC consoles perform the types of tasks that User Account Control (UAC) is designed to restrict. In the hands of someone malicious (or simply careless), consoles have the power to wreak havoc on your computer.

Therefore, when using an MMC console, you're likely to encounter a User Account Control request for permission to continue. If UAC is enabled on your computer, the type of request you get and the restrictions that are imposed depend on your account type and the console you're using. Some consoles, such as Device Manager (Devmgmt.msc), display a message box informing you that the console will run with limitations. (In effect, it works in a read-only mode that allows you to view device information but not make changes.) Others block all use by standard user accounts. To ensure that you don't run into an "access denied" roadblock when performing administrative tasks while signed in with a standard account, always right-click and then click Run As Administrator.

Running Windows 11 in a virtual machine or in the cloud

When you need to test a new app or online service, the last thing you want to do is risk the PC you rely on for daily work. But setting up a separate physical computer requires a significant investment in hardware, not to mention the desk or workbench space that a secondary system occupies and the maintenance it requires.

A much better alternative to setting up a separate physical machine is to use a *virtual machine* (sometimes called a VM), which enables you to build a simulated "computer within a computer" that you can use without investing in any additional hardware or using any additional space in your physical environment.

A virtual machine runs in an isolated session on the *host computer*, under the control of a system-level software layer called a *hypervisor*. The operating system running within the virtual machine is called the *guest operating system*. To connect to the VM, you open it in a window, which you can expand to occupy your full display, just as if you were connecting to a PC using a remote connection.

➤ **For more on how remote connections work, see "Connecting to another computer with Remote Desktop," in Chapter 11, "Configuring Windows networks."**

A VM can run the same software as a physical PC and can interact over a virtual network with other PCs and with web-based services. Crucially, a VM doesn't require any hardware beyond what's already part of the host PC.

Every business edition of Windows 11—Pro, Enterprise, and Education—includes a built-in hypervisor and associated management tools; an expanded set of virtualization tools is available in Windows Server. Collectively, these features are called *Hyper-V*.

NOTE

The Hyper-V feature set is included in Windows 10 as well. Using Hyper-V on a PC running Windows 10, you can install Windows 11 in a virtual environment without requiring an upgrade to the host PC's operating system.

Virtualization in Windows 11

Setting up one or more virtual machines with the help of Hyper-V is especially useful for developers, IT pros, researchers, and even authors of books on computer operating systems. Consider the value of a VM in scenarios like the following:

- **You need to run an app that was written for an earlier version of Windows and does not work properly in Windows 11.** Set up a virtual machine that runs the older version of Windows, install the outdated app in the VM, and use the VM exclusively for working with that app.

- **You're a web developer and you need to test your website in different browsers and under different resource configurations.** By setting up a virtual machine for each target configuration, you can reliably reproduce what your audience will see and adjust your code accordingly.

- **You've received a suspicious email attachment and you're curious about what it does.** Professional security researchers test software of unknown provenance or explore potentially dangerous websites using a virtual machine that's properly isolated from the host PC and the host network. That allows them to examine possible malware without jeopardizing the host machine.

- **You want to test a new Insider version of Windows 11 or experiment with a non-Microsoft operating system such as Linux.** You could set up a dual-boot configuration, but using a virtual machine allows you to switch between the alternative operating system and your host PC instantly, without rebooting.

Using a virtual machine makes it possible to capture images of screens that would be impossible to grab using ordinary screen-capture tools (for example, images showing sign-in screens or even Windows setup before Windows itself is fully functional). That's an invaluable feature for anyone producing documentation.

Virtual machines are also highly portable. You can move a VM to a new host by simply copying a few files.

There are, of course, some jobs for which Hyper-V virtual machines are inappropriate. Any task that requires direct access to physical hardware, such as the use of a discrete GPU to encode and decode video files, should be reserved for physical hardware. Likewise, any workload that depends on low latency and precise timing (including PC gaming) is likely to perform unacceptably in a VM.

To use Hyper-V, your system must meet certain minimum requirements, and you might need to enable the Hyper-V feature, as described later in this chapter. After those preliminaries are complete, you can use the Hyper-V Manager utility to create and manage virtual machines. With enough system resources, you can run multiple VMs simultaneously, each operating independently of the others. Because they function as separate computers, each VM can run a different version of Windows—32-bit or 64-bit, old or new, server or desktop—or even other operating systems that work on PC-compatible hardware.

NOTE

The hypervisor included in Windows 11 is also used to enable virtualization-based security features, such as Hypervisor-Enforced Code Integrity (HVCI). For more on this group of features, see Chapter 12, "Windows security and privacy."

In addition to the option to create a virtual machine running Windows 11 on your own local PC, Microsoft offers a subscription-based service called Windows 365, which enables IT administrators to create virtual PCs that are hosted in the Microsoft Azure cloud. To learn more about this service, see "Running virtual machines from the cloud," later in this chapter.

And if those options seem overly complicated or too resource-intensive, there's a simpler alternative. A feature called Windows Sandbox, which is available in all Windows 11 business editions, allows you to create a lightweight, temporary Windows 11 virtual machine in seconds, with no additional configuration steps required. You can read more about this feature in the following section.

Creating an instant VM with Windows Sandbox

When you just want to check out a suspicious web link or test an app or online service, you don't need to go through the time-consuming process of creating a virtual machine with Hyper-V and then deleting or resetting it after your experiment is complete. As an alternative, use the Windows Sandbox feature to build an extremely lightweight, clean, temporary virtual machine that's ready in seconds, without requiring any additional downloads. When you close the sandbox, every trace of it is discarded, and your next session starts from a clean baseline.

Windows Sandbox uses the same underlying technology as the Hyper-V platform but runs independently. To use the feature, you must be running Windows 11 Pro, Enterprise, or Education, and hardware virtualization must be enabled in your PC's firmware. If you satisfy both of those conditions, open the Windows Features dialog in Control Panel, select the Windows Sandbox checkbox, and click OK. (You do not need to enable any of the features under the Hyper-V heading to use Windows Sandbox.)

After you restart your PC, the Windows Sandbox shortcut will be available in the list of apps on Start. Click that shortcut to create and run a lightweight virtual machine immediately. The resizable Windows Sandbox window, shown in Figure 17-1, closely resembles a Hyper-V virtual machine, minus the toolbar and configuration options.

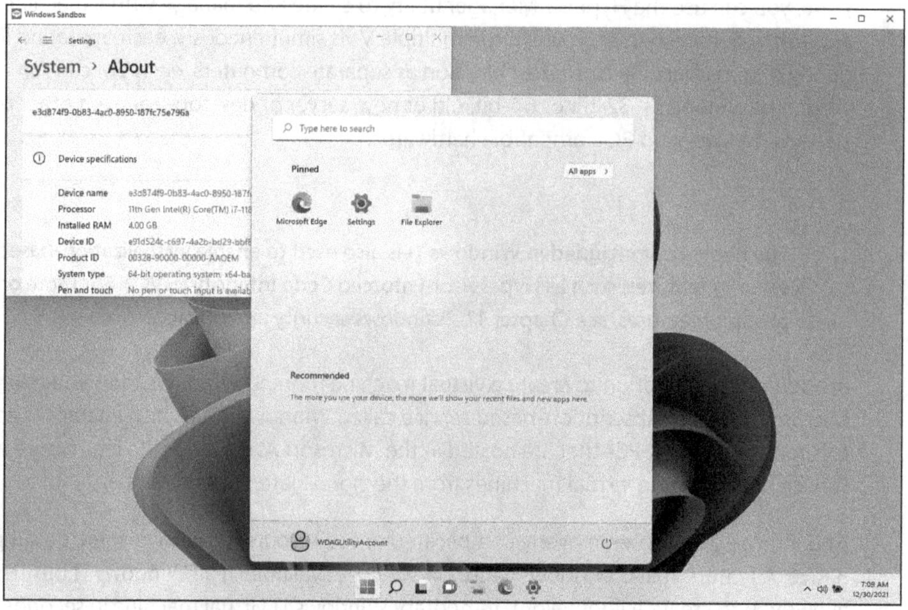

Figure 17-1 The Windows Sandbox runs the same Windows version and edition as the host PC but does not include any of the provisioned Windows apps except Microsoft Edge, File Explorer, and a handful of accessories like Notepad and Windows Media Player Legacy.

A few things are worth noting about these lightweight virtual machines:

- The sandbox runs an unactivated copy of Windows 11; the edition and version match those of the host PC.

- Windows Defender Antivirus protection is turned off. (Because the sandbox is not persistent or connected to the host, this means malicious code can run but can't cause damage outside the sandbox.)

- A small number of Windows accessories, administrative tools, and system utilities are available, including Notepad, Windows PowerShell, and Windows Media Player Legacy. With the noteworthy exception of File Explorer and the Microsoft Edge browser, however, no Windows 11 apps are installed or available.

- Many administrative functions are disabled, including the ability to install updates and inspect disks and network configurations.

- The default user account is a local administrator called WDAGUtilityAccount; that account is also used by the Windows Defender Application Guard feature for browsing web pages in an isolated environment.

- Virtual resources available to the sandbox include 4 GB of virtual memory and a 40 GB system drive, although the amount of actual memory and disk space used is much smaller. The sandbox image itself is contained in a small virtual disk file stored in C:\ProgramData\ Microsoft\Windows\Containers\Sandboxes\.

NOTE

Because the sandbox runs in a Hyper-V enhanced session, it shares the Clipboard with the host PC. As a result, you can copy links or executable files from the host PC and paste them directly into the sandbox window. For more on how enhanced sessions work, see "Running a virtual machine," later in this chapter.

By design, Windows Sandbox is lightweight and simple, without a point-and-click interface for customizing the sandbox environment. However, you can create a custom configuration by editing a simple XML file. Including the value <MemoryInMB>8192</MemoryInMB>, for example, increases the default memory for the sandbox from 4 GB to 8 GB. Sandbox configuration files use the .wsb extension to associate with Windows Sandbox, and you can launch a sandbox using a custom configuration by double-clicking a saved .wsb file. For details, see "Windows Sandbox configuration," at *https://bit.ly/windows-sandbox-config-files*.

To create a persistent virtual machine that you can modify and reuse, you need to use the full Hyper-V platform, as described in the next section.

Setting up Hyper-V on Windows 11

Hyper-V (or, more accurately, the Hyper-V role) has long been a power feature in server editions of Microsoft Windows, enabling IT managers to use a single physical machine to host various server roles, each in its own virtual machine. Since the release of Windows 8 in 2012, Microsoft has included so-called Client Hyper-V in Pro, Enterprise, and Education editions of Windows, to the great delight of IT professionals, developers, security researchers, and tech enthusiasts.

NOTE

Although this chapter offers a thorough introduction to Windows-based virtualization, there's plenty of technical detail that didn't fit in these pages. For a more comprehensive reference, see the official documentation, "Hyper-V on Windows 10," at *https://learn.microsoft.com/virtualization/hyper-v-on-windows/*. (Don't be fooled by the title: The core features of Hyper-V in Windows 10 and Windows 11 are essentially identical.)

The feature sets of Client Hyper-V and its counterpart in Windows server editions overlap but are not a perfect match. Client Hyper-V in Windows 11 has the ability to create virtual machines that support Secure Boot and virtual Trusted Platform Modules; they also include support for nested virtualization, which allows virtual environments to host additional virtual machines.

The Hyper-V platform includes the Hyper-V hypervisor and a group of services that do the work of managing virtual hardware, connecting to virtual networks, and running virtual machines. In particular, the Virtual Machine Management Service (Vmms.exe) and the Hyper-V Host Computer Service (Vmmcompute.exe) both run under the credentials of the currently signed-in user; other parts of the Hyper-V infrastructure run under local system and service accounts, allowing VMs to run even when no user is signed in.

Separate from the hypervisor and related Hyper-V services, Client Hyper-V includes a set of management tools. Two of them are worth calling out here:

- **Hyper-V Manager (Virtmgmt.msc)**   A Microsoft Management Console snap-in that provides management access to the virtualization platform. Using Hyper-V Manager, you can create a new virtual machine; adjust the configuration of an existing VM; configure virtual networking and storage hardware; import, export, and share VMs; and adjust the settings of the Hyper-V platform itself.

- **Virtual Machine Connection (Vmconnect.exe)**   A Windows desktop app that enables you to interact with a running virtual machine using the keyboard and mouse on the host PC. The application can run in a window, in which its contents act as a virtual monitor for the VM, or in full-screen mode, where the virtual machine's display takes over the host PC's display.

You'll find detailed coverage of both of these essential tools later in this chapter.

On hardware designed for earlier Windows versions, running Hyper-V required careful checking (and sometimes extra configuration steps) to ensure that the host computer's CPU supported the necessary virtualization features. On a PC that meets the hardware requirements for Windows 11, these features are enabled by default, and extensive hardware compatibility checks aren't necessary. The host PC must, however, be running Windows 11 Pro, Enterprise, or Education; Hyper-V features are unavailable on Windows 11 Home.

Beyond those basic compatibility requirements, the most important consideration is to ensure that the host PC has sufficient system resources (memory and disk space) to handle the intended workloads:

- Although it's possible to create and run a low-resource virtual machine on a host PC with 4 GB of total RAM, we recommend at least 8 GB of total RAM (and preferably 16 GB) for satisfactory performance with one or more virtual machines running Windows 10 or Windows 11.

- Each virtual machine is stored in files on your hard drive. The size can vary considerably depending on how you configure your virtual machines (for example, whether you use fixed or dynamically expanding virtual hard disks), how many checkpoints you save, and so on—but expect to use at least 20 GB of disk storage for each virtual machine.

With those prerequisites in place, the only additional step required is to turn on the Hyper-V features, which are off by default. To do so, open the Windows Features dialog, shown in Figure 17-2. (The executable file for this system tool, OptionalFeatures.exe, is located in C:\Windows\ System32. To open it quickly, click in the search box, type **features,** and then click Turn Windows Features On Or Off.)

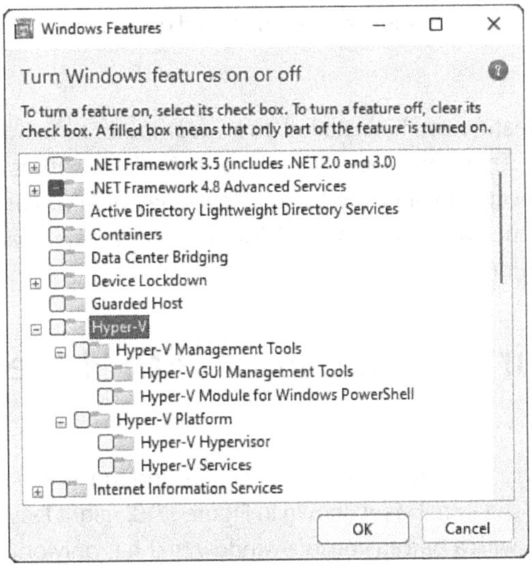

CHAPTER 17

Figure 17-2   To install the Hyper-V hypervisor and all related tools and services, select the top-level Hyper-V checkbox in the Windows Features dialog.

Click the plus sign by the top-level Hyper-V entry to show all available subentries. Select Hyper-V (which also selects all the available subentries) to enable it, and then click OK. After a few moments, Windows asks you to restart your computer.

Alternatively, you can enable Hyper-V by using Windows PowerShell. Use this cmdlet:

```
Enable-WindowsOptionalFeature –Online –FeatureName Microsoft-Hyper-V –All
```

TROUBLESHOOTING

You're unable to install the Hyper-V Hypervisor and Hyper-V Services

If your computer does not fully support Hyper-V, the entries under the Hyper-V Platform category will be dimmed and unavailable. The most common reason for this condition is that your computer is running Home edition, which doesn't support the full Hyper-V platform. The only fix in that case is to upgrade to a supported Windows edition.

You might also encounter this problem if your hardware doesn't have the required virtualization features enabled. The switches to configure hardware-based virtualization features are typically found in the firmware settings for a PC. To access those firmware settings from Windows, click Start, click Power, and then hold down Shift as you click Restart.

The Hyper-V Management Tools feature can be installed on any computer running any edition of Windows 10 or Windows 11. Therefore, even if the Hyper-V Platform entries are dimmed (which means your computer isn't capable of hosting virtual machines), you can use Hyper-V Management Tools to manage virtual machines that are hosted on a different physical computer (in most cases, a computer running Window Server).

Creating and managing virtual machines with Hyper-V Manager

Hyper-V Manager is the app you use to create, configure, manage, and run virtual machines. When you start Hyper-V Manager, the initial view, shown in Figure 17-3, might leave you scratching your head. You're faced with a barren console window that has only one available action.

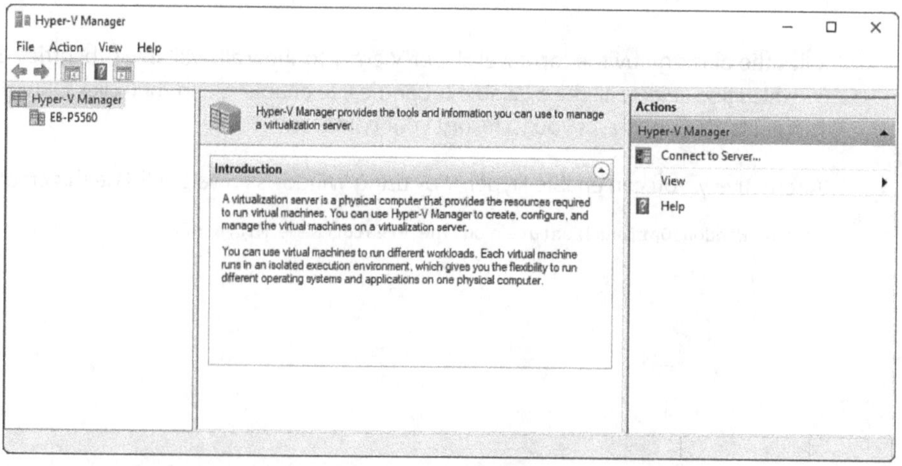

Figure 17-3   On a PC running Windows 11 Pro, you must select the PC from the pane on the left to work with existing VMs and create new ones.

The trick is to select a "server" (in this case, your local computer) in the left pane, the console tree. (On computers that do not have Hyper-V Platform enabled, the only option is to choose Connect To Server from the Actions pane, which enables you to connect to a different PC or server running Hyper-V.) That action reveals far more information and options, as shown in Figure 17-4.

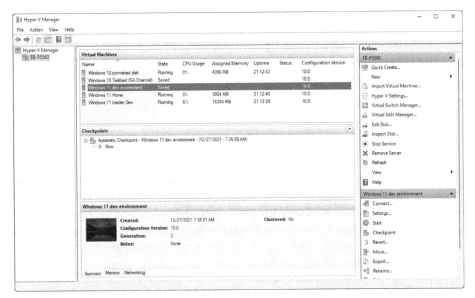

Figure 17-4 The bottom of the Hyper-V Manager window shows details about the currently selected virtual machine, with available actions for that VM on the right.

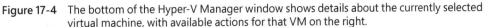

TROUBLESHOOTING

The name of your computer doesn't appear in the console tree

If your computer's name doesn't appear under Hyper-V Manager in the console tree, it's probably because either your account lacks the necessary privileges or your computer is not running the Hyper-V Hypervisor and associated services. The first problem can occur if you're signed in using a standard account. To fix it, right-click the Hyper-V Manager icon in Start, choose Run As Administrator, and supply credentials for an administrator account. To ensure that your computer is running the Hyper-V Hypervisor, be sure you're running a supported edition of Windows 11 and that the Hyper-V Platform features are enabled, as described in the previous section.

When you select a Hyper-V host in the console tree (in this case, your PC running Windows 11 Pro, Enterprise, or Education), the center pane lists the virtual machines available on that host and shows a bit of information about the current state of each one. Below that, you see a list of checkpoints for the selected virtual machine. (A *checkpoint* captures the configuration and data of a virtual machine at a point in time. For more information, see "Working with checkpoints" later in this chapter.) At the bottom of the center pane, the Summary, Memory, and Networking tabs show additional details about the selected virtual machine. Here you can see at a glance what IP addresses have been assigned to the virtual machine, how much memory is in use, and so on. The thumbnail image on the Summary tab also provides a convenient launching method for the virtual machine; double-click it to connect to that virtual machine.

As in other console applications, the right pane shows available actions for the items selected in the left and center panes. In Figure 17-4, shown earlier, you can see the actions that apply to the Hyper-V host running on the local computer named EB-P5560 and to the virtual machine named "Windows 11 dev environment."

Inside OUT

Add notes to help explain a virtual machine's configuration

In the settings for every virtual machine is a Name field that includes a free-form box where you can record notes about that VM. We recommend that you get in the habit of using these notes to record details that will help you or a colleague understand the details of a configuration (including the default account for signing on) without having to poke around in the VM's settings. Those notes can be especially useful when you're reopening a VM that's been unused for months or even years.

In Windows 11, you have two options for creating a persistent virtual machine from within Hyper-V Manager. The Quick Create option allows you to create a VM with just a few clicks by downloading a predefined virtual machine image from an online collection; if you're comfortable with the settings it makes on your behalf, this can be a useful tool.

The alternative is the traditional New Virtual Machine Wizard, which walks you step by step through configuring each virtual component. The process can feel tedious, but it also results in much greater control over the VM's configuration.

Before examining either of those options, though, let's look at the architecture of a Hyper-V virtual machine.

What's in a VM?

Creating and configuring a virtual machine doesn't require any tools, nor does it involve connecting physical components like motherboards, solid-state drives, and memory modules. To build a virtual machine, you use point-and-click Hyper-V management tools to select from an assortment of standard virtual components and add them to your PC build. With one noteworthy exception, the CPU, your virtual machine is unable to directly access hardware that's part of the host PC.

You can see all of the components that make up a Windows virtual machine by opening Device Manager within that machine. Figure 17-5, for example, shows Device Manager expanded to show a virtual disk, a virtual DVD-ROM drive, a virtual network adapter, two virtual storage controllers, and an assortment of virtual system devices on a virtual motherboard.

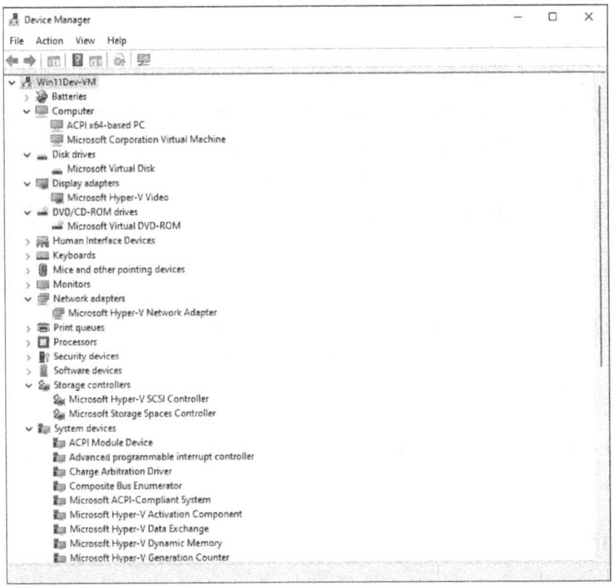

Figure 17-5   Virtual machines are made up of virtual components, as you can see when you open Device Manager from within a VM running Windows 11, as shown here.

It's considerably easier (and less expensive) to upgrade a virtual PC than it is to perform the corresponding task on a physical PC. To add more virtual memory or a second virtual storage device, for example, all you need to do is shut down the VM and adjust a few settings.

We discuss the tools for creating and reconfiguring VMs later in this chapter. The remainder of this section covers how Hyper-V stores the different pieces that make up a VM.

The most basic building block is the virtual machine configuration file, which is stored in a binary format using the .vmcx file extension. By default, these configuration files are stored in %ProgramData%\Microsoft\Windows\Hyper-V; you can specify an alternative location when you create a new VM, and you can move configuration files to a different folder or drive using Hyper-V Manager. (%ProgramData% is an environment variable that is set to C:\ProgramData on a standard Windows installation.)

CHAPTER 17

Inside OUT

Use PowerShell to work with a virtual machine directly

The simplest way to create and modify a virtual machine running on Windows 10 or Windows 11 is with the use of Hyper-V Manager. Any settings modified in this fashion are saved in the configuration file that has been registered with the current Hyper-V host. (Because those settings are saved as a binary file in .vmcx format, the file cannot be edited directly.)

For Hyper-V experts who work with virtual machines regularly, there's an additional option: Use the Hyper-V module for Windows PowerShell, which is installed along with Hyper-V Manager. Using cmdlets in this module, you can import, export, modify, and run virtual machines without having to touch Hyper-V Manager. The full documentation for this module is available at *https://learn.microsoft.com/powershell/module/hyper-v/*.

Other files stored in the same location include .vmgs and .vmrs files, which contain information about the current state of a running VM, and the smart paging file, which supplements dynamic memory when you restart a VM.

The information contained in the configuration file instructs Hyper-V how to allocate resources to specific types of virtual hardware, as outlined in the next four sections.

Machine generation

In Windows 10 and Windows 11, Hyper-V supports two types of machines, each of which represents a different generation of virtual PC hardware:

- Generation 1 supports a wide range of guest operating systems, including most versions of Windows (32-bit and 64-bit) and Linux. The virtual hardware in a Generation 1 virtual machine is typical of that found in BIOS-based PCs for many years.

- Generation 2 supports only 64-bit Windows versions, with support for modern technologies such as Secure Boot and UEFI built in. Among desktop operating systems, Windows 8, Windows 8.1, Windows 10, and Windows 11 are supported; it also supports Windows Server 2012 and later versions as a guest operating system. Generation 2 VMs also support all current Linux distributions.

NOTE

For a complete discussion of the differences between the two VM generations, including a list of supported operating systems, visit *https://bit.ly/Gen1Gen2*.

Generation 2 removes support for attaching physical DVD drives and other older hardware to a virtual machine, a feature required only for the most ancient operating systems. A Generation 2 virtual machine has modern UEFI-based firmware, which enables Secure Boot and booting from a network adapter, SCSI hard drive, or virtual DVD. In addition, Generation 2 virtual machines enable modern Hyper-V features, such as the ability to adjust memory or add a network adapter while the virtual machine is running.

You must make the choice of generation at the time you create a VM, and you can't change it after that initial selection.

Memory

Like its physical counterpart, a virtual machine needs memory. When a VM is running, the memory assigned to that VM is reserved by Hyper-V and can't be used by the host PC. If you assign a fixed amount of memory to a VM configuration, running that VM can put significant memory pressure on the host PC. If your host PC has 16 GB of RAM, for example, and you set the RAM value to 8 GB for a VM, your host PC is effectively limited to 8 GB for Windows and all other activities when that VM is running, even if the VM is using only a fraction of the memory assigned to it.

To ease this pressure, Hyper-V in Windows 10 and Windows 11 includes a feature called *dynamic memory,* which allows you to make more efficient use of the memory in the host PC.

When you enable the Dynamic Memory option for a VM, you assign memory in a range by setting two additional values: Minimum RAM and Maximum RAM. That configuration enables the VM to grab physical memory when it needs it (especially when starting up) but releases that memory when it's no longer in use so that it's available for the host PC.

Figure 17-6 shows memory usage in a VM that is configured with Dynamic Memory enabled and default settings in use, with Minimum RAM set to 512 MB and Maximum RAM set to 1 TB.

CHAPTER 17

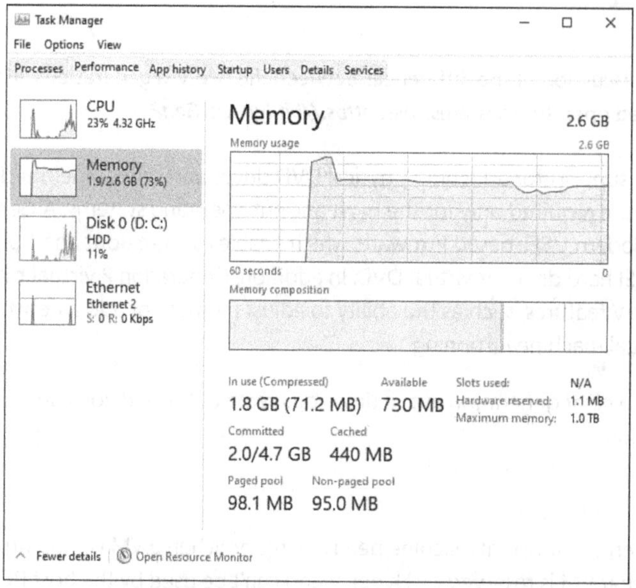

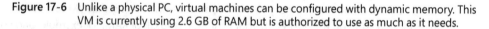

Figure 17-6   Unlike a physical PC, virtual machines can be configured with dynamic memory. This VM is currently using 2.6 GB of RAM but is authorized to use as much as it needs.

In that Task Manager window, you can see the current RAM usage, 2.6 GB, in the upper-right corner. That's slightly more than the 2048 MB of RAM that was allocated at startup, which means this VM has already taken advantage of its ability to ask for additional memory when needed. The Maximum Memory value at the bottom right shows that this VM is ready and able to increase its RAM to as much as necessary. No, the host PC does not have a terabyte of RAM available, but specifying that extremely high default value means that the VM has permission to use as much physical RAM as is available on the host PC.

Dynamic Memory is an excellent way to conserve memory when running Hyper-V on a system with limited physical RAM. If you have ample system resources and want a VM to run with a fixed amount of RAM, clear the Dynamic Memory checkbox to disable that option.

You'll find a discussion of the different ways to manage memory usage in VM configurations later in this chapter.

Storage controllers and virtual disks

Every Hyper-V virtual machine includes a virtual storage controller. On a Generation 1 VM, this virtual component mimics a legacy IDE controller. On a Generation 2 VM, it acts like a SCSI controller.

Part of the basic configuration of a VM is, of course, a virtual hard disk that attaches to that virtual controller. Hyper-V in Windows 10 and Windows 11 supports three virtual disk file formats: the legacy VHD format, the newer VHDX format, and a specialized VHD Set format for shared virtual hard disks.

The legacy VHD format is limited to a total size of 2 TB. VHDX files, on the other hand, can be as large as 64 TB, provide better data resiliency, and support advanced 4K sector technology; you can also expand a VHDX file on the fly without having to shut down the VM in which it's being used. (VHD Set files are an esoteric format primarily intended for use with failover clusters of multiple virtual machines running Windows Server editions and are not intended for use on desktop PCs running Windows 10 or Windows 11.)

An important attribute of a virtual disk that distinguishes it from a physical disk is the disk type, which can be one of the following three choices:

- **Fixed size**   This type of virtual disk uses exactly as much disk space on the Hyper-V host as its configured size. The size of the VHD file doesn't change based on the amount of data stored within it.

- **Dynamically expanding**   Choose this disk type when you want to conserve physical disk space on the Hyper-V host and the workloads you plan to use on the VM are not disk-intensive. The virtual disk file starts out small and grows as you add data to it within the VM. (You can't, of course, overturn the laws of physics; as your virtual hard disk expands, it uses a corresponding amount of physical disk space.)

- **Differencing**   This advanced disk type starts with a parent disk that remains intact; any changes you make in this virtual disk affect only the file containing the child disk and can be reverted easily.

On a Generation 2 virtual machine, you also have the option to use a shared drive by specifying a virtual disk file that already exists. If you have a spare physical disk partition available, you can attach that physical drive to it directly rather than using a virtual disk. This option offers excellent performance but is impractical on most desktop configurations.

Generation 1 VMs can directly connect to a physical CD/DVD drive. VMs of either generation can use virtual DVDs, which are most useful when you want to mount an ISO file to install a new operating system in the VM. If you're feeling especially nostalgic, you can even create a virtual floppy disk on a Generation 1 machine.

You'll find more about the mechanics of creating and managing virtual disks later in this chapter.

Inside OUT

Mount or unmount a virtual DVD quickly

Any disk image in ISO format can appear as a virtual DVD drive, and there's no need to go through the Settings dialog to mount or unmount a virtual drive. Instead, to attach an ISO file as a drive within a running virtual machine, click Media from the VMConnect console, and then click DVD Drive > Insert Disk. Choose an ISO file, and click OK. To unmount a virtual drive, use the Eject <*ISO filename*> option from the DVD Drive menu.

Networking

Support for basic networking in Hyper-V requires two components: a *virtual network adapter*, configured separately for each VM, and a *virtual switch*, which is managed by the Hyper-V platform. The default virtual network adapter is called a *Hyper-V specific network adapter* and is available for both Generation 1 and Generation 2 machines. In Generation 1 machines only, you can install a *legacy network adapter* capable of booting directly to a network and running unsupported operating systems.

By default, a new virtual machine is set up with a network adapter but is not connected to the network; this configuration is equivalent to a standalone computer with a wired network card (and no Wi-Fi adapter) that isn't plugged into a router or switch and thus can't connect to the internet or to other computers. That disconnected configuration might be useful for some testing scenarios, but for most situations, you probably want to give your virtual machines access to a network connection.

To do that, you must first configure the virtual network adapter to connect to a virtual switch; that action connects the virtual network adapter in your virtual machine to the physical network adapter in your physical computer, thereby allowing the VM to connect to the outside world. For each virtual switch you configure, Hyper-V creates a corresponding virtual network adapter on the host PC that handles communication to other hosts and to the internet.

In Hyper-V on Windows 11, every VM has access to a preconfigured default network switch that communicates with the host PC and other PCs using Network Address Translation (NAT). To use this switch, when you get to the point in creating a new virtual machine where you configure networking, simply select Default Switch from the Virtual Switch dropdown. (See "Configure networking," later in this chapter.)

You can create additional custom switches to accommodate other network configurations and then choose the type of virtual switch you need for each VM, at startup time or while the VM is running.

To create a virtual switch or make changes to an existing one, open Hyper-V Manager and then, in the Actions pane (or on the Action menu), click or tap Virtual Switch Manager. Then select the type of switch you want to create:

- **External**   This is the correct choice when you want your VM to behave as if it were another PC on your local network. This configuration binds the virtual switch to the host PC's physical network adapter so that you can access your physical network. Assuming the host PC's physical network adapter is connected to the internet, your virtual machines using this type of switch also have internet access.

- **Internal**   An internal virtual switch allows connections among other virtual machines using the same virtual switch on the host PC but isolates them from other devices on the host PC's network; those VMs can also connect to the internet using the virtual network adapter (vEthernet) on the host PC.

- **Private**   Use a private virtual switch to set up a network that comprises only the virtual machines running on your physical computer and using the same virtual switch. This network is isolated from all physical computers, including the Hyper-V host on which it's installed. Without additional configuration steps, it has no internet connectivity.

When you click or tap Create Virtual Switch, you're asked for more details, as shown in Figure 17-7. Click OK to complete the switch creation.

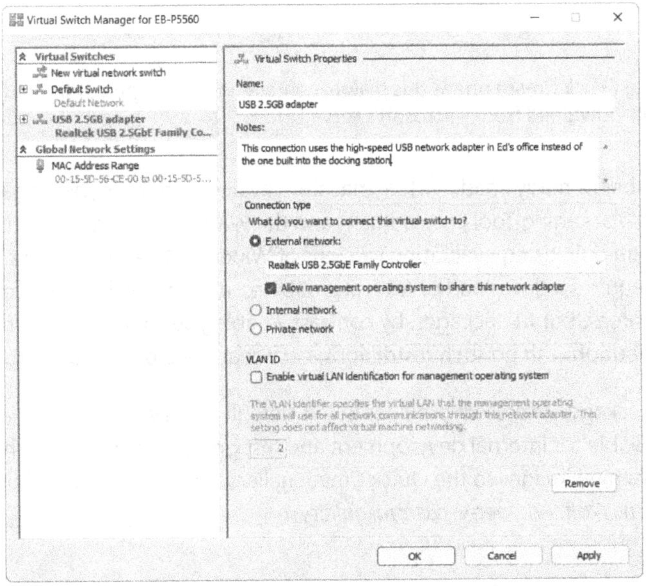

Figure 17-7   If your computer has more than one physical network adapter, you can specify the one you want to use for a new switch under External Network.

Using Quick Create to download and run a preconfigured VM

The Quick Create command appears at the top of the Actions pane on the right side of Hyper-V Manager when you've selected the host PC in the left pane. Clicking Quick Create opens a Create Virtual Machine dialog like the one shown in Figure 17-8. From this dialog, you can choose one of the predefined virtual disk images available from Microsoft, as shown here.

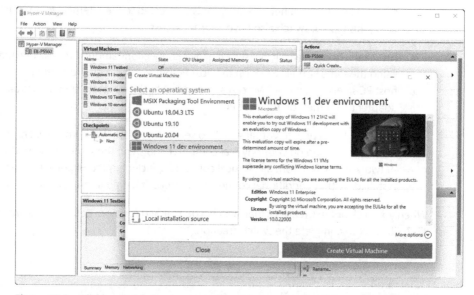

Figure 17-8   Clicking Quick Create opens this dialog, containing links to preconfigured VMs available for download from Microsoft's servers.

Over time, the number of ready-made virtual machines available in the Hyper-V gallery has increased. The MSIX Packaging Tool Environment and the Windows 11 Dev Environment packages, for example, are built using evaluation versions of Windows 10 and Windows 11 Enterprise, respectively. Each requires a download of several gigabytes, and the evaluation license expires after 90 days. The three Ubuntu packages, by contrast, enable you to set up a VM running this popular Linux distribution with no such restrictions; each requires a download of roughly 2 GB.

In addition to the packages Microsoft provides in this default gallery, IT professionals can make custom images available for internal development and test groups. For details on how to add your own virtual machine images to the Quick Create gallery, see this post from Microsoft's Thomas Maurer: *https://bit.ly/hyper-v-custom-gallery*.

Inside OUT

Get ready-to-run virtual machines

As part of its support for software developers, Microsoft offers free downloads of fully configured virtual machines that run evaluation versions of Windows 11. Each one includes Windows 11 with a suite of popular developer tools installed and is packaged for use with four popular virtualization platforms: Hyper-V, VMware, VirtualBox, and Parallels. These VMs are for testing and evaluation and expire after 90 days, but instructions provided with the VM files explain how to use the files after expiration. You can find these virtual machine files at *https://developer.microsoft.com/windows/downloads/virtual-machines/*.

If nothing in the Quick Create gallery meets your requirements, take advantage of the last option to create a VM using local installation media. From the Quick Create dialog, select Local Installation Source, click the Change Installation Source button, and navigate to the ISO file you want to use for installation or the virtual hard disk you want to use as a template. The file must be in the form of an ISO image or a VHD/VHDX disk image. Figure 17-9 shows this option in use with a previously created virtual machine running an Insider release of Windows 11.

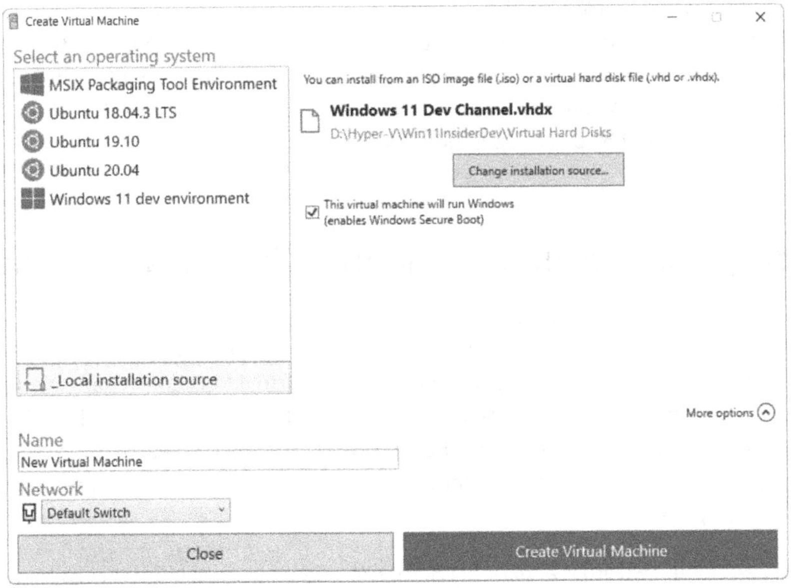

CHAPTER 17

Figure 17-9   Choosing the Local Installation Source option enables you to quickly create a VM with ISO-based installation media or using a virtual hard disk as a template.

The checkbox under Change Installation Source enables Secure Boot, a feature of UEFI-based computers. Click More Options to display controls where you can enter a descriptive file name and select a virtual network adapter. You can specify two settings from this dialog:

- **Name**   The text you enter here is used to identify the VM in the Virtual Machines list in Hyper-V Manager.

- **Network**   Here you select a virtual network switch for the VM. Unless you've created a custom network switch, choose Default Switch here.

With those details complete, click Create Virtual Machine. Hyper-V creates your new VM using default settings and displays a final dialog with two buttons. The first allows you to connect to the VM immediately; the second opens the Settings dialog for the new VM, where you can adjust the amount of memory, tinker with hard drives, and make any other necessary changes.

CHAPTER 17

Inside OUT

Don't use Quick Create for an older operating system

Quick Create always creates a Generation 2 virtual machine—a setting that cannot be changed. As described in the previous section, "What's in a VM?" a Generation 2 machine is the appropriate choice when the guest operating system you plan to use is a recent 64-bit version of Windows or a recent Linux distribution. When setting up a VM to run an older operating system, such as Windows 7, you're better off using the New Virtual Machine Wizard and selecting Generation 1, which has virtual hardware that's better supported by earlier operating systems.

Building a custom VM with the New Virtual Machine Wizard

If you want step-by-step control over the process of creating a new VM, the Quick Create option is not for you. Instead, open Hyper-V Manager and, in the Actions pane, click or tap New > Virtual Machine. That action launches the New Virtual Machine Wizard. Navigating through the wizard leads you through the process of setting up a virtual machine. Use the Next and Previous buttons or the links along the left side to step through each group of settings. At any point in the wizard, you can click Finish to create a virtual machine that uses default values for any wizard pages you skip.

The first page of the wizard is a text-only Before You Begin page, which you can banish for good by selecting Do Not Show This Page Again. The remainder of this section describes your options at each successive step of the wizard.

NOTE

For fast results, you can open the New Virtual Machine Wizard and immediately click Finish. As it turns out, however, that upfront efficiency is just an illusion, as is the corresponding Quick Create option. When using the wizard in this fashion, you'll need to spend time and effort later manually changing the generic default name for the VM and the virtual hard disk, adjusting the size of available memory, and attaching installation media. In addition, the default settings create a Generation 1 VM, which can't be changed to a Generation 2 configuration.

Specify name and location

After you step through the Before You Begin page, the wizard asks you to provide a name for your virtual machine. Replace the generic New Virtual Machine entry with a name that helps you differentiate this virtual machine from others you might create. (The wizard will use this entry again later, as the suggested name for the virtual hard disk you create.) If you don't like the proposed storage location for the virtual machine files, select the checkbox and specify another, as shown in Figure 17-10.

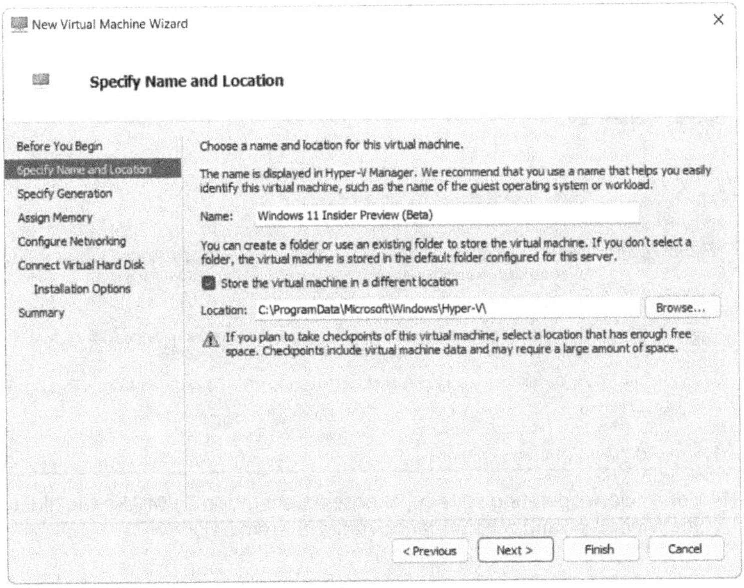

Figure 17-10   Use a descriptive name to help identify the VM in Hyper-V Manager. We recommend storing configuration files in the default location unless you have a separate, dedicated data drive.

The default location is %ProgramData%\Microsoft\Windows\Hyper-V\. If your computer has a small system drive and a larger data drive—a common configuration in some desktop systems that use a solid-state drive for system files and a large hard disk for data files—you might want to store the files elsewhere. Keep in mind that a virtual machine can occupy 10–40 GB or more, and each checkpoint can consume equivalent amounts of space.

It's possible to change the location where the virtual machine configuration files are stored after you create the VM, but it's not easy. The virtual hard disk can be moved by right-clicking the machine name and choosing the Move option, for example, and the paging file location can be changed by adjusting the VM configuration, but these options aren't available for the core configuration files. To completely move all the pieces of a virtual machine at a later time, you can export a virtual machine, copy it, and store it in a different location. You're much better off choosing a suitable location *before* you create the virtual machine.

Specify generation

On the Specify Generation page, shown in Figure 17-11, select either Generation 1 or Generation 2 for the style of virtual machine you need. (For a discussion of the differences, see "Machine generation," earlier in this chapter.)

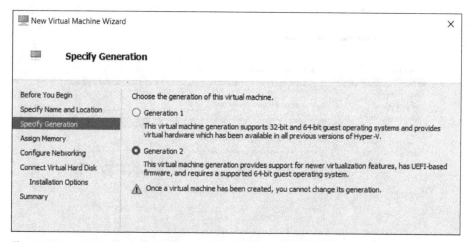

Figure 17-11 For modern operating systems, choose a Generation 2 VM. Use the older alternative for Windows 7 and other older operating systems.

If you're going to install a current, supported version of Windows in your virtual machine, select Generation 2 to enable additional features such as Secure Boot. For an older operating system, the default option, Generation 1, is probably a better choice.

Assign memory

On the Assign Memory page, shown in Figure 17-12, you specify the amount of RAM to assign to the VM during startup. This amount remains assigned to the VM when it's running unless you select the Use Dynamic Memory For This Virtual Machine option. (For an explanation of how dynamic memory works, see "Memory," earlier in this chapter.)

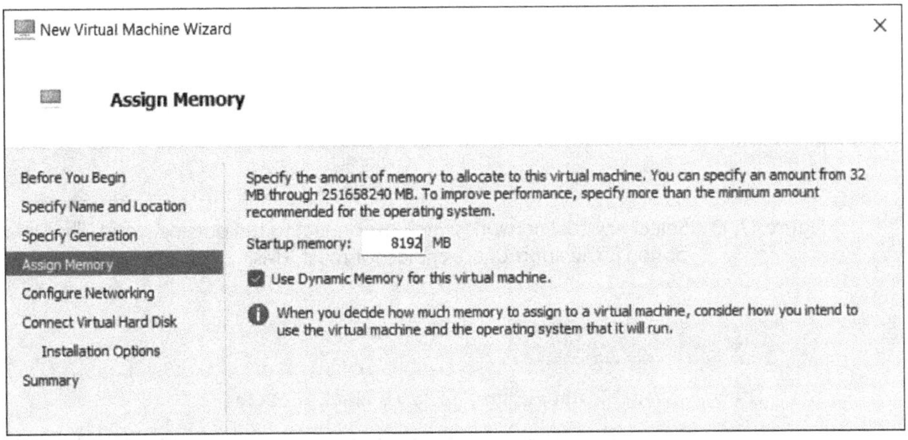

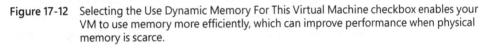

New Virtual Machine Wizard ☒

Assign Memory

Before You Begin
Specify Name and Location
Specify Generation
Assign Memory
Configure Networking
Connect Virtual Hard Disk
Installation Options
Summary

Specify the amount of memory to allocate to this virtual machine. You can specify an amount from 32 MB through 251658240 MB. To improve performance, specify more than the minimum amount recommended for the operating system.

Startup memory: 8192 MB

☑ Use Dynamic Memory for this virtual machine.

ⓘ When you decide how much memory to assign to a virtual machine, consider how you intend to use the virtual machine and the operating system that it will run.

CHAPTER 17

Figure 17-12   Selecting the Use Dynamic Memory For This Virtual Machine checkbox enables your VM to use memory more efficiently, which can improve performance when physical memory is scarce.

Note that the wizard does not allow you to specify values for Minimum RAM and Maximum RAM. Instead, if you use the New Virtual Machine Wizard and enable dynamic memory, Hyper-V assigns 512 MB and 1.0 TB, respectively. You can exercise far more granular control over memory by adjusting the settings for a VM after you create it, as explained a bit later in this chapter.

Configure networking

On the Configure Networking page, shown in Figure 17-13, you specify the virtual network switch where you want to connect your virtual machine's network adapter. The default option is Not Connected, which results in a virtual machine that's isolated from all other computers (physical and virtual) and from the internet. To connect to the host PC and to the internet, select Default Switch (which uses NAT to connect to your computer's network) or select a virtual network switch you created previously.

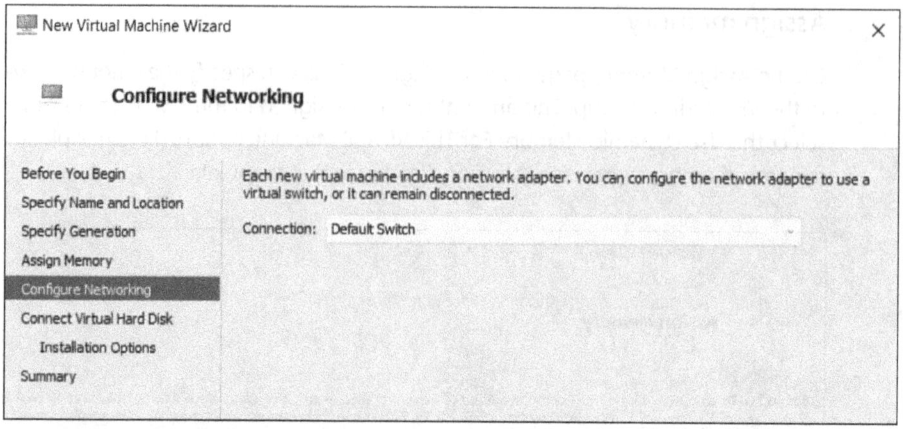

Figure 17-13   Select a virtual network switch to connect to the outside world. The Default Switch option is the appropriate choice for most VMs.

TROUBLESHOOTING

The only available networking option is Not Connected

If you're running a currently supported version of Windows 10 or Windows 11 and the Default Switch option is missing, the most likely explanation is that you or another administrator removed it. You can re-create this switch by shutting down any running VMs and then removing and reinstalling the Hyper-V Platform feature, as described earlier in "Setting up Hyper-V on Windows 11."

Connect virtual hard disk

Use the Connect Virtual Hard Disk page, shown in Figure 17-14, to set up the virtual machine's first virtual hard disk. By default, the New Virtual Machine Wizard creates a dynamically expanding virtual hard disk, using the VHDX format and a default name based on the name you entered in the first step. (You also have the option to specify the location of an existing file in VHDX format.) If you want to create a fixed-size virtual hard disk or use the older VHD format, choose the Attach A Virtual Hard Disk Later option and customize your VM after you complete the wizard.

Just as with a physical computer, a virtual machine can have multiple hard drives; the wizard allows you to create or attach the system drive only. By default, this drive is created in the Shared Documents folder for the Public user profile, where it's accessible to any user who signs in on the host PC. You can override that default and store the virtual hard disk on any physical disk that's accessible to the Hyper-V host.

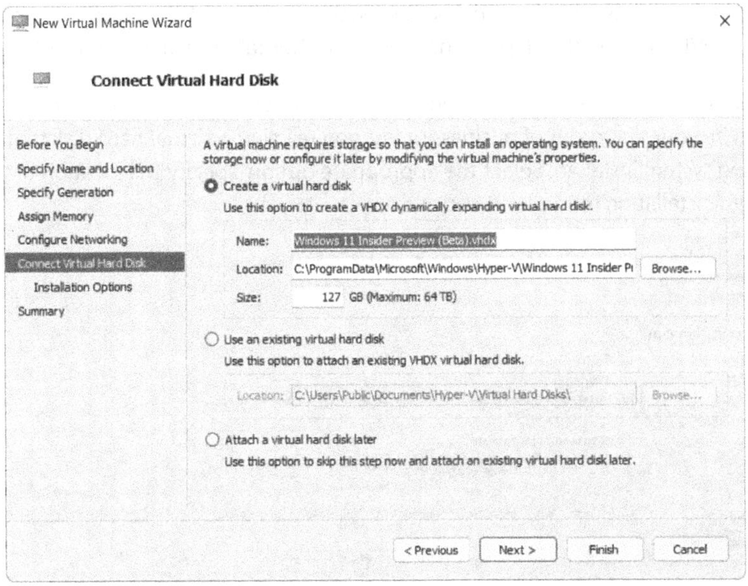

Figure 17-14   With the first option, you create a virtual hard disk. Choose the second option to use a virtual hard disk that already exists.

In addition to specifying the name and location of your virtual hard disk file, you must specify the disk's capacity, in gigabytes. Be sure you create a virtual hard disk that's big enough to store the operating system, apps, and data you plan to use on the virtual machine. Although you don't want to go overboard, don't worry too much about specifying a size that's too big. As noted earlier, a dynamically expanding VHDX file starts small and can grow as needed; just make sure the location you choose on the physical disk has enough space to accommodate the virtual drive file as it grows.

NOTE

Changing the name or location of a virtual hard disk is a tedious process that requires multiple steps. Likewise, resizing a virtual hard disk after it has been created involves tinkering with partitions in the virtual machine. To avoid those hassles, it's worth putting some thought into getting this setting right from the start.

If you have an existing virtual hard disk you want to use instead of creating a new one, select the second option on this wizard page.

Installation options

The Installation Options page, shown in Figure 17-15, enables you to specify how and when you want to install an operating system in your new virtual machine. Because this is a Generation 2 virtual machine, the only options available are to use an ISO image file or install from a network server running enterprise deployment tools. (Generation 1 VMs offer options to install from the physical CD/DVD drive on the Hyper-V host or from a bootable virtual floppy disk.)

Like a physical computer, a virtual machine is useless without an operating system, so installing one should be your first order of business unless you're using a virtual hard disk that already has an operating system installed. Select the appropriate option, specify the location of your operating system installation media, and click Next.

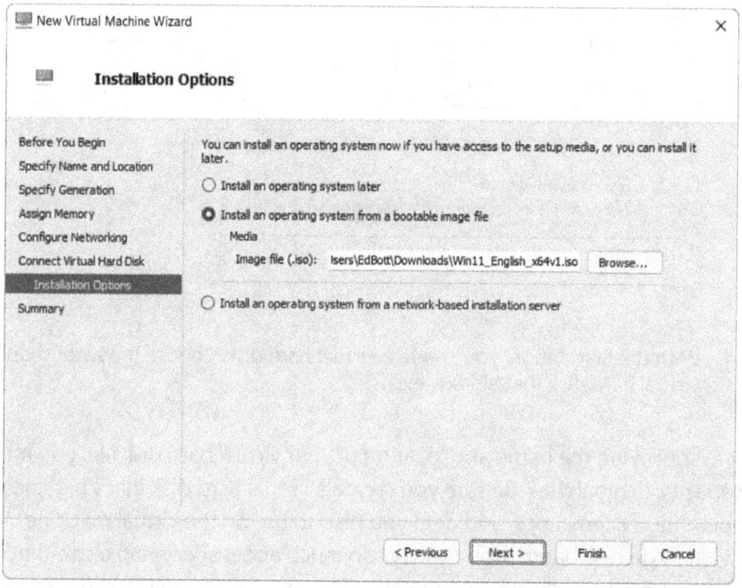

Figure 17-15   These options are available for a Generation 2 VM. Generation 1 VMs allow installation of an operating system from a physical DVD or a virtual floppy disk.

This brings you to a Summary page, where you can review your settings before clicking Finish to complete the wizard.

Even after clicking Finish, you still have a few choices to make before working with your new virtual machine. In Hyper-V Manager, you can select the newly created VM and then fine-tune its settings (as described in the following section). When you're satisfied with those settings, double-click the new virtual machine to open it in a Virtual Machine Connection window. Then click or tap the Start button on the toolbar or choose Start on the Action menu. This "powers on" your virtual machine. If you created a new, blank virtual disk and attached an ISO file containing Windows installation media, Hyper-V launches the operating-system setup from the location you specified in the wizard.

TROUBLESHOOTING

Your VM displays a network message instead of booting to a virtual DVD.

If you start your newly configured VM for the first time and see a message telling you that the VM is attempting a "PXE network boot using IPv4," you need to adjust the boot order for the VM to give the virtual DVD drive a higher priority than the network adapter.

Open the Settings dialog and click Firmware (if this is a Generation 1 VM, click BIOS). In the Boot Order list, select the Network Adapter entry and click Move Down until that entry is at the bottom of the list. Save the revised settings and restart the virtual machine. Click in the Virtual Machine Connection window and then tap a key when you see the "Press any key to start from DVD" prompt. Note that you may have to respond very quickly to enable this option. If at first you don't succeed, turn the VM off and try again.

Running a virtual machine

Double-clicking the name of a virtual machine in Hyper-V Manager opens that VM in a Virtual Machine Connection (VMConnect) window. If the VM is already running, you'll be taken to the machine in its current state. For a newly created VM that you're running for the first time, or for a previously created VM that's shut down or sleeping, you'll need to click Start to power on the machine. (You can use the button in the connection window or on the toolbar, or click Action > Start from the Virtual Machine Connection menu bar.)

When you run a session in a Virtual Machine Connection window, you can use one of two session types:

- Basic sessions run in the VMConnect console window, which can be expanded to any resolution supported by the virtual display adapter. This type of session accepts keyboard and mouse input and displays the contents of the VM display; however, there's no access to audio hardware or external USB devices. This is the only option available for VMs running Windows Home edition (regardless of version).

- Enhanced sessions provide a significantly richer experience, with the ability to share the Clipboard with the host machine, redirect audio from the VM to the host PC's speakers or headphones, share local drives and some USB devices in the VM, connect to a printer through the host PC, and sign in with a smart card. Enhanced sessions also support higher display resolutions and can use multitouch displays and multiple-monitor configurations.

Enhanced session mode uses Remote Desktop Protocol over the virtual machine bus (VMBus), which requires a supported guest operating system: Windows 8.1 or later (Pro, Enterprise, or Education edition) or Windows Server 2012 R2 or later. Remote Desktop connections do not have to be enabled in the guest operating system. For guest operating systems that don't support enhanced sessions, such as Windows 7 Pro, the only alternative to a basic session is to configure a network connection in the VM and use the Remote Desktop client to connect to it. That option, which is not supported on Home edition, provides several of the features available in an enhanced session, including a shared Clipboard and audio support.

Working with Virtual Machine Connection windows

As shown in Figure 17-16, a virtual machine running in a Virtual Machine Connection window looks (and, for the most part, acts) just like a separate physical computer, except that it's contained in a window on your desktop.

Figure 17-16   A Windows VM in a Virtual Machine Connection window enables you to create multiple user accounts and sign in using a password or a PIN.

Use the toolbar at the top of the window, as shown in Figure 17-17, to operate the virtual machine. Additional options are available on the menu bar above it.

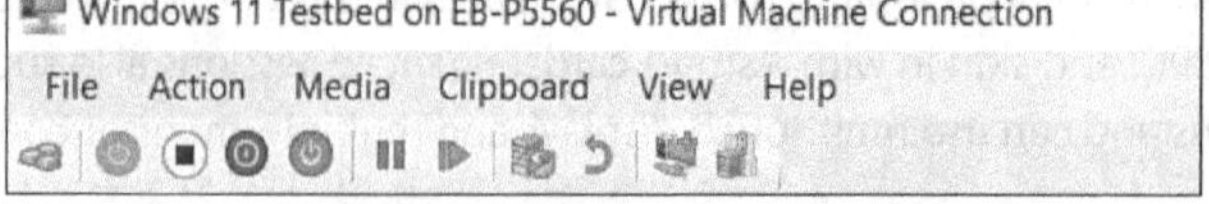

Figure 17-17   It's worth memorizing what each of the buttons on this toolbar does.

From left to right, the buttons have the following functions:

- **Ctrl+Alt+Del**   Because the Ctrl+Alt+Del key combination is reserved by Windows on your physical computer, when you press it while you're using a virtual machine, the key combination goes to your host computer. To mimic the effect of Ctrl+Alt+Del within a virtual machine, press Ctrl+Alt+End, or tap this toolbar button.

- **Start**   This button turns on a virtual machine that is currently not running. If the VM is running, it's grayed out and unavailable.

- **Turn Off**   This button turns the virtual machine off, but it does so in the most drastic manner possible, with the same effect as unplugging a physical PC. This is, of course, not the most graceful way to shut down a computer (even a virtual one), and you'll probably lose any unsaved data.

- **Shut Down**   Clicking this button is equivalent to using the Shut Down command in Windows 10 or Windows 11; it instructs the machine to go through the usual shutdown process. Note that some configurations (usually older, unsupported operating systems) do not allow the use of the Shut Down command in Hyper-V. For a virtual machine without this support, use commands within the virtual machine to shut down properly.

- **Save**   This button saves the virtual machine state and then turns it off, releasing all resources to the host PC. The process is much like hibernation on a physical computer. When you next start the virtual machine, you return immediately to where you left off.

- **Pause/Resume**   Pausing a virtual machine stops it temporarily but does not fully release its resources, as the Turn Off, Shut Down, and Save options do.

- **Reset**   Resetting a virtual machine discards any changes and reboots using the last saved version.

- **Checkpoint**   This button creates a checkpoint, which is a snapshot of the virtual machine's state and its data. For more information, see "Working with checkpoints" later in this chapter.

- **Revert**   This button restores the virtual machine to its condition at the previous checkpoint and restarts the virtual machine.

- **Basic/Enhanced Session**   On guest operating systems that support it, this button toggles the virtual machine between basic session mode and enhanced session mode. For more information, see the next section, "Using enhanced session mode."

- **Share**   Use this option to export the entire virtual machine configuration and data files (but not checkpoints) to a compressed file in VMCZ format. You can then copy that file to another PC running Hyper-V and double-click to import the VM. (For more details on this option, see "Importing, exporting, and moving Hyper-V VMs," later in this chapter.

Within the Virtual Machine Connection window, you use the virtual machine just as you would a physical computer, with only a few exceptions:

- When you run an older, unsupported guest operating system, using a mouse is not as fluid as it is when your guest operating system is Windows 7 or later. In those configurations, the mouse can become trapped when you click inside the virtual machine window. To release it, press Ctrl+Alt+Left Arrow.

- Not all of your physical computer's hardware is available in all virtual machines. For example, access to a physical DVD drive on the Hyper-V host is not available in Generation 2 virtual machines. (You can, however, mount an ISO image as a DVD drive.) For Generation 1 machines, only one virtual machine can use a physical DVD drive at any given time. (To release the DVD drive from one virtual machine so that you can use it in another, use commands on the Media menu.)

- USB storage devices, audio devices, and some other local resources work only in enhanced session mode. (For more information, see the following section.)

When you close the Virtual Machine Connection window, the virtual machine continues to run. By closing the window, all you're doing, in effect, is turning off the virtual monitor. To shut down or turn off the entire virtual machine, you should use the appropriate buttons on the Virtual Machine Connection window. If that window is closed, you can access these functions by opening Hyper-V Manager, selecting the VM's entry, and using the Turn Off, Shut Down, and Save options in the Actions pane.

Using enhanced session mode

Running a Hyper-V basic session in a window is convenient and adequate for simple tasks. But that option comes with significant limitations, including a lack of support for audio playback and an inability to share files between the host PC and the VM using the Windows Clipboard.

The solution to these and other problems is *enhanced session mode*, which allows you to connect to the following resources on your host computer from a Hyper-V virtual machine:

- Audio devices

- Printers

- Clipboard (which you use to copy and paste files and other information between the virtual machine and your physical computer)

Inside OUT

You can't connect to USB devices on the host PC

When reading some Hyper-V documentation, you might see references to a feature that allows VMs to connect to USB devices on the host PC when running enhanced session mode. Although this is technically true, the limitations are severe. You can connect to fixed storage devices, including USB drives, and printers in enhanced session mode. This capability is not enabled for removable devices such as USB flash drives, however, nor will you be able to connect to most other types of USB devices.

In enhanced session mode, you can't change the resolution of the virtual display using commands within the virtual machine. Within the VM, the Display Resolution option in Settings > System > Display is grayed out and unavailable, and this message appears: "Display settings can't be changed from a remote session." (Recall that enhanced session mode uses Remote Desktop Protocol to connect to the virtual machine, which explains the message about a "remote session.") There are two workarounds to this limitation:

- If the VM is running in a window, you can change the display resolution by dragging the borders of the Virtual Machine Connection window; when you do so, the guest operating system automatically adjusts to the dimensions. This solution, while convenient, makes it nearly impossible to choose a standard resolution—which might, for example, be a requirement for compatibility testing.

- To choose a specific display resolution, switch to basic session mode and then close the Virtual Machine Connection window. In Hyper-V Manager, click Connect to open a new Virtual Machine Connection window to be greeted by a dialog in which you can specify the screen resolution, as shown in Figure 17-18.

In this same dialog, clicking Show Options expands the dialog to show a Local Resources tab. There, you can specify which local resources—that is, printers, drives, and other devices from the host computer—you want to use within the virtual machine. For more information about these settings, see "Connecting to another computer with Remote Desktop" in Chapter 11, "Configuring Windows networks."

If your virtual machine is running an operating system that supports enhanced session mode, you can switch between basic and enhanced session mode by clicking or tapping the next-to-last button on the Virtual Machine Connection toolbar. (Use that icon as a shortcut to determine whether you're running in basic or enhanced session mode.)

You can enable and disable enhanced session mode on a per-server or per-user basis. To view or change either setting, open Hyper-V Manager and select the host name from the tree on the left; then, under the host name in the Actions pane, click or tap Hyper-V Settings. In the Hyper-V Settings dialog that appears, you'll find enhanced-session-mode settings under Server and User.

CHAPTER 17

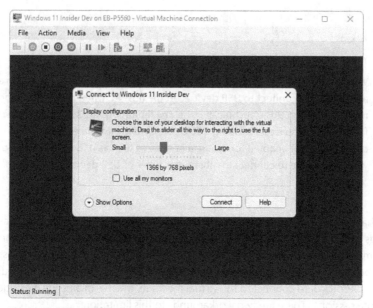

Figure 17-18   Use the slider to choose a specific resolution if you want your VM to run in a window. Move the slider all the way to the right if you want to use the host machine's display at its full resolution.

One of the most effective uses of an enhanced session is to work with a virtual machine as if it were a complete replacement for the host PC. To do so, move the resolution slider all the way to the right, until it reads Full Screen. If your host PC has multiple monitors, select the Use All My Monitors checkbox. Click Connect, and the virtual machine expands to fill the entire display (or displays). The only indication that you're working with a virtual machine is the connection bar at the top of the screen. That bar includes the name of the VM and the host PC in the center, as well as standard Minimize, Restore, and Close buttons on the right. If the status bar gets in the way of something on the screen, you can slide it left or right. To hide it completely, click the Pin icon at the far left. When the status bar is hidden, you can show it by moving the mouse pointer to the top of the screen and allowing it to remain there briefly.

> ### TROUBLESHOOTING
>
> **No sign-in options are available when you try to connect to a VM**
>
> This is a frustrating known issue that occurs when you try to sign in with a Microsoft account using an enhanced session. The fix is simple: Click the Basic Session button on the Virtual Machine Connection window to switch to a basic session and sign in using your password or PIN. Then, in the VM, go to Settings > Accounts > Sign-in Options. Under the Additional Settings heading, turn off the For Improved Security, Only Allow Windows Hello Sign-in For Microsoft Accounts On This Device setting. Click the Enhanced Session button, and your sign-in options should now be visible.

Working with checkpoints

A *checkpoint* captures the data and configuration of a running virtual machine—a snapshot in time. Indeed, in earlier versions of Hyper-V, checkpoints were called *snapshots*. A checkpoint can be restored so that you can quickly and easily return your virtual machine to an earlier time—this capability is particularly valuable for providing a consistent test environment. When evaluating competing software products, for example, you can install an app in a VM and conduct your tests and then revert to the previous checkpoint to start another round of testing with a different app under starting conditions that are exactly the same as they were in the previous test.

To capture a checkpoint from within a running VM, click or tap the Checkpoint button on the Virtual Machine Connection toolbar, or use the keyboard shortcut Ctrl+N. You can provide a descriptive name for the checkpoint, but no other interaction is necessary. The checkpoints you collect for a given virtual machine appear in the center of the Hyper-V Manager window, as shown in Figure 17-19. To revert to an earlier checkpoint, select the checkpoint and, in the Actions pane, click or tap Apply.

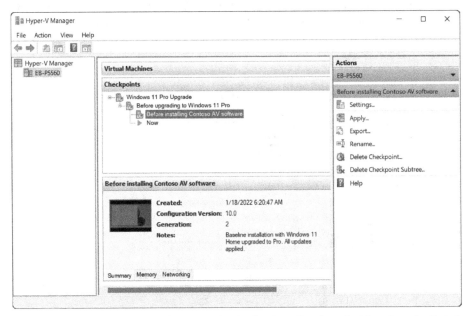

Figure 17-19 When you select the name of a checkpoint, a list of applicable actions for that checkpoint appears in the Actions pane for that VM.

Other options in the Actions pane enable you to rename a checkpoint, delete a checkpoint or checkpoint subtree, and export the saved checkpoint to a new VM, leaving the original undisturbed.

In Windows 10 and Windows 11, Hyper-V supports two kinds of checkpoints:

- *Standard checkpoints* include information on the virtual machine state, running applications, and network connections. That's useful if you're trying to return to a specific point in time. As a result, restoring a VM to its previous state from a standard checkpoint might take you to an unstable condition (for example, the same network connections might not be available).

- *Production checkpoints* use the Volume Snapshot Service (VSS) backup technology to save the data and configuration of a running virtual machine but not its state. This provides a solution that is much more useful as a backup alternative but is inappropriate when you're trying to start with a specific state.

Standard checkpoints are the default for new VMs you create; to check the current Checkpoint settings and make any changes, open Settings for a virtual machine and, under Management, click Checkpoints. That opens a dialog like the one shown in Figure 17-20.

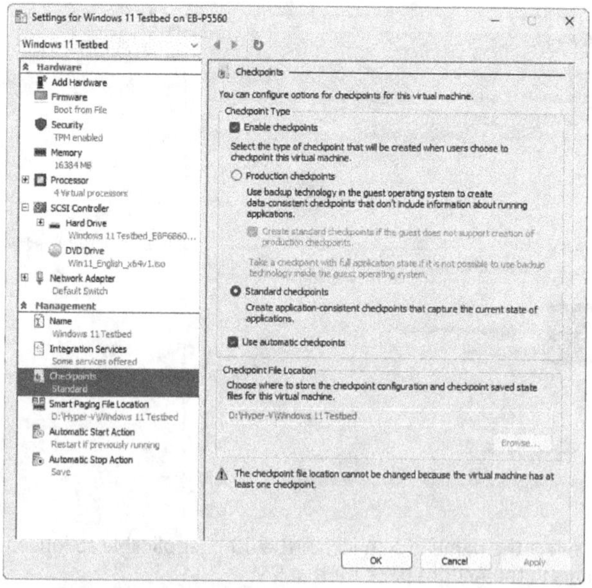

Figure 17-20   Use this page in the settings for a VM to enable or disable checkpoints and to choose a checkpoint type.

On that same dialog is a Use Automatic Checkpoints checkbox. This option automatically creates a checkpoint each time you start a VM, giving you the option to roll back any changes you make in the current session without having to remember to create checkpoints. The next time you shut down and restart the virtual machine, you'll have the option to revert to the previous checkpoint. This option is automatically on for new Windows 10 and Windows 11 VMs.

Checkpoints can use large amounts of disk space. On host PCs where storage is scarce, consider disabling automatic checkpoints and using them only when necessary.

Changing settings for a virtual machine

As noted earlier in this chapter, you can freely modify most of the virtual hardware associated with a virtual machine—for example, adding virtual memory, expanding a virtual hard disk, or connecting a virtual DVD drive. The one exception is the machine generation, which cannot be changed after its initial configuration. You can also perform management tasks, such as adjusting how the VM behaves when you shut down or restart the host PC.

To dive into these settings, open Hyper-V Manager, select the virtual machine you want to reconfigure, and then, near the bottom of the Actions pane, click or tap Settings. (If that menu is not visible, right-click the VM name to see a shortcut menu containing the same options.)

This Settings dialog (which we visited briefly in Figure 17-20 in the previous section) contains two groups of options: one for the virtual hardware and the other for management settings. Some of these settings can be changed even while a machine is running (which is important for virtual machines running critical tasks), especially on Generation 2 virtual machines. Other configuration changes, however, require that the VM be shut down and turned off (not just saved).

Note that some hardware options available here differ slightly, depending on the machine generation. The remainder of this section summarizes options available in the virtual hardware for Generation 2 VMs, which covers most mainstream uses for a Hyper-V virtual machine.

Firmware

This section enables you to define the boot order for a virtual machine. If you're working with a Generation 2 VM running Windows 10 or Windows 11, the boot order starts with an EFI Boot Manager file. If you want to boot from a virtual DVD by default, adjust these settings so that the DVD Drive option is first in the list.

Security

On Generation 2 VMs, the options available when Security is selected offer features that are equivalent to those you get with Windows 11 running on a UEFI-based physical PC. If you plan to run Windows 11 in a Hyper-V VM, you should start by enabling Secure Boot and the virtual Trusted Platform Module (TPM), as shown in Figure 17-21, before you run Windows Setup. (The latter option also allows the disks in a virtual machine to be encrypted with BitLocker Disk Encryption.)

CHAPTER 17

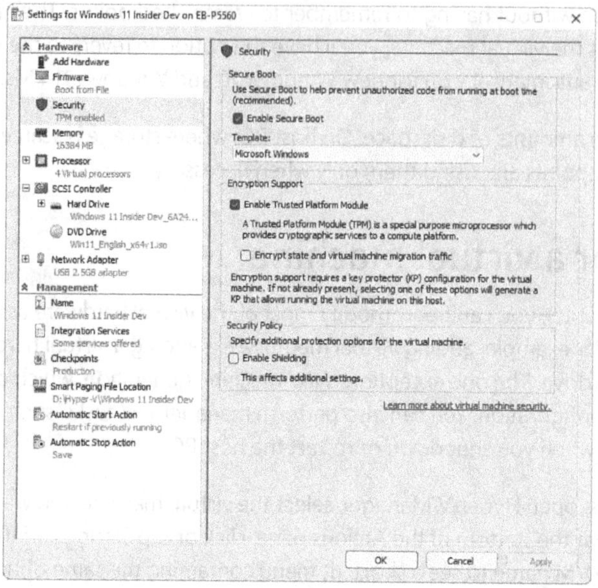

Figure 17-21   If you plan to install Windows 11 in a virtual machine, be sure to enable Secure Boot and the virtual Trusted Platform Module before you run Setup.

In this example, it's worth noting that Secure Boot is enabled using the Microsoft Windows template. For a virtual machine running a distribution of Linux that supports Secure Boot, choose the Microsoft UEFI Certificate Authority template instead. (The third option, Open Source Shielded VM, is available only on hosts running Windows Server 2016.)

Memory

As with a physical PC, adding memory is the single most important thing you can do to improve performance. The balancing act with a virtual machine is finding the right configuration that doesn't hobble performance on the host PC.

Options available when you select from the Hardware pane are identical for both generations of virtual machines. When dynamic memory is enabled, you can specify minimum and maximum amounts of memory to be available to that VM. If you're obsessed with memory tuning, you can also change buffer sizes for dynamic memory and adjust the priority for memory usage when multiple virtual machines compete for a limited supply of physical RAM.

Figure 17-22, for example, shows the memory configuration for a VM running an Insider Preview release of Windows 11. In this example, the Minimum RAM setting is increased from its default value of 512 MB to 4096 MB, and the default Maximum RAM value is lowered from its insanely high value to 8192 MB.

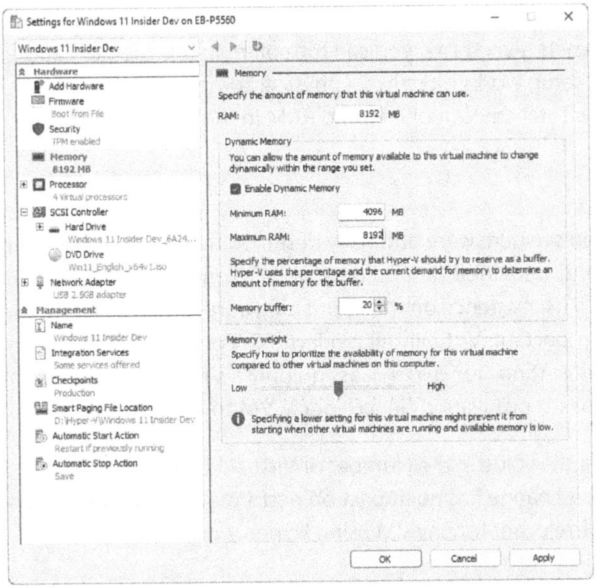

Figure 17-22   Using these dynamic memory settings, the VM will never have less than 4 GB of RAM available to it. When needed, it can use as much as 8 GB of memory but no more.

There's no right or wrong way to adjust these settings, which depend on how you plan to use the VM. For example, if you're testing a Windows Insider Preview build of Windows 11 and you plan to switch to that VM as soon as you start up your host PC, without running any additional apps on the host PC, you can safely allocate an amount of RAM equal to the total physical RAM on your system. By contrast, if your goal is to have two VMs running in the background at all times while you do your daily productivity tasks on the host PC, you'll want to restrict the amount of RAM for those VMs, even if that means they occasionally encounter some memory pressure.

Using dynamic memory ensures that each machine gets as much memory as it needs, but it doesn't reserve a fixed amount of memory (which would preclude other virtual machines or the host operating system from using that memory).

TROUBLESHOOTING

Installing a guest operating system fails with a memory-related error

In some configurations, the installation of the guest operating system might fail even though the dynamic memory settings appear to allocate sufficient resources. The problem occurs when the system assigns a minimal amount of memory to the VM at startup, and that amount causes the installer to believe the system doesn't meet minimum requirements. The solution is to increase the value for RAM so that it is at least equal to the minimum required for installing the operating system. After installation is complete, Windows reduces the amount of assigned memory, if appropriate, according to the Minimum RAM value for that VM.

CHAPTER 17

If you plan to run only one virtual machine, or if you know how much memory your virtual machine needs to perform its given tasks, you can turn off dynamic memory and specify a fixed amount of memory. This setup works more like a physical computer, in that whatever memory you specify is equal to the total amount of installed RAM in the virtual machine.

Processor

The Processor settings you see here were originally designed for Hyper-V on servers containing multiple processors and were irrelevant on desktop PCs running Windows 10. But with the release of Windows 11 and its insistence on minimum hardware requirements, these settings suddenly became more important. Virtually all modern PCs contain a single processor with multiple cores, but the default settings for Hyper-V assign only a single core to a virtual machine. That detail causes Windows 11 installations in a Hyper-V VM to fail almost immediately.

The solution is to increase the value in the Number of Virtual Processors field to at least 2, as shown in Figure 17-23. This change has no impact on performance, and the remainder of the settings on this page are irrelevant for any VM using Hyper-V on Windows 11.

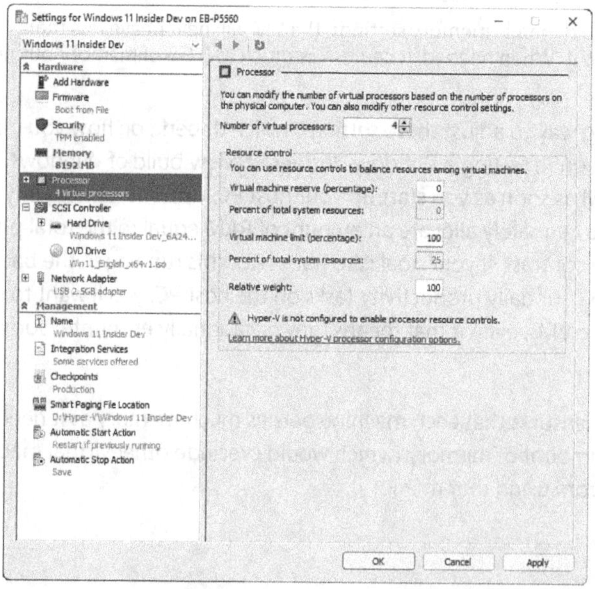

Figure 17-23   If you plan to install Windows 11 in a VM, you need to increase the number of virtual processors shown here.

SCSI Controller

Generation 2 VMs include a single virtual disk controller that uses the Small Computer System Interface (SCSI) and is capable of handling multiple virtual disks. For most garden-variety VMs, the default configuration is sufficient: a single virtual disk used as the system drive and a virtual

DVD available for installing software. For some tasks, however, you might want to add a second virtual hard disk, or you might need to change the size or format of an existing disk. This section covers your available options.

NOTE

Generation 1 machines by default use legacy IDE controllers, and the system disk must be attached to an IDE controller. (You also have the option to choose the legacy VHD disk format; for Generation 2 machines, the default format is VHDX and the older format is unavailable.) Each of the two IDE controllers on a Generation 1 machine can connect up to two devices. If you attempt to connect a new secondary drive to a controller that already has two devices attached, your attempt fails with an error message. If both of the default IDE controllers are full, use the SCSI Controller instead.

Adding a new virtual disk

To add a new virtual disk to an existing VM, make sure the VM is shut down and then follow these steps:

1. Open Settings and click the entry for the VM's disk controller: SCSI Controller on a Generation 2 machine, or one of the two IDE Controllers on a Generation 1 machine.

2. From the list on the right, choose Hard Drive and click Add. Hyper-V automatically selects an unused location on the controller and displays the settings for that location, as shown in Figure 17-24.

Figure 17-24   Clicking the New button on this page launches a wizard that walks you through configuring a virtual hard disk.

3.   Click New to open the New Virtual Hard Disk Wizard and complete its steps:

- **Choose Disk Type**   Dynamically Expanding is the default and is usually the correct choice for a VM running a modern operating system; you can also choose Fixed or Differencing. (For an explanation of how each type is used, see "Storage controllers and virtual disks," earlier in this chapter.)

- **Specify Name And Location**   Change the default filename ("New Virtual Hard Disk.vhdx") to something descriptive, and adjust the location if necessary.

- **Configure Disk**   Accept or change the default size of 127 GB and create a new, blank virtual hard disk, as shown in Figure 17-25, or select one of the other options to copy the contents of an existing physical or virtual disk to the newly created disk.

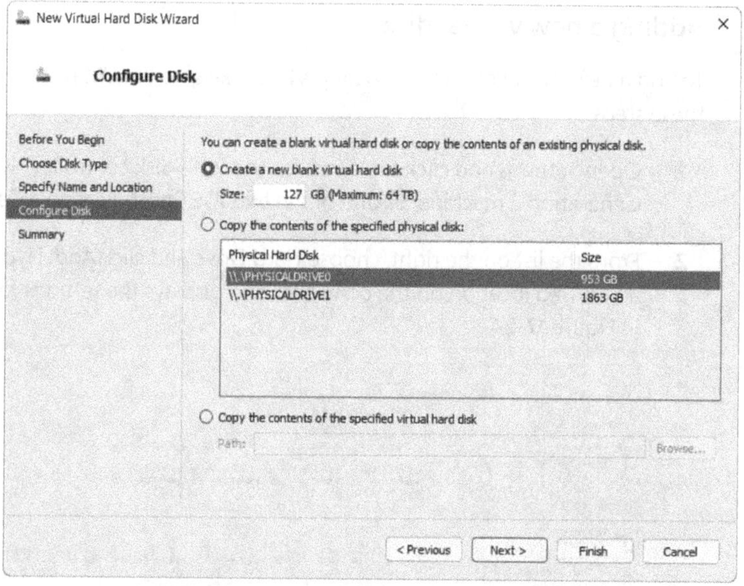

Figure 17-25   These settings create a dynamically expanding virtual hard disk that has a capacity of 127 GB within the VM but uses minimal disk space on the host PC.

4.   Complete the wizard to add your hard disk.

Note that this sequence is the equivalent of attaching a new, unformatted drive to a physical PC. If the virtual machine is running Windows, you need to use the Disk Management console to add the drive, format it if necessary, and assign a drive letter.

➤ For details on how to set up a new hard drive in a physical (not virtual) PC, see Chapter 8, "Managing local and cloud storage."

Removing or replacing a virtual disk

Removing a virtual disk from a VM configuration is a straightforward process. You might choose to do so if you created a secondary disk for test purposes and no longer need it. From the Settings dialog for the VM, click the drive in the Hardware pane on the left, and then click the Remove button on the right.

Although it's possible to remove the system drive from a VM, it's hard to imagine why you would want to do that. You're more likely to replace one virtual disk with another, a task you can complete by selecting the virtual disk, clicking the Browse button in the pane on the right, and then choosing the replacement drive. As an alternative, you can also click New to replace the existing disk with a blank disk for a clean start.

In either case, note that removing or replacing the disk does not remove the underlying VHD/VHDX file. If you want to reclaim that storage space on the host PC, you need to do so manually, from File Explorer.

Inspecting, expanding, and converting virtual disks

If you're curious about the size, format, and other details of a virtual hard disk, select its entry in the left pane of the Settings dialog and then, on the right, click Inspect. That opens a small dialog packed with all the essential details, including the current file size and the maximum disk size.

To expand a virtual disk or convert it to a different format or disk type, you need to first remove any checkpoints from the virtual machine (see "Working with checkpoints," earlier in this chapter). After doing so, shut down the VM, select the hard disk from the Settings dialog, and click Edit. That opens yet another wizard, with Compact, Convert, and Expand options that are relatively easy to follow.

CAUTION

Changing the format, disk type, or size of a virtual hard disk runs a small but meaningful chance of data loss. As a precaution, we recommend backing up the VHD/VHDX file before performing the conversion or resizing.

If you find you've run out of virtual disk space (or are in imminent danger of doing so), use the Expand option to increase the size of the drive. Note that the additional space you create is not automatically added to any disk volumes in your virtual machine. You need to open the VM and use Disk Management to expand the volume to use the newly added space.

Network Adapter

For just about any mainstream computing task, the default network adapter is sufficient, and there's no need to make any changes. The main reason to use this dialog is to choose a different virtual switch—if you're moving between wired and wireless networks on the host PC, for example. Networking experts might want to explore some of the options here, such as the ability to spoof a MAC address so that your VM's packets appear to come from another device on the network. You can find that option by expanding the properties under the Network Adapter heading and then clicking Advanced.

Automatic start and stop actions

Use the final two options under the Management heading to specify what happens to a virtual machine when you shut down or start the Hyper-V host PC. For most purposes, the correct setting for Automatic Stop Action is Save; for Automatic Start Action, you can configure a VM to start automatically (with or without a delay) or start the VM only if it was running when the system shut down previously.

Importing, exporting, and moving Hyper-V VMs

How do you move or copy a virtual machine from one Windows PC to another? Using Windows 11, you have two options.

The first is to use the Export function. Start by shutting down the VM you want to move or copy. Then, in Hyper-V Manager, select the VM and click Export in the Actions menu. In the resulting dialog, specify a location that has sufficient free disk space to hold all the files associated with the VM (a folder on a removable hard disk, for example, or a network share) and then click Export. This operation (which can take a long time depending on the size of the virtual disks associated with the VM) saves your files in three separate subfolders in the location you specified.

To import the VM on the new PC, open Hyper-V Manager and click Import Virtual Machine from the Actions menu. In the Import Virtual Machine Wizard, browse to the location that contains the exported files and then choose one of the three options on the Choose Import Type page:

- **Register The Virtual Machine In-Place (Use The Existing Unique ID)**   Use this option if you are permanently moving the VM to the new Hyper-V host and you want to use the exported files in their current location. This option makes sense if you copied the files to a dedicated Hyper-V data folder on the new PC, for example.

- **Restore The Virtual Machine (Use The Existing Unique ID)**   Use this option if you want to permanently move the VM to the new Hyper-V host and, as part of the import, copy the exported files to the default location on the new PC. The exported files remain in place on the storage device you used for the transfer.

- **Copy The Virtual Machine (Create A New Unique ID)**   This option is appropriate if you plan to continue using the old VM and you want to create an independent copy of the VM on the new Hyper-V host. For a Windows VM, note that choosing this method will probably require reactivation.

A slightly simpler alternative is the Share option. From a VM that's running in a Virtual Machine Connection window, click the Share button (the rightmost button on the VMConnect toolbar) or press Ctrl+H. That action copies the virtual machine configuration and data files (but not checkpoints) to a compressed file in VMCZ format. Copy that file to the new Hyper-V host and double-click to restore the VM to default locations.

Finally, if you've run out of disk space on the host PC and need to move all or part of a VM to a new, more capacious drive, shut down the VM and click Move. The resulting wizard enables you to move virtual disk storage or an entire virtual machine to a new location or locations of your choosing. The VM remains registered in Hyper-V Manager; only the location of associated data files changes.

Running virtual machines from the cloud

Client Hyper-V is the easiest way to work with virtual machines in Windows 11, but it's not the only way. Two relatively new options provide cloud-based alternatives that might make sense if you're a candidate for virtualization.

Windows 365 is a subscription-based product that uses virtual machines hosted in a cloud service run by Microsoft. Each Windows virtual machine, called a Cloud PC, is created with Windows 11 installed by default, although administrators can choose to use Windows 10 instead. A Cloud PC is assigned to an individual user and functions as their secure, dedicated work PC, with access available through a web browser, through Remote Desktop apps on a desktop PC or Mac, or through mobile clients available on iOS and Android devices.

The service is available in two subscription types: Windows 365 Business is for organizations with up to 300 users or Windows 365 Enterprise is for larger organizations. For more information, see *https://learn.microsoft.com/windows-365/*.

Microsoft Azure is a cloud-based service capable of running virtual machines that don't require local resources. Azure VMs are charged on a pay-as-you-go basis and are ideal for test environments and important servers where downtime is not an acceptable option. Every Visual Studio subscription includes a monthly allowance for Azure usage, with ready-made Windows and Linux VMs available. For more details, see *https://azure.microsoft.com/services/virtual-machines/*.

CHAPTER 18

Using Android and Linux on Windows 11

Over the past decade, Microsoft has tried running Windows on devices of every shape and size, including a long and ultimately unsuccessful attempt to establish Windows as a smartphone platform. The Windows Phone operating system officially reached its end of life in 2019, but that doesn't mean Microsoft has given up on the idea of bringing its technology to devices that are smaller than a laptop PC.

Today, you can find dozens of Microsoft productivity apps on the two most popular mobile platforms: iOS and Android. The Android operating system, which is based on the Linux kernel, has more than 2 billion active users. If you have an Android-powered smartphone, you can connect it to your Windows 11 PC to make both devices more useful. The secret is an app called Phone Link, which we cover in this chapter.

That's not the only Android connection, however. Windows 11 also offers an optional feature that allows you to run apps written for Android on your PC. Those apps run in a virtualized environment called the Windows Subsystem for Android. If that sounds intriguing, keep reading. In this chapter, we explain how this subsystem works and also describe some fairly significant limitations.

And finally, there's Linux, an alternative open source operating system favored by developers and tech enthusiasts. If you fall into either of these groups, you can read more about how to install Linux as part of Windows 11.

Linking an Android phone to your PC

If you have an Android phone, you can take advantage of a Windows 11 feature to link it to your PC for quick access to messages and notifications, as well as the option to place and receive calls, without having to take your phone out of your pocket and unlock it. Using the Phone Link app, you can also view, edit, and share any photos you've taken using your smartphone's camera. With the right hardware, you can even mirror apps from your smartphone, interacting with them using your keyboard and mouse or your PC's touchscreen.

NOTE

Sorry, iPhone owners, but this feature isn't available on your platform, and third-party options we recommended in previous editions in this series have been discontinued.

Figure 18-1 shows the Phone Link app in action.

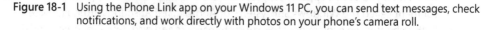

Figure 18-1   Using the Phone Link app on your Windows 11 PC, you can send text messages, check notifications, and work directly with photos on your phone's camera roll.

The upper-left corner of the Phone Link app shows most of the status icons you need, so you can check the strength of your network signal and remaining battery life. Below that region are buttons to turn on Do Not Disturb, mute the phone's audio, and show or hide the music player. The Notifications pane below that displays the same notifications you'd see if you were to swipe down on your phone's screen. Note the text message at the top of the list in Figure 18-1, which includes a box for entering a quick reply without having to change screens.

To make the Android-to-Windows connection, you need two pieces of software. The Phone Link app is installed with Windows 11. On certain smartphone models from Samsung and Honor, as well as on Microsoft's own Surface Duo, the Link To Windows service is preinstalled. On those devices, the connection options are available by swiping down from the home screen and

CHAPTER 18

opening Link To Windows from Quick Settings. On all other Android devices, you need to install the Link To Windows app. (A shortcut to the app's listing in the Google Play Store is available at *https://aka.ms/yourpc*. Note that you can only open that URL from an Android device.)

With both of those pieces in place, make sure your phone is connected to the same Wi-Fi network as your PC; then open the Phone Link app and click Get Started. Sign in with a Microsoft account and then follow the prompts to complete the connection. The Phone Link app can make the connection using a QR code that you scan using your smartphone's camera, as shown in Figure 18-2; if that option doesn't work, you can use a PIN code to complete the link.

Figure 18-2   The simplest way to link your Android phone to your Windows PC is to use a QR code like the one shown here.

The links above the contents pane allow you to switch between available phone features. Click Messages to split the pane in two, with all of your conversations in the pane on the left and the full history of the selected thread in the pane on the right, as shown in Figure 18-3.

Figure 18-3   The Messages tab gives you full access to every SMS/MMS conversation, complete with options to add animated GIFs and photos.

Note the search box at the top of the conversation list, which allows you to find specific text messages without a lot of scrolling. The icons below the reply box let you add emoji or animated GIFs or attach a photo to a message.

If you have a headset with a microphone connected to your PC, you can click the Calls tab and turn on the option to make and receive phone calls using your phone's connection. You need to go through a brief setup process and turn on Bluetooth to enable this feature.

The Photos tab shows thumbnails of up to 2000 photos and screenshots from your phone. Click any photo to see it in the full app window, and use either the toolbar or right-click shortcut menus to open the photo for editing on your PC, save it as a local file, or share it using another app.

And speaking of apps, on devices that include the Link To Windows service, you'll find an extra Apps tab, where you can open individual apps in a smartphone-sized window on your PC screen and work with them directly. Apps can be pinned to the Windows Start menu so you can open them without having to go through the Phone Link app.

Clicking the gear icon in the upper-right corner of the Phone Link app opens a Settings page where you can modify some interesting options. On the My Devices page, for example, you can connect a second phone so that you can switch between your work and personal devices. The Features tab in Settings has a bevy of options for controlling privacy features such as cross-device copy and paste and the ability to show photos and make calls from the PC. If you're annoyed by the quantity of notifications from the phone arriving on your PC, you can temper them with settings under the Notifications heading.

Running Android apps on Windows 11

When Microsoft announced Windows 11, the company promised that the operating system would be able to run Android apps alongside apps written for Windows. That feature arrived in early 2022 in the form of a feature called the Windows Subsystem for Android. It's an impressive technical achievement, but it also has significant limitations that make it more of a curiosity than a breakthrough.

The biggest limitation is that the Android subsystem doesn't run the vast selection of apps from Google's Play Store. Instead, it requires the Amazon Appstore, which has a far more limited selection. Figure 18-4 shows the Amazon Appstore running on Windows 11.

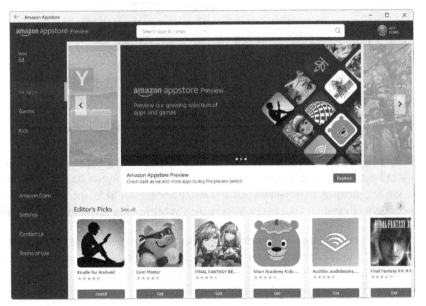

Figure 18-4   The Windows Subsystem for Android installs apps from the Amazon Appstore, which has a limited selection compared to the Google Play Store.

You'll also find listings for Android apps, including Amazon's Kindle reader and Audible audiobooks player, in the Microsoft Store. Where you would normally see an Install or Get button, however, you instead see a Get From Amazon Appstore button. If the Windows Subsystem for Android and the Amazon Appstore app aren't already installed, clicking that button begins the installation, as shown in Figure 18-5.

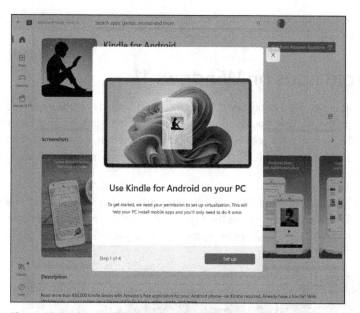

Figure 18-5   Compatible Android apps are listed in the Microsoft Store. Installing one of those apps also installs the Windows Subsystem for Android and the Amazon Appstore, if necessary.

The Windows Subsystem for Android runs only on Windows 11. Its hardware requirements are significantly more stringent than those of Windows 11 itself. In particular, it requires a minimum of 8 GB of RAM, with 16 GB recommended. In addition, the CPU requirements specify you must have at least an eighth-generation Generation Core i3, AMD Ryzen 3000, or Qualcomm Snapdragon 8c processor; that means you can't install and run Android apps on a PC equipped with an 8th Generation Intel Core m3 processor, such as Microsoft's Surface Go 2, for example.

And even if your PC meets the hardware requirements, not every PC can take advantage of this feature. The Windows Subsystem for Android feature is available only in select regions, including. (For the full list, see "Countries and regions that support Amazon Appstore on Windows," at *https://bit.ly/android-subsystem-support*.)

The final requirement is that your PC must have the Virtual Machine Platform feature enabled. Note that this feature is available on any edition of Windows 11 and does not require Hyper-V. Although you can enable this feature manually by clicking the Virtual Machine Platform checkbox in the Windows Features dialog (Settings > Apps > Optional Features > More Windows Features), there's no need to go to this trouble. When you attempt to install an Android app for the first time, the installer handles this task automatically, as shown previously in Figure 18-5.

The easiest way to install the Windows Subsystem for Android is to open the Microsoft Store, search for the Amazon Appstore app, and then click or tap Install. The installer runs an automated compatibility checker and, assuming your system passes muster, begins the installation process.

After setup is complete, any Android apps you install from the Amazon Appstore run in a window alongside Windows 11 apps and can be snapped into position or maximized the same way that Windows apps can. Figure 18-6, for example, shows the Kindle for Android app running alongside the Windows 11 Task Manager.

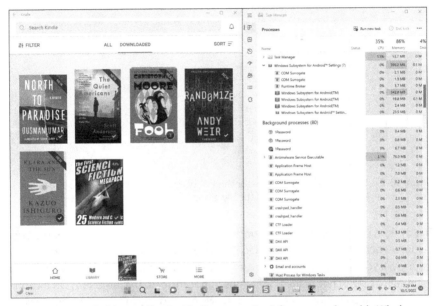

Figure 18-6   Android apps, like the Kindle app on the left, can run alongside Windows apps using the Windows Subsystem for Android.

Although Android apps and games run in windows that are identical to those of their Windows counterparts, you might notice some subtle differences. First, those apps don't get their own listings in Task Manager. Instead, they run under a single background process that controls the virtualized Android subsystem, VmmemWSA. This process can consume a significant amount of memory and disk space (which explains why Microsoft recommends at least 16 GB of memory if you plan to run Android apps). In addition, the thumbnails for individual Android apps don't show up as part of the snap layout options when you snap a Windows app into position. The workaround is to start by snapping the Android app into position first.

Because the Android subsystem runs as a virtualized container for Android apps, you can't open it directly. You can, however, manage its behavior using the Windows Subsystem for Android Settings app, which is installed along with the core components of the subsystem and is available by clicking Start > All Apps. Figure 18-7 shows this app in operation.

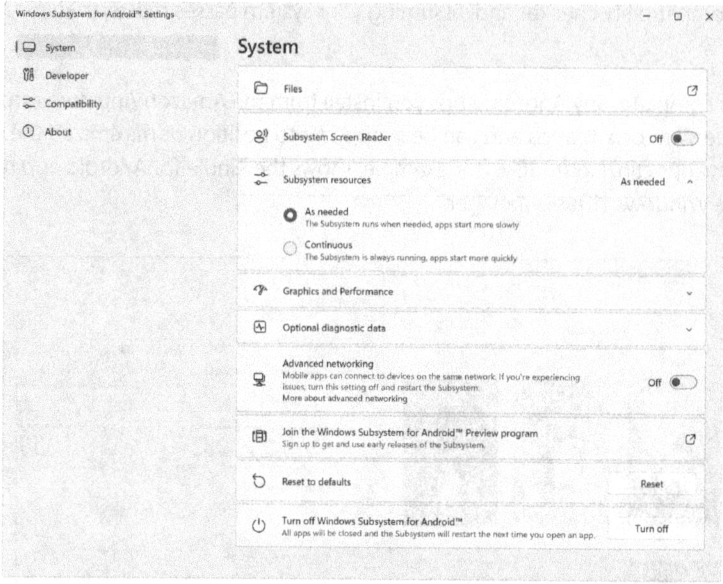

Figure 18-7   To adjust resource usage for the Windows Subsystem for Android, use this Settings app, which is installed automatically along with the other Android components.

Two options on the System tab are worth calling out specifically here. Under the Subsystem Resources heading, choose As Needed if you want the Android subsystem to run only when it's required. If you have ample system resources and you want Android apps to run immediately when called upon, choose the Continuous option instead. The large Turn Off button at the bottom of that page closes the Android subsystem and any running Android apps, freeing its resources immediately.

If, after experimenting with this feature, you decide it's not for you, you can remove it from your Windows 11 PC. Open the Windows 11 Settings app, go to Apps > Installed Apps, and scroll down to the Windows Subsystem for Android entry. Click the three dots to the right of the menu entry and then click Uninstall. Note that uninstalling the Windows Subsystem for Android also uninstalls the Amazon Appstore and any Android apps you've installed.

Using the Windows Subsystem for Linux

Once, not so long ago, Windows and Linux were archrivals. As a free, open source alternative to Windows, the Linux operating system gave PC owners a choice, although they could only run one operating system at a time.

Eventually, Microsoft added support for Linux to its Hyper-V virtualization platform, giving Windows PCs the option to run Linux in a virtual machine within Windows. That configuration requires significant system resources, however, and effectively it creates a second PC running alongside Windows, with very little integration between the two environments.

That all changed in 2017, when Microsoft officially released the Windows Subsystem for Linux (WSL). In 2019, Microsoft announced WSL 2, a newly architected version of WSL that runs the full Linux kernel in a highly optimized virtual machine, based on a subset of the Hyper-V architecture. WSL 2 uses relatively modest system resources and provides seamless integration between Windows and Linux. Although WSL 2 uses a virtual machine, it's managed and run in the background, without requiring you to perform any configuration or management tasks.

WSL 2 is primarily a tool for developers who want the benefit of working in a Linux development environment while still taking advantage of productivity apps running on the Windows platform. You can run such command-line software as grep, awk, and sed, and you can run Bash scripts that rely on these utilities. You also can launch Windows binaries directly from a WSL command prompt and even run Linux graphical apps on Windows.

The simplest way to install WSL 2 is to open a PowerShell window with an administrator's credentials and then issue this command:

```
wsl --install
```

That command enables all the features required to run WSL and downloads Ubuntu Linux. After restarting your PC, run the Ubuntu On Windows shortcut to complete the installation and set up your Linux user credentials in a Terminal window, as shown in Figure 18-8.

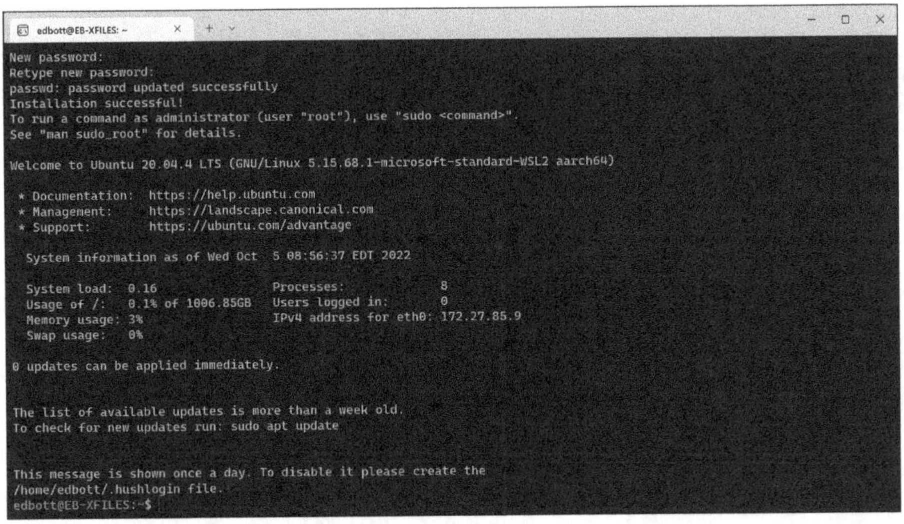

Figure 18-8   The primary operating environment for the Windows Subsystem for Linux is a Terminal window like this one.

We could devote an entire chapter to the inner workings of WSL 2 and barely scratch the surface. If you're interested in exploring this feature further, we recommend starting at the official documentation pages at *https://docs.microsoft.com/windows/wsl/about*. There, you'll find instructions on how to get started, a section of tutorials, details on how to change the default distribution, and much more.

Managing Windows PCs in the enterprise

Throughout this book, our emphasis has been on how individuals can get the most out of Microsoft Windows: learn how to use its many features, save time with shortcuts and work-arounds, and customize it to suit specific needs. Most of this information applies equally to a variety of devices—including tablets, laptops, and desktop PCs—in a variety of environments. Whether you use Windows as a standalone system, in a home network, in a small business net-work, or in an enterprise-scale operation, you can make use of this knowledge.

In this chapter, however, we depart from that focus on the individual to provide an overview of topics, products, and techniques that are useful primarily on business networks. Most require a business edition of Windows: Windows 11 Pro or Windows 11 Enterprise. (Windows 11 Education editions can also use most of these features, as can Windows 11 Pro Workstation.)

In addition, many of these features rely on Active Directory Domain Services (AD DS), which are available only on centrally managed networks running Windows Server. Azure Active Directory (Azure AD) provides a set of cloud-based management tools without the requirement to oper-ate a local server.

Of course, we don't have the space in this book—or any other single book—to fully docu-ment the wealth of business tools Microsoft makes available for Windows 11. Instead, our goal here is to provide a survey of some widely used tools, along with pointers to more in-depth information.

Using a domain-based network

Elsewhere in this book, we describe setup, configuration, and usage of peer-to-peer (or *work-group*) networks. This is the type of network usually found in homes and small businesses, and it doesn't require a server; each computer on the network is an equally empowered peer, and access to the device and its data is managed locally.

Windows 11 Pro, Enterprise, and Education editions can also be configured in an AD DS domain. This is sometimes called *on-premises Active Directory* or even *Windows Server Active Directory* to differentiate it from Azure AD, which operates as a fully managed cloud-based service.

The traditional AD DS domain-based network requires at least one computer running a version of Windows Server, although large networks typically contain many such servers. In addition, at least one server must be designated a domain controller, a process known as *promotion*. Most domain-based networks contain additional domain controllers to provide for load balancing and fault tolerance.

AD DS provides identity and access services, enabling users to sign on to any domain-joined device using a single user account. In addition, if an administrator integrates AD DS with Azure AD and synchronizes accounts, then users can not only access on-premises resources and apps, they can also access cloud-based apps using single sign-on (SSO).

NOTE

When users and devices are joined to an on-premises AD DS environment and also to Azure AD, the result is a *hybrid network*. We describe this configuration in more detail later in this chapter.

AD DS supports a logical structure based on forests, trees, domains, organizational units (OUs), and sites. These containers enable administrators to group users and computers in ways that reflect the structure of the organization—by geography or department, for example.

An on-premises domain controller offers full, policy-based management capabilities, and all computers and user accounts in the on-premises environment can be centrally managed through management tools available to domain administrators who connect (typically using remote connections) to the Windows Server.

NOTE

You can install the domain management tools on a Windows 11 workstation by adding the Remote Server Administration Tools (RSAT) feature. Open Settings > Apps > Optional Features. Next to the Add An Optional Feature heading, click View Features and then search for RSAT. Select the appropriate tools from the (long) resulting list; you must have administrative permissions to connect to the server using these tools.

When you have more than a handful of computers in a network, connecting (or joining) them to a Windows domain makes them much easier to manage, albeit at a significant cost. Windows servers are expensive, and they require skilled administrators to keep them running properly.

NOTE

To join a computer to a domain, you must sign in as an administrator on the local computer and provide appropriate credentials in the domain to perform the join.

A detailed description of domains and Active Directory is well beyond the scope of this book. However, here are two resources to get you started:

- Windows Server: *https://www.microsoft.com/cloud-platform/windows-server*

- Active Directory Domain Services Overview: *https://bit.ly/ADDS-overview*

Managing an Azure AD-based network

Azure AD provides authentication and authorization services for cloud apps hosted in Azure or Microsoft 365. It also supports widely used internet authentication protocols and standards, such as SAML and OAuth, which enables you to use Azure AD to authenticate your user accounts for access to third-party cloud apps. In addition, depending on the version of Azure AD you have, you can implement features such as multifactor authentication (MFA) and conditional access.

NOTE

Conditional access allows administrators to create and configure policies and conditions that users must satisfy to be able to access apps or resources. For example, an administrator can require that if a user signs in from an untrusted location, they must use MFA to authenticate before being able to connect to their Exchange Online mailbox.

While Azure AD has some fundamental similarities to AD DS, it's a very different beast. For example, instead of using security groups to define administrative access (administrators, standard users, and so on), it provides administrative access by using role-based access control (RBAC). This aligns with the approach taken by other cloud providers.

Azure AD allows management of devices as well as user accounts. Figure 19-1, for example, shows a list of devices for the fictional organization Contoso. For mobile devices running iOS and Android, the entry under the Join Type column is Azure AD Registered. By contrast, computers running Windows desktop operating systems are listed as Azure AD Joined, which provides users with a better sign-in experience. (Don't be fooled by entries under the Version heading. A version number of 10.0.22000 or higher represents a device running Windows 11.)

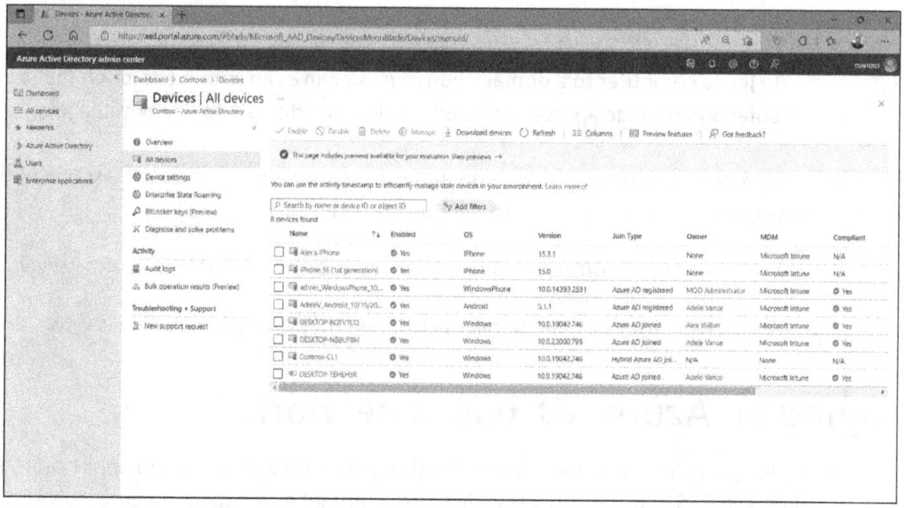

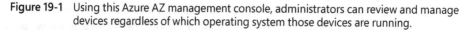

Figure 19-1   Using this Azure AZ management console, administrators can review and manage devices regardless of which operating system those devices are running.

You can add users by using the Azure Active Directory admin center, or by using Windows PowerShell. To review and modify the properties of a user account, select its entry under the All Users node. If the network is configured to use Azure AD Connect, an administrator can synchronize user accounts from on-premises AD DS to Azure AD. In this configuration, synced users are displayed with the Directory Synced value of Yes, as shown in Figure 19-2.

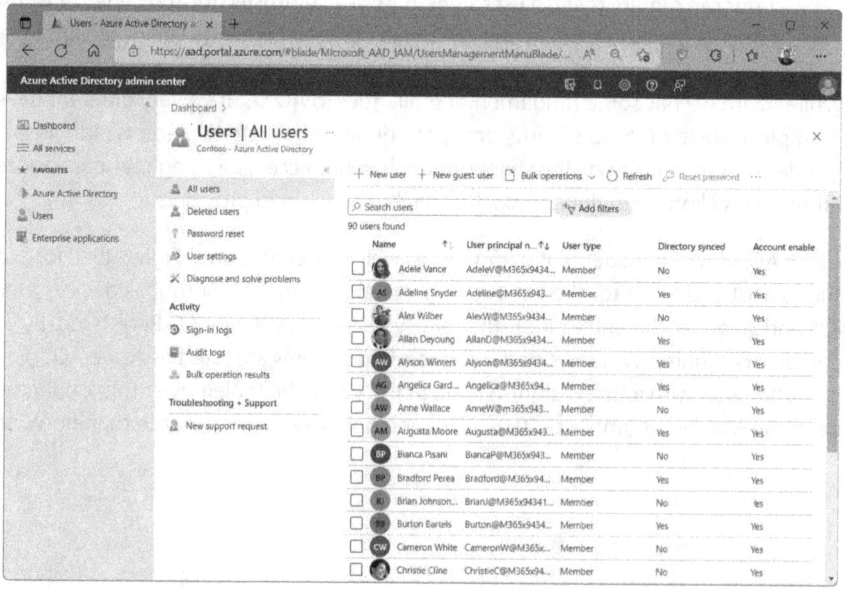

Figure 19-2   Users on an enterprise network can be added to Azure AD, or synced from on-premises AD DS.

There are a number of versions of Azure AD:

- **Free**   Included with any subscription to a Microsoft online app or service for business use.

- **Microsoft 365 Apps**   Included in specific versions of Microsoft 365 (formerly Office 365) subscriptions. Provides the same basic function as the free version, but also supports features like self-service password reset (SSPR).

- **Premium P1**   Available with Microsoft 365 E3 or Microsoft 365 Business subscriptions. Provides same capabilities as the free version but also includes features such as conditional access and on-premises synchronization.

- **Premium P2**   Available with Microsoft 365 Enterprise E5. Includes all the features found in Azure AD P1 and includes Azure Identity Protection and Privileged Identity Management.

NOTE

Premium editions of Azure AD are available as a separate subscription that can be added on to a Microsoft 365 subscription.

Learn more about Azure AD here: *https://bit.ly/AzureAD-intro*.

Managing hybrid networks

Over the past decade, an ever-growing number of organizations have begun replacing on-premises servers with cloud-based resources. This is generally a gradual process, involving a period when some apps and resources are in on-premises domain-based networks and also in the cloud. This type of deployment is known as a *hybrid network*.

Network administrators typically want users to be able to sign in to their computers using a single user account that unlocks access to apps and resources regardless of where they're located. There are two ways to set up a hybrid network.

A network administrator can choose to sync user accounts from AD DS to Azure AD using Azure AD Connect, as described earlier. In this configuration, users sign in with a single AD DS user account that enables access to on-premises resources and apps, while also providing access to cloud-based resources and apps. This is a convenient feature for administrators and users alike.

As an alternative, an administrator can join computers to both the AD DS domain and Azure AD. This configuration is known as Hybrid Azure AD Join and uses Azure AD Connect to complete the process. When configuring Azure AD Connect, an administrator can optionally specify to enable device synchronization, so that devices in the on-premises domain are synced as devices to Azure AD.

Co-management enables administrators to choose whether to manage hybrid devices using on-premises tools, such as Microsoft Endpoint Configuration Manager, or to use mobile device management (MDM) solutions such as Microsoft Intune. We discuss both of these tools later in this chapter.

Managing computers with Group Policy

Active Directory administrators use Group Policy to configure computers throughout sites, domains, or OUs. An administrator creates Group Policy Objects (GPOs), which are a collection of settings that are applied to a user's device when they sign in. Thousands of Group Policy settings are available, although administrators need to enable and configure only those they want to enforce in their organization. After configuring the desired settings, the administrator then links a GPO to an appropriate container, such as an OU.

Then, any computer and user objects stored in that OU are configured by the settings in the GPO. The Group Policy Management console is displayed in Figure 19-3.

In a domain environment, Group Policy enables an administrator to apply policy settings and restrictions to users and computers in a single step by linking the policy to a container. Contrast that centralized management strategy with a workgroup, where you must make similar Group Policy settings on each computer where you want such restrictions imposed.

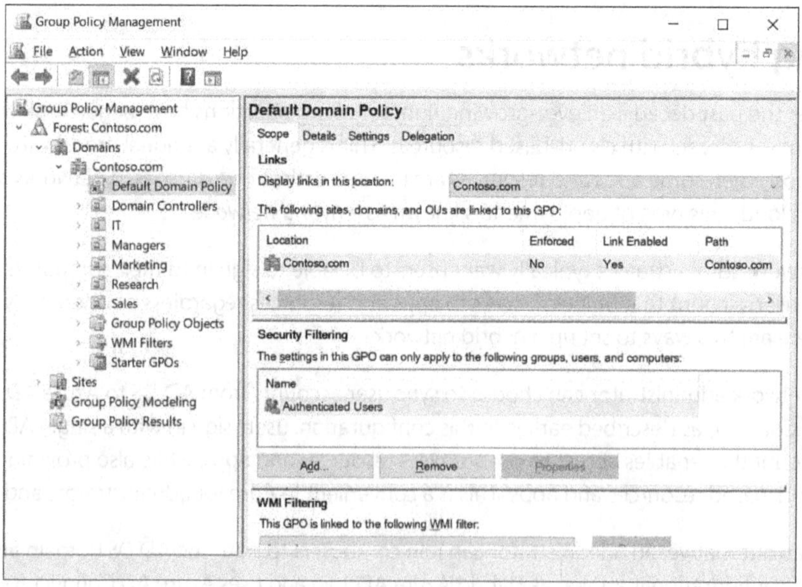

Figure 19-3   Administrators use the Group Policy Management console to create GPOs and link them to containers in Windows Server Active Directory.

Using Group Policy, an administrator can configure the following aspects of computer and user settings:

- **Software Settings**   Enables you to deploy apps to targeted computers or users.

- **Windows Settings**   Enables you to configure scripts that run during startup and shutdown or when signing in or signing out. Also provides access to important security settings.

- **Administrative Templates**   Provides access to many thousands of settings grouped into specific categories, such as Network, Printers, System, and Windows Components. Available settings can be updated when Microsoft releases a new version of Windows or Microsoft Office.

Figure 19-4 displays the Group Policy Management Editor for the Default Domain Policy in Contoso.com.

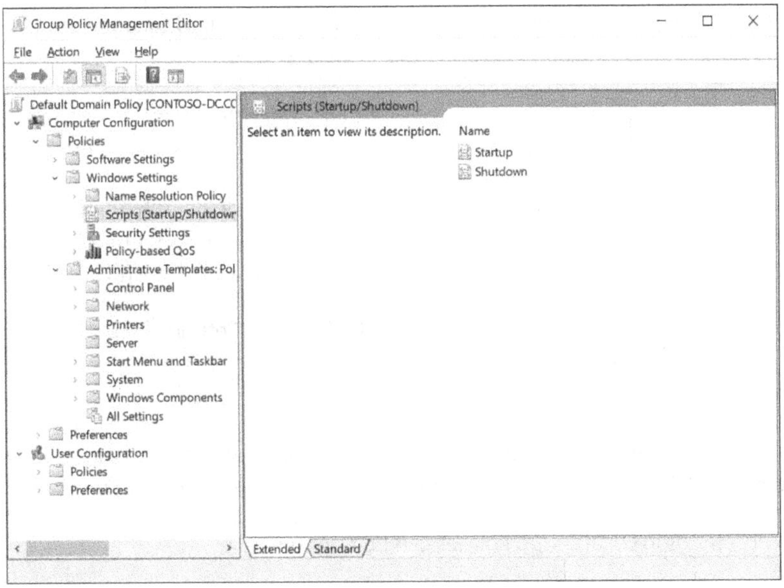

Figure 19-4   Administrators use the Group Policy Management Editor to modify the settings of a GPO.

As mentioned, the Administrative Templates node of a GPO can be updated. This requires an administrator to download and install the underlying template files, known as .admx files. For each .admx file, Microsoft provides a downloadable spreadsheet that lists the policy settings for computer and user configurations included with that version.

This spreadsheet is cumulative, so it includes all policy settings that apply to all versions of Windows 10 and Windows 11. The list also provides other details about each setting, such as the scope of the setting (machine or user), the registry value it controls, and whether a setting change requires a sign-off or reboot to take effect. The spreadsheet for Windows 11 22H2 is at *https://bit.ly/Win11-22H2-GPO-reference.*.

For more information about Group Policy, visit the following website: *https://bit.ly/Win11-22H2-GPO-reference.*

Using Local Group Policy Editor

You don't need a Windows domain controller or an Active Directory infrastructure to apply Group Policy. You can apply policies on individual Windows 11 devices using Local Group Policy Editor (Gpedit.msc). In fact, we use this tool to illustrate all of the examples in this book. You can do the same, even if you don't have access to the Group Policy Management console on a domain controller or don't need the power of Active Directory.

Setting policies using Local Group Policy uses fundamentally similar methods as those used in an Active Directory domain. However, there are a few differences, including the following:

- Domain-based GPOs support both policies and preferences. Preferences enable you to configure initial settings for the computer or user that a local user or administrator can choose to change. The Local Group Policy supports only policies and not preferences.

- In the Local Group Policy Editor, although the Software Settings folder is still visible, it's nonfunctional in a local context. You cannot configure app deployment settings using local Group Policy.

- Local Group Policies can be assigned to the local computer only, whereas GPOs in a domain are linked to containers that typically affect numerous computers.

- User settings in Local Group Policies can be targeted at

  - All users

  - A specific user account

  - Administrators

  - Nonadministrators

- Domain-based GPOs can be targeted at all users in an OU to which the GPO is linked. However, this behavior can be altered through a feature called Security Filtering.

- Any settings configured through a Local Group Policy on a computer that's AD DS domain-joined are potentially overwritten by GPOs linked to the domain or OUs in which the computer resides. In other words, Local Group Policies have a lower precedence than domain-based GPOs.

In general, you can use Local Group Policy Editor to explore available settings regardless of how you want to apply those policies. To begin exploring Group Policy, type **gpedit** in the Start search box, and then click Edit Group Policy. As shown in Figure 19-5, Local Group Policy Editor appears in the familiar Microsoft Management Console format.

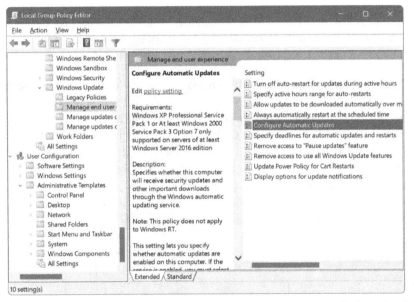

Figure 19-5   Selecting a folder or a subfolder in the navigation pane displays all policy settings associated with that group in the details pane. When you select a setting, a description of the setting appears.

The Computer Configuration branch of Group Policy includes various computer-related settings, and the User Configuration branch includes various user-related settings. The line between computer settings and user settings is often blurred, however. Your best bet for discovering the policies you need is to scan them all. You'll find a treasure trove of useful settings, including many that can't be made any other way short of manually editing the registry.

In the Administrative Templates folders are many hundreds of computer settings and even more user settings, which makes this sound like a daunting task—but you can quickly skim the folder names in Local Group Policy Editor, ignoring most of them, and then scan the policies in each folder of interest.

To learn more about each policy, simply select it in Local Group Policy Editor, as shown in Figure 19-3. If you select the Extended tab at the bottom of the window, a description of the selected policy appears in the center pane.

CHAPTER 19

NOTE

Some settings appear in both User Configuration and Computer Configuration. In a case of conflicting settings, the Computer Configuration setting always takes precedence.

Changing policy settings

Each policy setting in the Administrative Templates folders has one of three settings: Not Configured, Enabled, or Disabled. By default, all policy settings in the local Group Policy objects are initially set to Not Configured.

To change a policy setting, open Local Group Policy Editor and double-click the name of the policy setting you want to change or click the Policy Setting link that appears in the center pane of the Extended tab. A dialog then appears, as shown in Figure 19-6.

Near the top of the dialog for each setting is a large area labeled Comment, where you can add your own remarks about a policy, which can come in handy later when you are trying to remember why you changed a specific policy. The Help pane below the Comment area includes detailed information about the policy setting (the same information that appears in the center pane of the Extended tab). The pane to the left of the Help pane offers options relevant to the current policy. Previous Setting and Next Setting buttons make it convenient to go through an entire folder without opening and closing individual dialogs.

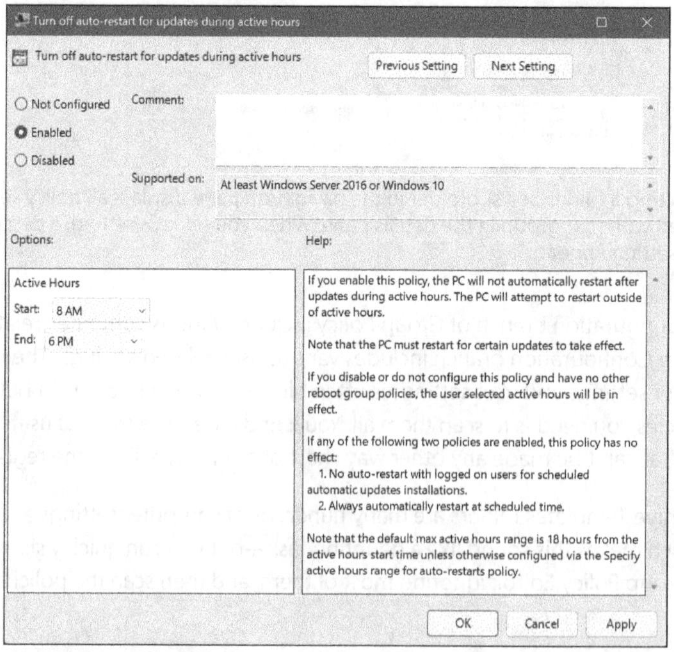

Figure 19-6   When a policy setting has configurable options, like the Start and End times shown here under the Active Hours heading, they're available only when the policy is set to Enabled.

Deploying Windows 11 in the enterprise

In larger organizations, managing PCs individually is impractical. For large-scale Windows deployments, administrators typically use centralized management software for a variety of tasks: to deploy Windows, to administer updates for Windows and other software, to manage hardware inventory and track software licenses, and to apply policies throughout an organization. These tasks traditionally apply to PCs that are owned and managed by the organization, but increasingly they're being applied to personal devices that are used to access company services and store company data. This option typically uses mobile device management (MDM) software, which can configure security policies on devices from a variety of manufacturers, including PCs running Windows 11. This option is often referred to as Bring Your Own Device (BYOD).

Enterprise administrators have a wide selection of third-party MDM and system management tools they can use for a network with a large number of Windows 11 PCs. This section lists a number of Microsoft tools you're likely to encounter in such an environment.

Microsoft Endpoint Configuration Manager

Microsoft Endpoint Configuration Manager describes a family of tools for administrators responsible for managing devices and users, both on-premises and in the cloud. Configuration Manager is a console-based application that enables an enormous range of capabilities, including allowing administrators to distribute applications, manage devices, and enforce network security.

Configuration Manager is a powerful but complex system that enables you to control all aspects of computer management. It integrates with other management tools, including Microsoft Intune, to give administrators excellent visibility into the status of their infrastructure. With the Configuration Manager console, shown in Figure 19-7, administrators can perform the following management tasks:

- Deploy and manage apps.

- Manage and distribute software updates.

- Deploy operating systems.

- Manage and deploy Windows and application updates.

- Gather and interpret desktop analytics data.

- Manage Microsoft Edge browser.

- Configure and perform Microsoft 365 Apps management.

CHAPTER 19

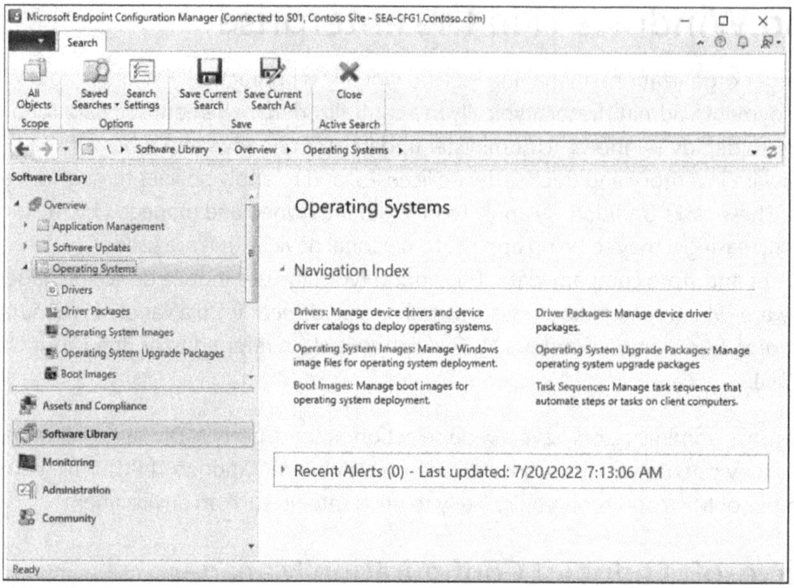

Figure 19-7   Administrators use the Microsoft Endpoint Configuration Manager console to manage an organization's computing infrastructure using Endpoint Manager.

Microsoft Deployment Toolkit

You can use the Microsoft Deployment Toolkit (MDT) to deploy Windows operating systems within an on-premises network of any size. Unlike Configuration Manager, MDT is useful only for deploying Windows; it's not a tool for ongoing management and maintenance. That said, it's pretty good at what it does, and doesn't require as much specialist knowledge as Configuration Manager.

NOTE

The MDT can be downloaded, free, from the Microsoft download website: *https://www.microsoft.com/download/details.aspx?id=54259.*

MDT uses files saved in the Windows Imaging File format (.wim) and supports two types of image files:

- **Boot images**   Used to start a computer that has no local operating system installed (sometimes called bare-metal computers). Sometimes, this image is distributed to the target computers using a memory stick. But perhaps more commonly, boot images can be accessed across the network by using a PXE-capable network adapter; in this instance, the boot image is stored on a deployment server. The boot image contains a runtime version of Windows called Windows PE, which is used to launch setup, or, in this case, to launch a program that is used to apply an operating system image.

- **Operating system images**   Hardware-agnostic images that contain a complete operating system. These OS images can be applied from the Windows product DVD, in which case they're generic; alternatively, you can capture the hard disk of a working computer to create a custom image, which might contain specific apps, drivers, and settings appropriate to your organization.

By using the MDT Deployment Workbench, shown in Figure 19-8, you can perform numerous management tasks, including the following:

- Deploy Windows operating systems.

- Upgrade Windows operating systems.

- Migrate user settings using User State Migration Tool (USMT).

- Deploy apps during OS deployment.

- Deploy drivers during OS deployment.

- Monitor current deployments.

- Apply local GPOs as a GPO pack.

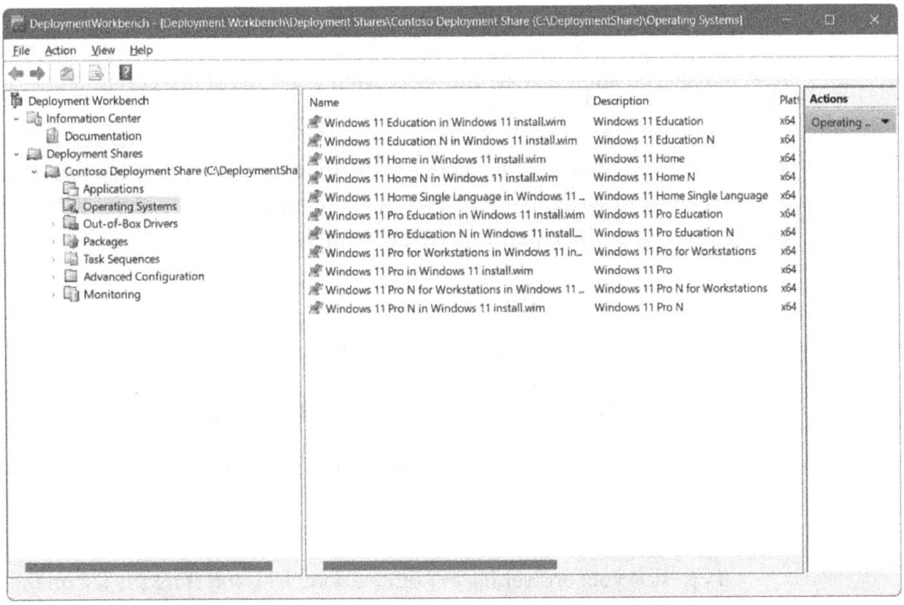

Figure 19-8   The MDT Deployment Workbench is used to upload apps, images, drivers, and other packages. The administrator then creates a task sequence to perform the desired deployment.

Full documentation for MDT is located at *https://bit.ly/mdt-documentation*.

CHAPTER 19

Inside OUT

Zero Touch deployments with ECM and MDT

MDT can be used to perform what Microsoft calls Lite-Touch Installations, which require minimal intervention from an administrator. However, when combined with Endpoint Configuration Manager, an administrator can create a task sequence to perform Zero Touch installations instead. This approach can be especially useful when an organization has a large number of Windows devices to deploy.

You can learn more about the Zero Touch installation architecture here: *https://bit.ly/ZTI-overview.* Although this documentation refers to Windows 10, the principles work just as well with Windows 11.

Windows System Image Manager

Windows System Image Manager (Windows SIM) is part of the free downloadable Windows Assessment and Deployment Kit (Windows ADK). In addition to Windows SIM, Windows contains application compatibility testing tools and deployment utilities.

Windows SIM works hand in hand with the Deployment Image Servicing and Management (DISM) tool and Windows Configuration Designer to create and configure provisioning packages that can be applied both after deploying Windows 11 to a computer, or during the Out Of Box Experience (OOBE) in Windows 11 setup.

You use Windows SIM to create answer files. These are XML text files used by Windows Setup to automate the responses to questions posed during the various stages of Windows Setup. You can use Windows SIM to perform the following tasks:

- Create and edit answer files.

- Validate your answer files against a Windows installation image.

- Review configurable settings in your Windows image.

- Include additional drivers, apps, and supplemental packages.

NOTE

If you save your answer file as Autounattend.xml, and store the file on the installation media in the root directory, Windows Setup automatically locates the file and uses the stored responses during setup.

To learn more about Windows SIM, go to *https://bit.ly/Windows-SIM-overview.*

Windows Autopilot

Windows Autopilot is a cloud-based deployment and provisioning tool, part of Microsoft's Mobile Device Management (MDM) and Mobile Application Management (MAM) system called Intune.

> ## NOTE
>
> **Businesses can license Microsoft Endpoint Configuration Manager with Microsoft Intune; this hybrid on-premises and cloud-based management solution is referred to as Endpoint Manager.**

Rather than relying on images to deploy Windows, Autopilot uses the default factory image supplied as part of a new PC from a hardware OEM. When the user turns on the PC, Windows Autopilot intercepts the (OOBE portion of setup and directs the device to the organization's server, which then provisions the device according to the organization's requirements. This provisioning process includes the deployment of configuration profiles, compliance policies, apps, and security settings.

Windows Autopilot works only on computers that are preinstalled with Windows 10/11 Pro, Enterprise, or Education. In addition, the devices must be assigned to an Azure AD group and the users must have permission to join the devices to Azure AD. Here's how Windows Autopilot works in practice.

An organization purchases a batch of new computers from a hardware vendor. That vendor in turn uploads the device IDs of these new computers to the Autopilot service and then ships the devices to the organization (or directly to the users). When the user turns on the computer, it connects to the Autopilot service and checks for the presence of its ID. Because the OEM previously uploaded the device IDs, OOBE now follows the prescribed settings of the organization's Autopilot profile.

After the user enters their Azure AD account credentials, their device is Azure AD joined, enrolled in Intune, and ready for use.

> ## NOTE
>
> **Although it's a requirement that devices have internet access during setup, it's important to note that this means the device must be able to connect to the Autopilot service and also to both Azure AD and Intune. This is not usually a problem, but can sometimes be an issue when devices connect through managed networks that control which URLs and IP addresses can be visited by users.**

Using Autopilot is straightforward for organizations already using Intune.

After new and existing devices are Autopilot-enabled, an administrator can sign in using a special keyboard combination and trigger an Autopilot Reset when needed. This reset removes any personal files, apps, and settings. It resets target computers to an approved state, ready for use by a new organizational user.

Windows Server Update Services

In the Windows-as-a-Service era, Microsoft expects most of its customers running Windows 11 PCs in homes and small businesses to connect directly to Windows Update servers. In large organizations, administrators typically want more control over the update process.

Windows Server Update Services (WSUS) provides that control by enabling administrators to manage their own update servers, approving updates to Windows and hardware devices only after they're confident that they'll install without issues.

NOTE

WSUS is implemented by installing the Windows Server Update Services server role on a Windows Server computer.

To use WSUS on Windows 11, you must modify a number of computer settings to point your Windows 11 devices to the internal WSUS servers. This is best achieved by using Group Policy.

Open the Group Policy Management console and then select the appropriate GPO for editing. Open the GPO in the Group Policy Management Editor and navigate to Computer Configuration > Policies > Administrative Templates > Windows Components > Windows Update > Manage Updates Offered From Windows Server Update Service. Then select the Specify Intranet Microsoft Update Service Location policy. Enable this policy, and then, as shown in Figure 19-9, specify the intranet server URL, the statistics URL, and optionally, the alternate download server URL.

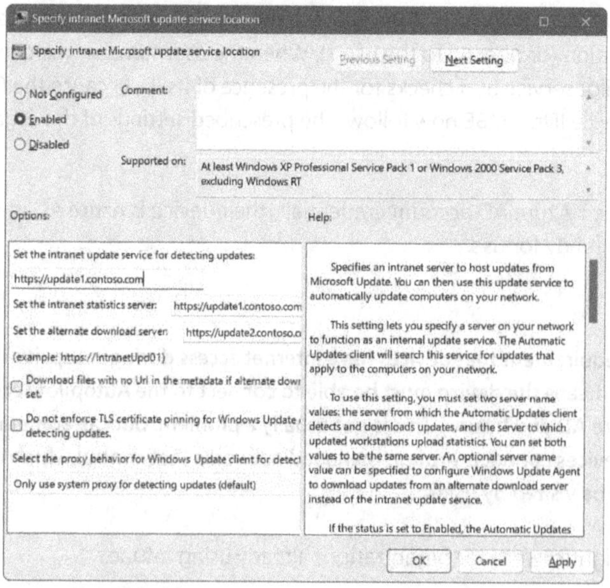

Figure 19-9   Edit these Group Policy settings to specify from which WSUS server the client computers will obtain their updates. You can also specify a secondary update server.

The official documentation for WSUS is at *https://bit.ly/WSUS-intro*.

Windows Update for Business

Windows Update for Business is not really a service; rather, it's a collection of configurable settings that you can use to determine when Windows Updates are applied to your Windows 11 computers. You can apply these settings using Group Policy or by using an Intune device configuration profile.

As we noted earlier, Windows updates are divided into two main categories: quality updates and feature updates. (For more details, see "Keeping Windows up to date" in Chapter 12, "Windows security and privacy.") Quality updates are delivered monthly (although some critical security updates are delivered "out of band"—that is, outside the regular schedule) and are cumulative; in other words, each new update package includes operating system fixes and minor changes from previous releases. Feature updates, as the name suggests, introduce new features and are now released annually in the second half of each year.

NOTE

Feature updates are now identified with a year prefix and a suffix that identifies when in the year the update was released. Windows 11 version 22H2, for example, was released in the second half of 2022.

To implement Windows Update for Business in an on-premises environment, you use Group Policy on a domain controller in larger networks; on small networks without a Windows domain, you can use local Group Policy settings. Open the Group Policy Management console or Local Group Policy Editor and then select the appropriate GPO for editing.

Navigate to Computer Configuration > Policies > Administrative Templates > Windows Components > Windows Update > Manage Updates Offered From Windows Update. Then enable and configure the following settings, shown in Figure 19-10:

- **Select When Preview Builds And Feature Updates Are Received**   Enables you to defer these updates for up to 365 days.

- **Select When Quality Updates Are Received**   Enables you to defer quality updates for up to 30 days.

- **Manage Preview Builds**   Enables you to opt into a Windows Insider channel for previews of upcoming updates. Choose between Dev Channel, Beta Channel, and Release Preview Channel.

CHAPTER 19

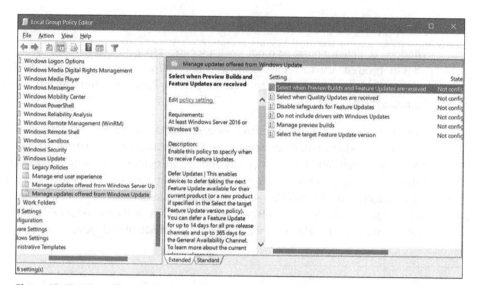

Figure 19-10   You will typically group your computers together and then use GPO security filtering to apply different Windows Update for Business settings.

On a domain-based network, an administrator can configure all computers with the same settings by creating a GPO and linking it to the domain object. To create different update settings for different groups of computers, use the following high-level procedure:

1.   Create a security group for each collection of computers and add the required computers to that group.

2.   Create a separate GPO for each collection of computers.

3.   Link the GPOs to the domain object in the organization.

4.   Use security filtering to ensure that a particular GPO only applies to a specific group.

5.   Configure the required update settings in each GPO.

In this way, administrators can ensure that specific update settings are applied to groups of computers that they want to manage in the same fashion. For example, an organization might want a small group of technically sophisticated users to install updates as soon as they're released by Microsoft, knowing those users will report any issues they encounter. Remaining devices can be configured to defer updates for 10 to 14 days, after they've been given the all-clear by those early adopters. It's also easy to reconfigure the update settings for a computer because all you need to do is remove that computer from one security group and add it as a member to another security group; this causes the computer to reconfigure its update settings.

Managing Windows 11 in the cloud

Many organizations are moving some or all of their IT infrastructure to the cloud. If you work for a small organization, it's entirely possible that all your services are delivered via cloud providers.

For larger organizations, and certainly for enterprise-level organizations, you'll probably find that your infrastructure is hybrid; in other words, some services are provided by servers and apps in on-premises networks while others are delivered through service providers in the cloud.

Microsoft offers a range of cloud services that can be used with Windows 11. We describe them in more detail in this section.

Microsoft 365 and Windows Enterprise licensing

Microsoft 365 (formerly known as Office 365) is often an organization's starting point to the cloud. Rather than manage and maintain Windows Server computers to host apps like Exchange Server and SharePoint Server, organizations choose to subscribe to a solution that provides these capabilities in a serverless, managed, pay-as-you-go subscription, with the option to add the traditional Office desktop apps (Word, Excel, PowerPointOutlook, and more).

Microsoft 365 Enterprise plans can include Windows licenses and other advanced features as well. Microsoft 365 Enterprise E3 plans, for example, include the following:

- Windows 11 Enterprise licenses for users.

- Device and app management through Intune.

- Advanced identity and access management features.

- Threat protection, information protection, and compliance management.

Microsoft 365 Enterprise E5 includes all the standard plan features, together with those for Enterprise E3, plus the following additional capabilities:

- Advanced analytics.

- Additional identity and access management features.

- Additional information protection.

- Additional compliance management features.

CHAPTER 19

Inside OUT

Subscription activation is automatic

If users in an organization have a Microsoft 365 Enterprise subscription that includes a Windows license, they can automatically upgrade a computer installed with Windows 11 Pro by joining the device to Azure AD using the credentials associated with that subscription. Doing so automatically upgrades the operating system to Windows 11 Enterprise; this upgrade does not require a product key, nor does it require a restart.

You can review the current Microsoft 365 Enterprise plans at the following Microsoft website: *https://www.microsoft.com/microsoft-365/compare-microsoft-365-enterprise-plans*.

Administrators can manage an organization's Microsoft 365 subscription from web-based portals, as displayed in Figure 19-11. They can also use Windows PowerShell to perform more granular administrative tasks.

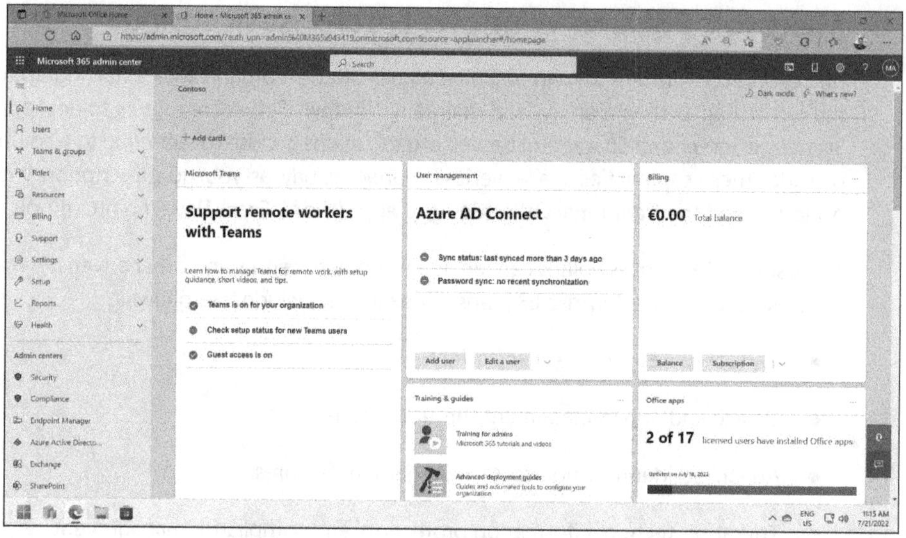

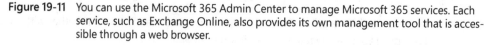

Figure 19-11 You can use the Microsoft 365 Admin Center to manage Microsoft 365 services. Each service, such as Exchange Online, also provides its own management tool that is accessible through a web browser.

To access these services, a user must sign in to Azure AD using a licensed account. For Windows 11, this typically means performing an Azure AD Join operation. Any user can do this during Windows Setup, or thereafter in Settings. An administrator can also automate the Azure AD Join process by using provisioning.

A Windows 11 computer that is Azure AD joined enables a user to sign in to that computer using their Azure AD user account. All installed client apps (such as Outlook or Teams) are automatically configured to use the signed-in user account details.

NOTE

Users cannot Azure AD Join non-Windows computers, such as Apple Macs running MacOS or phones or tablets running iOS or Android. However, these devices can be registered in Azure AD. As long as the user account associated with a device is licensed, the user can connect to the Microsoft 365 services, but they can't seamlessly sign in to services using that Azure AD account; instead, they must enter the Azure AD user account details for each app they want to connect with.

Azure Virtual Machines running Windows 11

Perhaps the first exposure many IT professionals have to Microsoft Azure is hosting infrastructure, such as file servers running on virtual machines (VMs). Over the past few years, organizations have increasingly used virtualization to support on-premises workloads. Moving to the cloud is often viewed as a means to run those same VMs in someone else's datacenters, as displayed in Figure 19-12.

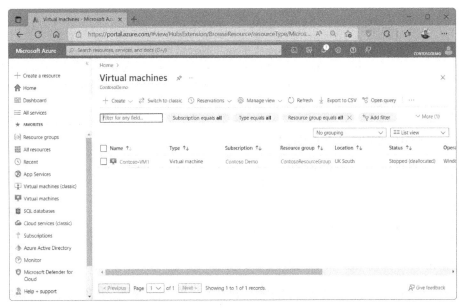

Figure 19-12   Adding VMs to Azure is straightforward. You can set up a cloud-based VM from scratch, or migrate your on-premises VMs to the cloud.

Installing Windows 11 on a VM in Azure is a fairly straightforward process and doesn't require advanced technical skills. When you create a VM in Azure, you define the operating system and virtual machine hardware characteristics using a wizard that guides you through the process.

NOTE

To create an Azure VM with Windows 11, you'll need an Azure subscription. The subscription is free, but the VM incurs charges when it's running.

Sign in as an administrator in your Azure subscription and select Virtual Machines. Click Create, and follow the on-screen instructions to define the characteristics of your VM. Some important ones, on the Basics page, are the following:

- **Image**   Choose an appropriate Windows 11 image from the extensive selection.

- **Size**   Choose a suitable virtual processor and allocate the desired amount of virtual memory.

- **Licensing**   You can select the I Confirm I Have An Eligible Windows 10/11 License With Multi-tenant Hosting Rights option if you already have a Windows 11 Enterprise E3/E5 per user or Azure Virtual Desktop Access per user license. This saves you from paying for a Windows 11 license for the VM. For more details, visit *https://bit.ly/deploy-win11-on-azure*.

It's important to note that because the VM with Windows 11 is running in Azure, you must connect to it remotely. For graphical access, you can do this using the Remote Desktop Protocol (RDP), which is enabled by default.

NOTE

Be prepared for a rude shock if you forget to shut down a running Azure VM after using it. You pay by the minute for any Azure resources you're using, even if a virtual device is simply idling. For Windows 11 Azure VMs, remember to shut down when the session is complete.

Windows 365 cloud PCs

Although installing Windows 11 on a VM in Azure has benefits, it's perhaps not the easiest way of accessing a cloud-based Windows PC. This is where Windows 365 can be beneficial.

Windows 365 is a fully hosted Windows desktop PC that runs in the Microsoft cloud, but is accessible from virtually any device that has an internet connection, including tablets and PCs running non-Microsoft operating systems. The service is independent of Azure and Microsoft 365 and is available for a free 30-day trial.

For a more detailed overview, visit *https://learn.microsoft.com/windows-365/overview*.

There's no technical configuration required; select the appropriate subscription and click Buy Now. You can choose a cloud PC by selecting from a list of configurations that vary from a basic model (2 virtual CPUs, with 4 GB of memory, and 64 GB of storage) to much more powerful devices with up to 8 vCPUs, 32 GB of RAM, and 512 GB of storage.

The Basic, Standard, and Premium configurations come inclusive with installed features and apps, such as Microsoft Endpoint Manager, desktop versions of Office apps, and integration with Intune for MDM.

Organizations can choose from two options:

- **Windows 365 Business**   For smaller companies and organizations of up to 300 seats. Provides a ready-to-use cloud PC with straightforward management.

- **Windows 365 Enterprise**   For large organizations that need unlimited seats for licensing. Enables administrators to build custom cloud PCs from images they create.

CHAPTER 19

Windows 365 cloud PCs are charged monthly on a per-user basis. You can review current pricing plans for Windows 365 at *https://www.microsoft.com/windows-365/all-pricing*.

Microsoft Defender for Endpoint

As an organization moves resources into the cloud, its security focus shifts toward the *endpoints*—the devices that employees use to access organizational data. Microsoft Defender for Endpoint offers a collection of security tools designed for enterprise administrators. It provides the following capabilities:

- **Endpoint behavioral sensors**   Built in to Windows 11, sensors monitor behavior of the operating system and collect related data. This data is then sent to the organization's instance of Microsoft Defender for Endpoint in the cloud.

- **Cloud security analytics**   The behavioral data collected from endpoints is presented in a meaningful way, identifying threats, helping security analysts understand what's happening, and providing suggestions for mitigating detected threats.

- **Threat intelligence**   This feature helps security professionals identify specific attacker tools and techniques, generating alerts when those tools and techniques are found in endpoint data.

As with most enterprise features, Microsoft Defender for Endpoint is available in a variety of subscription plans at different price points. It also requires configuration of the devices to be monitored, using Group Policy or management tools such as Intune.

Find out more at *https://bit.ly/ms-defender-for-endpoint*.

Microsoft Intune

As mentioned earlier, Intune enables administrators to perform mobile device management (MDM) and mobile application management (MAM) for their organization's devices. Intune performs a similar function to Group Policy in an on-premises network. However, Intune works in a different way. Whereas AD DS only supports Windows computers, administrators can use Intune to manage and configure a variety of devices, running a range of operating systems that includes MacOS, iOS, Android, and, of course, Windows 10 and Windows 11.

The Overview page in the Microsoft Endpoint Manager admin center displays summary information about managed devices, as shown in Figure 19-13.

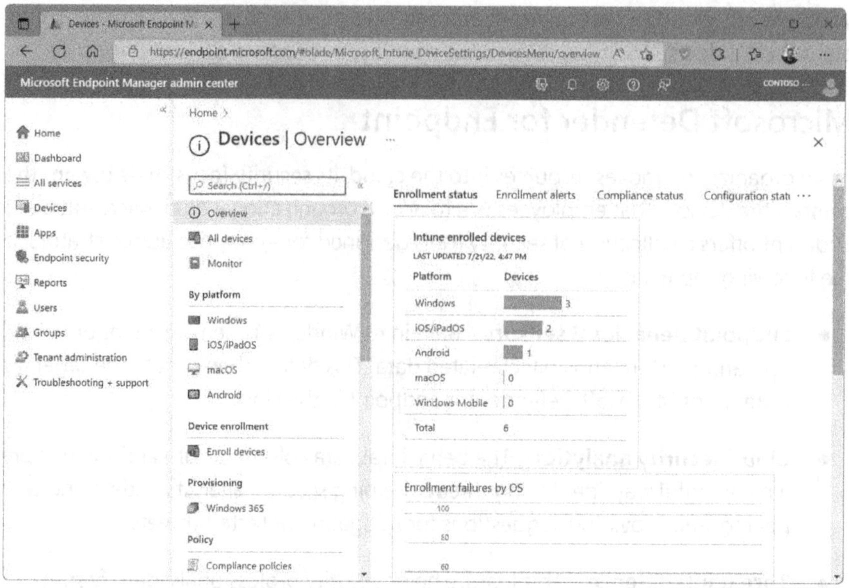

Figure 19-13   A view of the Devices page in Microsoft Endpoint Manager admin center. From here, administrators can review the enrollment status, compliance status, and configuration status of users' devices.

Administrators can use Intune to perform the following management tasks:

- **Configure devices**   Create and apply device configuration profiles that can configure firmware settings, device restrictions, email accounts, Wi-Fi and VPN connectivity profiles, and much more.

- **Verify compliance**   Create and apply compliance policies that require devices to meet specified security settings. Noncompliant devices can be removed from Intune. You can also use compliance status in Azure AD conditional access policies.

- **Deploy and configure apps**   Distribute, configure, and manage a variety of app types, including Windows desktop apps, Store apps, and line of business apps.

- **Secure devices**   Use endpoint security policies to configure the desired security settings for devices, including settings like disk encryption, firewall settings, account protection, and endpoint detection and response.

It's important to note that some management features require that users' devices be enrolled in Intune. However, not all features require this. It's possible, for example, to manage the settings in apps without device enrollment.

Generally, devices are enrolled in Intune when they are joined to Azure AD. However, you can also enroll into Intune in other ways, including as a separate task by using the Settings app in Windows 11.

NOTE

Enrollment creates a management relationship between the device and Intune.

After you've enrolled and configured devices, you can review their properties in the Intune console. You can review hardware, discovered apps, device compliance, device configuration (as displayed in Figure 19-14), app configuration, recovery keys (BitLocker), and other settings

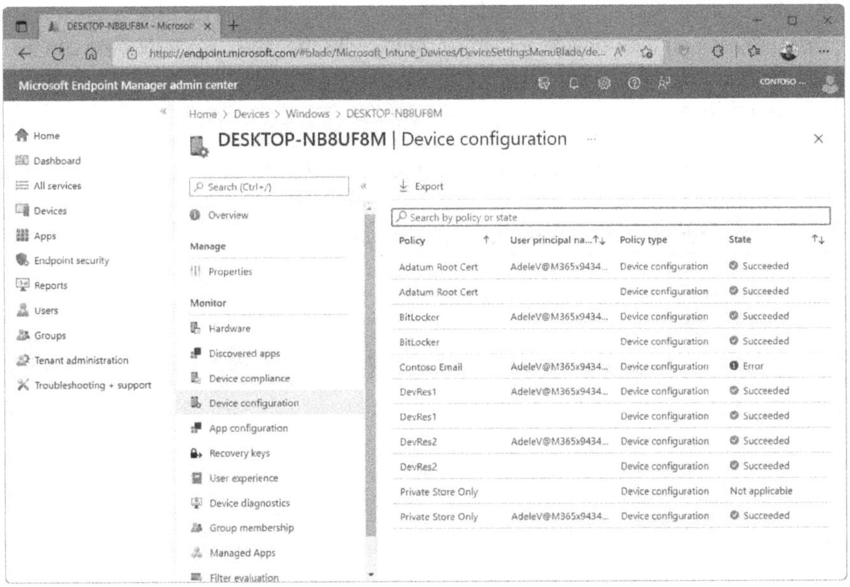

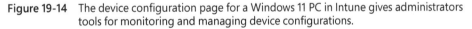

Figure 19-14   The device configuration page for a Windows 11 PC in Intune gives administrators tools for monitoring and managing device configurations.

Full documentation for Microsoft Intune is available at *https://learn.microsoft.com/mem/intune/*.

Managing apps with Intune

A signa feature of Intune is the ability to deploy and manage apps to a variety of operating systems. On Windows 11 PCs, administrators can deploy the following types of apps:

- **Store apps**   Rather than requiring, or even allowing, users to install apps from the OS store for their device, an Intune administrator can create a Store app deployment that points to the URL for the required app. They can then make the app available for users in the organization without additional intervention.

- **Microsoft 365 Apps**   Administrators can deploy Outlook, Excel, Word, and other Office desktop apps (collectively branded as Microsoft 365 Apps) to both Windows and macOS users. For Windows users, they can determine which specific components are installed.

- **Microsoft Edge**   Using Intune, administrators can deploy the new Edge browser to devices running macOS or Windows. They can deploy Edge to iOS and Android devices using the app stores for those platforms.

- **Other**   Includes web link apps, line of business apps, and Win32 apps.

After deployment, administrators can use App Configuration Policies to configure the apps' settings. They can also use App Protection Policies to stipulate requirements for the use of an app when connecting to corporate data. These settings determine what a user can do with corporate data on their device and, importantly, whether the corporate data can be decrypted and shared outside the organization. These policies vary based on the operating system of the managed device.

In Figure 19-15, the administrator has selected the All Apps node resulting in a filtered display of the available apps for the organization. For these apps to be delivered to user devices, an administrator typically assigns the apps to a group.

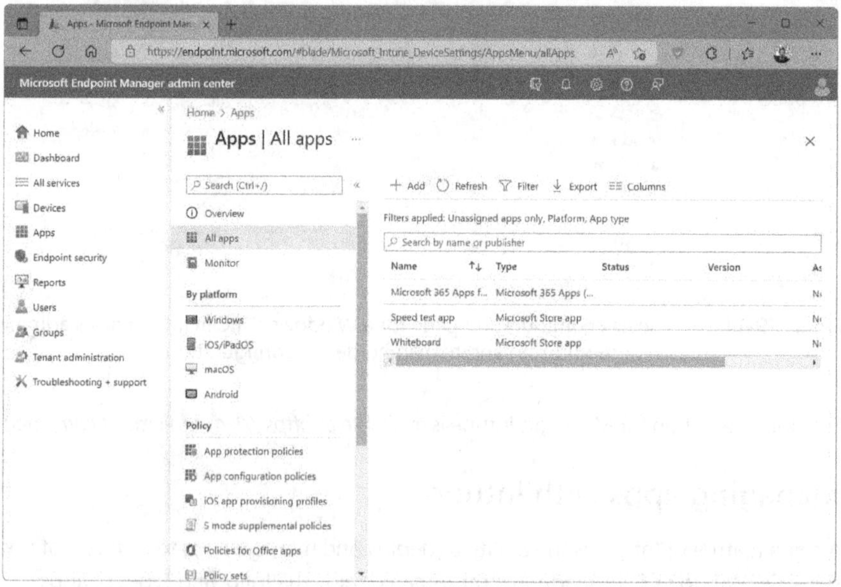

Figure 19-15   The Endpoint Manager admin center All Apps folder displays a list of all apps owned by the organization. The list can be filtered, as here, to apps for Windows only.

Managing special-purpose computers

Throughout this book, we focus almost exclusively on desktop and notebook PCs that are configured for use by a single primary user, with secondary accounts set up as needed for others in a family or business who occasionally need to use that device. In businesses, however, other scenarios are sometimes appropriate. In the following sections, we look at two specialized Windows configurations: shared PCs and kiosk devices.

Using shared PC mode

A school or business might find it useful to have a shared PC—one that can be used by any student or employee as needed or one that you want to make available for temporary use by customers and visitors. A feature in Windows 11 called *shared PC mode* makes this easier than in previous versions.

Shared PC mode requires that the computer be joined to an AD DS domain or to Azure Active Directory. After that step is complete, an administrator applies a series of customizations using mobile device management software, such as Microsoft Intune; as an alternative, they can use a provisioning package created with the Windows Configuration Designer (WCD), which is free in the Microsoft Store: *https://www.microsoft.com/store/productId/9NBLGGH4TX22*. Figure 19-16 shows the first step of creating a provisioning package using WCD.

Using either method, you can configure the shared PC to allow access by anyone with an account in the organization's directory, guests, or both. You can also configure what happens when a user signs off: automatically delete the account's local profile and data, or save the cached data for faster sign-in next time.

You can find step-by-step instructions for setting up and using shared PC mode at *https://bit.ly/shared-pc-mode*.

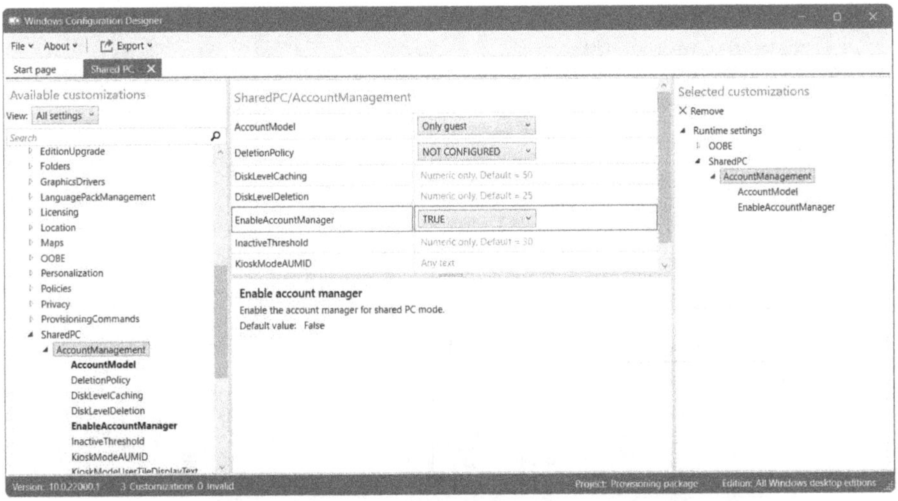

Figure 19-16   Smaller organizations that don't have access to MDM software can use the Windows Configuration Designer to create a Shared PC provisioning package.

Setting up a kiosk device

Another common scenario in business is to set up a kiosk device—a computer that is set up to do only one thing. An office might use this computer as a check-in device for guests; a retail business could put a kiosk PC on the retail floor and allow customers to use the device's touch-screen to view a product catalog or check prices. You could configure a device using these tools to run a single app, such as a banking program or an inventory app, while eliminating the risk that a worker will inadvertently allow the machine to be compromised by using a web browser or an email program.

Windows 11 supports several additional kiosk configurations, including multiapp kiosks, which display a simplified Start menu that makes it possible for kiosk users to choose from a list of allowed apps.

You can also configure a kiosk device to run Microsoft Edge in a variety of configurations—as a public browser with user data protected, for example, or as a digital sign or interactive display showing the contents of a single site.

To set up kiosk mode, open Settings > Accounts > Other Users. Under the Set Up A Kiosk heading, click Get Started.

Next, either specify to create a new account to run kiosk mode, or select an existing account, and click Next. We recommend that you choose the option to create a new account for kiosk use; when you do so, Windows automatically configures that account to sign in automatically at startup. If you choose an existing account, users need to sign in using that account's password.

After specifying the user account, choose the app that will run in kiosk mode, as shown in Figure 19-17.

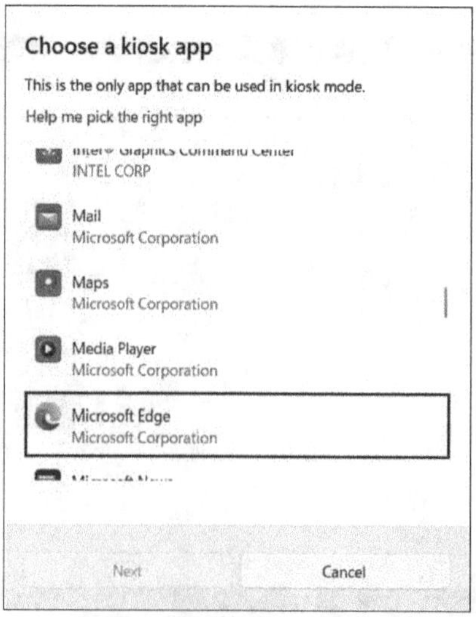

Choose a kiosk app

This is the only app that can be used in kiosk mode.

Help me pick the right app

Intel® Graphics Command Center
INTEL CORP

Mail
Microsoft Corporation

Maps
Microsoft Corporation

Media Player
Microsoft Corporation

Microsoft Edge
Microsoft Corporation

Microsoft News

Next   Cancel

Figure 19-17   You can choose any modern app to run that's installed on the kiosk computer. If you use provisioning to configure kiosk mode, you can also select a desktop app.

If you choose Microsoft Edge as the single app to run, the Set Up A Kiosk page in Settings offers these two options:

- As a digital sign or interactive display

- As a public browser

Click Next to specify the default URL where the browser will return after a defined period of inactivity, which will also reset the current browser session. Then click Next and Close. Kiosk mode is now set up.

You can configure a kiosk-mode device in multi-app mode or any browsing configuration using an XML file and mobile device management software such as Microsoft Intune, or you can create a provisioning package using Windows Configuration Designer, as discussed earlier in this section.

With your device thus configured, it launches directly to the configured kiosk app, running in a full screen and lacking most elements of the Windows 11 interface, including the Start button and taskbar. To exit kiosk mode, press Ctrl+Alt+Delete and sign in using another account.

To undo or adjust this setup, return to Settings > Accounts > Other Users. Click Assigned Access, click to select the user account configured for kiosk mode, and click Remove Kiosk. Click the app name to reveal a Change Kiosk App button that allows you to choose a different app.

CHAPTER 19

Appendixes

Windows 11 editions and licensing options

Like its predecessor, Windows 11 is available in a seemingly endless roster of editions. Each edition encompasses a specific set of features, sometimes coupled with licensing options and geographic restrictions.

Despite that apparently confusing assortment, however, most people have no problem sorting through their choices. When you purchase a new PC through traditional retail channels, you're likely to have a choice of two and only two editions: Home and Pro. (A relatively new option, Windows 11 Pro for Workstations, is available exclusively on powerful workstation-class hardware not normally found alongside PCs sold through typical retail channels.) Likewise, IT pros responsible for deployment of Windows PCs in large organizations typically upgrade PCs running Windows 11 Pro to some flavor of Windows 11 Enterprise; their choices are most often dictated by licensing agreements rather than individual features.

It's not technically an edition, but a feature called S mode is worth mentioning here. On a PC running Windows 10 or Windows 11 in S mode, configuration settings restrict installation of apps to those that are delivered through the Microsoft Store. Windows PCs running in S mode also set Microsoft Edge as the default browser and use Bing as the default search engine. Neither setting can be changed.

Some new PCs come preinstalled with Windows 11 Home in S mode, and PCs running Windows 10 Home in S mode can be upgraded to Windows 11. However, S mode is not supported on any other edition of Windows 11; if you attempt to upgrade a PC running Windows 10 Pro, Education, or Enterprise in S mode, you must permanently switch it out of S mode first.

To disable S mode in Windows 10, go to Settings > Update & Security > Activation and choose Switch To Windows 10 Home or Switch To Windows 10 Pro. That action leads to a link that takes you to the Microsoft Store and a Switch Out Of S Mode page.

To disable S mode on a PC running Windows 11 Home, the process is slightly more confusing. Open Settings > System > Activation and follow the Switch To Windows 11 Pro link, which takes you to the Microsoft Store. Do not choose the option to upgrade your edition of Windows; instead, choose the Switch Out Of S Mode option and follow the prompts.

Note that this switch, once made, is irreversible.

Windows 11 also includes IoT (Internet of Things) editions that are designed for use in specialized hardware such as automated teller machines and "smart" devices that lack a display. This appendix, however, focuses exclusively on editions of Windows 11 designed for use on desktop PCs, laptops, and PC-like tablet devices such as those in the Microsoft Surface family.

Windows 11 editions at a glance

Although the full assortment of Windows editions might appear confusing, their progression is, for the most part, consistent. Each edition contains all of the features of the previous edition, along with a higher price tag and a set of unique features that you can evaluate to decide whether the cost of upgrading is justified.

We start with a brief discussion of hardware configurations. Table A-1 lists technical limits related to CPU and memory support that might affect your purchase or upgrade decision. Note that these requirements apply equally to x64 and Arm64 architectures. (Windows 11 does not support x86 processors.)

Table A-1   Supported hardware configurations in Windows 11

Hardware component	Supported configurations
Number of CPUs/cores	Windows 11 Home: One physical processor Windows 11 Pro, Enterprise, or Education: One or two physical processors Windows 11 Pro for Workstations: Up to four physical processors All editions support multicore processors, up to a maximum of 64 cores per physical processor
Addressable memory (RAM)	Windows 11 Home: Up to 128 GB Windows 11 Pro, Enterprise, or Education: Up to 2 TB Windows 11 Pro for Workstations: Up to 6 TB

For our discussion of specific editions, we start with those available preinstalled on new PCs and in retail channels. We follow that with editions available for deployment within large enterprises, organizations, and educational institutions.

Retail and OEM editions

Consumers and businesses that acquire Windows on a new device or as a retail upgrade typically have their choice of two editions: Windows 11 Home and Windows 11 Pro. On a small number of high-end hardware devices intended for demanding workloads, some OEMs offer Windows 11 Pro for Workstations as an option. A new edition, Windows 11 SE, is designed for preinstallation on low-cost devices for the education market.

All these editions are available preinstalled on new PCs from original equipment manufacturers and are also available as retail products in shrink-wrapped boxes or as downloads from the Microsoft Store and third-party online stores.

NOTE

In some markets, you might find Single Language, KN, and N variations of the standard retail and OEM editions. A Single Language version doesn't allow you to install an additional language pack or change the base language unless you update to the full, language-neutral version. N versions are available in the European Union, and KN versions are offered in South Korea; both editions have had several media playback features removed as a result of legal proceedings between Microsoft and regulators in those jurisdictions. For most Windows installations in developed countries and regions, including the United States and Western Europe, the standard Home and Pro editions are the preferred choices.

Windows 11 Home

Windows 11 Home includes all the core features that are described in detail in this book. That includes the complete Windows 11 user experience, with its customizable Start menu and taskbar, as well as the modern Settings app that offers access to system settings formerly included in Control Panel. It also includes the technical architecture of Windows 11: the NTFS file system, TCP/IP networking, power management, and the Windows Search index, as well as compatibility with virtually all software designed for Windows 10 and Windows 11.

Except for some high-end configurations that include multiple processors and massive amounts of system memory, there's no difference in hardware support between Windows 11 Home and higher editions. Any device that has a compatible Windows driver works on Windows 11 Home, including multiple displays, touchscreens, and pens that support the Windows Ink platform.

Every edition of Windows receives security and feature updates through Windows Update, although the Home edition lacks some configuration options available in more advanced editions. Likewise, the security infrastructure of Windows 11 Home supports the use of a Trusted Platform Module and Secure Boot and, with the proper hardware, allows the use of Windows Hello biometric authentication. Some advanced security features, such as BitLocker Drive Encryption, require Pro, Enterprise, or Education editions.

And, of course, every edition of Windows 11 includes the same assortment of apps, including Microsoft Edge.

Windows 11 Pro

Windows 11 Pro includes the same core features as Windows 11 Home, with the addition of features that are primarily of interest to business users and corporate network administrators. All the features in the following list are also available in Enterprise and Education editions:

- **Client Hyper-V Platform**   With proper hardware support, enables users to create a virtual machine (VM), install Windows or another operating system on the VM, and use it as if it was a separate physical device.

- **Windows Sandbox**   Creates an instant virtual machine that uses minimal system resources and erases all traces of its activity when closed.

- **Language packs**   Changes the Windows 11 interface to add language packs and switch between languages for displaying menus, dialog boxes, and other elements.

- **Windows Update for Business**   Allows central management of security updates and new features delivered through Windows Update, with the option to configure limited delays for quality updates and longer delays (up to one year) for feature updates.

- **Mobile device management**   Supports the use of mobile device management tools, which allows administrators to configure security options, provision apps, and perform other management tasks from the cloud.

- **Encrypting File System**   Enables strong encryption of individual files and folders on an NTFS-formatted volume.

- **BitLocker Drive Encryption**   Allows an entire drive to be encrypted, protecting its contents from unauthorized access if the computer is lost or stolen.

- **BitLocker To Go**   Encrypts data on removable media such as USB flash drives and external drives. (Devices running Windows 11 Home can read from and write to storage devices encrypted using this feature but cannot manage BitLocker To Go encryption.)

- **Domain join/Group Policy management**   Allows the device to join a Windows domain and be managed by using Active Directory and Group Policy.

- **Azure Active Directory support**   Allows a Windows 11 device to join Azure Active Directory (AAD), with a single sign-in to cloud-hosted apps. In a Hybrid Azure Active Directory environment, devices enrolled in an on-premises domain can be joined to AAD.

- **Windows Autopilot**   Allows end users to connect to AAD and set up a new device using an organization's standard configuration, with Windows apps and settings applied automatically.

- **Windows Information Protection**   Provides advanced control over data files, including encryption and remote wipe.

- **IE Mode for Microsoft Edge**   Using network configuration files, administrators can define compatibility settings for sites accessed using Internet Explorer, including those on corporate intranets, enabling the continued use of older web apps that aren't compatible with Microsoft Edge.

- **Remote Desktop (server)**   Allows remote access to the full Windows experience on the current PC; the connection is made over the network using Remote Desktop Protocol from a client program running on any Windows PC, Mac, or supported mobile device. (Devices running Windows 11 Home can connect to a PC that allows incoming Remote Desktop sessions but can't share their own resources in this fashion.)

Windows 11 Pro for Workstations

Windows 11 Pro for Workstations is intended for use on "server-grade hardware" that is much more powerful than the average desktop PC. Devices intended for use with this edition typically have multiple CPUs and massive amounts of memory. By design, these workstations perform compute-intensive tasks such as computer-aided design, data analysis, and video rendering, which need hardware resources far beyond what even a high-end desktop PC can deliver.

The feature set for this edition is similar to that of Windows 11 Pro. Where it differs is in its hardware support, as described in Table A-1 at the beginning of this section.

Windows 11 Pro for Workstations includes support for devices with persistent memory (also known as non-volatile memory modules, or NVDIMM-N), the fastest data storage possible on workstations. It supports SMB Direct file transfers, over network adapters that use Remote Direct Memory Access (RDMA) for faster throughput and very low latency. As an alternative to the traditional NTFS file system, it supports the newer ReFS (Resilient File System), which is optimized for large data volumes spread over multiple physical disks.

Editions for organizations

Windows 11 Enterprise is available as an upgrade for PCs that already have an underlying license for Windows 11 Pro. Windows 11 Education provides equivalent features for large networks in academic environments (K–12 and university) and allows upgrades from Windows 11 Home or Pro editions. Historically, Enterprise updates required an organization to purchase licenses through a Volume License agreement. Those agreements are still available for larger organizations, but in recent years Microsoft has introduced new subscription options that make Enterprise upgrades available for small businesses and individuals as well.

APPENDIX A

Windows 11 Enterprise

The following list enumerates features that are available only in Windows 11 Enterprise editions. On corporate networks, you have the option to enable some additional features by upgrading to the Enterprise edition as part of a volume license agreement with Software Assurance:

- **Azure Virtual Desktop**   Supports cloud-based deployments of Windows applications and desktops. (This feature was formerly known as Windows Virtual Desktop.)

- **Microsoft Defender Credential Guard**   Supports multifactor authentication using smart cards and biometric information to prevent "Pass the Hash" exploits.

- **Microsoft Defender Exploit Guard**   Allows network administrators to create security policies that reduce the attack surface of a Windows PC, reducing the likelihood that network-based attacks will succeed.

- **Microsoft Defender for Endpoint (previously known as Microsoft Defender Advanced Threat Protection)**   Available only with Windows 11 Enterprise E5 and Microsoft 365 E5 subscriptions, provides detection of online threats and attacks.

- **DirectAccess**   Provides secure connections (without a virtual private network, or VPN) between a client PC running Windows 11 and a remote server running Windows Server 2008 R2 or newer.

- **Universal Print**   Helps network administrators manage printer security through a cloud-based portal, allowing users to quickly find and use the nearest printer without having to install drivers.

Windows 11 Enterprise E3 and E5

Microsoft has expanded the availability of Windows 11 Enterprise upgrades through a subscription offering called Windows Enterprise E3, available only through Microsoft partners who are part of the Cloud Service Providers program. The feature set for these editions is identical to Enterprise edition sold through volume license agreements and upgrades Windows 11 Pro. The most important distinction is that these subscription editions are licensed on a per-user basis and are tied to an Azure Active Directory account. Each user can install the upgrade on up to five PCs.

Windows Enterprise E5 is an upgrade to Windows Enterprise E3 that adds support for Microsoft Defender for Endpoint, an enterprise-based, cross-platform security solution.

Microsoft 365 E3, E5, and F3

In 2020, Microsoft rebranded most of its Office 365 subscriptions as Microsoft 365. Three of the Microsoft 365 offerings include Windows 11 Enterprise E3 as part of a package that also includes

Office apps and services, and a variety of management, analytics, security, and compliance tools collectively branded Enterprise Mobility + Security. (The F3 edition includes web apps only and is intended for use by so-called frontline workers—Microsoft's term for employees who work directly with customers or the general public.) The Windows 11 portion of these subscription packages contains the same feature set as other Enterprise edition offerings.

Windows 11 Enterprise LTSC

Shortly after the release of Windows 10, Microsoft announced its intention to release a version of Windows Enterprise edition designed for use on specialized equipment in mission-critical environments, where stability is a prime consideration and regular feature updates are unwelcome. Deploying this edition allows administrators to limit deployment of new Windows features, installing reliability and security updates only.

These releases are delivered as part of the Long Term Servicing Channel (LTSC), which was previously known by the equally awkward moniker Long Term Servicing Branch (LTSB). The two most recent releases in this channel are Windows 10 Enterprise LTSC 2019, which was released in November 2018, and Windows 10 Enterprise LTSC 2021, released in November 2021.

Each LTSB/LTSC release contains the same features as other editions from the same release cycle, with two noteworthy exceptions:

- LTSB/LTSC releases do not receive feature updates through Windows Update.

- These releases do not contain many in-box applications that are included with other editions, including Microsoft Edge, Microsoft Store, Cortana (limited search capabilities remain available), Mail, Calendar, Weather, Microsoft News, Photos, Camera, and Alarms & Clock.

In July 2021, Microsoft announced that its next release of Windows to the Long Term Servicing Channel would be based on Windows 11 but did not specify a date for its release. Given the two-to three-year intervals between previous LTSC releases, it's reasonable to expect that this version will not be ready until the end of 2023 or later.

Editions for educational institutions

At schools and other institutions of learning, administrators can enable advanced features by upgrading to Windows 11 Pro Education and Windows 11 Education. These specialized editions provide education-specific default settings but are otherwise essentially equivalent to the Pro and Enterprise editions.

Administrators in education environments can provision new devices with the Set Up School PCs app or Windows Configuration Designer. They can also deliver "digital assessments" with the Take A Test app; see *https://bit.ly/win11-take-a-test*. These features work with all desktop Windows editions except Windows 10 and Windows 11 Home.

Institutions that have deployed Windows 11 Pro and Enterprise in managed environments can configure the product to have similar feature settings to Windows 11 Pro Education and Windows 11 Education using Group Policy settings.

For specific details about these Windows 10 editions and configuration options, see *https://bit.ly/win10-education*.

Windows 11 Education

Windows 11 Education is effectively a variant of Windows 11 Enterprise that provides education-specific default settings. These default settings disable some features that are common to retail editions, including tips and tricks, as well as Microsoft Store suggestions. It is available only through Volume Licensing channels.

Windows 11 Pro Education

This edition is effectively a variant of Windows 11 Pro that provides education-specific default settings similar to those in Windows 11 Education. It is available on new devices purchased with discounted K–12 academic licenses through OEM partners. (These discounted licenses are sometimes referred to as National Academic or Shape the Future.) This edition is also available through Volume Licensing channels.

Windows 11 SE

This edition, which is new to Windows 11, is available preinstalled on new hardware for the education market. Its primary purpose is to provide a secure environment for use by students. As a result, it requires management through Microsoft Intune for Education and supports what Microsoft calls "a curated app experience" consisting only of "essential education apps." For more information, see *https://bit.ly/windows-se*.

The Windows Insider Program

If you have a hankering for new Windows features, all you have to do is wait. Microsoft has announced its intention to release new feature updates for Windows 11 once per year, typically in September or October. These full upgrades are delivered at no charge through Windows Update to devices running every OEM and retail edition of Windows 11. In addition, Microsoft regularly slips minor updates to features and apps in with its regular monthly security and reliability updates.

If you'd rather not wait for those updates, you can sign up for the Windows Insider Program, which is free of charge and open to anyone who wants to receive preview releases of Windows as they work their way through the development process. This open approach makes it easy to track the development process and see what's coming in a future feature update.

By running preview builds, you can try out new features as they develop. More importantly, the program gives you the opportunity to report bugs and provide feedback and suggestions that can influence the direction of those features.

Insider releases are ideal for Windows enthusiasts, of course, but they're also of value to IT professionals who want to avoid unpleasant surprises when new versions are rolled out to the public. This appendix explains how to enroll in the Windows Insider Program and manage your participation in a way that matches your tolerance for the glitches and occasional crashes that are inevitable with early releases that haven't been fully tested.

How the Windows Insider Program works

Microsoft introduced the Windows Insider Program in 2014 when it announced Windows 10, delivering the first preview release days later. The program has continued nonstop since then, expanding in 2017 to include business users as well as personal accounts.

You don't need to pay a fee or pass a test to join the Windows Insider Program. All you have to do is complete two steps. First, go to *https://insider.windows.com*, read the terms and conditions, and sign up using a Microsoft account or an Azure Active Directory address. After completing that prerequisite, you can take the second step by configuring any device running Windows 11 to install Insider Preview builds.

Inside OUT

What's different about the Windows Insider Program for Business?

To join a device to the Windows Insider Program for Business, use an Azure Active Directory (Azure AD) account to register; the Azure AD account option is available only if the device is connected to your corporate network using that account. When you install a preview build on an Azure AD–joined device using that Azure AD account, an additional My Company page appears in the Feedback Hub, where you can see and upvote feedback submitted by other members of your organization.

If you are a Global Administrator of an Azure AD enterprise domain, you can also register that domain with the Windows Insider Program. Doing so allows you to manage Insider builds on corporate devices by applying policies. It also ensures that feedback from your users is not shared with outsiders.

For details on how to participate in the Windows Insider Program for Business, see *https://insider.windows.com/for-business*.

Unless you're an experienced software tester, you should approach Insider Preview builds with caution. By definition, they are unfinished, with known and unknown issues that can potentially expose you to system crashes and data loss. The best test platforms are secondary PCs that are properly backed up; for testing software compatibility and previewing new Windows features, a virtual machine is an excellent choice, although it doesn't provide the real-world hardware compatibility information that Microsoft engineers rely on.

Another significant issue associated with setting up access to Insider Preview builds is the need to install feature updates far more frequently than the normal once-a-year schedule. The most aggressive Insider option involves installing a new feature update weekly during normal development cycles, and the pace of updates sometimes increases to multiple builds per week as developers reach the end of the cycle and prepare for the public release.

Joining a device to the Windows Insider Program is not a decision to be made lightly. If you decide you want to stop receiving preview builds and go back to the current release channel, you need to pay close attention to Microsoft's announcements and change settings as instructed. You can safely disconnect a device from receiving Insider builds without reinstalling

Windows only during the brief interval after a new version is released to the General Availability Channel and only if you previously made the appropriate configuration changes. If you miss those deadlines, you have to back up your data and perform a clean reinstall of Windows.

If you're cognizant of the risks and willing to accept the trade-offs, keep reading to learn how to set up a Windows 11 PC to receive Insider builds.

Inside OUT

Stop unauthorized users from switching to Insider builds

If you manage PCs in an office or home, you probably don't want to have preview builds installed on them without your permission. To prevent users from creating headaches for you and your support staff, take the following steps:

On any PC running Windows 10 Pro, Enterprise, or Education, you can apply a Group Policy setting to block changes to Insider settings on that PC. Go to Computer Configuration > Administrative Templates > Windows Components > Windows Update > Manage Updates Offered From Windows Update > Manage Preview Builds; set that policy to Disabled.

On devices running Windows 11 Home (which doesn't support Group Policy settings), your best option is to configure standard user accounts, which require permission from an administrator (you) to access Windows Insider Program settings.

In Microsoft Insider–speak, the process of running Insider Preview builds is called *flighting*. You control your participation by choosing one of three *channels* for each device that's enrolled to receive these early releases. The following section describes these channels in more detail.

Enrolling a device in the Windows Insider Program

After registering your Microsoft account at *https://insider.windows.com*, you're ready to configure a Windows 11 device to receive Insider Preview builds. First, confirm that you've configured Windows to send optional diagnostic data to Microsoft, so that engineers can investigate the cause of crashes and other issues. Go to Settings > Privacy & Security > Diagnostics & Feedback and make sure the Send Optional Diagnostic Data switch is set to On.

Next, go to Settings > Windows Update > Windows Insider Program and click Get Started.

The first step is to link your PC to the registered Insider account. In most cases, the Microsoft account you use to sign in to Windows 11 is the best choice here. Then click Continue, as shown in Figure B-1, to walk through the wizard's steps and configure your Insider settings.

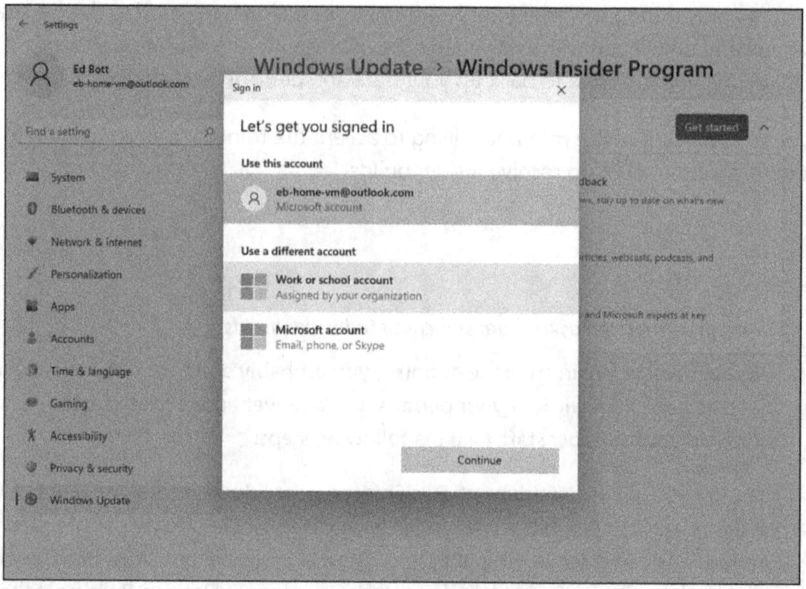

Figure B-1   If you're willing to accept the risks of installing preview builds in exchange for the opportunity to influence the direction of Windows, click Get Started and link an account that you previously registered with the Windows Insider Program.

After that step is complete, choose one of three Insider Preview channels. The names and general contours match those used for test releases of other Microsoft software and services, including Microsoft Edge, Microsoft 365, and Microsoft Teams:

- **Dev Channel**   New builds go to this group of Insiders first, and these preview builds are not synchronized to a future release of Windows 11. Microsoft uses this channel to experiment with new features and services, occasionally using A/B testing to roll out different versions of features to different groups of testers. Some features may never find their way into a release. The excitement of being among the first to experience new features should be balanced by the risk of being the first to experience a new bug. You can report those bugs using the Feedback Hub. Microsoft recommends this channel for "highly technical users."

- **Beta Channel**   Devices configured for this "early adopter" channel receive preview builds after they've had a chance to be well tested by the Dev channel. These builds are aligned to a specific upcoming release and are likely to be more stable and reliable because they incorporate fixes based on feedback from testers in the Dev channel.

- **Release Preview Channel**   This is the most conservative channel of all, offering new builds near the end of the development cycle for a feature update. Insiders who choose this channel also receive advanced quality updates and have early access to certain key features. These builds are fully supported. Microsoft recommends this channel for IT pros who want to preview and validate upcoming releases without a major risk of instability.

Before you can complete the configuration process, you must click through multiple warnings, which list the risks discussed earlier. After a restart, you're ready to begin receiving new builds. The current Insider Preview release that matches your preferences downloads and install automatically, just like a feature update from the General Availability channel.

After configuring a device to receive Insider Preview builds and restarting, you should see some new options in the Windows Insider Program section in Settings > Windows Update, as shown in Figure B-2. There, you can review your Insider settings, including which channel the device is currently enrolled in.

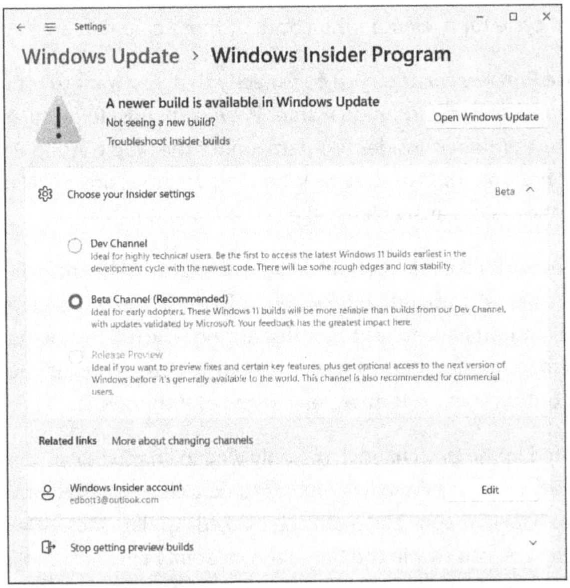

Figure B-2   Click the current channel or the Windows Insider Account to change Insider settings.

To use a different account with a specific device, first make sure that account is registered with the Windows Insider Program. Then click the account card at the bottom of that Settings page and use the Change or Unlink buttons.

Inside OUT

When can you change channels?

When you first enroll a device to receive Insider Preview builds, you're required to choose a channel. After installing that feature update, you'll continue receiving all new builds and updates from that channel. What happens if you want to change channels? That depends on where you're starting from.

Devices that are running builds from the Beta or Release Preview channels can move to a higher channel by choosing its option on the Windows Insider Program page in Settings. After making that change, the next update you receive will be from that channel. You can move from the Beta channel to Release Preview only during a brief window near the end of the development cycle for a release, when both of those channels are in sync.

From the Beta or Release Preview channel, you can specify that you want to return to the General Availability channel and stop running Insider Preview builds. To do so, go to Settings > Windows Update >Windows Insider Program; under the Stop Getting Preview Builds heading, turn on the Unenroll This Device When The Next Version Of Windows Releases switch. (This option is not available for the Dev channel.)

Note that this option does not take effect until the official release of the next version to the General Availability channel. Depending on where Microsoft is in the development cycle for that release, you might have to wait months, during which time you need to keep installing builds and minor updates from the channel you're leaving. If you don't want to wait, your only option is to perform a clean install of Windows 11.

If you're currently enrolled in the Dev channel, the only way to change to another channel (including the General Availability channel) is to do a clean reinstall of Windows 11, which also requires reinstalling apps and restoring backed-up data files. After the reinstallation is complete, you can stay in the General Availability channel or re-enroll the device in the Windows Insider Program, choosing your preferred channel.

Insider Preview builds arrive via Windows Update, just as they do in the General Availability channel. Major builds are the equivalent of feature updates; minor updates are analogous to monthly security updates, smaller and quicker to install. When running an Insider Preview build, you might notice a few changes. For starters, a watermark appears in the lower-right corner of the screen, above the clock in the notification area, with the words "Evaluation copy" and the Insider Preview build number. (This watermark disappears for some builds that are released near the end of a development cycle, as Microsoft prepares the final preview builds for the official release.)

As noted earlier, on a PC configured to receive Insider Preview builds, some privacy settings are mandatory. If you go to Settings > Privacy & Security > Diagnostics & Feedback, for example, you'll find that the Feedback Frequency options are set to the default levels, and a message on that page discloses that the Windows Insider Program has taken control of those options.

Those options return to normal when you change the configuration of a device so that it no longer receives Insider Preview builds and is back on the General Availability channel.

NOTE

When we began writing this book, Microsoft was about to release the version of Windows scheduled for release in the second half of 2022. Instead of a code name, this release was identified as 22H2 in its Insider flight details. To identify the current status of Insider Preview releases for Windows 11, go to the Flight Hub at *https://learn.microsoft.com/windows-insider/flight-hub/.*

When running an Insider Preview build, you can suspend delivery of new builds for up to seven days. Go to Settings > Windows Update and click Pause Updates. You might choose to make this change if you're in the midst of a big project and don't want your work to be interrupted by a large download that could take an hour or more to install. You might also choose to stop updates temporarily if you're traveling. As a member of the Windows Insider Program, however, that delay is limited to a week. (For a device in the General Availability Channel, you can use the same option to pause updates for up to 35 days.)

Keeping track of what's in each preview build

Every new Insider Preview release is accompanied by copious documentation. Visit the Insider Flight Hub at *https://docs.microsoft.com/windows-insider/flight-hub/* to catch up on just the highlights. That page lists each build in the active development cycle, in reverse chronological order, with a link to the corresponding set of release notes on the Windows Insider Blog, which discusses those features in more detail and includes detailed lists of general fixes as well as known issues. Visit *https://blogs.windows.com/windows-insider/tag/windows-insider-program/* to browse through all the release notes.

Inside OUT

Read the release notes when installing a preview build

Every preview release of Windows 11 is accompanied by detailed notes documenting features that are new or changed in the current release, as well as issues that have been fixed from previous builds and—crucially—known issues that might affect your PC's performance or stability.

It is, of course, human nature to ignore these notes and plunge headlong into a new preview release. As tempting as the prospects of new features might be, we strongly urge you to at least skim each set of release notes, especially the Known Issues section, before using a new preview release. Doing so can save you frustration and needless troubleshooting when you run into a feature that's not working correctly. In rare cases, it can also prevent the annoyance of a failed install when a known issue affects specific hardware or software installed on your device.

Links to those same release notes are also available in the Feedback Hub app, on the Announcements tab; click the megaphone icon in the navigation pane to see the full list, as shown in Figure B-3.

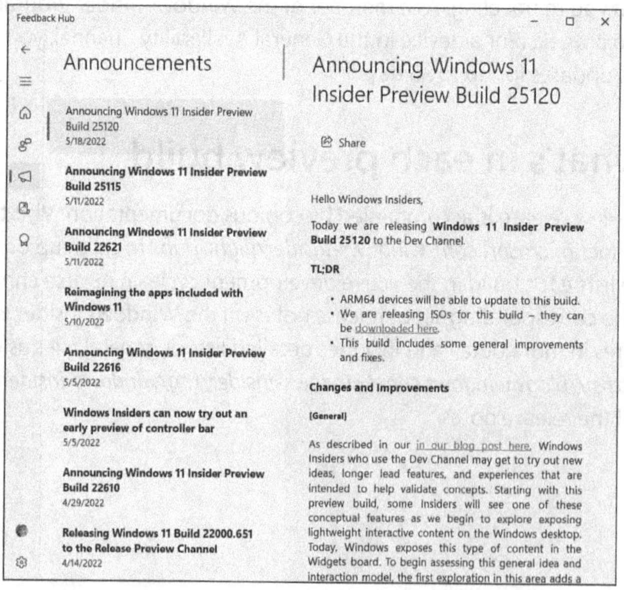

Figure B-3 Open the Feedback Hub and click the megaphone app in the navigation pane to see a full list of announcements, including details about each new Insider Preview build.

That's not the only purpose of the Feedback Hub app, of course, as we consider in the next section.

Submitting and tracking feedback

The Windows Insider Program is, by design, a feedback loop. Microsoft gathers a useful amount of information from online telemetry, of course, but the primary means for offering bug reports and suggestions to Microsoft is via the aptly named Feedback Hub app.

That loop is a crucial step in ensuring that serious bugs are caught and fixed before they reach the general public. A prime example of just how important that task is occurred when Microsoft released the Windows 10 October 2018 Update, version 1809. Only days later, the rollout of that feature update was paused for more than a month after early adopters reported two serious bugs with the new update.

Ironically, Windows Insiders had done the job they were supposed to do, with multiple Insiders reporting both bugs during the course of testing preview builds. Microsoft's engineers had missed those reports in the flood of data from the Feedback Hub. To help ensure that those reports are taken more seriously and avoid a recurrence of that embarrassing release cycle, the Windows team added a new Severity field to the feedback form and instituted new review processes.

The Feedback tab, shown in Figure B-4, allows you to view and search all items submitted by the Insider community, adding your own comments and upvoting items to make a suggestion more visible to the Microsoft employees designing and coding upcoming Windows releases.

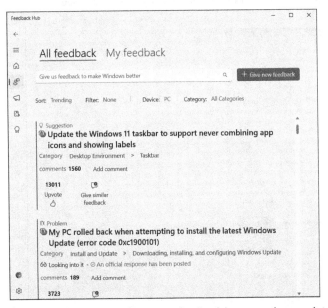

Figure B-4   Before creating a new feedback item, use the search tools to find previous reports.

Before you click the Add New Feedback button, use the search box to find previous reports on the same issue. If you find one that already covers the issue you were planning to report, consider clicking the Upvote button (to the left of a summary item and below the heading when you open the full feedback item) rather than creating a duplicate feedback item. If you have additional details that are relevant, open the item and add a comment. (You can also comment on comments.)

A few suggestions for getting the most out of the Feedback Hub app:

- Use the Sort options to change the display of search results. Choose Trending to see items that are getting the most current activity; click Upvotes to show feedback items that have already proven popular and might benefit most from your support.

- Choosing My Build from the Filter list can help you avoid seeing outdated feedback and confirm that an issue you're experiencing is also being reported by others using the same build. Clearing that option can help you report a longstanding issue that was reported in previous builds and is still occurring in a current build.

- Take advantage of Filter options to identify issues that have been addressed by the Windows development team. Select the Changes Made and Official Response categories to see items that contain these details.

If you can't find an existing feedback item, click Give New Feedback and fill in the four-part form. Provide clear details in the subject line so that others can find your issue and choose the correct category in step 2. Pay special attention to the Add More Details section, shown in Figure B-5, which includes a checkbox for prioritizing an issue as "high severity." For issues that you can reliably reproduce, consider using the options to attach screenshots and files or even record a series of steps to help an engineer understand exactly what you're seeing.

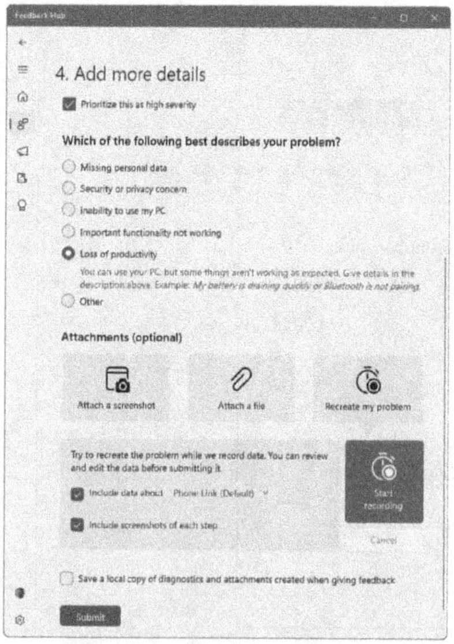

Figure B-5   The Start Recording option allows you to record a sequence of events that an engineer can reproduce, making a bug report or suggestion far more effective.

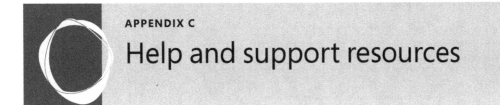

Help and support resources

This book is packed with details about how Windows works and how you can make it work better for you, but it can't possibly answer every question. That's especially true when you factor in the nearly infinite combinations of hardware and software that are possible in the diverse PC ecosystem and then add the updates that Microsoft delivers every month.

So, where do you find answers to those naggingly specific questions? That's the purpose of this appendix, which serves as a roadmap to places where you can find help, troubleshooting tips, how-to guides, drivers, utilities, and advice.

Our list starts with official resources, collated and curated by Microsoft, but we also include community-based resources where you're likely to find reliable answers.

Online help

It's been more than a decade since any new version of Windows included a local documentation file. Instead, modern versions of Windows make help accessible online, where it's easily updated and expanded.

In that spirit, your first stop for answering most basic questions should be the web—specifically, the Microsoft Bing search engine, which delivers results directly from Microsoft Help when you ask a question about Windows. Figure C-1 shows one such question, with the answer in a box above all other search results and the source clearly labeled as "Help from Microsoft."

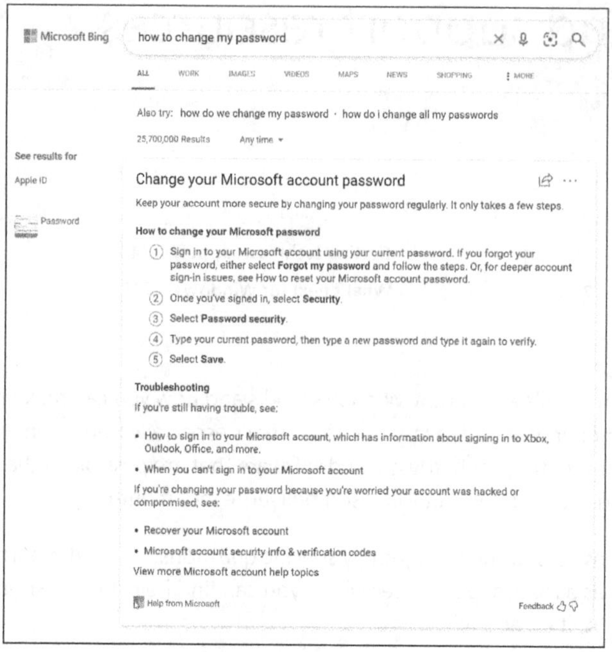

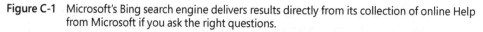

Figure C-1   Microsoft's Bing search engine delivers results directly from its collection of online Help from Microsoft if you ask the right questions.

Sometimes, of course, you're not looking for a detailed explanation or step-by-step instructions but simply trying to find a Windows setting without having to dig through menus or dialogs. For that type of chore, you have your choice of two places to start a search:

- **The search box on the Start menu**   Entering a search term (in the example that follows Figure C-2, the word *display*) in the search box on the taskbar returns a short but usually well-focused set of results.

- **The Settings search box**   Click Start > Settings (or use the keyboard shortcut Windows key+I) and enter a word or phrase in the search box above the navigation pane. Note that the results list might also contain entries from the legacy desktop Control Panel, although these options are increasingly rare in the Windows 11 era.

For traditionalists, one bit of local help is available on a Windows 11 device, courtesy of a Microsoft Store app called Tips. The app, shown in Figure C-3, is installed with Windows 11 and updated through the Microsoft Store.

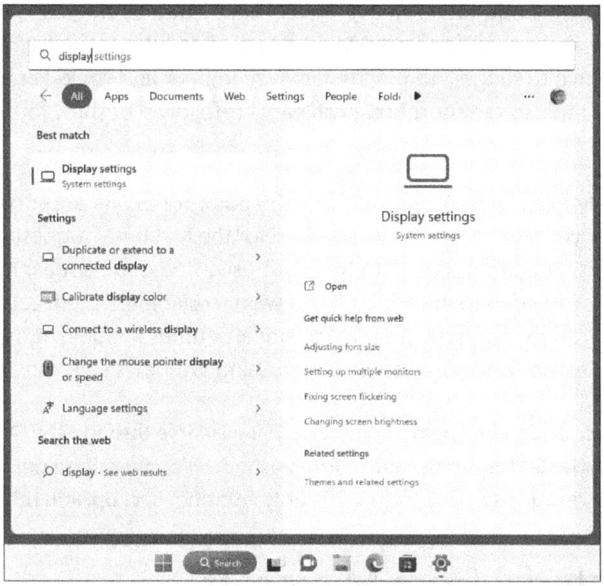

Figure C-2   Using the search box in Start is usually the fastest way to navigate quickly to a specific setting.

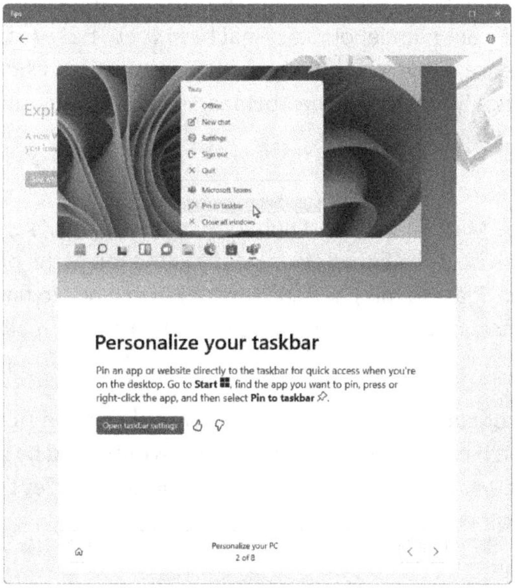

Figure C-3   The Tips app is installed with Windows 11 and is intended primarily for beginners and nontechnical users.

The content in the Tips app is basic, offers an overview of core features, and is aimed primarily at nontechnical users. Most readers of this book will probably find little new information there, but it's an excellent resource to suggest to friends, family members, and coworkers who could benefit from it. Click any topic to see short tips, in an easy-to-follow slideshow format, for that topic.

You can open Tips directly from Start. An alternative entry point comes via pop-up tips that appear occasionally after you sign in to a Windows 11 PC for the first time, suggesting that you try out new features. Those tips are designed to be unobtrusive and don't appear if you already used the feature the tip is intended to introduce. If you want to eliminate them completely, go to Settings > System > Notifications, scroll to the Additional Settings heading at the bottom of the page, and clear the Get Tips And Suggestions When Using Windows checkbox.

> ➤ **An additional source of detailed help in Windows 11 is available through the Other Troubleshooters section under Settings > System > Troubleshoot. We cover these guided tools as well as online Fix It resources in Chapter 15, "Troubleshooting, backup, and recovery."**

Online reference material from Microsoft

Microsoft's commitment to ongoing support of Windows includes an enormous library of training aids and reference material. This section lists the most important of these resources. Note that the process of updating documentation originally prepared for Windows 10 is ongoing, and you can expect to find a significant number of topics that have yet to be revised for Windows 11. In some cases, the differences are minor, but it's worth being cautious when relying on documentation that wasn't specifically created for the operating system you're using.

Microsoft Support

The most prominent feature at the Microsoft Support hub for Windows (*https://support.microsoft.com/windows*) is a large search box, positioned prominently at the top of the page. If a general web search is unsuccessful, navigate to this page and use that search box to find detailed instructions, troubleshooting advice, and links to apps and driver updates that match your search terms.

If you just want a tutorial that's more detailed than the superficial version in the Tips app, click any of the topics beneath the search bar to see collections of articles organized by subject. The Trending Topics section for Windows 11, near the bottom of the page, lists articles that have proven particularly popular with other visitors.

Inside Out

What happened to the Microsoft Knowledge Base?

For decades, Microsoft maintained an online resource called the Knowledge Base, filled with official support documents that provided details about known issues, workarounds, security updates, new features, and anything else that the Microsoft Support organization deemed worthy of formal publication. Every article in this repository had a unique identifying number, which was preceded by the letters KB, along with a string of keywords to help make the article easier to find.

And then, in 2020, the Knowledge Base archives simply vanished. Some articles have been republished on the Microsoft Support website, using a completely different naming system, but there's been no systematic effort to redirect old KB pages. If you run across an old reference to a KB article, you'll probably find that the link leads to an error page.

The KB syntax has survived in one area. Each monthly security update for Windows is identified by a KB number that accompanies its unique build number. If you want to know what fixes were included in the Windows 11 update released on May 10, 2022 (build 22000.675), for example, you'll find them in article KB5013943.

But with those noteworthy exceptions, the KB era has officially ended.

Microsoft Docs

The well-organized index at Microsoft Docs (*https://learn.microsoft.com/docs/*) offers just a hint of its scope, with links on the opening page to separate sections for every important product (and a few obscure ones) in Microsoft's catalog. Collectively, the site contains all of Microsoft's technical documentation, along with reference materials and tutorials for software developers, hardware designers, and IT professionals. The information is thorough, well organized, and expanding at an impressive rate. The Windows Client Documentation for IT Pros section, at *https://learn.microsoft.com/windows/resources/*, is likely to be of most interest to readers of this book.

Resources for IT Pros

Microsoft's Inside Track site (*https://www.microsoft.com/insidetrack/it-pro*) includes case studies, videos, and tutorials prepared primarily for IT pros. Many of the case studies and whitepapers feature IT experts from Microsoft, explaining how they deployed the company's own technologies.

Microsoft Learn

This online learning resource (*https://learn.microsoft.com/*) is an excellent source of free train-ing on a wide range of topics, including Windows 11. Available content includes prerecorded courses, live events (and archives of previous events), and books, with walk-throughs and demos bringing complex topics to life. If you're looking for a Microsoft certification, start here.

Getting technical support

If you can't find an answer in the technical documentation, or if a problem seems to be unique to your system configuration, you can turn to the Microsoft Community forums at *https://answers.microsoft.com*. These threaded message boards are organized into categories—choose Windows, select Windows 11 from the Versions dropdown, and then select an entry from the Topics list to narrow down the list of answers.

If that filtered list doesn't surface a useful article or discussion, click the search icon in the upper-right corner and enter a relevant search term to see whether anyone else has reported a similar issue or whether a member of the community has written an article on the subject. See Figure C-4 for an example of one such search.

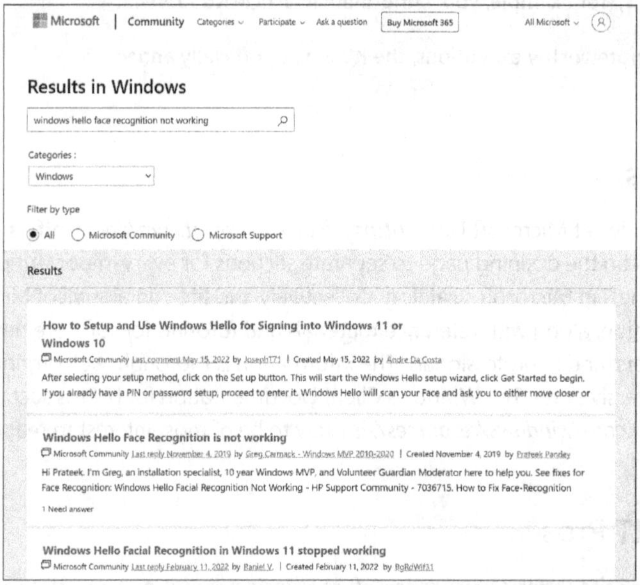

Figure C-4   Use the filter options beneath the search box to narrow the search results from the Microsoft Community forums.

If your search doesn't turn up the answer you're looking for, it's time to get specific. Click Ask A Question to begin composing a question of your own. (You can use this same form to start a discussion if you want to raise an issue that doesn't require an answer.) When posting to the Community forums, try to use a subject line that will clearly describe the problem to anyone scanning a list of topics, and be as specific as possible when describing your issue. It helps to provide relevant details about your system configuration and hardware as well the results of any troubleshooting steps you've already tried.

Note that support in these forums is provided by community members as well as Microsoft support personnel. You're also likely to run into an occasional Microsoft MVP (Most Valuable Professional). There's no guarantee you'll get a satisfactory answer, but we can testify from personal experience that this route has been successful for many people.

To keep track of a discussion, sign in with your Microsoft account and use the Subscribe link at the bottom of any message. You'll receive an email at the address associated with your Microsoft account whenever anyone replies to the message; this is true regardless of whether you started the discussion yourself or found an existing discussion that you want to follow.

Microsoft Q&A

If you're an IT pro and have a question or want to start a discussion with other like-minded and experienced individuals, go to Microsoft Q&A, which replaces the advanced forums formerly found on MSDN and TechNet. You'll find Windows-related discussions here: *https://learn.microsoft.com/answers/products/windows*. Scroll down to the Windows Client for IT Pros section to find links that lead to a dedicated Windows 11 section.

Topics available on Microsoft Q&A include a much broader range of Microsoft products and technologies than those covered in the Community forums, with a special emphasis on deploying and using Windows in the enterprise.

The basic rules of engagement for these more advanced message boards are similar to those that apply in the Microsoft Community forums: search first, and ask a new question only if you can't find an existing discussion that addresses your issue.

Search options for Microsoft Q&A allow you to filter by date and by content type. Filtering the results list to show only items posted in the last week can be useful—if you're looking for details about a known issue with a just-released update, for example, and you don't want to be distracted by earlier, unrelated discussion. Figure C-5 shows one such filtered search.

Figure C-5   Use the options on the right side of the results list to filter your search by date or article type. Click Refine Search after making your selections.

Free and paid support from Microsoft

Getting answers from fellow Windows users has the advantage of being free and easily accessible, but sometimes you need formal support from Microsoft engineers.

Microsoft provides free support for security issues. If you suspect your computer has been infected with malware, for example, you can request and receive support at no charge. Other support options might be covered under a product warranty that's provided if you purchase Windows directly from Microsoft, or you can open a support ticket (called an "incident") for a fee.

Visit the Microsoft Answer Desk online at *https://support.microsoft.com/contactus* to see your support options. Listings on that page direct you to the appropriate technical support resources for different business categories.

As an alternative, use the Get Help app, which is installed by default with Windows 10 and Windows 11. This app prompts you through an AI-powered chat session with a virtual agent. If that doesn't provide the answer you're looking for, you can chat with a support agent to get non-virtual support. Figure C-6 shows the options available when we asked for help with a possible ransomware issue.

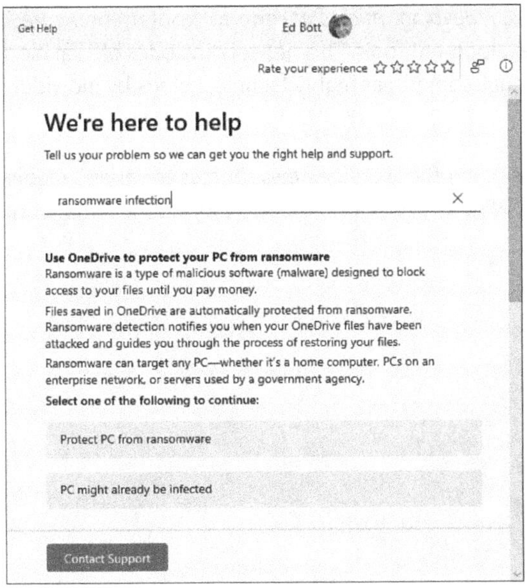

Figure C-6 Use the Get Help app to chat online or talk with a support representative. Note that some options might require payment.

What's next for Windows

If your organization uses Windows, you should make a special effort to stay on top of what's coming in current and future updates to Windows 11. The easiest way to keep track of what's new in each update (and to refresh your recollection about what arrived in earlier updates) is to read the Windows 11 Release Information page at *https://aka.ms/windowsreleasehealth*.

In addition to reading those engineering and support documents, you can check in regularly at Microsoft's network of official blogs covering the Windows ecosystem. The following represent valuable information sources we recommend adding to your reading list:

- Microsoft runs its own mini network of Windows blogs that includes blogs for Windows Experience, the Windows Insider Program, Windows Developer, Microsoft Edge, and Microsoft Devices. A central hub is located at *https://blogs.windows.com/*.

- The Microsoft lineup of business software is represented by the Microsoft 365 team, which runs a blog at *https://www.microsoft.com/microsoft-365/blog/*.

- You'll find a large assortment of technical blogs at the Microsoft Tech Community. Blogs cover business areas like financial services and healthcare as well as specific products. An index is available at *https://techcommunity.microsoft.com/t5/custom/page/page-id/Blogs*.

APPENDIX C

- Developers can go to *https://devblogs.microsoft.com/* for content on Azure, Visual Studio, PowerShell, and other development tools. This network includes official blogs from product teams as well as personal, sometimes highly technical blogs by individual Microsoft employees.

And, of course, there are dozens of unofficial online news sources of varying credibility that will happily keep you up to date on Windows rumors and news. (Sometimes what appears to be news is really just a rumor.)

Index

Symbols

* (asterisk) wildcard in searches, 322, 332

@ mentions in email messages, 184

| (pipe symbol) in Command Prompt, 620

? (question mark) wildcard in searches, 332

~ (tilde) wildcard in searches, 333

3D Objects folder, 305

802.11ac Wi-Fi standard, 393

802.11ax Wi-Fi standard, 393

802.11g Wi-Fi standard, 393

802.11n Wi-Fi standard, 393

A

AAC audio format, 195

abbreviating parameter names in PowerShell, 607

accent colors, changing, 119-120

access control, 366, 368-369

access control lists (ACLs), 369-370

accessibility settings, 132-135

access points (Wi-Fi), security, 397

accounts in Mail and Calendar apps. *See also* user accounts
  adding new, 179
  deleting, 180
  linking Mail account inboxes, 182
  managing, 178-179

  pinning to Start, 182
  renaming, 179
  syncing, 177, 180-181

ACLs (access control lists), 369-370

activating Windows 11
  advanced license management, 60-61
  antipiracy checks, 50-52
  corporate licensing, 59-60
  licensing options, 52-53
  managing activation, 55-56
  product keys, 53-55
  troubleshooting activation, 56-59

Active Directory domain accounts, signing in with, 343

Active Directory Domain Services (AD DS), 691-693

adapters for networking, 372-373

adding
  Calendar app accounts, 179
  calendars to taskbar, 131
  clocks to taskbar, 131
  contacts in People app, 187-188
  events in Calendar app, 186-187
  to Favorites list (Microsoft Edge), 237
  folders in Photos app, 198
  hard disks to existing Windows installations, 256-259
  Mail app accounts, 179
  registry values, 627
  secondary user accounts, 361-363
  virtual disks to VMs, 675-676

Address Space Layout Randomization (ASLR), 457

AD DS (Active Directory Domain Services), 691-693

administrator access. *See also* UAC (User Account Control)
  registry virtualization and, 631
  running desktop apps with, 156

Administrator account, 344

administrator accounts, 336, 343-344

Advanced Query Syntax (AQS), 321

Aero Shake, 98

airplane mode, enabling, 374

Alarms & Clock app, 175

aliases
  for Microsoft accounts, 339
  in PowerShell, 606

alignment of taskbar, 80, 83

alternate IP configuration, 381

alternative keyboard layouts, 105-106

Amazon Appstore, 685-686

Android apps, running on Windows, 685-688

Android phones, linking to PCs, 681-685

antipiracy checks, 50-52

antivirus programs
  Microsoft Defender Antivirus, 22, 455
  configuring, 455-456
  Controlled Folder Access feature, 457

J–K

Q

R

W

Hear about it first.

Since 1984, Microsoft Press has helped IT professionals, developers, and home office users advance their technical skills and knowledge with books and learning resources.

Sign up today to deliver exclusive offers directly to your inbox.

- New products and announcements
- Free sample chapters
- Special promotions and discounts
- ... and more!

MicrosoftPressStore.com/newsletters

 Pearson

Plug into learning at

MicrosoftPressStore.com

The Microsoft Press Store by Pearson offers:

- Free U.S. shipping

- Buy an eBook, get three formats – Includes PDF, EPUB, and MOBI to use with your computer, tablet, and mobile devices

- Print & eBook Best Value Packs

- eBook Deal of the Week – Save up to 50% on featured title

- Newsletter – Be the first to hear about new releases, announcements, special offers, and more

- Register your book – Find companion files, errata, and product updates, plus receive a special coupon* to save on your next purchase

Discounts are applied to the list price of a product. Some products are not eligible to receive additional discounts, so your discount code may not be applied to all items in your cart. Discount codes cannot be applied to products that are already discounted, such as eBook Deal of the Week, eBooks that are part of a book + eBook pack, and products with special discounts applied as part of a promotional offering. Only one coupon can be used per order.

 Pearson